This is a critical study of the *Twilight Saga* phenomenon: four *Twilight* books and seven *Twilight* movies (yes, don't forget the two *Twilight* spoof movies!). *The Twilight Saga* is a popular fantasy romance franchise which began in 2005 with the first *Twilight* book and in 2008 with the first *Twilight* movie.

MEDIA, FEMINISM, CULTURAL STUDIES

The Sacred Cinema of Andrei Tarkovsky
by Jeremy Mark Robinson

Liv Tyler
by Thomas A. Christie

The Cinema of Hayao Miyazaki
Jeremy Mark Robinson

Stepping Forward: Essays, Lectures and Interviews
by Wolfgang Iser

Wild Zones: Pornography, Art and Feminism
by Kelly Ives

'Cosmo Woman': The World of Women's Magazines
by Oliver Whitehorne

The Cinema of Richard Linklater
by Thomas A. Christie

Andrea Dworkin
by Jeremy Mark Robinson

Cixous, Irigaray, Kristeva: The Jouissance of French Feminism
by Kelly Ives

The Erotic Object: Sexuality in Sculpture
From Prehistory to the Present Day
by Susan Quinnell

Women in Pop Music
by Helen Challis

Sex in Art: Pornography and Pleasure in Painting and Sculpture
by Cassidy Hughes

Erotic Art
by Cassidy Hughes

Jean-Luc Godard: The Passion of Cinema / Le Passion de Cinéma
by Jeremy Mark Robinson

Genius and Loving It! Mel Brooks
by Thomas Christie

The Comic Art of Mel Brooks
by Maurice Yacowar

Marvelous Names
by P. Adams Sitney

Odd Couples
by P. Adams Sitney

The Art of Katsuhiro Otomo
by Jeremy Mark Robinson

Akira: The Movie and the Manga
by Jeremy Mark Robinson

The Art of Masamune Shirow (3 vols)
by Jeremy Mark Robinson

Julia Kristeva: Art, Love, Melancholy, Philosophy, Semiotics
by Kelly Ives

Luce Irigaray: Lips, Kissing, and the Politics of Sexual Difference
by Kelly Ives

Helene Cixous I Love You: The Jouissance *of Writing*
by Kelly Ives

FORTHCOMING BOOKS

Legend of the Overfiend
Death Note
Naruto
Bleach
Vampire Knight
Mushishi
One Piece
Nausicaä of the Valley of the Wind
Harry Potter

THE TWILIGHT SAGA

THE TWILIGHT SAGA

THE BOOKS, THE MOVIES, THE CULTURAL PHENOMENON

Jeremy Mark Robinson

CRESCENT MOON

Crescent Moon Publishing
P.O. Box 1312, Maidstone
Kent, ME14 5XU, Great Britain
www.crmoon.com

First published 2025.
© Jeremy Mark Robinson 2025.

Set in Times New Roman 10 on 14pt.
Designed by Radiance Graphics.

British Library Cataloguing in Publication data available for this title.

ISBN-13 9781861712011

CONTENTS

PART FOUR ♣ THE *TWILIGHT* MOVIES

ACKNOWLEDGEMENTS

To the authors and publishers quoted.
To the copyright holders of the illustrations.

ABBREVIATIONS

T	*Twilight*
NM	*New Moon*
E	*Eclipse*
BD	*Breaking Dawn*
TS	*The Twilight Saga: The Official Illustrated Guide*
CFA	*The Twilight Saga: The Complete Film Archive* (R. Abele)
NMC	*New Moon: The Official Illustrated Movie Companion* (M. Vaz)
BR	*Blood Rivals* (M. Howden)

PICTURE CREDITS

For Lauren

Niente sarà più
come prima.

twilight

SUMMIT ENTERTAINMENT PRESENTA "TWILIGHT"
UNA PRODUZIONE TEMPLE HILL IN ASSOCIAZIONE CON MAVERICK/IMPRINT KRISTEN STEWART ROBERT PATTINSON BILLY BURKE PETER FACINELLI
CASTING TRICIA WOOD, CSA DEBORAH AQUILA, CSA MUSICHE CARTER BURWELL SUPERVISIONE MUSICALE ALEXANDRA PATSAVAS COSTUMI WENDY CHUCK MONTAGGIO NANCY RICHARDSON, A.C.E. FOTOGRAFIA ELLIOT DAVIS
PRODUTTORI ESECUTIVI KAREN ROSENFELT MARTY BOWEN GUY OSEARY MICHELE IMPERATO STABILE PRODOTTO DA GREG MOORADIAN MARK MORGAN WYCK GODFREY
BASATO SUL ROMANZO "TWILIGHT" DI STEPHENIE MEYER SCENEGGIATURA MELISSA ROSENBERG REGIA CATHERINE HARDWICKE

www.eaglepictures.com

Il film Twilight è tratto dall'omonimo best seller di Stephenie Meyer pubblicato in Italia da Fazi Editore

On set, Twilight (2008).

PART ONE

❧

STEPHENIE MEYER

1

STEPHENIE MEYER

BIOGRAPHY.

Stephenie Meyer[1] was born on Christmas Eve, 1973 in Hartford, Connecticut. She grew up in Phoenix, Arizona (where *Twilight*'s Bella Swan hails from), along with five brothers and sisters (Heidi, Paul, Jacob, Emily and Seth).[2] Her parents were Candy and Stephen Morgan (a finance officer). Meyer studied in Scottsdale, AZ (Chaparral High School) and Brigham Young University in Provo, Utah (and also at Arizona State University), taking a B.A. in English Literature. She married Christian Meyer (an accountant) in 1994, aged 20, when she was at university (they have three sons).[3] She is a Mormon, and lives in Cave Creek, AZ.

Bella Swan, Stephenie Meyer's best-known creation, admits in *Twilight* that she's not a typical Arizonan girl. She's not tall,[4] blonde, sporty and tan, not a cheerleader or a volleyball player (T, 9). She's slender, soft, pale and unathletic.

> I didn't relate well to people my age. Maybe the truth was that I didn't relate well to people, period. (T, 9)

According to Forbes, Stephenie Meyer is worth about $125 million (in the 2020s). She is thus one of the most financially successful authors in the world, alongside Dean Koontz, Dan Brown, Tom Clancy, Jo Rowling, and Jackie Collins. Meyer has also been involved with film production on a minor scale (via Fickle Fish Films,[5] backing projects such as *Austenland* and *The Host*).

1 Morgan is her maiden name.
2 You'll notice that Meyer used their names in her signature work.
3 One is called Seth – the name of one of Meyer's brothers, and one of the werewolves in the *Twilight* series (her other sons are Paul and Gabe).
4 But Beau in the *Life and Death* rewrite is tall.
5 Meyer's film company is Fickle Fish Films (ficklefishfilms.com).

Never say never: after the *Twilight* books were out in the world, Stephenie Meyer said that was it. And she asserted that she wasn't going to publish *Midnight Sun* after it had been spoilt by a leak. But then in 2020 *Midnight Sun* was published. And in February, 2023, it was reported that Meyer was working on two new *Twilight* books (and an animated TV series was in the works).

Brothers are clearly an important influence for Stephenie Meyer: she has acknowledged her brothers Seth, Jacob and Paul in the *Twilight* books. Also, three of the werewolves are named after her brothers, Jacob, Paul and Seth. Brothers crop up in *The Host*. Meyer herself has three sons. It's no wonder, then, that Bella Swan is such a tomboyish personality, quite at home with guys fixing their motorcycles (and she's much more comfortable with Jacob and his working class pals than the bourgeois, cultured Cullens).

Stephenie Meyer enjoyed her character Jacob Black – an ordinary kid thrust into an extraordinary situation, she called him (which's how critics define Steven Spielberg's films – ordinary people in extraordinary circumstances). Jake is the boysy aspect of the *Twilight* series: 'I have been surrounded by boys, with my kids, my brothers, my father and uncles, so he was very familiar to write about'.

Supporters of Stephenie Meyer's fiction included Orson Card and Jodi Picoult. She was 'the superstar of young adult ficton' for the British newspaper *The Times* and 'the world's most popular vampire novelist since Anne Rice' for *Entertainment Weekly*.

Detractors included Stephen King (she 'can't write worth a darn'), and numerous critics and journalists. As Truman Capote bitched about Jack Kerouac: 'That's not writing, that's typing'. Blah, blah, blah... And both Jane Austen and Emily Brontë returned from the grave to visit a cabal of lawyers in New York to demand royalties.

But many famous authors disliked Jane Austen, including D.H. Lawrence, Ralph Emerson, Virginia Woolf and Mark Twain. It was Twain who bitched thus:

> I often want to criticize Jane Austen, but her books madden me so that I can't conceal my frenzy from the reader, and therefore I have to stop every time I begin. Every time[6] I read *Pride and Prejudice* I want to dig her up and beat over the skull with her own shin bone!

Critics regularly trash authors they think can't write well – Dan Brown, Jeffrey Archer, J.K. Rowling, Jackie Collins, Tom Clancy and

---

6 Eh? Twain here claims he read *Pride and Prejudice* more than once! Maybe there was nothing else to do in the 19th century.

Stephen King. Of course, those authors have out-sold your average critic and journalist by zillions (envy is certainly part of the mix).

Many readers and fans don't care. They're into the story and the characters, not whether an author weaves in hi-falutin' allusions to Marcel Proust's *Remembrance of Times Past*, or if an author can compose sentences with the lyrical precision of Samuel Beckett (very few can!), or if an author knows how to use brainy words properly, like ontology or hermeneutics.

Other fans/ readers recognize that the *Twilight* books aren't 'high art', but are lowbrow and a 'guilty pleasure'. These are the readers/ fans who begin their assessments with the announcement, 'I know these books are junk, but...' (I find that very odd, turning reading into a Guilt Trip. It's weird hearing readers always apologize for reading Jackie Collins! She's a *fantastic* storyteller!).

However, Stephenie Meyer's prose style is maddeningly boring at times, and her pedantic desire to explain every little thing is irritating. Of the authors derided by the critical academy, Meyer is one of the worst. But somehow Meyer has created characters, plots and situations that have thrilled millions of readers.

A BOOKISH GIRL.
Stephenie Meyer has remarked:

> I spent my entire childhood reading, and I think I was bit annoying because I was always living in a fantasy world.

Well, we knew that! Or we could guess it. Yes. Because that's what the *Twilight* series, on film or the printed page, represent: a fantasy world. It's what writers of fiction get hooked on: they love to spend time in the fantasy worlds they have created, and with the characters who sometimes amaze them by doing things they didn't expect. That is without doubt one of the chief appeals of writing novels, being swept up in the fantasy, living in your imagination.

Thus, it is the writerly self-absorption, the poetic trance, that is valuable to the author, even more, in a way, than the quality of the work they're writing. In this way, writing itself becomes a way of being alive that appeals to the writer. Some writers just love writing. It doesn't even matter, to a degree, what they're writing about. Thus writing as a drug, a hit, a daydream, a self-hypnosis.

So, it doesn't matter whether the *Twilight* novels are 'any good', technically or structurally, or if the characters are 'original' or clichéd, or if the prose style is or isn't enchanting and lyrical, or if the themes and issues are or aren't explored with insight and subtlety. Because, for the author, the *act* of writing the novels has been enough.

Twilight fans like to live in the world of *Twilight*, just like some folk like to sink into the worlds of *Harry Potter, The Matrix* or *Star Wars*. Raul Ruiz, in *The Poetics of Cinema*, offered an intriguing view of film consumption: instead of identifying with the hero of a film, and living vicariously through that character,

> in any film worth seeing you should identify with the film itself, not with one of its characters. You should identify with the objects being manipulated, with the landscapes, with all the characters. (119)

When I read the *Twilight* series, I am Bella, and Edward and Jacob. In this way, the film (or book) goes beyond being a spectacle, something you watch, to something you produce yourself:

> now it appears that the images are taking off from the airport of ourselves, and flying toward the film we are seeing. Suddenly we *are* all the characters of the film, all the objects, all the scenery.

SOME OF STEPHENIE MEYER'S TECHNIQUES.

Some of Stephenie Meyer's prose has the feel of a creative writing class, a university club, a college competition:

(1) Take a minor character and explore their back-story (*The Short Second Life of Bree Tanner*);

(2) Narrate the *Twilight* story from Edward's point-of-view (*Midnight Sun*);

(3) Narrate the story from Jacob's point-of-view (the *Jacob* book in *Breaking Dawn*);

(4) Switch the genders of every character (*Life and Death*);

(5) Find new ways of retaining the same villain from book one (Victoria) – in book two *and* book three;

(6) Create new obstacles for the lovers: marriage (he will, she won't)... pregnancy... death in childbirth... etc.

Stephenie Meyer is the sort of writer who composes character biographies for her charas. Meyer is the eager, dedicated student in a creative writing class, the girl who does her homework the same day as the class. (Yet Meyer didn't attend a writing course).

Yes: Stephenie Meyer is not a professionally trained writer: she started out, like most writers, as a keen amateur, writing for the fun of it, without hankering after fame and fortune. Writing for Meyer is 'still for the joy, when I actually sit down and write' (TS, 27).

The characterizations created by Stephenie Meyer in the *Twilight Saga* books are pretty thin. Meyer is not William Faulkner or Alexander Dumas! You have a vague idea of what her characters look like, but apart from that sketchy characterization, her people simply don't come to life; they are not flesh-and-blood (blood!) people. Meyer relies far more on what her characters *do* and what they *say* and how they *feel* (or rather, how they tell you how they feel).

However, those limitations don't matter too much – not every novel can be *The Rainbow* or *The Count of Monte Cristo*. Rather, the characterizations in the *Twilight* series are functional: they do the job and nothing more. Because the *Twilight* books are relationship books and romance books. 'My focus is the characters – that's the part of the story that is most important to me,' Meyer pointed out.

Stephenie Meyer acknowledged that 'some parts of Bella's experiences are modeled after real life (my life, to be exact) in order to ground the fantasy aspects of the story in solid reality'.

S. Meyer said she is a compulsive re-writer, and can't leave a page untouched. *Twilight* was revised many times, and in 2008 Meyer also fancied revising it again ('I could do such a better job now' [TS, 12]). If I had a recommendation for editing/ revising, it would be to cut down on the boring, everyday details of Bella's life, where every goddam thing is explained. But, *uhh*, that would mean cutting out 75% of the novel! (All you'd have left would be Bella gushing-gushing-gushing over Edward's super-incandescent beauty!).

Here's another example of one of the many writing exercises that Stephenie Meyer produced around the *Twilight Saga*: a short[7] exploration of the story from the viewpoint of Jacob Black. Composed in the first person, the wry, ironic banter of Jacob comes through, as it did in the segment of *Breaking Dawn* that he narrated:

> One day, the daughter of your dad's best friend shows up. She's really pretty in that girl-next-door kind of way, but, more than that, you're just instantly on the same page with her. Kindred spirits. Bella walks away from all her school friends, seemingly totally interested in everything you say. You are immediately infatuated, but you know that she's out of your league. She's a junior, you're a freshman – dream on. Still, you think about her a lot. Maybe someday, you tell yourself.

---

7 Well, 16 pages long.

TWILIGHT AND RELIGION.

Critics have also drawn attention to Stephenie Meyer's status as a Mormon (she is a member of the Church of Jesus Christ of Latter Day Saints), trying to find biographical links to the *Twilight* franchise. Well, yes, of course the *Twilight* books are steeped in the Judæo-Christian religious tradition, like the society of the contemporary U.SA. itself, to the point where it's impossible to separate them out. The *Twilight* books are wholly Western and Biblical and Christian and religious in that respect: they are productions of their time and place. And of course vampire lore too is soaked in Judæo-Christian mythology – indeed, vampire fiction offers wonderfully colourful and exaggerated expressions of Western culture, including Western religion (vampireology in the Western world can't exist without that religious context of Judaism and Xianity).

Critics have found plenty of Mormon tenets and influences in the *Twilight Saga*, tho' Meyer dislikes how her religious beliefs are emphasized in criticism of her fiction. But Meyer has acknowledged the significance of the Mormon faith in her life and work.

Mormonism, the Church of Jesus Christ of Latter Day Saints, was founded in the 1830s by Joseph Smith in Utah. There are many famous followers of the Mormon faith today, including Gladys Knight, Christina Aguilera, Jewel, Ryan Gosling, Aaron Eckhart, and the Osmonds (and one of Meyer's favourite authors, Orson Card).

Yet the spiritual and religious aspects of Western culture and society, including Mormonism and other facets of Christian religion (such as Gnosticism), are far less significant in the *Twilight Saga*, in the end, than the soap opera elements, the romance genre elements, or the teen-girl-growing-up elements.

Yet the spiritual and religious aspects of Western culture and society, including Mormonism and other facets of Christian religion (such as Gnosticism), are far less significant in the *Twilight Saga*, in the end, than the soap opera elements, the romance genre elements, or the teen-girl-growing-up elements.

STEPHENIE MEYER AND E.L. JAMES.

And then there's *Fifty Shades of Grey*.

If you told Stephenie Meyer's publishers and editors, back in 2005, when the *Twilight* novel was first released, that a frumpy, middle-aged British woman would produce a pornographic version of *Twilight* which would sell over 150 million copies and lead to a movie franchise grossing over $1.3 billion, they wouldn't believe you!

Who knew that fan fiction could generate so much $$$$?

It must be odd for Stephenie Meyer – to have a dedicated fan compose a version of her story that became so incredibly successful. In addition, while Meyer refused to add sex scenes to *Twilight*, this eager fanatic has added lots of sex! It's as if Meyer herself has been stalked by someone as brilliant at stalking as Edward Cullen! She created her own super-stalker with Christian Grey! (The stalking of Meyer by E.L. James continued when James copied Meyer's penchant for re-telling the *Twilight* story from the perspective of other characters. That I find genuinely creepy).

✐

This study of *Twilight* was written between 2013 and 2016. As usual, it was then put aside (tho' added to from time to time), until it was completely rewritten (again) in 2024-2025.

There are many fruitful theoretical and philosophical approaches one can take with the *Twilight* franchise. But, aside from a short chapter on feminism, and some sections about French feminist philosophers such as Julia Kristeva, I have left that to other writers.

Stephenie Meyer

2

OTHER BOOKS
BY STEPHENIE MEYER

THE SHORT SECOND LIFE OF BREE TANNER

The Short Second Life of Bree Tanner (2010) was a spin-off book from the *Twilight Saga* (in particular from the third book, *Eclipse*). *The Short Second Life of Bree Tanner* is a novella (178 pages in my Atombooks edition) focussing on a minor character in *Eclipse,* Bree Tanner. She is a young (15 years-old) girl from Las Vegas/ Idaho who's been seduced by Riley Biers (the lieutenant working for the villain Victoria) and turned into a vampire. Riley is tasked with breeding an army of newborn vampires in order to take on the Cullen clan, and Bella and Edward in particular.

The Short Second Life of Bree Tanner does comes across a bit like the creative writing exercises that Stephenie Meyer pursues, when she writes about characters (seen in the novels' outtakes on her website, and at the back of some of the *Twilight* books), to explore their background. In a creative writing class, the assignment might be:

> • *Pick one of the minor characters from the novel* Eclipse *and write a story about them.*
> • *5,000 words.*
> • *Hand-in date: September 13.* [1]

So, off the eager author duly goes. And *The Short Second Life of Bree Tanner* is the result:

---
[1] Bella's birthday.

(A) well-meaning, shy girl

(B) bad childhood

(C) got in with the wrong crowd (!)

(D) didn't wanna fight

and (E) ended up being killed by some vampire bullies.

Like the *Twilight Saga*, *The Short Second Life of Bree Tanner* is narrated in the first person: in many respects, Bree Tanner is the clone of Bella Swan: both are young, white, North American teenagers who get too close to vampires. The major difference, of course, is the big theme of the *Twilight Saga*: *choice*. Bella *chooses* to become a vampire, while Little Bree is enslaved into vampiredom against her will.

First person narration is Stephenie Meyer's usual approach: it's also found in *The Host* as well as all of the *Twilight Saga* books. It irks me, partly because the characters that Meyer chooses as her narrators are quite boring people, unimaginative, non-complex, and with a flat, muted way of seeing the world and people. And the way that Meyer uses the first person perspective is also rather predictable: we know how her characters're going to think and feel before they think or feel.

✏

The story of *The Short Second Life of Bree Tanner* is straight-forward: it concerns the short time when Riley Biers was gathering and training a makeshift vampire army to fight the Cullens for Victoria, in revenge for them (and Bella) dispatching her mate, James Witherdale, in the first *Twilight* book (so, yes, we are dealing with an issue from two books back). The vampires that Victoria and Riley pick are all young, rebellious, antsy, arrogant, surly, resentful and not happy with being a vampire (just as they weren't happy before).

So the story of *The Short Second Life of Bree Tanner* is a bit like a youth leader or Summer camp worker with a bunch of morose, irritated teenagers he's trying to whip into shape so they can perform a stage version of *Jesus Christ Superstar* (or, of course, *Romeo and Juliet!*) in the final week for the visiting parents and relatives, without beating each other up.

However, as with the other *Twilight Saga* books, it's not really the story and the vampirism that interests Stephenie Meyer in *The Short Second Life of Bree Tanner,* but the characters. There are three key charas in *The Short Second Life of Bree Tanner:* Bree manages to make a couple of significant buddies following her induction by Riley into the scuzzy, bloody world of modern-day vampirism (it's the opposite of Carlisle Cullen's calm, polite, clean and affluent form of a vampiric lifestyle).

One is Diego, Riley's right-hand man, who forges an uneasy but ultimately important (and sort of romantic) friendship with Bree. Diego's a rather blank older teen, invented partly so Bree can have someone to hang out with.

The other friend is Freaky Fred, a large, enigmatic vampire who has the special ability to become invisible (and to ward off onlookers). Fred's one of those characters that are scary and strange at first, but whose silent, undemonstrative facade hides a clever mind and a soft heart (there are echoes of classic American books such as *To Kill a Mockingbird* and *The Grapes of Wrath*).

We note that both of the boys that Bree Tanner attaches herself to, Diego and Fred, are older than she is, boys with more social assurance than she possesses (there are obvious affinities with Bella Swan, of course, and to the father quests and fatherly issues that Stephenie Meyer's young girls under-go).

Poor Bree Tanner! Her life prior to vampirism wasn't great: she hints at abuse from her father (and her buddy, Diego, was also having a lousy time of teenage, threatening to leave home). Yet one of the consequences of becoming a vampire is that their former life as a human fades into vagueness (tho' not for all vampires – when it suits the story, vampires like Edward, Carlisle and Jasper can recall their former lives clearly).

Like Bella Swan, Bree Tanner is another shy, bookish, modest and unassuming girl (she reads books!):

> If I were being honest with myself, I'd pretty much turned into a huge vampire nerd. I followed the rules, I didn't cause trouble, I hung out with the most unpopular kid in the group, and I always got home early. (24)

Bree is the same characterization as Bella Swan, really, tho' with a more troubled background (she's beaten by her father). Stephenie Meyer even includes the name Kristie in amongst the vampire gang (a reference perhaps to actress Kristen Stewart).

So Bree tries to keep her head down and stay out of the way of the jocks and the jerks in the newborn vampire army (Raoul, Kevin, etc). Like the little girl in a poor family of violent misfits, when all your siblings and relatives are jostling for scraps of food, Bree takes refuge on the floor next to the couch where your weird cousin resides, Freaky Fred.

✎

Some of the writing in *The Short Second Life of Bree Tanner* is clunky – there's a sequence where Bree Tanner and Diego are somehow able to jump thru the trees and get close enough to a solitary house in a field, so they're able to overhear Riley Biers and Victoria encountering Jane and the Volturi (without, of course, Jane, Felix, Victoria, etc, being able to sense them – and we know keen the senses of the Volturi mob are!).

It's in the final sequence that *The Short Second Life of Bree Tanner* really comes alive, when we view the Cullen coven (and Carlisle in particular) from a new perspective, when Bree Tanner arrives at the scene of the battle that climaxes *Eclipse* (in both the book and the movie). Now we see much more of Bree pleading not to fight, and more of her encounter with the Cullens, and Carlisle's attempts at saving her from the wrath of the vampire world's arch punishers, the Volturi.

In the *Eclipse* movie, all of this happens very quickly (Felix steps in and slays Bree swiftly, following Carlisle's pleas). In *The Short Second Life of Bree Tanner,* the outcome is never in doubt (once the Volturi arrive on the scene, we know they're going to clean everything up decisively), but it makes Bree's demise have much more dramatic weight.

The first person perspective means that Bree Tanner, without an overview of the battle (and told to keep her eyes closed by Jasper Whitlock), doesn't really know what's going on; she hears the werewolves but doesn't see them (she calls them howlers). Bree doesn't know everybody present, either (so she calls Edward 'the redhead').[2] There's an imaginative touch of using Edward's mind-reading capability, so that Bree is able to sneak past Jane's domination of the whole post-battle scene by telling Edward information in her head, knowing he'll pick it up).

THE HOST

THE HOST, THE BOOK.
Stephenie Meyer's follow-up to the *Twilight Saga* was *The Host* (2008), a laugh-out-loud, postmodern comedy romp about a sleazy, TV chat show host whose body is switched with a stripper after a *really* bad night in Las Vegas. No it wasn't! *The Host* was a sci-fi adventure story with a potentially intriguing narrative hook or gimmick: souls that can be transplanted into bodies. Essentially, *The Host* was a split personality/

---

2 Ironically, that's Jacob's name for Victoria.

Jekyll & Hyde sort of tale, where the soul (the Wanderer, a.k.a. Wanda), is placed inside the body of Melanie, another of Meyer's familiar young, female characters. The setting was a post-apocalyptic North America (with Arizona and the desert (Meyer's homeland) prominent).

The narrative structure was perhaps the most impressive aspect of *The Host* – it was a flashback structure, with the Wanderer being haunted by the memories of Melanie (including her romance with Jared), so that two female souls/ presences in one body are falling in love with one guy (an amusing twist on the erotic triangle of the *Twilight Saga*).

Meanwhile, as another book aimed at the teen market, the characters in *The Host* are playing out their emotions at Diva Level, where everything is always life or death: 'I'm not sure I can physically bear this looming goodbye' (84); 'It feels like he is part of me, that to separate us will tear the skin where we are joined' (95).

The Host also included some extras at the back of the book aimed at the teen audience: some topics for discussion (for a reading group), an interview with Stephenie Meyer, and another of Meyer's music playlists (featuring the usual suspects: U2, Linkin Park, My Chemical Romance, Foo Fighters, Placebo, the Killers, Travis and of course Muse, Meyer's own creative Muse).

I managed to get through only half of *The Host* (it's a long book, or it's cleverly printed to look like a long book). But I did watch all of the movie adaptation.

THE HOST, THE MOVIE.

The Host was duly filmed and released in 2013. Produced by Nick Wechsler, Steve Schwartz, Stephenie Meyer and Paula Mae Schwartz for Silver Reel/ Nick Wechsler Productions, written and directed by Andrew Niccol (b. 1964), *The Host* starred Max Irons, Jake Abel, Saoirse Ronan, Diane Kruger and William Hurt. Budgeted at US $40 million, *The Host* grossed a respectable $63m worldwide. It was filmed in New Mexico and Louisiana. Released: Mch 29, 2013. 125 mins.

Unfortunately, *The Host* was scuppered by flashy, ad agency visuals, a samey tone, a slow pace, boringly staged scenes and another bland girl at the centre.

Yes, once again, it was an S.M. story (a Stephenie Meyer story, not *that* sort of S. & M. story!) about a skinny, neurotic, white girl lost in America, encountering dodgy authority figures and with brothers/ guys in tow. Thus, again with the slow, melancholy music (courtesy of Antonio Pinto), again with the contact lenses, again with the slightly robotic acting, and again with the view of the future as a sleek, concrete-and-glass world. *The Host* was also marred by rehashed sci-fi ideas (we've been here before in many sci-fi novels, and in flicks such as *Invasion of the Body Snatchers* and countless possession and invasion yarns, like the *Men In Black* pictures).

And why do all futuristic, North American movies of late look and feel the same? Where the Haves (the villains), the bourgeoisie, the authorities live in classy, chrome-and-glass buildings, and where the Have-Nots (the heroes) struggle to survive in trailer parks and desert backwaters? (*The Host* inevitably recalls the truly awful *Hunger Games* movies, centring around whingeing, white, teenage girls).

The Host, crucially, didn't solve the problem of having two personalities reside in one actress. So it resorted to that age-old stand-by of the desperate screenwriter, the voiceover. Plus some moody close-ups of actress Saoirse Ronan wearing halo-ed contact lenses. Oh dear. Where is the imagination here?

In the novel of *The Host*, Stephenie Meyer uses her usual first-person narration, with the two voices dwelling inside Melanie. Easy to do in a book, of course. In a movie, there are many options, but the solution presented in the 2013 *Host* movie didn't really work, and certainly wasn't very cinematic.

So Melanie escapes the vaguely fascistic Seekers and stumbles thru the desert[3] (New Mexico does look lovely, as always), ending up at one of those futuristic communities that look like a Mormon/ Quaker/ Amish theme park. Yes, and look, here comes William Hurt playing a grizzled, old coot complete with shotgun and the no-nonsense 'tude of a grizzled, old coot out of a Sam Peckinpah Western. Phew! At least Hurt's Jebadiah can explain the plot to us! (Yes, he *is* called Jebadiah – there are too many names beginning with 'J' in this movie: Jared, Jeb, Jaime, etc).

✐

In 2016, Stephenie Meyer published a thriller, *The Chemist*. I haven't read *The Chemist* yet (tho' I'll happily watch the movie of it – far less painful than wading thru Meyer's prose, where every stupid little thing is explained).

---

3 Following a ridiculously OTT car crash in her Volvo which would kill any passenger.

the short
second life of
bree tanner

an eclipse novella

STEPHENIE MEYER
AUTHOR OF THE #1 BESTSELLING TWILIGHT SAGA

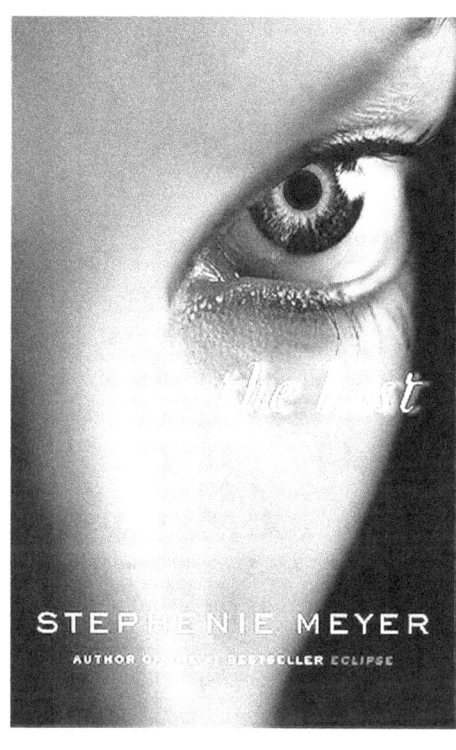

3

TWILIGHT AND *FIFTY SHADES OF GREY*

THE BOOKS.

Fifty Shades of Grey (2011) by E.L. James (Erika Mitchell/ Leonard, b. 1963, London) began as fan fiction about the *Twilight* series, but without vampires. Instead, the hook is portrayals of bondage and S/M sex, which're added to what is essentially a very formulaic romantic drama. (More books followed: *Fifty Shades Darker* (2012) and *Fifty Shades Freed* (2012), *Grey: Fifty Shades of Grey As Told by Christian* (2015), *Darker: Fifty Shades of Grey As Told By Christian* (2017) and *Freed: Fifty Shades Freed As Told By Christian* (2021). 125 million copies sold by 2015! 150 million by 2023!

Salman Rushie found *Fifty Spades of Grey* an awful book – it made *Twilight* look like *War and Peace*. Stephenie Meyer insisted that she hadn't read *50 Shades of Grey:* 'it's so not my genre. Erotica is not something I read. I don't even read traditional romance.'

It's a standard approach in fan fiction for relationships to be eroticized, or made more sexually explicit than in the original piece; it's also a familiar practice to employ homosexual, lesbian and queer takes on the original relationships. (Famous examples include homoerotic depictions of Dr Spock and Cpt Kirk in *Star Trek*).

Thus, *Fifty Shades of Cullen* and the *Twilight Saga* share numerous affinities – but many of them are elements of the romantic fiction genre: the mysterious, powerful (and rich) older man, the innocent, virginal, young woman, the fascination and the courtship, the aspects of danger or threat, and the power games. *The Twilight Saga* already contains many ingredients of dubious behaviour, from coercion, passive-aggressive manipulation and stalking to outright abuse: *50 Shades of Grey* merely exaggerates that (and sexualizes it).

Thus, *Filthy Shades of Grey* started out as a piece of fan fiction with the title *Master of the Universe*, published under the pseudonym Snowqueens Icedragon. 219,000 entries about *Twilight* are registered at the Fanfiction.net website.

So in *Fifty Shades of Black and Blue* Anastasia Steele is Bella Swan and Christian Grey is Edward Cullen, Katherine Kavanaugh is Rose Cullen, Mia is Alice, and so on. Even stranger: E.L. James has published versions of the *Fifty Shades of Grey* series from Christian Grey's point-of-view, as Stephenie Meyer had done with *Twilight* in *Midnight Sun*, from Edward's viewpoint: *Grey: Fifty Shades of Grey As Told by Christian*, *Darker: Fifty Shades of Grey As Told By Christian* and *Freed: Fifity Shades Freed As Told By Christian*.

✍

On paper, in theory, it shouldn't really be so successful: if someone suggested the idea back in 2005 or so – how about a bondage and domination version of *Twilight*? Same sort of characters, same sort of *milieu*, but with S/M? Back then, you might have predicted a niche market for such an item. Perhaps as fan fiction – which's how *50 Shades of Grey* began.

The massive success of *50 Sheds of Grey* is thus as inexplicable as that of the *Twilight Saga*.

The sex scenes and the bondage and sadomasochist ingredients in *Fifty Shades of Beige* are a side issue – they are gimmicks, marketing hooks, used to sell what is essentially another romantic drama. The really disturbing aspect of *Fifty Shades of Grey* is the power-gaming and exploitation in the central relationship: and not just that Christian Grey is a controlling, domineering personality, but that Anastasia Steele submits to him so completely.

The prose style in *Fifty Shades of Lame* is stodgy and dull. Phrases repeat with thudding regularity: *Crap. Holy shit. Oh my*, etc. Alas, the viewpoint is not only first person (like *Twilight*), it's also written in the present tense: the most irritating of all narrational voices (and depressingly common in contemporary fiction).

> *Oh my...* He wants me, Christian Grey, Greek god, wants me, and I want *him*, here... now, in the elevator. (78)
>
> •
>
> *Oh my.* I can barely contain myself, lying helpless, watching him move

1 Did James choose the name Christian because it's Stephenie Meyer's husband's name?

gracefully around my room. It's a heady aphrodisiac. (192)

•

Holy shit. He's looking at me expectantly, his eyes growing colder. *Shit.*

'Spank me, please... Sir,' I whisper...

'I want to see your face while I spank you, Anatasia,' he murmurs, all the while softly rubbing my backside.

His hand moves down between the cheeks of my behind, and he pushes against my sex, and the full feeling is... I moan. I, the sensation is exquisite.

'This is for pleasure, Anastasia, mine and yours,' he whispers.

He lifts his hand and brings it down in a resounding slap against the junction of my thighs, my behind and my sex. (364-5)

So, as with *Twilight* and Bella Swan, we have to spend time with the boringly predictable and predictably boring Ana Steele. She is much more than an observer figure, who can be ignored: she is the heroine of the piece. Everything is happening to her. We are stuck in Steele's mind a lot of the time – and it's not a great place to be. In fact, it's a lot worse than Christian Grey's infamous 'Red Room of Pain'.

The narrative structure of *Fifty Shades of Gay* follows the romantic drama model closely – and also the first *Twilight* book: the anxious, plain, young woman, the confident, handsome, older man, the difference in class, status and wealth, etc. In *Twilight*, the obstacle keeping the lovers apart is that one's human and the other's a vampire; in *Fifty Shades of Grey*, it's Anastasia's reluctance to commit, the differences in social status, and her confusion and anxiety about Grey and his lifestyle (embodied in the MacGuffin of the contract between 'the dominant' and 'the submissive', and Anastasia dragging her feet about signing it in blood).

So the moral dilemma for Anastasia Steele is: do I hook up with this guy or not? He's handsome and rich, but he's an asshole – and a controlling, aggressive, psychotic asshole, too. (And there's a secondary question: is this the best jerk out there, or can I do better? It's the age-old dilemma for a romantic heroine in a romantic story: do I wait for better, or do I shack up with this one?).

Fifty Shades of Snow White is a romantic fantasy. It's *Cinderella*, like *Twilight*, where a plain, clumsy, unremarkable girl can snag a powerful man (and be revealed at the end of the fairy tale as a Beautiful Princess). A bondage/ domination fairy tale, then, the Disney Princess brand of pretty dresses but with leather and chains. Ana Steele shares numerous traits with Bella Swan, including the submissive, masochistic persona. Steele is even a bookish girl like Bella – she's a wannabe journo, and later she works for a publisher. (Even her look is the same –

long, brown hair, frumpy clothes, and *Fifty Shades* also has a North-West U.S.A. setting, in the movie version).

✎

From a social, political position, *Fifty Shades of Grey* is a disturbing franchise in its glorification of masochism, of a person's assent to coercion and exploitation. Whether the victim is male, female, transgender, transsexual or squirrel, it's a horrible portrayal of enslavement.

From a feminist perspective, *50 Shades of Gravy* is rancid. And feminists have attacked the piece repeatedly (just as they targetted *Twilight* as another celebration of female victimhood). Some feminists have seen the *50 Shades* franchise, despite it being written by a woman (and the films partly scripted by a woman), as an exaltation of male predation and abuse.

'OH MY!' – THE *FIFTY SHADES* MOVIES.

The inevitable movie adaptation of *Fifty Shades of Grey* arrived in 2015. Produced by Michael De Luca,[2] Jeb Brody, Marcus Viscidi, E.L. James and Dana Brunetti (4 guys, 1 woman) for Focus/ De Luca/ Trigger Street/ Universal, wr. by Kelly Marcel (with Mark Bomback and another screenwriter polishing the script, uncredited),[3] and dir. by Sam Taylor-Wood, it starred Dakota Johnson[4] (daughter of Don Johnson and Melanie Griffith), and Belfast-born Jamie Dornan.[5] Music was by superstar composer Danny Elfman. Editing was by the legendary Anne Coates (and others). Released Feb 13, 2015. 125 mins.

Fifty Shades of Grey was based out of North Shore Studios in Vancouver, which the *Twilight Saga* also used. *Fifty Shades* also filmed around the city (as the *Twilight* series did), and used Vancouver to stand in for Seattle (as the *Twilights* did). It's likely that some crew in the production worked on both movie franchises.

Several in the production team[6] have since described author E.L. James as a pain in the neck on set, keen to control every aspect of her book, and there were many arguments. James was a novice writer out of her depth in amongst veteran film people who'd worked on numerous productions. In the 'making of' documentaries for the third *Fifty Shades* movie, James is standing right next to the film director watching the

2 De Luca is a veteran producer of numerous movies, many of which you will have seen (*Austin Powers, The Mask, Rush Hour, Boogie Nights*, the *Blade* series, etc). .
3 Other writers might've been involved, too, but they have been forbidden to put their head above the trenches unless they want to spend the rest of their lives in a rubber sack at the bottom of the Hudson.
4 An obvious casting choice was Kristen Stewart. But casting Stewart, as with Robert Pattinson, would be highly unlikely.
5 Charlie Hunnam had originally been cast, but left for several reasons, one being scheduling.
6 Including the director and one of the writers.

takes on a monitor. Some film producers visit the set occasionally (many don't), some deal with an issue then leave, but James is right there, keeping a beady eye on everything. (James later admitted to suffering from Impostor Syndrome, where you feel acute guilt and bottomless depression over earning million$ from inflicting garbage on punters).

Fifty Shades of Brown is a striking example of the gender of the people behind the camera not making any diff. whatsoever to the outcome: *Fifth Shades of Grey* may be a story centred on a woman, written by a woman, partly scripted by a woman, and directed by a woman, but the result is thoroughly masculinist and patriarchal. Worse, it is also regarded as anti-feminist and promoting chauvinism and even abuse.

This is because Western society is patriarchal thru and thru, and commercial cinema is also a part of that patriarchal society, with movies in turn reflecting that society. Thus, films can't be anything other than patriarchal, even if they determinedly and carefully aim to be otherwise (and that also includes *avant garde*/ experimental/ radical films, or films which consciously subvert the norms of patriarchal society).

When you watch *Fifty Shades of Clay* with *The Twilight Saga* in mind, it all fits into place. In a way, the *Fifty Shades of Grey* series is simply the *Twilight* series but with the sex scenes and 'adult' material that the Young Adult novels and the 'PG-13' movies couldn't show.

No matter how you look at it, how sympathetic you are with the characters and their plight, how forgiving you are, *50 Shades of Grey* is a truly terrible movie. It's a tepid, lame, limp romance where you just want to slap the two leads: he's an arrogant, spoilt pr*ck, and she's so passive, so wan, so weedy, and so excruciatingly *dim* and *stupid*, you wonder how she got this far through life. How she could even manage to open a door. How she could find her way to a busstop. (The way that Dakota Johnson plays Anastasia Steele is so aggravating – in every scene she's anxious and about to burst into tears.[7] Always biting her lip. And she's been given a 'no make-up' look[8] which, for some bizarre reason, includes pink cheeks, like she's a petrified five year-old in the scary adult world of spoilt, messed-up, white bachelors).

Fifty Shades of Oy Vey boasted an awful script (by Kelly Marcel, Mark Bomback and another screenwriter), dreary direction, and performances never juicier than daytime soap opera. The smug secondary characters (such as Kate) are especially nauseating. *Of course Fifty Shades of Hate* included a sprinkling of pop songs – aimed squarely at the target

7 And Johnson employs lots of breathing acting – over-dubbed breaths and gasps, as Kristen Stewart does in the *Twilight Saga.*
8 Courtesy of make-up artist Victoria Down.

market of middle-aged women ('wuss rock', as *The Simpsons* calls it).[9] *Of course* there're flashy cars and fancy restaurants and fashionable apartments decorated in the trendy, minimalist style. (The critics laid into the movie, tho' some bravely spoke up for it – they were later taken into the Red Room of Shame by Nazi stormtroopers, never to be seen again).

Further, the tone of *50 Shades of Greyscale* is samey throughout; the same scenarios repeat with little variation; the music (sorry, Danny Elfman!) dribbles and putters thru every scene to no effect;[10] and, needless to say, the staging and camerawork is hellishly dull.

Come on, this movie cost 40 million dollars! Can't the filmmakers do *something* a little cinematic? By comparison, the first *Twilight* movie, costing $38 million, was wonderfully inventive.

It took me a long time to get through watching *Fifty Shades of Grey* – I used my usual method for watching dreck: very short doses, with lengthy gaps for recovery. So, ten minutes of crud, followed by weeks of watching something – anything! – else.

Fifty Shades of Neigh is one of those abysmal movies which should have a Health Warning: *think carefully before you watch this movie because YOU WILL NEVER HAVE THOSE TWO HOURS AGAIN.*

This is probably the lowest point of Danny Elfman's amazing career (*Batman, Mars Attacks, The Simpsons, Edward Scissorhands, Spiderman*), cinematically and musically. Elfman delivers the default soundtrack of 99% of drama on TV and in film in the Western world: plinky, plonky piano (a disgusting form of music which should be outlawed on pain of death). And puttering electronica which meanders through scenes. Only once or twice does the Elfman Magic reveal itself, in a choral piece late in the movie, even tho' religious, choral music like this is totally out of place. (Also composing music were Peter Bateman and David Buckley).

A fantasy for manic depressives with low self-esteem – like the *Twilight* series, but without cool vampires and action scenes to change the pace. (*Fifty Shades of Grey* is a talky picture, like so many rom-coms and rom-dramas – it's actually conversation, not kissing or sex, which carries the courtship and romance in the romantic genre. A romantic movie boils down to a series of conversations. Hence, a Jane Austen or Thomas Hardy novel of 150 or more years ago can be supremely romantic, but there are no sex scenes (certainly no bondage scenes!), and often not much cuddling or kissing, either).

The 2015 *Shady* movie ends with a marvellous moment when

9 Ellie Goulding, Sia, Skylar Grey, Vaults, Annie Lennox, Jessie Ware, Beyoncé, Awoination, etc, plus a couple of oldies – the Rolling Stones and Screamin' Jay Hawkins.
10 The diaoramas, blue screen additions and car scenes look fake.

Anastasia Steele says, 'No' to her tormentor, as she walks out on him. But it's too little and far too late.

Many film critics found *50 Shades of Grey* awful, but this was one of those movies where the reviews – or even the general reaction to the movie in the media, or the movie's PR image – had no effect whatsoever on the box office performance.

So no matter how execrable *Fifty Shades of Grey* was, it did ma$$ive business for a romantic drama – and one without stars, and with sex scenes and nudity, and rated 'R' (making over $400 million overseas, but far less in the U.S.A. – $166 million. You can bet that the sophisticated audiences in Europe loved it – it's exactly the sort of movie that inherits the classy erotica label from *Emmanuelle* and *Last Tango In Paris* in thr Seventies). Not as big as *Basic Instinct* (1992), perhaps, but amazingly strong for a movie of this type, and for an 'R' rated flick (the producers were aiming for an 'R' rating, knowing full well that 'NC-17' rated movies die a death at the box office, and many distributors/ exhibitors won't touch them).

In many territories, it was a huge hit for Universal Studios. And so the *Fifty Shades of Fey* sequels followed rapidly (in 2017 and 2018) and all were released around Valentine's Day as date movies. And bearing in mind that the budget was $40 million, and the gross was $571 million, someone somewhere made lots of money). The next two *Fifty Shades* movies grossed in the region of $382 million and $372 million, stupendous numbers for an 'R' rated franchise.

Nobody could've predicted that the movie adaptation of *Fifty Shades of Grey* would do such great business, nor the books. Actually, movies with more graphic depictions of sex do occasionally break out of the niche markets and enter the mainstream: *Emmanuelle, Deep Throat* and *Last Tango In Paris* in the 1970s, for example, or, more recently, *Basic Instinct, 9 1/2 Weeks,* and the neo-noirs and erotic thrillers of the early 1990s (*Body of Evidence, The Last Seduction, Jade* and *Red Rock West*).

FIFTY SHADES OF BLACK

The garbage that is the *Fifty Shades of Grey* franchise has been spoofed many times. Thank the Movie Gods for send-ups like the parody *Fifty*

Shades of Black (2016), written by Marlon Wayans and Rick Alvarez, prod. by Rick Alvarez, Marlon Wayans, Megan Forde, Matt Johnson, Glendon Palmer, Michael Tiddes, Steven Squillante, Paddy Cullen, and Stuart Ford, and dir. by Michael Tiddes. Released Jan 29, 2010. 92 mins.

Here every single piece of the *Fifty Shades of Grey* schtick is skewered in a series of scattershot, crude and often very funny jokes.

Critics loathe movie spoofs of this kind (*Vampires Suck, Breaking Wind, Date Movie, Epic Movie,* etc), and many viewers seem to groan with despair (not ecstasy), but I love them. Every single one.

(Pretty much everybody seems to misunderstand what a movie spoof is – almost every professional review makes category errors in assessing send-ups from Mel Brooks, the Zucker-Abrahams-Zucker team, Jason Friedberg and Aaron Seltzer, and the Wayans Brothers).

It's delightful how little *Fifty Shades of Black* has to nudge the *Fifty Shades of Grey* franchise to reveal its idiocies and banalities. Like Black being a stalker, and turning up at the hardware store where Hannah Steele (Kali Hawk) works:

'Are you a stalker?' she asks.

'Yeah, but that's OK, right?' he replies.

The script of *Fifty Shades of Black* is happily crude, never giving up an opportunity to mention fist-fucking, or anal sex, or sex toys, or to include plenty of swearing (much more than the ridiculously prim original movie, *50 Shades of Hay*).

Marlon Wayans plays Christian Grey as a major weasel, coward, Momma's Boy, and generally useless guy. But it's not solely Wayans who's scoring jokes off Kali Hawk – in *Fifty Shades of Black*, she gets to play the gag man, too (and she also beats Hell out of him!).

Squeezed into *Fifty Shades of Black* is an impressive array of pop cultural quotations and allusions – many're delivered by Marlon Wayans. Indeed, part of *Fifty Shades of Black* seems like a stand-up routine cleverly shoe-horned into a rom-com format. Wayans' Grey is referencing U.S. Presidents, pop stars, actors, and of course 100s of movies (the Wayans Brothers, like Jason Friedberg and Aaron Seltzer, Zucker-Abrahams-Zucker and every director of movie spoofs, are major film buffs). Black icons such as cited, too: Tiger Woods, Denzel Washington, Barack Obama, Bill Cosby, etc. After all, this is a movie called *Fifty Shades of Black*, and it features two black leads.

Fifty Shades of Grey (2015).

PART TWO

◯

THE *TWILIGHT* SERIES

I couldn't believe the rush of emotion pulsing through me – just because he'd happened to look at me for the first time in a half-dozen weeks.

Stephenie Meyer, *Twilight* (63)

1

THE *TWILIGHT* SERIES:
INTRODUCTION

'You... made... me faint,' I accused him dizzily.
'*What am I going to do with you*?' he groaned in exasperation.
'Yesterday I kiss you, and you attack me! Today you pass out on me!'

Stephenie Meyer, *Twilight* (279)

THE *TWILIGHT* FRANCHISE

What is the *Twilight* franchise?

It is millions of fans (Twihards/ fang fans/ fanpires).

It is four novels (totalling 591,000 words), plus several spin-off books.

It is the books re-packaged, reprinted and translated in many formats.[1]

It is five movies and two spoof movies.

It is several TV documentaries.

It is a host of home entertainment releases and box sets.

It is a mass of merchandizing and tie-ins.

It is a vast pile of fan fiction.

It is an enormous amount of discussion online and in print.

A big North American/ Western movie franchise will often include some of the following: a Broadway musical (the *Twilight Saga* is tailor-made for a *Phantom of the Opera*-style musical); straight theatrical

---

[1] And a comic – a comic was produced of the *Twilight Saga* (2010) – with Korean artist Young Kim providing the visuals, and published by Yen Press.

adaptations; a TV series (live-action or animated – the *Twilight* series is ideal for an animated kids' show); soundtrack albums (including 'inspired by' and 'image' albums); pop singles and pop promos; video/ computer games; tie-in books and guidebooks; and of course the giant spread of merchandizing and toys (Tee shirts, calendars, jewellery, posters, duvets, lunch boxes, fangs, garlic, crucifixes, fake blood, coffins, cloaks, etc). The *Twilight Saga* as a franchise included many of these items.

The *Twi*-books have sold 160 million copies (by 2020), and *Twilight* spent 235 weeks on the bestseller list of the *New York Times.*

The *Twilight* movies were huge hits: *Twilight* grossed $402 million worldwide, *New Moon* $687m, *Eclipse* $706m, *Breaking Dawn 1* $684m and *Breaking Dawn 2* $829m. (A total gross of about $3.3 billion).

What Hollywood loves best of all is a modestly priced movie (or even a cheapo) that does great business: *Pretty Woman, Home Alone* or *American Grafitti*. At a rumoured $38 million, *Twilight* could be placed in that category: a modestly (or medium) budgeted flick that went ballistic at the box office.

THE *TWILIGHT SAGA* BOOKS
(Year of first edition)

Twilight, 2005
New Moon, 2006
Eclipse, 2007
Breaking Dawn, 2008
The Short Second Life of Bree Tanner, 2010
Twilight Saga (comic), 2010
The Twilight Saga: The Official Illustrated Guide, 2011
Life and Death, 2015
Midnight Sun, 2020

THE *TWILIGHT SAGA* MOVIES
(Year of first release)

Twilight, 2008
New Moon, 2009

Eclipse, 2010
Breaking Dawn, Part 1, 2011
Breaking Dawn, Part 2, 2012
Vampires Suck, 2010
Breaking Wind, 2012

The word count for the four *Twilight* books:
Twilight 118,501
New Moon 132,807
Eclipse 147,930
Breaking Dawn 192,196
(591,000 words in all)

PUBLISHING *TWILIGHT.*

Stephenie Meyer had written the first *Twilight* book for herself, with no publisher or agent in mind. As she has often related (on the *Twilight* PR circuit), the idea started from a dream she had June 2, 2003 (when she was 30), involving a girl and a vampire in a meadow (in the dream, he talks, she listens, he loves her but he wants to kill her [TS, 3]). The *Twilight* story unfolded to describe what came before and after the meadow scene. Meyer said she kept writing, following the story, only going back to the beginning later, fleshing out aspects of the story that led up to the meadow scene (TS, 5). *Twilight*'s first draft was finished on Aug 29, 2003.

At the time, Stephenie Meyer was a full-time Mom with a young family. She didn't go to writing classes, wasn't trained, and didn't study a course (however, she studied English Literature at Brigham Young University). Meyer has since recalled that her elder sister Emily persuaded her to do something with the novel once it was finished. The journey from first-time writer to published author seems to have been relatively swift (Meyer wasn't sending round her manuscripts for years like many wannabe writers). Meyer mailed 15 letters to literary agencies and it was Writers' House that bit (her agent was Jodi Reamer, assistant Genevieve Cagne-Hawes replied to Meyer's initial letter, and Megan Tingley decided to go ahead with publication). The book was in a bidding war among publishers, with Little, Brown and Company winning (the deal, made in Nov, 2003, was for three books for $750,000 – not bad for a new author).

✎

Of the title *Twilight*, Stephenie Meyer noted on her website: 'It isn't absolutely perfect; to be honest, I don't think there is a perfect title for this book (or if there is, I've never heard it)'. *Forks* was an early title. The *Twilight* novel have the one-word chapter titles of airport fiction: 'Family', 'Killer', 'Visitor', 'Flight', 'Cheese', 'Jelly', etc.

Stephenie Meyer likes to include the title within the books; so, in *Twilight*, Edward ruminates on twilight being the best time for a vamp; in *Eclipse,* Jacob Black points out that his sun has been eclipsed by Edward (Bella regards Jake as the warm sun in her life – Edward is the 'midnight sun', the title of the book of the romance told from his point-of-view published in 2020).

The book covers of the *Twilight Saga* for the North American and British editions featured black backgrounds with photographs of objects in white and red hues: a red apple for *Twilight*,[2] a white and red flower for *New Moon*, a red ribbon for *Eclipse,* chess pieces for *Breaking Dawn*, and an hour-glass for *Bree Tanner* (authors don't usually select their book covers, publishers do). The book covers were sombre, rather abstract and thematic, hinting only allusively at their contents. (Book covers for foreign language editions and for markets outside of the U.S.A. changed the covers considerably – *The Twilight Saga: The Official Illustrated Guide* features a selection of foreign language book covers: some are abstract and allusive, but many include photographs or illustrations of young women, staring out at the reader with solemn expressions).

The *Twilight* books became a publishing phenomenon. And this was for a new writer with no track record. 100 million sales! According to Stephenie Meyer's website, 29 million *Twilight* books were sold in 2008 and 26.5 million in 2009. But every so often, the book publishing world will do this: it will go nuts for a particular project, creating a bidding war. The author (and her agent) sit back and watch the wolves fight. The *Twilight* book was sold to the big American publisher Little, Brown for $750,000. It's occurred recently with *Fifty Shades of Grey* (E.L. James)*,* John Grisham's thrillers, and Dan Brown and *The Da Vinci Code.*

Stephenie Meyer, like many authors before her, must've been stunned. Meanwhile, veteran hacks, who've been writing for years, were fuming. They attacked the books – Stephen King called Meyer 'not very good': 'she can't write a darn'. It's true, tho' – the *Twilight* books aren't great pieces of literature, as with the books of Dan Brown and Jeffrey Archer.

But what the ticked off pundits and resentful writers forget, of course, is that these over-the-top publishing deals and phenomena – the *Harry Potter* series being the most lucrative of recent times – throw light

---

2 The apple can have any symbolic meaning you fancy. Meyer referred, of course, to the apple in the *Bible* ('forbidden fruit'), the apple in *Snow White*, and in Greek mythology,

on books again, and they get people reading books, and buying books.

TRUE LOVE: FANTASY: INNOCENCE: MARRIAGE.

The *Twilight* series is founded on some simple but very important elements from the romance literary genre: (1) true love, (2) fantasy, (3) innocence, and (4) marriage.

(1) True love – *above all*. This is paramount, and comes at the top of the list of attributes of the traditional romance genre (rather than the modern romance genre, or the postmodern romance genre). True ❤❤❤ above all – for Stephenie Meyer, this means unconditional love, and selfless love. It means giving your all to the other person, even if it means hurting yourself (this is where the masochism comes in), and Bella Swan denying the creepier or downright offensive aspects of her beloved.

Critics have complained that the *Twilight* series enshrines an abusive relationship in Bella and Edward, which includes psychological as well as physical coercion. Stephenie Meyer's answer is the same answer she gives to everything, through the books themselves: *true love*. She means: in true love, you give everything.

(2) *Fantasy*. But we are dealing with *fantasy fiction*, folks: this is the *dream* of true love, the *idea* of true love, the *yearning* for true love. It's the *idea* that true love *should* exist, and *ought* to exist, even if it actually doesn't! Even if it has never existed anywhere in any relationship! At any time in history! In this or any other dimension!

The *idea* of love. The *idea*.

We are discussing the *fantasy* end of the enormous romance genre, which takes in a huge variety of forms of romantic fiction. The *Twilight* series is fantasy fiction *par excellence*. It's got vampires and werewolves! It's got immortal beings! It's got people who can fly, resurrect, use telepathy, predict the future, the whole schmeer! It's not 'realistic' fiction, urban fiction, crime fiction, or, Hell, cowboy fiction. It's fantasy, and it's romance.

(3) *Innocence* is a key element in *The Twilight Saga*. The series is not intended to be 'gritty' or 'realistic'. Thus, the Cullens live a fantasy lifestyle of upmarket luxury, the love shared between Edward and Bella is 'pure', and the sex is not raunchy and sleazy.[3] Stephenie Meyer is writing for young adults, and isn't interested in delivering something nasty and crude (leave it up to the spoof movies of the *Twilight Saga* to do that!). The *Twilight* series is *fantasy*, and *romance*, and a *romance fantasy*, and

---

3 The lovers kiss and caress, but not beyond first base! After a few meetings, in many another love story, they would've progressed to more than chaste kisses, or Edward stroking Bella's jaw. But no, the *Twilight* series plays it very innocent: hands stay above the waist! Stephenie Meyer declined to provide the sex scenes that her editor asked for.

a *fantasy romance*. It's not *meant* to be 'real life', to be a 'gritty', 'dark', 'realistic' tale. It's Jane Austen Lite not Fyodor Dostoievsky Heavy.

> Next to being married, a girl likes to be crossed in love a little now and then.

Jane Austen, *Pride and Prejudice*

Stephenie Meyer consciously avoided graphic depictions of sex in the *Twilight Saga*: she just wasn't interested: 'There's a reason my books have a lot of innocence. That's the sort of world I live in.' Meyer was asked by her editor Rebecca Davis or Megan Tingley[4] to include some sex scenes, but Meyer refused. Meyer doesn't read erotica, and hasn't read the *50 Shades of Grey hommages* (steals) of her work. Meyer insisted that *Twilight* was about 'love, not lust', about 'life, not death'.

Anyway, there was no need to Stephenie Meyer to add graphic scenes to her *Twilight* novels, because other people did it for her, including Erika James with the *50 Shades of Grey* cash-in series. And the *Twilight* movies added multiple layers of sensuality with luscious photography, beautiful stars, fashionable clothes, and more kissing and cuddling than fifty other romantic films.

(4) *Marriage.* Tie a bow, chime the bells, cut the cake, whisper the vows, wear the dress, live the dream... The *Twilight* series enshrines traditional marriage just like the romance genre does. Yes, it's Fairy Tale Time, it's Cinderella Time, it's finding your Prince and falling in lerrrve with him and getting married at the end of it all.

Bella Swan's an old-fashioned girl, ultimately. She valorizes romance and marriage. She would've preferred if it if her Ma and Pa had stayed together (in an ideal world), and she wants to be Mrs Edward Cullen. Bella wants to be a wife (even tho' throughout *Eclipse* she's unimpressed by wedlock).

So sue me! This isn't a postmodern, radical, left-wing, lesbian, separatist, feminist series of books and movies! It's not about challenging patriarchal society from a feminist stand-point, or about establishing an enclave of radical, lesbian, separatist women in rural Oregon, or about encircling the Pentagon with hundreds of thousands of peace protesters and melting the War Machine into pink goo from the sheer power of love.

It's a romantic story about two teenagers set in a high school in small-town U.S. of A., and one of them happens to be a vampire. That's all. It's not radical, feminist fiction, it's not an incendiary ideological

---

4 Meyer's other editors include Aysa Munchnick and Megan Tingley. I'm not sure if the editor referred to by Meyer is Davis or Munchnick or Tingley. In the *Twilight* novel, Tingley is cited.

attack on Western civilization, and it is not a novel aiming to bring North American capitalism to its knees (you wish!).

Perhaps even more prominent as a genre than romance in the *Twilight Saga* is *relationships* – these are relationship novels, where family relationships and friendships (at school and at home) are as significant as romance (so it's not only 'Team Edward', 'Team Jacob' and 'Team Bella', it's also 'Team Swan', 'Team Cullen', 'Team School', etc). And in blockbuster popular fiction, relationship fiction is everywhere. Sometimes 'family saga' is used as another term for a relationship story. The *Twilight* series has been dubbed a 'saga', but actually it isn't, really: a proper saga is a story that explores several generations, often with rival clans and institutions, and with a wider, socio-political scope.

STRUCTURE.

The *Twilight* books are simple, structurally, in terms of romantic relationships:

Twilight	Bella and Edward
New Moon	Bella and Jacob
Eclipse	Bella, Edward and Jacob
Breaking Dawn	Bella and Edward (and Renesmee)

TWILIGHT AND CLASSIC LITERATURE.

The form and the influences and the model for the *Twilight Saga* is not contemporary fiction so much as 19th century fiction – *Twilight* is Jane Austen or Charlotte Brontë in modern dress. The models for Stephenie Meyer's *Twilight* stories are authors such as Emily Brontë, Charlotte Brontë, Jane Austen and Thomas Hardy. But it's using modern, 21st century fashion, with modern dialogue, modern cultural references, contemporary props like cars and cel phones, etc.

Thus, the *Twilight* tales include archaic, 19th century tropes such as women staying virginal until marriage (despite both sides wanting to), women refusing men even when they appear in their bedrooms (and they are both tempted), marriage, sex after (and within) marriage, death in childbirth, and so on.

The *Twilight Saga* are *fiction*, not 'real life'. Altho' the outward attributes appear contemporary, and approximating to 'real life' in North America in 2005 – like the clothes, the schools, the vocabulary in the conversations – the fundamental relationships, the concerns, and the goals are distinctly 19th century.

Or put it like this: we know that Edward Cullen would be very happy in 1870s Europe or North America… And Bella Swan would be, too.

TWILIGHT AND *JANE EYRE.*

Stephenie Meyer has cited *Jane Eyre* as an influence on *Twilight*: of course, Edward makes a decently gloomy, brooding Mr Rochester, and Bells is a Jane Eyre figure, someone who 'does what she thinks is right, and she takes it – and she doesn't mouth off about it', Meyer remarked (TS, 41). There is also some of Jane in Edward, Meyer reckoned (TS, 44). Meyer admitted that 'Jane Eyre was one of my best friends growing up. She really was a big part of my life' (TS, 41). (Snobby critics carped that some of the audience of the *Twilight* series wouldn't recognize the *Jane Eyre* references. Maybe, but surely some readers of *Twilight* have gone on to explore the classic works of Austen, Brontë, Eliot, Shelley *et al.* And for that alone Meyer has to be applauded).

The links btn Charlotte Brontë's novel of 1847 and the *Twilight Saga* are easy to see: the heroine is an outsider,[5] an orphan, proud but moody, passionate but also depressive, a fish out of water (no one understands her), but she's the star of her own melodramatic story (her life).

> 'And this her voice,' I added. 'She is all here: her heart, too. God bless you sir! I am glad to be so near you again.'
> 'Jane Eyre! – Jane Eyre!' was all he said.
> 'My dear master,' I answered, 'I am Jane Eyre: I have found you out – I am come back to you.'
> 'In truth? – in the flesh? My living Jane?'
> 'You touch me, sir – you hold me, and fast enough: I am not cold like a corpse, not vacant like air, am I?'
> 'My living darling!'

Charlotte Brontë, *Jane Eyre*

Jane Eyre is also a fighter and a survivor – key elements of Stephenie Meyer's central charas. Meyer's young women will be pushed around, have to do things they don't want to do, but they always survive. Eyre struggles through, too, despite several set-backs. And she gets her man – yes, it's really Eyre who snags Edward Rochester (altho' the domineering and rather sarcastic master of the house thinks he's in charge and in control all the time).

> Why was I always suffering, always browbeaten, always accused, forever condemned?

5 There is no mention of Bella Swan's friends in Phoenix, and she doesn't contact them in the movies.

Why could I never please? Why was it useless to try to win any one's favour? (46)

MORE LITERARY REFERENCES.

The four *Twilight* novels were linked to literary classics: *Pride and Prejudice* in *Twilight*, *Romeo and Juliet* in *New Moon*, *Wuthering Heights* in *Eclipse*, and *The Merchant of Venice* and *A Midsummer Night's Dream* in *Breaking Dawn*. Other literary references in the *Twilight Saga* include the *Bible*, Jean-Jacques Rousseau, Montague Summers, and Geoffrey Chaucer. (Many of the authors and the texts are staples in English Literature classes).

Charlotte Brontë, Emily Brontë, Jane Austen, William Shakespeare, L.M. Montgomery (*Anne of Green Gables*), and Orson Scott Card were some of Meyer's favourite authors.

A Midsummer Night's Dream was one of two William Shakespeare plays alluded to in the novel of *Breaking Dawn*. Because *A Midsummer Night's Dream* is about loving the wrong person, and mistaken identities (which is 'made right in this glittery instant of fairy dust' at the end, Stephenie Meyer noted [TS, 41]). *A Midsummer Night's Dream* was used as an inspiration for the visual design of the wedding in the *Breaking Dawn* movie (the play has been adapted for the movies many times).

Oddly, Stephenie Meyer has remarked that she doesn't enjoy *Wuthering Heights* as a whole, but rather some of the characters, and some of the sections. The relation to the *Twilight* series for Meyer was the element of choice (choice being absolutely primary among the issues the *Twilight Saga* explores): in *Wuthering Heights*, it was Cathy's choice between Edgar Linton and Heathcliff: 'I think about that part a lot. It's one of those things that stays with you' (TS, 49).

And of course our resident Eng. Lit. geek Bella S. says she's already read the reading list handed out by the English tutor (Emily Brontë,6 Geoffrey Chaucer, and the two Williams, Faulker and Shakespeare).

The 2008 *Twilight* movie toned down portraying Bella Swan as a bookish girl from the 2005 novel – she visits a bookstore to buy a book, sure, and she is sometimes shown writing, but she isn't consuming classic novels by the truckload. So it's a Jane Austen romantic movie but the heroine isn't the Book Geek of the 2005 text. (Similarly, the movie doesn't get into other classes at school, such as literature or mathematics. However, the *New Moon* rectified that by introducing an English class early on, with its evocations of *Romeo and Juliet*.)

(In Japan, Bella Swan would be classed as a 'shut-in', an *otaku* or

---

6 Bella re-reads *Wuthering Heights*, one of the intertexts with *Twilight* (T, 30).

geek who stays in their bedroom with computers, video games, TV and cel phones, rather than venturing outside. It's a social problem that has drawn a good deal of media attention. (And in *New Moon*, Bellsie becomes a major 'shut-in').)

ITALY.

Among the Italian influences in the *Twilight Saga* are: the Volturi; scenes set in Italy; the soon-to-be-lovers go to an Italian restaurant; the Cullens cook an Italian meal for Bella (they think she's Italian with a name like Bella); *Romeo and Juliet* (which's set in Verona – tho' of course William Shakespeare never left England); Alice drives a Ferrari (and her high fashion outfits bear Italian influences, as do some of the other characters); Carlisle is the 'Stregoni benefici' (and spends time in Italy, including with the dreaded Volturi); in the *Twihard* movies there are Italian dress and suit designers (and a counterpart are the Latin influences: the honeymoon's in Brazil and Rio, Edward holes up in Rio during his *Romeo and Juliet* 'Mantua' exile, etc).

LOVE IN *THE TWILIGHT SAGA*.

Losing Edward for Bella was like losing her whole life: she was living so much in and through the beloved, like classic lovers in poetry and romantic fiction. As Bella puts it in *New Moon*:

> It *was* like someone had died – like *I* had died. Because it had been more than just losing the truest of true loves, as if that were not enough to kill anyone. It was losing a whole future, a whole family – the whole life that I'd chosen… (398)

One of the key forerunners of this kind of heterosexual love in literature is courtly love poetry, composed by mediæval troubadours in France in the 12th and 13th centuries, the *Minnesängers* of Germany, and the *trouvères* of Northern France, later refined and polished to perfection by the Italian *stil novisti* ('new sweet style') and the great Italian poets Dante Alighieri (in the *Vita Nouva*) and Francesco Petrarch (in the *Canzoniere*). In the *Rime Sparse* (*Canzoniere*), the Petrarch-poet exalts Laura's eyes as nothing less than the way to Heaven, as one of the great *canzoni* (number 70), explains:

> Gentil mia Donna, l'veggio
> nel mover de' vostr' occhi un dolce lume
> che mi mostra la via ch' al ciel conduce
> (My noble Lady, I see in the moving of your eyes a sweet light that shows me the way that leads to Heaven) (7: 1-3)

This is love poetry (*fin amor*) as a highly sophisticated cultural pastime, where the lyrical praise of the beloved enhances the literary skill of the poet. Thus, the more passionately the love-poet glorifies the beloved woman, the greater it elevates his art (and ego). Stephenie Meyer draws on this ultra-romantic approach to celebrating the beloved, how Bella is madly in love with Edward and extols his virtues all the time: he's 'perfect and beautiful to an excruciating degree'; 'his beauty stunned my mind'.

Love in the *Twilight Saga* is all or nothing, it's life or death, it's now or never. It's the lover living wholly for the other person. It's the lover doing anything for their beloved. Love or death, and nothing in between (what's in between is the limbo of in-betweenness[7] that Bella lives in during the months following Edward's departure).

As director Jean-Luc Godard says, we are all in-between – between cultures, between places, between people. The *Twilight Saga* depicts a woman between two men, two choices, two lifestyles, but also in the in-betweeness of love and death (or love and non-love). And when the issue of possibly becoming a vampire emerges, then it's a choice between life and death, or change and being immortal = not changing (as Bella explains in her important monologue at the end of *Eclipse*).

As the Ancient Greek poet Sappho had written of love:

It brings us pain
and weaves myths.[2]

Like all romantic heroines, and all love poets, Bella Swan is also in love with love itself – the idea of love, the experience of love. She's hooked on the feeling of being in love. She's subsumed her identity in the other person so much that her own identity is fraying at the edges, is becoming unstable (the wound in her chest is a gaping hole into which parts of her self/ soul/ identity tumble – some never to return).

✎

One girl, two boys – and it's easy to see, if you leave out the monsters and mythical ingredients of vampires and werewolves, that Edward C. and Jacob B. are classic stereotypes of teen romance stories: Jake is the earthy, warm (literally!) working class kid, kind-hearted, sensitive, a six-foot-seven hunk who rides motorcycles and dresses as the bad boy (much more is made of this James Dean/ Marlon Brando 'wild one' aspect of Jacob in the books, especially in *Eclipse*).

---

7 Bella is also the perfect 'in-betweener' herself – between being a child and an adult, between being a teenager living at home and a young woman living independently, etc.

Edward Cullen is the upper-class, sophisticated, fashion-plate boy, the rich kid from a good home with wealthy parents. He's smart, highly educated, snooty, supercilious, sarcastic, with Adonis looks and an expensive car. He's Ferris Bueller or Jay Gatsby to Jacob's Tom Sawyer.

Edward's the smarmy, aloof, well-off, brilliant-at-everything guy you love to hate in school; while Jacob's down-to-earth, one of the boys, easy to be around (but also easily hurt!). Edward's also scarily controlling and possessive[8] (tho' he professes all the time that he has his beloved's interests at heart first and foremost). Edward's the kind of guy who sneaks into your bedroom to whisk away all the relics of your love affair when he vanishes from your life (eh?! Waaa?!). He's the kind of guy who trails you in his car all the way home, just to make sure you get home safely (like the most protective father ever!).

The class barrier between Bella and Edward is a stronger element in the 2005 novel, where Bella's often quietly resentful that her family has far less wealth than the Cullen clan (and out at the res the Quileute Tribe seem even poorer). For Natalie Wilson, in the *Twilight* series, 'a white, working class human chooses between an ultra-white, ultra-privileged vampire and a far less privileged wolf of colour' (in M. Parke, 2011).

It's also noteworthy that romantic triangles link together two men (or, here, two boys) in a homosocial manner. It's an aspect of love triangles that critics (and Hollywood movies) prefer to ignore (the film adaptations of the *Twilight* series avoided the homosocial subtext, even though they eroticized both youths even more than the novels).

THE PREGNANT HEROINE.

Bella Swan's pregnancy and death in *Breaking Dawn* are part, too, of the common narrative of a hero's story: the descent and the return. You'll find thousands of stories where the hero/ine reaches an incredibly low point, with major obstacles to overcome, towards the end of the tale. S/he has to defeat an impossible-to-kill villain, or Save The World against all odds.

Stephenie Meyer acknowledged that she was thinking in terms of the 19th century (and 19th century literature) when she portrayed the childbirth sequence in *Breaking Dawn* (where, in the 19th century, there was a strong possibility that you could die giving birth [TS, 36]).

For Bella, the final battleground is (in) her own body, and is her life itself. Not Edward and her romance, not her and the second choice lover, Jacob. But just her, on her own. The love that Bella feels for Edward is

---

8 Feminists were critical of 'Edward's controlling nature and Bella's willingness to submit'.

true love, in the romance genre, but now Bella has another love – for her child. (The baby is an *addition*, a *complication*, that I'm sure some readers resented, because it distracts from the Grand Opera of the Love Story, and takes the *Twilight* series into other areas, and away from the fairy tale form of young romance culminating in marriage and Happy Ever After. Or as the books put it: *f-o-r-e-v-e-r*).

So Bella gets what she wants; and there's even the added reward of a second guy who's utterly devoted to her – Jacob Black – *and* the priceless bonus of a child.

In an action-adventure story, you push you hero/ine to the maximum, when it seems impossible that they can overcome the hurdles. In the action-adventure genre, the mantra for your hero is: obstacle, obstacle, obstacle! In the romance genre, it's the same, but the arena and the context, is different. In the *Twilight* series, the genre is romantic fantasy, so the battleground is relationships and emotions. It's one individual relating to another.

In *Breaking Dawn*, Stephenie Meyer pushes her hero/ine to the point of death, then has her return. The vampire motif comes into play here, with her lover/ husband bringing her back to life with his blood/ venom, and quick thinking during the birth sequence. But take away the magical/ vampiric layers (which are gimmicks, really), and you have a story of a man helping a woman come back to life thru love. It's love, not the literary/ fantasy trick of vampirism, that resurrects Bella. What does she say after her rebirth (in part two of the movie)?: *I love you*, the Most Sacred Three Words in the entire romance genre (and in all Western poetry, you might say). 'There was something I needed to say. The most important thing', coos Bella in the book (BD, 363). Oh boy, how people are *desperate* to hear those three magical words directed at them! And to be able to say those Three Magical Words to someone else! (Without them going, '*meh*!', or 'Eh?', or 'Oh no, no, *no*!').

Indeed, in the *Twilight Saga*, lovers hurl the Three Magic Words at each other like it's a badge, a trophy, a totem, a spell that can justify anything and explain anything. If you say, 'I love you' you can get away with anything, and no matter how much you wind up the other, or yell at the other, they will forgive all if you also intone/ whisper/ mutter, 'I love you' (the 2015 rewrite of *Twilight, Life and Death* chucks the phrase 'I love you' all over the shop).

Stephenie Meyer knew that some readers would find the new direction of *The Twilight Saga* a problem – the pregnancy and childbirth sections (certainly it takes it out of the immediate experience of many readers in the Young Adult market).

SULKING, POUTING AND HUFFING OFF.

There is a *lot* of sulking, huffing off and pouting in the *Twilight Saga,* which detractors complained was masochistic, where anger is negatively expressed with charas sinking into lengthy sulks (Bella in *New Moon*), or contemplating suicide (Bella in *New Moon* again), or performing ritual suicide (Edward in *New Moon*), or embarking on weeks-long sulks and rages (Jacob in *Breaking Dawn*), etc. If there's an opportunity for a character in the *Twilight Saga* to mope about, to get angry then suppress it, to seethe and simmer, they will take it.

Can't get your own way? Storm off into the forest!

Spurned by your lover? Collapse and weep, you pitiful loser! (Oh yes, make sure it's in the forest again!).

Imagine your girlfriend's dead? Offer yourself up to a nest of vampires!

Meanwhile, the other characters in the *Twilight Saga* look on in bewilderment and sorrow as the central trio of J.B., E.C. and B.S. fret an' fume an' rant an' rage. Can't they just order a beer in a bar and chill out already? Can't they shrug and go *meh!*, like Lisa Simpson from *The Simpsons*?

What's the big deal? Oh yes – love, passion, desire, getting *that* girl, dating *that* boy. Mike Newton, Eric or Tyler won't do – and, no, not even Jacob Black!

It's got to be Edward!

It was hard to believe that someone so beautiful could be real. (T, 75)

BELLA IN THE BOOKS.

In the *Twilight* book, Bella Swan has every neurosis and mental illness going: self-absorption > self-pity > paranoia > obsessive compulsive disorder > and of course manic depression. In *Breaking Dawn* Bella says she's had 'a lifetime of insecurities' (80). Well, we sort of knew that! (So when the Bookish Mouse becomes an Adrenalin Junkie in *New Moon*, it really stretches belief).

The Swanster is also a worrier *par excellence* – she would win the Gold Medal in the Neurotics Olympics (without even trying). She is 10 on the scale of the Angst-o-Meter (in the *Vampires Suck* movie). Give Bella a subject, and she will find a way of fretting about it. That beat-up old truck? Sh¡t, what if the engine blows up on the way back from La Push and I'm stranded in the middle of nowhere? That tree over there?

Hell, what if a freak lightning strike hits it and it crashes into my bedroom?! As for the internet, darn, honey, *do not* look up weird diseases on it! Never Google words like 'death'!

Jeez, thinks Jacob Black, Bella Swan is such a martyr! She beat herself up about everything, about hurting Edward's feelings. It was sickening. 'She'd totally been born in the wrong century. She should have lived back when she could have gotten herself fed to some lions for a good cause' (BD, 172).

(Meanwhile, Edward Cullen matches Bella Swan's neuroses beat-for-beat, and sulk-for-sulk. Their depressions are perfectly matched. It's a marriage of neurotics. Edward, as Stephenie Meyer noted, tortures himself (never coming to terms with his vampire status), over-thinks everything, and feels every emotion to the max [TS, 23]).

On her website, Stephenie Meyer provides a more detailed portrait of Bella Swan:

> In my head, Bella is very fair-skinned, with long, straight, dark brown hair and chocolate brown eyes. Her face is heart-shaped— a wide forehead with a widow's peak, large, wide-spaced eyes, prominent cheekbones, and then a thin nose and a narrow jaw with a pointed chin. Her lips are a little out of proportion, a bit too full for her jaw line. Her eyebrows are darker than her hair and more straight than they are arched. She's five foot four inches tall, slender but not at all muscular, and weighs about 115 pounds. She has stubby fingernails because she has a nervous habit of biting them.

Bellsie Swan is one of the poster girls for Young Adult fiction (and their movie adaptations); other girls include Katniss Everdeen in *The Hunger Games,* Lyra Belacqua in *The Golden Compas/ His Dark Materials,* Meggie in the *Inkheart* books, and Hermione Granger in the *Harry Potter* series.

JACOB AS EXPOSITION BOY.

It's Jacob Black who tells Bella Swan that Doctor Carlisle and the Cullens are 'blood drinkers', 'cold ones', vampires (T, 108). And that they've been around for a long time.

Stephenie Meyer invented Jacob Black partly so he could be the one who told Bella Swan about Edward and the vampires:

> Bella needed a way to find the truth out about Edward, and the conveniently located Quileute Tribe, with all their fantastic legends, provided a cool option for that revelation. And so Jacob was born – born to tell Bella about Edward's secret.[9]

9 Quoted in M. Howden, 71.

That's because Stephenie Meyer thought that Edward would never come right out and confess to Bella: 'I'm a vampire' (TS, 19). But after Jacob Black had been invented, he became an easy character to write, and added some humour to the piece. (The Quileute Tribe had a werewolf/ wolf legend, which fit the story, so the conflict of werewolves vs. vampires could be included: 'it felt like, *Now* it's on!', Meyer recalled, 'Now I know how it has to be!' [TS, 20]).

In the novel of *Twilight*, Jacob Black gives Bella Swan strong clues as to the identity of Edward Cullen; the 2008 movie follows the 2005 book, but it's more that Bella comes up with the realization herself. It occurs in the scene where she returns from Port Angeles with Edward, and stops at the police station to see her Dad (and Edward meets his Pa, too). As Bella exits the building, and sees the corpse of Waylon being wheeled out to an ambulance, there is a rapid montage of images of what Bella's thinking about. Here she puts two and two together: this leads into the online research sequence.

In the movie version of the beach scene, where Jacob Black tells Bella Swan about the myths and legends of the 'cold ones', which gives her the first hints that Edward Cullen might be a vampire, Taylor Lautner plays the scene with a grin, as if Jacob's completely confident that Bella wouldn't fall for a vampire.

Wrong, Jake!

(And it's *already* too late, dude – the romance is a done deal in the *Twilight* film after the first act – after 30 minutes.)

Notice how the 2008 movie switches directly from the beach scene into the marina scene, where Charlie's pal Waylon Forge is killed by the three outlaw vampires, illustrating immediately the hints that Jacob's offered (and reminding us that vampires are dangerous, even when they're as beguilingly delectable as Edward C.).

MUSIC.

In *Twilight*, Bella Swan uses music as therapy, to stop herself from thinking (about – what else?! – Edward Cullen and vampires). The Queen of Twilight doesn't name the band, just says that they used 'too much bass and shrieking' (T, 112).[10] Altho' music is linked by Meyer to certain scenes in the *Twilight Saga*, she very rarely identifies a real pop act in the books, for obvious reasons (but Meyer has provided lists of music and pop bands which go with certain scenes, for each book – so diehard (I mean, Twi-hard) fans can create a playlist to play on their cel or I-Pod

---

10 So it could be anybody, but not Taylor Swift or the Osmonds.

when they read the books. And Meyer's done this again for *The Host*).

For the first *Twilight* book, Stephenie Meyer's soundtrack includes: Dido, Orchestral Manœuvres In the Dark, the Cranberries, Travis, Coldplay, Radiohead, Linkin Park, My Chemical Romance, David Gray, Collective Soul, and Billy Joel – and of course Muse (note the proportion of British pop acts).

There's a strong tradition of pop music in Washington State in the Pacific North-West: the Riot Grrrl movement, for instance, was based in Olympia, WA (as well as Washington, DC). The 'Riot Grrrl' movement occurred in the 1980s and early 1990s. It began in North America, partly as an off-shoot of grunge. Riot Grrrl acts included Hole, Bikini Kill, the Lunachicks, L7, Huggy Bear, Japanese band Shonen Knife, Blood Sausage, Limpstud, the Furbelows, Linus, and Seven Year Bitch.

CARS.

Cars are a big deal in the *Twilight Saga*. A silver Volvo S60R and Aston Martin Vanquish for Edward. Bella's beat-up 1953 Chevvy truck. Carlisle: Mercedes S55 AMG. Emmett: Jeep Wrangler. Rosalie: BMW M3 convertible. Jacob's V.W. Rabbit. Alice: yellow Porsche 911 (several German makes, note: Merc, Porsche, B.M.W., and V.W.). In the acknowledgements section of the *Twi*-books, Stephenie Meyer credits her brothers (Paul and Jacob) for being car nuts, and advising her on cool cars to put in the stories.

Meanwhile, in the official guide of *The Twilight Saga*, there is a section on cars. (The movie adaptations duly reproduced the car fetishism. And you can bet the car companies like Volvo, Merc and Porsche loved having their cars in the movie – at times, the helicopter shots of cars racing thru tree-lined, winding roads are interchangeable with car commercials. Volvo were one of the sponsors of *New Moon*).

Why all these cars? For the same reasons that late teens want to have cars! Many scenes in *Twilight* are set in cars – not only romantic, making out scenes, but many dialogue scenes (and there're action scenes involving cars, too). After all, these teen charas live with their parents, and cars represent a non-parent-space, a non-school-space, and a non-friend's-space. (We're in the rural Pacific North-West, after all, where trains and buses and trams can be thin on the ground).[11]

SCARY AND VIOLENT.

The element of real violence – and the threat of violence – in the

---

11 Bella's Dad realizes that his daughter will need a transport of her own.

male characters in the *Twilight* series is way more disturbing than, say, the emphasis on sexual abstinence. Nobody can miss the fact that the two men in Bella Swan's life have a monsterish side to them. They both warn Bella that they don't want to hurt her. They both warn her that they are potentially violent, to the point where they can't control themselves.

'*I would never hurt you*' always seems a very odd and sadistic thing to say to some you love (well, don't hurt me then, *baka*!). But it's found everywhere, including in many pop songs. Even Prince sings it in the astounding, immortal song 'Purple Rain':

> I never meant to cause you any sorrow,
> I never meant to cause you any pain.
> I only wanted to one time see you laughing,
> I only wanted to see you laughing in the purple rain.

Yes, it's *Beauty and the Beast*, of course, and part of the romance genre in its fantasy mode, but the *Twilight* texts do emphasize the threat of violence in men to a striking degree (even tho', in a *Beauty and the Beast* narrative, the Beast does have to be beastly, and in a movie that means the beastliness has to be *shown*). And it's not only Jacob and Edward – Sam Uley loses his temper for a second and scars his beloved Emily for life, so he (and she) is perpetually reminded of his uncontrollable nature (this subplot clearly evokes marital abuse). And Jasper Whitlock is so incensed by the smell of blood when Bella cuts herself, he goes berserk, which persuades the entire Cullen clan to up sticks and leave the neighbourhood (among other factors). (But it was only a paper cut! Rarely has so much pandemonium arisen from a simple snick of a finger! Come on, Jasper, that's no way for a courteous Texas gentleman to behave in front of a lady!).

'The word *scared* didn't really seem to cover it.' (*New Moon*, 314)

Love is dangerous, right? *You might get hurt*, right? Yes – the *Twilight* novels trot out those platitudes all the time, as do 10,000,000 pop songs. *Love hurts, love causes pain, to love is to suffer* – Hell, poets have been dining out on such clichés since forever! (In the *Twilight Saga*, the pain of lerrrve has a *physical* aspect – suffering leads to real scenes of wounding, like Bella leaping into the ocean and getting knocked out. The masochistic aspects of *The Twilight Saga* are taken to a rather silly and too-literal degree).

And nobody can miss the fact that many of the 'good' vampires in the *Twilight* series, as well as the 'bad' vampires, have *very* violent histories and origins. Jasper and Edward have killed many people; meanwhile, Rosalie slaughtered her rapists, tho' apparently she doesn't feed on humans. Edward tells Bella early on in the first *Twilight* book that he might be the villain – and he is: he is a serial killer. Oh sure, he 'only' slew bad guys and murderers (so, he's like the Judge as well as Executioner, now? *He* decides who must die?). But he's still killed *a lot* of people. So Bella's married Jack the Ripper or Ed Gein (well, *shoot*, popular culture in the U.S.A. does secretly admire its serial killers!).

THE FINALE OF *TWILIGHT*.

Why does, all of a sudden, the narrative of *Twilight* alter? We have to buy a lot of reversals and dramatic turns here, in the aftermath of the baseball game: that, altho', as Edward states, there are 'seven of us and two of them', the heroes are still going to run (even when we can see that Emmett, for one, is a vampire who is busting for a fight!); that James Witherdale is an obsessive tracker who will stop at nothing to hunt down James – we have only Edward's word for that, as he informs Bella in the car as they flee the baseball scene (in other words, we don't *see* James's compulsion to hunt, we are only told it); and that Victoria is also not to be under-estimated (we have only Laurent's word for that).

Seven vampires against one vampire (or two at most) – the 2005 *Twilight* book's finale does seem unconvincing. That the Cullens are immediately on the run, *reacting* to the villain vampire James Witherdale instead of turning round and facing him head-on seems just silly. We've just observed them playing baseball in a thunderstorm! – they're all more'n physically able, and Edward is so insanely furious, he could probably take James on his own. Not only that, they have a woman with them (Alice) who can predict the future! Not only that, they have a guy (Edward) who can hear what people're thinking! Not only that, but each of the Cullens can sense when a vampire is nearby! Not only that, Bella's Dad is the Chief of Police, and must have plenty of ways he could call on help in order to protect his beloved daughter.[12] But instead, ironically, *vampires* are posted at his house to protect *him*!.

But no, the Cullen family flees, to regroup at their mansion, before devising schemes to out-wit the two vamps James and Victoria with decoys (for Bella Swan) and the like. It's all far too complicated and unconvincing. It doesn't mix well, either, with the romance plot, which, after all, is the primary plot of *Twilight*.

---

12 He rustles up some local boys to help with the bear hunt, for example.

That this action climax to the *Twilight* book comes out of nowhere is also easy to spot. There are no hints of it (except in the prologue), and the characters of Laurent, Victoria and James come out of the blue. So they have no weight as characters, except as obstacles/ adversaries. (Laurent's characterization, for instance, is minimal). Thus, for the *Twilight* movie, many of their scenes were added to the book,[13] to remind us of their presence (and they were introduced much earlier) – all of which is geared towards providing the *action* finale in a movie that's essentially a romantic drama.

Further, the *motivation* of James Witherdale the Naughty Vampire is unconvincing. He wants Bella Swan because... well, it's a game to him, he's a hunter, he's selected her as his quarry. Presumably there are thousands of seventeen year-old girls just as juicy and innocent and cute as Bella in the Pacific North-West of the United States of America (we *know* there are! And some of them are *Twilight* fans!). But no, James wants *Bella*, and *only* Bella.[14]

Yes, I know that James W. is a thematic counterpoint to Edward Cullen (who also wants Bella – and to eat! – but not like *that*!). But I don't buy it. The fact that James has very little characterization (no background, no history), means we are not interested in him in the slightest. He is *merely* an obstacle, an antagonist, an adversary. That's all. As such, he can be killed at the end without any of us worrying at all. We don't *care* about James because the 2005 *Twilight* novel doesn't want us to be! (And neither does the 2008 *Twilight* movie!).

A big deal is made of James Witherdale the villain vampire in *Twilight* being a hunter. But in fact, all of the vampires in the *Twilight Saga* are hunters, they all have acute senses, they can smell and track people over great distances. Even the newborn vampire army bred by Riley and Victoria in *Eclipse* (they are untrained, naïve, inexperienced vampires) are able to track down Bella Swan from a distance (Riley picks up Bella's clothing to give them the scent, like dogs).

The finale in the first *Twilight* book does link up psycho James with Alice Brandon and Alice's origins as a vampire (she can't remember being human – it happens to all of us from time to time!). So Alice is a victim of James's that got away, so he's going to make good that loss by slaying Bella (eh? Does that make sense?!). The link connects Bella and Alice. A pity that the 2008 *Twilight* movie didn't really make this clear, or use Alice's back-story (partly due to time, of course, and the focus is

---

13 There were a few more scenes, or bits of scenes, involving the nomadic vampires in *Twilight*, but they were cut out.
14 Yes, the official *Twilight* guidebook explains this in more detail.

always on li'l Bells).

(Alice's origins are intriguing, connected to James the psycho in the first *Twilight* book, and involving mental illness, but not really explored in the movies. In the *Twilight* texts, Alice's forgotten much of her former life, including her time in an asylum of the old type, where electro-shock therapy was used (T, 390f). An old vampire who was fond of Alice turns her into 'a strong new vampire', as James tells Bella, so there was no need to kill her anymore (tho' he slays the old vampire).)

twilight
THE GRAPHIC NOVEL   VOLUME 1

STEPHENIE MEYER
ART AND ADAPTATION BY YOUNG KIM

twilight
GRAPHIC NOVEL   VOLUME 2

STEPHENIE MEYER
ART AND ADAPTATION BY YOUNG KIM

2

THE CHARACTERS IN
THE TWILIGHT SAGA

BELLA SWAN.

Li'l Isabella S. is our narrator and heroine, a girl of 17 from Phoenix, AZ (population: 1.445 million in 2010), who moves to live with her Pa Charlie in Forks (population: 3,532 in 2010, plus 7 undead) in the Pacific North-West, a (real) small town where it's perpetually cold and raining (La Push has 95 inches of rain annually on average, and it rains 120 days in the year).[1] Bella is quiet, withdrawn, bookish,[2] intelligent, and permanently depressed. *Twilight* is a portrait of a self-obsessed and introspective girl who's close to autism.

Bella is not a City Girl: she lives in Phoenix, sure, but in the suburbs, not downtown. When she visits cities, Bad Things Happen: in Port Angeles she's menaced by street punks and goes joyriding with bikers; in Seattle she meets dodgy fixers; in Volterra she encounters deadly vampires; and back in Phoenix she's attacked and bitten by a vampire.

Bella Swan is unusual in some simple respects: she is not a popular culture junkie, she hardly watches television, doesn't listen to music, doesn't read magazines or newspapers, isn't into fashion, doesn't have a cel phone (!), and doesn't follow popular trends. She only occasionally consults the internet, and sometimes refers to classic fiction (she is a reader, yes, but doesn't reference anything she's reading very often. Jane Austen is top of her list, as well as *Wuthering Heights*. So, few or no references to modern American giants such as Faulkner, Stein,

---

1 The location was selected, Stephenie Meyer said, because vampires need cloud cover.
2 'In high school, I was a mousy, A-track wall-flower', Meyer admitted.

Hemingway, Wharton, Salinger, Fitzgerald, or Le Guin).

By contrast, the *Twilight* movies present a more switched-on Bella, culturally (while the Cullens are certainly media and tech savvy). Yet the *Twilight* movies too pull back from, say, crowding Bella's bedroom with pin-ups from boy bands, posters, CDs, magazines, LCD tablets, I-Pods, cel phones, computer games, *manga*, make-up and fashion accessories. (The movies also depict the kids at Spatula Academy of Fictional Excellence *not* using their cel phones and tablets at every possible second when they're not in class, as teens all over the Western world do – and in class, too!).

Bella Swan's anti-pop culture (or non-pop culture) status is curious in the *Twilight Saga*, as if her teenage rebellion consists entirely of being *against* pop culture in all its manifestations. She is among the most un-hip/ un-trendy/ un-switched-on of teenage characters. While her chums might be expected to sit around the table during lunch and chat about TV or pop music or whatever, Bella is notable for her complete lack of interest in anything like that.

Bella doesn't watch TV. Charlie does (the average is 2 to 4 hours a day in the U.S.A.). And, after Edward's jilted her, she doesn't listen to music, either.

The truth is, Bella Swan is appearing in… a *book*! A *what*?! Yes, a *book*, a real paper-and-print object, not something postmodern and digital and virtual, like a website, a cel phone message, an online image, an MP3 file or a TV show.

EDWARD CULLEN.

Fans have wondered if the attraction of Edward Cullen is that he is an old-fashioned gentleman. This is justified within the text by Edward growing up in the Edwardian era, but actually it's more than that. Edward is a guy who hurries around the other side of the car (deliberately walking at human pace) in order to open the door for his girl.

Fans responded to Edward Cullen's old-fashioned, old timey attitude – plus the fact that Edward has plenty of $$$$, comes from a warm, loving family, respects his parents, dresses like a fashion model, has a nice car, a sumptuous house, and is drop-dead gorgeous! Oh yes, what's not to like about Edward? Oh, ah, of course: the prima donna pouting, the centuries-long sulks, the glowering, Byronic brooding, the childish stubbornness, the physical aggression, and the admission of serial killing. (Half of the Cullen clan are serial killers – Rosalie, Jasper and Edward.)

(Personally, I don't find Edward Cullen sexy as a person in the books – the narrator continually describes his skin as freezing cold, and his body is hard as stone. It'd be like cuddling a block of ice! Of course, the way that Robert Pattinson embodies Edward in the *Twilight* movies is va-va-voom!)

However, Robert Pattinson was well-known for disliking the *Twilight* series, finding the concept weird, and the fans scarily intense. Pattison didn't mind who heard his views on the *Twilight* phenomenon. It seems ill-advised to publicly criticize the fans. But Pattinson was happy to take the millions of dollars in acting fees – a rumoured $25 million for the last *Twilight* movie (for each of the three stars), plus additional revenue – rather than, say, donating his salary to charity.₃

SMELLS GOOD! OR, MORE ON EDWARD.

Smell is a big deal in the *Twilight* series: the narrator and Bella Swan are always emphasizing the scents of the lovers (and their breathing/non-breathing).₄ Scents are key plot devices in chases, pursuits and hunting in the vampire world. And heartbeats: like a heroine out of Victorian romantic fiction, Bella's often acutely aware of how strongly her heart is beating (well, I guess it's good to check now and again if your heart is still beating). This literary cliché is given a new twist – because a beating heart means pumping blood, which's what vampires crave. (And when Bella's in hospital at the end of *Twilight*, a heart monitor that's hooked up to Bella is used for jokey asides, as she gets all hot and bothered when pretty boy Edward starts nuzzling her neck. But not in the movie). When Bella becomes a vampire in *Breaking Dawn*, out goes the heart motif (tho' it's deployed to the max in the transformation sequence). But vampires, oddly, retain breathing (even tho' they don't need oxygen). Because breathing is a handy attribute for a novelist (I mean, if you take away a lot of the characteristics linked to blood – blushing, beating hearts, bits of the body swelling – you are limiting yourself a tad).

Indeed, Stephenie Meyer employs many of the clichés of romance fiction, including embarrassments, misunderstandings, blushings, hesitations, and Bella even faints at one point (because she's just so *in lerrrve* with Edward Cullen).

The slightest scent of blood drives the vampires in *Twilight* nuts – so presumably the women and girls menstruating in Sporks would be torment for the *Twilight* vamps. Half of the population of the planet

---

3 And it didn't stop Pattinson appearing in more Dumb Hollywood Movies, such as the *Batman* franchise.

4 The *Twilight* movies also mix the sound of breaths high – Kristen Stewart adds huffing and sighing to her many actorly tics.

bleeds every month for decades of their lives. The links between menstruation and vampire mythology have been noted by several writers, but most vampire fictions and fantasies tend to pretend it doesn't exist. (And TV and movies prefer to erase it completely).

In the *Twilight* books we learn that Edward was born in Chicago, Illinois in 1901 (T, 251), making him 104 by the time of the book (it was published in 2005); in the *Twilight* movie, he says he's 109. He's a white kid who was dying of Spanish flu in 1918 when Carlisle Cullen found him. His parents were already taken by the disease (which killed more people than World War One. Media interest in the Spanish flu epidemic grew during the C.O.V.I.D. crisis of 2020). So Edward is changed into a vampire at age 17 (and he sort of remains eternally seventeen); thus, Bella isn't much older when she is transformed (which's a nagging concern for her – being older than her boyfriend. In the novel *New Moon*, the back-story of Edward is expanded a little, so now we find out that Edward's Mom was dying, and she pleaded with Carlisle to do what he could to save her near-dead son, as if she knew that Carlisle was a vampire).

One of the most striking elements of conventional romance literature that the *Twilight Saga* uses is Bella's constant and breathless enshrinement of Edward. Numerous times Bella calls him god-like, perfect, a male model advertizing raincoats, an angel, a beauty, etc. Bella's got it *bad*. Love at first sight, right? Yes, and Bella never recovers from that initial sighting. She never lets up loving Edward from that first moment (the story is all over, in a way, by a third of the way into the first *Twilight* book, when Bella tells Edward that it's too late: she's hooked).

So our five-foot-four heroine is hopelessly over-the-new-moon about Edward, gushing over him in *New Moon* as 'excruciatingly lovely and forever seventeen… a marble tribute to some forgotten pagan god of beauty'.

> I was consumed by the mystery Edward presented. And more than a little obsessed by Edward himself. (T, 57)
> •
> I wasn't *interesting*. And he was. Interesting… and brilliant… and mysterious… and perfect… and beautiful… and possibly able to lift full-sized vans with one hand. (T, 67-68)
> •
> …what was my other choice – to cut him out of my life? Intolerable. Besides, since I'd come to Forks, it really seemed like my life was *about* him. (T, 220)
> •
> The meadow, so spectacular to me at first, paled next to his magnificence.

(T, 229)

•

He threw a mocking smile in my direction, and my breath caught in my throat. Would I ever get used to his perfection? (T, 419)

To make the reader understand that Edward Cullen is incandescently gorgeous, Stephenie Meyer reminds us throughout the whole *Twilight* series: that crooked smile! those golden eyes! those bronze, wavy locks! that perfect body! oh, and did I mention his lovely smile?!:

I looked at his concerned, innocent expression and was disoriented again by the force of his gold-colored eyes. (T, 49)

•

He was smiling, relaxed – and, as usual, perfect and beautiful to an excruciating degree. (T, 199)

•

He'd never been less human... or more beautiful. Face ashen, eyes wide, I sat like a bird locked in the eyes of a snake. (T, 232)

•

His beauty stunned my mind – it was too much, an excess I couldn't grow accustomed to. (T, 246)

Why Bella? Why *this* particular girl, after a century of abstinence and withdrawal? Well, if you have to ask that, don't read any more romance novels! You see couples everywhere you go where you think, eh? I don't get it – *she's* dating *him*!?

Edward tells Little B. that she fascinates him, like he fascinates her. 'You're not like anyone I've ever known. You fascinate me' (T, 214). The term *fascination* would sum up the themes in the first *Twilight* book.[5] Without desire you don't really have a romantic story of any kind.

However, Edward Cullen is not a well-adjusted guy. He's jealous, possessive, controlling (and a control freak), very angry, a manic depressive, a stalker, has murderous fantasies, and has been (and therefore *still is*) a serial killer.

For Robert Pattinson, it was really Bella who was making all the important contributions to the romantic relationship:

when you actually look at the story, Edward had nothing. He was really gone, down and out, and every time it's always Bella saving the day, but she refuses to acknowledge it. She gives all the credit to Edward. (CFA, 30)

One aspect of Edward Cullen's personality nobody can miss in the 2005 North American novel is how sarcastic and derogatory he is towards Bella Swan. He chuckles in almost every single scene he has with Bella,

5 Thomas Hardy uses the term for the third Book of *The Return of the Native* (and it's the heroine, Eustacia Vye, who fascinated).

he makes smart-ass quips which put her down, he doesn't take her seriously... he is, in short, an arrogant fool, the kind of guy that Bella should walk away from. But she can't, because he has those golden-ochre-brown eyes (*oooh!*), and that super-angelic face (*aaah!*), and that so-sensational, super-gorgeous, to-bite-for smile (*Oooh la la!*).

> I was stunned by the unexpected electricity that flowed through me, amazed that it was possible to be *more* aware of him than I already was. (T, 191)

HE'S 104; SHE'S 17. *CREEPY!*

The Twilight Saga is also a joke on the younger woman and the older man. The man is so old, he's 104! (109 in the movies). Which makes Edward Cullen another father figure for father complex girl Bella Swan. Or, rather a great-great-great grandfather figure!

One of the very odd things about the romantic relationship of Bella Swan and Edward Cullen in the *Twilight Saga* is the age difference. People freaked out about Woody Allen dating Soon-Yi Previn (or ageing rockers Chuck Berry, Bill Wyman, Jimmy Page and Jerry Lee Lewis and their teen brides/ lovers), but Edward is 104, and Bella is 17! He's not twenty or thirty years older than her, he's 87 years older!

So it would be like dating someone as old as your great-grandfather or your great-great-grandfather, rather than as old as your grandfather or your father or your older brother! This guy is *ancient*! Yes, it's part of the vampire mythology, of course, but, Hell, it's also *so creepy*! So creepy you can't believe it: he's a guy who's been around as a 17 year-old for, like, 87 years! And he's dating a 17 year-old girl! (And we're supposed to believe that he's also a virgin, and hasn't dated anyone! A *lot* of guys would be very happy staying perpetually 17 years-old!).

In *Breaking Dawn*, Bella complains that Edward has been seventeen for over ninety years (while she is getting closer to nineteen with 'every stinking day' [BD, 14]). Mortality is a *big* deal with Bella, and it's one of her chief reasons for wanting immortality (this would normally put Bella into the villain category – what do villains crave in countless stories? Immortality!).

There's also the very strange aspect of Edward Cullen's *psychological* age. If he is actually 104 years-old, then surely he is also *psychologically* that old! He isn't a seventeen year-old kid any more! Oh, sure, he *looks* like a seventeen year-old youth, but he *can't be*, if he was born in 1901. No! (The last time that Edward was a 17 year-old was in 1918!).

So Edward Cullen's youth was spent in the 1910s not, like Bella

Swan's youth, in the 2000s. That means his key years, the years of his *real* teenage, the time when his personality, his cultural tastes, his attitudes, his morals and all the rest, were formed in the 1910s. And the 1910s were *very* different, socially and culturally, from the 2000s.

So Edward Cullen isn't simply old-fashioned, like 1990s old-fashioned (compared to the 2000s), or even 1980s or 1970s old-fashioned – he is positively prehistoric, spending his teens in the years before the First World War! (Occasionally Edward's old-fashioned manners and speech are remarked upon, but usually it's portrayed as if he's a 1980s guy in a 2000s setting; when in fact he's a 1910s guy in a 2000s setting!). But that, of course, is partly what appeals to readers – you've got a *genuinely* 'old-fashioned', romantic lover here!

Ken Gelder pointed out in *New Vampire Cinema*: 'why he is still in high school remains the film's biggest mystery' (87). We know that Edward Cullen attends universities during his 100-odd years, but would you go back to *high school* after studying at a much higher level in colleges and universities? Err... well, the *Twilight* novels answer that by explaining that the Cullens need to fit in with wherever they live (in which case, wouldn't attending a university in nearby Seattle make more sense? Or getting one of numerous jobs suitable for a 100+ year-old guy? Why does it have to be high school? – oh yes, I know: *bite me!*).

HE'S SINGLE.

One of the most obvious questions to ask in the first *Twilight* novel and movie is this: why hasn't Edward got a girlfriend/ wife/ boyfriend/ husband? After all, he's clearly handsome (!), highly educated, charmingly old-fashioned, comes from a wealthy family, and boasts a line in smooth patter. He could probably pick and choose amongst the girls (and boys!) at Norks High School (you can bet that a few guys wouldn't say no to having Edweird bite them!). Even Jessica Stanley might try going out on a date with Edward, just for the Hell of it! (There's a hint in the *Twilight* book that Jessica has tried but – *no way!* – been rejected).

> 'That's Edward. He's gorgeous, of course, but don't waste your time. He doesn't date. Apparently none of the girls here are good-looking enough for him.' (T, 19)
>
> •
>
> 'W-o-w.' She exaggerated the word into three syllables. 'Edward Cullen.'
> 'I know,' I agreed. 'Wow' didn't even cover it. (T, 178)
>
> •
>
> ...when I thought of him, of his voice, his hypnotic eyes, the magnetic

force of his personality, I wanted nothing more than to be with him right now. (T, 121)

And the Cullens, too, are all paired up: there are seven Cullenses, comprising three couples: Rosalie and Emmett, Carlisle and Esme, and Alice and Jasper. Edward is conveniently the only one without a 'mate' (they call lovers 'mates' in Stephenie Meyer's vampire mythology). And there's no mention of any previous girlfriends for the virtuous and virginal Edward (we find out in a later novel that Carlisle hoped that Rosalie might be The One).

I say 'conveniently', because that's what it is: it's part of the conventions of fiction (and movies) that beautiful people just happen to be single, so the hero/ine can have a relationship with them. That's why, when you see Halle Berry or Tom Cruise or Scarlett Johansson or Johnny Depp in a movie, they are helpfully (but unbelievably) unattached (and not only unattached, they don't have ten kids by several partners (or adaopted kids) trailing behind them).

Two characters are intimately linked to Bella and Edward – Mike Newton and Jessica Stanley. Mike asks Bella for a date, and Jessica was (presumably) turned down by Edward. And then Mike and Jessica start dating (but not before Edward has expressed his jealousy several times about Mike, even tho' Mike is presented as a buffoon and no serious threat to his courtship of Bella).

Two teens in the *Twilight* movie warn Bella Swan away from Edward Cullen. Of course, they are also boys who are attracted to her (and are turned down). But the girls (principally Jessica and Angela) don't express any reservations; rather, they seem delighted that one of their own has managed to draw the unreachable, infuriatingly aloof Lord Edward's attention.

MORE ON THE ROMANTIC TRIANGLE.

One woman… two guys…

In the Hollywoodization of romantic fiction, it's typically a guy and two women. One will be cast as blonde, the other brunette, one will be funky and friendly (or kooky/ weird), the other'll be be haughty and snooty and unapproachable. Uh-huh. So, in the *Twilight* movies, there's a guy who's pale, the other one's dark; one is cool, prissy and uptight, while the other is friendly, casual and earthy…

So it goes on. And on…

The *Twilight* franchise also adds a couple of differences of its own: one's physically cold, the other's hot! One's a white, preppy, East Coast type, the other's a Native American! One's a vampire, the other's a werewolf! (In *Breaking Dawn*, Bella admits that 'our triangular relationship seemed impossible, three different kinds of heartbreak that could not be avoided' (BD, 626-7).)

Jacob makes up for what Edward lacks, Stephenie Meyer pointed out (TS, 22). Edward isn't the perfect boyfriend, admitted Meyer – he over-thinks everything, and every emotion is over-wrought (you could say the same of Bella – and of many of Meyer's chief characters).

THE CULLENS.

'Carlisle had created Edward, Esme, Rosalie and Emmett', we are told (BD, 519). Alice and Jasper join the Cullen clan later. Edward's first described as a lanky, boyish youth with 'untidy, bronze-colored hair', as he steps into Forks High School, who stands out from his buddies Jasper Whitlock (tall, lean, honey blond hair) and Emmett McCarty (big, muscley, dark, curly hair) (T, 16). Rosalie Hale is depicted as a tall, statuesque blonde, the kind that models swimwear and makes every woman jealous of her voluptuous figure. Alice Brandon is portrayed as skinny, small, black-haired and pixie-like (T, 16). The Cullens all have dark eyes, shadows under their eyes, perfect noses, chalky, white skin, and faces right out of a fashion magazine (as well as exceptional clothes). The Cullen kids have an unreal air about them – when they're playing in the snow, Bella thinks that 'they looked more like a scene from a movie than the rest of us' (T, 35).

The Cullen clan advertize themselves locally as adopted children, with Carlisle as in his early thirties, too young to have children who're 18 (most of the Cullen kids, we note, are in the 17 or 18 range when they were changed into bloodsuckers). They are 17 or 18 for the same reason that Bella and Edward are 17 – to play to the teenage target audience of the books (and the movies); the characters are a year or two *above* the target market age, because teens are growing *up*, looking towards adulthood (and younger teens look up to older teens).

The Cullens are hi-tech vampires, too: they have facilities for forging passports and documents, and hacking into computer systems (necessary to keep up the disguise of being humans). They have their own company (C.E.E.), a private island, a fleet of classy cars, expensive medical gear, and a blood bank as back-up (for when the abattoirs are closed).

Bella Swan is attracted to opposites, it seems – vampires/ werewolves, Americans/ Native Americans (colonizers/ colonized), cold/ hot, rich/ poor, South/ North, Arizona/ Washington. Bringing in Native

Americans and First Nations culture into the mix politicizes the *Twilight Saga* beyond the usual romantic fantasy outing. The vampires are aligned with the invaders, the colonizers, the white (European) forces, arriving in the Pacific North-West unwanted and causing mayhem.

They don't work for a living. Well, among the Cullens, Carlisle does a proper, decent and vital job – he's a doctor. But the others? They go to school... Even though they're decades old.

CARLISLE CULLEN.

Carlisle Cullen as a doctor is described by Bells in *Twilight* as young, blond and 'handsomer than any movie star I'd ever seen' (T, 52). Carlisle is the conscience of the Cullen family, the moral leader, and its patriarch. In *Breaking Dawn*, Bella calls Carlisle the Cullens' 'creator, their center, and their guide' (BD, 30). He's the original 'good vampire' in the *Twilight* cosmos – he's the one who comes up with the idea of living as a bloodsucker without eating humans. Aro Volturi in particular is fascinated by Carlisle's attempt at an alternative, New Agey lifestyle for vampires (Lord Aro is distinctly 'old school' – we're talking 3,000 years old!).

Sympathy, sweetness, kindness – Carlisle Cullen embodies the helpful, healing aspects of the vampire world – he is far and away the gentlest of the vampires (along with Esme), and the one who makes the move towards violence and aggression the slowest and the most reluctantly. If there's a way of avoiding violence or confrontation, Carlisle will explore it (it's Carlisle who offers sympathy to Bree Tanner, for instance, while the first instincts of the visiting Volturi is the newborn vampire's termination).

Even Jacob Black grudgingly admires Carlisle Cullen: 'He was good. Good as any human we protected. Maybe better' (BD, 188). So, no, Jake's not going to take a bite out of Carlisle.

In the 2005 *Twilight* novel, we find out that Carlisle is a Brit, born[6] in London in the 1640s (so he's now 362 years old). He was changed into a vamp in 1663 (when he was 23). And Carlisle's father was a witchfinder (!) in the witchhunting era of 1600s Britain (with allusions to the wars between Protestants and Catholics in Reformation/ Enlightenment Europe). So Cullen senior was an intolerant, Anglican priest who 'led hunts for witches, werewolves... and vampires' (T, 289). Carlisle is handed the job of witchhunting, and gets bitten by an ancient vampire during a night when a coven of vamps is flushed out of London's sewers.

---

6 His Mom died in childbirth, as Bella does.

To escape being burned alive by the witchfinding mob, Carlisle hides in a basement, trying to keep quiet while he undergoes the horrendous transformation into a vampire.

All of this is riddled with clichés from the fantasy and horror genres – you'll find the same Gothic material of Wichfinder Generals, witchhunts, and internecine wars between religious factions such as Catholics and Protestants in many a Western comicbook and Hammer horror movie. But clichés work – that's why people continue to use them (and there are solid reasons why these motifs became clichés in the first place).

Anyway, Carlisle Cullen's journey of self-discovery as a vampire – eventually leading towards his calling as a doctor – is a key thematic ingredient in the vampire lore of the *Twilight* series. Not least is Carlisle's development of the 'humanitarian' idea of feeding off the blood of animals rather than humans, so that the vamps in *Twilight* can be regarded as 'good' vampires. Because humans eat animals all the time, don't they? Millions and millions of them! (Calling eating animals the vampire version of 'vegetarianism' is an amusing send-up of trendy, New Age fads).

Subsequently, Carlisle Cullen swam to France, studied in Europe, and spent some time with the Volturi clan in Volterra (from 1700-20). Of course, Lord Aro, Caius and the ancient Volturi vampires couldn't understand why a vamp who prefer to go 'veggie', when humans were the tastiest meal of all (and in plentiful supply in Italy). So Carlisle strikes out for the New World (as you do): 'he dreamed of finding others like himself. He was very lonely, you see,' Edward tells Bella (T, 297). Carlisle's back-story is a whole movie on its own, but was only partially evoked in the *Twilight* adaptations (in *New Moon* we see some of it).

In the *Twilight* movies, Peter Facinelli skilfully delivers the characterization that Stephenie Meyer created in the books. You can believe that the movie-Carlisle really did create the haven for the alternative vampire lifestyle described in the *Twilight* novels. And Facinelli suggests the angelic looks of the most gorgeous movie star ever, tho' far more important is the emphasis on healing and empathy.

ESME.

Esme is the 'mother hen' (as Jacob Black puts it) of the Cullen coven. She committed suicide when she lost a baby; she jumped from a cliff (which Bella does in *New Moon* – 'classic martyrs' think alike!).

'…my first and only baby. He died just a few days after he was born, the poor tiny thing,' she sighed. 'It broke my heart – that's why I jumped off the cliff, you know,' she added matter-of-factly. (T, 321)

Carlisle Cullen found her in the morgue of the hospital (where it was assumed she was already dead), and transformed her into a vampire (T, 252). In the *Twilight* series, humans have to be living in order to be changed into vamps.[7]

In keeping with her image as the Earth Mother of the Cullen tribe, Esme is a kind-hearted vamp, a non-fighter, who cooks for Jacob Black when he's visiting (even managing to remind him of his dead Mom). Esme's absence is very notable, however, during the pregnancy and birth scenes in *Breaking Dawn* (in fact, there are scenes where you'd expect Esme to play a much bigger role as the Mother Hen, but instead Alice (usually) or Rosalie (sometimes) step in).

ALICE.

Mary Alice Brandon is described as having 'short, inky hair in a halo of spiky disarray around her exquisite, elfin face', with a 'willowy, graceful' and slight frame (T, 216). She is a quirky, wilfully eccentric person, more pixie-like than human. Alice is one of those people who're devoted to Having a Good Time, at whatever cost (as if Alice is hiding some tragic secrets).

In many respects, Alice is employed in the familiar manner of novelists as representing a characterization that's the *total opposite* to the heroine, Bella Swan. In every respect, Alice differs from Bella: she is glamorous; immaculately dressed; mesmerizingly attractive; socially out-going; clean; neat; well-organized; wholly contemporary; and very high maintenance. Edward comments that Alice 'rarely allows us to wear the same thing twice', and they have piles of clothes to go to the thrift store (BD, 251). Alice would *never* been seen out in public in old sweat pants and a Tee shirt; she would *never* drive a 1953 Chevy truck; and she would *never* consider a werewolf as a decent boyfriend! Alice is up-to-the-minute fashionable, while Bella couldn't care less. Alice represents the jet-setting, woman-about-town character out of a Jackie Collins block-buster novel that Bella might wish to be on her more vulnerable days. Bella's never had the confidence to *be herself* the way that Alice is so supremely Alice (that might be Alice's chief job or pastime: Being Alice).

Stephenie Meyer squeezes as much of the clash of opposites out of

7 There's an amusing joke in the *Wednesday* TV series (2022) where the heroine hides in a morgue, and she's so good at playing dead she fools the physician.

the Alice-and-Bella relationship as possible. Bella tolerates Alice and her crazy schemes often because she's part of Edward's family; if she wasn't, Bella would have nothing to do with her. Alice exasperates Bella, and Bella exasperates Alice. Bella calls Alice 'an unstoppable force of nature' in *Breaking Dawn* (58). Once tiny Alice gets an idea into her head, there's no way of stopping her. It's easier just to let her have her own way than to say no. (Alice is also bossy, and at times over-bearing; in a Jackie Collins novel, she would act as a bitch from time to time).

Alice Brandon is one of those people who try very hard to educate and develop their friends, but with Bella Swan it's a losing battle. Yet Alice never gives up the attempt. Bella is the kid sister that Alice never had, whom Alice can use as a doll to dress up. (Stephenie Meyer has said she would love to have Alice as a friend).

There's a little flirtation bubbling underneath between Alice and Charlie Swan. The Police Chief might take an instant dislike to Edward (no guy's good enough for any father's daughter!), but Alice's supermodel looks coupled with her flighty, light-hearted manner win him over from the off.

CHARLIE SWAN.

One aspect of the *Twilight Saga* is very prominent, but doesn't receive as much attention as the Bella-and-Edward or Bella-and-Jacob relationships, or the teen romance angle, or even the vampire and werewolf element, and that's Bella's relationship with her father Charlie Swan.

In fact, there are, really, *three* guys in Bella Swan's life: her One-True-Love, Edward, her Best-Friend-Almost-Lover Jacob Black, and her father, Charlie Swan. In *Eclipse,* for instance, there is a *lengthy* sequence at the top of the novel where Bella is talking to her father. Bella's been grounded (following going A.W.O.L. in Italy in the finale of *New Moon*), her Pa wants her to start seeing some of her friends (and Jacob most especially). There is a *lot* of father-daughter talk, as each side negotiates with the other in their best interests. And this is *way* before the Twin Hunks, Edward and Jacob, enter the foreground of the *Eclipse* novel.

Or, to put it another way, the *Twilight Saga* is a literary series with a *major* father issue, a father fixation, an œdipal tangle with consumes quite a bit of the time and energy of the protagonist, Bella Swan. Of course, a stern but loving parental figure is part of the Young Adult fiction format, and Charlie Swan is necessary to the plot of *Twilight*

Saga (for all the obvious reasons). He is a classic Dad, naturally: grumpy, taciturn, protective, hard-working, terrible cook, adores sport, beer and watching TV.[8] A big, undemonstrative but lovable bear, Charlie exasperates Bella often, and she also mothers him (that there isn't a woman in Charlie's life stretches belief a little, but it is part of the dramatic formula for this kind of story).

Charlie drinks Rainer beer, wears check shirts over Tee shirts, and jeans, and has a moustache. He fits right into the Pacific North-West. (In the movie, Bella is dressed like her Dad – check shirts, jeans, etc, which's very cute).

In *Eclipse,* Bella Swan herself acknowledges the fatherly aspects in her relationships with her two lovers, Edward Cullen and Jacob Black: when Edward is driving Bella over to meet Jacob, Bella likens it to the time when her parents were divorced, and she was ferried between them (E, 209). That Bella regards Edward and Jake as parental figures is telling (and much is made of the boundary of the territory between Forks and La Push, where hand-overs occur, and which Alice can't see past with her future visions).

THE VOLTURI.

The Volturi clan have been around for 3,000 years (plenty of time for the decadence and weirdness to flourish!). The Twilight Lexicon has Lord Aro *et al* being born around 1,300 B.C.

You don't irritate the Volturi, unless you want to die, Edward tells Bella (NM, 418). Vampires tend to keep out of their way as much as possible: they are the K.G.B., the C.I.A., the F.B.I., the M.I.6 and the security services of the vampire world. (They are also aligned with Roman Catholicism, pitting them against the Mormonism of the Cullen clan – so it's one branch of Christianity versus another, religious conflicts are just as strong today as 500, or 1,000 years ago).

The Volturi mob may be a vampire organization akin to the Vatican City, with global, hi-tech connections, but they can't ascertain whether Renesmee is an immortal child or not from their HQ in Volterra, Italy. And they don't even bother to have at least one independent source confirm it before going to battle! Instead, from one word from Jane, they go to war! Boredom, I guess. The Volturi do enjoy an opportunity to be sadistic.

---

8 In *Eclipse,* Charlie heads 'for the TV, just like every other night' (E, 46).

ARO.

The most dangerous vampire in the *Twilight Saga* (by some way!) is Lord Aro (you do *not* want to have Aro as your enemy!). Transformed in his mid-twenties (like Carlisle, his counter-part among the N. American vampires), and born *c.* 1300 B.C. in Greece, Aro possess the unusual gift of being able to see every thought someone's had when he touches them.

Lord Aro is an arch manipulator and schemer – part-Iago and part-spymaster – this comes over much stronger in the *Twilight* books than the movies (which simply don't have time to explore that). In the books, Aro is portrayed as one of the oldest vampires in existence who is continually on the look-out for new talent to add to his Volturi Empire. Lord Aro won't use force or coercion at first, but will scheme and flatter his way into situations, biding his time before making his move (tho' violence is never too far away from the Volturi operation, and everybody knows that it can be deployed at any moment).

The Volturi mates/ wives/ lovers (Sulpicia, Athenodora, etc), meanwhile, play little part in *The Twilight Saga*, and are kept out of the way (literally – they are practically prisoners, rarely leaving Volterra. Lord Aro uses a number of other vampires and their gifts to keep the female mates happy while he and the boys perform the real business of running the Volturi organization. It's a reflection of the archaic, chauvinist, patriarchal make-up of the Mafia, where the women are expected to stay home, keep house and cook).

Compared to Lord Aro, the other members of the Volturi coven (Marcus, Caius, Felix, Demetri, Jane) aren't particularly interesting (indeed, Aro in the *Twilight* books isn't that riveting, either – but in the *Twilight* movies, he's played by Michael Sheen! Wow! Sheen is sensational – he can take a boring piece of business in a script and turn into magic on-screen). And Daokta Fanning certainly makes something of her role as Jane (where her catchphrase is 'Pain').

3

TWILIGHT AND
POPULAR CULTURE

What is *Twilight* about?

Not vampires. Not werewolves. Not horror. Not the Pacific North-West. It's about first love, it's about falling for the bad boy in skool. It's about being awkward, aloof and snooty but still falling for the guy that all your friends warn you about (and then the schmuck jilts you! *So bite me!*). Bella can't resist that pale, glowering face, those dark, golden eyes… Forget that he's a vampire – that's the least of it – because he's vain, stuck-up, supercilious, brutish and violent. And he's a stalker! He creeps into Bella's bedroom and drools over her sleeping!

Twilight's a romance of two outsiders, two misfits, two intellectuals.⁹ Two lonely (but oh-so-sensitive) souls who find solace in the solitude they share with their significant other. Yet both Bella and Edward remain curiously lonely even after their relationship has been cemented (cemented tho' not consummated). They are lovers for whom love is *not* the all-encompassing, all-healing balm they hope it will be. Bella, at the end of the first *Twilight* movie/ book, isn't any happier than she was at the beginning. Neither is Edward, tho' he has at least found someone who can drag him out of his perpetual narcissism momentarily.

But *Twilight*'s also about disaffected youth; it's about the younger generation feeling isolated and not fitting in; it's about growing up and finding your parents' generation disappointing (your folks get divorced,

---

9 Look at the books and CDs in Edward's room and how Bella is bookish.

they're actually quite boring, and they're not the wonderful people you looked up to after all – your Dad can't even cook!); it's about the Sins of the Fathers (in this case, the fathers are also perpetual sons, the vampires being their fathers from generations back); it's about the decline of contemporary North America, socially and politically; it's about the deadening boredom of small-town life; and it's about finding escapism in archaic fantasy about vampires and ill-advised romances.

Bella Swan is from a broken home, which further encourages our sympathy for her. It's a familiar way of life for children of divorced parents, the shuttling from one home to another. That provides the motivation for Bells to move house from Arizona to Washington, where she was born (from the hot/ dry to the cold/ wet, from the desert to the forest).

The most interesting thing about *Twilight* is that it's a movie and book about youth and romance with a young woman at its centre. Yet the *Twilight* movie (and the novel) don't do anything with that promising premise. It squanders it, it throws it all away. In the end, *Twilight* is a thoroughly conservative, reactionary story, on screen and in print. These vampires definitely vote Republican! But then, right-wing ideology (close to fascism) has always under-pinned vampireology, even in the hippest, trendiest, most socially-conscious vampire outings. After all, vampire tales are all about blood, aristocracy, decaying families, the survival of the fittest, the law of the jungle. Nietszchean Supermen in black Gothic clothing.

THE *TWILIGHT* CULTURAL PHENOMENON

The *Twilight* series became a phenomenon in popular culture. To the point where it spawned its own spoof movies, jokes, enormous numbers of fan websites,[10] fan fiction by the ton (and inspiring the lucrative *50 Shades of Grey* franchise), and a vast merchandizing operation. And of course a sizeable groundswell of negative reaction: along with the fang fans, they were plenty of people who loathed the *Twilight* movies (such as boyfriends who were dragged along to see the flicks by their girlfriends).

10 Have a look at Stephenie Meyer's website, which contains a *long* list of the fan sites devoted to all things *Twilighty.*

Mad, The Muppets, Robot Chicken, The Hillywood Show and *Saturday Night Live* are among the shows that have spoofed the *Twilight Saga*. For the short *Saturday Night Live* skit (called *Firelight*), Taylor Swift appeared as Bella in amongst the Cullen family, who were parodied as Frankenstein's monsters. (Swift had wanted to appear in *New Moon*, but the producers declined). Other parodies include *TwiLite* (by Stephen Jenner), *The Twishite Saga* (by Stephford Mayo), *Nightlight* (by the *Harvard Lampoon*), *Twilight: The Musical* (by Gliff Productions), and *Almost Night* (by Jacob Wallace).

Critics, as expected, had very mixed views of the *Twilight* phenomenon (they automatically do whenever something becomes a cultural phenomenon, or what they regard as way too popular). But then, they weren't the target audience, as with *Harry Potter* or spoof movies or Japanese *animé* or 'chick flicks'. The *Twilight* movies were enjoyed by massive audiences, but not by the intelligentsia, not by film critics on the East Coast, or by any male, or anybody over the age of 15.

Or that's how it seemed.

The acrimony that the *Twilight Saga* received from film critics and media watchers was striking. You saw the same thing with the *Harry Potter* phenomenon, or the *Pokémon* craze, or the glut of superhero movies, or the blockbuster novels of Jackie Collins and Dan Brown... Critics often drew attention to the second-rate nature of the books by Stephenie Meyer (and, as with J.K. Rowling or Jackie Collins, there was certainly an element of jealousy: 'how did this author get so rich with such poorly-written tripe?' lies behind the complaints of the cognoscenti). And yet author S. Meyer has often talked up literary classics, acknowledging her debts to Jane Austen, William Shakespeare and Charlotte Brontë, and also encouraging readers to seek out the classic texts.

The Twilight Saga was derided by some quarters of the media in the same way that other products aimed at teenage girls have been: the critical academy typically scorns pop music, romantic fiction, lifestyle magazines and women's magazines, television soap operas, etc. As some observers noted, society just doesn't like teenage girls.

Those outside the *Twilight* phenomenon (poor, unloved things) didn't understand it. They saw only 'emo', Goth-a-like teenagers mooning over lerrrve and vampirism (as opposed to 'grown-up', 'intellectual', critically-acclaimed fare like *Romeo and Juliet* (by William Shakespeare), where teenagers moon over lerrrve, or *Sense and Sensibility* (by Jane Austen), where young women moon over lerrrve, or any Thomas Hardy novel, where youngsters moon over lerrrve, or the poetry of Dante Alighieri and Francesco Petrarch (where youths moon over lerrrve), or for a change, *Hamlet*, where a young prince moons over being depressed).[11]

The truth is, the literature and cinema vaunted by the critical academy and the 'highbrow' media is founded on precisely the same base/ primal desires (love, folks, is a key factor in pretty much every classic movie and novel – yes, and most classic poetry, and operas, and ballets, and plays, and, well, pretty much everything), the same clichéd situations (you're telling me that *War and Peace* or the *Divine Comedy* don't contain 10,000 clichés?), the same stock characters (as in the fiction of Mark Twain or George Eliot), and the same issues (love, lust, power, money, race, exploitation, injustice, etc).

Let's remember that many of the Big Name Authors and the Classic Books of the past three thousand years use clichés, sleaze, unbelievable plot twists, unconvincing coincidences, dumb dialogue, out-size characters and everything else that the 'trashy' novel uses (and is castigated for). Dante does. The *Beowulf*-poet does. Cervantes does. Shakespeare does. Gogol does. Eliot does. Twain does. Homer does.

TWIHARDS AND TWILIGHTERS: THE FANS

The *Twilight* fans have been dubbed 'Twihards', 'Twilighters', 'fang fans' and 'fanpires'. The franchise developed into a well-known media brand, alongside Disney, *Star Wars, Harry Potter,* Hello Kitty and Barbie. The level of fan interest in the *Twilight* movies took many by surprise. Stephenie Meyer commented on how *Twilight* changed her life: 'the massive amount of fans that I hadn't expected, and the massive amount of people who hated it, which I also didn't expect'. Some in the first movie's cast thought they were making a low budget, indie sort of movie for the fans of the books, and hadn't anticipated quite that level of hysteria.

'The wonderful thing about this is our audience and fan base, which is primarily women and girls. Women, in general, are very passionate fans, and that's what you love about them', noted screenwriter Melissa Rosenberg (2012).

Taylor Lautner remarked that the fans could be 'pretty intense': 'They

---

11 Edward Cullen is a Hamlet clone.

are very intense, but it's cool that they're so dedicated and so passionate. They're the reason we're here doing this sequel [*New Moon*]'. Robert Pattinson found that fans identified very closely with the characters and their situations: 'I guess this story is just so intimate that people think they really know the characters and can feel the emotion'.[12]

The internet (and later social media) played a key role in the creation of the fan base of the *Twilight Saga*, and how the franchise was consumed and perceived. For Stephenie Meyer, the publication of the books was compromised somewhat when spoilers came out (for instance, the two spoilers for *New Moon* – that Edward leaves and that Jacob is a werewolf).

Of the *Twilight* series, film critics often complained that 'only fans will understand these movies', or, 'these movies are only for fans'. What those remarks really mean – and we've heard them about many popular/ fantasy franchises – is: 'I can't be bothered to follow the story and the characters'; or: 'It's yet another fantasy franchise like all the others, but not for the general public'; or: 'only nerds who need to get a life will enjoy these flicks'.

But the story and the characters of the *Twilight* movies are easy to comprehend. It's a love story, that's all! It's Romeo and Juliet (heard of them?!), it's Cathy and Heathcliff, it's Elizabeth Bennet and Mr Darcy, it's Jane Eyre and Mr Rochester, it's the Princess[13] and the Prince, or it's Little Red Riding Hood and the Wolf, or it's Beauty and the Beast[14] of countless fairy and folk tales. (And many of those characters from literature are consciously referenced in the *Twilight* texts, making them perfect for high school essays).

The devotion that the pin-up stars of the *Twilight* movies have drawn from fans veers on the alarming. As Robert Pattinson has noted, for months he seemed to travel around the world being screamed at, during the promotional tours for the *Twilight* flicks. Women offered their underwear for Taylor Lautner and Pattinson to sign, and four women had their necks bitten and bleeding, presenting themselves to Pattinson, saying, 'this is for you!' (These are some of the stories printed in the media – presumably *way* wackier propositions have been made to the *Twilight* stars that nobody has dared to reveal!).

12 Even Melissa Rosenberg received attention from the fans, as she found out when she attended Comic-Con, and fans knew who she was (CFA, 40).
13 Observers noted that the *Twilight Saga* tapped into 'Princess culture', which was marketed to young girls (*Twilight* has a Damsel In Distress who's saved by a Prince).
14 *Beauty and the Beast* is a model for so many horror movies: the fairy tale can be discerned everywhere in the horror genre (including the vampire genre and its sub-genres). The other great ancestor of horror movies is of course *Frankenstein* – both the Gothic novel of 1820 and the many movies (one of the classic *Frankenstein* flicks is directly referenced in *Breaking Dawn*, in Edward's flashback).

The obsessive interest that the *Twilight* movies generated in the media spilled over into real life: Robert Pattinson and Kristen Stewart wanted to keep their relationship private, for instance, and refused to confirm it (or to discuss it afterwards). But for the publicity department promoting the *Twilight Saga*, that was gold dust! To have a screen romance in a big franchise of movies being reflected in a real life liaison was the kind of PR you can't buy (or engineer!).

And it got to the point where fans and followers were upset when Kristen Stewart was discovered kissing middle-aged director Rupert Sanders in public (she was working on the mind-bogglingly cretinous *Snow White and the Huntsman*). When audiences are mixing up reality and fantasy, marketing departments, studios and filmmakers know they've got them right where they want them.

2008 was a Big Year for Twihards: the release of the first *Twilight* movie and the publication of the final book, *Breaking Dawn* (publishers and movie distributors seek out this kind of synergy – the *Harry Potter* franchise is a good example, with the later J.K. Rowling books being released around the time of the movies). By 2008, then, the *Twilight* book series was over – but no, wait! There was a further installment, with the *Bree Tanner* novella in 2010 (which coincided with the release of the second sequel, *Eclipse*).[15] And altho' the book series was done by 2008, fans still had movies to look forward to in 2009, 2010, 2011 and 2012. (And in between times, the merchandizers were exploiting the *Twilight* market with 100s of items). And there were further books from Stephenie Meyer, including the gender reversal *Life and Death*, and *Midnight Sun*. (And more texts were announced in Feb, 2023).

The town of Forks has capitalized on the success of the *Twilight* franchise. Logging and wood was the chief business in Forks; but after the success of the *Twilight Saga*, it became 'the *Twilight* Town', with a new tourist economy (there was 'a *Twilight* Symposium' in 2009, which allowed fans to visit Forks High School. Later, an annual bloodsucking festival, Forever Twilight, was established). Some 8,000 Twi-hards were visiting the town every month at the height of *Twi*-fever (and they still visit today).

Actress Ashley Greene was a keen devotee of all things *Twilight* – she inaugurated a series of podcasts (*The Twilight Effect*) with her chum Melanie Howe about the *Saga* (highly recommended). In 2022, Greene noted that there was a resurgence of interest in the *Twilight Saga* (the movies had appeared on Netflix and Peacock).

---

15 Originally, the story of Bree was going to be part of *The Twilight Saga: The Official Guide.*

The vitriol that some viewers and readers have expressed is disturbing in its ferocity, as if the *Twilight* novels and the *Twilight* movies had committed horrendous crimes (perhaps the vampires smashed their way into the homes of the complainers and ripped apart their familes right in front of their eyes, while leaving them barely alive and psycholoigically scarred for life). Similarly intense responses from viewers are found in the *Star Wars* fan community and other franchises. *Star Wars* fans will talk in terms of 'betrayal', or having their childhoods 'ruined' by this or that *Star Wars* movie or sequel.

(Well, screenwriter Melissa Rosenberg knew they weren't making *Dr Zhivago.* But the romantic theme was a universal one, which would apeal to men and women: 'the fantasy being to be loved and cherished for exactly who you are' [2012]).

Here is a smattering of loathing about *Twilight* culled from the Internet Movie Database website:

'I absolutely hated this movie';	'so boring';
'boy was I disappointed';	'this movie was horrible';
'the movie was terrible';	'worst movie I ever saw'.
'it was so cheesy and corny and awkward';	

So some of the consumer reviews and user reviews of the first *Twilight* call it the Worst Movie Ever Made ('this movie is simply awful!'). And they hated it – hated, hated, hated it! Clearly these viewers haven't seen *Where the Wild Things Are* or *Hannibal* or *Quantum of Solace* or *Chocolat* or *About a Boy* or *Billy Elliot* or *Unbreakable* or *Emmanuele 5* or *Bridget Jones* or *X-Men Origins: Wolverine* or *The Avengers* (1997) or *Charlie's Angels* or *Speed 2* or *Alien vs. Predator* (there are 1,000s of others – we could be hear til twilight next December coming up with just a few of the titles of godawful movies).

Let's have a look at the debate about high art versus low art as it relates to *The Twilight Saga* and similar works. (This short section is taken from my critical study of Jackie Collins,[16] an author often derided like Stephenie Meyer).

The æsthetic oppositions in the critical debate about blockbuster/ airport/ 'trashy' fiction include:

High art	Low art
Highbrow	Lowbrow
Elitist	Popular
Culture	Trash
Royalty	Celebrity
Old money	New money
Bourgeois	Working-class
Tradition	Modernity
Europe	North America
Classical music	Pop music
Art cinema	Popular cinema
Letters	E-mails/ Messages/ Social media
Novels	Internet
Classic novels	Blockbuster novels

The snobbery surrounding critical views of blockbuster/ popular novelists, including Stephenie Meyer, can be found everywhere. Have a look on the internet and anti-social media, and you'll see reviews and writing by fans and readers which talk about 'guilty pleasures', about Meyer's books being 'trashy' and badly written – but enjoyable. ('Cringe' is a term that crops up a lot in *Twilight* criticism among consumers; so the books and the movies feature cringeworthy scenes. Yes, but so what? The books are about clumsy, shy, confused teenagers! Come on, even you, dear reader, were sometimes unsure, evasive or just plain annoying when you were a teenager!).

Readers seem to feel 'guilty', they always apologize, they always talk down reading *Twilight* – as if they should be reading Hermann Hesse or Torquato Tasso or Mikhail Bakhtin or Gayatri Chakravorty Spivak (what's stopping them? Go read Slavoj Zizek or Michel Foucault

---

16 *Jackie Collins: Queen of Hollywood*, Crescent Moon Publishing, 2022.

already!). Or doing something useful like Saving The Earth.[17]

I'm writing a book about *Twilight*, so I have to read the books and watch the movies! But you, dear reader, don't need to waste your time on something you hate! For instance, how many of the classic novels have you read? – *The Magic Mountain, The Counterfeiters, The Outsider, Candide, Heart of Darkness, The Rainbow, The Three Mustketeers, Frankenstein, Dracula, Eyeless In Gaza, The Catcher In the Rye, The Maltese Falcon, Alice's Adventures In Wonderland, Great Expectations, Tom Sawyer, A Wizard of Earthsea, Fire From Heaven, Wolf Solent, Thérèse Raquin* and *Tess of the d'Urbervilles* – all fantastic.

Yes, but reading novels isn't *homework*, folks, it isn't meant to be a chore. If you're not in school or college, you don't *need* to read novels to pass exams or write essays. Nobody's going to test you on the ideological, post-deconstructionist themes in the *Twilight Saga* or E.L. James's *50 Shades of Grey*!

So why all this guilt?

Why all this embarrassment or shame surrounding populist/ airport/ blockbuster novels? You could say that readers are demeaning themselves – that they are 'lowering' themselves in reading what they regard as 'trash'. But why feel 'guilty', and why call it 'trash'? It's fiction, it's entertainment – come on, folks, reading is just another one of 10,000 things you could be doing. But don't feel 'guilty' about it!

If you feel 'guilty' about reading the *Twilight Saga*, then *read something else*, by the Gods! There are at least two or three thousand novels that are regarded as classics in the Western tradition. Read them, dear, sweet reader, and don't feel 'guilty' about reading 'junk'. Why waste your time? You only have 80 years (if you're lucky!).

If you want to read a classic, literary novel with plots that resemble a Stephenie Meyer book, try *Tess of the d'Urbervilles* or *Jane Eyre* or *Pride and Prejudice* or *Wuthering Heights*. Then you won't feel shameful!

And if you think the *Twilight* movies are baloney, well then, go and watch masterpieces such as *Shoah, Night and Fog, The Battle of Algiers, Histoire(s) du Cinéma, Day of Wrath, The Magnificent Ambersons, Mirror, Sunrise, Intolerance*, and *The Gospel According To Matthew*.

✐

So you die.

You go to Heaven (somehow, you didn't manage to get bitten by a vampire, so you ain't immortal, and you die).

17 Earth doesn't *need* saving – I mean the *planet* itself, not *humanity*; the planet's been around for 4.6 billion years!

St Peter's right there at the Gates (with 2,000 bouncer-angels wearing dark glasses and armed with holy spears).

He asks you, 'Did you or did you not[18] read a Stephenie Meyer *Twilight* book during your life? When you should have been reading great Christian texts such as St Augustine and Dionysius the Areopagite?'

You mumble that maybe you glanced at *Twilight* once when you were fifteen and on vacation and it was raining.

St Peter sighs heavily. Then thunders, 'DAMN YOU TO HELL, YOU HERETIC!'

And down to Hell you go.

✐

This will not happen.

✐

Some of the consumer reviews online complain about spending too long reading the *Twilight Saga* when they *really* didn't like it or enjoy it. But what sane, conscious human *chooses* to spend six hours doing something they don't enjoy?! (Was an Italian-American wise guy holding a gun to their head?!).

I'm reminded here of genius film director Jean-Luc Godard: when someone says, 'I saw a bad film', Godard's retort is to say, 'it's your own fault. What did you do to improve the dialogue?' Only Godard could tell someone it was their own fault if they saw a bad film! And then go on to suggest that they improve the dialogue! Applying this crazy Godardism to the disgruntled readers of *The Twilight Saga* – why didn't they start rewriting the books? In six hours, you could rewrite several chapters of *Twilight*! (And of course some *Twihards* have done just that, created their own fan versions. And some fans even went on to publish their work and sell millions!).

At the Fanfiction.net website, the numbers of stories by fans based on best-selling books include the following at the top of the list:

Harry Potter (783,000 entries),

Twilight (219,000),

Percy Jackson and the Olympians (73,900),

The Lord of the Rings (56,300),

and *The Hungover Games* (45,600).

Critics attack books all the time, but they never offer to rewrite them or to propose 100 ideas for changing a story. A review might be 500 words of bile, but it is never 200 words of bile and 300 words of ideas

---

18 For some reason, St Peter sounds like Senator Joseph McCarthy at the H.U.A.C. trials.

for improvements. Any decent writer can come up with plenty of ways in which a text or a story could be altered, but critics never bother.

LOW AND HIGH ART.
This complaint is often trotted out:
   – It's trash.
   – So? And your point is?
   – It's trash.
   – But so is 99.99% of *everything* the global media churns
     out, in any era, any nation, anywhere.

If you regard the *Twilight Saga* as 'trash' or 'low art' or 'populist culture', then you might have to apply that same simplistic judgement to everything else you consume that is also 'low art' and 'popular culture'. It means that all of the following must also be seen as trash:
   • Pop music
   • Movies
   • Television
   • Radio
   • Magazines and newspapers
   • Theatre
   • Internet
   • Advertizing

This means, using your simplistic terms, that *all* of pop music is trash – pop music meaning soul, hip-hop, rap, rock, jazz, folk, metal, dance, drum and bass, whatever genre. It means that 99.99% of the movies you love are junk. It means *all* of television. It means 99.99% of radio. It means *all* of magazines and newspapers, lifestyle mags, consumer mags, whatever mags, except maybe some academic journals, which are 'high culture' (but even upscale newspapers are filled with 'low culture' – and they certainly advertize and review low culture). It means nearly all theatre, except Shakespeare, Ibsen, Chekhov, and 'serious' plays, etc. It means 99.99% of the internet. *All* of advertizing and anything commercial, naturally.

If you were serious about avoiding all kinds of 'trash' and 'low culture', you would only partake of: ballet, opera, classical music, art, museums, and straight theatre. You would never enter a supermarket, never surf the web, never glance at a billboard, never go to the cinema, never watch TV, never listen to the radio or pop music, never go to a pop concert, never read a magazine or newspaper, never consume advertizing of any kind, and so on.

BEYOND GENRE.

The *Twilight* series has been part of a trend in recent Hollywood cinema for productions based on fiction in the teenage or Young Adult market: *Percy Jackson, His Dark Materials, The Hunger Games, Divergent, Eragon* and of course *Harry Potter* and J.R.R. Tolkien. (Stephenie Meyer was a big fan of *The Hunger Games*, and Lionsgate, who bought up Summit, backed the *Hunger Games* movies).

Like the blockbuster-campy-airport-beach-vacation-tune-out novel, Young Adult fiction is not a genre or a format. It's more a way of approaching and selling fiction (that is, it's a marketing construct, because booksellers – and the media – like to know where to put the books on the shelf, and how to categorize their products). Thus, one finds all sorts of Young Adult books beside each other on the bookshelves, in different genres. The marketing devices meld the genres together. There are some genres suited to the Young Adult novel: thrillers, sci-fi, historical romance, family saga and Gothic horror.

Of all the genres among all bestselling books, thrillers out-number everything else. In 1995, a list of the genres for the 100 top-selling books included: thrillers: 27, crime: 7, romance: 6, sagas: 5, autobiographies: 5, humour: 4, fantasy: 3, TV tie-in books: 3, film tie-in books: 2, horror: 2, science: 2, gardening 2, short stories: 1, with genres such as travel, drink and biography having 1 book each. In the 1990s, thrillers took between 20% and 25% of the share of bestselling novels each year. Thriller/ crime fiction continues to dominate fiction publishing. (And in movies and television, yes, thrillers are everywhere).

The *Twilight* series isn't 'realism', is not meant to be 'realistic' – it's romantic fantasy. All fiction is *fiction*. Made-up stuff. Play-acting. Putting on silly clothes and fooling around (look at the *Twilight* movies! They are supremely dressing-up movies).

(Or put it like this: a term like 'realism' is pretty useless (like naturalism). Instead, think of fiction as building different worlds, of worlds-within-worlds. Some worlds might relate to the so-called 'real world'. But they don't have to, or need to. As Ursula Le Guin commented, writing about the 'real world' in a slanted or altered manner (sometimes in reverse), as in science fiction and fantasy fiction, is a great way of looking at it). The *Twilight Saga* has created a world which readers want to visit (some repeatedly).

Trashy, pulpy, populist novels draw together fictional forms such as the epic, the saga, the romance and the soap opera (the *Twilight* series has been given the title of 'saga', tho' it's not quite as far-reaching across generations, themes and locations as the family saga).

The airport/ populist/ blockbuster novel is a yarn, a tale, a story in the time-honoured tradition (i.e., they are very conventional novels, as the novels are in the 18th century or 19th century tradition, and many Young Adult novels are, and not in the modernist or *avant garde* tradition). There are also many elements of the fairy tale and the folk tale, of getting the prince, of overcoming obstacles, of achieving a quest, and being rewarded with wealth and marriage. Trashy/ airport/ populist novels also update the 'bodice-ripper' (a sub-genre of romantic fiction), infusing it with titillation and sex.

The Penny Dreadful, the 'blood and thunder' and the 'bloods' of the Victorian era and Victorian melodrama are also ancestors of Stephenie Meyer's *Twilight* books – quick, cheap, sensational and lurid publishing in weekly installments.

The 19th century 'penny dreadfuls' and the 'penny bloods' were deliberately shocking and gory, and lowbrow and populist (just like TV and cinema – indeed, television and movies took up the same sort of area of lowbrow entertainment, and has continued to exploit the same territory for 115 years).

The 'penny dreadfuls' or 'bloods' were at the height of their popularity in the 1840s and 1850s. It was quick, cheap and sensational publishing in serial (often weekly) form in periodicals and newspapers.

The 'penny bloods' and 'penny dreadfuls' exploited new printing technology which could produce thousands of copies of magazines and newspapers, as well as cheap distribution, which fed into the rise in literacy as well as the huge acceleration in population in London. (The comics industry in Japan is a comparable phenomenon).

One of the tendencies of the lowbrow/ populist novel is towards the soap opera, a day-to-day story of the lives of the Rich and Famous (or the Weird and the Down-trodden. Or, in the case of *Twilight*, the Awkward, Plain and Unloved). Not surprisingly, blockbuster/ populist novels are eminently suitable for TV and film adaptation. They become television 'mini-series', extended fairy tales in modern dress.

But airport/ populist/ blockbuster novels are *already* their own TV and movie adaptations: they don't need to be turned into movies and television: they are already there. *The Twilight Saga* is vivid enough as storytelling that it doesn't need a movie adaptation.

TWILIGHT
THE COMPLETE JOURNEY

PLUS
5 PULLOUT MAGAZINE COVER POSTERS

STUNNING PHOTOS, CANDID INTERVIEWS & INSIDE SCOOP ON ALL 5 MOVIES, INCLUDING BREAKING DAWN PART 2

FROM THE EDITORS

entertainment

FINAL COLLECTOR'S ISSUE

OVER 200 AMAZING PHOTOS

SPECIAL

OK!

THE ULTIMATE GUIDE

TWILIGHT

25

WIN! THE ULTIMATE 6TH BIRTHDAY GIVEAWAY!

UP FOR GRABS!
DVD MICRO SYSTEMS
COLOUR PRINTERS
MOVIE PREMIERE
WATCHES
DVDs
MOVIE TICKETS
CHAMPAGNE
PC GAMES

FIRST

asia's premier movie magazine

NOVEMBER 2008 ISSUE 73

BLONDE CONFESSION #1
"Studying law does *not* make me a bimbo"
ANDREA FONSECA

LEONARDO DICAPRIO & RUSSELL CROWE
Body Of Lies' Brothers to Charm

BLONDE CONFESSION #2
"It's fun to have boobs!"
EVA MENDES

FREE!
SIX YEARS
NINETY-NINE COVERS
ONE GIANT POSTER

Big Bloody Deal

Twilight: The Next Harry Potter
+ Exclusive interviews with Kristen Stewart & Robert Pattinson

TWILIGHT
Collector's Covers
No.1 of 9

Entertainment WEEKLY

ISSUE #1078 · DECEMBER 4, 2009

How the Fans of NEW MOON Are Shaking Up Hollywood. Inside the Phenomenon.

TEAM EDWARD

SPECIAL EDITION

WIN A TRIP TO LONDON AT

Tribute

www.tribute.ca

OCTOBER/NOVEMBER 2009

TAYLOR LAUTNER   KRISTEN STEWART   ROBERT PATTINSON

the Twilight saga
new moon

HOLIDAY MOVIES 2012, The Box, Nine, A Christmas Carol and more!
PLUS: Scarlett Johansson, Jessica Alba, Robert Downey Jr., Sarah Jessica Parker, Leonardo DiCaprio

Twilight stories in King Magazine and Bravo Magazine (Germany).

Sie sind jung, sie sind hot,
sie sind die neuen Überflieger Hollywoods:
Robert Pattinson und Kristen Stewart!
Doch trotz ihres **Erfolgs** mit
„Twilight" fürchten sie sich:
davor, ihr altes Leben aufgeben
zu müssen . . .

Robert & Kristen

Robert und Kristen spielten in den
USA mit ihrem Film „Twilight" in sieben
Wochen schon knapp 130 Millionen
Euro an den Kinokassen ein!

Wir haben

TEXT: Yvonne Huckenholz, Yao Ni

Plötzlich Superstars! Für Robert Pattinson (22) und Kristen Stewart (18) ist dieses Märchen wahr geworden. Doch wirklich glücklich sind die beiden Hauptdarsteller aus „Twilight" (ab 15. Januar in unseren Kinos) nicht darüber! Im exklusiven Doppel-Interview mit BRAVO erzählen Robert und Kristen, wie sehr der Ruhm ihr Leben verändert hat, wovor sie Angst haben und warum sie es mit der Körperpflege nicht so genau nehmen . . .
BRAVO: Wo immer ihr jetzt auftaucht, herrscht Fan-

Robert: „Ich verlasse nur noch ungern das Haus!"

ROBERT: Es ist echt verrückt! Ich werde mich nie daran gewöhnen, dass mich Fans bitten, in meine Vampir-Rolle zu schlüpfen und sie in den Hals zu beißen. Ich war sogar mal kurz davor, mich als Edward vorzustellen, weil mich so viele Fans mit meinem Rollennamen ansprechen . . .
BRAVO: Das zeigt: In eurem Leben hat sich seit „Twilight" viel verändert . . .
ROBERT: Allerdings! Um ehrlich zu sein: Inzwischen verlasse ich nur noch ungern das Haus (lacht). Wer wird schon gern am Flughafen fotografiert, wenn

Kristen und Robert beim BRAVO-Besuch

BRAVO: Im Film seht ihr immer toll aus, musstet dafür Stunden in der Maske verbringen. Wie lang braucht ihr denn privat im Bad?
KRISTEN: Ich mache morgens fast gar nichts, brauche vielleicht fünf Minuten im Bad. Zähneputzen, das war's auch schon . . .
ROBERT: Ich brauche nicht mal fünf

BRAVO: Immerhin gehst du überhaupt ins Bad, Robert! Schließlich hast du doch mal gestanden, dass du dir manchmal wochenlang nicht die Haare wäschst!
ROBERT: Das stimmt (lacht). Haarewaschen nervt. Eigentlich geh ich nur ins Bad, wenn ich aufs Klo muss!
BRAVO: Jetzt mal Hand aufs Herz:

4

TWILIGHT AND FEMINISM

Stephenie Meyer has asserted that she is a feminist. Maybe she is, but she is fundamentally a conservative author, and the feminism that emerges from her fiction can be termed liberal feminism or mainstream feminism. Meyer is definitely not a radical feminist, a separatist feminist, or a revolutionary feminist. She is a devotee of Jane Austen and Charlotte Brontë, not Joanna Russ, Ursula Le Guin, Mary Daly or Julia Kristeva. And her books do not advocate living apart from men in lesbian, radical feminist communes or 'womyn's lands', and they do not hope to revolutionize masculinist culture, and they do not wish to avoid, transcend or destroy men and patriarchal society.

Many feminists and critics have attacked the *Twilight* books and movies for their reactionary, conservative and patriarchal depictions of young women in contemporary, Western society. For the detractors, Bella Swan is a drippy, droopy, low self-esteem girl who swoons over Edward Cullen, staking everything in her life on him. She becomes the Passive Princess who has to be protected by a Prince (she's a Passive-Aggressive Princess). She believes wholly in the idea of true love (and romance, and marriage).[1] She can't be happy or fulfilled without Edward in her life.[2]

Worse: for some critics and feminists, the *Twilight* series exhibits disturbing images and motifs of abuse and sadomasochism. One of the most obvious (and physical) expressions of abuse is the morning after the wedding night scene, where Bella Swan is bruised (and, even creepier,

---

[1] One wonders if the *Twilight* series has been used as an example in domestic discussions about relationships: *see, honey, she turned into a vampire so she could be with him. Would you do that for me?*

[2] But remember too that the *Twilight* movies play with the issue of sexuality and masochism in a humorous manner. For ex, Bella, during the honeymoon, knowing that Edward is withholding himself from her sexually, dresses provocatively in sexy numbers. She flops on the bed in front of him wearing lingerie. It's lighthearted and innocent, it's not about sadomasochism and psychological abuse.

likes it – it's the badge of true love). Thus, as soon as she becomes a wife, she is a battered wife (there's another abused wife/ girlfriend scene, when Sam Uley 'accidentally' injures Emily, and Rosalie was raped).

It was pointed out that the central relationship in the *Twilight* series exhibits 15 signs of abuse as listed by the National Domestic Violence group in the U.S.A. (As Tanya Gold noted in the *Guardian* newspaper, 'there is the controlling male, the female with low self-esteem, the threats of suicide and murder, and so on').

Feminists have criticized the *Twilight Saga* for its portrayal of Bella Swan as a teenage girl who must undergo several sacrifices and renunciations in order to remain with Edward Cullen, culminating with transforming herself into a vampire so she can stay with him. M. Carmen Gomez-Calisteo noted that 'even more harmful, being more than willing to make costly personal sacrifices, and losing friends in the process are seen as indicators of love'.

We can say there isn't a price paid in the *Twilight* series, but there is: *death.* Bella has to die in order to achieve vampirehood. It's a symbolic death, followed by a miraculous rebirth. It's a rite of passage, a transformation from one state (life) thru another (death) into a heightened state (vampiredom). For the feminist critics who scorn the *Twilight Saga*, Bella has to give up too much – she sacrifices too much. (That Bella is dead the movie of *Breaking Dawn* makes absolutely sure (as does the novel): we see Edward and Jake trying to revive her many times, to no avail. We see Edward desert her corpse and go to fight the werewolves.)

Camille Paglia, by contrast, rejects (in *Vamps and Tramps*) the emphasis on the victim in recent feminist debates:

> I *hate* the victim-centred nature of contemporary feminism! It's *loath-some* to me. I believe woman is the *dominant* sex, okay? And that everyone knows this, *everyone* knows throughout world culture that woman *dominates* man. Everyone but feminists knows that! And I think it's absolutely perverse and neurotic to insist that history is nothing but male oppressors and female victims. This is *ridiculous*, all right? (240)

Author Stephenie Meyer insisted that Bella Swan had to be wounded physically to pay off the idea that Edward Skullin refused to make love with her because it would be too painful (for her). That is, Edward's reluctance (or avoidance) of having sex with Bella was because he thought he would harm her. It's a version of the man with unbridled lust, who can't contain himself (yet, throughout the *Twilight Saga* books/ movies, Edward is an incredibly restrained, buttoned-up guy, who can't even handle blood without getting hysterical or violent). It's the man who's so passionate he might hurt the woman he loves. Edward also represents a threat, then, at a physical level, as the object of desire for Bella.

Stephenie Meyer claimed that a key part of the feminism she propounded in the *Twilight* books was based in freedom. Bella Swan has a choice. Libertarian projects were increasingly an important part of ideology in the West in the 21st century.

OK. What else? Edward Cullen certainly exhibits plenty of other forms of disturbing behaviour. That he's a stalker in all but name is clear to anyone (he admits he is an obsessed stalker in *Midnight Sun*): he creeps into Bella's room, he watches her while she's asleep, he follows her in his car,[3] he fills in application forms for her, and he pokes thru her belongings.[4] Creepy? Very!

Edward Cullen employs psychological tactics and coercion a number of times in the *Twilight Saga*. He can tell what people are thinking, and uses this against Bella Swan (and Jake Black). He issues threats to get what he wants. He places Bella often in the role of the submissive Princess who must be protected and/ or saved.

The thought of hurting Bella Swan tortures Edward Cullen. So he says. Many times in the *Twilight* opus Edward tells Bella, 'I couldn't live with myself if I ever hurt you. You don't know how it's tortured me' (T, 239). He states in *Twilight*, 'I could kill you quite easily, Bella, simply by accident' (T, 271). *By accident?!* What's this about 'accidentally' killing someone?! What's with all this talk about hurting people and torture? Oh right, Edward's a *vampire*. I get it! Yes, but take away the vampirism, and it becomes very creepy very quickly.

She's a lamb, he's a lion: a stupid lamb, Bella admits, and 'a sick, masochistic lion', Edward adds (T, 240).[5] A sadist *and* a masochist, in one, glittering mix.

> Would he rather *die* than change me?
> Stephenie Meyer (*New Moon*, 479)

Presumably Edward Cullen is 'redeemed' by... by what, exactly? He's a serial killer, but somehow that's OK ('it doesn't matter', claims Bella Swan at the end of the *Twilight* novels). Robert Kolker, talking about *Schindler's List* in *A Cinema of Loneliness: Penn, Stone, Kubrick, Scorsese, Spielberg, Altman*, made comments about redemption which can also apply to how the *Twilight Saga* treats Edward:

---

3 'I wondered if it should bother me that he was following me; instead I felt a strange surge of pleasure. He stared, maybe wondering why my lips were curving into an involuntary smile' (T, 152).
4 When he ends their relationship in *New Moon*, he sneaks into her bedroom and squirrels away everything that he'd given her, including the CD of his music and the photos.
5 Meyer was keen to have these lines in the movie.

The redemptive event that so obsesses Spielberg and American culture in general achieves a number of results: it provides narrative closure without having to reach any definitive conclusions; it totally evades politics and history; it gives men an excuse for their behavior; and, most obviously, it hails the redeemed character (and presumably the spectator) into the ideologies of testing, heroism, love, marriage, and family – without the audience having to act on anything but their ability to look at the screen. (2000, 324)

The redemption is fake, ultimately. It isn't earned, it doesn't make sense. It's imposed on awfully violent events by a conservative ideology which would seek to make everything better.

And how about Bella Swan? Well, certainly there are elements of masochism in her relationship with Edward Cullen in the *Twilight Saga*. Certainly she stakes so much of her soul and well-being on happiness in love with Edward (tho' that is part of the romance genre – look at the history of poetry! Plenty of male poets have depicted themselves in their works undergoing dubious masochistic relationships with their beloveds. And a million contemporary pop songs depict boys and men who're nothing without their women; again and again, across the whole history of pop music, we hear singers griping about their missing 'babies', how they can't function with them, how their lives have gone to pieces because *she* or *he* isn't there no more). Certainly Bella allows herself to be pushed around by Edward (and the other Cullens). Certainly she acts in a scarily submissive manner during her pregnancy, and in her attitude towards the child inside her that's breaking her bones.

But those elements of masochism in the *Twilight Saga* are also part of the romance genre, and of love stories everywhere. Come on, look at any of the classic love stories in the history of world literature, and I bet you can discern elements of masochism and sadomasochism in all of them! Courtly love poetry of the twelfth century, Elizabethan love poetry, Ancient Greek love poetry, William Shakespeare's plays, the revenge tragedies of Thomas Middleton, John Webster and John Ford, the great 19th century novels of the Brontës, Hardy, Eliot, Austen – S/M is all over those classic texts! Sometimes it's psychological sadomasochism, and occasionally it's physical.

Because those elements of sadomasochism exist in many relationships, including throughout the social realms of the real, Western world. You and your government. You and the police. You and the military. You and your neighbours. You and your work colleagues. You and your college/ school. You and your family!

The *Twilight* series is no different from classical literature in simply exaggerating what is already there, and siting it within a particular genre (never forget the *genre* elements of the *Twilight* series, it is *wholly* a genre-based text. Genre meaning the form of the text, the shape, the structure, the boundaries, the themes, the characters, the events, etc).

Because that's what literature (art/ drama/ entertainment/ whatever) is, that's what it does: it exaggerates what is already there. The *Twilight* series couldn't have become a pop culture phenomenon if it didn't resonate deeply with audiences in book or movie form. Forget the vampire and magical stuff, audiences can relate to the *Twi-lite* books and films on a relationship and psychological and emotional level.

Having said all of that, there's no doubt that the primary character in the *Twilight* series does exhibit masochistic thoughts and behaviour that is disturbing. But then so does Tess Durbeyfield (*Tess of the d'Urbervilles*), or Elizabeth Bennet (*Pride and Prejudice*), or Cathy Earnshaw (*Wuthering Heights*), or Juliet (*Romeo and Juliet*), or Cleopatra (*Antony and Cleopatra*), or any of the great heroines of world literature.

It's not only Edward Cullen who comes across as a stalker at times: Jacob Black is also overly-protective, to the point where, as with Edward, it's suffocating. Does Bella really need 'protecting' that much? (Her Dad's a cop! With a gun! And in the movie, several guns! He's cleaning a rifle right in the foreground of one shot!). According to Jacob and Edward, yes she does need protecting! So they are prowling around her house, or shadowing her truck, or calling her to make sure she's OK.

For J. Aubrey *et al* (in the essay "The romanticization of abstinence: Fan response to sexual restraint in the Twilight series"), 'Edward represents a 'safe' sexuality: his simultaneous passion for Bella and his protection of her virtue result in a romantic hero who is both sexually charged and chaste'. Aubrey *et al* found that some teenage girls (aged 15 and 16) responded positively (and unexpectedly) to the emphasis in the *Twilight* novels on abstinence, on waiting until marriage for intercourse. For Sarah Seltzer (in the *Huffington Post*), the hero insisting on waiting until marriage to consummate their romance emphasizes his desire to protect her: so Bella's 'physical safety becomes a symbolic substitute for her virginity, and Edward guards it with overprotective zeal' (2008).

Critics have attacked the depiction of love and sex in the *Twilight* series as 'abstinence porn', for making a big thing of no-sex-before-marriage. 'Abstinence porn'? Isn't that a contradiction?! (It sounds like another 'Only In America' phrase). Much more potentially damaging is the emphasis on masochism, on corrupt, exploitative relationships, on Edward's stalker tendencies, and on marital abuse and violence against women (plus the unsettling references to suicide, and the veiled suicide attempts from both Bella and Edward – and the real one from Esme).

In an article on *Twilight* and the television shows it influenced, such as *True Blood* and *The Vampire Diaries*, Sara Klein explored the sexualization of the heroine:

> These shows, popular among women of all ages from tweens to women, emphasize female sexuality by focusing on the heroine as a sexually active protagonist. However, while women appear to maintain control of their identity in these stories, the male gaze within the show continues to behold them as hyper-sexualized beings. Thus, *Twilight* began the phenomenon of the hyper-sexualized protagonist female, a larger movement toward a sexually saturated femininity, which remained visible in cinematic and televisual vampire tales. (2022)

Thus, although the *Twilight* series seems to exalt a young woman as a pro-active heroine taking control of her destiny, she is also sexually objectified by the men in her life, and by her society, and at times she is literally controlled by the two boys who are romantically involved with her.

The question of *choice* is a Big Issue in the *Twilight Saga* – what are Bella's choices? They include:

- being human
- being vampiric

- dating Edward
- dating Jacob

- living in Forks
- living in Florida

- living with Dad
- living with Mom

- getting old
- being immortal

This is where Stephenie Meyer's form of second wave feminism is grounded – in the concept of choice, and freedom (linking to the libertarian project found in much of 21st century popular culture).

Feminists and critics have wondered what sort of messages the

Twilight novels and movies are sending to teenage girls. Well, yes. But there are many assumptions, some patronizing, in how some critics and feminists have judged the *Twilight* series. Assumptions about *how* teenage audiences consume books and movies, as if all audiences take everything literally and seriously. As if audiences (of any age) can't tell when something is meant to be fantastical, and thus received as high fantasy and entertainment. As if audiences consume movies and novels with their minds and souls opened, vulnerable and impressionable. As if audiences don't have defences against fantasy fiction and cinema. As if audiences don't have brains and minds and can separate reality from fiction, and real boys from fictional vampires.

But they can! Audiences are *incredibly* sophisticated! Indeed, they *have to be* to make sense of the *Twilight* movies and books in the first place! The *Twilight* series doesn't make a jip of sense if you don't have a very sophisticated understanding of what stories are, how they are delivered culturally, how they work – or why you enjoy them.

Or put it like this: there are *many* levels of involvement, imagination and, to use a trendy word of today, 'immersion' in the *Twilight* series, as in any fiction, fantasy or otherwise. I find the idea that audiences can't separate the levels out really patronizing and demeaning. Yet you'll find commentaries on the *Twilight* franchise which wonder what sort of 'messages' the *Twilight* series is sending to young people couched in those parental, auntie, moral guardian frameworks. Media watchdogs, social commentators, librarians, schools, and educationalists (left-wing or right-wing or radical), put on their granny hats and pretend to be concerned about the damaging lessons that *Twilight* or *Harry Potter* or *The Hunger Games* are promulgating.

You can also counter the negative criticism of the *Twilight* brand from feminists and critics by pointing out that Bella Swan, for all her drippiness and passivity and fatal masochism, does have times when she is assertive, when she acts, when she makes decisions. Let's not forget that Bella is the *heroine*, the primary character, of this fantasy romance series. Yes, there is a bunch of strong men in her life who affect her – Edward, Charlie, Carlisle, Jacob, Aro, her Pa Charlie etc – and often Bella's simply reacting to events and people (and not driving the events), but it's Bella who makes many of the decisions, and performs many of the acts, that helps her to win through. (Screenwriter Melissa Rosenberg said she thought of Bella as an assertive heroine who goes after what she wants. Maybe Rosenberg had to think like that, to be able to write the scripts for the movies, and didn't want to think of Bella as a submissive, masochistic girl).

No, Bella Swan is not a radical, lesbian, feminist super-bitch who decimates all men in her path with a chainsaw, and goes about creating a lesbian, separatist paradise. Bella Swan doesn't travel to rainy Washington State to set up a commune of radical, lesbian women! (You wish! That's another novel!).[6]

No: this is a set of romantic novels and movies. With love ('true lerrrve') as its heart! You can't expect a traditional, heterosexual, romantic fiction heroine aged 17 (and in the Young Adult fiction market) to be Camille Paglia or Andrea Dworkin combined with Tank Girl or Lara Croft! (That would be something, though!).

But Bella Swan does assert her sexuality often in the *Twilight Saga*, which's unusual for any heroine (at least in the movie world). It is also unusual for a teenage woman to do that (for example, when Catherine Trammell does it in *Basic Instinct* (1992), it's not so striking, because Trammell's a supremely confident, self-assured and economically independent adult woman). And it is Bella – against Edward's repeated, increasingly anxious protestations – who goes *towards* vampirism, who demands, in the end, that Edward (or – Hell – anybody!) change her into a vampire (if Edward won't do it, Bella would go straight to Carlisle and he, being such as nice guy, would oblige).

But it is also outside the stories of the movies and books of *Twilight*, in the economic and social sphere, that a pro-woman (if not feminist) stance is certainly asserted. The *Twihard* movies were based on novels written by a woman. Not so unusual. That the pictures were scripted by a woman is far rarer.[7] That the first *Twilight* movie was directed by a woman is very rare (you try naming more than ten living, female film directors!).

But *way* more significant than that was this: a giant movie franchise with a young woman at the centre (and not a name actress, like, say Sigourney Weaver (*Alien*)), but a young actress. How many of those are there? Like, hardly any! I'm talking about franchises, not single movies; I mean movies that have generated billions of $$$$, not tens of millions.

One of the only comparable movie franchises (not single movies) would be the *Underworld* series starring Kate Beckinsale, the *Lara Croft* series featuring Angelina Jolie, *Resident Evil* with Milla Jovovich, and

---

6 There are several minor genres which link vampirie stories and lesbian love and eroticism, with forms of feminism.
7 Melissa Rosenberg has the primary screen credit, tho' it's common in Hollywood for many writers to be attached to a project, to come and go over the years, as the project shifts from producer to producer, as actors sign on then get cold feet, or go off to make other movies, as movies go into turnaround, or get sold off to other companies. However, in the case of *Twilight*, there wasn't time for the project to go thru many writers.

Kill Bill with Uma Thurman (and *Charlie's Angels*, perhaps, but that's an ensemble franchise*,* and *The Hunger Games* perhaps. The *Star Wars* sequel movies (2015-2019) featured a young, white woman in the lead role (Rey, played by Daisy Ridley), but they were once again ensemble pieces (but focussing on a young woman in *Star Wars* was certainly inspired by the recent movies, cited above, including *Twilight*).)

Yet Kristen Stewart is not only much younger, she doesn't play a kick-ass heroine, but a regular girl (until she becomes a vamp, but that's in the final *Twilight* movie of a five-movie set). In fact, Bella in the books and the movies is definitely *un*athletic: she's clumsy, can't play ball without falling over or hitting someone, hates sports, swimming, and even dancing. (That's her appeal, partly – she's not only the 'girl next door' character, she's also a nerdy, plain, loser girl next door. According to *Twilight* fan Karla (from Indianapolis), 'Bella is the awkward, misunderstood girl in high school that gets the unattainable boy, it's a classic fantasy for any age girl').[9]

On feminism's plus side, the *Twilight* series portrayed a woman looking at a man as a love object, reversing the usual network of looks in cinema (*pace* Laura Mulvey's famous 1975 article on looking and voyeurism in cinema). When we see Edward walking in slo-mo in the movies, we are taking Bella's point-of-view. This is *her* man, we look at him through her. It's fun, it's rare, it sexualizes/ feminizes Edward, and objectifies him, as women are objectified and sexualized by men's looks in all movies. Add to that the many scenes of partial male nudity – where Bella's a fully dressed woman in amongst a bunch of topless men – and you have further examples of gender reversal.

---

8 *The Hunger Games* features a dour, so-serious teen girl who's a sister to Bella Swan.
9 The *Twilight Saga* captures another aspect of high school stories – the transfer student. Bella Swan is the new girl, an object of fascination for the kids who've spent all their lives in this little, provincial town.

5

TWILIGHT AND VAMPIRE MYTHOLOGY

Being a vampire didn't look like such a terrible thing – not the way the Cullens did it, anyway.

Stephenie Meyer, *New Moon* (10)

VAMPIRE LORE.

The *Twilight Saga* took up some traditional vampire lore, but not all of it (in fact, Stephenie Meyer deliberately ignored/ avoided much of it). Of course – because there's plenty to draw upon, and few vampire stories use *everything*. Stakes thru the heart, acute sense of hearing (and smell), the ability to move fast, immortality, cold flesh, fear of sunlight (and of crosses, of holy water, of garlic), inhuman strength, Existential weariness, piercing red eyes, shape-changing (including into mist), the list of the attributes of vamps in traditinal vampireology goes on and on (even *Dracula* by Bram Stoker didn't use everything in vampire mythology).

In Stephenie Meyer's vampire lore, which consciously ignores many of the accepted legends about blood-suckers, the moment of trans-formation from human to vampire is absolutely central.[10] Significantly, the *age* which Meyer picks for most of her vampire characters is young – late teens or early twenties (at the latest) for the major vampire characters (such as the Cullens and Bella). Why? Because the *Twilight Saga* is aimed at the teen market (it's put on the shelf in bookstores with other Young Adult fiction), and a series populated entirely by vampires in their 60s and 70s isn't quite the same! (Certainly not as glamorous! Bella in

---

10 Meyer admitted that Bella loses some of her 'relatability' when she becomes a vamp.

her 60s isn't the story!).

For Melissa Rosenberg, 'the vampire lore lends itself to the ultimate unattainable love. The longing we have felt, that delicious longing. I think that's why the lore itself is so popular' (2008).

In the *Twilight Saga*, the vampires' attributes are summed up by Bella Swan: very cold, stony, graceful, black/ gold eyes, old-fashioned speech, no food, superstitious about blood, fashion-plate clothing, movie star beauty, fast movements, and other-worldliness (T, 119).

When a human is bitten, they become frozen at that age – after the vampiric transformation, their bodies don't change, they don't age, and don't sleep (outwardly, it's their eyes which change – they have red/ black/ gold eyes, depending on when they've fed).

The *Twilight Saga* vampires are pale, beautiful, graceful, quick, and glisten like diamonds in the sunlight (which they avoid),11 on top of being being immortal and nearly indestructible, living on drinking blood, and flammable (TS, 80-81).

Most Meyeran vampires live in small covens (a coven can be two vamps), and most are nomadic (partly by necessity, and partly because of boredom [TS, 81]). They mate for life – 'and once they fall in love, that feeling never fades' (ibid.). Yes, because the key word in the *Twilight Saga* is *forever*, and it's a romantic fantasy. (So that when a vampire loses their mate, they never recover from it – Marcus among the Volturi and Victoria among the North American Nomads are examples). Thus, they don't fall out of love, or drift over to other lovers. And that means no divorce, either. It's all or nothing (one of the definitions of the teenage psyche in fiction).

The kiss (or bite) of the vampire can be interpreted any way you like. Sham mage/ clown/ madman Aleister Crowley, for instance, developed his own form of sex magicke in which the 'serpent's kiss' meant biting the wrist or throat (Crowley had his teeth filed down to perform this vampiric act!).

In the film adaptations, *The Twilight Saga* was unusual in vampire cinema in *not* using blood as a key *visual* motif. But blood features prominently in the dialogue, and some of the motifs in the background. This being a 'PG-13' flick, there was a limit to the amount of blood allowable (altho' horror filmmakers have got around censorship rules in numerous ways).

Instead, Edward Cullen *talks* about blood, and looks like at Bella Swan like he wants to devour her. By contrast, many famous vampire

---

11 But it would be a great look for parties.

pictures have happily celebrated the flow of blood (and Japanese animation has a long tradition of portraying blood in huge quantities, including in family shows such as the incredible, all-conquering *One Piece* series).

Blood is of course absolutely central to vampirism, and the portrayal of vampireology in literature, movies, *manga* and popular culture. In *Twilight*, blood is, as usual, what is craved above everything. Yet this is precisely what the Cullen regime has attempted to do without, relying on animals instead of humans (and reflecting a trend towards vegetarianism in Western societies. The Cullens are hippy, New Age, 'veggie' vampires).[12]

From the astonishing depictions of blood and the exchange of blood in Bram Stoker's *Dracula* novel of 1897 (the blood-soaked scenes are genuinely disturbing and scary), the red stuff has been such a key element in the portrayal of vampirism in popular culture, to the point where it can be a metaphor, a symbol, a motif, a theme, an issue, an ideology of or for anything you like. Race, ethnicity, origins, diaspora, immigration, alterity, class, power, gender, disease, plague, pollution, drug addiction (any addiction), Sexually Transmitted Diseases, A.I.D.S. and of course sex – the ways in which ketchup is deployed in popular culture's vampire narratives are countless. But the *Twihard* series isn't about blood or vampires in the end, it's about relationships and being a teenager.

Sunlight is such an integral element in vampireology in the mass media; the *Twilight* series consciously stepped away from using sunshine as a major obstacle for vampires. Instead, their skin turns pretty and diamond-like (to the point where Bella gushes over Edward's beauty – even more than usual, that is!). If you've seen any of the classic vampire movies, you'll know that the tiniest shaft of sunlight means decay and/ or death to a vampire. Peter Cushing's Van Helsing tearing down the drapes to reveal the sunlight to Christopher Lee's Count Drac in the Hammer horror movies, or the burning skin in the lesser-known but wonderful 1987 flick *Near Dark*.

The mythology of sunlight in vampireology was given a major boost in the classic 1922 movie *Nosferatu*, where many of the filmic motifs originated – aided by the Hammer *Dracula* movies. (However, vampires in *Twilight* are careful to emerge only on overcast days. Their remote house's overshadowed by giant cedar trees. And they selected the Olympic Peninsula in Washington, 'one of the most sunless places in the world', because of its rainy, dark climate, so they can go out during the

---

12 I don't know how different animal blood is from human blood; I mean, many animals and humans are mammals, right? No doubt some enterprising Twi-hards have found out.

day).[13]

A vampire that glitters irritated some fans, as well as actor Kellan Lurtz (Emmett) when he read the script for *Twilight*. But why not? Vampires are already fantastical creatures; it's an amusing variation on the notion that vampires can't bear sunlight.

Clearly, Stephenie Meyer decided to come up with her own variations on the 'rules' of vampireology. But they're not laws in the conventional sense; rather, they are accepted as the done thing in some areas of fiction, comics and films. Those guidelines or forms or 'rules' have developed over time, but an author can do what they like. There are no rules in art. In popular cinema and televison, for example, there are plenty of variations on what a vampire might be.

Beheading vampires is gory and extreme (and then burning them), but it is at least a convincing way of dealing with a monster. It tends to work with humans in 'real life'.[14] In a fantasy book or movie it offers a suitably impressive and final flourish to a fight (tho' in fantasy fiction, anyone can come back from the dead any which way). For 'PG-13' rated pictures, the *Twilight* series contained a surprising number of beheadings. One way of slipping them past the M.P.A.A. ratings board was the lack of blood. And that the victims are not real people, they're naughty vampires (so, like, who cares?).

I've always found the action in the *Buffy the Vampire Slayer* TV series feeble – where tiny, too-glam Sarah Michelle Gellar 'kickboxes' demons. Gellar never convinced as a 'vampire slayer'. Punching off a vampire's skull in the *Twilight* series is far more convincing as a means of destroying a monster (plus instant immolation – keep those torches burning, guys!). *The Twilight Saga* is very wispy and wimpy in many areas, but you have to admit that Stephenie Meyer gets the destruction of villains right: decapitation and burning.

Scouring the internet for info on vampires, Bella Swan stumbles upon 'Stregoni benefici', a good Italian vampire (T, 117).[15] The concept of a 'good vampire' is not confined to the *Twilight Saga*, of course. There are other stories about 'good vampires' who fight against 'bad vampires' – the *Hellsing* and the *Vampire D manga* and *animé*, for instance, or the *Blade* and *Underworld* movies (and plenty of children's stories and picture books). In Japanese pop culture, it's pretty much mandatory for a demon or monster slayer to be either part or wholly

---

13 We could get really picky here: there must be times when Carlisle has to walk from his car to his doctor's surgery or the hospital when it's sunny.
14 Head chopping has been used to terminate kings and queens many times, for example.
15 In *Breaking Dawn*, 'Stregoni benefici' is linked to Carlisle and his time with the Volturi (BD, 113-4).

demon or monster themselves (as in the excellent *Ogre Slayer* or *Bleach* series).[16] Edward is very much like 'a good vampire' type (as Carlisle, his mentor, is), a monster who's struggling with being a monster, a monster who doesn't want to be a monster, a monster who didn't choose to be a monster, a monster who falls in love with a human girl (ah, it can't end well, can it?! But this time, it does!).

★

The Twilight Saga: The Official Illustrated Guide is a useful volume for fans who want to know more about the vampires and the vampire world that Stephenie Meyer created. It includes descriptions of vampires; short biographical portraits of the key vampire characters; information on the werewolves; biographies of the human characters (including the pupils at Forks High School); a timeline of the events in the *Twilight* novels; music playlists to go with the books; key plot points of the books; some fan art; a gallery of book covers of the foreign language editions; some F.A.Q.s; and even info on the cars the characters drive.

By far the most entertaining elements in *The Twilight Saga: The Official Illustrated Guide* are the back-stories of the vampire characters (some of which, but not all, are included in the novels themselves). The most useful sections in the guide are the lengthy interview with Stephenie Meyer, and the timeline of the events in the novels.

TWILIGHT AND DRACULA.

The *Twilight Saga* is an entertaining reworking of the *Dracula* mythology, told from the point-of-view of one of the Count's victims, who's fallen in love with him. In Bram Stoker's incredible 1897 novel of *Dracula*, the authority figures (Van Helsing, Dr Seward, Jonathan Harker *et al*) are trying to protect damsels in distress (Lucy and Mina) from the predatory vampire. The *Twilight Saga* rewrites that scenario, and has Bella as Lucy/ Mina hopelessly in love with Edward/ Dracula, to the point where she wants to live with him forever, and *wants* him to bite her and make her immortal.

Bite me! The *Twilight Saga* is thus the story of girl who wants to become a Bride of Count Dracula (jeez, I think there's a movie in there somewhere!).

Dracula by Bram Stoker is the absolutely mandatory novel to read if

---

16 *Ogre Slayer* (a.k.a. *Onikirimaru*), by Kei Kunosuke, and published in *Shonen Sunday* in 1988, is a charming and unusual variation on the monster killer/ demon hunter theme. It features a magical youth with a magical sword whose chief goal in life is to slay *oni* – demons and giants (which can often only be dispatched with the magical sword). If he kills all of the *oni* in the world, he will be redeemed, and become fully human (because he is part-demon). In Kunosuke's version of the folktale, *oni* are created from human corpses. (Katako or Kozuna comes from an early Shinto folktale, where a half-human, half-demon boy struggles with his semi-demonic nature.)

you enjoy vampire stories. And no wonder: it still packs a visceral thrill even after you've seen thousands of vampire movies, TV shows, cartoons, comicbooks, *manga*, stage plays and all. If you really enjoy the *Twilight Saga*, try Stoker's novel *Dracula*.

(*Bite me!* Yes, Bella really does say that in the *Twilight Saga* books (but not often enough! Handily, Jacob Black in his section of *Breaking Dawn* is quicker to deliver quippy remarks. Jake's a much funnier narrator than Bella). Instead of opting for Edward's point-of-view (in *Midnight Sun*), we'd much rather see all of the *Twilight Saga* from Jake's p.o.v.)

VAMPIRE MOVIES.

Dracula movies (or movies which feature the Count) have been produced in 1922, 1931, 1936, 1943, 1944, 1945, 1948, 1958, 1960, 1966 and pretty much every year since. Meanwhile, vampire movies go back to 1896, and were produced in 1909, 1910, 1913, 1914 and every year since then. Comedy vampire movies, lesbian vampire movies, homosexual vampire movies, and pornographic vampire movies are sub-genres. Vampires (and Dracula) have been mixed in with numerous ensembles of monsters in movies (such as the Universal sequels to *Dracula* and the *Abbot & Costello* series).

Some well-known vampire movies of the 1970s to the present day include (this is a condensed list): *The Omega Man*, the Hammer horror flicks, *Salem's Lot*, *Countess Dracula*, *Blacula*, the *Nosferatu* remake, *Love At First Bite*, *Bram Stoker's Dracula*, *Near Dark*, *The Hunger*, *Rabid*, *The Keep*, *Fright Night*, *Vampire Hunter D*, *Lifeforce*, *The Lost Boys*, *Vampire In Venice*, *The Lair of the White Worm*, *Buffy the Vampire Slayer*, *Love Bites*, *Chronos*, *Interview With the Vampire*, *Dracula: Dead and Loving It*, *From Dusk Til Dawn*, *Nadja*, *Vampire In Brooklyn*, *Vampires*, *Dracula 2000*, *Shadow of the Vampire*, *Queen of the Damned*, *The Little Vampire*, *Dark Shadows*, *Underworld*, *Night Watch*, *I Am Legend*, *Vampires Suck*, *Blood: The Last Vampire*, *League of Extraordinary Gentlemen*, *Van Helsing*, *Blade*, and *The Vampire Hunters* (and TV series such as *Vampire Knight*, *Hellsing*, *True Blood* and *The Vampire Diaries*).

Twilight can't help but remind the viewer of numerous other vampire outings, in books, TV, cartoons, cinema, etc. For Ken Gelder, in his *New Vampire Cinema*, the vampire movie endlessly recycles itself: it

> is always derivative, paying a kind of perpetual tribute or homage to itself. It is a very particular kind of genre that – for all its fascination with origins – is condemned at the same time to re-make and reycle, to

copy, to plagiarise, to cite and re-cite... (vi)

Every vampire movie feeds off other vampires movies, for Ken Gelder: 'every vampure film is to some degree a self-conscious remake or sequel or restaging of other vampire films that have preceded it' (30), so that it seems as if each new vampire movie simply rehashes previous vampire pictures. And *Twilight* led to its own remakes or sequels or cash-ins – such as the two TV series *The Vampire Diaries* and *True Blood.*

Critics noted that the romance in the *Twilight Saga* drew on the on-off romance between Buffy and Angel in *Buffy the Vampire Slayer* ('a teenage girl and handsome, sensitive, angst-ridden vampire who tries, not always successfully, to restrain his carnal appetites in order not to become monstrous', as Ken Gelder put it in *New Vampire Cinema* [83]). Among the other affinities between *Buffy* and *Twilight* include: both were about white, American, teenage girls; both from single parent families; both arrive in a new town and high school; 'good' and 'bad' vampires; a high school Prom; an emphasis on teen fashion; indie rock music,[17] etc.

VAMPIRES VS. WEREWOLVES.

Notice that the Cullen vampires in the *Twilight* series are aligned with white, middle class North America: they might be a New England family with aristocratic origins in Europe. It's the Old World enduring into the New World. They have a lavish home in the forest. Carlisle Cullen, for instance, the father vampire, has a heritage going back to at least post-Renaissance Italy (where he lives in Volterra with the decadent but vicious aristos, the Volturi, tho' quite why this mild liberal who likes helping and healing people hooks up with them isn't explained. He'd much more likely be living quietly in some rural village, rather than the global centre of vampire power – the vampire equivalent of the Vatican City and a crime syndicate's HQ in Gotham or Hong Kong). Carlisle is a doctor, suave and highly educated (and Edward listens to Claude Debussy at home,[18] also plays the piano, and can recite William Shakespeare and Emily Brontë).

The Cullen offspring are spoilt rich kids with flashy cars and a smug, arrogant attitude. None of them have to work, and thus neither does Bella Swan (indeed, in the finale of the last *Twilight* flick, she stuffs bundles of dollars into a backpack for her daughter). (To be fair, you'd have to be a stupid immortal not to benefit from financial deals spread across centuries! The Cullens have Alice, too, with her predictions, for the stock

---

17 Some of Meyer's favourite pop acts include Muse, My Chemical Romance, Linkin Park, Blue October and Coldplay.
18 'Claire de Lune', of course (T, 90).

market and the lottery. The Rupert Murdochs, Donald Trumps and Bill Gateses of this world would probably pay billions to be immortal! Then they could out-last mega-corporations such as Warners and Disney and make a killing in 500 years' time!).

The werewolves, meanwhile, headed up by Jacob Black (Taylor Lautner in the movies), are aligned with Native American culture (down to the casting[19] of the actors in the adaptations from First Nations, the *mise-en-scène*, and cultural references). They live on a reservation (which was inspired partly by the real Quileute Indian Reservation, based in La Push,[20] Washington).

The werewolves are earthy, sensual, and straightforward. The guys hang around outdoors stripped down to shorts (making the on-screen transformations into werewolves in the movies so much easier!). They are boysy boys, rough and tumble, frat house types, with their motorbikes, pick-up trucks, male bonding, joshing, enormous appetites, and cliff-jumping antics.

But there is also a female werewolf! Oh yes, the *Twilight* series evens things up a tad when it includes the first female werewolf in many a year in the form of Leah Clearwater. The *Breaking Dawn* novel includes some moments when the wolf-boys find having a *girl* in their pack a little disconcerting (like when they transform, they are naked. Ugh! And the guys so *don't* want to deal with 'women's issues' in their pack!). And Leah isn't some dumb girl, she's a chip-on-the-shoulder, resentful woman who's in love with pack leader Sam Uley (who's devoted to Emily, the 'wolf girl', as Bella calls her). So it's yet another love ▲ [triangle] in the *Twilight Saga*.

No one can miss, either, the classist and political aspects of the werewolves and Quileute tribal communities, on top of the racial issues: they are working class, and have far less social agency and prestige – and money – than the Cullens and the other vampires. The Cullens have private islands, a luxurious mansion and cottage, expensive cars and they can hire private jets. One critic described Jake Black as the Poor Guy in a fairy tale, unable to attain the Princess, which the Rich Man does: 'he is essentially a trailer-park mythical creature from the wrong side of Grimm' (T. Gold). Yes, Jacob and his chums can't compete with the upscale lifestyle of the Cullens (or the Volturi), vampires who embody 'old money', power, prestige, wealth, and influence. (Carlisle – or Edward – might be a future President, but the most that Jacob could aspire to

---

19 Casting was overseen by Lana Veenker, who had also worked on shows like *Dances With Wolves.*
20 La Push is described as 'the tiny Indian reservation on the coast' (T, 6).

might be to have his own garage and car maintenance business).

The real Quileute Native American Tribe (numbering around 400)[21] were not keen on their depiction in the *Twilight* movies, according to some reports. They thought the pictures had misinterpreted their legends. And they didn't receive any compensation from the production companies.

In movies, werewolves enjoyed a renaissance in the 2000s-2010s: they appear in *Harry Potter, Van Helsing, Red Riding Hood,* and the *Underworld* series.

Ken Gelder reckoned that the *Twilight Saga* was about the only vampire mythology which put together Native Americans with vampires structurally, in a 'coloniser/ colonised paradigm', so that the two groups, like Edward and Jacob, mirror each other:

> No wonder Edward and Jacob shadow each other so closely, each taking up long periods of screen time when the other is not there. And no wonder – when they do see each other – that they react so hysterically, so anxiously. (2012, 88)

For readers who wish to explore vampire fiction and vampire cinema, there are numerous critical studies. I would recommend Ken Gelder's books, *Reading the Vampire* (1994) and *New Vampire Cinema* (2012). These are good general introductions.

---

21 Other sources say the Quileute Tribe today is about 2000 people.

Two of the great vampire
movies, Nosferatu (1922)
and Dracula (1931).

Some more recent vampire outings.

PART THREE
✤
THE *TWILIGHT* BOOKS

About three things I was absolutely positive. First, Edward was a
vampire. Second, there was part of him – and I didn't know how potent
that part might be – that thirsted for my blood. And third, I was
unconditionally and irrevocably in love with him.

Stephenie Meyer, *Twilight* (170-1)

1

TWILIGHT, THE BOOK

'Mostly I dream about being with you forever.'

Stephenie Meyer, *Twilight* (433)

I have to admit to getting halfway thru the first *Twilight* novel before abandoning it. Two chief reasons: (1) the quality of the writing, and (2) the character of Bella Swan. The prose in *Twilight* was irritatingly dull. And repetitive. And just, well, not especially engaging or worth the time.

Altho' I consume books by the ton, I found *Twilight* lacked a good editor (too much was left in which should've been cut), and there just wasn't enough dramatic/ romantic juice in the scenario of Bella Swan falling in love with Edward Cullen from afar and then up close. I didn't believe in either Bella or Edward as fictional characters. I couldn't get caught up in their romance at all.

The personality of Bella Swan in the *Twilight* novel is self-absorbed to an almost autistic level. She is so snooty – nothing is good enough for her! She complains about Forks,[1] the Pacific North-West, the weather, being away from home, about her Dad, about her Mom, about her friends, her teachers, her school, and, like, everything. She feels superior, she thinks she is above everyone. She is so serious. She lacks a sense of humour.

I could go on! (But Bella Swan is not meant to be an anti-heroine or an ambiguous figure, someone you don't necessarily have to like, or root for. She is clearly meant to be Cinderella, the Princess, the one you're hoping will find Happiness and True Lerrrve.)

Another aspect of the *Twilight* novel grated with me: not liking

---

1 Stephenie Meyer visited Forks in Summer, 2004 (as related on her website).

Isabella Marie Swan and finding her unappealing meant that the choice of the first person narration for the story was, like, very annoying (the story, as Stephenie Meyer noted in *The Short Second Life of Bree Tanner,* 'was her experience only', so that 'anything that Bella couldn't see or hear or feel or taste or touch was irrelevant'). Bella is simply not a very charming, interesting or entertaining person to be with (or inside of) for a whole novel. (Yet I can imagine that it is precisely this aspect that many readers enjoy. I can imagine plenty of the millions of readers who's enjoyed the *Twilight* series thinking, 'yeah, I think that, too!', or, 'yeah, it *is* like that for seventeen year-old girls!').

Stephenie Meyer acknowledged that it was sometimes limiting to write everything from Bella Swan's point-of-view (TS, 30). Of course – that's the trade-off you make when you select that subjective viewpoint.

Because Jacob Black's section of *Breaking Dawn* is the most entertaining, and the best-written part of the *Twilight Saga*,[2] I kind of wish that Stephenie Meyer had rewritten the *Twilight* books completely from Jake's point-of-view (rather than the obvious point-of-view, Edward's – which Meyer did in *Midnight Sun*, or by reversing the genders in *Life and Death*). Of course, it wouldn't completely work – you'd have to miss out plenty of the story, if you pedantically stuck to Jacob's point-of-view.

I have picked up *Twilight* since, tried to carry on reading it, but again have given up. I can read *Jude the Obscure* (Thomas Hardy), or *King Lear* (William Shakespeare)*,* or *The Iliad* (Homer), or the *Canzoniere* (Francesco Petrarch), and any number of classic texts, or any number of silly novels (I love Jackie Collins, for instance). But *Twilight* and Stephenie Meyer… No, I can't do it! (In the end, I found a solution: read *very* short chunks, which are just about bearable, before exasperation kicks in, and you hurl the book across the room/ canyon/ beach/ plane. But it was watching the movie that solved the problem).

That's why I am not exploring the *Twilight* books in great detail here, or the relation of the books to the movies. Suffice to say, in contrast to the usual way of thinking, and in contrast to many fans, I found the *Twilight* movies far superior to the books. As entertainment, as fun, and as a way of spending time. (For some Twi-fans, that is heresy. Or is it? The movies were endorsed by Stephenie Meyer, and she acted as co-producer on the later movies. The *Twilight* movies are thus 'canon', they are gospel, they are sacred texts just like the novels).

---

2 Of the three narrators of the *Twilight Saga* – Bella, Jake and Edward – Jake is by far the funniest, and Edward is the most serious. Bella and Edward are pretty much siblings in the commentary stakes – they both have a cool, distanced, and self-absorbed quality to their first-person narratives.

Of course, the *Twilight Saga* movies have pretty people like Kristen Stewart, Taylor Lautner and Robin Pattinson to look at. And fun character actors like Billy Burke and Anna Kendrick, and incendiary actors like Michael Sheen. And they are not related solely in the first person. They have music. They have action. They have lovely images of mountains and forests. And they are told by storytellers who don't have Stephenie Meyer's clunky, boring prose style.

For quite a bit of the narrative of *Twilight* (the book), Bella Swan is surrounded by men – at least in relation to her growing friendship with Edward Cullen. Which is, after all, the central relationship of the *Twilight Saga*. There's her Pa, Charlie (Bella is worried about how he'll react to her dating the youngest Cullen, then she worries about what he'll think of her hanging out with Jake Black); there's Jake; there's Billy Black, Jake's Dad, who issues ominous warnings to Bella; there's Carlisle… Meanwhile, Stephenie Meyer doesn't use the motif of a young woman surrounded by a group of female friends, who are supportive, encouraging, and protective.[3] Instead, the two lovers become a self-enclosed world, and Bella only accepts advice and such from Edward and Charlie (she ignores Billy's warnings, for instance).

The *Twilight* movies reproduce this masculinist orientation: altho' characters such as Alice, Rosalie, Esme, Jessica, and Bella's Mom René are important secondary characters, this is a patriarchal world, filled with guys: Charlie, Carlisle, Jake, Billy, Jasper, Emmett, male teachers, the werewolves, and of course Edward (who is everywhere, doing the work of ten men in influencing the heroine).

The *Twilight Saga* is a school story, too. Well, hell – in a school scenario, you have teachers and pupils, and rules, and dorms, and a social hierarchy, and they constitute a readymade format that will keep stories ticking over for centuries. Add to that friendships and rivalries between students, plus of course high school romances, and sports, and competitions, and parties, and Prom Night, and school trips – and you can see why authors and filmmakers have been using school settings since forever. (You'd have to be a terrible author not to be able to write a decent school story. Indeed, it's good advice for young writers: set your story in a setting with a strong sense of social hierarchy).

Another aspect of stories set in high school is the new girl, the transfer student. Bella Swan is something exotic – from Arizona – in the

3 Bella has an uneasy friendship with Jessica Stanley, until Jessica cools off following the dis-astrous night out in Port Angeles; as the narrator quips, 'as far as I could tell, Jessica has crossed over to the dark side' (NM, 232). Bella has a more intuitive relationship with Angela, but that is very minor.

little town of Forks (with its tiny population of 3,532).[4]

Some *Twilight* timelines[5] have Edward being born in 1901 and turned into a vampire in 1918, when he's seventeen, with the books being set in 2005. The *Twilight* timeline on the Twilight Lexicon website has the main action taking place from January, 2005 to January, 2007. Two years. That's all. Bella Swan was born in 1987, so she's seventeen in 2005, when the story starts.

4 In 2010.
5 At the Twilight Lexicon website.

twilight

STEPHENIE MEYER

THE INTERNATIONAL BESTSELLER

2

NEW MOON, THE BOOK

What kind of place *was* this? Could a world really exist where ancient legends went wandering around the borders of tiny, insignificant towns, facing down mythical monsters? Did this mean every impossible fairy tale was grounded somewhere in absolute truth? Was there anything sane or normal at all, or was everything just magic and ghost stories?

Stephenie Meyer, *New Moon* (293-4)

INTRODUCTION.

New Moon (2006) was an easier book to read for me because I had resigned myself to some of the unavoidable issues of the *Twilight* series. Such as Isabella Marie Swan's unlikeableness and uselessness, and the boring prose style. I'd seen the seven movies (don't forget those two excellent spoof movies!), and as part of the *Twilight* phenomenon, *New Moon* the book isn't too taxing an experience (indeed, no one would pretend that you have to read the *Twilight* books with the careful attention of great fiction. They are light in the sense of being candy, disposable, undemanding, and superficial).

So, Stephenie Meyer's *New Moon* continues the story of the first *Twilight* book directly, with, thankfully, only minor summaries of the plot of *Twilight* for those who haven't read it. *New Moon* is More Of The Same (which, for many fans, is just fine, thank you very much!).

The novel of *New Moon* is 563 pages in my Atom Books edition (an imprint of Little, Brown), picked up from a Sunday market (for 75 cents) – the one with the black cover and the red and white flower (a tulip?)[1] on the front. However, the typeface is large (13 point Sabon), so there are far

---
1 Not a tulip according to La Meyer.

fewer words per page than a typical novel (this book is in 10 point Times). Also, the paper's thick. All standard ploys from publishers to make a book look much longer than it actually is. (This is, of course, a book aimed at the Young Adult market. But what is a 'young adult'? Is there such a thing? A grown-up, but somehow still young, and not fully grown? A teenager who wants to look forever young – if they can find a vampire to bite them?).

LOVE AND LOSS.

New Moon is built around a massive and cataclysmic separation of the lovers. Unfortunately for Bella S., *she* is the jilted one, when Edward C. walks away from her in the forest near her home. He acts high and mighty and noble and *sooo* sensitive (it's for her good, too, he insists: it's better that she just forget all about him).

But she goes to pieces – literally.

To sum up:

He leaves *her.*

This is the key event in *New Moon* – a loss and a separation from which everything else in the narrative flows. Bella Swan reacts *so* strongly, it becomes a sulk and depression of prima donna proportions, literally (and physically) debilitating her.

Stephenie Meyer said she hadn't been in Bella's situation in *New Moon*, experiencing that level of depression and withdrawal. But when she was writing *New Moon* it was 'like I was really there, like I really was her' (TS, 31). Which is a very familiar feeling for authors (but remember too that authors identify with all of their characters, and the places, the situations, etc).

Act two of the 2006 *New Moon* book is dramatized similarly in the 2009 movie of *New Moon* as a continuous bout of self-induced depression, so painful that Isabella Swan dreads being alone, fears not being busy so she has time to think, and spends each night in such agony she stays awake until exhaustion sets in and she sleeps. (Or, in the *New Moon* movie, she has nightmares and yells in her sleep, until her Dad comes in with a mallet).

Thus, love becomes suffering on a grand, sulky, pouty scale – in true, 19th century literature style, *à la Withering Plights,* or 12th century, French courtly love poetry, or Elizabethan tragic plays, or many an opera, or any pop song from 1956 to the present day.

You've all heard the pop songs:

My baby's left me! She's gone! He's gone! I feel so alone! Where's mah baby? Come back honey! Baby, come back!

You can hear this self-pitying baloney in 800,000 pop songs any day and any hour on radio stations across the entire planet (and most pop songs were and are written by people in their twenties and thirties and older, *not* by 13 year-old teenagers! How did they think they could get away with such inane lyrics?! And, incredibly, pop acts in their middle-age are still on stage today singing this sort of adolescent claptrap).

'Could I betray my absent heart to save my pathetic life?' (NM, 376). There is a hole in Bella Swan, symbolic, emotional, psychological – the withdrawal of Edward's love is likened to a gaping wound in her body, the Lacanian lack made visceral. Bella takes to clutching her chest, trying to keep herself together (it's good that Kristen Stewart didn't do that in the *New Moon* movie). The hole is described so often, with its bloody, frayed edges, it takes on an unmistakable vaginal form. Stephenie Meyer stretches the poetic tropes of the heart, and the hole in the heart, and the wounded body, to an exaggerated degree.

✐

LACAN AND THE LACK.

Sidenote on Lacan and the lack: From Plato to Sigmund Freud and Jacques Lacan, the desire and the lack has been central to Western sexual metaphysics: in this negative model, one is doomed feel a lack, to a desire for more and more consumption, which leads to dissatisfaction. Freudian-Lacanian desire can never be satisfied: dissatisfaction is built-in (the Lacanian lack is always there). Desire is never annihilated: for Georg Wilhelm Friedrich Hegel, only another desire can satisfy desire and also perpetuate it. Desire thus desires more desire (this has a vivid expression in late capitalist consumerism, where it is always the *next* commodity that will truly satisfy and stop the hunger for more objects. But it never happens).

For French feminists such as Hélène Cixous, Jacques Lacan's (1901-81) philosophy of the Lacanian 'lack' is ridiculous. As she writes in "The Laugh of the Medusa" (1975): 'what's a desire originating from a lack? A pretty meagre desire'.[2] Woman is man's dream, his desire, Cixous asserts in *The Newly Born Woman*, because she is absent: 'man's dream: I love her – absent, hence desirable, a dependent nonentity, hence adorable. Because she isn't there where she is' (67). And Luce Irigaray and other feminists (Sarah Kofman, Elizabeth Grosz, Michèle Montrelay and Mary Ann Doane) have criticized the Freudian-Lacanian emphasis on the phallus as the 'transcendental signifier', as the measure of authentic sexual

---

2 Quoted in E., Marks, 262

pleasure. What woman lacks is lack itself, says Montrelay, an inability to create distance and representation.

The psychoanalytic theories of French feminist Julia Kristeva (b. 1941) throw some light on the withdrawn, depressed state of Bella Swan. In her *Soleil Noir* (= *Black Sun* – a very *Twilighty* title!), Kristeva developed her psychoanalysis of melancholy. For Kristeva, the melancholic is reduced to one basic meaning – despair and pain (*douleur*), rather than a search for meaning. The melancholic fails to develop a sense of the imaginary and the symbolic. The inability to mobilize the imaginary and symbolic in the melancholic makes melancholia a kind of living death. Kristevan melancholia is not neurosis, for melancholia does not eroticize the death drive, which results in hatred, and melancholia prevents an eroticization of the separation from the mother. The mother is not the lost object – instead, the subject dies in her place. The artist, though, is able to deal with states such as melancholia because s/he can control signs. An artwork, Kristeva suggests, can be the mark of a 'vanquished depression' (*Black Sun*, 76).

John Lechte, discussing Julia Kristeva's concept of melancholia, points out that the depressive person is still able to use signs, has not become dissociated from language, but that language 'is always foreign, never material', that language has become detached from energy drives, and emotions have become 'separated from symbolic constructions'. So that Kristevan melancholia is 'the reverse of love with its synthesis of idealization and affect'. For Lechte, 'melancholia is considered by Kristeva to be the equivalent of a mourning for a partial loss which cannot be symbolized. The individual is that loss, weighed down by tears and silence'.[3]

THE BIRTHDAY PARTY.

The theme of time and mortality is introduced in *New Moon* using the motif of the birthday (the 2006 book opens with a premonition dream where Bella Swan sees herself as an old woman who looks just like her Gran – that is your fate, to become your parents, or, if you're really lucky to live long enough, your grandparents).[4] Edward isn't getting any older, but Bella is now eighteen. Like many of us (!), Bella resents ageing (as well as changing). Part of her drive to immortality is to stop changes as well as ageing.

This is an aspect of the *Twilight* series that critics – and fans – tend

3 J. Lechte, 1990, 34-35.
4 In *Twilight*, Bella is seventeen (her birthday is September 13). There's a push towards getting married before her nineteenth birthday, so she can remain 18, not too much older than Edward (who's 17 physically, but 104 really).

to overlook: Bella is absolutely determined to avoid getting old. It's not solely about avoiding dying, it's also about not ageing. Thus, it's not immortality she hankers after so much as *not* being old and boring and decrepid. And being in a romantic relationship with someone who stays young while *she* gets old irks Bella something rotten! It would be completely possible for Bella to simply accept her fate and date Edward as a human girl.

(And the very ironic thing about all this is that Bella Swan is *already* a very middle-aged teenager. She is *already* old and boring. To the point where her idea of a good day out is to visit a library or a bookstore. And she also looks after her Mom Renee, including shopping and cooking, so she's a Mom to her Mom, and a Mom to her Dad).

✐

The birthday party at the Cullens' place is a disaster,[5] when Jasper Whitlock goes ape over Bella Swan cutting herself, which leads on to the separation. Bella's reaction to Edward ending their relationship is exactly as expected: she collapses totally.

The scene with Jasper[6] exploding over the sight/ smell of blood is there to demonstrate how crazed vampires become around humans and blood, to remind us of the danger involved in dealing with vampires, to provide a powerful reason for the Cullens to leave Forks (among others), and to show what Edward might be capable of if he failed to rein himself in. (In the movie adaptation of *New Moon*, the Jasper-and-blood scene provides a little bit of action, too, in a rather talky first act, leading up to the Big Separation).

Ah, to be a teenager!

To be in love!

To love someone *so much* your very well-being and health depends on it! To love somebody *so badly*, you will ruin your health when you react badly. Yes, it's been part of the romantic genre for, like, millennia, right? Sure! It worked for ancient poets such as Ovid and Catullus, in the *Bible*, in Ancient Egyptian mythology, in Homer's *Odyssey*, so it's going work here, right? It does!

Isabella Swan's predicament in *New Moon* is wholly clichéd, wholly familiar, and easy to identify with. To make herself ill because *he* is gone.[7] To seethe with resentment and anger because *he* is gone. To wallow in self-pity because *he* is gone (Bella is a prima donna among and

---

5 It's also an embarrassing scene for Bella – ignoring the moment where Jasper gets crazy when Bella cuts herself, it's an awkward moment for a shy teen like Bella, being the centre of attention in this posh family.

6 So Jasper's vampire ability to make everybody around him calm doesn't work on himself.

7 As Bella has enough time for moping about for months on end in bedroom, how about getting a part-time job? Everybody does it.

self-pitiers!. To sulk to the max because *he* is gone (Bella was Number One Sulker in the U.S.A.'s Emotional Olympics every year from 2006 to 2012!).

We are in a pop song here, folks:

Love hurts... love is pain... I love you, come back to me...

Bella's 'Angst-O-Meter' (from *Vampires Suck*) is in the red! *New Moon* is a novel of *loss* and *lack*. Separation all the way.

SUICIDE.

However, altho' Bella Swan sulks and pouts and basks in self-pity and cries and curls up in the foetal position in bed in agony (night after night), she doesn't self-harm, doesn't lash out at other people, and doesn't brood on suicide.

Well, not at first.

Suicide – the issue is raised during the disastrous girlie night in Port Angeles with Jess, when Bella ponders: 'I wasn't suicidal. Even in the beginning, when death unquestionably would have been a relief, I didn't consider it' (110).

But as Bella's all-consuming depression deepens, she contemplates acts that're so reckless they amount to self-harm and/ or suicide. (Indeed, suicide is a disturbing element in the *Twilight Saga*: Esme committed suicide following the death of her baby, for instance, and Edward decides to commit a vampiric 'suicide' at the end of *New Moon*).

At least I could be with him again before I died. That was better than a long life. (NM, 459)

Bella Swan fears loneliness, inaction, the cold death of being depressed: 'suppose I got depressed again, even with Jake? I had to keep occupied' (195).

Talk about low self-esteem! (Hence the title *New Moon* – it refers to the darkest of nights, as Stephenie Meyer explained, and to Bella's dark night of the soul: 'this is the darkest kind of night. *New Moon* is the darkest period of Bella's life').

Halfway thru *New Moon* Bella Swan thinks of herself as 'damaged goods' (NM, 213), 'truly messed up' (353), 'I was broken' (375), and so emotionally wounded she's not worth anybody bothering with, let alone a super-warm hunk like Jacob Black ('he was much too good for me' [375]). Poor Jake can only ever be her best friend and her brother, but never her lover. The middle acts of *New Moon* explore the scenario of the Rebound Guy, the Second Choice Guy, the Best Friend Guy, the guy who can never as delicious as the first choice. (And the First Choice Guy is absent, so he's fantasized about, and built up into something even more gorgeous and desirable).

NEW MOON AS *ROMEO AND JULIET* FOR TEENS.

The *Twilight Saga* is *Romeo and Juliet* for kids: *Romeo and Juliet* (1597) has of course been a staple of school and college classes since forever; students still watch the movie versions of William Shakespeare's 1590s play, study the texts, and go see the theatrical productions on school trips.

And *Romeo and Juliet* has probably been adapted for the screen more than any other William Shakespeare play, along with *Hamlet* (so that the movie of *New Moon* can be seen as another remake).

New Moon makes explicit the references to *Romeo and Juliet* when it prints a quotation from it at the beginning of the novel:[8]

> These violent delights have violent ends
> And in their triumph die, like fire and powder
> Which, as they kiss, consume...

The words are spoken by Friar Laurence in act two, scene six, as the romance of Romeo and Juliet is growing apace:

> ROMEO:
> Amen, amen! But come what sorrow can,
> It cannot counterfeit the exchange of joy
> That one short minute gives me in her sight.
> Do thou but close our hands with holy words,
> Then love-devouring death do what he dare;
> It is enough I may but call her mine.
>
> FRIAR LAURENCE:
> These violent delights have violent ends
> And in their triumph die, like fire and powder
> Which, as they kiss, consume. The sweetest honey
> Is loathsome in his own deliciousness,
> And in the taste confounds the appetite.
> Therefore love moderately: long love doth so;
> Too swift arrives as tardy as too slow.

There isn't really an adviser/ helper figure like Friar Laurence in *New Moon* (Bella Swan could definitely do with one – her Mom is notably absent), but the old Friar does make an important point here: *love moderately.* And of course, that's what Bella – and Edward – cannot do! It's All Or Nothing for them!

---

8 Stephenie Meyer considered using a different quotation.

There are further references in the *New Moon* novel to the Immortal Bard, such as watching the famous *Romeo and Juliet* movie of 1968,[9] and Bella and Edward being compared to William Shakespeare's star-crossed lovers (however, Edward is critical of Romeo's actions – tho' he then proceeds to exile himself, just like Romeo!). Later, there's a passage in *New Moon* where Bella turns into a literary critic, pondering on the events in *Romeo and Juliet*, and wondering if the character of Paris (linked to Jacob Black) might've had more impact (after all, Romeo – Edward – wasn't coming back from Mantua/ Brazil). This part of *New Moon* (chapter 16: "Paris") has the feel of a high school essay that Bella might write for her English class (and it also comes across as a section added to the novel that doesn't quite fit in):

> I wondered what she would have done if Romeo had left her, not because he was banished. but because he lost interest? What if Rosalind had given him the time of day, and he'd changed his mind? What if, instead of marrying Juliet, he'd just disappeared? (NM, 370)

Julia Kristeva's observations about William Shakespeare (in her essay "Romeo and Juliet: Love-Hatred in the Couple") ring true for many melodramas of love, including the *New Moon* story. For example, Kristeva notes that Shakespeare's lovers in *Romeo and Juliet* spend more time getting ready to die than loving. This death-wish is at heart of Western depictions of love (it is evoked in the classroom in *New Moon* where the students watch the *Romeo and Juliet* film). Meanwhile, in Francesco Petrarch's *Canzoniere*, the poet spends much more time whingeing about love than loving. Petrarch dwells obsessively on the death of his beloved Laura de Sade (who died young, in 1348). As if, in dying, she attains mythic status. Similarly, Shakespeare's young lovers dwell manically on their obsessive, accursed affair (*Tales of Love*, 210). The *performance* of their love, played out against the warring families, against their peers, against the socio-political world of the play, becomes more significant than their love itself. The experience is not enough. There must be performance and dialogue. Love becomes a discourse. Metaphor takes over.

The plotting of *New Moon* in the finale is clearly meant to evoke *Romeo and Juliet* on a number of levels. The most obvious one is the suicidal acts of the two lovers (Bella's close-to-suicide in the cliff-jumping sequence, and Edward 'suicide' of provoking the deadly Volturi clan, knowing that their reprisal will mean his destruction). Another level

---

9 Thousands of school kids will have watched this Italian/ British movie, tho' more recently they would probably prefer the 1996 version starring Leonardo Di Caprio.

is the conflation of Juliet-with-Bella and Romeo-with-Edward and the comparison of their teen love affair with that of the famous tragic lovers of William Shakespeare's play. Another level is the complex and far-fetched plotting: both the finales of *Romeo and Juliet* and *New Moon* have hard-to-believe narrative paths and twists. The climax of *Romeo and Juliet* has so many things that can go wrong (with the Priest coming up with really stupid ideas); similarly, it takes *a lot* of effort for Stephenie Meyer to manœuvre her players in the final drama of *New Moon* (and into something close to the plotting of the finale of *Romeo and Juliet*. And in the *New Moon* movie, the plotting is even clunkier, making sudden, juddery leaps).

It pivots around Edward Cullen acting like a complete moron.[10] He calls up the Swan residence in Dorks and is informed by his arch rival in love (Jacob Black) that Bella is dead, and that there's a funeral. Edward – an apparently smart guy (remember, he has been around a bit – he's 104!) – immediately jumps to the wrong conclusions (and he buys what Jacob tells him, his rival in lerrrve). And then he also believes Rosalie that Bella's died; and Rosalie, as Edward should know, has always disliked Bella intensely (the lesson here, folks, is: *don't* trust your rivals or hearsay when it comes to life-and-death decisions!).

What a chump! And this guy is the Most Fabulous Boy In The Universe that Bella Swan is desperate to the point of suicide to be with?

But, as you vamp fans know well, if the theme of suicide is evoked in a love story, it usually means the plotting has to be ridiculous. And in *New Moon*, it is utterly stupid. We are in the 21st century, guys! It's not 16th century Verona or Mantua![11] We have cel phones! The internet! Land lines! Pagers! I-Pads! Laptops! Radios! Television! Hell, even the United States Postal Service! Are you really telling me that someone amongst the wealthy, hi-tech Cullen clan *can't* get a message to Edward, or that Edward *can't* double-check Bella Swan's death? Did he at least stop in an internet cafe for an hour, the dweeb, relax for a moment, have a latte, and do a Google search for recent news in the Porks area? Or log onto Facebook or similar websites (or local, Forks sites), and ask around about Bella? Didn't he have five minutes to make some calls to confirm Bella's demise? To call a hospital? The police? At least to call Carlisle. (After all, Edward is 104 years-old – he must've learned a few things in that time! Like, before embarking on a major act of self-destruction, *think*! But where Bella is concerned, apparently not).

---

10 Even Bella has to admit: 'I still couldn't believe that he was capable of reacting like this. It made no sense!' (NM, 426).
11 Or a British author's idea of what Italy would be like – Shakey hadn't been there.

The thing is, to stage a grand, operatic double suicide sort of story in the contemporary, Western world which relies on misunderstandings and miscommunications is a lot more difficult to pull off than it was in, say, the romantic tragic novels of Thomas Hardy of the late 19th century (when communications in rural England were not instant), or in late 16th century Italy.

I mean, these days, if they buy a copy of *Twilight* on Amazon, people are announcing it on Twitter/ X, Instagram, TikTok or F***book within seconds!

I guess the audience buys the OTT climactic plots of both *New Moon* and *Romeo and Juliet* because they are played so straight and so intensely: in *New Moon*, the finale just about works because Alice Sullen is so passionately earnest all the way through (we know that Bella Swan is head-over-heels in love with Edward Sullen, so her intensity is a given). The way that Alice's depicted in the *New Moon* novel, for instance, is essential in making the ditzy final act work (and the 2009 adaptation of *New Moon* uses all of the resources of cinema to persuade us to buy this baloney – the music (by Alexandre Despla) is working over-time, for example, and Ashley Greene's Alice sells the life-or-death dramatics).

The movie version of *New Moon* escalates the action from the novel, as the *Twilight* movie did with the *Twilight* book; this is a natural tendency in movie adaptations in the recent, Hollywood film industry. The movies have the audience in mind when they added car stunts in the first *Twilight* outing, for example, or more werewolf action in *New Moon*.[12]

BELLA THE ADRENALIN JUNKIE.

Bella Swan becoming an adrenalin junkie just so she can hear Edward Cullen's voice remonstrating her as a stern parent in her head is a sort of bizarre twist on romantic passion: 'the truth was that I wanted to hear his voice again' (NM, 160). There is a masochistic streak here that is disturbing (and throughout the *Twilight Saga*), and it's more disagreeable than the sexual abstinence issue. The twisted thing is that Bella's craving to hear Edward fuels her friendship with Jacob Black. So all the time that poor Jacob thinks that Bella is enjoying hanging out with him at La Push, behind it all is Bella's yearning for the 'Cold One' (talk about emotional manipulation! Bella would make a great politician!).

And while Bella's hanging out with Jake in the middle chapters of

---

12 Apparently 75 pages about the werewolves were cut from *New Moon* before publication.

New Moon, she's secretly hoping she might hear Edward's spectral voice again. 'This might be a very bad thing. But it would be worth it, if I got to hear *him*' (NM, 197). It's always all about *Edward*, for Bells, no matter what Jacob or Mike Newton or anybody else does or says. (However, the book (and the author) is clear that Bella is conjuring up Edward herself. And, because teen romance is operating at the extreme levels of All Or Nothing, Life Or Death, only life-threatening scenarios can work the magic. The idea of Bella sitting down and conjuring Edward's voice by sheer force of will or imagination (not too difficult for real poets, artists and visionaries), or obtaining help from a Native American shaman, or a psychotherapist, or popping pills, no, that's too easy!).

There are much safer and more effective ways of obtaining a vision of your absent boyfriend than jumping off cliffs into the freezing and dangerous Pacific Ocean! For example, there must be plenty of shamen about among the First Nations in the Pacific North-West of the U.S.A. (I just had a quick look online – there are plenty). They are experts in visioning, in counselling, and in healing. Not to mention that there are all sorts of magical practitioners, and holistic healers of many kinds. Or, aside from New Age therapy, there are psychotherapists, psychiatrists, counsellors, and many professional folk who deal with such issues.

Scary movies become part of Bella Swan's quest for adrenalin and thrills, just like the *Twilight* movies themselves. So there's the zombie movie (*Dead End*) that Bella goes to see with Jessica in Port Angeles, and another horror flick (*Crosshairs*) that Bella wants to see on her double date with Mike and Jacob (Mike suggests a romantic comedy (*Tomorrow and Forever*),[13] but Bella's like, *urrgh*, no, give me blood and guts! Mike thinks Bella's weird, but in fact teenage girls are one of the prime audiences for horror movies, and the vampire/ horror elements in the *Twilight Saga* play just great with a female teen audience).

Dawn of the Dead (1978) was referenced in the scene in *New Moon* where Jessica and Bella exit the theatre (in the spoof movie *Vampires Suck*, this becomes *Breaking Dawn*, a brilliant, self-reflexive concept, where the characters spoil the plot for the punters waiting in line – 'thanks for the spoiler, dipshit!'). In the *Twilight* book it's a zombie movie (*Dead End*), but not one of the George Romero-directed classics. However, it's a genuinely scary movie (that rare item), which frightens both Jessica and Bella. Thus, it becomes part of Bella's quest to shock herself back to life. The trip to the theatre is also part of Bella's attempts

13 In the *New Moon* movie, it's a rom-com called *Love Spelt Backwards Is Love*. You can also glimpse other fake movies on the film posters in the cinema foyer.

to be sociable and lead a normal life, when she promises her Pa Charlie that she'll go out to Port Angeles with Jessica and do normal girl stuff, like go see a movie. (But in the adaptation of *New Moon*, neither Jessica nor Bella seem upset by seeing the zombie movie afterwards (Jessica loudly dismembers it) – indeed, Bella is up for more thrills afterwards, when she goes for a ride with a biker).

BELLA THE ANTI-ROMANTIC.

Bella Swan herself doesn't like romance, doesn't want to watch romantic comedies, and doesn't draw hearts 'n' flowers on her school books. No. Faced with the choice between a horror movie and a romance, she opts for horror every time. (Part of the reason that Bella can't bear to see Emily and Sam Uley acting so affectionately around each other in *New Moon* is that it reminds her of the gaping lack in her own life. Yes, seeing lovers all over each other does make you puke).

The irony is that Bella Swan is starring in one of the drippiest, gooiest, dumbest and heart-and-floweriest of recent romances in either print or celluloid form.

Another irony is that Bella would *not* read the *Twilight* novels! (Badly-written teen junk with a victim heroine).

And she would *not* watch the *Twilight* movies! (And neither would Edward! And *definitely* not Jacob!).

Indeed, Bella would take pity on the Twihard fans; she'd look down on them. She'd think that the fanpires were deranged losers. She'd rather do her Calculus homework than watch *Buffy* or *Charmed*![14]

Yes, even tho' our Bells swoons and moons and moans and weeps like the flimsiest, wispiest Disney Princess, she'd never catch a re-run of Disney's *Cinderella* on TV or carve Bella {♥} Edward on a tree!

BELLA THE DORK.

At times, Bella Swan acts like someone so obsessed and haunted by her failed love affair she becomes truly strange: like a murderer lurking around the scene of the crime, Bella takes to haunting the places she and Edward visited. She goes to the abandoned Cullen home in the forest by the river (surely a property that appealing would've been snapped up by now),[15] where she meets some fans from Philly taking selfies, and signs some autographs; she spends ages trying to find the secret meadow (hiking in the hills with Jacob); and she hates going home precisely

---

14 Note the lack of a TV in her bedroom, no piles of DVDs of *Angel*, *Practical Magic* and *Underworld*, and that she isn't depicted watching TV much.
15 Maybe by a clan of centaurs.

because she doesn't want to be in her bedroom. But she discovers that:

> There was nothing special about this place without *him*. (NM, 234)

The 2009 film adaptation wisely cut down on some of Bella Swan's stranger acts, not only due to time, but it would be just too odd to see Bella loitering around the empty Cullen mansion (even if a voiceover explained her eccentric behaviour). Instead, the movie picked the more spectacular aspects, such as the motorcycles and the cliff-jumping (and motorbikes means more Jacob!).

Bella Swan is also a dork: she invites both Mike Newton and Jacob Black to the cinema, on the disastrous double date, which she pretends isn't a date – the others she invited bail or are ill (thus there's another romantic triangle in *New Moon*, between Bella, Jacob and Mike). Bella reasons with herself that she'll get a group together to go to the cinema, but of course by then she is regarded as an outsider by the school kids, and everyone declines.

'IT'S A JACOB THING' – HE'S A WEREWOLF!

Jacob Black is a naturally warm, happy person, a total contrast with both Bella Swan and Edward Cullen.

> Jacob was simply a perpetually happy person, and he carried that happiness with him like an aura, sharing it with whoever was near him. Like an earthbound sun, whenever someone was within his gravitational pull, Jacob warmed them. It was natural, a part of who he was. (NM, 145)

The werewolf elements would've originally come much later in *The Twilight Saga*, according to Stephenie Meyer (in *Breaking Dawn*). But Meyer's editor (presumably Megan Tingley or Rebecca Davis) preferred to keep the story in high school longer (TS, 21).

The narrative elements of Jacob Black being a werewolf were altered in the 2009 movie of *New Moon*. The 2006 book plays the werewolf clan much creepier, with suggestions that it is a (religious) cult. Jake scares Isabella Swan by talking about the sinister influence of Sam Uley and the boys who are part of his group (meanwhile, the adults in the area reckon that Sam is doing good things in the community). Jacob is afraid of being drawn into the Sam-cult, and Bella is worried about her best friend.

Bella Swan stands to one side, unable to do much except to listen to her friend Jacob Black talk about the Sam Uley sect; of course, in contemporary, North American society, religious cults are well-known (the Branch Davidians, the Sullivanians, the Children of God, Heaven's Gate, etc). But exactly what the Sam-cult entails, how he seduces victims, what rituals are involved, and what the goals or modes of operation of the coven might be, are left unspoken (there are hints of lycanthropy throughout the book of *New Moon*, of course, such as the big, black bear that's been scaring hikers,[16] and Jacob's warmth).

'So, you're the vampire girl.'
I stiffened. 'Yes. Are you the wolf girl?' (NM, 332)

Leaving aside the werewolf and horror genre components, what you have in the middle of *New Moon* (in fact, taking up the bulk of the 2006 novel), is a portrait of a growing friendship between two teens in a brotherly-sisterly/ best friend manner which's derailed halfway thru by some mysterious and powerful force. It's the change in Jacob's personality that's the really scary aspect, not the werewolf or horror genre elements. So it's the scenario of a friend getting into something that they don't want to talk about, that seems to upset them, that doesn't seem to bring them much joy, that they don't want to share with you. It could be anything – drugs, violence, dodgy politics, petty crime, gangs, terrorism, etc. What it actually is isn't as significant as how it affects the friendship, and how it alters someone's personality for the worse.

The 2009 movie of *New Moon* plays it differently: it drops the more menacing aspects of the Sam Uley creed, changes the way that Jacob B.'s affected by becoming a werewolf, and finds much more dramatic and exaggerated ways of depicting how Bella Swan responds to the dilemma (for instance, in the *New Moon* novel, she drives up to the Quileute Indian Reservation, and hangs around, waiting for Jacob; they have a long talk in the rain. Plenty of that's in the movie of *New Moon*, but now Bella's doing crazy stuff like walking up to the boys and whacking Paul in the face! The Bella of the novels would never have the guts to do that! Or the physical co-ordination!).

EVERYONE HAS 'ISSUES'.

No one can miss the fact that both of the guys in Bella Swan's life in *New Moon* seem intent on ruining her life, or their relationships with her (all three of them are experts at self-sabotage. Indeed, one of the recurring themes of the *Twilight* series is this: *if you want someone to mess up your life, you can do it better than anyone!*).

16 Animal attacks, bear attacks and wolf attacks (or serial killers) are sometimes raised as the reasons for the disappearances in the Pacific North-West; Bella thinks it's Sam Uley and his gang in *New Moon*, and the authorities (including Chief Swan) reckon it's animals; but it's the Nomad vampires.

At the start of the 2006 *New Moon* novel, Edward walks out of Bella's life, inducing a deep depression that cripples her for months (in a way, she never recovers from this agony, which exists thru to the end of *Breaking Dawn*. Even when she has Edward back and in her arms, it's still there). And Jacob, her New Best Friend, suddenly turns cold and nasty and withdrawn following an unspecified illness. (Yet both boys stress that they would never hurt her, and want to protect her).[17]

It seems as if what's causing Bella Swan's suffering is the men in her life, not anything in her personality, or anything she does. She wants Edward, but he's jilted her; she wants Jake as a friend, but he too distances himself (not returning her calls, avoiding her, etc).

> 'there was something deeply wrong with me. Why else would my life be filled with characters from horror movies?' (NM 294)

Jeez, even the guy who seemed friendly and warm, Jacob Black, turns out to have Major Issues of his own! Can't a girl find a guy who's not complex or troubled or neurotic?![18] Oh yes, here he is: how about Mike Newton, the Mr Average Guy?! Unfortunately, Bella feels absolutely nothing for him (but, bless him, he does keep trying! But a boy who vomits over a scary movie is probably not the guy for Bella (as Jacob sarcastically points out).)

JUMPING OFF CLIFFS.

Bella Swan is a selfish brat and an idiot. One of the silliest things that Bella does in *New Moon* is to jump off a high cliff into the ocean. It doesn't convince on any level: it's the last thing a timid mouse like Isabella would do. And she wanders off on her own, knowing there's a vampire out to kill her! "'I've never seen anyone so prone to life-threatening idiocy'", Alice complains (NM, 386). On the psychological level, she's addicted to her hallucinations of Edward's voice ('I was addicted to the sound of my delusions' [NM, 352]), so, yes, that's a motivation. But not for something so foolish! Bella insists that it's not suicide, that she's doing it for kicks. But it doesn't convince on that level, either. (Bella would self-harm, try drugs, use one of Daddy's guns, maybe have sex with inappropriate guys, maybe even try martial arts, before getting anywhere near cliff-diving!).

Once Bella Swan's in the water, it becomes a kind of suicide. Well, the whole act has all of the hallmarks of suicide[19] (even tho' Bella tells

---

17 Something that boys and men repeat to the women in their lives *ad nauseam*. Yet they still do it!
18 Despite being complex, neurotic and troubled herself!
19 'I was almost happy that it was over. This was an easier death than others I'd faced. Oddly peaceful... Happiness. It made the whole dying thing pretty bearable' (NM, 361).

Alice Cullen afterwards that she wasn't trying to drown herself). But what Bella *says* and *thinks* aren't the same as what Bella *does*! (Notice that Esme commits suicide by leaping from a cliff in the back-stories of the *Twilight Saga*, after which she is vampirized by Carlisle Cullen).

Well, from an *author's* point-of-view, the cliff-diving sequence does allow the heroine to apparently kill herself and be rescued (it's the Prince and the Princess of fairy tales – as Jacob Black rescues her), and to push herself to the limits, and to test the boundaries between life and death. (And in *Breaking Dawn*, the author has the heroine 'die' and not die. Taking a protagonist to the borders of death is a common trope in fiction – not only fantasy or horror fiction).

There are elements of the cliff-jumping sequence of psychology and emotion and theme that resonate, of course, but as a piece of action and narration, it's utterly bonkers. And you wish La Meyer could've found a more convincing piece of storytelling.

JACOB AND BELLA.

The Bella-Jacob relationship reaches an emotional climax during the teen's werewolf transformation and Bella's realization that he is a werewolf (which comes to her, yet again, in a dream. We have to suspend disbelief that Bella is able to recall a conversation that took place months before in great detail. But that, of course, is a device employed by every novelist – and people writing their memoirs).

After Bella has *accepted* Jacob's werewolf status, the book of *New Moon* is largely over. That is, the emotional and psychological meat of Ms. Meyer's book has been resolved, and the narrative shifts into the third act, featuring Victoria the Nomad vampire aching for vengeance, and the return at the end of the Cullen clan (in particular Alice and Edward).

Sorry Twihards and fanpires, but Victoria is completely uninteresting – even when she's played in the *Twilight* movies by two attractive actresses who've been babed-up by the hair, make-up and costume departments (Rachelle Lefevre and Bryce Howard). No amount of lavish make-up and funky, furry fashions can disguise the fact that Victoria, like James before her in book/ film one, is simply a function of the plot that's been deployed to add some action and suspense to the final act of *New Moon* (and of each *Twilight* book, actually – Victoria hangs around for too long. She should be vanquished in this book, and not linger on to the other novels; ditto with the movies).

In the revelation scene in *New Moon* (set on the beach at La Push), Bella S.'s not scared/ amazed/ put off by Jacob B. being a werewolf, but the fact that people in the woods're being killed (at first, she thinks it's Sam Uley, Jacob, Paul and the crew who're committing the murders). Stephenie Meyer stretches out the misunderstanding between the would-be lovers as much as she can, to make the relief when they both realize they've misunderstood each other so much the greater.

The *Twilight* series is certainly operatic in the way that it exaggerates the emotions in these teen characters up to the level of opera divas playing Romeo and Juliet (or Faust and Mephistopheles).

But that *is* teenage romance in fiction, isn't it? Or it's love stories in general. Why hold back, why suppress emotion until it's frittered away in boring conversations? (Actually, there are plenty of those in *The Twilight Saga*!). No, it's much more entertaining to have the lovers/ would-be lovers embarked upon hysterical, weepy scenes, or lengthy sulks, or blushing embarrassments, or agonized confessions (once again with plenty of weeping and gnashing of teeth!).

EDWARD.

As soon as the slightest, quiveringest mention of Edward Cullen's name, or even the tremblingest, shiveringest suggestion that someone might be going to refer to Edward in the next sentence, Bella Swan goes into hysterical freefall. She grabs her chest and torso to stop herself literally falling apart. She can't breathe: "'It's like I can't breathe... like I'm breaking into pieces", Bella confesses to Jacob (NM, 349). His response is:

> 'We're a pretty messed-up pair, aren't we?' Jacob said. "Neither one of us can hold our shape together right.'
> 'Pathetic,' I agreed, still breathless.
> 'At least we have each other,' he said, clearly comforted by the thought.
> (NM, 349)

Some readers of the *Twilight* books and viewers of the *Twilight* movies thought that Edward really was there, helping Bella Swan in ghost form. No – it was her subconscious helping her out (Stephenie Meyer was clear about that). Yet vampires, of course, do have magical powers – Count Dracula above all (and the way that the movie of *New Moon* portrayed the spectral appearance of Edward did suggest his presence, the way that spirits have been depicted in other movies).

THE FAIRY TALE RETURNS.

In *New Moon*, as soon as Bella Swan hears from Alice Cullen that Edward C.'s in trouble (or, more accurately, that he's being a total jerk), she drops Jacob Black *completely*, and hurries off to save her poor Romeo ('my heart was far away, wandering and grieving after my fickle Romeo' [NM, 375]).

Jake is dumped so rapidly he doesn't know what's hit him. *Whoooosh!* One minute Bella's there, in his arms in the truck, and the next instant, she's hopping around the Swan house like Road Runner, in a hysterical state, desperate to *ziip* as fast as possible to her beloved Cold One. She shoves Jacob out of her way as she leaves in Alice's black Merc.

Following the encounter with the Volturi in Volterra, Italy, there are lengthy *dénouement* scenes in *New Moon*, even tho' the lovers are united and the story is essentially over (over for the second time). Now Edward gets to present his side of the story: Bella thinks that Edward has acted like this because he's been on a huge guilt trip[20] ('the same guilt that compelled him to come here to die when he believed that it was his fault that I'd killed myself' [NM, 459]). No, Edward insists, like Romeo in Bill Shakespeare's play, that he can't exist in a world which doesn't include Bella. So he opted to kill himself rather than continue living. An ultimate romantic reason, then.

F-o-r-e-v-e-r is one of the mantras of the *Twilight Saga*: even more than the word *love* or the word *romance, forever* sums up the aching towards impossible, attainable but so-seductive eternity. Love is *f-o-r-e-v-e-r*, right? Being together is *forever*, isn't it? Got to be! Two years, three years, five years (the lovers argue over dates and times), doesn't do the trick. It has to be Immortality Or Nothing.

> I couldn't keep my eyes off of Edward's face for long. I stared at him, wishing more than anything that the future would never happen. That this moment would last forever, or, if it couldn't, that I would stop existing when it did. (NM, 489)

In the *dénouement* scenes at the end of *New Moon* (chapters 22: "Flight", 23: "The Truth" and 24: "The Vote"), Bella Swan insists that she wants to become part of the Cullen family and to be turned into a vampire. Two people offer to do it for her (Carlisle and Alice, of course), but one person is resisting big time: Edward (who's the one that Bella would prefer to transform her). So we know that this is going to be a Big Obstacle in future installments of the *Twilight Saga* (and it is – it's the major disagreement between the lovers).

The fairy tale was back on. Prince returned, bad spell broken. I wasn't

---

20 Bella tells Edward that he's the sort of person who thinks he's to blame for everything (NM, 507).

exactly sure what to do about the leftover, unresolved character.[21] Where was *his* happily ever after? (NM, 550)

But there's no mistaking that now that Edward is back, and he and Bella have cleared up their misunderstandings, and they are together again. An item. Two-are-one. And Jacob Black – well, poor Jake, is simply cast aside.

So all of the narrative work of the previous four hundred pages in *New Moon*, is junked in one fell swoop! Those thousands of words expended on depicting the developing friendship between J. and B. as it inches towards romance, all for nothing! The epilogue of *New Moon* ("Treaty") is especially harsh on Jacob Black. Because Jake doesn't stand a chance when Edward is standing right next to Bella Swan (which he is throughout *New Moon*'s epilogue). It seems as if the narrator, too, has sided completely with Edward, and the Bella-and-Edward relationship. The way that Bella puts down Jake (and in front of Edward) in their final confrontation is pretty cruel.

Anyhoo, *New Moon* closes with the lovers re-united but a bunch of issues for the heroine to deal with: her best friend alienated; Victoria still on the loose (*still?!*); the Volturi gunning for her; and being grounded by Charlie (NM, 562).

(When the lovers're re-united at the end of *New Moon*, Edward is pretentious and prissy enough to quote from *Romeo and Juliet*: 'Death, that hath sucked the honey of thy breath, hath had no power yet upon thy beauty' (NM, 452). What boy would quote from William Shakespeare in the middle of a love scene?! Well, remember, he's *not* a boy – he's a 104 year-old man!).

THE VOLTURI AND ITALY.

It's in *New Moon* that the vampire world of the *Twilight Saga* is expanded: the first novel focussed on the Cullen coven and the North American Nomad vampires. That was sufficient to provide plenty of vampire-related material, as well as some powerful antagonists with the Nomads. In *New Moon*, Stephenie Meyer opted to extend the world of her alternative/ indie vampires to include many covens, with the Volturi clique at the top of the chain, in Italy.

This is a typical narrative manœuvre for a sequel: to increase the threat, to thicken and deepen the back-stories and the history, and to make the secondary world more complex and multi-layered. It's not essential: *New Moon* could've continued by wheeling in a new threat, using the

---

21 This might be Meyer-as-Bella talking.

'Monster of the Week' format of television and comics everywhere, with a new one for *Eclipse,* and so on, to be disposed of by the end of each book.

The trip to Italy does offer a change of location for the *Twilight Saga*, of course, a welcome respite from the rain and gloom (and predictability) of Sporks, La Push and the Olympic Peninsula (which's precisely why tourists go to Italian hill-towns in the first place!). Because the plotting is so hopeless, and the threat so minimal in *New Moon* (what, like Stephenie Meyer is going to sacrifice the lovers like this?! No!), about the most amusing part of the Italian escapade is seeing Alice Cullen in her element as the Audrey Hepburn of the 2000s, with her fashion plate wardrobe, her head-scarf, her million-dollar smile, and her handy ability to see what Edward's doing from halfway across the Atlantic Ocean (more is made of this by actress Ashley Greene in the adaptation of 2009 movie, of course, than the novel of 2006, which's so much more desperate).

Of all of the Cullens making a return at the end of *New Moon*, Edward and Carlisle, the two obvious choices, are left aside (until very near the end): instead, it's the lovely, visionary Alice who materializes at the Swans' residence in the Pacific North-West in her black Mercedes car. Why did Stephenie Meyer pick Alice? For all the obvious reasons – not least Alice's ability to see into the future, one of the handiest tools for an author – none of the other Cullens can connect with Edward without needing cel phones, etc (Alice also brings a little glamour and girlieness to what has been a predominantly boysy book, with all those 'really big half-naked boys'!).

It's amusing that Edward Cullen's idea of antagonizing the Volturi clan is to take off his shirt! It's like his version of the werewolves going topless, like he's copying Jacob! (He takes off his shirt, and just stands there, looking beautiful and glittery! That might work for a male model, but this guy's a mass murderer! And a supernatural creature!).

Far better than going topless, for a vampire, would be to grab one of the kids milling about in the square in Volterra and attack them. Bloodsucking and fangs and death might do the trick in exposing yourself as a vampire better than taking off your shirt.

new moon

STEHPENIE MEYER
AUTHOR OF THE NEW YORK TIMES BESTSELLING TWILIGHT

3

ECLIPSE, THE BOOK

Mike grinned. 'Anyone in the mood for a bet?'
'Ten on Jacob,' Austin said at once.
'Ten on Cullen,' Tyler chimed in.
'Ten on Edward,' Ben agreed.
'Jacob,' Mike said.

Stephenie Meyer, *Eclipse* (81)

INTRO.

The novel *Eclipse* (2007) by Stephenie Meyer, published by Little, Brown, was structured around a series of conversations, like the other *Twilight* books (and like many romantic stories – a romance yarn is essentially a series of dialogues with some kissing at intervals (and some pouting and sulking, if things aren't going well). But *not* like the Hollywood movie versions of the *Twilight* books, which emphasized *action* far, far, far more than the *Twilight* books do).

So, *Eclipse* is a series of conversations:

(1) *Eclipse* opens with a *very long* chat between Bella Swan and her Dad Charlie.

Followed by:

(2) A *very long* talk between Bella and Edward Cullen.

Followed by:

(3) More *long* conversations between Bella and Edward.

Followed by:

(4) A *long* conversation between Bella and Jacob Black.

In fact, it's not until around chapters 3 and 4 of *Eclipse* that the villains' plot of Victoria & co. causing trouble in Seattle, WA is given more'n a passing mention (the Seattle murders news story is cited a couple of times). The *Eclipse* movie of 2010, however, completely altered the structure of a series of conversations, and turned the novel of *Eclipse* into a romantic drama with plenty of action (and stepped away from Bella's point-of-view to depict the development of the newborn vampire army in Seattle).

To be picky, Victoria the Vampire should be seeking vengeful satisfaction from Edward Cullen – or all of the Cullens, not Bella Swan. It was the Cullens as a group who killed James. Bella was merely the victim: so kill the murderers already, not the victim! (and, besides, it was *James* who chose to hunt Bella, to steal her away from the Cullens. Actually, Victoria ought to be furious with James for being such a psycho – and such a creepy guy, with his preposterous, movie-villainous plan of editing video tapes to play back to Bella on the phone, in order to trick her and lure her to her old ballet school! Instead, Victoria seems to regard Bella as a romantic rival for James, which is also twisted).

However, *Eclipse* is not about the vampire Victoria seeking revenge, or the Volturi Vampire Government pursuing punishment for her daring to cause a nuisance for them, and *Eclipse* is not about werewolves, or vampires, or werewolves versus vampires: it's about le*rrr*ve! It's about r-r-romance! It's about being a teenager and arguing with your Dad! It's about going to high school! It's about growing up! It's about choice!

Yes, *Eclipse* is a teen romance story aimed at the Young Adult market (or 'YA' as Stephenie Meyer insists on calling it).

Three characters, that's all:

Bella Swan ••• Edward Cullen ••• Jacob Black

One girl <—> two guys.

Wait a minute – two *gorgeous* guys! Two *to-die-for* guys! (In the *Twilight Saga*, the guys out-shine the girl for glamour and beauty!).

'I had what I wanted. I couldn't have them both' (E, 459). Two hot hunks fighting over an awkward, plain girl – that's part of the appeal of *The Twilight Saga*, isn't it? That Bella Swan is actually quite boring (and neurotic, shy, clumsy, etc). That she stands for any girl – or anybody who feels unremarkable, plain, overlooked and unloved.

ECLIPSE AND WUTHERING HEIGHTS.

Wuthering Heights (1847) is one of the intertexts with the *Twilight* series, with Bella Swan as Cathy and Edward as Heathcliff and Jake as Edgar Linton – or vice versa[1] (continuing the lit'ry theme from *New*

---

1 Stephenie Meyer noted that they would be either Linton or Heathcliff.

Moon with its intertext of *Romeo and Juliet*).

The *Twilight Saga* contains a few mini-essays at a high school-level, where the charas discuss literary texts: in *New Moon*, B.S. and E.C. talk about *Romeo and Juliet*, and in *Eclipse* they muse for a page (a page of dialogue, of course) about *Wuthering Heights* (notice that Bella doesn't spend hours dicussing 19th classic novels with Jacob!). Edward dismisses Emily Brontë's hyper-passionate novel and its self-destructive characters,[2] while Bella is an ardent admirer (her paperback copy is well-read. I'm with Bella – Emily Brontë wipes the floor with Jane Austen).

It's noted, tho', that much of the trouble in *Wuthering Heights* derives from Cathy, not from Heathcliff. (While the *Romeo and Juliet* subtext appeared in the movie adaptation of *New Moon*, the *Wuthering Heights* subtext isn't really included in the adaptation of *Eclipse*). Stephenie Meyer remarked that she liked to read parts of *Wuthering Heights*, was attracted to the characters, but disliked the novel as a whole – too depressing.

Later, Bella Swan compares her situation to Catherine Earnshaw's again:

> I was selfish, I was hurtful. I tortured the ones I loved.
> I was like Cathy, like *Wuthering Heights*, only my options were so much better than hers, neither one evil, neither one weak. (E, 459)

And, as Bella and Edward're reunited at the end of *Eclipse*, Miss Swan once again consults the most passionate novel in the English language for a quote about Cathy that sums up her feelings:

> If all else perished, and he remained, I should still continue to be; and if all else remained, and he were annihilated, the universe would turn to a mighty stranger. (E, 541)

Not to be out-done in the prissy-and-pretentious stakes, Edward also snags a quote from Emily Brontë (which he knows by heart, of course):[3] 'I *cannot* live without my life! I *cannot* live without my soul!' (E, 541). The book and film of *Eclipse* led to increased sales of the Emily Brontë novel. Did Brontë get royalties? Yes, every Friday).

---

2 The charas are not on the level of Elizabeth Bennet and Mr Darcy (*Pride and Prejudice*) or Romeo and Juliet, Edward complains (E, 25). Bells defends *Wuthering Heights*, saying that 'it's something about the inevitability. How nothing can keep them apart – not her selfishness, or his evil, or even death, in the end' (E, 25).
3 But why would Ed memorize parts of a novel he dislikes? Even if he's got a lot of time in his 104 years!

ROSALIE.

The back-story of Rosalie Hale related in *Eclipse* is the story of a beautiful but shallow young woman who has ambitions to become the wife and mother of one of the neighbourhood's successful businessmen, Royce King the Second ('I was eighteen, and I was beautiful. My life was perfect' [E, 138]). Rosalie in the present day (as a grouchy vampire many decades old) critiques her bland, predictable ambitions when she was a human of 18 years-old, when she was more like a Disney Princess, fatally naïve, and unable (or unwilling) to see the faults in her beau.

Rosalie Hale's story is a sad fairy tale: she's telling it to Bella Swan in *Eclipse* in order that the human might reconsider her desire to become a vampire so she can live with Edward Cullen forever and ever. A sorrowful fairy tale, because it ends very badly, with Rosalie gang-raped on the streets of Rochester, N.Y., at night, by her drunken fiancé and his cronies (the rape is elided by Rosalie, just like the movie of *Eclipse* left it out [E, 143]). That Rosalie is on the verge of marrying Royce King also offers a contrast with the impending marriage of Edward and Bella.[4] (Rosalie's miserable story is also another instance in the world of *Twilight* of people becoming vampires when they're in extreme situations: Rosalie being raped and saved by Carlisle Cullen;[5] Emmett being attacked by a grizzly bear; Alice in a mental institution; Esme after jumping off a cliff; and Edward dying of Spanish flu. It's grim stuff – Jasper is one of the few characters in the vampire world who's changed into a vampire out of nowhere, when he encounters Maria and her chums Lucy and Nettie (the Mexican coven) in the middle of the American Civil War. For Jasper, it's very, very bad luck).

Rosalie Hale is a bitter soul, a victim of men's predatory nature, the harsh, patriarchal world of the 1930s, Western world. She feels that her life was stolen from her, that she didn't have any *choice* in becoming a vampire (the issue of *choice* is perhaps the key ethical dilemma at the heart of the *Twilight* books: the choice to become a vampire, the choice of this lover or that lover, the choice of sex before marriage, the choice of wedlock, etc).

Rosalie Hale's beauty (and innocence) works against her, in the end: her story has affinities with classic novels such as *Tess of the d'Urbervilles*: men become wolves, taking advantage of Little Red Riding Hoods (like Alec d'Urberville with Tess Durbeyfield). And Rose's middle-class environment (being the daughter of well-off parents), with

---

4 In *Twilight*, Edward hints that Carlisle was hoping that Rosalie might be a mate for him (T, 252).
5 Rosalie somewhat resents Carlisle saving her (a recurring reaction in the *Twilight Saga*), and says she didn't really like Carlisle and his brother Edward (as Edward pretended to be at the time).

its comfort and safety, is also not enough to protect her. (That Rosalie's back-story in *Eclipse* closes with vengeance, as she slaughters the men who violated her, is a classic case of turning the tables on the oppressors. Everyone cheers when the victim becomes a monster herself, and is able to slay the wolves one by one – leaving Royce King for last, of course).

EMMETT.

Rosalie Hale saving Emmett from a bear attack is an amusing spin on fairy tale motifs (such as *Little Red Riding Hood*), and of course it makes good, in a way, her own experience at the hands of her fiancé Royce King and his buddies (so that now, as a vampire, Rosalie is able to save someone in distress – to do a Carlisle Cullen). In *Twilight,* Edward recounts how Rose found Emmett near-dead in the Appalachian mountains, and carried him 100+ miles back to Carlisle (there is more of this story in the extras included on Stephenie Meyer's website).

JASPER.

One of the lengthiest back-stories in *Eclipse* concerns Jasper Whitlock and his very troubled, violent life with Maria the Vampire back in the 19th century. There's a clear echo of Scarlett O'Hara in the characterization of Maria (and her vampire cohorts) and their craving to regain their estates during the American Civil War (the flashback acts as a vampire version of *Gone With the Wind*, just as *Eclipse* itself is a vampire version of *Wuthering Heights*). The details of Maria and her plots aren't explored much in the movie adaptation.

Jasper Whitlock's story offers parallels, of course, with the present-day situation in Seattle with the newborn vampire army (the 2010 novel *The Short Second Life of Bree Tanner* explores the newborns' side of the story in more depth). And Jasper's uneasy relationship with his mistress Maria also echoes that of Riley Biers with Victoria.

In the world of *Twilight*, the Southern United States of America is a hotbed of dissent, grudges and internecine conflict among vampire clans. It's impossible to miss the digs at the present-day U.S.A., with its struggles of politics and religion.

Jasper Whitlock's story of becoming a vampire is in keeping with his human life as a soldier in the American Civil War: he is portrayed as a Texan gentleman, who might've ridden on horseback out of a classic cowboy movie. That he is given the job of protecting women and children, as they're evacuating from the advancing armies of the North, is significant.

An intriguing aspect of Jasper's vampirism is dissatisfaction and depression. Altho' he was with Maria as long as Carlisle was with Edward (87 years or so), he never felt the bond was strong (E, 266). And he becomes depressed, disillusioned, and unhappy with breeding and killing newborns. (But his back-story has a happy ending, when he wanders into a diner in Philly and meets the tiny but gorgeous Alice – and she's been waiting for him (having foreseen their meeting): '"You've kept me waiting a long time"', she tells him [E, 268]).

BELLA AND ALICE.

Angela Weber is one of the few young women of Bella Swan's age that she can talk to; there's an uneventful and bland scene in *Eclipse* where Bella helps Angela to write out her announcements for the school Prom (it's a deliberately flat and unexceptional scene perhaps because it follows a volatile encounter between Bella and Jacob Black on the beach).

> And yet, with a strange, sudden intensity, that's exactly what I wanted. I wanted to talk to a normal human girlfriend. I wanted to moan a little bit, like any other teenage girl. I want my problems to be that simple. It would also be nice to have someone outside the whole vampire-werewolf mess to put things in perspective. (E, 120)

In *Eclipse,* among young women, Bella Swan actually spends more time with Alice Cullen than anyone else. And Alice is a quirky, wilful, stubborn personality whose character is diametrically opposed to Bella's far more reserved, cautious, introspective personality. Alice comes from a completely different world – a glamorous, frothy *milieu* of sports cars, parties, shopping, and expensive clothes. Bella is a frumpy, stay-at-home in old sweats, while Alice is a social gadfly in Chanel (Alice is a super-model character from a Jackie Collins novel). But it's easy to see why Stephenie Meyer would be keen to include plenty of Alice, if possible, because she's a fun character to write for (certainly, Alice might have a fantasy romance series of her own (she's a sister to the characters in *Charmed*). Indeed, actress Ashley Greene auditioned initially for the role of Bella).

WEREWOLVES.

In *Eclipse, The Twilight Saga* really gets into werewolves (or wolves – the novels differentiate between the two, using shape-changing for the Quileute creatures) – what it means to be a werewolf, how Jacob Black is different from the others, how the wolf pack works, how they share thoughts, how 'imprinting' works, and of course how the werewolves team up with the veteran vampires to defend the rural, small-town Pacific North-West from a newborn vampire army from scuzzy, urban Seattle (the *Twilight Saga* is utterly small-town, suburban Middle America, and it's no accident that the threat (of the newborns) comes from a Big, Bad City. Or, at other times, from a bunch of decadent aristocrats in another country – for God's sake, not New Jersey! – no, Italy!).

Anyhoo, one of the long back-stories in *Eclipse* is a round-the-campfire storytelling sequence as Billy Black and the Quileute tribal elders relate the myths and legends of the werewolves and the Quileute Tribe. Now we get to find out some of the origins of the werewolf/vampire set-up, and, crucially, how the werewolves come into existence because the 'Cold Ones' appear (the symbiotic relationship has a fatalistic, somewhat masochistic aspect to it, which's reflected in the two relationships in Bella's love life, Bella-and-Jacob and Bella-and-Edward).

COURTLY LOVE.

Incredibly, Bella Swan doesn't have a cel phone! You're kidding, right? No – she borrows Edward's cel when she wants to make a call! Come on, even a kid of five is desperate for a cel phone! You can get them for twenty bucks in any Walmart or Target! Well, I guess Stephenie Meyer likes the idea of more traditional forms of communication – like people meeting face to face, in the flesh. And like letters (written with a feathered quill dipped in violet-hued ink, of course), as if we're living in a 19th century novel.

So in *Eclipse* we've got the publisher Little, Brown reproducing the handwriting of Jacob Black (boyish and functional), Edward (perfect calligraphy, of course!), Bella (girlie and functional), and even Charlie (manly and functional).

> If I had my way, I would spend the majority of my time kissing Edward. (E, 38)

> [Jacob's] familiar husky voice sent a wave of wistfulness through me. A thousand memories spun in my head, tangling together – a rocky beach strewn with driftwood trees, a garage made of plastic sheds, warm sodas in a paper bag, a tiny room with one too-small shabby loveseat. (E, 63)

According to Rosalie in *Eclipse,* Edward Cullen wasn't interested in dating anyone, not even the glamorous clan of Tanya's in Denali (E, 147). Nevertheless, Bella can't help feeling jealous. She imagines her 'gorgeous immortal rival' (E, 172).

'Is it really so impossible to wear clothes, Jacob?' I asked. Once again, Jacob was bare-chested, wearing nothing but a pair of old cut-off jeans. Secretly, I wondered if he was just so proud of his new muscles that he couldn't stand to cover them up. I had to admit, they were impressive... (E, 191)

'What's it like – having a vampire for a boyfriend?'
I rolled my eyes. 'It's the best.'
'I'm serious. The idea doesn't bother you – it never creeps you out?'
'Never.' (E, 193)

The concept of 'imprinting' among werewolves is an amusing twist on the ancient concept of 'love at first sight' in the *Twilight Saga*. Jacob Black explains it to Bells in *Eclipse:*

When you see *her*, suddenly it's not the earth holding you here anymore. she does. And nothing matters more than her. And you would do any-thing for her, be anything for her... You become whatever she needs you to be, whether that's a protector, or a lover, or a friend, or a brother. (E, 156)

'Imprinting' would be instantly recognizable to mediæval poets, such as the troubadours and the poets of the courtly love poetry tradition, and the *stilnovisti* poets like Dante Alighieri, Guido Cavalcanti and Guido Guinicelli.

In the Middle Ages, the concepts of 'love at first sight' and the eyes as 'the windows of the soul' were commonplace. The idea of Venus's cherubic assistant Cupid firing arrows of love into the beloved's eyes was sort of taken literally. Look at love poetry in the mediæval era, and eyes and looking are evoked all the time (as they are in love poetry of any era). And similarly in movies, and in romantic movies, the eyes and the looks do much of the talking. Certainly that's true in *Twilight,* where eyes are the subject of very close scrutiny).

Once imprinting has been introduced (a third of the way into the book of *Eclipse*), Stephenie Meyer teases the audience as they wonder whether Jacob Black has 'imprinted' on Bella Swan (only in *Breaking Dawn* is that mystery explained). But of course, true lovers don't need mysterioso concepts like wolfish 'imprinting' to go all-out in love! (Indeed, the culture of love evoked in the *Twilight* books is actually ancient – going back to the Middle Ages, and way beyond, to the Ancient Roman and Greek eras).

'there's no point to forever without you. I wouldn't want one day without you' (E, 245)

In *Eclipse,* Bella Swan muses that it would be easier to tell her Mom, her Dad and friends Angela, Ben and Mike that she was becoming a vampire than getting married. Bella has major hang-ups concerning wedlock (E, 288).

> 'I'm in love with you, Bella,' Jacob said in a strong, sure voice. 'Bella, I love you. And I want you to pick me instead of him.' (E, 290)

Jacob is pretty confident that Bella loves him back: 'You love me, too,' he tells her (E, 292). Bella of course resists, but by the end of the 2007 novel she's realized that, yes, she does love Jake. To the point where she's seriously contemplating a life with him.

> 'I love you, Bella,' he murmured.
> 'I love you, Jacob,' I whispered brokenly. (E, 465)

Cleverly, Jacob Black plays upon Bella Swan's vulnerability – that Edward Cullen left her once, and he might do it again (E, 296). That was Bella's most terrible time, which Jake knows full well.

Later, in their final, heartbreaking conversation in *Eclipse,* as Jacob recovers at the Quileute Res in La Push and Bella visits him, he tells her that he is right for her and she is for him. 'I'm exactly right for you, Bella. It would have been effortless for us – comfortable, easy as breathing', if the world didn't contain monsters and magic (E, 530). Bella knows that Jake is right, that he is her soul mate in a natural or non-magical world (E, 531).

Two guys, one girl – two soul-mate pairings – with Bella Swan caught in the middle. Both are right, both fit. So there's two Bellas – 'Edward's Bella and Jacob's Bella' (E, 539). Unfortunately, you can't have both, can't have it both ways, can't have your cake *and* eat it, can't have one lover for one part of your personality and life and another for the other parts (well, not in a conventionally moral and traditional romantic novel aimed at teenagers! So, no threesomes in the *Twilight Saga!*).

HEADING TOWARDS THE FINALE.

About two-thirds into *Eclipse,* the newborn vampire army threat is brought into the foreground, when the romantic triangle of Bella-Edward-Jacob has played out to the point where Jacob's tried to kiss Bella and they've fallen out. During the Graduation Party (where Alice, bless her, inevitably, goes OTT in turning the Cullen mansion into a flashy, L.A. nightclub), the newborn vampire plot is re-introduced, as Bella realizes that the newborn bloodsuckers have been created by Victoria and are coming for her.

Anyhoo, the newborn army threat in *Eclipse* is a mere backdrop to the much more interesting scenes where the vampires and the werewolves decide they could work together. Because the viewpoint selected by author Stephenie Meyer stays wholly with Bella Swan, we don't know anything about the Seattle vampire newborns (other than occasional grisly news reports on TV). Thus, Bella has to be stubborn enough to want to stay up until three in the morning so she can tag along with Edward to the training sessions at the baseball field, overseen by Jasper. Because if Bella falls asleep, we wouldn't see anything of Jasper teaching the werewolves and the vampires on how to slay newborn vampire kids. (In the *Eclipse* movie, there's no baseball field, and the scene occurs in daytime in a forest – where, yes, hikers and backpackers could easily walk thru the trees and spot vampires and werewolves! But, somehow, as in all movies, the general public mysteriously vanishes).

As the plot of *Eclipse* progresses in the final third part of the Young Adult novel, the narrative makes some jumpy shifts, and there's quite a bit of finagling of the plot by the Twilight Queen in order to put Jacob, Bella and Edward together, up on that snowy mountain in a storm (they could be anywhere – a Taco Bell, a sleazy bar, a motel).⁶ Well, sure, it *is* pretty contrived, but the reader goes along with it because it is, after all, the romantic soap opera that is the compelling aspect of the *Twilight Saga*, not the horror genre or action elements.

So all of that business with the scent – to mask Bella's scent, and also to lead the newborn vampires onto the battlefield – is an artificial (and rather tiresome) means for putting Bella and Jacob together (and not only that, but also to have Bella being carried by Jake, which she finds a little too intimate).

THE FINALE OF *ECLIPSE*.

When *Eclipse* reaches its action finale, it amounts to one of the longer sequences of action in the *Twilight* series. It's a re-run of the previous two books' finales, of course: Edward protecting his beloved Bella from vampire attacks (including from some of the same vampires!).

The battle with the newborn vampires is a major guilt trip for Bella Swan, because she reckons, in her egotism, that she is the cause of everything:

What if it was Emmett, so brave and thoughtless that he was never the

6 Even a crummy motel would be warmer!

least bit cautious? Or Esme, so sweet and motherly that I couldn't even imagine her in a fight? Or Alice, so tiny, so fragile-looking? (E, 277)

Sticking strictly to a first person p.o.v., Stephenie Meyer stages the climax of *Eclipse* entirely in the snow on the mountain, where Bella's stationed with Edward and Seth. Handily, Edward is able to see via Seth to the battle raging below, in the baseball clearing, using wolfy connections (yes, the narrative devices are being *really* stretched here! – linking up mind-reading with wolf telepathy!).[7] So Edward is able to bring parts of the conflict into the Bella-space on the mountain (of course, that isn't enough for the Hollywood movie of *Eclipse,* which stages the battle with the newborn vamp army up close and personal. And if you read the *Bree Tanner* side-story, you get a fuller picture of what happened in the baseball clearing).

The finale of *Eclipse* is never in *any* doubt, of course: Riley Biers and Victoria are soon history and, no surprises here, Bella's in a state of hysteria and shock. Jacob Black is taken away following the Big Kiss Scene, so he can be injured in the battle; thus it's Seth as a werewolf who helps Edward take down Riley and Victoria (Seth working with Edward as a team comes out cooler in the *Eclipse* novel than in the 2010 movie, where they don't really work together). And of course, Bella gets to do her bit, with the third-wife-shedding-blood gag from the werewolf legends told around the Quileute tribal fire (but – *wait a second* – this is the *U.S.A.*! God bless America! A nation where it's in the goddam *constitution* to have the right to bear arms! ('the right of the people to keep and bear Arms shall not be infringed' – Second Amendment). Didn't anybody in the Cullen clan think of arming Bella, just in case? Like, couldn't Bella have a handgun or two? Are you telling me that the Cullens, with all their hi-tech gadgets, haven't got some firearms? Maybe a lightsabre? Couldn't Bella aim at Victoria's skull during the fight on the mountain and unload a clip into it? That might slow the harpy down, surely? Why does Bella have to be the pale, quaking, unarmed, useless girl-victim? Why can't Bella kick ass too?! At least give her a knife so can protect herself at close quarters, and maybe slit her arm open to do the third-wife-blood-shedding-thing instead of scrabbling about in the dirt for a stupid sharp-edged stone? And – *come on!* – her Dad's the Chief of Police! Surely Bella can be a tomboy who's handy with a gun, having been taught by her Pa as a kid to fire a pistol when Mom wasn't watching?)[8]

---

7 In the movie, it's assumed that Edward can now read minds from miles away.
8 Charlie gives her pepper spray! Come on, Charlie, don't be such a wuss! Give her the girl weapons training!

The argument –> the Big Kiss –> the departure –> the jostling of two guys crazy about the heroine –> and the battle. At least in terms of dramatic structure, the ending of *Eclipse* is more readerly satisfying than the finales of both *New Moon* and *Twilight* (even tho' it simply replays them in essence). That is, for readers, the action's better staged and more slickly described.

But it's not as emotionally satisfying, in a way, even tho' the agony of Jacob B. finding out that Bella S.'s planning to marry Edward C., plus Jake getting injured, enhances the emotional catharsis. And Bella zooms from hysteria to paranoia and guilt with astonishing speed. She wants to disappear, wants to make up with Jake, wants to placate both guys (impossible!), and wants to stop *hurting people*.

Bella Swan's on the guilt-trip-to-end-all-guilt-trips at the close of *Eclipse* (which's what the emotional climax of *Eclipse* is all about, really).[9] She feels terrible about the way she deals with Jacob Black, feels bad about Edward Cullen, hates being the (partial) cause of Victoria's fury and the newborn vampire invasion, loathes putting the Cullens and the wolves in the line of fire, and is torn between craving the vampire's life and being simply human. For Bella, becoming a vampire is 'the key to what I wanted more than everything else in the world put together' (E, 21).

Poor Bella: it ain't easy being a teenager! She seems, from her point-of-view, to hurt everybody around her: Charlie and Renée and Jacob when she decides to become a vampire, and Edward and the Cullens when she stubbornly maintains a relationship with Jacob Black and the Quileute Tribe members. Stephenie Meyer concocts a scenario where Bella is at the centre of a bundle of conflicting groups and individuals, so that whatever she does, she always ends up hurting somebody.

As Bella Swan tries to seduce Edward Cullen at the end of *Eclipse,* as if she can trick him into making love to her, she – inevitably! – runs thru a host of conflicting emotions. She's guilty, she's confused, she's unsure, and she's horny.

Why wasn't I stopping this? Worse than that, why couldn't I find in myself even the desire to *want* to stop? What did it mean that I didn't want *him* to stop? That my hands clung to his shoulders, and liked that they were wide and strong? (E, 468)

The biggest loser in the *Twilight Saga* is probably Jacob Black, closely followed by Charlie and Renée. In terms of the romantic story, Jacob loses most, in not getting the Princess in the end (the runner-up

---

9 Bella Swan is much more hysterical about her guilt than she is in the movie.

prize of the Heroine's Daughter just doesn't count!). But in *choosing* Edward, Bella also *loses* Jake. The issue of *choice* is absolutely fundamental here: if you chose *one* path, it automatically deletes *all other paths*. You pick one guy (or lifestyle), and you instantly exclude billions of others.

✐

The emotional finale of *Eclipse* wraps up the romantic triangle (mostly), as Bella Swan says goodbye to Jacob Black, and pledges herself to Edward Cullen. Essentially, *Eclipse* ends the whole *Twilight* story right there, and it would be perfectly satisfying as a trilogy of books. But there's another book in the *Twilight Soap Opera* to come, *Breaking Dawn*, the longest book, which takes Bella's story into marriage, a honeymoon, sex, pregnancy, birth, motherhood, washing, cleaning, ironing, cooking, shopping and washing the car and darning socks and fixing the toaster (just kidding!), and becoming a vampire.

Of course, Jacob Black doesn't disappear from the *Twilight* story at the end of *Eclipse* (tho' he does flee into the wilderness when he receives the wedding invitation in a major sulk, as he tries to forget all about Bella Swan getting hitched to a bloodsucker and romantic rival). Actually, Stephenie Meyer makes a major dramatic shift at the end of *Eclipse,* by having Jake narrate the epilogue from his point-of-view (this wasn't taken up in the 2010 movie adaptation).

This leads the way for the first big change in the narrative structure of the *Twilight Saga* in book form, when Stephenie Meyer opts to have an episode of *Breaking Dawn* narrated by Jacob Black (which's the most entertaining section in the four and a half *Twilight* books – five and a half if you include the gender-reversed *Life and Death In Teen-Romance Land*. No, six and a half if you include *Midnight Sun*).

SEXUAL POLITICS.

Edward Cullen giving Bella Swan the ultimatum of marriage in return for having sex with her is an amusing twist on 19th century literature's representation of wedlock and the ethical choices available to young women in Western society in that era (turning about the morality and ethics of the fiction of Jane Austen and the Brontë Sisters). As Bella tells Edward, 'you are bizarrely moral for a vampire' (E, 475).[10] It's amusing, too, because it reverses the gender expectations, with Bella wanting intimacy, and Edward insisting on marriage first (tho' – Heaven forfend! – the word 'sex' *is not* used by Stephenie Meyer in the *Twilight*

---

10 Actually, he's basically 1910s, morally.

books! Instead, Meyer employs euphemisms like 'human experience'. Of course, because in the romance literary genre, love can't be reduced to sex, it must always be Something More, something spiritual 'n' magical 'n' infinite).

So, every time Bella Swan raises the issue of sex – *oops*! – I mean, the issue of making love, or 'human experience', Edward Cullen always declines. 'Not tonight' is his recurring mantra: "I'm not saying no,' he reassured me. 'I'm just saying *not tonight*'' (E, 399). Edward is the uptight nursemaid with a permanent headache. *Not tonight, hon,* he'll be repeating forever. (Edward is conscious of the gender reversal: 'Tradition-ally, shouldn't you be arguing my side, and I yours?' [E, 400]).

Bella Swan is opposed to marriage for lots of reasons: she thinks she's too young, she wants to pursue her education, she reckons marriage is old-fashioned,[11] she doesn't want to repeat the mistakes her folks made, etcetera. All of the familiar reasons that late teens/ early twenties people give for preferring not to marry.

> 'Isabella Swan?' He looked up at me through his impossibly long lashes, his golden eyes soft but, somehow, still scorching. 'I promise to love you forever – every single day of forever. Will you marry me?' (E, 408)

The pro-women, quasi-feminist stance of the *Twilight Saga* is expressed in *Eclipse* in several ways. One is obvious: among the vampires, *Eclipse* is keen to promote women as powerful figures. Thus, the people who run the newborn vampire armies in Jasper's flashback are Maria and two women; it's the female mate of the vampire in the Quileute Tribe flashback who runs amok much more than the male (after the wolves dispatch him); and in the present tense, it's Victoria, who's orchestrating the newborn vampire in Seattle.

---

11 Altho' she's picked the most old-fashioned guy in Forks!

eclipse

STEPHENIE MEYER
THE INTERNATIONAL
NUMBER ONE BESTSELLER

4

BREAKING DAWN, THE BOOK

I felt like – like I don't know what. Like this wasn't real. Like I was in some Goth version of a bad sitcom. Instead of being the A/V dweeb about to ask the head cheerleader to the prom, I was the finished-second-place werewolf about to ask the vampire's wife to shack up and procreate. Nice.

Stephenie Meyer, *Breaking Dawn* (170)

INTRO.

Breaking Dawn was published on Aug 2, 2008 by Little, Brown (with one of those *Harry Potter*-esque midnight releases at 4,000 stores in the U.S.A.). *Breaking Dawn* (756 pages in hardcover) was a massive hit from the outset (6 million copies sold in 2008). It was the biggest-selling children's book of 2008, and stayed on the top-selling charts of *U.S.A. Today* for 58 weeks. The reviews of *Breaking Dawn*, as you can guess, veered from enthusiastic ('a wild but satisfying finish to the ballad of Bella and Edward' – *Time*), to vitriolic ('shockingly, tackily, sick-makingly sexist' – *Independent*). And the book reviews didn't affect the sales one iota.

Breaking Dawn had its origins in *Forever Dawn*, the sequel to *Twilight* which Stephenie Meyer planned in 2003, and completed in February, 2004 (Meyer said she changed the title because *Forever Dawn* was too cheesy).

In *Forever Dawn*, Bella's pregnancy was narrated from her point-of-view, in the usual first person. By *Breaking Dawn*, Stephenie Meyer had switched to Jacob's viewpoint, which allowed for a new perspective and, of course, more humour.

Most of the plot turns that the novel *Breaking Dawn* makes are familiar. Editing would benefit parts of *Breaking Dawn*. Two or three of the conversation scenes in the book *Jacob* (between the werewolves) go on and on. The New Mom scenes, where Bella gets to know her daughter Renesmee, are rather long.

THE NARRATIVE STRUCTURE.

Marriage -> a wedding -> a honeymoon -> sex -> pregnancy -> birth -> motherhood... *Breaking Dawn* continues the Life and Times of Isabella Swan as she moves from being a teenager to a young woman (she's keen to be married before she hits nineteen, partly because her beloved, Edward Cullen, remains seventeen (well, seventeen going on 104!). Her Mom Renée says Bella's never been a teenager (and is a rather middle-aged teenager – and Edward is a rather old-fashioned teenager), but actually Bella prefers to stay her age – 18 years-old – forever. This is the key to the *Twilight Saga*: f-o-r-e-v-e-r).

The story of *Breaking Dawn* can be summed up like this:

Wedding
Honeymoon
Lovemaking
Pregnancy
Birth
Death
Rebirth
Vampirism
Motherhood
Happy Ending

Added to this very traditional range of issues, which millions of people face every day (dealing with in-laws, undertaking a splashy wedding, getting pregnant, arguing with your spouse, etc), are the vampiric ingredients of the *Twilight* series: becoming a vampire, and dealing with the vampiric world (such as the vampire police, the Volturi mob). And not forgetting the small matter of death and rebirth.

But the *Twilight Saga* could end with *Eclipse,* where the romantic triangle is largely resolved (tho' Bella Swan's guilt over causing Jacob Black so much pain threatens to consume her. That might fade with time, however). Indeed, there was talk of the *Twilight Saga* being a book trilogy: it would have been easy to end *Eclipse* with a big wedding, followed the heroine transforming into a vampire:[1]

---
1 There's no need for the lovey-dovey honeymoon.

My eyelids fluttered open. I saw his shining, crooked smile.
'Did it...? Am I – ?' I whispered.
'Yes, Mrs Cullen,' he said softly.
'So... I am a vampire now?'
Edward smiled again and kissed me.
Now we could spend our lives kissing forever.

In venturing into areas like (1) getting married, (2) setting up a home with your hubby, (3) getting pregnant and (4) having kids, *The Twilight Saga* moves away more than a little from the usual province of fiction for young adults (the *Twilight* series could become pretty boring at this point, when our heroes turn into a married couple with a kid and a home. Instead of crooked smiles and golden eyes and endless kisses, there'd be chores like taking out the trash, tax forms to fill in, changing diapers, and bickering about whose turn it was to wash up. Bella and Edward would become just like every bored, married couple in the history of the world).

Luckily, there is still some mileage to be squeezed out of the Jacob Black plot in the *Twilight Saga*, and the werewolf plot – which, added to the Bella-becoming-a-vampire plot and the vampire world/ Volturi/ Renesmee plot, means that *Breaking Dawn* can be stretched out quite a ways (Hell, to become *two* movies!).

But as Bella Swan and Edward Cullen have pledged to be together forever at the end of *Eclipse* (including quoting from *Wuthering Heights* and seriously comparing themselves to Cathy and Heathcliff), and the last word of *Eclipse* is *eternity*, well, shoot, that's the romantic-erotic-love plot of the *Twilight Saga* all tied up.

But, to be fair, it was already set in stone that Bella-and-Edward would be together by a third of the way into the first *Twilight* book (when Bella acknowledges, 'it's too late' – meaning, she's already committed 100% to Edward romantically).

THE JACOB BOOK.

The Jacob Black story takes up a third of *Breaking Dawn*, representing a major shift not only in style and viewpoint but also, thankfully, humour: the *Jake Book* in *Breaking Dawn* is much funnier than the Bella-narrated sections of any part of the *Twilight Saga*. Jake cracks jokes (there's a whole series aimed at Rosalie Hale about dumb blondes), reacts in a direct, casual and earthy manner to events, and is so much more *alive* than Bella. Even the chapter titles are amusing in the *Jacob Book*: instead of the boring, airport fiction, one-word chapter titles of the *Twilight Saga* ('Burgers', 'Blood', 'Soda', 'Turnips', 'Pasta',

---

2 The obvious viewpoint to take is Edward's; Stephenie Meyer had done that in *Midnight Sun*.

'Disney', 'Hairdryers', etc), there are chapter titles like "Sure As Hell Didn't See That One Coming" (9) and "Why Didn't I Just Walk Away? Oh Right, Because I'm an Idiot" (10). (And several unused chapter titles: "Why Am I Still In Love With This Emo Loser Bella?" and "But Stephenie, Why Do I Have To Lose Out To This Stuck-up Bloodsucker?").

To the point where, when the point-of-view shifts backs to Bella ('I *Am* Pouting and Sulky, So Sue Me!') Swan in *Book Three* of *Breaking Dawn*, it's a bit of a let-down. *Uggh*, darn, we *knew* we'd have to return to the Bella-Point-of-View, but, Hell, she can be so, like, *serious* (and the way she sees the world, even in her new vampirized state is so, like, predictable. Whereas you don't always know what Jake is going to do or say. Who would you rather hang out with? Team Bella? Team Edward? Or Team Jacob?).

In his book in *Breaking Dawn*, Jacob Black realizes that he's being masochistic, that he's being a jerk, that he can't get enough of his fix – Bella Swan – for his drug addiction. So he hangs around the Cullen household, resented by some (Rosalie), but welcomed by others (Esme, Alice, Carlisle, even Edward). Jacob will put up with the snarks from Mopey Rose just so he can be close to Bella. Emmett and Jasper are notably absent for much of the *Jacob* book.

Indeed, a good deal of the action in the *Jacob* section in *Breaking Dawn* is based in and around the white bread, upper-class Cullen mansion, with Jake Black sticking around partly because he can't stay away from Bella S., partly because she wants him to be there, partly because he knows she's dying and hasn't got long for this world, partly because he's now an outcast from the Quileute Tribe (and can't go home for the time being), and partly because some of the vamps (Edward in particular) find uses for him (it's Jake, for instance, who comes up with the solution to Bella wasting away – offer her some blood!).

Unable to handle the stifling claustrophobia of the lovey-dovey mother-and-baby duo, Jacob Black flees the Cullen stronghold (in an Aston Martin Vanquish, no less! Yes, the *Twilight Saga* is the Jackie Collins version of a modern vampire yarn!). So Jacob hares off at 200 mph towards Tacoma and Seattle (as you do),[3] winding up at a local park. He's searching for... yes, the usual thing: love/ romance/ a soul mate. Surely one of the young women in the park would do for the time being while you're waiting for True Love to come along? (which would be Woody Allen's view). No, not for Jacob! Even tho' a girl (Lizzie)

---

3 Rather than South to Cali.

approaches him who offers sympathetic words (and she knows her cars, too!, recognizing the Aston Martin), Jake can't get Bella out of his mind.[4]

Well, *duh*, of course not – you can't find your soul mate in 35 minutes in a Seattle park! Or maybe you can! (This is a fantasy, after all). Anyhoo, Jake simply jumps in the car and, with his wolf tail between his legs, hurries back to the House of Pain and Misery and a Woman Dying In Childbirth in Sporks, WA. No surprise that this unconvincing and inconsequential side-story didn't appear in the double helping movie version of *Breaking Dawn* (it's a no-brainer to cut this going-nowhere-fast side-story).

In *Breaking Dawn*, Edward Cullen is so desperate to save Bella Swan's life that he makes a bizarre offer to Jacob Black, which Jake can't believe: if Bella wants a baby, then she could have one with Jake. Edward suggests that Jake could hint to Bella that she could lose this particular, monstrous baby, and they could try for a real, human child (while she is still human). Needless to say, this plot point didn't make it into the movie versions of *Breaking Dawn*!

THE MIDDLE CHAPTERS.

The narrative proceeds for much of the 2008 novel along conventional lines: there's the wedding, of course, which includes the usual ingredients of nuptials (parents, friends, dances, gifts, speeches, surprise visits from quasi-boyfriends, etc), followed by the secret honeymoon on a South American island. This part of *Breaking Dawn* reads like any one of a million romance novels. It's Stephenie Meyer doing Barbara Taylor Bradford Lite for a teen market.

The lovemaking in *Breaking Dawn* is also completely as expected (tho' some fans found it a bit too passionate, as if Edward and Bella suddenly become sex fiends.[5] Not really – their passion has been signalled all the way thru the *Twilight Saga*, and has been foreshadowed, for instance, in the scene in *Eclipse* where Bella tries to seduce Edward into letting down his defences. In *Breaking Dawn*, Bella says she wants to try sex (*oops*, not 'sex', the dreaded 'S' word – I mean, making lerrrve), before becoming a vampire: she wants 'a *real* honeymoon', 'the complete experience before I traded in my warm, breakable, pheromone-riddled body' [BD, 19]).

So they make out on an idyllic island retreat near Rio de Janiero. It's perfect, right? Yes, for most of the time, it is a ridiculously, self-

---

4 'Did I *want* to imprint on some girl who hung out in a mall all day?' (BD, 304).
5 The dread word 'sex' is carefully stepped around like a snake in the grass in *Breaking Dawn*.

indulgently perfect honeymoon (no *Wuthering Heights* or *Romeo and Juiliet* gloom in sight). Which's right – Edward Sullen's happy now they've got married (being an strictly conventional, tradition-bound gentleman), and that he's shackled to Bella Swan for eternity (even if she's human). And Bella Gets Her Man. (The movie of *Breaking Dawn* portrays how tiresome romantic, idealistic perfection can be – that perfect honeymoon becomes so boring after a while. In movie terms, that is. It's great to live in romantic perfection, but it's boring to watch it as an observer, from the outside. It's one reason why fairy tales end with Happy Ever After. It's not that Happy Every After is full of problems and set-backs, if viewed 'realistically' or in 'real world' terms, it simply becomes boring life).

When Bella Swan becomes pregnant, the shift in psychology and theme in *Breaking Dawn* is palpable. Stephenie Meyer has recounted that she always wanted Bella to have a baby, and to take the *Twilight* series beyond a conventional trilogy, and into a fourth book, which would include babies and pregnancy and motherhood. (Which I'm sure some readers found disappointing or irritating – why not end with the Absolute High of Bella Getting Her Man, and Edward Getting His Girl?). Meyer said there was a 'very hard fought battle' with her editors over wanting to go beyond *Eclipse* into *Forever Dawn* and motherhood.

The emphasis is still wholly on Bella Swan in this part of *Breaking Dawn*, not Edward Cullen: to those readers who asked Stephenie Meyer how Bella got pregnant from a vampire, she replied that she focussed on Bella, on what changed in a woman's body when she was with child, and left the mechanics of it mysterious. But if you have *already* bought into the idea that the *Twilight Saga* is a *fantasy romance* and contains vampires and werewolves (which are highly fantastical creatures – unless you live in New Jersey), then a human woman getting pregnant by a male vampire isn't so far-fetched.

▲

At this point, *Breaking Dawn* switches from Bella Swan's story to Jacob Black's story. The journey of the newly-weds back to the Pacific North-West is elided (like, say, how Edward travelled to Italy in *New Moon*), and we are now in Jake's mind-screen, seeing events wholly from his perspective. There is a minor plot about the rivalry between the vampires and the werewolves, and Jacob breaking away from Alpha Dog Sam Uley because he thinks it's wrong to go attack the Cullens and to kill his beloved Bella (this subplot arises due to Bella becoming a vampire, which goes against the vamp-and-wolf Treaty). Seth and Leah, the newer werewolves in the ensemble, also opt to flee the Tribe's pack, led by Uley, and follow the new Alpha Hound, Jacob (handily allowing some interaction for Jake, so he's not doing things all on his lonesome).

However, Seth and Leah – entertaining as they are – aren't really needed here.[6] Because this part of *Breaking Dawn* is, yet again, about Jacob Black and Bella Swan, and Bella Swan and Edward Cullen, and – surprisingly – Jacob and Edward. Yes, we're back to the love triangle in the *Twilight* series, folks, for its ten millionth milking! ('Milking'? Shouldn't that be 'bloodsucking'?! Or something!).[7]

You're kidding? *Not* the romantic triangle *again*?

Wait, will you cool it?! – this is what *The Twi-Saga* is all about! You knew that! And you *love* it! So now we've got Jacob Black hanging around the Cullens' house, feeling somewhat uncomfortable as he's a lone wolf in a nest of vampires; but, Hell, he just can't enough of his deep fix – li'l Bella Swan. (Bella thinks: 'in Jacob's eyes – by choosing Edward, I was choosing a fate that was worse than death, or at least equivalent to it' [BD, 59]).

There are gruesome moments in *Breaking Dawn* – like both Edward and Jacob having to witness their beloved Bella declining towards d-e-a-t-h. Every day, sometimes every hour, she is getting worse. So thin, so frail, so helpless (and she was skinny as a stick before that anyway!). The cup of blood is a yuk moment in *Breaking Dawn* (very gross in the movie, too), as is the vampire creature inside Bella cracking its mother's ribs (*ouch!*). The image of the bruises on Bella's belly made by the vampire monster punching her from the inside is especially revolting (why is everything to do with vampires violent?! Or creepy?! Or scary?! When is the first Buddhist, peace-loving, *properly* vegetarian vampire going to hit the world's movie screens or bookshelves?!).

Meanwhile, in the *Jacob* section of *Breaking Dawn*, Edward Cullen has lost it completely: he is no longer the assertive, in-command, brilliant, beautiful vampire of the *Twilight Saga*. He is a torn-apart man, someone clinging onto hope but facing death. He is exhausted, on the verge of losing everything. He won't leave Bella's side for a second. Edward is near-suicidal, too. He can't – he won't – live without Bella (like Heathcliff in *Wither and Wuther*):

> 'The moment Bella's heart stop beating, I will be begging you to kill me.'
> 'You won't have to beg long.' (BD, 168)

6 And they're not that interesting as charas – Leah's the chip-on-the-shoulder ex-girlfriend who doesn't want to hang around Sam anymore, and Seth's just an eager, innocent kid who idolizes Jacob.

7 Or maybe 'bloodening', as in *The Simpsons*' joke horror movie *The Bloodening*.

Edward is Mr Rochester in *Jane Eyre* at his lowest ebb; he's Jude Fawley in *Jude the Obscure* not long before his shuffling, pathetic demise; he's King Lear when everybody has abandoned him except his loyal jester. Jacob calls Edward 'a burning man', a ghost of his former self.

Phew – heavy stuff, isn't it? We've got (A) our heroine dying as a monster inside her tears her apart and eats her alive. We've got (B) the hero unable to do anything to help, and beating himself up for putting that thing inside her. We've got (C) the other boyfriend hanging around feeling equally lost and helpless. And we've got (D) a bunch of werewolves beyond the perimeter aching to slaughter some bloodsuckers.

Grim, grim, grim – but all is not a suffocating blanket of desperation and depression in the middle section of 2008's *Breaking Dawn* novel. For a start, Jacob Black is indomitable, and never gives up (which's one of the absolutely fundamental attributes of a hero, of course). He also has a keenly commonsensical and matter-of-fact way of looking at things (Jacob thus assumes some of the dramatic functions of Carlisle). He also has a sense of humour (vital!). And he has a job to do (to protect the Cullens and his beloved Bella from Sam Uley's boys). Edward's mind-reading is used extensively, so that conversations take place partly in Jacob's head.

And then there are minor but pleasing subplots in the Cullen mansion section of *Breaking Dawn*: the Rosalie vs. Jacob plot is one. He's got her number: unable to have children herself, Rose covets the thing⁸ inside Bella Swan with a scary obsession. *She wants that baby!* And she doesn't care if Bella Swan (whom she's never liked) dies in the process of getting it out. (Yet Esme too is linked with children and babies – she is the 'mother hen' of the Cullen clan (as Jacob dubs her), and she committed suicide when her baby died. So you might expect Esme to be hovering around Bella too. But Esme is often curiously way in the background in *Breaking Dawn*).

Jacob Black dubs Rosalie Hale 'Blondie' and 'ice-cold Barbie' (BD, 222). He finds it creepy and spooky how Rose is all over Bella Swan. So there's the Hopeless Husband on one side (stroking her feet and looking up in despair at her face), and the Blonde Bitch on the other side, cradling Bella's head in her arms and feeding her cups of blood (as a power play of emotional masochism and passive-aggressive manipulation, and seeing who can be the biggest victim, this is vivid material!).

---

8 'Thing'?

It's a pity that the two 2010s movie versions of *Breaking Dawn* didn't make more of the seething antagonism between Jacob Black and Rosalie Hale, or the way that Rose has taken over the role of Midwife and Protector, so that Edward Cullen himself is somewhat sidelined, along with Carlisle and Esme (and even when split into two flicks, so there *was* time!). At the level of psychology and familial relationships, the Rosalie-Edward-Bella-Jacob subplot is convincing and satisfying. It's also an amusing portrait of how someone spots an opportunity and muscles in.

▲

When the vampire witnesses turn up in *Breaking Dawn*, a new perspective on the vampiric world is opened up in the *Twilight Saga*. It is rather predictable, tho', with visiting vamps all conforming to racial and cultural stereotypes: the Amazons (Kachiri, Senna and Safrina, strong, tall, fearless warrior women) • the Romanians (Vlad and Stefan, creepy, old school Count Draculas hoping for payback against their arch enemies, the Volturi) • the Oirish vamps (Liam, Maggie and Siobahn, charming but eccentric losers) • the American Nomads (Garrett the cowboy-style adventurer – Sam Peckinpah by way of Venice Beach) • the other U.S. Nomads (Peter, Makenna, Charles, Charlotte) • Alistair (the unsociable, loner Englishman who prefers the attic, a latter-day Dorian Gray out of Oscar Wilde) • the Egyptians (nature wizard Benjamin, stern patriarch Amun, and their mates Kebi and Tia) • and not forgetting the faithful Denalis from up North in Alaska (Carmen, Eleazar, Irina, Katrina and Tanya, the vamps most closely aligned with the Cullens).

Oh, and if you're planning on writing a school paper on the visiting vampires in *Breaking Dawn*, there's a handy index to them at the back of *Breaking Dawn* (and even more info in the *Official Illustrated Guide* to the *Twilight Saga*). Note that many of the vamps have special gifts, and also that less than a third have mates (but all of the Olympic Peninsula coven have partners – that's because the Cullens are the closest to good, ol', warm-hearted, regular folk in the *Twilight Saga*, living the Great American Dream. The Cullens comprise nicely-matched romantic couples: Carlisle and Esme, Jasper and Alice, etc. But the Denali coven only have Eleazar and Carmen as a couple (even tho' there are some attractive women among them); the American Nomads only have Peter and Charlotte; and the European Nomads have Charles and Makenna. Yet the high-ranking Volturi are couples: Aro and Suplicia, and Caius and Athenodora).

▲

THE BIRTH.

As the birth approaches, *Breaking Dawn*'s narrative becomes by necessity artificially constructed. So, the one person that is absolutely essential to be present at the birth, the person with the most experience, and the wisest of them all, Carlisle Cullen, is of course absent (he's out fetching more blood). Well, that's part of the clichéd melodrama of birthing scenes, isn't it? The damn Doctor's absent (it's surprising, perhaps, that Stephenie Meyer didn't use that other staple of dangerous, melodramatic birth scenes, especially of the 19th century kind – the raging thunderstorm, the rain lashing down so Carlisle loses his way in the dark).

Similarly, it takes a little engineering on Stephenie Meyer's part to have not Esme, Alice and Rosalie overseeing the birth (as one might expect in a traditional scenario, and certainly in Meyer's 19th century literary models), but Bella Swan's two boyfriends! Edward and Jacob! Yes, Esme has been mysteriously A.W.O.L., and Alice has been lurking in the background. Rosalie hasn't left Bella's side but, when it comes to an emergency situation and Bella goes into rapid decline, Rosalie goes nuts at the sight/ smell of so much blood (well, *duh*, you'd think the vamps would've thought of *that* eventuality and done something to circumvent it – I mean, you do tend to find that blood's a part of many births! I mean, four babies are born around the world *every second*!). Which allows Jacob to attack Rose and get her out of the way.

This leaves our two devoted, teenage (and totally clueless) boyfriends to deliver the baby! Ah, don't you just *love* traditional melodrama, with its preposterous twists and turns? (And it took quite a bit of finagling from Stephenie Meyer to make this work!). Anyhoo, I guess the birth scene in *Breaking Dawn* is more fun (*ooops,* I mean, dramatically challenging) than having a vampire version of a busybody, Mary Poppins Nanny/ Mid-wife turning up, and shoo-ing the boys out of the birth room and taking over.

And this, inevitably, is where the magical ingredient of the vampire venom is deployed, as a last resort. So Bella Swan (and Stephenie Meyer) gets to have her way: she marries her vampire, she takes her vampire sexually, she gets pregnant, she gives birth and, to top it all, she gets to be turned into a vampire (and she dies and is reborn!). Which's all a girl ever wants, right?! Especially a girl hooked on romance and romantic fiction such as Brontë and Austen. (*Breaking Dawn* is very much about Having Your Cake And Eating It – for Bella, but also for Meyer).

'Frozen forever at eighteen,' He whispered.
'Every woman's dream come true,' I teased. (BD, 25)

However, as this's all been narrated in *Breaking Dawn* by the appealingly easy-going Jacob Black, the focus is not on a gloating Bella Swan, or on the desperate Edward Cullen, but on a devoted lover in agony because he can't save the life of the woman he loves (and he knows he's not going to Get The Girl even if she survives! Oh Jake, just *walk away, walk away!*).

BELLA THE VAMPIRE.

The transition section in *Breaking Dawn*, after Bella Swan becomes a vampire, took Stephenie Meyer a long time to write – she said she put more than ten times the effort into writing that half a chapter than the rest of the book. Understandable – that part of the novel has to really work. After all, it's what Bells has been yearning for throughout the *Twi*-series.

It has to be said that Bella Swan as a vampire is far less interesting than Bella Swan as a shy, awkward, clumsy Average Girl from Phoenix, AZ. In spite of Bella becoming a sort of superhero, what with her magic shield that saves the day, her super, newborn, vampy strength, her new, fashion plate looks (with tailored clothing courtesy of Alice) and all, Bella has far less to do or achieve in the second half of the novel of *Breaking Dawn*. Partly because once you're an immortal vampire, with all of those to-die-for powers (literally worth dying for!), what can possibly go wrong in your life? (Apart from a visit from the World Vampire Police, the Volturi, which turns out to be nothing but a *very* long conversation in a snowy[9] field). Yes, the Vampire Cops turn up, check you've done nothing wrong, tell you off sternly, then they slink away! Eeeh?![10]

Bella S. is an average, gauche, gawky girl, as she admits in *Breaking Dawn*: she has low-esteem to the max, calling her life 'eighteen years of mediocrity':

> I'd never been best at anything... I was a good student, but never the top of the class. Obviously, I could be counted out of anything athletic. Not artistic or musical, no particular talents to brag of. Nobody ever gave away a trophy for reading books. After eighteen years of mediocrity, I was pretty used to being average. (BD, 484)

The special gifts that some of the vampires possess become tiresome

---

9 And vampires can't feel the cold, and the wolves are super-hot, so even the snow isn't a problem!
10 As Emmett says at the end of the extended scene in *Eclipse* when the Cullens discuss the newborn vampire army – we are going to kick someone's ass, right? Well, not here, Emmett, no!

after a while in *The Twilight Saga*. Jasper's ability to chill everyone out is useful, for instance, but Edward's mind-reading is employed way too often, as is Alice's seeing into the future. Meanwhile, Renesmee's gift of replaying memories as soon as they've occurred is just plain irritating.

It's amusing that weedy nerd Bella Swan becomes a more powerful vampire, as a newborn vamp halfway thru *Breaking Dawn*, than any of the Cullens, including ace warrior Jazz, beefy hulk Emmett, and perfect cheekbones Edward (Stephenie Meyer gets some comedy from the girl being stronger than the boy in a romantic scenario, pulling him into rib-crushing clinches).

MEET THE KID – RENESMEE.

Following the intense scenes of the birth, *Breaking Dawn* slows the storytelling down to a striking degree, so that every scene is milked (blooded) to the fullest extent. For instance, when Isabella Marie Cullen comes round and encounters Edward and the Cullens in her new vampire state, much is made of Bella possibly being a ravenous beast. There is a *long* scene where Jasper, Emmett and Edward are very wary of Bella, expecting her to freak out and start attacking everybody.

Following this, the hunting scenes in *Breaking Dawn* are tighter, re-instating the central romance of Edward 'n' Bella (taking them back to the first days of their relationship). But the sequence where Bella finally gets to see and meet her baby Renesmee[11] are some of the most extended passages in the *Twilight Saga*. It takes forever for Bella to cross the room and meet her baby, for instance (while the Cullens look on warily).

But this *is* the storytelling pace in *Breaking Dawn*, this *is* what interests the author, Stephenie Meyer. Not the vampire stuff, not the magical stuff, not the vamp vs. wolf stuff, and not even, anymore, the Edward-and-Bella relationship (because that is now tied up and set in stone 'forever').

No, this section of the last *Twilight* novel is about being a Mom and getting to know your offspring. Of course there's the complication of Jacob Black 'imprinting' on Renesmee (which irks Bella S. majorly. It's like everyone else knows Renesmee except Bella). Indeed, *this* is the new romance in Bella's life: between her and her child (and *of course* Renesmee is absolutely beautiful (alabaster skin, rose petal cheeks, blah blah), with the rather irksome vampire gift of replaying memories as soon as they've happened, a baby vampire as a tape recorder).

The section following the bonding of mom-and-half-vampire in

11 Why did Stephenie Meyer choose a girl for Bella's baby? To come up with a suitable mate for Jacob Black, of course. But also perhaps because she has three sons.

Breaking Dawn gets a little smug, as Bella Swan receives birthday presents like a whole house (with the flashy car appearing later). Indeed, the *Twilight* series sort of becomes a Jackie Collins, capitalist love-fest and money-fest, as the new Mr and Mrs Cullen congratulate themselves on being such a Cool Couple, having a Great House, a Great Love and Marriage, and the Beautifullest Daughter In All the World. ('Not many people get every single thing they want, plus all the things they didn't think to ask for, in the same day', gloats Edward [BD, 447]).

Do you want to vomit? Do you want to slap them? (And Edward most of all?!).

These chapters of *Breaking Dawn* – 21 to 24 – slow the storytelling down to a sluggish wade thru treacle and sentimentality. Because the love story, the romantic triangle, the dramatic tension that was keeping the *Twilight Saga* simmering along, has vanished (it was over in *Eclipse*, really). And now you've got two lovers who've got everything they have hankered after (both Bella and Edward state this plainly – the vampire cats that got the cream – I mean, the blood).

Self-satisfied, conceited, complacent, and so totally in *lerrrve*. If you want to throw up, now is your opportunity! Ah, folks, what can possibly go wrong? – because Bella's got: (A) her man, (B) her marriage, (C) her baby, (D) her house, and even (E) her damn classy car! Oh, and let's not forget, Bells's also got (F) immortality and vampirehood! Tick those boxes, baby!

It's all a girl ever wanted, right? Sure! This is *romance*! This is a *romance* novel! This is *fantasy* romance. Where 'happy ever after' is pretty much mandatory and built-in.

Nobody can miss how *Breaking Dawn* meanders somewhat following the birth of Nessie and the realization from Mrs Cullen that she's got all she wants, and the admission from Edward Cullen that he's got all he wants. (Once again, when you return to Bella after being in Jake Black's head for 198 pages of *Breaking Dawn*, you remember that she is quite boring).

Luckily, there's still Jacob (about the only 'normalish' or part-way 'human' character in the Cullen mansion) to throw a spanner in the works. So our favourite werewolf invites Charlie Swan to see Bella (after revealing his wolfy nature to Charlie first, and telling the Police Chief that he is no longer in good, ol' Kansas – this is Oz, a Gothed-out, fashion plate Oz). Jacob does this partly to keep Bella around (and Renesmee, of course, whom Jake is doting on like a wide-eyed, gormless Disney rabbit). Bella and Edward are *furious* that Jacob has pushed events wildly out of control (but Bella manages to appear something close to human). What is 'human' anyway? The Cullen vamps offer some suggestions to Bella when Charlie is five minutes away, on how to act like a human:

> 'The main thing is not to sit too still or move too fast,' she told me.
> 'Sit down if he does,' Emmett interjected. 'Humans don't like to just stand there.'
> 'Let your eyes wander every thirty seconds or so,' Jasper added. 'Humans don't stare at one thing for too long.'
> 'Cross you legs for about five minutes, then switch to crossing your ankles for the next five,' Rosalie said. (BD, 464)

THE FINALE.

Making Mary Alice Brandon Cullen such an important character in the second half of *Breaking Dawn* is intriguing and entertaining, but it also takes away a lot of agency and influence from Bella Swan. It also means that Bella is *reacting* to events (as the Volturi mob loom on the horizon), rather than driving the story. Now Bella's chief goal, it seems, is to become the shield necessary to protect her loved ones. Instead of being a fighter, Bella becomes a defender.

Alice C., lovely, graceful, enigmatic, infuriating (for Bella Swan) as she is, is also a secondary character in the *Twilight Saga*, and her elevation to the principal organizer of the Cullen coven's plans to safeguard themselves against the onset of the entire Volturi army in *Breaking Dawn*, sidelines both Bella and Edward (and Jacob). Now everybody seems to wondering what Alice is doing, what Alice was intending, what Alice was thinking when she acted so mysteriously and quickly (vanishing with her mate Jasper Whitlock).

It's a trade off, tho' – because once Alice and Jasper leap across the river and disappear in a cloud of dust (tho' leaving, as all vampires do, a trail that can be followed), the narrative of *Breaking Dawn* still stays with Bella Swan and her entourage. Why? Because the *Twilight Saga* is firmly (pedantically) a first-person narrative structure, so we're always with Bella (meanwhile poor Jacob Black, after the fracas surrounding him imprinting on li'l Nessie is over, sinks into the background, offering only a resentful growl here and there as vampires from around the globe turn up in the Pacific North-West as witnesses).

So Bella Swan frets and worries and frets some more – she's in a state of perpetual anxiety for most of the second half of *Breaking Dawn* (well, angsting has been her default setting for most of the *Twilight Saga*! She can angst and fret at an Olympic Games level. Bella, you have to admit, is someone who *needs* anxiety in her life – and if there isn't any there, when she has achieved everything she ever wanted – Hell, she will *manufacture* some! So that, even after the 'Happy Ever After' of the *Twilight* fairy tale and the 'forever' of *Twilight*, Bella will be finding stuff to worry about).

Eventually, the Volturi mob turn up in the snowy baseball field, and the long-awaited confrontation takes place. (There are 32 Volturi, including their guard, their wives (!),[12] and a bunch of witnesses at the back, and there are 26 Cullenses[13] and their witnesses (plus 16 were-wolves [BD, 632, 634]).

The confrontation involves *lots* of talk, then *more* talk, then *even more* talk.

Lord Aro talks. Edward talks. Carlisle talks. Caius talks.

Bella Swan is pretty much an observer (a *very* angry and distraught observer, however!), while the two sides talky-talk (notice that it's mainly the men who talk). This goes on from page 631 to page 687 of *Breaking Dawn*.

Bella Swan's daughter Nessie is one of the causes (or the pretexts) for this encounter with the Volturi brigade, but neither Renesmee nor Bella have much to contribute; instead, Lord Aro and Caius for the Italian vamps and Carlisle and Edward for the Olympic Peninsula vamps have the most to do.

The finale of *Breaking Dawn* is dominated by Lord Aro, everybody's favourite crazy, vampire lord. In the 2008 novel, however, altho' Aro is a major villain, he isn't the total psycho depicted by the incredible Michael Sheen in the *Twilight* movies, the sort of movie super-villain who's inches away from exploding into murderous rage and violence. Instead, Stephenie Meyer splits up the villain into three components: Aro, Caius and Marcus. Aro is actually something of a scientist or botanist or historian, fascinated by unusual phenomenon – 'histories', he calls them, which he collects and studies (Aro is more the spymaster, the behind-the-scenes schemer – being out in the open like this is a little too exposed and uncomfortable for him, with so many foes facing him, some of whom are confirmed murderers. However, he is an egotist who loves the sound of his own voice, and he enjoys having an audience different from the people who've surrounded him for millennia. It must get a little boring being entombed below Volterra year and year – they've heard all of his jokes and tall tales).

---

12 We have been told that the Volturi never bring their wives along, and that they *very* rarely leave Volterra. So the presence of both the chief Volturi and their spouses is an indication of how big this is.
13 Tho' only 19 will fight.

It's Caius, not Aro, who is the big bruiser aching for a fight. Throughout the finale of *Breaking Dawn*, Caius is looking for any means of starting the smackdown, while Aro is constantly reining him in (Caius gets to waste Irina, the squealer who got it fatally wrong about Renesmee being an immortal child), but that isn't enough to satisfy his bloodlust (or should that be 'dustlust' or 'ashlust' or 'crystallust', or whatever vamps're made of?). Meanwhile, Marcus is simply bored. Bored, bored, *bored* – after 3,000 years, it takes more'n a confrontation between two bunches of vampires in a field in Washington State to generate a spark of interest for him (besides, Marcus's never been the same since Aro dispatched the love of his life, Loretta – I kid, her name was Shirelle. No, I kid again, it was Didyme).

So the two sides gather, trade information, witnesses, speeches, and veiled threats and… and Bella Swan gets to finally reveal her gift: her magical shield. Thus, Bella throws out that shield and ends up protecting everybody from those nasty Volturi vampires. Even the pint-sized, offensive weapons of the Volterrans, Jane and Alec, the 13 year-old psycho twins, can't do anything against Bella's defensive shield.

However, it's Alice Brandon who has orchestrated much of the finale of *Breaking Dawn*, and takes some of the agency out of Bella's hands (wrongly, I think: the way that Alice foresees everything, and has time to set up numerous events in motion, is unconvincing. Alice is just too irritatingly perfect. And the *Twilight Fairy Tale* isn't about *Alice*, it's about *Bella*).

Also, Jacob Black has very little to do in the finale of *Breaking Dawn*, and in the confrontation scene in the baseball field, which's a pity. Oh, he's there, all right, and he's protecting his beloved Nessie, but he, like the wolves, doesn't contribute much of anything to the finale (hence he's given the job of protecting Renesmee in the movie version, with a big chase sequence).

And there's a smugness to the finale of *Breaking Dawn*, and it's such a let-down after the apprehensive (and prolonged) build-up, when nothing really happens apart from Irina's death (but nobody sheds tears over that, really[14] (not that vampires can weep!), because Irina's mate Laurent was a nasty S.O.B. who tried to kill our heroine, Bella Swan).

No wonder, then, that the film producers of the two-part *Breaking Dawn* movies decided that, no, no, *no*, following the book at this point, being 'faithful' and all, while laudable and noble, just isn't going to satisfy the global movie audience (who are much more ravenous and

---

14 Aside from the Denali clan.

demanding than any vampire or monster depicted in any movie).

The *Twilight* movies had emphasized *action* and *spectacle* far, far more than the *Twilight* novels. The previous three *Twilight* movies had added numerous pieces of action, spectacle and violence (particularly in the finales), which *Breaking Dawn* seemed bound by duty to pay off. No way could a grand gathering of the good vampires and the bad vampires culminate with a single sacrificial victim, and then everybody cheers and air-kisses and goes home happy! ('I love a happy ending,' as Aro puts it in *New Moon*).

So the filmmakers cleverly found a way of having their cake and eating it, by staging a Grand Battle that never occurred! It was both a smart move, and such a Big Cheat that it beggars belief. But if you forget the storytelling and just enjoy the visions of seeing all your favourite charas going into battle, it works terrifically well. (It's worth noting that the *build-up* to a Big Battle can be just as compelling as the Battle itself, and many great movies have dwelt at length on the preparations, the doubts and fears, the training, the organization of the forces, the last-minute reinforcements, etc, to wonderful effect. However, they do usually pay-off all of that narrative work with the battle itself).

And then, it's all over, the Volturi armada leaves the battlefield 'the picture of remorse' (BD, 686), cloak-tails flapping, and it's whoops and hugs all round for the Cullens and their witness friends (however, there is the subplot of the old vampire Joham who's trying to breed a sort of 'super-race' – thus giving the Volturi something to focus on.[15] So Caius can get to play the bully. And of course, the Volturi won't let this lie – they will be back!).

So with a *lot* of behind the scenes work by author Stephenie Meyer in *Breaking Dawn*, it's Bella Swan who gets to be the superhero who saves her family and friends from annihilation. Bella has also become the beautiful swan of her name (*Bella Swan* = 'beautiful swan'): a number of times the book notes that Bella is now not an ugly duckling, but an alluring woman (the waiter at the restaurant where she goes to meet J. Jenks, and Jenks' fixer, finds Bella attractive). Even Lord Aro admits that vampirism fits Bella very nicely:

In truth, young Bella, immortality does become you most extraordin-arily,' he said. 'It is as if you were designed for this life.' (BD, 647)

Chapter 39 of *Breaking Dawn*, "The Happily Ever After", is, unironically and straightforwardly, just that: the happy ending that the

---

15 A minor plot dropped from the movie.

Twilight series was *always* going to have. Always.

F-o-r-e-v-e-r...

What? Did you *really* think that Bella Swan and Edward Cullen and Renesmee and Jacob Black and all the others would be slaughtered? Or not get what they want? Did you really imagine that the *Twilight Saga* could end any other way? There is no dramatic suspense in the confrontation with the Volturi crew in *Breaking Dawn* because there is no suggestion at any point – no matter how much Bella frets and worries and seethes[16] – that they pose a *genuine* threat. Yes, as readers, we like to *pretend* that Caius will get his way and persuade Lord Aro to authorize a Vampiric Pogrom. But, no, come on dude, it was *never* going to happen!

You don't have a four-book romance story ending with mass bloodshed of the lovers and the heroes! Even if you do allude to *Romeo and Juliet* or *The Merchant of Venice* or *Wuthering Heights*. Even if you spend page after page underlining the jeopardy and the threat. (Authors – and filmmakers – know that they are slaving away for *months* at conjuring up the direst threats and the nastiest possibilities, under-standing completely that *the price will never be paid*. This is part of the mechanisms of a contemporary Hollywood movie, and of the romance fiction genre).

In the end, *Breaking Dawn* closes with foreverness as the key theme (as it was in the last *Twilight* movie of 2012): yes, these lovers will be together F❤O❤R❤E❤V❤E❤R (it's the last word of *Breaking Dawn* – and the original title of the novel was *Forever Dawn*):

> 'We have plenty of time to work on it,' I reminded him.
> 'Forever and forever and forever,' he murmured.
> 'That sounds exactly right to me.'
> And then we continued blissfully into this small but perfect piece of our forever. (BD, 699)

And two pages before the end of *Breaking Dawn*, Bella S. sums up all the Good Things That Have Come To Pass:

(1) her family is reunited,

(2) Renesmee is safe, and will live a long time,

(3) Jacob's still her best friend,

(4) Nahuel is happy,

(5) she gets her vamp lover, Edward,

and (6) even her Pa Charlie has found companionship (in the arms of Sue Clearwater)[17] (BD, 697).

---

16 She would be fretting and angsting anyway, dire threats or no dire threats. And becoming a vampire won't cure Bella of her tendency towards anxiety.

17 That further forges links between the white Americans and the Native Americans.

Stephenie Meyer's favourite Bella-and-Edward moment in *Breaking Dawn* is 'the last two pages of the book. That was it, when Edward really sees how Bella feels about him, there's just no match for that'.

breaking dawn

STEPHENIE MEYER
THE INTERNATIONAL
NUMBER ONE BESTSELLER

5

LIFE AND DEATH: TWILIGHT REIMAGINED

In 2015, for the tenth anniversary of the publication of the first *Twilight* book, Stephenie Meyer released *Life and Death: Twilight Reimagined*. (In a gimmicky publishing move, the two *Twilight* books were printed back-to-back, with one upside-down, so you could read the original *Twilight,* then flip the book to peruse the weird rewrite, a gimmick also used for a Robert Pattinson and Taylor Launter biography).

I found the first *Twilight* novel a challenge to get through, until I saw the *Twilight* movie (it's much shorter as a life experience than reading the book, for a start!). The thought of reading *Twilight* with the genders reversed didn't appeal much – maybe I'll wait for the *Twilight* remake in which Bella-is-now-Beau is played by a scrawny, neurotic, twitchy actor,[1] and Edward = Edythe is cast as a skinny, paranoid starlet on the rise.

So, of course I gathered up my garlic, phials of holy water, cloak and wooden stake, and descended through the myriad layers of the Underworld to read *Life and Death: Twilight Reimagined* (it might be a while before the movie adaptation comes out). It's *déja vu* all over: this is a ghost book, a faint, barely-there spirit text which's overwhelmed by both the *Twilight* novel of 2005 and the *Twilight* movie of 2008 – and the whole *Twilight* franchise. As the story in *Life and Death: Twilight Reimagined* unfolds and we inhabit the wild and wacky mind of transfer student Beaufort Magnifico Swan (!), moving to Forks, WA from AZ and falling head over fang with Edythe, we can't help experiencing the story

---

1 Maybe Kristen Stewart in drag? The tiny, tomboyish Stewart could appear in a movie version as Beau Swan in *Twilight Reimagined* (she's boyish enough, tho' of course not tall enough).

thru the vivid images of the *Twilight* movie, and we constantly hold the story of the 2005 novel in our heads, too. (Am I the only reader, too, who has to remember the switched names? – that 'Jeremy' is really Jessica, that 'Jessamine' (!) is Jasper, and so on). 'Try not to get caught up in antiquated gender roles', Edythe sneers at Beaufort (135).

Reversing the genders in a rewrite of a novel automaticially invites explorations of all sorts of theoretical and philosophical themes, which queer theory, feminist theory, identity poltics and gender politics have addressed. Transgender identity politics, for example, has been a hot topic for decades (even famous film directors have been switching genders – Michael Cimino and the Wachowskis), and *Life and Death* offers plenty for critics, feminists and philosophers to get their teeth into.

For actor Robert Pattinson, *Twilight* had already reversed the usual gender roles, so that it was Bella saving Edward, who

> was really gone, down and out, and every time it's always Bella saving the day, but she refuses to acknowledge it. She gives all the credit to Edward (CFA, 30)

And this is what La Meyer did: *Life and Death* was a rewriting of the *Twilight Saga* with the genders reversed. So now Jacob is Julie, Edward is Edythe, Alice is Archie, Rosalie is Royal, Esme is Earnest, and Bella is Beau (short for Beaufort!).[2] Once again, it came across like a writing exercise for a Creative Writing class: –

ESSAY QUESTION:
1A. 'How does changing the genders of the principal characters in *Wuthering Heights* affect the story?'
(2,000 words max).

Stephenie Meyer had already tackled this exam question: –

ESSAY QUESTION:
2A. 'Write *Twilight* from the point-of-view of Edward Sullen' (which became *Midnight Sun*).

So, *why*?

---

2 You can't help noticing that the re-naming of the characters in the *Twilight* anniversary edition is even more eccentric: Royal-Earnest-Jessamine-Beaufort-Carine-Archie-Edythe-McKayla, etc.

Stephenie Meyer explained that she was keen to counter the negative criticism of the *Twilight Saga*, how Bella Swan was portrayed as a victim, how she always had to be rescued by Edward, etc. But wait, reversing the genders *does not* answer that criticism! Because Bella has to become a *guy* so she's not a victim anymore!

Twilight fans received *Life and Death: Twilight Reimagined* with mixed feelings. Some Twi-hards were hoping for an official release of *Midnight Sun* (unlikely for years, as that text had been 'spoilt' by its pirating for Meyer, until it was finally published in 2020), or some extension of the existing *Twilight* story (the further adventures of Jacob and Renesmee, for example, or how many cans of beer Charlie consumed while watching TV on the night of Thursday, September 13, 2008).

But Stephenie Meyer had *already* reversed the gender roles in her *Twilight Saga:* for instance: the girl wants to have sex, but the boy doesn't; the boy wants to wait until they're married before they do it, but the girl doesn't care, and so on.

For some fans, *Life and Death* was as if Stephenie Meyer was writing fan fiction of her own novel. I bet there have already been some stories written by fans which have reversed the genders (it's apparently a standard move in fans' stories).4 *Twilight* in drag or *Twilight* cross-dressing seems an obvious ploy.

For other fans, it seemed snippy and lame that Stephenie Meyer should try to answer critics by going back and rewriting the novel.

Why Stephenie Meyer didn't write a new novel of romance from a male point-of-view is a mystery (having already written *Twilight* from two viewpoints). Instead, more *Twilight* stories from Meyer were announced in 2023.

In the *Foreword* of *Life and Death: Twilight Reimagined*, Stephenie Meyer sheepishly admitted that she knew fans were hankering after *Midnight Sun*, and that twisting around the boy-girl thing in the *Twilight* story did seem perverse (it is – it's unnecessary, un-asked-for, and wilfully eccentric). Meyer also insisted that it didn't matter about the gender issue. *Twilight* was about love, first and foremost, so that the gender of the participants was beside the point:

> I've always maintained that it would have made no difference if the human were male and the vampire were female – it's still the same story. Gender and species aside, *Twilight* has always been a story about the

---

3 Writers sometimes regret the way their books turned out. J.K. Rowling famously changed her mind and wanted Harry dating Hermione. Meyer wished she had added other elements to her *Twilight* books. For example, she wanted to go back and add Edward confessing his love to Bella much earlier.
4 After checking online, yes of course gender-swap versions of *Twilight* have been created.

magic and obsession and frenzy of first love. (2015)

In which case, *why bother* to rewrite *Twilight* with the genders changed? Why not just write a paragraph to suggest how it might be done and leave fans to imagine it all? (In fact, next time Meyer could post ten new ways in which *Twilight* can be reworked on her official website, and let the fans do the rest).

Ah – Stephenie Meyer puts forth her reasons in the *Foreword*. I knew it! Meyer is a *rewriter*, an author who enjoys rewriting her work. Thus, the real reason for tackling *Twilight* again was another chance to *rewrite* the book, to correct mistakes, to add little bits of business, to embellish with a detail here and there… *'it was glorious'* to have another run at *Twilight,* Meyer admitted, to fix all of the elements that had been irritating her (*Foreword*).

About 70% of the *Life and Death* book comprised editing and rewriting, Stephenie Meyer reckoned, with 10% for ideas of dialogue which she'd thought of later, 5% for correcting Alice's visions, and how they impacted on the story, 5% for the changes from Bella to Beau, 5% for how altering the gender affected the story, and 5% as a catchall for further changes. (So the gender elements comprise only 10% of the new novel (5% + 5%).

So now it's: are you 'Team Julie' or 'Team Edythe'? (Well, in the re-imagined *Twilight*, Team Julie barely makes an impression – in the *Twilight Saga* franchise, the PR concept of Team Jacob or Team Edward only kicked in from the second movie of 2009 onwards).

Notably, the 2015 *Twilight* rewrite was longer: *Life and Death: Twilight Reimagined* runs to 387 pages, while the original *Twilight*, when you flip the book over, is 341 pages (in the two-in-one anniversary edition). Also, the ending was changed: now Beau-Boo decides to move to New York and audition for *Saturday Night Live.* Just kidding! – now Beau becomes a vamp much earlier. As Ms Meyer explained in the *Afterword*:

> As a human, Bella had to endure a lot more pain than Beau did, but in the end I know she would tell you it was all worth it. Beau will be fine – more than fine, he'll be very happy – but he'll always have the one big regret. (388)

So this is the *third* version of the *Twilight* story (the first two were: the novel of 2005 and the *Midnight Sun/* Edward Cullen text (unpublished until 2020). To go from a Bella-centric book to an Edwardcentric book to a gender-switch book suggests that narrative viewpoint is primary for Stephenie Meyer. Yes – and she prefers the first person. (What's next? *Twilight* seen from the point-of-view of Bella's beat-up, ol' Chevy truck? Well, that truck has had some adventures! Actually, we have to add Bree Tanner to the dance of viewpoints in the *Twilight Soap Opera*. But the most enjoyable p.o.v. was definitely that of Jacob Black in the *Breaking Dawn* novel. Why? Better jokes, more humour, and a somewhat cynical, 'duh, whatever' approach which sticks it to the so-serious, so-mopey Bella-and-Edward Charade).

Ultimately, *Life and Death: Twilight Reimagined* is the same story. Swapping over the boy for the girl is a mildly interesting exercise, but any reader can imagine it for themselves, without having to consume a whole novel.

Simple reversals can be a good way of producing parody. Feminist writers, for instance, have generated a lot of mileage out of rewriting traditional fairy tales (from the 1970s onwards) by simply reversing the genders. So princesses become heroes, kingdoms're ruled by queens, and men take on women's roles. It's striking just how much parody can be squeezed out of role reversals and gender switches. But parody is not Stephenie Meyer's goal (she's too straight as an author for that).

In swapping the genders, Stephenie Meyer opted for even sillier names than usual: so now we have Archie (Alice), McKayla (Mike), Jessamine (Jasper), Royal (Rose), Carine (Carlisle), and perhaps dumbest of all: Edythe (Edward). Some charas stayed the same gender: Aro, Caius, Marcus, Sulpica, Phil Dwyer, Renée Dwyer and Charlie Swan.

One of the aspects that the gender switch definitely altered was the portrayal of Edythe (Edward). The sinister aspects of Edward's character – the stalking, the domineering and controlling, the sarcasm and hostility, the gloating, the jealousy and the possessiveness have a new inflection when they emerge from a young woman. We know that guys act as stalkers (guys are hopeless, right?), but when Edythe confesses to following Beaufort to Port Angeles, it seems extra creepy.

How would you feel if someone followed you to a town and drove around trying to find you? Well, both 2015-Beau and 2005-Bella are flattered and delighted!

And when Edythe Sullen admits that she has been spending her nights watching Beau Swan sleep (229),[5] he doesn't go ballistic, doesn't threaten legal action, doesn't dive for the baseball he keeps hanging in the

5 'She sighed. 'I'll come back here after you and your father are asleep. It's sort of my routine lately.' I blinked. Then I blinked again. 'You come *here*?' 'Almost every night.' 'Why?' 'You're interesting when you sleep,' she said casually. 'You talk.' My mouth popped open. Heat flashed up my neck and into my face…'

corner of his bedroom, doesn't get Charlie to throw this freak out of the house and into jail, he's... embarrassed, surprised and... yes, flattered... Indeed, the only thing that pops into Boo-Boo's mind is that he might've been been talking in his sleep, and that could be awkward if Edythe, bless her perfect, porcelain ears, heard him.

Whether Edward was a virgin before meeting Bella Swan isn't made wholly clear in *Twilight*, but in the 're-imagined' *Twilight*, with its *female* vampire, oh yes, Edythe certainly is a virgin (after 90 years!). The key scene where all of this is discussed and mulled over (everything is *talked about* in the *Twilight Saga* rather than *done* – talking comes first, then there's talking during, then there's even more talking afterwards; indeed, talking is doing in *Twilight*) – is where Edythe is invited into Beau's bedroom for the first time. She's on his bed, they are embracing, so inevitably Beau brings up the issue of s—e—x (this comes after an important day spent together, when they visited the Garden of Eden (the Meadow), and kissed for the first time. Hell, even Charlie notices that Beau seems 'keyed up' [234]).

As with the original *Twilight* book, when the three-vampire-hunters-chasing-Beau plot device kicks in, it has the same feeling of being from a different novel. It's clumsy, it's over-written, it's too-complicated and, as with the first *Twilight* novel, the story is already over anyway (Beau and Edythe are now an item forevermore – as Beau's new family confirms in several ways, not least in the lengths to which they go protect to Beau from the hunters).

But is anybody really interested in the thriller plot, in the to-ing and fro-ing, the long drives and the plane flights, the phone calls, between Forks, Seattle, Phoenix, Florida, etc?

Get back to the romance already!

Even the switch-around of the genders – so that now Beau is the Princess/ Prince Who Must Be Protected, instead of pale, skinny Bella – doesn't go anywhere in *Twilight Re-Crossstitched*. There *are* things that can be said about girls protecting boys, about girl power, about girls being the masculinist, aggressive ones in a relationship, but not, alas, here.

•

Life and Death ends with the biggest changes, story-wise, from *Twilight*: Beaufort Swan is transformed into a vampire as he lies dying from being bitten by the vamp tracker Joss in the Phoenix ballet studio.[6] The experience is pretty much the same that Bella Swan underwent in

---

6 So we go back to the ballet studio – but did Beaufort have ballet classes as a boy? Oh no! It was his Mom who taught ballet lessons for a (short) while.

Breaking Dawn. Another change is that Beau dies publicly – his death is announced, and his parents lead the funeral procession (which Beau and Edythe watch from afar). The funeral is a slice of Victorian Gotharama (Meyer doing Mary Shelley or Emily Brontë), complete with another cadaver being buried in Beau's stead. Meanwhile, the encounter with Sam and the werewolves, back at the Sullens' mansion (over the issue of the vamp-wolf Treaty), and later at another meeting, is a brief side-story (Jules and Bonnie Black and the wolves haven't played much of a role in *Life and Death*).

So *Twilight Reimagined* closes with our lovers together – as vampires – ready to enjoy 'forever' together (the last line includes the magic word 'f-o-r-e-v-e-r': 'Forever we will drink blood! Forever will we stain the Universe red! Huzzah for vampires!' or, more accurately: 'Forever was going to be amazing' (387).

COMPARING *TWILIGHT* WITH *TWILIGHT REIMAGINED*.

Many of the changes between the two *Twilight* novels of '05 and 15 are very minor, cosmetic, the sort of polishing that writers like to do (if they have the chance), but which many readers wouldn't even notice. For ex:

> Because when I thought of him, of his voice, his hypnotic eyes, the magnetic force of his personality, I wanted nothing more than to be with him right now.
> •
> Because when I thought of her, of her voice, her hypnotic eyes, the magnetic way her body pulled mine toward her, all I wanted was to be with her right now.

Or:

> His hair was dripping wet, dishevelled – even so, he looked like he'd just finished shooting a commercial for hair gel. His dazzling face was friendly, open, a slight smile on his flawless lips. But his eyes were careful.
> •
> Her hair was dripping wet, tangled – even so, she looked like she'd just finished shooting a commercial. Her perfect face was friendly, open, a slight smile on her full, pink lips. But her long eyes were careful.

Altho' there are numerous changes, nearly all of them are minor: thus, the *story* is pretty much the same in both *Twilights*. As you read the book, the narrative unravels in the same way, at the same pace. There are few surprises, once you've got used to the swapped genders.

As the re-imagined *Twilight* unfolds, there is a mild amusement in seeing familiar scenes play out with the twist of reversed gender. Like meeting Jules' Mom instead of Jake's Dad (tho' Bonnie Black still comes over to the Charlie's place to watch sport on their TV).

Life and Death In Forks added some scenes not in the *Twilight* novel (or the movie): in one, Beau announces to Taylor, in front of the whole table in the school café, that he's had enough and, no, he won't be going to the Prom with her, and can she please stop being so beautiful. A Drama Queen Scene like this is not something that Bella Swan would have the guts to do (afterwards, Beau realizes that it will take a lot of living down).

The origins stories of Carlisle and the Volturi are altered a little in the 10th anniversary edition of *Twilight* – the tale of Carlisle's transformation is fleshed out a bit, and Edythe's explanation of the painting of the Volturi in the Cullen mansion is embellished a tad (now, tho', the mates of the Volturi are the leaders, with a bit of ancient world *grrr*l power, tho' Lord Aro and Caius and the rest haven't switched genders).[7] Indeed, of the many off-shoots and side-stories suggested by the *Twilight Saga*, going back to Carlisle's origins, or to the early days of the Volturi, appeal more'n most ideas. (Certainly, Carlisle, as with Alice, could sustain a whole *Twilight* book of his own).

As it appeared in 2015, after the *Twilight* movies had been made and released (3 years after *Breaking Dawn*), some of the *Re-imagined Twilight* book referenced the films (for ex, Tyler now becomes Taylor, a nod to Taylor Lautner). Bella now has blue eyes (a nod to Rob Pattinson, perhaps). Edythe mentions that Beau's hair sticks up and is like his own superpower, a reference to the famous Rob Pattinson hair (245).

Beau Swan doesn't seem as mopey and depressed as Bella Swan: he has the same awkward, nerdy, introspective personality, but he doesn't seem to get as hung up about it. Or are we simply immune to the evocations of low self-esteemism of *The Twilight Saga* by now?

As to the gender reversals of the other characters in the *Twilight* universe – Carlisle, Alice, Jasper, Emmett, Rose, Jacob, Mike, Jess, etc – it was mildly amusing to see what changed and what didn't. Carlisle, for instance, is already a motherly, feminized 'father' to the vampire coven,[8] so changing him to Cutie (no, Carine) didn't seem to adjust much.

More significant, perhaps, was making the distinctly 'feminine'/girlie Alice into the fey Archie (certainly, the re-shaping of Alice's

---

7 No doubt some of the additions intrigue *Twilight* fans – like the servant girl Mele who's in the painting.
8 And he was played as a feminized man in the *Twilight* movies by Peter Facinelli.

visions in the anniversary edition has more of an effect on the narrative, altho' it's in the later *Twilight* novels that Alice's glimpses of the future become over-used and somewhat problematic). More pertinent, perhaps, is Archie's more involved relationship with Beau (such as where Archie talks about being friends with Beau). So that, when the vamp couple and Beau run to ground in Phoenix, Archie is prominent in the narrative (and in the ballet studio).

One of the minor rewritings had the group of ruffians that threaten Bella in Port Angeles being armed with guns, and it includes women. In *Twilight*, the possibility of rape is clear (the *Twilight* movie made that even clearer); well, male rape isn't going to feature in *Twilight Re-imagined*! So in the 2015 rewrite, it's more like a scene in a TV cop show, as minor (drug) criminals threaten a cop's son (parts of the *Twilight* movies, you have to admit, come across as a TV cop show).

Truth is, no matter how you slice it, the *Re-imagined Twilight* isn't especially compelling. If you're going to rewrite and rework the first *Twilight* book, how about a full-on, stops-all-out satire and comedy? It might've been entertaining to see Stephenie Meyer send up her vampire saga with some outrageous jokes.

6

MIDNIGHT SUN

On her website, and in the official guide, Stephenie Meyer has provided some outtakes from the *Twilight* novels, extracts which were discarded by her editors, or rewritten by the author (including humorous pieces).

Among the sections left out of the published editions of the *Twilight* books are Emmett's account (to Bella) of his death and vampirization; Bella in the gym; more about Alice (shopping with Bella); more about Jake; and Bella and a scholarship. *Midnight Sun* (2008/ 2020) is a lengthier alternative take on the *Twilight* story.

Midnight Sun is Stephenie Meyer's laugh riot send-up of the *Twilight Saga* that makes the spoof movies *Breaking Wind* and *Vampires Suck* look tame (I wish!). No: it's the story of the first *Twilight* book (2005) rewritten from Edward Cullen's point-of-view. It was officially released in 2020, though for years Stephenie Meyer had decided she wouldn't publish it after it was leaked. (Meyer was disappointed when an incomplete version of *Midnight Sun* escaped online, and decided to shelve the book for the time being. Later, Meyer made a partial draft available. Meyer also recalled that writing the book was a struggle and not a pleasant experience).

Midnight Sun came about, according to Stephenie Meyer, when she 'started to wonder how the first chapter of *Twilight* would read if it were written from Edward's perspective', when she was supposed to be doing some editing work. The more she wrote of Edward's story, Meyer said, the more engrossed she became in the concept: 'the more I wrote, the more I became convinced that Edward *deserved* to have his story told.'

Like some other Stephenie Meyer works, it has the feel of a Creative Writing Exercise: you've written your teen vampire story from the girl's point-of-view (and in the first person), now do a 180° turn, and tackle it from the guy's viewpoint. *Yes, Ma'am! Right away, Ma'am!*

And off we go.

Thus, in *Midnight Sun*, we have the tale of the Girl and the Vampire, Beauty and the Beast, seen from the Monster's point-of-view, as if the 1897 novel *Dracula* by Bram Stoker had been written from the Count's p.o.v. (instead of the multiple viewpoints of the novel).

Midnight Sun is mildly entertaining, but it *is*, no matter how you look at it, the *same story* as *Twilight*, essentially – which we've already experienced in novel form and in movie form. Part of the problem with *Midnight Sun* is obvious: Edward Cullen is not yet heartthrob Robert Pattinson.

❍

The 'midnight sun' of the title is Bella Swan.

Yes, folks, Bella becomes the sun of light and warmth in Edward Cullen's long, cold, dark night of the soul. He is suffering, agonizing, until he has a revelation.

The scene, a critical one, occurs halfway through *Midnight Sun*: Edward has crept into Bella's bedroom for the first time, at night, while his Goddess sleeps (this is one of many creepy, stalker scenes in the *Twilight Saga*).

So she lies there, vulnerable, unprotected, and beautiful. And she says his name in her sleep. That, plus her scent, and her Botticelli-like beauty, anoints (or damns) Edward for life as Bella's Number One Admirer. His mind is made up.

Before this, Edward has been indulging in a months-long angst-o-thon – his brothers and sisters have looked on in bewilderment (or derision, in Rose's case), as Edward makes an utter fool of himself in pursuing the impossible (Esmé has of course gently encouraged him). He has considered leaving Forks, or worse, teetering on making a decision for a long time, until the 'midnight sun' episode.

❍

The erotic fascination that Edward has for Bella Swan is intense – he's the brooding, moody lover of every romantic novel ever written. To the point where his infatuation becomes rather one-dimensional and tiresome. Even Edward realizes that he's turning into a bore (as his brothers and sisters also find). It's 'Bella this' and 'Bella that'.

The Edward-point-of-view of *Midnight Sun* underlines just how possessive and controlling the vampire is, and just how angry he seems when he can't get what he wants. Edward Cullen resents his fascination with Bella, but he can't help himself. Edward's rage threatens to burst out all over – he loathes Mike Newton, for instance, whom he derides as a boring, generic human. When Newton circles around Bella, trying to summon up the courage to ask her out on a date (to the school dance), Edward has to work hard to prevent himself from slamming Newton across the room and into the wall.

Yes, for much of *Midnight Sun*, Edward Cullen is in a foul mood (rather like how Robert Pattinson is in the *Eclipse* movie).

Sometimes Edward C.'s wry sense of humour rises to the surface, such as when he can hear the thoughts of charas such as Mike Newton, one of his arch rivals for the affection of La Swan. Ed hears Newton complaining that he's a freak. At the same time, the very idea that Bella has agreed to go to the beach with Newton and the group sends Edward into a frenzy of jealous resentments. Later, as Newton tries to ask Bella for a date, Edward rips up the tree he's standing beside, and fantasizes about ending Newton's life (Edward adds murderous fantasies to his list of seriously psychotic attributes. Stephenie Meyer couldn't explain away Edward being a mass murderer – except to claim that it's fictional world, not our world: 'for me it's just a fantasy that doesn't exist'. Meanwhile, for Rob Pattinson, it was a story that was Meyer's sexual fantasy and should never have been published).

○

Among the elements that don't appear in the *Twilight* novel are Edward Cullen deciding he's going to slaughter the whole class in order to get Bella Swan. In *Midnight Sun*, Edward is a more violent proposition.

Another scene added to the *Midnight Sun* novel has Edward moping in the snow up in Alaska, and Tanya approaching him and sort of trying to seduce him. This is Tanya who's had, according to Edward, many lovers, and has seldom been rejected. But she is – because sulky Edward can't get that skinny nerd from the Grand Canyon State out of his mind.

There is much more of Edward's mind-reading in *Midnight Sun* – so that conversations with his Cullen cohorts are conducted partly as interior monologues (which the *Twilight* novel doesn't have, and which the movies only deliver in small amounts). In *Midnight Sun*, often whole conflabs occur half in Edward's mind. He can hear the vamps' thoughts, so he only has to speak (which he can do under his breath, because the vampires have super-acute hearing), and the replies come as thoughts.

○

We get to see, in *Midnight Sun*, more of Edward away from the love of his life, Bella Swan: a hunting trip with Emmett, for instance, where the Emmett-plus-bear motif is revived. We accompany Edward back to his home, where his family considers his predicament (they each have their thoughts, which Edward can perceive). Esme is happy for him (he doesn't want to let her down), Emmett can't understand the attraction, Alice is happy to imagine Bella as her new chum, and Rosalie is scornful, as usual. Edward seldom tries to explain how he feels to the rest of the Sullens – well, he does attempt it with Emmett, but he fails to persuade Emmett of Bella's charms.

There are added scenes to the *Twilight* novel – such as more of Edward stalking Bella Swan. He follows her outside in the yard, where she is reading a book (no, not William Burroughs, but Jane Austen – what else?). And when she falls asleep, she's murmuring, 'Edward'.

It's as if Edward Cullen has given himself with a new job: Stalking Bella Swan. Oh no, not stalking – I mean, *admiring* Bella from afar, I mean *worshipping* the ground she walks on, and *loving* the way she pins back her hair, and *adoring* the way she deflects Mike Newton's fumbling attempts at asking her for a date.

THE CULLENS.

For *Twilight*-ians, *Midnight Sun* is fascinating for its inside look at the Cullen clan, without having Bella Swan (winner of the Miss Angst, West Coast Competition in 2005) throw her all-encompassing manic depressive worldview over everything. Now we see the Sullen household from the inside, the Sullens as a vampire nest without having eight pints of fresh, virginal blood being wafted under their super-sensitive noses.

We hear more from the other Cullens – they don't get why Edward is so smitten with the boring human Bella Swan. For Emmett, she's just ordinary, while Rosalie dislikes her from the outset – because, reasons Edward, she is a threat to Rose's supremacy as the Number One Beautiful Woman On Earth (or at least in the Pacific North-West). Edward sees Rose as supremely vain, while she can't understand why Edward is going ga-ga over Bella but not over *her*. That Edward has been indifferent to Rose from the get-go drives Rose nuts.

A key scene that only exists in *Midnight Sun* is a big family conference at the Cullen compound, following Edward saving Bella from being crushed by the van. Inevitably, Rosalie (and Jasper) are vehemently opposed to Edward having anything to do with the human; Carlisle plays the peacekeeper and mediator, as usual; Esme is maternal desire, willing the family to stay together; Emmett is caught in the middle (not wanting to go against Rosalie); and Alice is confused by futures which're vague.

The issue? The survival of the Cullen clan in the contemporary, ordinary world. They don't want to move, now they've found a locale on the N. American continent which has few sunshine hours and plenty of rain. Edward will agree to leave, though, if that's the view of the conference (or if Carlisle asked him privately). But Carlisle, like Esme, wants to keep the family together (Carlisle is certainly one of the kindliest patriarchs in vampire mythology, the polar opposite of the venal, lethal fathers/ leaders in vampire yarns such as the *Underworld* movies).

Indeed, this aspect of the *Twilight Saga* is appealing: what if vampires in the contemporary era actually wanted to live like regular folk? (albeit, up-market, highly-educated folk?). What if they didn't want to haunt the night as ghouls feasting on unsuspecting souls? What if they preferred to go to school, work in jobs, and hang out like ordinary people?

What upsets the equilibrium,[9] in *Twilight* and *Midnight Sun* at least, is the arrival of Bella Swan in Sporks. Or, rather, Edward falling for Bells. Or, rather, the relationship between Bella and Edward culminating in an accident which threatens the security of the Cullens.

9 Which's revealed as a rather anxious equilibrium as the novels progress.

life and death

TWILIGHT REIMAGINED

TENTH ANNIVERSARY EDITION

THE *NEW YORK TIMES* BESTSELLER BY
STEPHENIE MEYER

midnight
sun

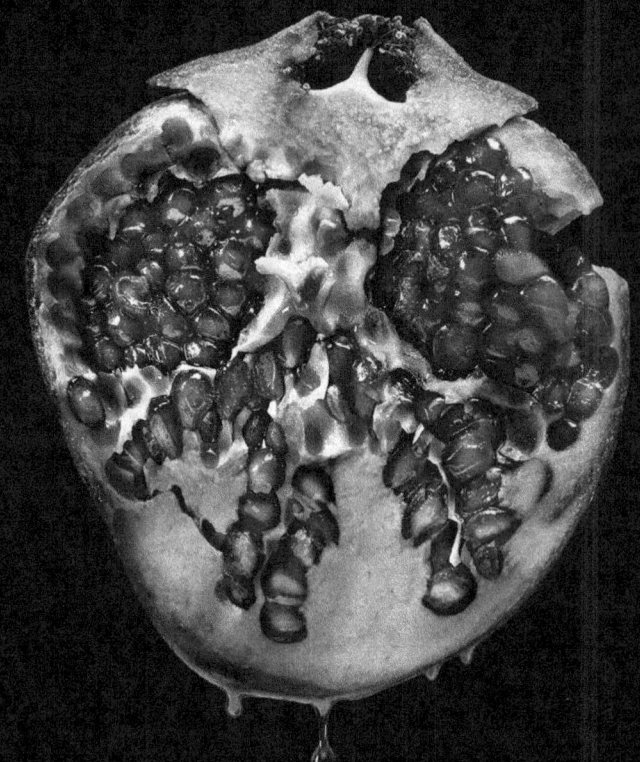

STEPHENIE MEYER
AUTHOR OF THE #1 BESTSELLING TWILIGHT SAGA

PART FOUR

O

THE *TWILIGHT* MOVIES

'So what you're saying is, I'm your brand of heroin?' I teased, trying to lighten the mood.

He smiled swiftly, seeming to appreciate my effort. 'Yes, you are *exactly* my brand of heroin.'

Stephenie Meyer, *Twilight* (234-5)

Stephenie Meyer with the director and star of Twilight (above).

1

THE *TWILIGHT* MOVIES: AN INTRODUCTION

I thought, 'If I can make you feel what it's like for that first super-passionate love, other people might like that too', and, of course, they did.

Catherine Hardwicke

ADAPTING *TWILIGHT.*

Some of the *Twilight* fans focussed on the directors of the movies, though it was the producers, as usual in the Hollywood film industry, that had more impact in so many areas on the final product than the directors.

But if there's one single person who's the most influential on the *Twilight* movies themselves, after Stephenie Meyer, it's screenwriter Melissa Rosenberg. Whatever you might think of Rosenberg as an author, it was Rosenberg who turned the books into scripts. It was Rosenberg who created the narrative structures of the movies (perhaps the toughest part), who defined the tone and the attitude, who translated the characters from the novels, who decided what to retain (and, even more crucially, what to leave out), and, very unusually, Rosenberg was the sole author of all five of the screenplays (unless possibly ghost writers also added to them).

It was Melissa Rosenberg, for example, with her instincts for writing for American television and movies, who argued for exaggerating the action quotient – adding more action to each of the novels (no doubt the many of the producers also agreed with that approach). It was Rosenberg, too, who had to come up with the scenes that Stephenie Meyer left out because she was stubbornly tied to the concept of seeing all events from Bella's point-of-view. That meant that Rosenberg invented numerous scenes for the *Twilight* movies.

Melissa Rosenberg (b. 1962, Marin County), was the daughter of a lawyer and a psychotherapist. Her television work included *Dexter, The O.C., Birds of Prey, Red Widow, Ally McBeal, Hercules, The Magnificent Seven,* and *Dark Skies*. Her film scripts included *Step Up, Alyx* and the *Twilight* movies.

Melissa Rosenberg's chief task was to condense the novel, she recalled, partly compressing the lengthy conversations, while 'making sure the characters' arcs and emotional journeys are the same'. One of the challenges was to turn Bella Swan's inner life into drama. Rosenberg acknowledged that 'a novel is a completely different animal' from a movie (2010), as numerous directors, writers and producers have pointed out. Some characters in *Twilight* were combined (such as among Bella's friends at school).

You can't simply walk onto the set carrying a copy of *Twilight* and announce, OK, Scene 1, James hunts a deer. There are a multitude of ways of adapting a novel. One of the classic methods is this: you decide what the novel is about, or what the main story is that you want to tell that's in the novel. Then you leave out all of the elements that are not part of that central narrative spine (which might be huge chunks of the novel if it's as a big as *The Count of Monte Cristo* or *War and Peace*. Inevitably, that will mean that plenty of ingredients that readers enjoyed will bite the dust). After that, you create numerous scenes, characters and bit of business which will link together the parts you have retained (because you can't simply smash together the parts you have selected end-to-end). This process might also include combining characters (very common), and deleting scenes which repeat information or are redundant (there isn't time in a movie for repeated visits to, say, a restaurant, for instance).

Finally, you still won't have a script that will work as a movie – the script will require further sculpting. For example, if your screenwriting contract is to compose an action-led movie in the contemporary Hollywood mode, the script will require action climaxes to acts one, two, three, etc, plus all of the other elements of action-based drama. It might be altered again for a particular actor, or at the request of a producer or director.

So you can see how the really challenging part of adapting the *Twilight* novels was to fashion the initial narrative structure (some writers buy two copies of a novel, cut out the pages and paste them into the script facing their own text (a method Francis Coppola has employed). Some start by writing a long treatment, which relates the adaptation in prose. Some just dive straight into writing the script, scene by scene).

Another approach to movie adaptations is the Orson Welles and Hayao Miyazaki method: the original work is used as an inspiration but is *not* adapted straight or 'faithfully' (a 'faithful' aadaptation is imposs-ible for many reasons). Welles insisted that a movie was a work *in its own right*, if you regard cinema as an artform. A movie is *not*, Welles asserted, simply an illustration of a novel or play, but a work of art on its own.

A simple question to ask in considering scenes in movies is: who is leading the scene? And the writer's question: where is the point-of-view? Thus, altho' the *point-of-view* is Bella's in *Twilight*, it's often Edward who is *leading* the scene. And often Bella is *reacting* to events, rather than driving them (particularly as she encounters new groups of vampires, from the Cullens to the Volturi, as her world widens). That further complicates the screenwriter's task (a common task in film adaptations is how to incorporate and dramatize observer characters, people who sit on the sidelines, or passive characters who are reacting to events).

The screenwriter of *The Silence of the Lambs*, Ted Tally, makes a vital point about the approach to a movie adaptation:

> So really the most fundamental decision you have to make in an adapt-ion is the primary point of view. Whose story is it more than anyone else's? Or, in Hollywood terms, who are we rooting for? It seems like such an obvious, simplistic question, but you'd be amazed how often it doesn't get asked or answered. It will determine every other choice you make in the adaption.[1]

It's striking how much of *Twilight* is being led by Edward in the second half of the movie. Altho' the movie stays with Bella Swan's point-of-view, it's Edward who taking control of many scenes, and whose emotions are leading the scenes.

▶

This is a break-down of a three-act action movie running 80-90 minutes. The first act is typically the regular length (25-30 minutes), but the second act in an action movie is often shorter (20-25 minutes, rather than 25-30 minutes). This is partly because the second act usually

---

[1] S. Katz, "A Conversation With Ted Tally", *Journal of the Writers Guild of America, West*, 9, Jan, 1996.

explores characterization, back-stories and subplots, which can take a movie too far from action (it's also because the second act is by far the most challenging to write). Thus, the third and final act in an action movie might run for 35-40 minutes – partly because action movies are all about action and climaxes.

An action movie will typically have three big action set-pieces and three additional, smaller set-pieces – this applies to action movies everywhere:

Act 1 climax
Act 2 climax
Act 3 climax
In addition, there will be further action sequences:
• The opening scene.
• Halfway thru act one.
• Halfway thru act two.

The finale of act three is often a reprise of the first act finale (on a bigger scale, with more at stake). The act two action set-piece might push the heroes back, have the villains triumphant for a moment, with all being staked in the final showdown. (They might steal the MacGuffin, or kidnap or injure one of the heroes).

Action movies which open with an action set-piece sometimes use it to introduce the characters, and sometimes it will be a stand-alone sequence (the opening scene of the first *Twilight* movie is a stand-alone sequence, and doesn't really introduce James the hunter vampire, but it evokes the themes of danger and hunting, and the forest setting). After the opening action scene, the exposition is delivered, as well as the narrative set-up or quest. This will be played out in the act 1 climax.

The action sequence halfway thru act one is often a reversal of fortunes for the heroes (it might split them up or injure one of them). If the movie didn't start with action, this is usually the first big action scene.

The action sequence halfway thru act two is often a chase or a raid or a heist – something to bring the heroes and the villains together. But nobody is a clear winner, and no one is sacrificed (sometimes more action scenes are added to act two).

▶

The above explanation of a typical process of adaptation from a novel in action terms explains many of the dramatic decisions we see in the final versions of the *Twilight* movies – why certain scenes occur when they do, for example, and why certain characters or scenes had to be dropped. Sometimes it's not only because there isn't time in a two-hour movie for every scene in a novel, it's because a scene in the book doesn't suit the adaptation that the production team is aiming for.

As Jacob complains in *New Moon*:

'Hollywood's version doesn't get much right.' (312)

For fang fans who disliked how the movies tackled the *Twilight Saga*, that's an under-statement!

Melissa Rosenberg said she didn't write for teenagers, but for adults – or, really, for herself:

I never got into the young adult headspace. With *Twilight,* they are pretty adult themes, aside from maybe the first one, but even that. They're very adult themes, actually, particularly as the characters age. I never wrote for young adults. I wrote for myself, as an audience. (2012)

The first *Twilight* movie streamlines the 2005 novel to a striking (but inevitable) degree, so that numerous interactions with secondary charas fall away, because the movie – rightly – focusses on the lovers (and because there's no time for much else). It's true, tho', that the secondary characters in the *Twilight* novel are under-written, completely routine and pretty dull (yes, in this respect, *Twilight* is a badly-written book). Really, only Jessica makes a strong impression (partly due to Anna Kendrick's performance). So the actors playing Mike, Jessica, Eric, Angela, Tyler, etc, struggle to flesh out their characters (with Kendrick as Jessica faring the best – Kendrick pops out of the screen; she might've stepped right out of 1978's *Grease*). Some of the characters in the novel were combined.

Melissa Rosenberg enjoyed writing for Bella's Dad, for James the hunter, and for Jessica and Eric, and coming up with the scenes which departed from the novels, because the novels stuck with the viewpoint of Bella Swan, such as introducing the new vampires, and Jacob revealing himself as a werewolf to Charlie, etc.

Every now and then, I'll look at an Internet fan site and someone will refer to something about Edward as, 'It's a fact.' Fact? He's a fictional character! (Melissa Rosenberg)[2]

Introducing James Witherdale and the American Nomad vampires

---

2 In M. Vaz, 2011, 81.

much earlier in the timeline of the novel of *Twilight* serves not only to act as threat to our heroes, according to Melissa Rosenberg, it also indicates that there are other kinds of vampires in this story (murderous ones – so you don't know if Edward might be like that), and it also brings Chief Swan into the story in his capacity as a cop (CFA, 13).

STEPHENIE MEYER AND THE MOVIES.

Stephenie Meyer got involved with the *Twilight* movies at a more hands-on level than many authors (most writers take the money and run. But if they're Jane Austen, William Shakespeare or Saint Matthew, they don't get paid at all! I mean, Alexander Dumas, Mark Twain and Charles Dickens haven't seen a cent from the hundreds of adaptations of their books! They would be millionaires many times over! As Spike Milligan quipped, does Beethoven get royalties? Yes – every Friday).

Stephenie Meyer has a producer credit on the later *Twilight* movies;[3] she worked with screenwriter Melissa Rosenberg on the scripts; and she joined the productions for some of the shooting schedules.

The choice for an author having their work adapted for movies and TV is generally between: (1) taking the money and handing over control to the filmmakers; or (2) taking less money, but having more say over casting and script (the two areas that are utterly crucial to any production). J.K. Rowling, for instance, took the More Control choice for the *Harry Potter* movie adaptations (Rowling is, like many writers, a self-confessed control freak. And Stephenie Meyer has described herself as a Nazi when it comes to logic in the film scripts). Thus, Meyer took the option of having More Input in the *Twilight* productions (and with zillions of books sold by that time, maybe she didn't have to worry about $$$$ so much).

Stephenie Meyer said she had drawn up a series of provisos which she wanted the filmmakers to stick to (such as how the characters would be depicted, that movie would be 'PG-13'-rated, and who dies. Oh, and no fangs). Advising on the *Twilight* script gave Meyer the opportunity to fix some of the narrative development in the novel. (Unfortunately, both Meyer and Rosenberg are rather humourless authors).[4]

When he's in the Cullens' place, Jacob Black thinks he's 'in some Goth version of a bad sitcom' (BD, 170). That of course sums up the *Twilight Saga* nicely. But Stephenie Meyer was adamant that the vampires in *Twilight* shouldn't be clad in stereotypical black cloaks and

---

3 Altho' exactly what some producer credits mean is not always certain.
4 Rosenberg said she prefers to write humour for adults, and had to tone down her humour for the *Twilight* scripts.

Gotharama. The filmmakers rightly opted for contemporary, street clothing, but with the colours and the tailoring carefully controlled. Most of the clothes for the vampires were fitted, for instance, emphasizing the actors' figures. Most of the costumes for the vampires tended towards darker hues, with greys, blues and blacks predominant (partly reflecting the colours of the Pacific North-West). The wolfy characters were pushed towards reds and warmer hues. The Cullens were conceived by costume designer Wendy Chuck (and Trisha Monaghan and others later) as an ensemble, with their costumes co-ordinated to match each other (the same approach was taken with the other groups in the *Twilight Saga*, such as the wolves, the newborns and the Volturi).

MORE ACTION, MORE VIOLENCE.

How *do* vampires fight? The *Twilight Saga* books are not always clear about that (partly because the viewpoint stays with Bella Swan, and she doesn't see everything, and isn't a warrior herself – she's a screamer, as Woody Allen would say). For the movies, made in the 21st century and within the context of a Hollywood franchise, where audiences expect out-size action and silly stunts and whooshy sound fx, a combat style had to be created. Instead of punches, boxing, karate or martial arts, the fighting styles in the *Twilight Saga* featured plenty of bodies slamming into each other, characters pinning each other against walls or floors, and lots of props smashing to create the impression of mayhem (tables, glass, trees, etc). The influence of Hong Kong action cinema, with its incredible wirework, its manipulation of props and environments, and its peerless portrayal of bodies in motion, is all over the *Twilight Sagas* (as it is pretty much every recent, Hollywood action movie), and no wonder, because stunt co-ordinator Andy Cheng was from that school of filmmaking. The *Twilight* movies added plenty of visual effects to the practical stunts and moves (such as blurring, speed ramping, etc), and the sound supervisors made sure the sound team came up with the mandatory OTT sound fx.

The *Twilight* movies are, as one would expect, *far* more violent than the books. For the first *Twilight* movie of 2008, the filmmakers added plenty more for the villains to do, so the audience's reminded of them all the way thru; and when the finale arrives, the filmmakers expanded enormously on the fights between James Witherdale and the Cullens.

By the time of the second movie, *New Moon*, the filmmakers were

---

5 The action in the *Twilight* movies is impressive, exaggerating the violence in the books to a crunching, visceral level. But it's not a patch on even an average Chinese action movie. Compare the *Twilight Saga* with classics of Hong Kong fantasy cinema, such as *The Bride With White Hair*, *A Chinese Ghost Story* or *The Swordsman*.

adding large chunks of action and conflict to the *Twilight* novels. When Jacob transforms into a werewolf in front of Bella's eyes, for instance, and defends her honour by scrapping with Paul, it's described in a rather impressionistic manner by Stephenie Meyer. But in the 2009 movie of *New Moon*, the werewolf fights are ferocious, filled with many elements and beats, and they last a lot longer than they do in the 2006 book.

New Moon also added much more for the Volturi to do – so instead of the exposition of the Volturi being handled with one character explaining it to another while contemplating the painting of the Volturi, the 2009 movie plumped for a full-scale flashback (with, inevitably, the Volturi being depicted as very nasty folk). Why? Because (Hollywood) movies reckon we need to *see* characters doing something: if they're villains, they've got to *do* something villainous. In that respect, the *Twilight Saga* movies improve upon the books, which rely on Edward's ominous explanations about the Volturi.

One of the biggest additions in terms of action to the *New Moon* novel in the adaptation occurred (as one would expect) in the finale. In the 2006 novel, the scene in the Volturi's inner sanctum amounts to nothing more exciting than a conversation between a group of people: Bella, Edward & co. arrive, they chat to Lord Aro, Jane & co., then they're allowed to leave (which is repeated in the finale of *Breaking Dawn*, a Cullens-and-Volturi chat). Prior to that, Bella races up to Edward, rescues him from making a jerk of himself, and then they embrace.

Well, shoot, that isn't enough for a Hollywood movie costing millions of $$$$ that's going to play around the world! And a movie that's the second entry in a franchise that by then was fast developing into a bonanza! Oh no – so we have plenty of action in the finale of *New Moon*, including scenes of our Edward being soundly beaten by the Volturi and their henchmen. Even so, the dramatic elements are sort of the same as in Stephenie Meyer's book, with our heroes being allowed to walk free, thus setting up future installments.

However, these additions made by the *Twilight* movies to the books do alter the narrative structure and the point-of-view dramatically: because in the books we are with Bella Swan pretty much all the way. We simply *don't* see characters acting on their own, away from Bella; we *always* encounter them when they interact with Bella in some way.

Thus, we *hear* about the Volturi from Edward Cullen, when he tells Bella Swan about them. But in the 2009 *New Moon* movie, we shift into flashbacks into their cruel ways, and we cut back to them at intervals, to remind us that they're still around. The first *Twilight* movie did the same, with its short scenes of the American Nomad vampires being *baaad*.

The ultimate addition of action and spectacle to the *Twilight Saga* texts is of course the super-twist and super-cheat in *Breaking Dawn, Part 2*. A Giant Battle is staged, only to have the whole thing being nothing but a dream, a vision. It's the most extreme version of expanding the *Twilight* novels up to the scale and spectacle of a Hollywood blockbuster movie, yet afterwards crumbling the scale back down to the size of the novels. Judging by the bussine$$ that *Breaking Dawn, Part 2* did at the box office, the strategy seems to have worked.

However, Stephenie Meyer asserted that the climactic battle in *Breaking Dawn was* in the novel, though only noted briefly in Aro's thoughts. So it wasn't such a big change from the book:

> it didn't feel like such a huge departure. For me, this moment is already in the book. However, we don't get to see it in all its exciting and gory detail because we are seeing the world only through Bella's eyes.

Meyer also said that if she had written the scene, not Melissa Rosenberg, 'I would have killed more Cullens. I do think the Volturi would have won the day'.

THE PRODUCERS.

Altho' movie fans tend to focus on (1) the stars, and very occasionally (2) the directors, it's the *producers* of movies, and the film studios, who have much more influence over a movie. The Hollywood film industry is a producer-led business. It's the producers who seek out new properties, option them, hire writers, develop them, try to interest backers and studios, and sometimes only when the production is green-lit are actors and directors and everyone else hired. Sometimes of course directors are attached to projects (but they also come and go). Sometimes actors act as their own producers (with their own companies), developing projects for themselves. But most of the time it's the film producers who are on the show first, and they stay right thru to post-production and release and beyond.

The *Twilight* movies, for instance, had four different film directors. Can you tell them apart? Not really. None of them are *auteur* directors, none of them are great names like, say, Francis Coppola or Martin Scorsese, and in the end it really didn't make much difference who they were. However, there were producers (such as Wyck Godfrey, Bill Bannerman, Marty Bowen, Karen Rosenfelt and Greg Mooradian) who stayed on for all five of the movies.

The *Twilight* movies were based in Vancouver in British Columbia before *Breaking Dawn* shifted production to Louisiana (*Twilight 1* had also been based in Portland, OR). Vancouver is known as 'Hollywood North', the third largest film production centre after Gotham and Tinseltown. Vancouver boasts several large studio complexes, including North Shore Studios (Lionsgate Studios), Bridge Studios, and Vancouver Film Studios, where the *Twilight* films were made.

THE FILM DIRECTORS.

The *Twilight* movies are franchise movies. They are not 'artistic' works or *auteur* works. The filmmakers are interchangeable, as with other franchises like *James Bond, Barry Trotter* or *The Avengers*. Twilighters focussed on the film directors to a degree, tho' not as much as other groups of fans of pop culture. Far more significant for fans were questions like: *who was going to play Edward?*, or: *were they going to change the book too much?*

Neither Chris Weitz, Bill Condon or Catherine Hardwicke were big names as film directors, and David Slade was a relative newbie. Hardwicke and Weitz, tho', had directed sizable movies just prior to their *Twilight* jobs: Hardwicke had helmed a Biblical story, *The Nativity Story*. And Weitz had directed the troubled *Golden Compass* adaptation. (Both movies involved lots of visual effects). Condon, meanwhile, was one of the screenwriters of *Strange Invaders*, and had directed *Dreamgirls* and *Chicago*.

But they are not *auteurs* – as they would be the first to admit; they don't have the lengthy credits, the themes and issues, the psychology, the philosophy, the stylistic and technical attributes, of true *auteur* cinema. The *Twilight* movies are thus not 'A Catherine Hardwicke Movie' or 'A Film By Bill Condon' (even if those credits appear in the pictures).

CATHERINE HARDWICKE.

If her interviews and PR are to believed, Catherine Hardwicke (b. Oct 21, 1955, Cameron, TX) is a bundle of energy who was perfect to helm the first installment of the *Twilight Saga*.[6] According to Erik Feig of the studio Summit, Hardwicke 'was the first director I met with and the only director for that movie' (M. Vaz, 2009, 135). The single most significant fact about Hardwicke for some observers is that she's a woman in the very masculinist world of film directing (can you name ten female directors of

---

6 Catherine Hardwicke became the most succe$$ful female director ever for the opening weekend returns of *Twilight*.

big budget movies?! Or, as Melissa Rosenberg noted, can you identify any women writers of the biggest grossing movie franchises? It's nearly all guys, apart from *Alice In Wonderland* (which was scripted by Linda Woolverton, and grossed $1 billion). The highest paid screenwriters are nearly all male).

The *Twilight* production became female-oriented to a degree: well, they started out leaning towards women in key roles, but the subsequent movies returned to business as usual (though with some women in important positions, such as Virginia Katz, who edited *Breaking Dawn*).

Anyway, *Twilight 1* had a female director, female screenwriter, female author, female editor and female star, along with the usual jobs filled by women in movies, such as casting, wardrobe, hair, make-up, etc (however, the key players among the studio and producers were male, and among the film producers of each movie, the men out-numbered the women).

Catherine Hardwicke has commented recently that she was hired because the backers reckoned it was a modest movie, and not a blockbuster movie. If it had been a franchise movie or a blockbuster production, they would've hired a guy, Hardwicke said. And when the *Twilight* movie did become a blockbuster, the studio subsequently hired male directors. However, there *are* female film directors who could've helmed *New Moon* and the other movies.

Catherine Hardwicke's enthusiasm for the *Twilight* subject matter and for making the movie comes over strongly in all of the material surrounding the project (she spends a lot of time during the DVD audio commentary laughing, for instance, where many filmmakers are so dull and serious. She's lively and funny in interviews, and in the 'making of' documentaries you can see Hardwicke's delight when a scene goes well – like the one in the forest, where she knew they had captured Movie Stardust).

Catherine Hardwicke was raised in South Texas (in McAllen, on a farm); she studied at the University of Texas (in Austin, which has a strong film community);[7] her background was in architecture (which she studied at degree level in Austin); Hardwicke later attended the University of California's film school in L.A.. (famous alumni include James Dean, Francis Coppola, Tim Robbins, Steve Martin, Rob Reiner, and Penelope Spheeris). Hardwicke's movie work prior to *Twilight* included production design (she worked on movies such as *Vanilla Sky, Tank Girl, Tombstone, The Newton Boys* and *Three Kings*).

---

7 Richard Linklater is the best-known film director from Austin.

Thirteen (2003) was an important early work (co-written with actress Nikki Reed – *Twilight*'s Rosalie), about the trials and tribulations of being a teenager. *Thirteen* boasts three terrific performances – from Evan Rachel Wood as the main character, a somewhat straight and squeaky clean girl, her single Mom played by Holly Hunter, and the bad girl who leads her astray, Nikki Reed (the movie isn't only about a teenager discovering life outside the family home via the local no-goods, it was also a vivid portrait of a tumultuous, love/ hate relationship between a mother and a daughter, in which the fear of embarrassment is uppermost). The setting is suburban North America (*Thirteen* was based in L.A., with trips to familiar places in Catherine Hardwicke's world – Melrose Avenue and Venice Beach).

The events and themes in *Thirteen* are very familiar – a teen being inducted into the wild world of drugs, sex, shoplifting, smoking, body piercing, and staying out after dark. *Thirteen* offers nothing new in those oft-explored areas, but it did have a lively energy and an up-for-it cast, and offered an entertaining voyage thru teen angst, ambitions, thrills and fears. (*Thirteen* foreshadowed the themes in the *Twilight Saga* in many ways).

In 2005 Catherine Hardwicke directed *Lords of Dogtown*, a skate-boarding movie among a group of kids in California, scripted by Stacy Peralta and produced by John Linson, Art Linson, David Fincher, Ginger Sledge and Joseph Drake for Columbia TriStar (once again drawing on Hardwicke's surroundings in Venice Beach).

As to Catherine Hardwicke's work before *Twilight*, her biggest movie was the Biblical production *The Nativity Story* (produced by M. Bowen,[8] T. Emmerich, J. Funk, M. Rich, T. Van Rellim, C. Boyter, and M. Disco for New Line Cinema, 2006).[9] *The Nativity Story* is a solid piece of work, skilfully put together, with some entertaining and insightful updates of the ancient stories from the *Gospels*. Altho' the script of *The Nativity Story*, as with the *Twilight Saga*, is the most significant single element (aside from the casting) – it was written by Mike Rich – the direction is accomplished and confident: Hardwicke's directorial style emphasizes the performance of the actors, with the camera getting in close right away (the first *Twilight* movie is marked by an

8 Several of the producers also produced the *Twilight Saga*.
9 *The Nativity Story* was part of a recent cycle of TV movies with religious/ Biblical topics which included *Mary, Mother of Jesus* (1999), *Cleopatra* (ABC, 1999), *Jacob* (1994), *Joseph* (1995), *Moses* (1996), *Samson and Delilah* (1996), *David* (1997), *Jesus: The Bible* (Roger Young, 1999), *Mary Magdalene* (2000) and *The Gospel of John* (Philip Saville, 2003). These were TV movies (sometimes mini-series) with high production values often made as international co-productions. (*The Passion of the Christ* (2004) was one of the few, like *The Nativity Story*, that had a theatrical release).

enormous number of very big close-ups).[10]

Thirteen, plus the emphasis on young people in *Lords of Dogtown* and *The Nativity Story* (which focussed on the young Virgin Mary and the troubled Joseph), probably encouraged the producers and studio of *Twilight* to entrust Catherine Hardwicke with the movie (because of the young cast). Hardwicke had also worked with Summit before.

Many in the crew of *Twilight* had previously worked with Catherine Hardwicke, including Elliot Davis,[11] Mary Ann Valdes, Jeann Van Phue, James Lin and Gene Serdena.

There were rumours that Catherine Hardwicke had been fired by Summit Entertainment from directing *New Moon*; no, she insisted that her contract specified that she had first look at the *Twilight* sequel. One of the reasons she gave for walking was the schedule, which was too tight (Summit wanted the movies released on a yearly cycle). The pre-production for *Twilight* was much longer – some 15 months (Hardwicke likes to rehearse, to storyboard, to shoot the script first with stand-ins, etc, which all takes time).

The studio (Summit) might've preferred to retain Catherine Hardwicke as director, because in the Hollywood industry, when something is a hit, repeating it is absolutely mandatory. And the concept of bumping up the female presence behind the camera, which the publicity highlighted, could continue. On the other hand, the *Twilight* franchise is bigger than any of the directors or the producers – and even the Goddess of *Twilight* herself, Stephenie Meyer. Thus, it wouldn't matter if the director was male, female or hamster.

Anyway, Catherine Hardwicke opted to leave, and to make *Red Riding Hood* (2011) instead (another of a bunch of recent reworkings of fairy tales in live-action, alongside *Gretel and Hansel*, *Enchanted*, *Malficent*, *Beauty and the Beast* and *Snow White and the Huntsman* – which starred *Twilight*'s Kristen Stewart). *Red Riding Hood* took a werewolf approach to the fairy tale; Amanda Seyfreid and Gary Oldman appeared (however, *Red Riding Hood*, seeming to exploit similar fantasy territory to *Twilight*, was not a hit, and critics mauled it). *Plush* (2013) followed, an erotic thriller with Cam Gigandet (James the hunter from *Twilight*), Xavier Samuel (from *Eclipse*), and Emily Browning, a TV pilot, *Reckless* (2013), and *Miss You Already* (2015).

---

10 Wyck Godfrey remarked that Hardwicke's directorial style was about getting in close: 'very handheld, close to the faces, everything is looks and touches, very sensual' (CFA, 10).
11 Elliot Davis had worked with Catherine Hardwicke as DP on *Thirteen*, *The Nativity Story* and *Lords of Dogtown*.

CHRIS WEITZ.

The director of *New Moon*, Chris Weitz (b. Nov 30, 1969, New York City), grew up in Gotham, and studied in England at St Paul's School in London and Cambridge University (he took a degree in English Literature at Trinity College). Weitz has credits that include *Antz* (1998, as co-writer),12 *American Pie* (1999, as co-director with his brother Paul),13 *Nutty Professor 2* (2000, as co-writer), *Down To Earth* (2001, as co-director), a remake of *Heaven Can Wait* starring Chris Rock, *About a Boy* (2002), a Hugh Grant romantic comedy based on a Nick Hornby book (co-written with Peter Hedges and Paul Weitz), and *Cinderella* (2015, as co-writer). Weitz had only three credits as (co-)director prior to *The Golden Compass* (*Down To Earth*, *American Pie* and *About a Boy*).

Adapted from the *His Dark Materials* books by British author Philip Pullman (b. 1946), *The Golden Compass* was by far the biggest production that Chris Weitz had been involved with (and far larger than *New Moon*). The movie was produced by New Line Cinema/ Ingenious Film Partners/ Scholastic/14 Depth of Field.15 The cast included Nicole Kidman (Mrs Coulter), Daniel Craig (Lord Asriel), Eva Green (Serafina Pekkala), Jim Carter (Lord Faa), Tom Courtenay (Farder Coram), Sam Elliott (Lee Scoresby), Jack Shepherd as the Master, Clare Higgins (Ma Costa), Ben Walker (Roger), with cameos by Christopher Lee and Derek Jacobi.

Chris Weitz was signed up as writer of *The Golden Compass* (in May, 2004), and then also as director, but walked in December, 2004;16 British director Anand Tucker (*Hilary and Jackie*) was hired as his replacement, and developed the production until May, 2006, when he left, apparently over 'creative differences' with the studio, New Line Cinema (the budget was also an issue). Which meant the movie was in pre-production limbo for a year and a half.17 An unplanned extension of pre-production would also have driven up the costs.18

In the end, Chris Weitz came back to *The Golden Compass* (it doesn't augur so well when two directors resign from a production, but it

---

12 Chris Weitz, along with his brother Paul, was one of the writers on *Antz* (1998, DreamWorks/ P.D.I.), along with Todd Alcott. *Antz* was a computer animated children's adventure film, directed by Eric Darnell and Tim Johnson, in the manner of *Toy Story* and *A Bug's Life*.
13 And exec. prod. on the *Pie* sequels.
14 Scholastic, the book's publisher in the U.S.A., had ventured into film and TV, with projects for PBS Kids.
15 It was produced by Deborah Forte and Bill Carraro; Michael Lynne and Bob Shaye of New Line Cinema were executive producers; Toby Emmerich, Mark Ordesky, Ileen Maisel, Andrew Miano and Paul Weitz were also executive producers (some of them were also at New Line).
16 One reason given was the inexperience of Weitz as a director in helming a big, complex movie.
17 The hiatus would also have meant many personnel would have left for other jobs.
18 For instance, when New Line Cinema picked up the *Lord of the Rings* movies (2001-03) after Miramax had dropped them, they also had to pay the $10.1 million that had already been spent by the production, and this was a long time b4 the cameras rolled.

is quite common; however, it's rarer for a director who walked to return).[19] Unfortunately, most of the pre-production was already underway by the time Weitz returned, which isn't an ideal situation by any means.[20]

Making *The Golden Compass* had been a difficult experience for Chris Weitz, as he has related.[21] Although the 2007 movie was made with the blessing of Philip Pullman, as with the *Twilight Saga* and Stephenie Meyer (indeed, Pullman was on set, and helped in many ways), it was a very disappointing movie in itself, and was a confused adaptation of the much-loved books, with a re-arranged ending. (According to Weitz, about 30 minutes was cut from the filmmakers' version of *The Golden Compass*, and in particular the ending was re-ordered. It's happened so many times.) And, saddest of all, despite good box office returns (tho' New Line Cinema didn't agree), the sequels didn't appear (*The Golden Compass* was intended to be the first in a three-film set). After *New Moon*, Chris Weitz helmed *A Better Life* (2011), and co-wrote *Cinderella* (2015).

DAVID SLADE.

David Aldrin Slade (b. Sept 26, 1969, Sheffield, Great Britain), tho' touted by the PR department as an 'acclaimed' and 'stylish' director, had only directed two pictures, *Hard Candy* and *30 Days of Night*. That Slade was hired not long before the pre-production of *Eclipse* suggested that either a director had walked from *Eclipse*, or that the producers and the studio had tried other directors but had been turned down (directors tend to be very reluctant to step into another director's shoes). Apparently, Drew Barrymore, Paul Weitz (brother of *New Moon* director Chris Weitz), and Antonio Bayona had also been considered (Summit Entertainment announced Slade's hiring on April 22, 2009). The lead-in time is very important on complex productions, but clearly the backers and the studio wanted to move fast with both *New Moon* and *Eclipse* (so that *Eclipse* was going into pre-production while *New Moon* was still in post-production).

BILL CONDON.

Bill Condon (b. 1955, New York City) has credits including, as writer, *Strange Invaders*, *Murder 101*, *F/X 2*, *Chicago* and his breakthrough work, *Gods and Monsters* (1998), about the last years of

19 Most directors would *not* return, for many, many reasons.
20 On the other hand, the much longer pre-production period might have meant a better movie in the end – because the more pre-production you have, especially for big, complicated shows, the better. Usually. But not in this case.
21 'It's one of the great sadnesses of my life that it didn't turn out the way I intended it,' Chris Weitz remarked of *The Golden Compass.*

Frankenstein film director James Whale (which Condon also directed). *Gods and Monsters* was a critical hit. As a director, Condon helmed a *Candyman* sequel, several TV movies, *Kinsey, Dreamgirls* and, after *Breaking Dawn, Mr Holmes, The Fifth Estate*, and a huge hit for Disney Studios, *Beauty and the Beast*. Condon was known for his love of Hollywood musicals, and he brought some of that to the two *Breaking Dawns*. As he explained in a Q and A with the Twilight Lexicon in June, 2011:

> I have a reverence for old Hollywood films, you know, and it seems to be this also reflects the kinds of movies that Vincente Minnelli would make. You know romantic melodramas that are really heightened with a great use of color and style to tell a woman's story.

MUSIC.

Music is a big deal in Stephenie Meyer's world of writing, according to the acknowledgements in the *Twilight Saga* books (where she raves about her favourite band, Muse),[22] and the 'writing inspiration' playlists she's compiled to accompany the books online and in print.[23]

So it's expected that the music in the *Twilight* movies would also be significant. It is. The soundtracks are full of single songs[24] from mainly indie/ alt rock/ emo/ heavy rock bands like Arcade Fire, Linkin Park,[25] Death Cab For Cutie, Travis, Elbow, My Chemical Romance, the Killers, the Strokes and Armor For Sleep.[26]

Music supervisors Adam Smalley and Alexander Patsavas contributed a good deal to the selection of the music in the *Twilight* movies. This is a challenging task, because the music supervisors have to deal with lots of record companies, lots of music publishers, and lots of artists. The deals to license songs for a movie can take months to finalize.

Music supervision is also difficult because everybody has an opinion about the choice of songs in a film – the producers, the director, the studio executives, the studio's Music Department, etc. During post-production, it's common for the producers, the executive producers, some studio executives and other executives to come in and have their say about the music for a movie. As composer Mark Macina remarked, talking about films like *The Lion King* and *Tarzan* for the Disney Studios:

---

22 Meyer cites Muse again in the acknowledgements of *Breaking Dawn*.
23 In *Breaking Dawn*, Meyer added Interpol, Motion City Soundtrack and Spoon to her playlists.
24 One of the rules was that the songs had to be unreleased.
25 Linkin Park's 'Leave Out All the Rest' plays over the closing credits.
26 'When a song and a scene are forever linked, that's when they're most effective', noted Alexandra Patsavas (CFA, 24).

There's not just one guy that comes in and listens to what I do, there's a group of guys. There's the director, the producer, the executive producer of music, the V.P of theatrical, Michael Eisner, Joe Roth, the Charman of the Board. All of 'em. They're all going to hear it! They're all going to have their own opinions on every note of the music, every frame of film – and they're all going to have something to say about it.[27]

Producer Wyck Godfrey mentions in one of the DVD audio commentaries that there were arguments about the music.

Alex Patsavas (b. 1968, Chicagoland) is one of the best-known music supervisors; her influence on the *Twilight Saga* is considerable. One of Patsavas' specialities is introducing new or unsigned pop acts to movie and TV scores.

British band Muse, one of Stephenie Meyer's favourites, provided songs for the *Twilight Saga*: 'Supermassive Black Hole' for *Twilight,* 'I Belong To You' for *New Moon*; and 'Neutron Star Collision' for *Eclipse.*

Atlantic Records released the soundtrack album, which included Iron and Wine, Muse, Paramore,[28] the Black Ghosts, Perry Farrell, Collective Soul, Blue Foundation, Robert Pattinson, Linkin Park, Mutemath, and Carter Burwell. The soundtracks for each of the *Twilight* movies were hits.

Songs that Robert Pattinson wrote with his friend Sam Bradley were used in *Twilight* ('Let Me Sign' in the finale, during Bella's death scene, and 'Never Think'). Kristen Stewart suggested the song 'Flightless Bird, American Mouth' by Iron and Wine for the Prom scene.[29]

Yet there are also lengthy sections of the *Twilight Saga* which *don't* feature music – not pop music, and not an under-score, either. And not even the low, burbling music or the low, tinkling piano cues that Western film producers and studios insist run underneath almost every scene in every movie of recent times (which is *so* irritating, where music is treated as wallpaper or muzak, with no dramatic function whatsoever – where music is used simply because film producers and studios seem to be terrified to the point of going insane by silence or near-silence in cinema).[30]

There is *far too much* music in some Hollywood movies, as if film producers and studio executives reckon that audiences will be bored if

27 M. Macina, in R. Davis, 1999, 188.
28 Hayley Williams of Paramore was a big fan of *Twilight*. Female vocalists were prominent in *Twilight*: Paramore, Florence and the Machine, Lykke Li, Sia, etc.
29 Iron & Wine's Sam Beam heard that Stewart was listening to their new album (*The Shepherd's Dog*) when they were filming the Prom scene, and suggested the song.
30 The score of *Breaking Dawn, Part 1* includes some 80 minutes of music – far, far too much (there is vaguely percussive music or that all-pervasive raindrop piano puttering underneath too many scenes). But, alas, that is typical for a contemporary, Hollywood movie, where, because silence is *so scary*, studio executives and filmmakers fill up scenes with music. Plus a batch of alt-rock/ indie pop/ soft rock tunes.

they haven't got something to listen to in between the dialogue and the sound effects. That's rubbish! – but it's amazing how many filmmakers stick to the maxim of continuous music (so that composers are now having to write scores for three-quarters of a film's running time – 90 minutes or more of music, which puts immense pressure on them).

So it's a delight to find that the first act of the first *Twilight* movie (the all-important act, really, in the whole vampire romance franchise), is surprisingly devoid of incidental music or pop music. Yes, there is a music cue over the opening titles, of course, and there is a slice of pop music ('Full Moon' by British band the Black Ghosts), underneath the montage sequence depicting Bella's departure from Arizona, and some other songs, but much of the romantic fascination between Bella and Edward occurs without music.

Because there's plenty of dialogue, and Kristen Stewart and Rob Pattinson are delivering plenty of busy, tic-filled acting, so the developing erotic fascination they have for each other doesn't need a full, classical orchestra mickey-mousing underneath every frown or flick of hair.

THE COMPOSERS.

For incidental music, the producers of *Twilight Saga* selected three well-known composers who really know their craft inside-out: Alexandre Desplat for film 2, whose credits include the *Harry Potter* movies, and *The Golden Compass*; Howard Shore, for film 3 (best known for scoring the movies of David Cronenberg and the *Lord of the Rings* trilogy, as well as many others); and Carter Burwell (for films 1, 4 and 5), whose credits include movies helmed by the Coen Brothers. While Burwell provided some more unusual cues which included percussion (the biggest cue occurs in the vampire reveal sequence on the mountain), most of the scores for the *Twilight* movies were traditional, orchestral scores.

Carter Burwell (b. 1954, New York City) has credits that include: *Conspiracy Theory* (1997), *Hamlet* (2000), *And the Band Played On* (1993), *In Bruges* (2008), *Where The Wild Things Are* (2009), *Doc Hollywood* (1991), *Rob Roy* (1995), *Wayne's World 2* (1993), *Velvet Goldmine* (1998), *Gods and Monsters* (1998), *Kinsey* (2004), *Three Kings* (1999), *A Knight's Tale* (2001), *Psycho 3* (1986) and the Coen Brothers' movies. Burwell had already scored a vampire flick before *Twilight* – and one that perhaps influenced Stephenie Meyer: *Buffy the Vampire Slayer* (1992). And a horror movie: the second *Blair Witch Project* movie (2002). Burwell also composed music for six movies directed by Bill Condon (who helmed *Breaking Dawn*) by 2015.

Alexandre Desplat (b. 1961, Paris) is a French composer of over 100 film scores (as well as theatre work). It's an impressive list of film credits: *The Queen, Girl With a Pearl Earring, The Golden Compass, The Curious Case of Benjamin Button, Godzilla, Fantastic Mr. Fox, Harry Potter and the Deathly Hallows – Part 1* and *Part 2, The Tree of Life, The King's Speech* and *Argo*. Desplat has worked with directors such as Roman Polanski, Terry Malick, Nora Ephron and Ang Lee.

Canadian Howard Shore (b. 1946, Toronto) was best known for scoring most of David Cronenberg's films (including *The Brood, The Fly, Dead Ringers, Naked Lunch, Crash, A History of Violence, Maps To the Stars, Crimes of the Future,* and *Videodrome*). Shore also wrote scores for Martin Scorsese (*After Hours, Gangs of New York, The Departed, Hugo* and *The Aviator*); Tim Burton (*Ed Wood*); Jonathan Demme (*The Silence of the Lambs* and *Philadelphia*); David Fincher (*Seven* and *The Game*); and Penny Marshall (*Big*). The *Lord of the Rings* score was Shore's highest profile job up to 2001 (it meant around three years of work, off and on, for Shore).[31]

---

31 Howard Shore remarked that scoring *The Lord of the Rings* had 'gone *way* beyond cues! It's written in suites and, all told, we're talking about more than two-and-a-half hours of music! 'There were 200 musicians on the soundtrack, a 200-piece orchestra (it was a 100-piece symphony orchestra, a 60-voice mixed choir, a 30-piece all-boy choir, and 10 vocal and instrumental soloists). The mixed choirs sang in the Quenyan, Sindarin, Black Speech, Adunaic, and Dwarvish, the languages of Middle-earth. And English.

Stephenie Meyer's cameo in Twilight (above).
On location (below).

Twilight (2008): the cast with screenwriter Melissa Rosenberg.

STYLE.

Cinematically, *Twilight* is filmed in a regular continuity, shot-counter-shot manner; fancy camera angles and camera moves are reserved for the occasional set-pieces or heightened moments (however, the camerawork is allowed to tilt off the horizontal from time to time). But because the story is essentially a series of conversations (like most of the romance genre), being too fancy isn't necessary (and can be distracting). During the high school scenes, the background is filled in most shots with background action which includes many of the secondary characters (so that scenes are staged with compositions favouring foreground and background action, and interaction between the two).

Notice how the secondary characters (Eric, Mike, Jessica and Angela) are placed in the centre of the car lot,[1] with the camera looking past them at Edward or Bella. The 2008 film doesn't forget the secondary characters, including them in compositions where they aren't necessary for the romance to unfold (the actors have been blocked so they are part of many scenes). Notice the subtle performances, too – such as Jessica glancing back at Edward when she approaches Bella to talk, as if encouraging Bella to say something about attracting the school's hot idol (or reminding us that Edward turned Jessica down).

Surrounding the lovers with their classmates reminds the audience that their courtship is partly being conducted in public; that they are also schoolkids; that there is a social element to their romance; and that they are meant to be young (altho' Edward definitely isn't! But we don't quite know that yet).

Notice how the camera is right in the actors' faces, emphasizing how the romance is being conducted in the middle of a crowded school, where everybody can see everything (sometimes there are cuts from Edward and Bella to the others, watching them). This enhances the romance, reminding us that these are schoolkids, always surrounded by their classmates (you could stage the romance in a million other environments, where the gaze of their contemporaries is absent). The busy social context of a high school also allows for the essential ingredients in any young romance story to come to the fore – the embarrassments, the misunderstandings, the awkwardness and the comedy (the script was originally more comedic, but was toned down when Pattinson and Stewart were cast. You can see how much of the romance-at-school could be played for comedy, as it has been in thousands of TV shows and

---

1 It's surprising how many scenes are set in the car lot at the school, including parts of the romance plot, the secondary charas interacting, and of course Edward saving the heroine from the sliding van.

movies. I would love to see the John Hughes take on *Twilight*, or *Twilight* as *Grease*).

Multiple cameras were often employed – a key reason being to grab as much footage as possible within the tight schedule (this was a movie filming in Spring which had to be ready for November, so the production office was acutely conscious of time). Often the camera is handheld, and often it's a Steadicam shot (director Catherine Hardwicke preferred the *cinéma verité* approach, where handheld camera is often employed).

But altho' there is plenty of handheld camera and mobile camera in *Twilight,* some scenes are covered with a fixed camera on a tripod. The police station scene, for instance, comprises only two shots: (1) a medium long shot of Charlie Swan at his desk, with Bella entering to talk to him; and (2) a medium close-up of both characters (from the same position). Because, partly, often there's no need (or reason) for fancy camera moves, and putting the camera on a tripod works fine. Also, in filming on a tight schedule, it's much quicker (and thus also cheaper) than laying tracks and rehearsing camera moves. Also, the emotional content of the scene – Charlie's down because a friend has died – doesn't need distracting camerawork.

Each *Twilight* movie opens in a rather boring manner, with second unit images of landscapes. Well, yes, this kind of intro does set the scene, of course, but it doesn't represent what the *Twilight* movies are about at all. And altho' the movies also open with moody music, and ominous motifs, that too doesn't truly embody the *Twilight Saga* series. And if there's a violent incident, like the beginning of the third flick (*Eclipse*), or the hunting scene in the first one (*Twilight*), that too isn't what the *Twilight Saga* is about.[2] To be more accurate, the movies should open with giant close-ups of Kristen Stewart (the first shot of *New Moon* is of course Stewart). Failing that, the two hunks, Boy Band Edward and Boy Band Jacob! (Chris Weitz said he asked editor Peter Lambert to insert the neutral imagery of the moon and landscapes at the top of *New Moon* precisely because he reckoned the audience in the theatre would be screaming!).

✦

It was unusual for the crew shooting the *Twilight* movies in that, for once, they were waiting for the sun to go *in*. Like Woody Allen (who's famous for liking rainy, overcast days, even if it costs thousands of $$$$!),[3] the *Twilight Saga* preferred rainy, windy, cloudy skies. The

---

2 True, it honours the prologue in the book.
3 Sometimes film crews were kept waiting around for days for the right weather on Woody Allen productions. One shoot, when Allen took his film crew out to a location for a day, was scrapped due to the weather being too bright and sunny, at a rumoured cost of $200,000.

Matrix movies replaced blue skies with flat white skies, and you didn't see the sky at all in *Blade Runner.*

Often DP Elliot Davis and the camera team filmed from a higher angle or with selective framing, to cut out sunny skies.₄ Silks and cloths were hung up to obscure the light/ sky.₅ Or the post-production teams were called on to replace the skies₆ with gloom and clouds (digital grading also allows for scenes to be taken down visually, or for day-for-night scenes).

However, in one scene in *Twilight,* despite all of that hard work in filming in overcast weather, despite the amount of effort (and expense) in developing the diamond, glittering skin visual effect, the filmmakers jettisoned everything and filmed Edward in full sun, surrounded by lots of schoolkids. To acknowledge their complete defeat at the hands of the weather gods, the filmmakers put Edward in sunglasses (and Edward also announces, directly to the audience, 'we're breaking all the rules here!'). It does seem wilful and unnecessary – the triumphant parade of the romantic union of Bella and Edward in this scene could be achieved in the cafeteria or one of the school corridors just as well, out of sight of the sun. (It's one scene that really needs reshooting).

Many, many scenes that you'd expect to see set at night in all of the *Twilight* movies were filmed in full daylight. The scenes where James, Victoria and Laurent menace and kill hapless victims in the first *Twilight* flick cry out to be filmed at night. The big action finale of *Eclipse,* in the clearing and up on the mountain in the snow was also staged in daylight. And the biggest, most costly scenes in all of the *Twilight* movies, the non-existent battle that climaxes *Breaking Dawn, Bite 2*, was also set in daytime (but what if it the sun broke thru the clouds for a moment?! You'd have bands of glittery vamps – *Twilight* does Vegas!).

✚

Each director and actor of the movies had to deal with the 'vampire mythology' of the *Twilight* series which laid down the law (courtesy of the Twilight Queen, S. Meyer, and developed by the filmmakers on the first *Twilight* movie): that these vampires didn't move much (or even sit down), didn't blink, breathe, fidget, drink coffee, eat regular food, smoke, etc.₇ Clean-livin' vampires! Oh yes!

So *Twihard* scenes were often staged as *tableaux*, with the vampires

---

4 'We had to keep a cloudy look at all times', Elliot Davis, DP, said, and that included sunlight in the background of shots.
5 Plenty of cloths and silks were used around the set to diffuse direct light, and create the clouded-over effect the *Twilight* series needed.
6 Done by C.I.S. Vancouver.
7 Maybe they're immortal because they don't smoke, drink, take drugs or debauch themselves. Except on blood – which all mammals have.

standing about in groups.[8] Static. Unblinking. Unbreathing. No nose scratching, coughing, itching They've got great hearing, so they don't need to yell. Which tended to give some of the vampire scenes the look of a classic play on TV or an arty Michelangelo Antonioni movie.[9]

Not a great gig for a Method actor, then! All of the quirks that Method actors love to employ – the gestures, the self-conscious tics, the props, the immersion in a character for months on end – couldn't be used (how are you going to learn to act like a vampire? Start hunting and eating deer in a forest?!).

But Kristen Stewart makes up for the Method acting in the *Twilight Saga*. For the scene where she rescues Edward in Volterra, for instance, at the end of *New Moon,* she ran up and down the corridors of the set (the Town Hall in Montepulciano), in order to achieve the breathlessness of her character, having run thru the town.

COSTUMES, HAIR AND MAKE-UP.

In the *Twilight* series, it's all about the hair and the make-up. And the clothes.[10] Of course! Look at the stylized hair on display, for instance, from the Jasper's Johnny Depp do *circa* 1994 and dirt-blond wig to Alice's feather-cut, pixie bob. And Carlisle Cullen's neat-as-pie, hair cream side parting. And Bella's straight, shoulder-length hair (which was altered and enhanced with hair-pieces, and was a partial wig and later a whole wig in the third movie). And Victoria's curly, red-ginger locks. And of course Edward's boy-band, male model hair (which Robert Pattinson unconsciously strokes all the time during the publicity tours and premieres). Pattinson must've increased sales of hair products for boys.

The characters were divided into three looks by costume designer Wendy Chuck: Bella and her Forks High School chums; the Cullen vampire coven; and the Native American characters.[11] The costumes were a combination of off-the-rack clothes and specially-made outfits.[12] Chuck dressed the vampires according to their personalities and origins. So Jasper had cowboy boots and jeans for the Southern U.S. image; Alice sported lots of accessories and rings; Esme's costume harked back to the Thirties, with a frilly blouse, a pencil skirt and a 1930s hair-do (CFA,

8 Director Chris Weitz referred to the conversation piece genre in painting.
9 The Cullens would fit perfectly into the world of *Blow Up, Red Desert* or *Identification of a Woman*, or the icy, bland, lifeless bourgeoisie in Jean-Luc Godard masterpieces of the 1960s such as *Weekend* or *Contempt.*
10 Thermals and layers were added underneath against the cold.
11 Chuck recalled that there wasn't enough prep time for the costumes, and that they couldv'e done with more crew and a bigger budget.
12 At times the cast of the *Twilight* movies look like the cosplay (costume play) fans of their own characters at a comicbook conference.

84). Edward's costume included lace-up boots, well-cut jeans[13] and Tee shirts (often in a grey/ pale blue palette [CFA, 86]). For Chuck, the costumes in *Twilight* were very much about the fit and the silhouette.[14]

Bella Swan's costumes change as *Twilight* progresses, explained Wendy Chuck – from a tomboyish look in warm hues (reflecting her Arizonan background, and her Mom being something of a hippy), to cooler hues and softer, more romantic clothes.

One idea was to have the vampires dressed against expectations – in white. This was tried, but it was found that it didn't always work with the make-up,[15] so the palette shifted into creams and pale grays (Carlisle often wears light blue).[16] DP Elliot Davis envisaged a 'cool, pale tone, which reflects the Pacific Northwest' (CFA, 128).

The colour palette for the Quileute Tribe was warm – with reds and oranges for Jacob (his house, his car, his shirt, Bella's pick-up truck from the Blacks, Jake's wolf-form, etc). Which contrasts with the Cullens and the vampires, in dark blues, blacks, greys ('blues, blue-grays, silvers, whites, blacks' for the Cullens, explained Catherine Hardwicke, 'to make them nice-looking kids but also, in a way, different' [CFA, 9]).

Costume is a big deal for director Catherine Hardwicke, as with directors such as Ken Russell, Walerian Borowczyk and Vincente Minnelli – to the point where some of the actors wore Hardwicke's own clothes (Kristen Stewart wore Hardwicke's Tee shirt in the kissing scene, some of her shoes, and Rachelle Lefevre had on Hardwicke's Henry Durante 'rock star' pants).

The costumes for the Volturi denoted rank: the *Twilight* movies followed this hierarchy of colour, with Lord Aro being the darkest and blackest, and those lower down the pecking order were slightly lighter.

Accessories were another minor element in the *Twilight Saga* costumes: the Cullens wear the family crest, an idea of Wendy Chuck's (she was fond of jewellery and accessories: Alice and Rosalie wear them as pendants around their necks,[17] and the boys on leather wristbands).[18] Bella wears a bracelet with saints on it that Catherine Hardwicke bought in her natural habitat, Venice Boardwalk, for a couple of dollars. Then there are tattoos (sported by the Quileute werewolves).

Meanwhile, the vamps (and some others) in the *Twilight Saga* have

13 The brand of jeans was important for Pattinson.
14 Universal Studios in Studio City was used for costume fitting on one, manic day.
15 According to Chuck, the costumes had to be altered from white with only a few days to go.
16 Peter Facinelli had the idea that Carlisle would protect his neck, a vulnerable spot for vampires, so he covered it with high collars and scarves.
17 Jewellery has been a popular item of merchandizing from the *Twilight* movies – some pieces are produced by licensed sellers (Artisan Designs created the silver jewellery and the crests for the movies).
18 We see the wristband (a perfect merchandizing item!) in close-up in the biology class scene.

contact lenses [19] (which the actors hated wearing!).[20] *Twilight* is one of many movies which use modern contact lens technology to give characters different eye colours. And digital additions are often added to eyes (as they were to Edward's eyes in *Twilight*). You have to admit, tho', that *Twilight* goes over-board with the contact lenses (even Kristen Stewart wears them, to make her green eyes brown, and darker).

Wigs were used for Kristen Stewart – a human hair wig (made by Victoria Wood) which employed the front part of Stewart's hair. It took 15-20 minutes to apply the wig. Stewart's hair in the first *Twilight* movie was dyed chestnut brown, and thickened with a hairpiece; Mary Ann Valdes oversaw the process.

Hair was dyed to match the characters (Nikki Reed, Jackson Rathbone and Peter Facinelli went blond, Kellan Lutz went dark. Long hair was tried out for Robert Pattinson (using hair extensions, overseen by assistant hair stylist Nicole Frank), but it hid the jawline (and Pattinson didn't like it).) It took about two hours to apply the make-up and hair to actress Ashley Greene. (According to Chud.com, *Twilight* was 'filled with dialogue that beggars belief and performances driven more by haircuts than by any school of acting'. But that's fine for many Twilighters – and hey, what's wrong with haircuts? or hair acting? But can you even have acting 'driven' by haircuts? Anyway, the hair wasn't created by the actors, but by the hair department, headed up by Mary Valdes).

THE CULLENS – CLEAN-LIVIN' VAMPIRES.

Take away the fact that the Cullens're vampires, and you have a nice, polite, clean-livin', grown-up, highly educated family of white New Englanders who've moved to the Pacific North-West because they've heard you can buy a mansion for half the price of Greenwich, Connecticut or downtown Boston. They have a tasteful mansion with paintings on the walls, they listen to classical music, books line their bedrooms, they play a shiny, black, grand piano in their leisure time (which's all the time!), they have flashy cars (Mercedes, Volvo, Porsche),[21] tailored suits and expensive dresses, and they are well-spoken, deferential, respectful, and tactful.

Darn it, any white, Republican Mom would be delighted to have them as children! (Well, Jasper Whitlock would have to lose his silly,

19 Grading was used to enhance the look of the vampires (such as employing blue filters [CFA, 33]).
20 In the book (and movie), Bells asks Edward if he's got contact lenses (T, 39).
21 And their garage is 'an ultra-modern, very cool James Bond garage', as set decorator Gene Serdena noted (CFA, 98).

curly locks! However, his Old Texan manners would surely enchant many a New England matriarch!). But you could invite them over for dinner without anyone batting an eyelid (these vampires don't blink!). And there wouldn't be any fear of the Cullens saying something tactless or crude[22] – because they hardly speak at all! (In which case, a riotous, frat house, beer-and-pizza party is probably *not* the time to invite the Cullens. They are not, how to say it diplomatically?, a whole lot of fun. Well, they *do* let their gold-blond, blow-waved hair down from time to time – with a little baseball – but they are definitely not party animals. They're just not warm-blooded souls (they don't have souls or blood!). For instance, in *Breaking Dawn*, when the witnesses arrive – the rebellious, anti-Volturi vampire friends of the Cullens – they stand around the living room like statues. This is one of the *very* few times that vampires get together in such numbers, but it seems like a wake, a funeral, as Jacob wryly comments in the book).

Yes, you could relate the Cullen lifestyle to the tenets of Mormonism, if you insist on taking the biographical approach – no drugs, drink, smoking, enshrining the family and marriage, etc. But isn't it more that the Cullens have found a way of integrating with everyday society as vampires, without standing out too much? They are good, law-abiding citizens. (However, they are much wealthier than average. But money is the foundation of the Great American Dream, right?).

The Cullens are depicted as polite, affectionate folk when Bella Swan first meets them at their mansion. In the kitchen scene, each vampire couple stands beside their partners. Either the Cullens like cuddling, or maybe they're encouraging their partners not to leap on Bella and devour her. (The touchy-feely aspect of the Cullen clan continued in the sequels).

For Jackson Rathbone, the Cullen family's strength is their devotion to each other: 'they're a tight-knit unit, and everybody wants that in their lives' (CFA, 26). Viewers have appreciated the *Godfather* movies for similar reasons: they may be heartless killers, crooks and exploiters but – hey! – they're a *family*.

That Bella Swan is babyed by the Cullens is striking: Edward Cullen carries her (often); Emmett carries her into the house during the finale (in the *Twilight* book); Alice carries her out of the house; Esme and Alice carry her downstairs... And later on, Jake seems to be carrying her often (and Charlie does, too. It was a good job, then, that Kristen Stewart was a skinny kid!). Bella is surrounded by parental surrogates, and people who want to mother her.

---

22 Except for Rosie, of course.

The Cullen mansion in the Twilighting novels is a white house about 100 years old. That makes more sense than the impressive but modernist building the location scouts (James Lin and others) found on the first *Twilight* movie. The Cullens should really be living in an old house ('old' for North America, that is – where anything older than 30 years is deemed 'old') – old but immaculately furnished and spotlessly clean, like a heritage museum in Virginia.

The back of the Cullen mansion was seen for the first time in the later *Twilight* movies, as well as Alice's bedroom, and Carlisle's study (the indoor set was re-built in Baton Rouge, and the exteriors were filmed in Squamish, British Columbia).

VISUAL EFFECTS.

The *Twilight* movies are stuffed with visual effects, some obvious, but many are either invisible (wire removal) or very subtle (digital make-up). Among the 100s of effects shots that the *Twilight* movies employed were sky replacement (got to have those moody skies over Sporks!); cable and rig removal (for the stunts); digital and practical make-up (used for Bella in her pregnancy); a Bella puppet (operated from the neck down) for the pregnancy scenes;[23] animated doubles for impossible stunts (like leaping over river chasms, or changing into wolves); face replacement (for the young girls playing Renesmee); digitally animated flames, and so on.

There are more cartoon Bellas and Edwards in the *Twilight* movies than audiences might realize: that is, digitally animated figures made to look like Bella and Edward. If the actors or the stunt doubles or the practical teams can't produce a particular movement, the animators can do it on a computer. (For example, the scene where Bella tries out her new vampire powers, and races thru forests and up mountains were augmented with animated versions of Kristen Stewart).[24]

And 100s of practical effects and live, on-set effects, such as gags like the treadmill pulled by a truck to simulate vampires running at high speed, or the 'magic carpet' which the vampires walk on, again for vampire speed (a huge number of effects were deployed to give the impression of vampires running fast. The mixing-up of techniques approach is typical of Hollywood cinema).

---

23 'It was very complicated', John Bruno recalled, 'and in the end people couldn't tell if it was the puppet or Kristen'.
24 As visual effects supervisor Ralph Maiers at Zoic explained: 'we knew we could improve some of the performances from the physical stunt team, simply because we didn't have to deal with the physics and safety requirements of the real world. We could animate Bella to perform some of her leaps, and her single-minded race up the cliff face, more gracefully and powerfully at the same time. This sequence gave our animators a chance to strut their stuff'. (J. Wolfe, "Zoic Creates VFX For 'Breaking Dawn 2':, Animation World Network, Dec 5, 2012).

For vampire speed, a number of special rigs and devices were developed: a 'carpet' pulled by a winch (and a truck) upon which the actors walked; actors were hung from harnesses and pulled along wires (with the camera dollying beside them); and there's plenty more wire-work as vampires are flung about all over the place.

Some detractors of the *Twilight* movies are harsh: they have called the visual effects terrible. Are they? But the people who produced the vfx in the *Twilight Saga* are the same companies who do all of the other TV shows and movies and commercials and corporate videos that everybody sees. Tippett Studio, for example, who handled the wolves in the *Twilight Saga* (based in Toronto and Berkeley), also produced visual effects for the *Star Wars* franchise (including the sequels), the *Jurassic Park* series, the *Starship Troopers* films, the *RoboCop* movies, the *Transformers* movies, *Hellboy*, *The Golden Compass*, *The Matrix: Revolutions*, *Armageddon*, *Willow*, *Evolution*, *Immortals*, and numerous other movies. If the visual effects produced by Tippett Studio and the other fx houses who worked on the *Twilight Saga Twilight* were genuinely awful, they'd go out of business within one financial quarter (visual effects firms have to be *really good* to get work – and really fast).

By the time of the final two *Twi-hard* flicks, *Breaking Dawns 1* and *2,* a huge proportion of the shots were visual effects shots, requiring a large number of visual effects companies to create them.[25] More green screen shots than *Avatar*!, quipped director Bill Condon. (The budget of the two *Breaking Dawns* was higher – at $110m and $120m – which reflected that, along with increased costs for actors, producers, locations, fees, studios, etc).

For *Breaking Dawn,* an extensive digital make-up job was performed (by Lola VFX) as well as as practical special make-up effects (by Legacy Effects) on actress Kristen Stewart to depict her emaciated state in the later stages of her accelerated and scary pregnancy (the effects teams also experimented with making Stewart look even worse than how she appeared in the film). This also worked the other way, during the resurrection scene, with digital make-up simulating Bella's body becoming fuller.

'We don't have faces transforming into demonic looks; we didn't film actors on a greenscreen stage and create environments behind them,' explained producer Wyck Godfrey.[26] The production wanted actors in real places doing real things. Ultimately, it doesn't matter, and probably

25 At least 16 visual effects houses worked on the *Breaking Dawn* movies.
26 However, there *are* some green screen shots in *Twilight*. But later in the *Twilight Saga*, greenscreens would be used extensively.

wouldn't have affected the impact that the *Twilight* movies made on the viewers. All an audience wants is a good show, to be entertained. *The Wizard of Oz* or *Singin' In the Rain* aren't any less enjoyable for being created largely on soundstages in Tinseltown. For the feeling of being in Forks and the Pacific North-West, however, filming on location certainly enhanced the *Twilight* productions with an agreeably outdoorsy flavour.

Andy Cheng was a Hong Kong stunt co-ordinator who came to the U.S.A. in 2001. In Hong Kong cinema, scenes are captured in-camera as much as possible (and as cheaply as possible!). This fitted in with the film producers' aim in *Twilight* to film in real locations and to avoid too many visual effects in post-production (the lower budget than comparable movies was partly behind the drive towards achieving effects on set).

When he met with the director Catherine Hardwicke, Andy Cheng said they had to work out what vampires were capable of – how fast they could move, how high they could jump, etc (and then to stick to that).

Choreographer Dee Dee Anderson worked the actors playing vampires to develop movements in a 'Cat Class' (this was seen at its best in the baseball game).

MALE NUDITY.
Take off your shirt, dude!
Yes, the topless thing became an issue in the *Twilight* movies, to the point that Taylor Lautner became a star as much for his beautiful, gym-honed body as for his acting. He became known as the 'star abs'.[27] He was a pin-up for both girls and boys (he was an idol and inspiration for boys, encouraging them towards health and fitness). Some gay male audiences also presumably enjoyed having so much male flesh on display (no one can deny there is a *huge* camp value to the *Twilight* movies!).

By the time of the two final *Twilight Saga* movies, Taylor Lautner (or his agent) decided that the topless gimmick had gone far enough (even tho' it was clearly part of the appeal of the *Twilight* series, and some reckoned that Lautner must take credit for some of the giant box office success of *New Moon*). And so the toplessness was cut back (and some viewers reacted like this: *awww*, what a pity!).

That Taylor Lautner was under-age in the earlier movies adds a further element to this erotic issue: indeed, the *Twilight* movies were sexualizing a 16 year-old actor, just as they were eroticizing a 17 year-old actress (both Lautner and Kristin Stewart were under-age when they began

27 The wolf pack actors were working out all the time during filming, in between takes: they had dumbbells on the set and also ate 6 meals a day (chicken, fish, vegetables and protein shakes, according to actor Chaske Spencer).

filming. And in *New Moon*, Lautner was still under eighteen). There are restrictions on how under-age actors can work on a film set, but even so there is an undeniable element of creepiness in the way that the filmmakers made use of both Lautner and Stewart.

Actually, though, it's Cam Gigandet who starts the whole topless thing in the *Twilight Saga*, when he appears shirtless (for no particular reason!) in the second killing scene in *Twilight*.

That we're talking about male sexuality and the display of the (partially naked) male body in relation to a massively successful and well-known movie series is very interesting. The reversals of gender and identity, in relation to sexuality and nudity (where it's nearly always women who are on display, who are sexually objectified, who are examined (and lusted after) by millions of viewers), is fascinating (no need, then, for Stephenie Meyer to turn the genders about in her tenth anniversary version of *Twilight*).

That the male nudity issue is attached to the chick flick genre, in which women (and young women in particular) are presumed to be the primary audience, makes the issue even more compelling. These are movies where male bodies are put on display specifically for young women.

It's a very different issue from your typical movie, from any filmmaking centre, whether it's Bombay, Sydney, Hong Kong or L.A.

Jacob is also a werewolf: *Twlight* was one of a number of movies which revived werewolves in the 2000s-2010s: they appear in *Harry Potter, Van Helsing, Red Riding Hood,* and the *Underworld* series.

There are some jokes about the nudity of werewolfing – when you shape-shift (called 'phasing' in the *Twilight* books and 'fan service' everywhere else), of course your clothes get ripped to shreds (so the guys take to carrying jeans or shorts on a string tied to their leg – this is taking the literalism of fairy tales and magic and the tiresome urge to explain stupid, little thing *too* far! Stephenie Meyer can't help herself, but *nobody cares* in fairy tales (or movies) if the werewolf magically has clothes! But it does lead to a creepy but amusing scene, where Jake takes off his clothes to reveal his wolfishness to Chief Swan).

(Sidenote on *300:* in recent movies which feature a good deal of male nudity or eroticized male bodies, such as *300* (2007),[28] the issue is very different from the *Twilight Saga*: it's placed usually within genres aimed at general audiences, or male-oriented audiences. A movie such as *300* is fascinating for different reasons: without question *300* is the most openly

---

28 *300* was based on the comicbook by Frank Miller and Lynn Varley, inspired by the 1962 movie *The 300 Spartans* (an excellent movie). It was published in the U.S.A. by Dark Horse in 1998.

homoerotic movie of recent years (and astonishingly camp, too!). Yet it is also very much a male-oriented action movie, with an emphasis on violence, blood, suffering and aggression that is very disturbing. Psychotic would be my description of *300* (and similar movies which fetishize pain and violence to a sickening, sadomasochistic degree: *Black Hawk Down, Saving Private Ryan, The Passion of the Christ*, etc). *300* is sinister and rotten ideologically: after watching *300* you'll be tempted to invade Poland. *300* definitely does flirt with fascism – or, Hell, it's a two-hour advert for fascism. *300* comes over as a replay of American conflicts such as the Vietnam War – yes, the Yanks lost, but they lost heroically!).

NOTES ON THE PRODUCTION OF THE FIRST MOVIE.

Twilight's shooting schedule was tight (only 45 days),[29] with a budget of $38 million,[30] and was plagued by weather problems (filming took place in Portland, Oregon, several places in Washington State,[31] L.A. and Pasadena). Shooting began in March, 2008. Nobody in the cast was a name,[32] which kept costs down (tho' some became stars afterwards, notably Kristen Stewart, Taylor Lautner and Robert Pattinson[33] – by the time of films 4 and 5, they were earning rumoured fees of $25 million), and cameos were avoided (altho' author Stephenie Meyer has a cameo, flipping burgers in Denny's – just kidding!).[34]

Ideally, shooting would've taken place earlier for a Nov, 2008 release date. One of the key reasons for principal photography not starting until March, '08 would be casting. As the producers comment, it took a long time to cast *Twilight*. (And the studio wanted the budget cut again).

The first *Twilight* movie production was based in Portland, Oregon (which is 245 miles from Forks). Locations featured in the *Twilight* novel, such as the real Forks and La Push, had been scouted (by James Lin), photographed and discussed, (Hardwicke joined a scouting trip in Sept, 2007) but it was decided that there wasn't enough in Forks and its environs to support either the large film crew or the locations they would require. Big, complicated movies demand a lot of resources (even modestly budgeted ones like *Twilight* at $38 million), as well as hotel

---

29 38 days in some accounts.
30 There was apparently some issue to do with the contract and the budget. The studio wanted the budget cut again.
31 The mountains of Washington were also used in *The Deer Hunter* and *Twin Peaks*.
32 Which would've kept salaries down.
33 Casting Edward was a big challenge: in the *Director's Notebook*, Catherine Hardwicke listed the casting requirement for Edward Cullen: pale skin, looks 17, great actor, 'great chemistry' with Kristen Stewart, and 'best-looking guy in the world' (27).
34 Stephenie Meyer is in the diner, with a laptop. How predictable. The author appearing in her work… as an author! (Is Meyer writing *Breaking Dawn*? Writing her own reviews? Checking her movie contract?). Meyer was dead certain she wasn't going to speak any dialogue in her cameo.

rooms, offices, cover sets, and studio spaces.[35] So the travelling circus of film production for *Twilight* set up in Portland, and employed many locations in the area: the ballet school, for instance, was built in a warehouse (the exterior was in Portland, standing in for Phoenix); the beach at La Push was filmed at Indian Beach in the Pacific Rim National Park, B.C.

CULTURAL REFERENCES.

William Shakespeare's plays were intertexts with the *Twilight* series: Stephenie Meyer employed *Romeo and Juliet* in *New Moon*, and *A Midsummer Night's Dream* and *The Merchant of Venice* in *Breaking Dawn*. *Macbeth* is referenced in *Twilight* (T, 95).

There are also giant close-ups of words in the *Twilight* movies (most poetically in the final frames of the final flick, a big C.U. of the word 'forever', the single word that sums up the romantic theme of the *Twilight Saga*). A page from a text is part of the wall decorations in the Cullens' home.

The Cullens are portrayed as bookish types – the art directors added plenty of books in their home in the *Twilight Saga* movies (and a ton of CDs, vinyl, cassettes, etc in Edward's room). You can see Jasper reading Keith Richards' autobiography in *Breaking Dawn*;[36] there's a *Vanished Civilizations* book on the coffee table in the Cullen mansion (as if they're researching the Volturi).

Yet one book is glaringly obvious by its absence in the *Twilight* movies: the *Bible*. The first quote in the whole *Twilight Series* is from the *Book of Genesis*, of course. The one about Eve and the Tree of Knowledge, the apple[37] and the temptation (typing Bella Swan as a modern Eve, tho' Edward isn't only the serpent – the temptation (and apple) is also vampirism, it's growing up, it's love and sex, it's life itself).

Absent, yet everywhere: the *Bible* is alluded to in many ways in the *Twi-Saga*. And religion, too: the Volturi, for example, are linked to Catholicism (with Lord Aro as the Pope flanked by two Cardinals), and

35 Had the budget been bigger, the crew might've simply built a lot of things they needed.
36 Apt because of the significance of music behind the scenes in the *Twilight Saga* (and actor Jackson Rathbone is a musician, so maybe that was his choice). Keith Richards' autobiography had generated sales of apparently $12 million in the U.S.A. (making him one of the most successful authors of recent times). It's certainly an entertaining book about a true survivor.
37 There's a brief bit with an apple in the first *Twilight* flick, where Edward juggles one (you can see in the 'making of' documentary how long it took to film that gag!). The apple, the *Official Illustrated Guide* tells us (as if we didn't know!), is about knowledge: are you going to bite the apple and 'discover the frightening possibilities around you or refuse and stay safe in the comfortable world you know' (TS, 539).

to an archaic, cruel, twisted and witchfinding form of Catholicism. (It's no surprise that the Catholic Church should have criticized the *Twilight* books. Like the *His Dark Materials* series or the *Harry Potter* books, there is plenty here for the Catholic Church *not* to like! But it's likely that many ordinary Italians also enjoy the *Twilight Saga*, just as they take to send-ups of Catholic religion or the Mafia).

CENSORSHIP ISSUES.

Sometimes you *don't* want to see graphic violence; you don't 'need' to see it, you can imagine what's going on anyway, which's the Alfred Hitchcock approach (the filmmakers used that technique in the birth scene in *Breaking Dawn*. In Hitchcock-style, they opted for point-of-view images, so that the audience would only see what Bella S. could see). And the scene is already intense and upsetting enough, without close-ups of placentas, vaginas, slicing scalpels, and biting vampire teeth! It's the painful demise of the heroine!

Indeed, many women in movie audiences in general are put off by extreme violence and horror (as any audience survey will tell you: you try marketing *The Texas Chainsaw Massacre* or *Saving Private Ryan* to women over 40!). However, the *Twilight* series was aimed partly at teenage girls, an audience more used to graphic imagery, perhaps, or more accepting of it. (Indeed, in horror cinema, girls in their teens are a key market. The horror genre is often seen as having a predominantly male audience. Not so. In the 1980s and 1990s, with the rise of the 'postmodern' or 'ironic' horror film such as *Scream*, the female audience increased: *Scream, Silence of the Lambs* and *Alien 3* had a female audience between 42% and 48%).

And kissing – lots and lots of kissing (some of the cast, such as Kristen Stewart, drew attention to the over-abundance of kissing). As Bella says in the books, she wants to spend the rest of her life kissing Edward. One of the running gags of the first *Twilight* movie is that everybody around Bella is smooching – Sam and Emily, Jasper and Alice, etc (while she looks on, embarrassed). It's not only Edward and Bella who kiss a lot in the *Twilight* movies: the Cullen coven are a bunch of good-lovin' vampires: there are *many* scenes where Esme and Carlisle or (most often) Alice and Jasper're kissing or embracing. It's sweet. It's unaffected and child-like. These guys actually *like* each other! Hell, they *lerrrve* each other! It's the opposite of how you might expect a nest of vampires to act (and they don't even go for the neck when they kiss! So *bite me!*).

Similarly with the sexual material: there is kissing, embracing, and some soft focus-style lovemaking in the *Twilight Saga* on celluloid (C.U.s of parts of bodies, few whole body shots, and no frontal nudity). But it's all quite virtuous: indeed, one of the appeals of the *Twilight* series for its target audience is that it *isn't* sleazy and gritty. This is a *fantasy* of sex, of love, of romance. The movies are *entirely fantasy*!

And, look at this – the romantic hero, bless him, is so caring, he withdraws from acting the usual, horny young guy. Yes – when things start hotting up in Bella's bedroom, Edward leaps away from the clinch. He can't, he won't, he mustn't – because he might hurt Bella, true, but also because he loves her so much! In the muddled gender roles and the twisted masochism of the *Twilight* franchise, it's the *man* who draws back from the brink of erotic love: it's the man who says 'no'!

And audiences responded to that – it was a different take on the usual date movie or romantic yarn. An attractive, young man who wants to but *won't* – wow! A glittering, boy band sort of guy[38] who has thrown himself at the girl's feet, who rides to her rescue from street punks in a shiny car, who saves her from being crumpled by skidding vans, yet who will step away when scenes get steamy – *oooh, fang me*! Is Edward Cullen for real?!

No sex scenes in the first *Twilight* flick? Actually, there is a pretty racy moment for a 'PG-13' rated movie: a boy and girl (she's 17) in her bedroom at night, in a hot clinch, and she's in her underwear. Remember what the director, Catherine Hardwicke, wanted the audience to do: 'I want them to grab their boyfriend or girlfriend and go and make out'.

(And audiences in the *Twilight Saga* movies are drooling over two under-age actors, who're presented as sexual objects: Kristen Stewart was under-age for most of the *Twilight* shoot, and Taylor Lautner was under-age for *Twilight* and *New Moon* (he was born in 1992).)

THE 'PG-13' RATING OF THE *TWILIGHT* MOVIES.

The *Twilight Saga* movies were rated 'PG-13' – a carefully considered decision (with $$$$$ at the top of the list of reasons). 'PG-13' would chime with the target audience, of course, including the Young Adult fiction audience of the *Twilight* books (tho' 'PG' rated versions as well as 'R' rated versions would have been easy to conceive and execute. In terms of violence, some disturbing and threatening scenes – and some

---

38 We have to suspend disbelief that a pretty boy like Edward hasn't dated at all in his 100-plus years (he's 109 in *New Moon* [540]). What, you're telling me that this guy that Bella and the narrator gush over as the most angelic angel ever to grace the planet with his presence hasn't had a single romantic relationship? Come on! And if Jacob Black looks like Taylor Lautner, he won't have any problem dating, either!

sexual content in *Breaking Dawn* – the *Twilight* movies could be rated 'R' (what's known as a 'soft R'). But not for language, which only occasionally strays into the terrifying zone of words such as 'crap' or 'shit').

The ratings system in North America in the 2000s was run by the Motion Picture Association of America (M.P.A.A.). The ratings are 'G' (general audience); 'PG' (parental guidance suggested); 'PG-13' (parental guidance suggested, some material not suitable for under 13 year-olds); 'R' (anyone under 17 must be accompanied by a grown-up[39] vampire); and 'NC-17' (no children under 17 admitted on pain of death).

The 'PG-13' rating was added in 1984, due largely to the second *Indiana Jones* movie (*Indiana Jones and the Temple of Doom*, 1984), which drew complaints for being too scary for a 'PG' rating. (Director Steven Spielberg admitted that the scenes of torture, beating and human sacrifice might be unsuitable for ten year-olds and under tens (a heart being ripped out of a body was cited by censors, as well as Short Round burning Indy Jones with a flame, and the gruesome feast. There were also scenes of children being beaten and whipped, and Indiana is tortured at length, and whipped). Spielberg suggested a 'PG-12' or 'PG-13' category, to bar pre-teens. Not only was *Indiana Jones and the Temple of Doom* deemed too violent, it was also criticized for being sexist and racist.

Paramount put a note on their *Indiana Jones and the Temple of Doom* ads, saying that the film might be 'too intense for younger children'. This wasn't enough for some parents; the National Coalition on Television Violence issued a formal protest. Barry Diller, Paramount's Chairman, suggested creating a 'R-13' category. The 'PG-13' rating was duly invented by the Motion Picture Association of America on July 1, 1984.

According to the Motion Picture Association of America's head honcho Jack Valenti, any reference to drugs would require a 'PG-13'; 'sexual nudity' or repetitive violence would take a film into 'R' rating. A single expletive is allowed in a 'PG-13' film, for example: the single use of the word fuck in 'PG-13' movies such as *Titanic, Minority Report* and *Armageddon*. Any more uses, and it becomes an 'R' movie).

THE *TWILIGHT SAGA* DOCUMENTARIES.

The documentaries on the production of the first *Twilight* movie included with the home entertainment releases emphasized principal photography (as usual), with the stars and some of the crew discussing

---

39 No newborns.

the characters and the story. Many aspects of film production were *not* explored in the documentaries, however. Such as: how much everyone was getting paid, how much the film cost, details of the contracts, the casting process, the auditions (touched on, but no tapes or photos or accounts were included), the rehearsal process, the hotels, the tie-ins and the merchandizing, the make-up (a huge ingredient in the *Twilight Saga*), the costumes (again, only touched on), and the personal relationships and love affairs that developed during production (there are many during every movie).

Meanwhile, aspects of the making of the *Twilight Saga* that fans might love to see were sidestepped: such as: the development of the script, the meetings between the producers, the author and the screenwriter, the meetings of the heads of production during pre-production (there are tons of meetings), interviews with the backers (Summit Entertainment), and so on. For example, Stephenie Meyer issued a bunch of points that she wanted the filmmakers to stick to – a discussion of those would've been fascinating.

As to the look and style of the *Twilight Saga*, the documentaries included a little bit on the costumes, but these characters have a look that's so important, along with the make-up and the hair styles, you could spend an hour of a documentary just exploring how the filmmakers and the designers created the appearance of the characters and what they wore. (There were, for instance, many sketches produced, including concept ideas for costumes and looks for each character). Luckily, *The Twilight Saga: The Complete Film Archive* covered some of these topic.

THE TWILIGHT SAGA: THE COMPLETE FILM ARCHIVE.

The *Twilight Saga* has the full complement of tie-in books and guides – for the books and for the movies. One of the most lavish of the tie-in books is *The Twilight Saga: The Complete Film Archive* by Robert Abele. It includes the usual accounts of the production of the films, interviews with cast and crew, plenty of on-set photos, publicity photos, profiles of the key actors, etc, but also much more: pages from the scripts, blueprints and sketches of sets, costume sketches, storyboards, etc.

But the most extravagant aspect of *The Twilight Saga: The Complete Film Archive* are the numerous elements pasted into the book (this book would be an absolute swine to put together for the design team at Insight Editions and Little, Brown). There are invites to premieres, a wolf maquette, the wedding invitation, all-access passes, costume sketchbooks, and pages of the script.

One of the most revealing paste-ins are the call-sheets: these are issued to everybody in the production team for each day of principal photography. They give you an insight into the enormous amount of preparation and organization that a high budget film requires. For March 25, 2011 (day 86 of 99 days of *Breaking Dawn*), the call-sheet tells us that the crew're due on set at 7.00 a.m. (some from Best Western and Executive Suites hotels in Squamish); 2 2/8th pages of the script will be filmed (the backyard of the Cullen mansion scene, where Bella fumes over Jacob imprinting on Renesmee); the actors are listed, plus stunt doubles, stand-ins, tutors for Mackenzie Foy, etc; the technical requirements (VistaVision cameras for the vfx of the wolves, rain covers, etc); and the cover set for bad weather (the tent interior for Bella and Renesmee, Carlisle's study for two scenes – Bella's revival as a vamp, and Carlisle measuring Renesmee).

MARKETING MOVIES.

Why would the studio/ backers of the *Twilight* movies (Summit Entertainment *et al*) want to have the pictures made and released quickly, after the success of the first *Twilight* flick? The most obvious reason is $$$$$, of course. But also to capitalize on the *Twilight* phenomenon before it abated; and to keep the young cast together (before they grew older – not essential, but a bonus). So while many movie sequels are released at least three years apart, and often more, the *Twilight* series followed recent examples like the *Harry Potter* movies, the *Lord of the Rings* movies, and the *Avengers* moves (among others), in compressing production and releases patterns to a year or so apart.

Another reason for the movies being produced and released each year was to exploit the youth market – it's an audience which will grow out of *Twilight* and move on to something else. The same approach to business occurs with the cycles of superhero movies in the 21st century, and the *Harry Potter* series.

As director Robert Zemeckis remarked of the *Back To the Future* sequels: 'the trick to writing a sequel is that people want to see the first movie but they don't want to see the first movie. They want the same except different'.[40]

Sequels often contain family members – the hero now has a kid, or a wife, or a relative, so now his family is under threat. Often the hero is tempted to join the baddies. The villain is humanized a little. Sequels

---

40 T. Shone, 159.

also explore the passage of time, and its effect on the heroes.

The *Twilight* series also helped to encourage movie studios to consider the female audience – 80% of the audience of *Twilight* was female. Other film studios took note, and delivered movies aimed at a similar market, including the *Hunger Games* series and *Divergent.* And women a little older than the audience of *Twilight* turned out in droves for the *Fifty Shades of Grey* movies (around 70% of the audience was female).

So boyfriends were dragged along to see the *Twilight* movies by their girlfriends. But those same girls were also taken to see war movies, superhero movies, thriller movies, sports movies, action movies, historical movies, sci-fi movies and many other genres of movies associated with boys and men (some of which are not only just as dumb as *Twilight,* but far more violent, more disturbing, and more offensive).

✦

Film promotion in the 1990s might include a 'making of' documentary (costing $75,000-150,000), a featurette of 3-7 mins (cost: up to $30,000), and 60 and 90 second news wraps. TV is the most expensive element of ad-pub (advetizing and publicity): in 1992, for a 30-second network TV spot on *The Simpsons* and the *Cosby Show*: $300-350,000. During *Cheers*: $350,000-400,000. During the Super Bowl: $800,000 ($7 million in 2024!). Press kits contain 10 or so b/w and 10 or so colour prints, plus info; some 2,000 journalists receive them 6-8 weeks ahead of the movie's opening. Stories are continually pitched to the press. Stars' interviews are co-ordinated. Local radio promotions, local tie-ins, competitions and giveaways are organized 6-12 weeks ahead of opening. Merchandizing goes into toy stores. During the opening weekend, box office grosses are closely tracked, and exit interviews are conducted by market researchers. Every film studio has a vast database of grosses at every theatre in the U.S.A. going back years. By 11 p.m., the numbers are in (from E.D.I. – Entertainment Data). A film that's not doing well might make it to a 2nd or 3rd weekend, but a strong rival picture on the 2nd weekend might help to kill it. If a film opens badly, not much can save it. A new marketing strategy can be created, but it might be cheaper to let it fade away. If a movie opens better than expected, more ad-pub money will be spent, but might be saved for later on in the film's run. Factors affecting release would include any similar films opening at the same time; any other big films on the same weekend; weather; competition from TV; and current events.

A film's title is turned by the marketing dept into a logo, which is its brand image. Crucially, it has to be, like any logo, easily and instantly recognizable. It has to embody the basic appeal and content of the movie. And it has to be easy to replicate in a variety of technological outlets, from print ads and DVD covers to TV spots and toy tie-ins. For *The Twilight Saga*, a classy logo was created, using an old-fashioned typeface (Thom Schillinger designed the logo; Ben and Karen Dale designed the logo for the novel).

A 'woman's film' might be marketed in a different way from a male action movie: demographics suggests that women have less disposable income than men, have more social obligations (such as children), and for a 'date visit' to the cinema, the male usually pays and chooses the film (but not in the case of the *Twilight Saga* movies!). But the 'women's film' may last longer in theatres, taking longer to find an audience, but the audience keeps coming back (the *Twilight* movies certainly benefitted from repeat viewings, like other giant franchises such as *Harry Potter* and *Star Wars*).

In the 1990s an increasing number of movies addressed a female audience – partly due to the increasing number of female studio executives.[41] Another reason was that 'women's films' – *Waiting To Exhale, While You Were Sleeping, Clueless* – could be made on smaller budgets ($15-25m) than blockbusters, and so could return a bigger cost-to-profit ratio (the first *Twilight* movie had a budget of $38m – a medium-priced picture[42] – but the theatrical gross was huge: $392 million. As Scott Mendelson noted, in a 2012 piece in the *Huffington Post*, 'Summit pulled off the ultimate coup, creating a top-tier blockbuster franchise for budgets usually associated with Oscar-bait prestige dramas or Adam Sandler comedies'. Catherine Hardwicke pointed out that the studio didn't want to spend lots of money, because it was a women's film. 'There were very low expectations for *Twilight*, because every other studio had turned it down').

Another term for the core market of 10-24 year-olds was the 'teen and pre-teen bubble'. This audience made up about a quarter of the total audiences for movies from the 1980s onwards, but also generated the biggest proportion of the total box office. Young males in the 10-24 category had more leisure time than many other groups, as well as spending money, and 'a burning desire to be first in line for the hot new pop sensation'.[43]

For Melissa Rosenberg, *Twilight* was unnusual in being a Holly-

---

41 B. Wintraub: "What do women want? – Movies", *New York Times*, 10 Feb, 1997.
42 Robert Pattinson said that the movie 'sort of got bigger and bigger and bigger' as they were filming it.
43 P. Golstein, "Hollywood Stoops To Conquer", *Los Angeles Times*, July 11, 1999.

wood tent-pole movie led by a young women, departing from most Hollywood movies of that kind being aimed at 13 year-old boys. But *Twilight* proved 'how women/ girls can drive box office and they can support a tent-pole movie'.

Films are market researched before they're made; concepts, images, adverts, titles, stars and stories are tested on the target audience (usually in shopping malls). The responses range from 'definitely want to see' through 'might' to 'not interested'. Sometimes market research consists of showing punters a tiny TV screen of an ad in a shopping mall. Other methods include phone polls, exit polls, and surveys.

Previewing will not only be perhaps the first time the filmmakers will have seen their film with an audience, resulting in editorial alterations, it's a key time for the ad-pub department and studio executives. If a film previews well, the studio might decide to open it wider than planned; if it previews badly, it must be opened quickly, because reviews and word-of-mouth will kill it; if it previews much better than expected, it might be released in the key cities – L.A., N.Y.C., D.C. and Philly are the top 4 in the U.S.A. – to build up strong reviews and word-of-mouth, before going national. A film might have previewed or market tested badly, but the exit polls at theatres might be great: a new marketing strategy, perhaps capitalizing on favourable critical reviews, might push the film much further than expected. Sometimes films are recut. The Hollywood studios preview some 25 movies every year, at least twice. Some previews are focus groups, with a question-and-answer session afterwards.

National Research Group (N.R.G.) is one of the main market testing agencies employed by the major American studios since it was founded in 1977. National Research Group field test not only preview screenings, but also print ads, trailers, posters, TV ads, sell lines, plots, concepts, titles, etc. Marketing research tracks the awareness of a picture throughout its life, from concept to production to release. National Research Group might screen 12 films per day. A prestige project from a studio might have 10 previews. Up to $250,000 might be spent previewing a movie. When the screenings are over, the market researchers study the comments and the 'numbers'. The idea is to predict the advertizing spend, the kind of marketing campaign, the film's primary audiences, and the sort of grosses the film might make. (National Research Group's Joe Farrell, perhaps the key figure in the preview process in the U.S.A. in the contemporary era, says he can predict a film's gross to within 10%).

The questionnaire from the audience research at previews will include categories such as Excellent, Very Good, Good, Fair, Poor; and Definitely Recommend, Probably Recommend, Probably Not, and Don't Recommend. The questionnaires will take in each character in the movie, including secondary characters. Also, the music, the ending, the action, the pace, the mystery, the suspense, the setting, the story, the acting, the slow parts, confusions, the scenes most liked or disliked. Percentages will be worked out for each segment of the audience: males under 30, females 30 and over, etc.

The logistical problems of launching a movie around the world include: organizing travel, flights, limos, taxis, hotels and tickets for the stars and talent; organizing premieres and press conferences; booking cinemas; inviting celebrities and press; putting on parties; planning magazine and newspaper interviews and photo shoots months in advance; booking appearances on chat shows on radio and TV; striking thousands of film prints and ensuring their delivery; dealing with companies in a variety of currencies, and so on.

✢

The Comic Convention in San Diego was employed by Summit Entertainment as a marketing tool for the *Twilight Saga* (excerpts from the cast visiting the Comic-Con appear on the DVD releases). Many fantasy and sci-fi franchises use San Diego as a publicity platform (*Star Wars*, *Indiana Jones,* every superhero movie, etc).

Whoever came up with the 'Team Edward' and 'Team Jacob' gimmick was a genius! It was a brilliant identification and codification of fandom. But surely there should be a 'Team Bella', at the very least (plus of course a 'Team Alice', a 'Team Carlisle' and a 'Team Rosalie', etc. There are other fan favourite teams aside from Team Edward, Team Jacob and Team Bella – Team Carlisle and Team Charlie are popular, as are Team Jasper and Team Alice.)

Few middle-aged film critics came out in favour of the *Twilight* movies, as Mark Kermode[44] noted:

> very few reputable critics have dared to put their head above the parapet and admit to tolerating, let alone actually liking, this massively popular teen-orientated franchise. (19)

And some critics put the *Twilight* phenomenon down, as with *The Da Vinci Code* and the *Harry Potter* series, without reading the books or watching the movies.

Many of the mainstream film critics didn't buy *Twilight*: 'a

---

44 Critic Mark Kermode is a Twi-fan, calling the first movie 'a very decent tale of high-school angst and teen alienation given an alt-lite grungey edge' (20).

disappointingly anemic tale of forbidden love that should satiate the pre-converted but will bewilder and underwhelm viewers who haven't devoured Stephenie Meyer's bestselling juvie chick-lit franchise' (*Variety*); 'questionable casting, wooden acting, laughable dialogue and truly awful make-up' (*U.S.A. Today*). Owen Gleiberman (*Entertainment Weekly*), Steven Rea (*Philadelphia Inquirer*) and *Slate* were amenable to *Twilight*. On her website, Stephenie Meyer stated about the first movie: 'I really liked the movie a lot. It wasn't perfect, but it was extremely good' (Nov 19, 2008).

TWILIGHT ON TV.

The *Twilight Saga* cries out to be turned into a giant, Broadway musical – it's got the lot! And the first *Twilight* movie, with its soundtrack filled with alt./ indie rock music, is perfect for a teen and post-teen Broadway musical audience. (Several of the parodies and *hommages* of *Twilight* have taken a musical movie approach – such as *The Hillywood Show*).

The *Twilight Saga* also begs to be turned into a long-running TV show (I bet this possibility has been discussed at length. Rumours of a TV series emerged in 2023). In fact, *The Vampire Diaries* is essentially *Twilight* on television.

For my money, the most satisfying rendition of *Twilight* on television would be in Japanese animation. Beautiful boys (*bishonen*) suffering in love (*shonen ai*), pretty, innocent maidens who fall in love with monsters (*yokai, oni*) – Japanese *animé* has this world evoked to perfection. Imagine *Twilight* produced in the style of an *animé* masterpiece like *Death Note* (2006-07)! Or the obvious choice, *Vampire Knight* (2008), which's already virtually the *Twilight* story anyway (if you love romantic vampire stories – set in a high school, of course! – I highly recommend *Vampire Knight*. For vampires, try *Rosario and Vampire* and *Hellsing 2* (a.k.a. *Hellsing Ultimate*); for love triangles try *Ichigo 100%* and *Macross Frontier*; for horror try *Demon Slayer* and *Ninja Scroll*; and for schools and comedy/ horror try *Highschool of the Dead* and *Blue Exorcist*).

In fact, the anticipated live-action TV series of *Twilight* was later revealed (in 2023) to be an animated adaptation in conjunction with Netflix – and of *Midnight Sun*, the story of the *Twilight Saga* from the point-of-view of Edward Cullen. This wasn't what many observers and *Twilight* fans were expecting. (Actually, many elements of the *Twilight* movies were animation).

To promote women in the film business, Stephenie Meyer backed a short film competition in 2014-2015, along with Lionsgate, Volvo, Tongal and Facebook. The seven winning entries of *The Storytellers: New Voices of the Twilight Saga* appeared on Facebook in 2015.

UNDERWORLD.

The *Underworld* movies of 2003, 2006, 2009, 2012 and 2016 (which might be described as *The Matrix* with vampires), pre-empted the *Twilight Saga* in many respects: they had a werewolf vs. vampire plot, a young white woman as the lead, they had the Goth-meets-high fashion look (clearly derived from Kym Barrett's sensational outfits for *The Matrix*), they drew on real science, they had scenes in medical facilities, and they had the vamp vs. wolfie rivalry going back centuries.

How much do you think the first *Underworld* cost to make? $100 million? $150 million? It certainly looked like those ultra-high budget movies: it's got the look, the stunts, the visual effects, the extras, the special make-up, and the extravagant sets. But according to some reports, *Underworld* was a $23 million production. Which's a bargain, like *Twilight*'s $38m, compared to far too many very high budget flicks which stink.

In visual effects, the *Underworld* flicks, which pre-dated *Twilight*, used a 'magic carpet' pulled along by a truck for high vampire speed, they had blood bubbling thru the interior of a body (Viktor's) in a re-animation sequence, they used Hong Kong stunt choreographic techniques (including wirework), they had vampires with contact lenses, and so on.

A NOTE ON HOLLYWOOD ACCOUNTING: *BATMAN*.

1989's blockbuster movie *Batman* throws some light on how the U.S. film industry works (Robert Pattinson starred as Batman in 2022). *Batman* was exposed by the *Hollywood Reporter* for using a 'rolling break even' financial system: the gross profits offered to the stars was added back onto the film's production cost, plus interest, plus studio overheads. *Batman* could therefore hardly turn a profit.

The figures for *Batman* run thus:

advertizing: $60 million;
prints: $9 million;
preprint, dubbing, editing: $1.1 million;
taxes, duties: $3.6 million;
trade associations: $2 million;
freight, handling, insurance: $1.4 million;
guild, union and residual payments: $2.4 million;

cost of making the film: $121 million;
distribution (inc. prints): $89 million;
interest: $14 million.

The gross receipts were:

domestic rentals (U.S.A.): $152 million;
foreign rentals: $71 million;
TV: $3 million;
Pay TV: $24 million;
videos: $34 million;
music: $500,000;
records: $500,000;
merchandizing: $9 million.

According to Warner Brothers, the total expenditure for *Batman* was $305 million, with total gross receipts at $285 million (remember, these are 1989 figures – you could double or triple them (or more) for the present day). Thus, the film made a loss of $20 million (1991 figures). The gross points participants were thought to be director Tim Burton, producers Peter Guber and Jon Peters, and stars Michael Keaton and Jack Nicholson. The five men would have made around $60 million. For his hammy turn as the Joker, Bad Jack gained $50 million (some said it was $75m: $6 million upfront, with 15% of the gross, and escalator clauses up to 20%).

The 'Bat-suit' was a 1994 case, with Michael Uslan and Benjamin Melniker claiming they were frozen out of the deal they made with producers Peter Guber and Jon Peters. They said they were forced to sign net profits contracts, instead of the more lucrative gross profits contracts, even though they had conceived the idea for the *Batman* film, and had bought the rights from Detective Comics in 1979.[45] Warner Bros. had spent plenty of money b4 *Batman* went b4 the cameras in 1988, but Melniker and Uslan were locked out by Warners. In the event, Uslan and Melniker took screen credits (as executive producers),[46] making them $300,000 each.

The key to the scandal of Hollywood accounting was net profits and contracts. The studios' Standard Profit Definition terms were lengthy, arcane documents which differed significantly from ordinary accounting. The different areas included overheads, distribution fees, interest, home video receipts and gross profits participation. The Hollywood studios had a special way of doing the accounts: on a typical, successful movie the

---

45 M. Bygrave, 1998.
46 Jim Miller of Warners' accounts department gave Uslan and Meniker the option of signing a contract which changed the agreed terms. If they didn't, they wouldn't get anything. Uslan and Milniker signed on Sept 6, 1988.

studio might get half the box office, with the cinemas having the other half. (Rental was the key figure, not box office gross, rental being about half the box office). From their 50%, the studio takes: 35% for distribution (even though it might really be 12%); a 10% surcharge on advertizing (for the studio's expenses, which might actually be zero); the negative cost (making the film); a 15% surcharge on the negative cost; and an over-budget charge. Plus interest, of course (the studios charge interest, even though they often borrow nothing). On average, a picture had to make 2.5 times its production cost (including publicity, prints, distribution) theatrically to break even (a different scenario now, with DVD, online, cable, satellite, streaming and home entertainment sales). The internal rate of return was between 0% and 20% (the average being between 8% and 15%). At the start of the 1990s, if a film made its negative cost back on theatrical release, ancillary markets would take it into profit. In relation to the sale of video cassettes (and now streaming, DVD and Blu-ray), Hollywood's accounting enables the studios to keep 80% of the receipts, with the other 20% being declared as part of the film's accounting. Some movies can make 8 times their theatrical take from home entertainment rentals. A flop at the box office could still notch up rentals of 100,000 (worth $5 million in the early 1990s). For example, in 2000, the top 50 video rentals included many films that didn't make it into the top 50 movies in theatres: *Stir of Echoes, Deuce Bigalow, Lake Placid, Messenger: The Story of Joan of Arc,* and *The Whole Nine Yards*).

Very few movies make a profit on their box office release: hence cinema exhibition is a loss leader and advertizing campaign for the 'back end' exploitation of a film. However, since the early 1980s, 'back end' has increasingly become 'front end', with the ancillary exploitation of broadcast television (network and syndicated), satellite television, cable television, pay-TV, streaming, DVD and video sales and rentals, and projection on cruise ships and aeroplanes. The bigger a movie is at the box office, the bigger its success in ancillary markets, such as video sales. (The *Twilight Saga* is a massive seller on home entertainment formats).

Thus, the $259 million that *Batman* made in domestic (U.S.A.) gross (about $150m in rentals) was but a part of the overall revenue generated for Time-Warner. This included: Time-Warner Licensing Corporation of America, which managed the copyright on the *Batman* characters; the merchandizing department took a percentage of every item of merchandizing sold; Time-Warner owned Cinemax and Home Box Office, which showed the film; Time-Warner owned the cable systems which delivered the broadcasts; Warner Home Video released the video cassette; and the tie-in soundtrack CDs were released by Time-Warner record companies.

With the *Twilight Saga*, each of the five movies were major box office hits, which would drive the sales in the ancillary markets considerably. When you add up all of the ways in which movie franchises like the *Twilight* series can generate revenue, you can see how it became a franchise worth billions.

The *Twilight Saga* movies broke box office records (at least with figures unadjusted for inflation): *New Moon* broke the records of *Harry Potter and the Half-Blood Prince* for an opening weekend; *Eclipse* had a best-ever Wednesday opening.

Twilight (2008), on set.

2

THE CAST OF THE *TWILIGHT SAGA*

'This looks like a horror movie waiting to happen,' I snickered.

Stephenie Meyer, *Twilight* (424)

CASTING *TWILIGHT*

It took a *long* time to cast the *Twilight* movies, as the producers acknowledged (Trisha Wood and Deborah Aquila cast the production). Suggestions came and went; Stephenie Meyer had her heart set on certain actors (such as Charlie Sheen for Edward – just kidding!), but auditions continued, there were scheduling problems, the fans had their own ideas (the producers considered what the fans thought), and finding the right people took much longer than your average production. (Meyer reckoned that Emily Browning, Ellen Page or Danielle Panabaker would be suitable for Bella, and Logan Lerman or Henry Cavill for Edward). Kristen Stewart was announced on Nov 16, 2007 by Summit Ent., and Pattinson's casting was announced on Dec 11, 2007.

Having done quite a bit of casting myself, I know (1) how difficult it is, (2) how long it can take to find *exactly* the right person, and (3) how much hard work it is. Casting is not something that the general public, or film critics, or anybody outside the industry really understands. Yet, apart from the script and the initial concept, it is probably the single most important element in producing a movie. And if you're trying to make something special, something you're going to be putting *a lot* of effort into creating, you want to make sure you've considered everybody, and have looked everywhere.

A casting session or audition typically involves some of the following: you turn up at an office, studio or theatre (making sure you look great and have done your homework about the production); you meet the casting people (or their assistants); you usually meet other hopefuls; you get called in (eventually) and chat with the casting team; you might read some script pages or get to do your party piece (your monologue as the Grinch pretending to be Lady Macbeth, whatever); you leave a photo and CV; you might have your photo taken, or be filmed; and then you wait… and wait… and wait…

The *Twilight* flicks were unusual because of (1) the kind of characters needed (vampires and werewolves), and (2) the amount of media and fan attention the books were gaining. The vampire family (the Cullens) had to look like a family, and had to play well together (and there were also romantic pairings within the Cullen clan). And the lovers had to work together well.

Finding Edward Cullen was one of the biggest challenges. He has to be:

(1) super-gorgeous,

(2) look seventeen,

(3) he has to be other-worldly,

(4) to look pale and vampiric,

(5) be a convincing romantic lead,

and (6) dangerous.

Finding a romantic lead actor is actually quite a challenge (not only a lead actor, but a *romantic* lead): he has to be someone that a lot of people will find attractive. It seems like there are loads of actors around like that, but actually, no, there aren't. Finding a romantic lead who can play 17 years-old is especially difficult. And someone who can *act* as well as look delectable. Then you add in the requirements of the material – the pale-skinned, vampire look, and add that Edward has to be a threat and somewhat dangerous, and has to do action, and you can see why ticking all of the boxes ain't easy. (A very young Marlon Brando, oh yes! Or perhaps a young Leonardo DiCaprio). Then there are the issues of availability, schedules, visas, agents, etc.

What happens in casting is an actor will tick *some* of the boxes, but not *all* of them. And the actor *must* satisfy all of the requirements. A pretty boy isn't enough (there are plenty of those!), a pretty boy who can play a romantic lead is much rarer. And one who looks like a beautiful but scary vampire is even rarer! Plus one who hasn't been snapped up by five movies and TV shows going into production. Plus someone who *wants* to do the role. Plus someone who can work well with the lead actress. Meanwhile, all of the key personnel (the producers, director, studio, etc) have to agree on the casting.

It can get very frustrating, as the start date approaches, and you still haven't found your leads (especially with *Twilight* which the studio Summit Ent. didn't want to drag on for years in pre-production). On the *Twilight* show, there was clearly much anxiety behind the scenes as actors came and went, as producers wondered, 'what about so-and-so?', but they weren't available, or they couldn't play 17 years-old (meanwhile, fans were reacting to every casting suggestion with their passions and hates: not Peter Facinelli, they cried, he's not blond! And yet, after the fans had seen the *Twilight* movies, they became fond of the actors, including Robert Pattinson, so that when they were suggestions of re-casting the movies, the fans now came out in support of the actors they'd originally scoffed at!). Lurtz and Facinelli were not the first choices for their roles, but got them when the actors chosen left; some actors had auditioned for roles but were offered others (such as Ashley Greene, who went for Bella).

Ultimately, the *Twilight* movies were bigger than their casts, as with the *James Bond, Harry Potter* or *Star Wars* movies: these were the sort of event movies that became pop culture phenomena, that went way beyond who plays who, who directs what, who wrote what, who scored the music or who designed the posters for Transylvania.

However, as the first port of call for audiences, and because so much of the *Twilight Saga* movies consists of giant close-ups of the three leading roles, the actors chosen were very important. Indeed, the special effects in these movies weren't dinosaurs (*Jurassic Park*), or aliens (*E.T.*), or lightsabre duels and spaceships (*Star Wars*), or superhero action (any recent action movie), they were faces and bodies. (Ignoring, of course, the vampire elements of the *Twihard* movies, which are, in the end, entirely secondary to the primary issue of love, sex, romance and teenage angst).

Ashley Greene has described part of the audition process for the *Twilight* movie, with the repeated visits – actors are called back again, sometimes several times, sometimes to read with other actors to check out their chemistry (Greene says she was determined to get the part – yes, but so were 10,000 other actresses! The competition for roles like this is *fierce*, to say the least!).

To prepare for the role, Robert Pattinson learned to drive, trained for fights and stunts, and how to play baseball. Some of the American actors learned baseball, too (such as Ashley Greene, cast as the pitcher; tho'

Jackson Rathbone, as you can see in the movie, was already there; he had horse-riding skills, too).

In January, 2008, an open casting call was put out for the role of Jacob Black: as Oregon-based casting director Lana Veenker put it:

> Besides being an authentic Native American, he needs to have charm and charisma. At this point, Catherine is more concerned about finding someone with the right looks and personality, than she is about prior acting experience. And he needs to be available for sequels! This will be an amazing opportunity for one lucky teenager.

Like many other Hollywood movies of recent times, the *Twilight Saga* casting included token ethnic minorities. Altho' the Pacific North-West community of Forks is predominantly white in the Stephenie Meyer books (as are most of the major vampire characters), the *Twilight* movies deliberately stepped away from that: thus, Laurent, who in the books is a Frenchman in the court of one of the King Louises, was played by black actor Edi Gathegi; Tyler was also cast black (Gregory Tyree Boyce); and Eric was played by Asian-American actor Justin Chon.

However, Stephenie Meyer had envisaged John Stamos playing Laurent rather than Edi Gathegi. This kind of casting seems one of those attempts at counter-acting criticisms of ethnic representation in cinema, where all of the key roles are taken by white actors. However, according to Catherine Hardwicke, she wanted even more ethnic actors in *Twilight* (her Alice would be Japanese), but Meyer disagreed.

THE *TWILIGHT* CAST

KRISTEN STEWART.
Kristen Jaymes Stewart (b. April 9, 1990, Los Angeles) was the first actor to be cast for *Twilight* (announced by Summit Entertainment on Nov 16, 2007) – which would immediately set the tone for the rest of the casting choices (when Stewart and Robin Pattinson were cast, for instance, the screenplay was altered, lost some of its comedy, and became more serious).

Stephenie Meyer praised the lead actors:

> I would like to make a few comments about Rob and Kristen, who are the

true heart of this movie. First, they are both amazing actors. Second, they are channeling Edward and Bella like nobody's business. Third, you might want to bring a paper bag to the movie, because their on-screen chemistry may cause hyperventilation.

Kristen Stewart grew up in a show business family (both her parents – John Stewart and Jules Mann-Stewart – worked in the industry; her Mom was Australian). They lived in the Valley (San Fernando). Stewart wasn't keen to become an actor and the centre of attention – she thought she might become a writer or director (she directed her first feature movie in 2024-25, *The Chronology of Water*).

Prior to *Twilight*, Stewart had appeared in *Panic Room, Catch the Kid, Fierce People, Zathura, In the Land of Women, Into the Wild,*[1] *What Just Happened,* and *The Messengers.* Following the 2008 *Twilight* film, Stewart was in *The Yellow Hankerchief, Welcome To the Rileys, The Runaways, On the Road, Snow White and the Huntsman, Camp X-Ray, Still Alice, Clouds of Sils Maria, Personal Shopper, Charlie's Angels, Happiest Season, Lizzie, J.T. LeRoy, Underwater, Crimes of the Future, American Ultra, Equals, Certain Women, Cafe Society,* and *Spencer.*

Thus, as this (incomplete) list shows, Kristen Stewart is a serious actress who had appeared in movies and television before she was cast in *Twilight*. Stewart was not, therefore, a total unknown who had done only one or two bits part for TV and some amateur theatre. Stewart also had more professional experience than probably all of the young cast (and some of the older actors, too).

Kristen Stewart is an actress who takes her work seriously – she's one of North America's Method-style actors, rather than a Hollywood starlet (Stewart recalls a young Jodie Foster, the actress as a dedicated, professional performer – she appeared with Foster in *Panic Room*). Stewart's Bella is a rather humourless, nervous mouse. Stewart was known for swearing a lot on set, which not everybody appreciated.

Fans liked Kristen Stewart possibly because she *wasn't* the usual Hollywood babe, she wasn't the All-American, blonde beauty with the to-die-for, curvaceous figure (she is small (5'4") and scrawny), and she didn't play the celebrity game (indeed, Stewart went out of her way to come over as a regular girl, but that she was also rather spoilt and indulged couldn't be hidden).

Melissa Rosenberg acknowledged that the depiction of Bella and Edward changed when Kristen Stewart and Robert Pattinson were cast. 'I had started with more of a comedic edge and it wasn't appropriate for

1 Hardwicke had been impressed by Kristen Stewart in *Into the Wild* (CFA, 17).

those actors and the tone,' Rosenberger recalled (as the movies showed, Stewart isn't great at playing comedy – but, luckily, Taylor Lautner is!).

Kristen Stewart and Robert Pattinson, according to Catherine Hardwicke, were a great match: 'from the moment they met, you could feel the magnetic pull and sexual tension': that was important – in casting the two leads for *Twilight,* you have to consider how they will work together. Of course, the heat generated by Stewart and Pattinson on-screen turned out to be off-screen, too. (Which was a publicist's dream come true! In fact, the press insisted on putting Stewart together with Pattinson for years after their romance was over in 2013. Why? Because that sort of on-screen-off-screen relationship fascinates the press – and the readers. And it has done since the 1920s).

Personally, I'm not fond of Kristen Stewart's highly self-conscious, Method form of acting. You're always aware that this is a performance monitoring itself (as with famous Method actors such as Robert de Niro and Harvey Keitel), but Stewart is unable to prevent those annoying tics and quirks to unbalance the role.

Breathing acting – where actors are encouraged to gasp and pant to emphasize the drama, melodrama, hysteria of scenes (even in simple dialogue scenes between two people in a room) – occurs throughout the *Twilight Saga.* Kristen Stewart is given nervous gasps and pants and in-breaths or sighs everywhere. You find this style of acting in many dramas of recent times (the *50 Shades of Grey* series, for instance, and many an action movie, such as the *Star Wars* sequel movies from *The Force Awakens* onwards). The pants and gasps are dubbed, or they're live, but they sound loud because dialogue is often delivered quietly throughout contemporary cinema and television, but when it's mixed high, it sounds loud.

Linked to breathing acting is mouth acting – biting the lip (coupled with a frown). Again, Kristen Stewart, bless her, is a key player. My favourite Stewartism is when she says 'no' or doesn't want to do something: she scrunches up her nose and mouth and shakes her head slightly.

So from the outset the filmmakers allowed Kristen Stewart and Robert Pattinson to go all-out, to include as many tics, squints, frowns, grimaces, and incredibly self-conscious bits of actorly business[2] as they wanted. One wonders if director Catherine Hardwicke and producers Wyck Godfrey, Mark Morgan, Greg Mooradian *et al* thought of asking the two lead actors to tone it down (some, including Stephenie Meyer, have said

2 Stewart has a curious habit of emitting a small gasp/ sigh/ 'huh?'.

that Kristen Stewart under-played Bella Swan! *Under*-played!?). These performances are extremely mannered (and Pattinson is just as quirky in his performance as Stewart – he is doing *a lot* of very unusual bits of business, emphasizing that it's just as difficult for Edward to be around Bella as it is for her to be around him).

Yet somehow, once you get past the desire to slap both of them hard, it sort of works. And there is definitely a chemistry between them (and also between Stewart and Taylor Lautner, and between Pattinson and Lautner), that certainly enhances the movie (and the subsequent *Twilight* movies. Here's where taking care and time during pre-production to cast exactly the right actors pays off. If this trio hadn't been just right, the whole *Twilight* franchise in movie form would be much less impressive).

A relatively unknown actress would've been fascinating to see as Bella Swan – Daisy Ridley in the *Star Wars* sequel movies is a good example of someone who's done some bit parts in boring TV shows and some short films who becomes an incredible presence in a series of giant movies.

If you want to imagine how Bella and Edward might've come across had they been played by different actors, two performers featured in the *Twilight* movies are a good illustration: Jackson Rathbone (Jasper) and Ashley Greene (Alice). For some fans, Rathbone and Greene are a more golden couple than Pattinson and Stewart.

ROBERT PATTINSON.

Robert Douglas Thomas Pattinson (b. May 13, 1986, London) was not a professionally trained actor. He was part of an amateur drama group (in Barnes, London), where he appeared in *Macbeth, Tess of the d'Urbervilles, Anything Goes* and *Guys and Dolls*. Pattinson also acted as a model in his teens; he later modelled for Dior.

One of Robert Pattinson's best-known roles prior to *Twilight* was playing Hogwarts School's golden boy Cedric Diggory in *Harry Potter and the Goblet of Fire* (2005). Pattinson called Diggory a genuinely nice guy, quiet, but also competitive. (In *Goblet of Fire*, Pattinson's Diggory is chiefly a function of the plot – he's someone for Harry Potter to battle against in the finale, and a heroic sacrifice (and handsome corpse) when he dies at the hands (and wands) of Peter Pettigrew and Lord Voldemort).

After *Twilight*, Robert Pattinson appeared in movies directed by David Cronenberg (*Cosmopolis* and *Maps To the Stars*), and in *The Batman* (2022). Other films included *Little Ashes, How To Be, Remember Me, Water For Elephants, Life, The Childhood of a Leader,*

Damsel, Tenet, Waiting For the Barbarians, The King, Good Time, High Life, The Lighthouse, The Rover, and *Queen of the Desert.*

Among the actors who auditioned for Edward Cullen were Dustin Mulligan. Tom Welling (*Smallville*) was a fan favourite. Around 5,000 boys were auditioned for the role of Edward. Robert Pattinson was concerned, going in for the audition, that *Twilight* was going to end up silly: 'there would be a bunch of big muscle guys outside [the building] and there'd be a really silly little girl there' (M. Howden, 63).

> He grinned his crooked smile at me, stopping my breath and my heart. I couldn't imagine how an angel could be any more glorious. (*Twilight*, 211-2)

But many fans of the *Twilight* books didn't want Robert Pattinson[3] to play their beloved Edward Cullen: 75,000 Twilighters signed a petition against him (that's a *lot* of fans! And a *lot* of fans who got together to protest, and a *lot* of fans who felt strongly enough about the issue to contribute to it). The ever-realist Pattinson was expecting it. He was almost talking himself out of wanting the part. (And yet, of course, once fans saw Pattinson on the silver screen, many became converts!).

> He was too perfect, I realized with a piercing stab of despair. There was no way this godlike creature could be meant for me. (*Twilight*, 224)

Catherine Hardwicke said that the role of Edward Cullen was the toughest casting challenge:

> How do you find the best-looking guy in the whole world that everyone is going to think is great-looking, but he has to be believable to be a 17 year-old in high school? That takes out almost every hot actor you can think of.

Plus they have to be pale, other-worldly, and tortured. And scary – they have to represent a believable threat (M. Howden, 57). Catherine Hardwicke remarked:

> Edward loves Bella and wants to protect her – that's everybody's fantasy. And there's sexual tension. They can't go too far or he'll kill her, which is this tingling, exhilarating thing! (M. Howden, 56)

The heart of the piece was the love affair for Catherine Hardwicke: 'she loves him and he's a killer' (CFA, 58). The casting process whittled down the candidates for Edward to four actors: they tried out the kissing

---

3 That Robert Pattinson was British helped, partly because Stephenie Meyer had the idea that Brits should be playing Americans.

scene at Catherine Hardwicke's house, and Robert Pattinson got the role. (There was some doubt at Summit Ent. about Pattinson, including his looks, but Hardwicke convinced them that he was right choice; Hardwicke said in 2018 that she had more freedom with casting and didn't have big-shot producers telling what to do).

Stephenie Meyer and Robert Pattinson disagreed about how Edward Cullen should be played: Meyer thought that Edward wasn't depressed or bored or lonely, but Pattinson insisted that he was. 'Yet in the performance he did what he wanted, and yet it was exactly what I wanted,' Meyer acknowledged. Meyer did admit that Edward was 'such a pessimist', someone who tortures himself (TS, 30).

For Stephenie Meyer, Edward started out as a pessimist, expecting the worst to happen, but by the end of *Breaking Dawn*, 'he has faith in their future'.

The anguished aspect of Edward was important for Robert Pattinson: he saw Edward as someone at the end of his time, who has nothing to live for, yet who can't end it all: 'all he wants to do is either become a human or die. The only reason that he hasn't died is because he is too scared; he doesn't think he has a soul' (M. Howden, 69). 'I really tried to make him an incredibly strong and powerful character,' Pattinson continued, 'but at the same time self-loathing and extremely vulnerable' ((ibid., 69).

For Robert Pattinson, Edward was someone who couldn't help messing things up in relationships. Edward is

> so... lost. He doesn't know what to do. It's this typically male attitude when you find somebody you're in love with and you just continuously, through your own doubts, keep messing up again and again and again.[4]

'Rob played the character as being tortured, which is really the metaphor for young love – it hurts, it's great, it's maddening,' explained producer Wyck Godfrey. 'He becomes obsessed with her, the same way she is with him' (CFA, 60). As American filmmaker Bette Gordon observed, 'usually the object of your obsession is less important than the fact of being obsessed.' It's the obsession that counts.

A sub-genre of Japanese animation is called 'boys in pain', where pretty boys suffer agonies in silence (or they're buddies (or lovers) with other pretty boys in doom-laden situations, such as war-time). The way that Robert Pattinson played Edward Cullen was very much like the *bishonen* (beautiful boys) in *animé*, all haunted expressions, pained

---

4 In M. Howden, 133.

looks, and perpetually troubled moods.

Robert Pattinson has commented several times in interviews about how strange the *Twilight Saga* was for him, as an actor, and also how odd it was as a story: 'It's a really weird story', Pattinson said in 2017, but somehow it became mainstream, and successful, and accepted. Pattinson was not a fan of the material, in short: it was weird for him being part of something he didn't particularly like. Pattinson also spoke critically of *Twilight* fans and their fascination with the *Saga.*

And Robert Pattinson went public with his critical views of the Goddess of *Twilight,* Stephenie Meyer : 'It was like reading her sexual fantasy'; Meyer thought she was Bella, Pattinson reckoned, 'in love with her own fictional creation'.

Well, in show business, it's known that personal attacks on colleagues can be professional suicide. It's just not done. Robert Pattinson lambasting the *Twilight* books and the *Twilight* movies is one thing, but directly criticizing the fans and Stephenie Meyer is ill-advised. (And Pattinson later starred in the *Batman* series, which, for twisted and creepy material far out-does *Twilight*!).

TAYLOR LAUTNER.

Taylor Lautner (b. Feb 11, 1992) was a sporty kid from Grand Rapids, Michigan (where he was born), who was into martial arts (karate) and sports (football, basketball), from an early age. Lautner was winning awards in national martial arts competitions (for karate) before he was ten. Lautner moved into acting and modelling at a young age, too (his pretty boy looks got him noticed). He appeared in the Steve Martin comedy *Cheaper By the Dozen 2* (2005), and was Shark Boy in one of the digital animated adventures directed by Robert *Spy Kids* Rodriguez (*Sharkboy and Lavagirl,* 2005).[5] Eventually, as offers and auditions came in, Lautner had to decide between devoting himself to sports/ martial arts or acting. He chose acting. His family upped sticks and moved to the Golden State, rather than have Lautner commute on the red eye flight from Michigan to Tinseltown. As well as appearing in movies and television, Lautner also did voiceover work (for *Rugrats Go Wild, Scooy Doo, Duck Dodgers*), and photographic modelling.

On January 18, 2008, an open casting call went out in Portland, OR:

> Lana Veenker Casting announced today that it is seeking a 16-18 year old Native American male to play a significant role in the upcoming Summit Entertainment film "Twilight," directed by Catherine

5 *Sharkboy and Lavagirl* was one of the early green screen, computer-generated movies. I saw it in Brighton, and can't remember much about it, excerpt that it was enjoyable!

Hardwicke...

"Director Catherine Hardwicke is keen to find the right teenager for the role of Jacob," says Casting Director Lana Veenker, owner of the Portland, Oregon-based casting company. "Besides being an authentic Native American, he needs to have charm and charisma. At this point, Catherine is more concerned about finding someone with the right looks and personality, than she is about prior acting experience. And he needs to be available for sequels! This will be an amazing opportunity for one lucky teenager."

Taylor Lautner noted that anyone who played Jacob Black would be loved by the fans, and that he was lucky enough to be the actor who did.

As the publicity and documentaries for the *Twilight Saga* showed, Taylor Lautner was also a superb ambassador for the *Twilight Saga* movies, with an appealingly easy-going personality (and looks that the camera just loves!).

The *Twilight Saga* movies play Jacob Black a little dumber and naïver than he is in the books. In *New Moon*, Jake's devoted to Bella, agreeing pretty much with whatever she wants to do, but he is also more mature and wiser than she is in many ways (they play a joshing game of adding on years to their ages for skills like fixing cars). But in the movie adaptation of *New Moon*, the way Taylor Lautner plays Jacob makes him goofier and more innocent. *New Moon* also needed a strong actor to play Jacob, as Robert Pattinson is A.W.O.L. for much of the movie. And Lautner's looks no doubt helped *New Moon* to become such a hit financially.

Catherine Hardwicke described Jake Black as the boyfriend from the wrong side of the tracks, if *Twilight* were being made in the 1970s, and he'd be a biker (in the event, Jacob became associated with black clothing and motorbikes). And he does have a 'bad boy' name – Jake Black.

Following *New Moon*, Lautner appeared in *Valentine's Day*, *Abduction*, *Tracers*, *Run the Tide*, *The Ridiculous 6*, *Home Team*, *Scream Queens* and hosted *Saturday Night Live*. The press also fed off the rumour Lautner was dating singer Taylor Swift (around 2009); Lautner was also linked romantically to actresses Billie Lourd, Lily Collins and Marie Avgeropoulos.

CASTING THE CULLENS.

In casting the Cullens, casting directors Trisha Wood and Deborah Aquila had to find people who (1) matched the books' characters, (2) could play vampires, (3) would work well as a couple (each Cullen is part of a romantic pair), and (4) would suit the overall family look and dynamic (altho' the Cullen family aren't related by blood (!), they do have to look like they fit together – Jasper and Rose, for instance, look like brother and sister). When you're casting lovers, you have to make sure that the two actors can work together. (Needless to say, the Cullen kids do look quite a bit older than the 17 or 18 they're meant to be, whereas at least Kristen Stewart and Taylor Lautner were close to the ages they played).

Several actors in *Twilight* came from the U.S. TV series *The O.C.* (= Orange County, 2003-2007), such as Reed, Gigandet and Rathbone. *Twilight* scripter Melissa Rosenberg wrote two episodes of *The O.C.*

Peter Facinelli (b. Nov 26, 1973, Queens, N.Y.) was a producer as well as an actor. Facinelli had appeared in numerous productions, including *An Unfinished Affair, Touch Me, Can't Hardly Wait, Damages, Arc, Reaper, Supernova, Fastlane* and *The Scorpion King* (b4 *Twilight*), and *Nurse Jackie, Loosies, Accidentally In Love, 13 Minutes, The Vanished, Countdown, Asher, Running With the Devil, Gangster Lord, The Damned, The Unbreakable Boy, Gallow's Hill* and *Freezer* afterwards.

The look of Peter Facinelli seems to evoke Tom Cruise *et al* in *Interview With the Vampire* – another vampire flick where the vamps are pretty, white boys. Carlisle is styled as a handsome man in his early middle age (which follows the novel – tho' in the book Carlisle is pretending to be 30). Altho' Carlisle is English, Facinelli plays him (like all of the other Cullens), with an American accent.

Carlisle Cullen required an actor with authority as well as glamour: Carlisle has to deliver a lot of exposition in each *Twihard* movie. He is the go-to person for information about vampires (especially their history and origins) – and in the *Twilight* books, too. Carlisle is also the go-to guy in any emergency or life-threatening situation (of which there are plenty).[6]

Elizabeth Reaser (b. June 15, 1975, Bloomfield, M.I.) has appeared in movies such as *Young Adult, Stay, The Family Stone, Sweet Land* and *Against the Current,* and TV shows like *True Detective, Saved, Grey's Anatomy, The Ex-List,* and *The Good Wife.*

As played by Jackson Rathbone, Jasper, with his curly, yellow-blond locks (a wig), and balefully staring eyes, kept reminding me of Harpo Marx (in the first *Twilight* movie). That he didn't say much in the first couple of *Twi-Lite* movies made him seem even more like Harpo.[7] It's in 2010's *Eclipse*, with its multiple flashbacks, that Rathbone shines (when

---

6 But of course, in the most important life-threatening emergency in the *Twilight* series, the birth of Bella's baby, he just happens to be AWOL!
7 Ah, if only Harpo, Chico and Groucho were creating mayhem throughout the *Twilight* movies! The so-seriousness would last about 1.5 seconds!

we get to see Jasper's colourful back-story).

Jackson Rathbone (b. Dec 14, 1984, Singapore) had appeared in many TV and movie productions, including *The O.C.*, *Travis and Henry*, *Beautiful People*, *Molding Clay* and *Close To Home* before *Twilight*, and in *The Last Airbender*, *No Ordinary Family*, *Girlfriend*, *Aim High*, *The Concerto*, *The White Collar*, etc, afterwards. Rathbone is also a keen musician, with a band (100 Monkeys) that have recorded several albums and toured.

Actress Ashley Michele Greene (b. Feb 21, 1987, Jacksonville, F.L.) was a model: Alice, as described in the *Twilight* book as a willowy, slender, graceful and ethereal soul, called for someone light on their feet and amazingly attractive (altho' fans complained that Greene wasn't exactly like Alice; Greene was auditioning for Bella Swan). But she certainly had the look (and the feather-cut bob hair).[8]

Alice is the most out-going of the Cullens, and Ashley Greene emphasizes her simple wishes for everyone to get along (and for organizing parties). Alice is upbeat, optimistic and carefree (as much as is possible for these sullen-Cullen vampires). Yet Green's Alice also gets to kick some butt when necessary: she is given major action gags in the battles. Alas, there wasn't time in the *Twilight* movies for Alice's troubled back-story.

Prior to *Twilight*, Ashley Greene had appeared in *Otis*, *Crossing Jordan*, *Punk'd* and *Mad TV*; after it, in *Skateland*, *Summer's Blood*, *Pan Am*, *Rogue*, *Bombshell*, *Aftermath*, *Urge*, *Kristy*, *Burying the Ex*, *A Warrior's Heart*, *LOL*, *Wish I Was Here* and *The Apparition*.

Filming *Twilight* was 'a rollercoaster', Ashley Greene said in 2022: 'it was a rollercoaster of emotions. We did have up ands downs, and it wasn't perfect all the time'.

Nikki Reed (b. May 17, 1988, L.A.) had worked with director Catherine Hardwicke on the movie *Thirteen* (2003); co-written by Reed, *Thirteen* featured Reed leading teenager Evan Rachel Wood astray in the world of contemporary Los Angeles. Reed had appeared in *Lords of Dogtown*, *Man of God*, *Cherry Crush*, *Justice* and *The O.C.* prior to *Twilight*, and in *Intramural*, *In Your Eyes*, *Pawn*, *Snap*, *Animal*, *Chain Letter* and *Privileged* after it. Reed has a media image of a quirky, sexy young woman, linked to pop culture and pop music (she has made music with her husband Paul McDonald, and their song 'All I've Ever Needed' appears in the *Breaking Dawn* soundtrack).

Rosalie Hale is described in the 2005 *Twilight* novel as beautiful

---

8 Greene was the tallest amongst the girls, but was supposed to be 4' 10".

(along with most of the other vampires). But she has a bee in her black hood about Bella, about being human, and she hasn't wholly embraced the vampire lifestyle. Nikki Reed captured the antsy, irritated nature of Rosalie. (The first time we see some ruffled feathers in the Cullen clan is when Bella spots Carlisle, Rose and Edward talking in low, urgent tones in the hospital corridor; it's Rose who's most upset, suggesting that Edward should've let the girl expire).

Kellan Lutz (b. Mch 15, 1985, North Dakota) was a curious choice for Emmett Cullen: chosen perhaps so that he wouldn't take away the spotlight from Edward (Stephenie Meyer wanted Lutz as Emmett, and fought for his casting). Emmett is basically the Hulk, a guy you'd want fighting alongside you, not against you, in a skirmish (he's bold and fearless). Lutz plays Emmett with a wry sense of humour that takes time to emerge; Emmett is first to make crude or sexual jokes. (Emmett, like Jasper, has a rather under-written characterization in the *Twilight* movies, where it was partly down to the actor to do something more with the role). Prior to *Twilight*, Lutz had appeared mainly on television (*C.S.I., Heroes, The Bold and the Beautiful, Six Feet Under*, etc), and after in films such as *Hercules, Immortals, Java Heat, The Expendables 3, A Nightmare On Elm Street,* etc).

Cam Gigandet (b. Aug 16, 1982, Tacoma, WA), playing the Nomad vampire James Witherdale, was a favourite actor with director Catherine Hardwicke, appearing in other projects she directed, such as *Reckless* and *Plush* (both 2013). Prior to *Twilight*, Gigandet had apeared in TV series (*The O.C., The Young and the Restless* and *Jack and Bobby*), and movies such as *Never Back Down* and *American Crude.* Gigandet is great casting as the main antagonist in the first *Twi*-movie, and relishes playing the bad boy vampire (Gigandet also leads the charge in going topless in the *Twilight* movies).

THE VOLTURI.

The Volturi might live in Italy, but they were played by a mix of Brits and Yanks (with British actors yet again being cast by Hollywood productions as villains or foreigners. Why not cast some real Italian actors? There are some terrific Italian performers to choose from – yes, and they are experts at playing mean S.O.B.s!). To be picky, the Volturi rulers (Aro, Marcus, Caius and their spouses) are actually *Greek* (they were born in 1400-1200 B.C., in the Mycenaean period, according to *The Twilight Saga: The Official Illustrated Guide*, 405).

The casting of the Volturi was altered from the *Twilight* books. For instance, the ambitious, eccentric head of the Volturi, Lord Aro, was in his mid-twenties when he became a vampire, but Michael Sheen is cast (and plays the role) older. The Volturi Guard twins, Alec and Jane, were 12/ 13 when they were transformed, but Dakota Fanning and Cameron Bright were cast older (once again, finding suitable teenage actors who are the actual age of their characters is very, very difficult).

For the Volturi in the *Twilight* series, an Italian accent was suggested, but not strongly, so that the villains in an American movie were yet again Brits (or at least headed up by a Brit).

MICHAEL SHEEN.

Michael Sheen (b. 1969, Newport, Wales) appeared as Lord Aro, the chief Volturi. Director Chris Weitz said that he 'aggressively went after' Sheen for the role of Aro. 'I see this great British actor as being capable of anything... I think he's quite brilliant and conveys an extraordinary intelligence'.

Michael Sheen is a sensational, explosive actor, with a mercurial energy – when he's on screen, no one else stands a chance! Sheen's star rose considerably in the 2000s, where he appeared in *Midnight In Paris* as a smart-ass college professor, as the British Prime Minister in *The Queen*, and David Frost in *Frost/ Nixon*. Sheen's other films include *The Deal, Fantabulosa, The Damned United, Underworld* and *Tron: The Legacy*.

Michael Sheen, a Welsh stage actor of the same cloth as Richard Burton and Anthony Hopkins, is a performer who can do anything (he has played many of the classical parts in the theatre, including Hamlet and Romeo). Sheen has won numerous awards for his theatre, television and film work.

One of Michael Sheen's more recent roles was the werewolf Lucian in the *Underworld* series: he played the lead role in 2009's *Underworld: Rise of the Lycans* (the *Underworld* franchise has several affinities with the *Twilight* series, such as ancient feuds between vampires and werewolves, and a vampire-werewolf, *Romeo and Juliet* romance). A superbly physical actor (he was a sporty kid and footballer), Sheen plays most of the *Underworld* movie topless (every luvvie should do a Topless Movie – Kenneth Branagh in *Frankenstein*, Taylor Lautner in the *Twilight Saga*, and Scarlett Johansson in the *Avengers*. Just kidding). Sheen is terrific as the Spartacus-like werewolf Lucian leading a revolt in the vampire castle, grabbing the scenes and making them his own (and with his large, wide eyes, ringed with kohl – big as an *animé* hero – he pops out of the screen).

Michael Sheen remarked that he enjoyed the variety of roles – to be able to play Tony Blair (in *The Queen*), David Frost (in *Frost/ Nixon*), and Lucian, the commander of the werewolves (in *Underworld*). Sheen said his daughter Lily (his daughter with *Underworld* star Kate beckinsale) was a fan of the *Twilight* books (in the documentaries on the home releases of *New Moon* he relates an amusing story of how he told Lily he was going to play Aro).

Rachelle Lefevre (b. Feb 1, 1979, Montréal) has credits that include *Big Wolf On Campus, The Summit, Casino Jack, White House Down, Charmed, Bones, Life On a Stick, C.S.I., Swingtown, Boston Legal,* etc.

Bryce Howard (b. Mch 2, 1981, L.A.), daughter of director Ron Howard, appeared, prior to *Eclipse*, in *As You Like It, The Village, Spider-man, Terminator 4,* and after it in *Pete' Dragon, Help, Jurassic World, Gold, Restless, Rocketman,* and *Argylle*.

THE HUMANS.

Casting according to ethnicity was added by the movies to the *Twilight* books (by casting directors Trisha Wood and Deborah Aquila): thus, Tyler (Gregory Tyree Boyce) is black in the movies, and Eric is an Asian American kid (the only really significant ethnic element in the *Twilight* novels is of course the Native American element).

The very wonderful Anna Kendrick (b. 1985) was Jessica Stanley: Kendrick effortlessly outshines anyone else who dares to share the screen with her; Kendrick's Jessica is feistier and wittier than the Jessica in the books. Kendrick's been in Broadway musicals (*High Society*) and *A Little Night Music*. Following *Twilight*, Kendrick appeared in *Up In the Air, Into the Woods, Scott Pilgrim vs. the World, Cake, Mr Wright, Pitch Perfect* and *End of Watch*.

Billy Burke (b. 1966, Bellingham WA) was Charlie Swan, complete with moustache, tins of beer, check shirt and a weary, long-suffering demeanour. Burke appeared on TV in *24, Karen Sisco, Revolution, Law & Order, Star Trek* and *Gilmore Girls,* and in movies such as the wonderful comedy *Jane Austen's Mafia, Ladder 49, The Fallen, Final Jeopardy* and *Red Riding Hood*.

The relationship between the father and daughter in *Twilight* is nicely played – cute, even: how they both don't do small talk, how they find it difficult to say what they want to say, how it's awkward for both of them when Bella moves to the North-West. Billy Burke and Kristen Stewart are great in those early scenes as Bella arrives in Sporks to start a new life.

MORE ON CASTING.

One of the pluses of being the first out of the door in a movie series is that you get to be the first to do the casting, the designs, the location scouting, the costumes, the hair and make-up, the look, the attitude and the tone. Everything in Movie One of the *Twilight Saga* franchise was created from scratch, and the subsequent *Twihard* movies had to work with that. Even if they rejected everything, and re-cast the sequels (a silly idea), and changed the tone and the look (a waste of time and all the money/ effort that had already been spent), they would still be working, as far as the movie audience was concerned, with that first *Twilight* movie.

Thus, casting directors Trisha Wood and Deborah Aquila and the producers (Bowen, Rosenfelt, Stabile, Godfrey *et al*) got to cast the *Twilight* series first. They chose Kristen Stewart, Taylor Lautner and Robert Pattinson to head up their cast, and the *Twi*-sequels had to live with that.[9] But the casting was in the main just right for the *Twilight* series. And that helped *enormously*. Because you can't say the same of many other movie franchises (some of which, we all know, often have roles that are hopelessly miscast – it would've been disastrous for the *Twilight Saga* to have two out of the central three roles perfectly cast, but one terribly cast!).

Greg Morradian, one of the producers of *Twilight,* recalled that 'it took forever to cast this movie', but he was happy once they had Bella and the Cullens signed up: 'I realised we finally had it. When I actually got to see them together performing in a scene, it took my breath away' (M. Howden, 61).

Avoiding big name actors was a key decision, of course. No Tom Cruises as Carlisle, or Vin Diesels as Emmett. As with high profile fantasy projects such as *The Lord of the Rings* or *Harry Potter*, the property itself was the biggest selling-point (because by the time the rights[10] were optioned by Summit Entertainment in 2007, the books were fast becoming a cultural phenomenon).[11] Avoiding stars is not only to do with cutting down on $$$$ – it can be about wanting to use fresh faces for a new story/ franchise, about avoiding clichés (of existing stars), and it gives you a wider selection to choose from (schedules are tougher to nail down with stars, for instance, who are often busy. In fact, scheduling is often a reason why a particular actor can't do the job).

---

9 Replacing Lautner was considered.
10 The rights to the next three *Twilight* books were acquired by Summit Ent. in Nov, 2008.
11 However, the *Rings* and *Potter* flicks did cast higher up the scale than the *Twilight* series. Michael Sheen was one of the bigger names to be cast, but, as he was playing the chief villain, that made sense.

Plus, the lead roles in *Twilight* are teenagers, so whoever you pick is probably not going to have much film experience (unless you cast older, and go the *Grease* (1978) route, having people in their late twenties or older playing teens). Also, *Twilight* is an ensemble piece – altho' it's a love story, there are two groups of characters in the first movie that form ensembles: Bella and her chums and the Sullens. So you need to cast actors who work well as an ensemble (and stars can unbalance an ensemble).

There are some obvious places where a film star could appear in the first *Twilight* movie – Carlisle Cullen, for instance, or Bella's father Charlie. Correctly, the casting team avoided that, and they also rightly declined to have cameos, which would distract from the piece (altho' there are cameos from some of the production team, including author Stephenie Meyer).

The cameo from Stephenie Meyer is in her own shot in the café, sitting at the counter, and she's addressed by name by the waitress (Katie Powers), as if she's a regular there. It's a much more prominent cameo that usual from the production team, who typically appear in disguise or in the background. And it's an in-joke: Meyer has her computer and is writing the additional dialogue for the day (to be photocopied on pink pages, of course).

FAME.

Some of the cast of *Twilight* had an ambiguous attitude towards the *Twilight Saga*, such as having to deal with the fame, the *paparazzi*, and the intense attention of fans. Robert Pattinson made no secret of his dislike of the *Twilight* series and his character, Edward Cullen, and also criticized the films for their plot holes, their weird view of life, and the fans (most actors do *not* directly and publicly criticize their work, the movies they appear in, or their colleagues, for all the obvious reasons. Pattinson has never held back, even calling *Twilight* a book that shouldn't have been published). Taylor Lautner spoke of the discomfort of having to film so many scenes topless.[12] Kristen Stewart was also unsure about the rewards the *Twilight Saga* brought, such as the fame (however, she accepted the millions of dollars in fees happily). After *Twilight*, Stewart distanced herself from it partly by pursuing roles and movies which were the polar opposite.

Ashley Greene, however, was a huge fan before she was even cast in the role (she was auditioning for Bella Swan). Greene later put together a

---

12 Lautner resented at times being the only actor on set who was shirtless.

podcast (*The Twilight Effect*) where some of the actors joined her (and fan Mel Howe) to discuss the movies.

Some of the *Twilight* actors are happy that they've been part of the franchise – they don't all dismiss it like Robert Pattinson. Certainly it helped many of their professional careers. Some of the actors did public appearances even years after the *Twilight* movies (I've seen Jackson Rathbone, Ashley Greene and Kellan Lutz at Comic Con).

Kellan Lurtz found waiting around on set tiresome, and contemplated not returning for the last two *Twilight* movies. Unfortunately, it goes with job: waiting is the primary activity on a film set for many in the crew as well as the cast. Or, put it like this: apart from a few individuals working at the centre of activity, filmmaking can be very, very boring.

The young stars of the *Twilight Saga* had to contend with being very famous (David Bowie once commented that he wouldn't wish fame on his worst enemy). Kristen Stewart found the attention that the role of Bella Swan brought was unnerving: 'the most uncomfortable, terrible weird' time, she said on the *Ellen DeGeneres Show* (2016). But in a 2015 interview with pop musician Patti Smith, Stewart also asserted that the *Twilight Saga* had some value for her: 'there's something there that I'm endlessly, and to this day, fucking proud of'. And Smith reminded Stewart not to take any notice of critics and complainers, because the *Twilight* series was much loved:

> Never apologize for your work. If people don't accept the *Twilight* series for what it is, well, fuck them. Millions of people loved that series. It gave them something.

The cast and crew of Twilight.

The cast of Twilight.

3

TWILIGHT, THE MOVIE

I want them [someone who's seen the movie] to grab their boyfriend or girlfriend and go and make out, then turn around and go back and see the movie again, then make out again!

Catherine Hardwicke (CFA, 134)

INTRODUCTION.

The *Twilight* series on the silver screen was launched by *Twilight*, released on November 21, 2008,[1] and produced by Summit Entertainment. It was, unusually, directed by a woman (Catherine Hardwicke, b. 1955), adapted from a book by a woman (Stephenie Meyer), with a woman (Kristen Stewart) in the lead role (and the movie is from her point-of-view), and with a woman taking sole screenwriting credit (Melissa Rosenberg (b. 1962) – it's typical for many writers to be involved in previous drafts.

Of the first *Twilight* production, Stephenie Meyer commented:

It was almost an entirely female production, which is so rare, and to be able to work with female writers and female directors and even our co-producer was a woman – it was a totally different feel than you would have on a more traditional, male-centric set.

Twilight was produced by Temple Hill/ Maverick/ Imprint for Summit Entertainment; Greg Mooradian, Mark Morgan and Wyck Godfrey were the producers; executive producers were Karen Rosenfelt, Marty Bowen, Guy Oseary and Michelle Imperatio Stabile (5 guys, and 2 women among the producers, then – and men out-number women among

---

1 The release dates was brought forward from December 12 so it wouldn't clash with the rescheduled release of *Harry Potter and the Art of Making Even More Money.*

the producers of the subsequent *Twi*-flicks); Melissa Rosenberg wrote the script; Nancy Richardson cut it; Trisha Wood and Deborah Aquila cast it; Wendy Chuck was costume designer; Jeanne Van Phue was make-up head; Mary Ann Valdes was hair dept head; Richard Kidd and Bill George were visual effects supervisors; Andy Weder oversaw the special effects; Carter Burwell,[2] Adam Smalley and Alexander Patsavas[3] composed and supervised the music;[4] Kenny Woods was music producer; Elliot Davis was DP; Ian Phillips was art director, Gene Serdema was set decorator, Andy Cheng (also known as Kai Chung Andy Chang) was second unit director and stunt co-ordinator; and James Lin was supervising location manager. Released: Nov 21, 2008. 122 mins.

Technical specs: filmed using Arriflex and Panavision cameras; Super 35; Eastman Kodak film (35mm); aspect ratio: 1:2.35; edited using Avid; Dolby Digital and D.T.S.

The *Twilight* project had originated at M.T.V. Films (a division of Paramount) in April, 2004. When the project came from Paramount, Stephenie Meyer wrote a couple of pages of elements that she insisted were in the new script, including having the same characters, defining the attributes of the vampires, and ensuring no deaths appeared in the movie that weren't in the book (these are common requests from authors to filmmakers, sometimes made legally binding). Meyer did that to protect her work after it had been changed at Paramount (into a 'completely different story', according to Melissa Rosenberg). The first movie was rushed along partly because a strike of the Writer's Guild of America was looming on Oct 31, 2007. Another reason for hurrying up the movie sequels of *Twilight* and producing one a year was that it featured a young cast who were getting old fast (as with the *Harry Potter* series). But the chief reason was to maximize the audience before *they* got old. That's why the sequels of recent hit movies are released closer together than the typical three or so years. (And there's only seven months between *New Moon* and *Eclipse*).

Summit Entertainment, which bought the options for the *Twilight* novels, was founded in 1991, originally as a sales/ distribution company. It moved into production, ultimately becoming a mini-studio by 2006. Lionsgate acquired Summit in 2012.

---

2 The film was edited using temp music (as usual on a movie), including some of Carter Burwell's other scores.
3 Patsavas and Smalley were responsible for selecting many of the rock/ pop acts in *Twilight*.
4 The score was recorded in London, at Air Lyndhurst Studios. The sound mix was done at Wildfire Studios.

THE PRODUCTION COMPANIES AND THE PRODUCERS.

One of the companies behind *Twilight* and *New Moon*, Maverick, was founded in 1992 by Madonna, Frederick DeMann and Ronnie Dashev (however, Madonna was bought out in 2004, and wasn't involved with the *Twilight Saga).*[5] Mark Morgan was C.E.O. Maverick's parent company was Warners. Maverick's movies included *Dangerous Game, Canadian Bacon, Alanis Morrisette, Agent Cody Banks, Material Girls, Hit and Run* and *The Stepfather.*

Imprint was founded in 2008 by Michael Becker and Mark Morgan, with *Twilight* as its first movie production (Morgan was one of the producers). Other Imprint films include *Percy Jackson, The Stepfather, Pawn, Kid Cannabis* and *My Man Is a Loser.*

Temple Hill Entertainment was founded in 2006 by Wyck Godfrey and Marty Bowen (both were producers on the *Twilight Saga*). Temple Hill's movies include *The Nativity Story* (helmed by Catherine Hardwicke)*, Alien Invasion Arizona* (which sounds like a Stephenie Meyer script), *Dear John, Everything Must Go, The Maze Runner* and *Tracers.*

Producer on all five *Twilight* films, Mark Morgan, has credits that include the *Percy Jackson* movies, the *Agent Cody Banks* movies, *Frostbite, Material Girls, Cruel World, The Wedding Planner, Slackers, The Gravedancers* and *Hit and Run* (some of these were as head honcho of Maverick). Morgan also co-founded Imprint in 2008, to produce the *Twilight* movies.

Wyck Godfrey's credits as a film producer prior to *Twilight* include: *Daddy Day Care, I, Robot, Behind Enemy Lines, Flight of the Phoenix, Eragon, The Nativity Story* and *Management.* After *Twilight*, Godfrey produced *Safe Haven, Revenge* (TV), *The Maze Runner, The Longest Ride, Tracers* and *Tipping Point.* Greg Mooradian has producer credits which include *Percy Jackson, The Stepfather, The Fan, Sugar & Spice* and *Drumline.*

For film producer Greg Mooradian (who read *Twilight* in galleys, before it was published), *Twilight* has a great hook – using vampirism as

> a metaphor for teenage lust, for that feeling 'I want you but I can't have you.' I thought that was such a wonderful metaphor to express teenage longing.[6]

'The vampires are really nothing more than a hook,' Mooradian asserted, 'the vehicle to tell the story of forbidden love' (CFA, 16). But

---

5 Amidst legal wrangles over – what else? – money.
6 In M. Howden, 29.

there was no way that you could predict that *Twilight* would resonate so strongly with teenage American girls, to become 'an anthem for young girls as much as anything in contemporary culture' (ibid.).

In *New Vampire Cinema,* Ken Gelder noted that the first *Twilight* movie had many women in key creative/ production roles, which may have been why the *Twilight* movies were 'so routinely disparaged by 'serious' cinema commentators' (85).

Certainly, the *Twilight Saga* was perceived by some in the critical community as trashy, lowbrow, superficial, unworthy of serious attention, etc – which's often how female art or feminine art or women's art is received in patriarchal culture; as if all of Hollywood's output made by male producers and directors in recent years is at the level of *King Lear* or *Citizen Kane.* Yeah, *right.*

Melissa Rosenberg was surprised by the vehemence of the criticism of the *Twilight* movies: 'When you start to read the criticism of *Twilight,* it's just vitriol, it's intense, the contempt' (2012). For Rosenberg, the feminine aspects of *Twilight Saga* were part of the negative criticism: 'because it's female it's worthy of contempt. Because it feels female, it is less than' (20120.

PRE-PRODUCTION.

The first *Twilight* movie enjoyed a long pre-production period. Usually, that makes for a better movie, because the filmmakers have had sufficient time to explore all aspects of the production, to try out stunts and props, to shoot tests, to develop the script, and to cast the movie, etc. (By contrast, a hurried pre-production schedule puts pressure on the crew to deliver what should take three months in a shorter time).

According to Catherine Hardwicke, the pre-production of *Twilight* was about 15 months, between scriptwriting and casting. That tells you a lot about filmmaking: 15 months for preparation, scripting, casting, etc, and only 38 or 45 days (9 weeks) for shooting. Thus, you can see how a huge proportion of every film is *really* made in preproduction, and in post-production – which would have run all the way from principal photography (the movie would be edited as soon as rushes were printed), up to the release date (some movies have been worked on right up to the very, very last minute).

It was a very short shooting schedule – the average for a romance or drama feature film is between 80 and 90 days; meanwhile, action, adventure and fantasy movies are 120-130 days.[7]

---

7 S. Follows, stephenfollows.com, 2018.

Pre-production is when a movie is really made. It's when all of the really important decisions have occurred. As Jean-Luc Godard pointed out, shooting isn't when the movie is made, because everything is already done.

The development fund covers everything a film requires before it officially begins preproduction.[8] To develop the project, budget it, research it, scout locations, shoot tests, and so on. A typical development budget for a film would include the following items:

- payment for the script (including option deals, rights, etc);
- the producer's fee;
- legal fees for the producers;
- travel and accommodation expenses for the writer and producers to attend meetings with investors (also for organizing pre-sales financing);
- admin costs and office overheads (usually not more than 15% of the budget);
- camera tests;
- location scouting;
- script editor;
- script readings with cast;
- putting together a budget and a schedule;
- producing artwork;
- expenses for research.

Pre-production for *Twilight* included a lot of drawings and paintings for storyboards, design concepts, costume ideas, etc. Oksana Nedarniaya created looks for the characters; Kathy Shorkey painted watercolours for the main roles; Marc Vena and Philip Keller did concept sketches; Keller and Trevor Goring produced the storyboards. (Thus, the look and style was created in great detail).

It's striking just how much of the first *Twilight* movie was rehearsed and planned in pre-production – beyond what many filmmakers would do. Sure, complex action scenes like the van crash in the school lot, or the treetops escapade, would require planning.[9] But Catherine Hardwicke, if the *Director's Notebook* of *Twilight* is to be believed,[10] likes to visit locations and photograph and film scenes using doubles,[11] to plan out the angles. Even simple scenes, like the simplest scene of all in drama – a two actors in conversation – would be storyboarded, or photographed at

---

8 E. Grove, 2004, 346-7.
9 But not in Hong Kong cinema – they would just go to the location and start shooting right away!
10 One wonders if Catherine Hardwicke's preference for taking a lot of time with pre-production and planning contributed towards her decision to decline to direct the second *Twilight* movie, which Summit Ent. wanted out only a year after the first *Twilight* movie.
11 In some shots stand-ins were used, played by Katie Powers and Logan Welch (such as the tree shots, whikle Helena Barrett abd Paul Darnell performed as stunt doubles).

the location using stand-ins. Hardwicke's team had a floor plan of the Swan household created, in which they worked out how to stage scenes (but this is a simple house, and most of the scenes were simple conversations – dead easy to go in, block the scene with the actors, light the set, get into costume and make-up, switch on a camera and shoot the scene). But the preparation was necessary partly because the shooting schedule was so tight, and Hardwicke probably felt that the preparation she did the better, because once shooting began, things would have to move *very* raidly.

And yet most of the first *Twilight* movie is filmed in the standard shot-reverse-shot manner, with shots consisting of singles, two-shots and over-the-shoulder shots (plus some point-of-view shots). A romance plot is mainly a series of conversations: you can film two people talking in all sorts of ways, but some approaches can be distracting, or too fussy, or too self-conscious, or too expensive. So, over-the-shoulders, one-shots and two-shots are used, as throughout the whole history of cinema.

Because they do the job.

Even movies celebrated as leftfield or experimental or *avant garde* employ the same standard shots that have been around for 120 years.

Part of the reason for such extensive planning in pre-production for *Twilight* was because principal photography would be on a short schedule of 38 (some say 45) days (discounting re-shoots and additional photography).[12] This might've been one of the reasons why Catherine Hardwicke declined to direct the sequel, *New Moon*, because the pre-production schedule was too short. (Kristen Stewart was a minor for much of the filming of *Twilight*, which meant that her hours on set had to be reduced compared to the adult actors). There were rumours that the production was asked by Summit Entertainment to reduce the budget (a common request) by $4 million or they wouldn't green-light it.

Among the first scenes to be filmed for *Twilight* were the baseball game and the ballet studio finale (partly because of the schedule of actor Cam Gigandet). Principal photography ended on May 2, 2008. Re-shoots in Tinseltown included the kissing scene, parts of the Prom (including Jacob and Victoria), the Native American flashback, the meadow scene, the high speed running gags, and more.

All four *Twilight* books were published *before* the first movie was released in November, 2008. So the *Twilight* fans knew how it was going to play out.

---

12 The Prom featuring Jacob was one of the scenes added to the schedule (it wasn't part of principal photography), and was filmed in L.A.

LOCATIONS.

Film in American and Canada, *Twilight* employed between 50 and 60 location sets; about 25 were real places adapted by the film crew. Most were in the Pacific North-West (including Oregon and Washington), some were in Canada, and some were in the Golden State. James Lin, Beth Melnick and Don Baldwin scouted locations in the Pacific North-West for two months during pre-production. There were also scouting trips with other location scouts, and for the heads of department, too. Some locations had been picked (like the vampire revelation scene), but weather prevented the locations from being used, so new ones had to be found. There was further location scouting for the re-shoots and the additional shoots. Filming was attended by many Twihards, who travelled from far and wide to watch the film crew and to meet the stars.

St Helens and Vernonia stood in for Port Angeles and Forks. Bella Swan's house was in St Helens (at 184, South 6th Street),[13] as were most of the Port Angeles locations (including the dress store, the bookstore, and the restaurant). Hoke House, Forest Park, Oregon, was the Cullen mansion[14] (it was designed by Jeff Koval from Skylab Architecture). The Cullen mansion was found by Beth Melnick; owned by a Nike executive (and dubbed 'the Nike house' by the crew), there were other houses nearby (which were hidden by the filmmakers – the Cullens live in the forest on their own).[15] Kato's Marina was the setting for the death of Waylon (Ned Bellamy), in a boat.[16] The prologue with the deer chase was also filmed in Oregon (in Silver Falls State Park), as was the mill murder (filmed at the Oregon City Mill near Portland), and the school trip (at Clackamas Community College, Oregon City).

The production didn't film much in Forks, WA. For instance, the real Forks High School wasn't used in the *Twilight* movie, but the production did recreate elements of it – such as the wooden sign ('Forks High School: Home of the Spartans'), letterman jackets, yearbooks, and newspapers.[17] Instead, Forks High School was filmed at Kalama High School, Kalama, WA (for the exteriors, including the many scenes in the parking lot), and Madison High School, Portland, Oregon (but later *Twilight* movies used the David Thompson Secondary School in Vancouver). The vampire confession scene was filmed in Okbow Park,

13 In later installments, it was filmed in Surrey, B.C.
14 Catherine Hardwicke said she added another storey to the Cullen mansion partly because she knew that in *Breaking Dawn* it would need to be a big house.
15 There are shots of Edward's car snaking along a small country lane to emphasize this (when Bella goes to meet his family for the first time).
16 The first murder occurs at Grisham Mill (the security guard); the second is at 'Kato's Marina' (Charlie's buddy Waylon).
17 The principal of Forks High School, Kevin Rupprecht, helped with material.

Portland. The diner was filmed in Forks, at the Carver Café (where Stephenie Meyer has her cameo, working at a computer, rewriting the dialogue – on-set and on-camera!).[18]

The Columbia River Gorge provided many of the impressive images of the landscape (such as the helicopter shot of the lovers in the giant tree). The production secured permission from the Historic Friends of Columbia River Gorge to film there (it's one of those locations where you can point your camera anywhere and get a great image, and one of the reasons that filmmakers visit the Pacific North-West or British Columbia). The outdoor part of the Prom was also set near Columbia Gorge (filmed in late April, towards the end of the schedule); View Point Inn near Portland was the location for the Prom's hotel. The gym in the high school just wasn't romantic enough for Catherine Hardwicke: 'no, no, no, that's not a beautiful, romantic, gorgeous location!' (CFA, 35). The baseball field was near Multnomah Falls. La Push Beach was filmed at Indian Beach in the huge Pacific Rim National Park, B.C., which stretches along the West Coast of Vancouver Island. The Blacks' home on the res was filmed in a Vancouver suburb (in Coquitlam).

Bella S.'s bedroom set was one of the weather cover sets – duplicates of the set were built in a shed in the Columbia River Gorge, so the crew could continue to work when the weather was bad (which it was sometimes). The bedroom set itself went thru several changes, to reflect the course of time and the changes in Bella's character. (Cover sets are necessary because once a movie starts production, it's an express train, and has to be doing stuff all the time. It's very expensive to keep all of those highly-paid people in one place).

The room chosen for Edward's bedroom had French windows (glass doors) which opened out onto a sheer drop (not ideal if you have toddlers!). It was perfect for Edward, and the space was used in the movie, when Edward grabs Bella and they fly out to a tree. There's no bed (it raises a laugh when Bella mentions it – that was Catherine Hardwicke's idea). The art directors filled the bedroom with music (CDs, vinyl, cassettes, 8-tracks, 78s, radios, etc), lots of books and journals, giving Edward a back-story of scholarly research (indeed, with all that music and all those CDs, it might be a room that the young Stephenie Meyer would enjoy).

Some of *Twilight* was filmed in California – in Los Angeles, for instance: there were extra shoots at Griffith Park, where numerous movies have filmed, such as *The Birth of a Nation* (at the golf course), for

---

18 Meyer visited the production 3 times during shooting.

instance (for the meadow scene), and also the scene added to the schedule where Jake pays an unexpected visit to Bella at the school Prom (this was filmed in Pasadena). The Arizona scenes were staged in Santa Clarita[19] and Valencia, California, with houses and streets dressed with cacti and palm trees.

When it came to shooting what should've been a day of surfing and a picnic round a campfire on the beach, the weather was atrocious, nixing the picnic (the crew found out that the States of Washington and Oregon are not California!). The scene filmed in the car lot, amongst the surfers' vans, isn't not quite the same thing. But there are images of surfers in the water, in the background, and some of the secondary charas in wetsuits. Plus some extras (Krystopher Hyatt and Solomon Trimble) were included as Jacob's buddies among the Native Americans. 'Portland is too cold. For anyone. But especially for Arizonans', Stephenie Meyer noted after visiting the film set.

(The beach scene was the worst day of filming in *Twilight* (a Tuesday late in the schedule), with the crew complaining of the tough conditions (rain and more rain, and wind, and cold). What was supposed to be a fun day at the beach[20] in Oregon became a struggle to film anything at all. (Catherine Hardwicke recalled that someone at Summit Entertainment had told her they were amazed she didn't cancel the day, and Hardwicke didn't know she had a choice).)

The kissing scene, on Bella Swan's bed, was re-shot in August, 2008 (in Pasadena, CA, in an Elk's Lodge), because it was a key scene that hadn't been captured fully during principal photography. Was the scene made more erotic in the re-shoot? Or less? (Hardwicke said the kiss could've been staged better, and they weren't able to film Edward's stunt, too).

As with all film franchises, plenty of elements changed from movie to movie in the *Twilight Saga*: even tho' the principal actors stayed pretty much the same (happily – the casting – by Trisha Wood and Deborah Aquila – was strong), the hair and the wigs, the cinematography and the colours, the interiors and exteriors of sets, the costumes, were all shifted about (heads of dept and other crew, too). Filming began on film one in Portland, Oregon, Washington, Vancouver and California, moved to Vancouver Film Studios for films two and three (plus they also filmed in many of the previous locations), but had shifted to Louisiana for the final two flicks (because of... you can guess why),[21] as well as

---

19 22301, Cataro Drive.
20 Equipment had to be carried down to the beach, and it wasn't possible to use the usual geear.
21 I'm sure many viewers had no idea that much of *Breaking Dawn* was filmed in Louisiana and not Washington state or Oregon. Didn't matter, did it? No.

Vancouver.

❧

On many DVD commentaries and in many interviews, actors in the *Twilight Saga*, and in many other movies, go on and on about the cold. Filming in the Pacific North-West in March was certainly a challenge, weather-wise. However, as anybody knows who's been involved in filmmaking, it is often very, very cold wherever you shoot. About the coldest I've ever been is on film shoots (especially if you wear tattered jeans with holes in them that you think look cool (as I have done) but then the wind rips thru them! Look at what Stephenie Meyer is wearing on the set in one of *Twilight* documentaries – lots of layers).

Filming is cold too because it involves *a lot* of waiting around. Fans and audiences who haven't been on film sets would be stunned at just how much waiting around there is. And if there's a big scene to do like a car blowing up, or a complicated crane or tracking shot, you can bet you'll be hanging around all day while it's set up and rehearsed.

On the *Twilight* shoots, tho', there was an added challenge – for Team Jacob, the guys had to appear topless (and shoeless/ sockless!), and in shorts, in freezing cold, and often in rain, too. In the scene where Bella and Jacob have an intense and lengthy conversation in the rain (in *New Moon*), you can see the actors shivering as the rain towers drench them (no, that water was not warmed up!). In those scenes, the actors want to yell at the director, 'you come here and do this, you bastard! And look good doing it!' (In movies with a lot of physical work, there are many times when the actors want to say that! Because the director, producers and assorted crew/ visitors/ assistants are under a tent (in 'video village'), dressed in warm, padded jackets ('biohazard suits', as Bella calls her coat in the *Twilight* novel), sipping hot coffee, crowded round the monitor, and chatting about what they're going to have for dinner that evening).

THE COSTUMES, HAIR AND MAKE-UP.

Kristen Stewart was given, rightly, a 'no make-up' look (by Jeanne Van Phue) for the role of Bella Swan (except of course it takes quite a bit of make-up, sometimes, to achieve that 'no make-up' look). Bella's not a girl for false eyelashes, eyeliner, blusher, lipstick, hair spray, curlers, manicures, etc. She only really Goths up in the final. outing, *Breaking Dawn 2*, when she becomes a vampire. But with the hair, the contact lenses,[22] and the make-up, Stewart's Bella is not quite the frumpy, ordinary schoolgirl of the *Twilight* novels.

---

22 Digital grading enhanced the special make-up and contact lenses of the vampires (Kristen Stewart was also fitted with contacts to make her green peepers brown).

Kristen Stewart hated wearing the contact lenses and the hair extensions. Stewart was given straight, brown, just-over-shoulder-length hair (as in the book; hair was by Mary Anne Valdes). Robert Pattinson was tried out with long hair additions, but Pattinson disliked them. Hair is often one of the chief areas of debate between filmmakers and actors, along with make-up and costume. If an actor isn't happy with other areas of the production (the script, how they're being directed, etc), their dissatisfaction is sometimes expressed in relation to their hair, make-up or costume.

Similarly with the costumes for Bella Swan (by Wendy Chuck): in the *Twilight* books, Bells likes to wear well-worn sweat pants and old, favourite Tee shirts (hell, don't we all?!). She is not a keen clothes shopped like Alice. In the *Twilight* movies, her clothing is not glam or showy, but it is certainly not formless and loose and non-descript (and it's definitely not old sweat pants and frayed shirts). Most of the costumes that Kristen Stewart wears are tailored or close-fitting, emphasizing her form. Most of the top that Stewart wears are tight. Pale greys, pale blues, and occasionally mid-greens are used (her costumes consciously complement Edward's wardrobe, which also leans towards greys, blues and blacks).

By contrast, you can see from any photo or screen shot that the vampires in the *Twilight Saga* have complicated make-up jobs (and their wardrobe is similarly highly stylized). As with the famous monster movies of yore, such as *Frankenstein* and *The Wolf Man*, it's likely that the look of the vampires in *Twilight* went thru many variations (including sketches and make-up tests – five artists produced concept art and storyboards) before the final look was settled upon (again, that would be part of the pre-production process, before the cameras rolled). And several people would have an opinion about the characters' look, as well as the director.

The trick with the Cullen clan was to make them appear charismatic and other-worldly enough to convince (and appeal) as vampires, but not to go too far overboard, because they have to be part of the real world (and not a glamorous city, but a backwater town in rural America). These are vampires who go to high school or work in hospitals.

They are also *beautiful* vampires – they are fashion plate vampires, vampires that would be picked for the vampire equivalents of the cover of *Vogue* or *GQ* magazines. The make-up was sophisticated and took a long time to apply – it wasn't simply a case of slapping on some white make-up, eyeliner and lipstick, and shoving in some contact lenses! Similarly, the hair is teased, curled and carefully primped to look exactly right (and there are many wigs, too). Also, the vamps aren't pure white, like Japanese *Kabuki* actors (pure white often doesn't work photographically in movies, and sometimes to have something come across as white it's painted a different colour).[23] Instead, as Norma Hill-Patton explained, they are pale.

The *Twilight* movie plays the North American Nomad vampires differently from the 2005 book: it appears that Laurent, not James, is the leader of the coven (Laurent does the introductions and most of the talking at the baseball game; he is also seen walking at the front of the group). The costumes are very different from backpacking outfits the Nomads wear (to blend in with the other outdoorsy folk in the mountains). Catherine Hardwicke wanted something 'rock 'n' roll'[24] for the Nomad bloodsuckers (very much like the kind of fashions you can see any day of the week in Venice Beach, a favourite spot for a fashionista like Hardwicke):[25] fitted jackets[26] and jeans for James, with dirty, blond hair (a wig) pulled tight into a ponytail (and Cam Gigandet as James started the trend in the *Twilight Saga* for going topless); long dreads, turn-of-the-century pants, a vest (waistcoat) and a silk cravat (but no shirt), and a flamboyant, pink-orange, 1970s jacket for Laurent (the Jimi Hendrix vampire look); a green Tee shirt,[27] long, ginger-blonde hair, tight, black pants (Rachelle Lefevre is wearing the director's own 'rock star' pants by Henry Durante), and a wild, white, sheepskin cape[28] for Victoria (you can bet that fur isn't fake! – for the character, that is!). The Nomad vampires wear clothes/ trinkets stolen from their victims.

Catherine Hardwicke has drawn on Venice Beach culture in her movies (as well as shopping for costumes for *Twilight Saga* there); so when she discovered that people surfed at La Push beach, she and Melissa Rosenberg added the references to surfing (a little bit of sunny, California culture in rainy Washington State).

It's not a director's job to go shopping for clothes for the actors! But Catherine Hardwicke is clearly fanatical about clothes – she had some of the characters wear her own clothes (including Bella and Victoria), drew sketches for the characters, and brought in clothes to use as models for the wardrobe dept (such as James's jacket).

---

23 Such as beige. The walls of the outdoor set at Pinewood Studios for *The Devils* (1971) were painted beige so they would photograph as white.
24 You can see from *Director's Notebook* that Hardwicke enjoyed dressing the Nomad vampires.
25 The Nomad vampires might stand out in the sleepy, rainy Pacific North-West, but not on the Venice Boardwalk!
26 James takes Waylon's jacket as a trophy.
27 It was worn by Waylon, and said, 'Kiss me, I'm Irish'.
28 Catherine Hardwicke had the idea that Victoria might wear a boa.

VISUAL EFFECTS.

Catalyst Media (based in L.A.), P.I.C., Industrial Light and Magic and C.I.S. Vancouver provided the visual effects for the first *Twilight* movie.

Part of the pre-production of *Twilight* involved the testing of practical rigs and visual effects devices to portray the heightened abilities of the vampire characters (in the baseball game, for instance). The vfx crew (headed up by vfx supervisor Richard Kidd), the stunt team (led by Andy Cheng), and the special effects crew (led by Andy Weder)[29] went to a forest near L.A. in December, 2007, to run a bunch of tests.

The filmmakers were keen to produce many of the effects practically, if possible (i.e., in front of the camera), rather than relying on green/ blue screens and digital animation. There *is* plenty of post-production visual effects work in *Twilight,* but much of it wouldn't be noticed by audiences: it comprises sky replacements (typically adding moody skies), added rain, added foliage, the removal of wires, rigs and harnesses, etc. (However, with the second *Twilight* movie and the other sequels, digital animation was required to create the werewolves and digital doubles for stunts, among other effects. But aspects of the wolves were practical, such as puppeteering the sets).

Director Catherine Hardwicke wanted to limit the amount of digital effects: 'if what you're seeing is real, it's going to feel real' (CFA, 26). Hardwicke preferred to use real locations, not green screens. Even so, quite a lot of *Twilight* was filmed in a studio (the bedroom scenes, including the re-shoot of the bedroom kissing scene, for instance, and the ballet school fight).

The *Twilight* movie was storyboarded throughout (by Phil Keller and Trevor Goring). The visual effects teams created animatics (animated storyboards, often filmed on video with a camcorder) of complex sequences like the baseball game. Among the challenges from an effects point-of-view were vampire speed and vampire athletics, the baseball game, and Edward sparkling like a diamond in the sunlight.

Vfx supervisor Richard Kidd said the glittering skin was the trickiest effect in *Twilight* to pull off ('a very difficult effect'). It's tricky partly because it's on the face, and it's on your lead actor, and it's in daylight (i.e., there's nowhere to hide the trickery). Industrial Light and Magic eventually did it (it's one of those rather abstract effects that seems easy to visualize in prose, but much harder to achieve in reality. It looked like

---

29 Andy Weder oversaw some of the practical effects (such as vampire speed). His previous movie was *Pirates of the Caribbean 3.*

Twilight's version of a blinged-up vampire).[30]

Bill George at Industrial Light and Magic developed the effect of the sparkling skin for Edward: it went thru a number of iterations and tests, being a rather vague concept (and also because visual effects is a trial and error process. Typically, a visual effects house will receive a commission, come up with ideas, send them to the production, who might suggest changes. Sometimes shots go back and forth several times until everyone is happy).[31] There were several visits to Industrial Light and Magic for the filmmakers.

THE BOOK VS. THE MOVIE.

The usual view of film adaptations is that 'the movie wasn't as good as the book', that the book is 'sacred', untouchable, perfect, that 'the filmmakers messed up the book', that 'they cast it wrongly', or that 'they missed out my favourite bits!'

Harry Potter, The Lord of the Rings and *His Dark Materials* – these are fantasy books that fans and readers adore, and they loathe it when filmmakers come along and change everything. It's the same with books for teens (such as *Percy Jackson* or *Lemony Snicket* or *The Hunger Games*), or romance classics such as *Jane Eyre, Emma* and *Wuthering Heights*.

With the *Twilight* series, the books were much newer, and hadn't gained the status of 'classics'. And, despite the controversy of some of the choices the filmmakers made, the *Twilight* film adaptation of 2008 was surprisingly close to the book (a 'faithful' adaptation is impossible for many reasons. Producer Greg Mooradian reminded viewers that the movie would be 'a separate piece of art', but it would try to be faithful to the novel). And of course Stephenie Meyer was available for advice and the like (and later on she has a producer credit on the movies). As Mooradian put it, 'She really is the franchise' (CFA, 129).

The 2008 *Twilight* movie captured Bella and Edward and their romance, first and foremost, pretty accurately from the 2005 book. The casting (by Trisha Wood and Deborah Aquila) was strong throughout. The material that the script added was in the style and manner of the novel (i.e., nothing was tacked on that didn't fit the world of the novel). And the film was even staged in areas very close to the settings for the 2005 novel (unlike many movie adaptations).

Time for a confession:

I prefer the *Twilight* movie to the *Twilight* novel.

30 It might look better on Ashley Greene.
31 Some filmmakers like Woody Allen find working with vfx frustrating and slow.

Heresy! Burn that heathen!

No: I think the *Twilight* movie is a better story better told.

With Kristen Stewart as Isabella Marie Swan, you can accept the heroine as a character and as a narrator much more easily than in the *Twilight* novel, where she comes across as a whiny, self-absorbed, snooty kid. In the book, Bella's a white, middle-class girl with self-centredness as her primary attribute (and job). She is useless at sports, bookish, and, tho' the novel doesn't say so, I imagine she has bad skin, bad hair (which she doesn't wash very often), and nobody gives her a second glance (except the school's unattainable hottie, Edward Cullen!).

Ah, but in the *Twilight* movie, Bella is Kristen Stewart, a movie-star-in-the-making, far more attractive and better-dressed (she has costume designers, make-up artists and hair stylists fussing around her!) than the Bella of the novel (who is much plainer), and, thankfully, and crucially, we are not in her head the whole time.

(Another reason why the *Twilight* movies are to be preferred over the *Twilight* books (sacrilege! blasphemy!) is because the books explain every darn thing, and the movies haven't got time to do that. There are many instances in film history where the movie version is superior to the book. Take a film that's regarded by many critics as the greatest ever made, *The Godfather* (1972), which also influenced the portrayal of the Volturi. The *Godfather* book, as author Mario Puzo admitted, is unsatisfactory, but the movie is gold dust).

STYLE.

The first *Twilight* movie is striking in its uses of several forms of cinematic narration. It isn't a straightforward drama at all. First, there are some flashbacks, illustrating the vampires vs. werewolves sub-plot, and how Carlisle vampirzed Edward. Second, there are editing patterns which elide the dramatic flow in a self-conscious manner (often employed to get the point of a scene across in a shorter time). Third, there are multiple montages, some of which are elegant (such as the internet montage about the history of vampirism),[32] and some are highly stylized (such as Bella's near-death experience in the finale). Fourth, the flow of time is shifted around: we hear James's use of the childhood home video over shots of Bella exiting the hotel. Fifth, there is plenty of voiceover (a common cinematic form in adaptations of novels, to preserve the authorial voice in the text).

(There's a brief flashback to the Native American/ wolf/ vampire

---

32 The movie features some rapid montage sequences to add further exposition – such as the internet montage when Bella Swan is researching the 'cold ones'.

legends in *Twilight,* featuring the Quileutes in wolf masks encountering four of the Cullen coven looking sheepish as they're caught feeding on a wild animal they've just killed. Set in – where else? – yet another forest, the scene included real wolves, and was filmed in August, 2008, during the re-shoots. The flashback (narrated by Jacob Black) shows the Cullen clan clad in 1930s clothing. Here we see the political Treaty being agreed between Carlisle and the Quileute Tribal Chief. The flashbacks are depicted in the familiar sepia-and-white tones of old photographs, which suits the era (1918 for the Carlisle flashback and maybe the 1930s for the Quileute Tribe flashback).)

▶

Among the many cinematic devices employed in the first *Twilight* movie are: slow motion (introduced early on, in the first day at school sequence, and for the first glimpses of the Cullen coven). Handheld camera – this is one of Catherine Hardwicke's signature devices (it's used throughout her earlier *Thirteen,* for instance). It gives the footage a jerky, mobile dynamism (and can also speed up shooting). The *Twilight* movie also employs the usual range of cinematic devices, from dollies, cranes, Steadicam, from hard, unfiltered light to soft, diffuse, ambient light. A really obvious factor is daylight (with cloud cover): this is a vampire love story which is filmed mainly in daytime (without the usual Gotharama, the deep shadows, the German Expressionist graphical qualities, and without extensive night shoots. One reason is simple: Kristen Stewart was a minor for most of principal photography (except the last 2 1/2 weeks), which meant that night shoots were out.[33] But even scenes that don't feature Bella, like the two murder scenes featuring the American Nomad vampires, were filmed in daylight, when in almost any other movie, they'd be night scenes).

DP Elliot Davis had lights placed all around the Cullen mansion to simulate the soft, ambient light the vampires preferred: silks were hung outside windows, in front of the lights, to soften the light, using cherry pickers (CFA, 100).

More significant, however, than all of the cinematic approaches in the camerawork,[34] is the use of subjective viewpoint: the *Twilight* movie takes up Bella's point-of-view throughout (often with the camera literally occupying the space where Bella would be, so we are literally sees events

---

[33] Filming with minors limits the amount of time they can spend on set; they also have to be educated during the shoot.

[34] It's a pity that some stretches of the *Twilight Saga* movies are directed in such a pedestrian manner. This material calls for an operatic, heightened approach at times – especially when you have Italian ingredients such as the Volturi and Volterra, and vampires, and werewolves, etc.

from her viewpoint).[35] A good example is in the car lot, when poor Mike Newton is trying to ask Bella to the school Prom, and there's a Bella subjective shot, where Newton's so uninteresting to her he's literally out-of-focus, and Edward is standing some way behind him, in focus (and smiling smugly. We don't know at this point that Edward has exceptional hearing, but he can guess from way off what Newton is up to).

As Stephenie Meyer noted in the introduction to *The Short Second Life of Bree Tanner*, the first person narration took precedence in *Twilight,* so that

> anything that Bella couldn't see or hear or feel or taste or touch was irrelevant. That story was her experience only. (2010)

The *Twilight* movies opted to stay with Bella throughout, but not to stick to a first person narrative approach. So the viewpoint steps away from Bella (most obviously to offer perspectives on what the villains're up to. The sequels stepped away even more often). And, even though the movie retains the subjective viewpoint for Bella, it's actually Big E. who's driving many scenes, making decisions, and being the Alpha Male Vampire.

THE PROLOGUE.

The prologue of the *Twilight* movie sort of follows the Stephenie Meyer novel, with the evocation of a deer[36] in the forest that's being hunted (the editing pattern adds jittery cuts to the loose camerawork, delivering the familiar form of storytelling of the horror film genre).[37] In the *Twilight* novel, the prologue refers to the hunter vampire James Witherdale, who provides the tacked-on finale (the movie opens with some voiceover adapted from the novel's prologue). However, the hunter might also refer to Bella Swan (yes Bellsie, not Edward!).[38] Because it's Bella who goes a-hunting for boys, and finds one in the form of Edward Cullen. Bella is the hunter in *Twilight*, she is the heroine, the chief protagonist. And altho' she is cast in the role of the hunted in the finale, we are never in doubt over her safety at all (there is no possibility whatsoever that Bella will be sacrificed).

The theme of hunting also refers, of course, to the 'vegetarian'

---

35 So there's a 'Team Jacob' and a 'Team Edward' in *Twilight*, thanks to the clever publicity department. But is there a 'Team Bella'? Yes there is – the whole of the *Twilight Saga* is 'Team Bella'.
36 Two of the most famous movies featuring deer hunts are *Bambi* (1942) and *The Deer Hunter* (1979).
37 When Edward grabs the deer, that was done with visual effects.
38 If it's Edward in the prologue, it should be a mountain lion, Edward's preference for blood (in the novel), not a deer.

vampires, who drink animal blood. And to the more threatening aspects of hunting within the context of romantic stories – the hunter and the hunted. And the theme of hunting also applies to other aspects of the *Twilight Saga*, such as later scenes of vampires hunting their prey, or Bella finally getting to be a vampire, and going out hunting for blood for herself.

ACT ONE.

The storytelling in the first act of the *Twilight* movie is very rapid – after the prologue, the 2008 film quickly introduces Bella Swan (in the desert suburbs), her Mom, her step-dad, the flight from Arizona to the Pacific North-West (using ærial photography, blurring from the desert and canyons to the snowy mountains), the drive home with her Pa, her first night in her new home (and old bedroom), and before only a few minutes have passed, the story really starts with Bella's first day at school (shifted to March from January of the novel).[39]

At this point, when the story of *Twilight* really begins, the voiceover falls away, and the storytelling slows to the regular pace of movies (as if to literally slow the narrative pace down, there is a slo mo shot of Bella, just before she meets the over-eager Eric, in the school corridor.[40] Slow motion[41] will of course be a recurring motif in the *Twilight Saga* – there is a huge amount of slo mo in the *Twilight Saga*, where it's used for all the usual reasons – to highlight a particular moment, to evoke unreality or subjectivity, to suggest high speed, etc).[42]

When the 2008 *Twilight* movie introduces Bella Swan in the first minutes, it's in a familiar cinematic manner: the camera trucks into a close-up as Bella lifts her head. She is depicted in the Arizonan desert, by day, on her own, digging up a little cactus. This part of *Twilight* is edited in a montage style, with Bella providing the voiceover[43] which knits the images together (the narration delivers some exposition). Following this, we are introduced rapidly to her Mom Renée, her step-dad Phil, and her departure from sunny Phoenix on a jet plane.

The first time you meet a character in a movie (or any story) is absolutely crucial: Darth Vader strides onto a spaceship in the midst of a battle in *Star Wars*... Don Corleone listens calmly and patiently like a

39 Perhaps because the movie was filmed from March (2008) onwards.
40 Why slo mo here? To emphasize that we are in Bella's mindscreen? To highlight her subjectivity, or anxiety, on her first day at this new school?
41 But filming in dark forests meant that the preferred 96 frames per second couldn't be used, so 48 f.p.s. was (M. Vaz, 2009, 97).
42 As *Vampires Suck* puts it, slo-mo is part of 'Hardwicke 101'.
43 But we hear Bella speaking in voiceover in the prologue before we meet her, so at that point,w Edward don't know who she is, tho' the tone of voice and the language tells us she's isn't a clichéd, omniscient movie narrator.

King while a guest attending the wedding of his daughter pleads for assistance in *The Godfather*...

So Bella Swan might be introduced chatting to her Mom in the kitchen, or hanging out with her friends in a shopping mall in Phoenix, and any number of ways. But no, she's on her own (her pals in Phoenix are simply erased completely from the movie), and doing something cute – taking a plant with her to remind her of her homeland. (Notice that it is daytime, and a neutral setting, not the usual stormy night of vampire cinema),

Twilight sticks closely to a first person point-of-view for much of the duration, staying with Bella Swan, but it also cuts away from Bella many times. One of the first scenes occurs in the opening act, when the nasty Nomad vampires're introduced chasing down a hapless victim in a generic industrial zone (the victim (a security guard played by Bryce Flint-Sommerville) is barely glimpsed, and the vamps are only seen in medium long shot). We get our first good look at the vampires in the second murder scene, at the marina.

Much of the first act of *Twilight* includes scenes without music, even though the soundtrack contains a large number of songs, plus under-score from Carter Burwell and company. So there are songs, and under-score, but it's refreshing to find a movie that doesn't feel pressured to add under-score every darn moment, so that the flickerings of romance between Bella and Edward occur with a focus on the dialogue.

THE TWO KEY ROMANTIC SCENES.

There are two crucial scenes in the *Twilight* movie, as far as the central romance plot is concerned: the first scene is the biology lab scene, the moment when the erotic fascination really digs its claws into the two lovers (emphasized by the camera travelling over the faces of the actors in extreme close-up). This is perhaps the most important scene in the whole *Twilight* franchise.

The biology class scene is part of a sequence involving several scenes in the biology lab: in the first, Bella Swan is led[44] by the teacher Mr Molina (José Zúñiga) to the table where Edward sits. This is the moment where Edward looks as if he's going to vomit, clutching his hands to his maw, when he seems to catch Bella's scent blown over by a fan. Altho' the scene is played straight (and focusses on Bella's alarmed reaction – no one's ever held their nose when they've met her before!), it is ridiculous (so there's no need for a Mel Brooks or Zucker-Abrahams-Zucker spoof

---

44 She's guided to the classroom by Mike Newton.

for this moment!).

The aftermath of this scene has both Edward Cullen and Bella Swan visiting the school office to have their class schedule changed. Yes, this is Romantic Novel Writing 101 – have your protagonists deeply fascinated by each other, yet also winding each other up. As the fascination shifts towards romance (he warns her off repeatedly, she tries to get past his cool, prickly exterior), there are further biology class scenes. Why? Because this is where Bella gets to sit at the same table as Edward – so they can be intimately close legitimately, without, say, her going over to the Cullen table in the cafeteria (way too scary!).

But Edward Cullen is absent (the reason is not explained for some time), and we stay with Bella turning up to find Edward gone A.W.O.L. Voiceover knits together some of these montages, until we reach the all-important romantic scene in the *Twilight Saga*, the first flourishing of romantic/ erotic feelings (on both sides). The emotional change in Edward is signalled by him saying (awkwardly) 'Hello', swiftly followed by some introductions. This is the first polite thing that Edward has said to Bella.

And from here (in the first act of *Twilight)*, it's a done deal, the love story is sewn up tight and neat – right up to the end of the second *Breaking Dawn* movie (no matter what happens, no matter that Bella 'dies' in the childbirth, that she becomes a vampire, no matter there's a giant battle (that never happened!), and no matter what poor Jacob Black tries!).

Stuffed animals are arranged around the soon-to-be lovers in the biology class, including a white owl behind Edward – this is Edward as angelic, perhaps, or Edward as wise and owl-like, or Edward as nocturnal, or Edward as predator, with Bella as a teeny mouse, his prey. (I always thought that owls only ate small creatures such as mice, but I've met animal trainers recently who've told me, oh no, owls are predators that will attack dogs and even deer! It's all about those super-sharp claws, which they dig into their prey).

The 2008 *Twilight* movie 'opened out' the novel a little, such as adding a biology trip to a horticultural centre big on recycling. Not necessary,[45] but it does offer a change of scene for yet another conversation between the nearly-lovers.[46]

❯

The second key romantic scene in *Twilight* is the mountain reveal

---

45 Some fans have complained, why bother?
46 A romance plot is often essentially a series of conversations – talk – then kissing – then more talk – which could take place anywhere.

sequence (it's actually multiple scenes running together – it's pages after page of dialogue and interaction): it begins at the high school, as Edward follows Bella up into the forest, while music ('The Skin of a Killer' by Carter Burwell) plays. There is a curious atmosphere to this part of the sequence, which is slightly ominous (enhanced by the use of slight slo-mo, and how Edward follows Bella without a word).

When Bella Swan tells Edward Cullen she knows what he is, it is staged with her Bella having her back to him, and Edward glaring at her and rather aggressively demanding that she says the fearsome word, *vampire.* The blocking allows us to see both actors in the same shot, but not facing each other (thus, it's less distracting that using the usual shot-counter-shot editing pattern).[47] The camera glides around the pair with skewed, unusual moves (using a Technocrane), as well as circling them in the over-used Steadicam style. (The sequence was filmed in several locations, including Oxbow Park, Portland, and a quarry).

The sequence continues with the first proper reveal of vampire speed (which seems rather ridiculous), as Edward Cullen hurtles Bella Swan on his back up into the misty mountains, to a spot above the cloudbank filled with glacial boulders (the *Twilight* movie doesn't really capture Bella's subjective experience of being carried at high speed by her vampire lover in the book. Other filmmakers might've emphasized Bella's feelings as she rushes through the forest).

The most challenging visual effect on the *Twilight* show occurs next, Edward's diamond-like skin glittering in the sunlight. Edward feels himself ugly and a killer, but Bella thinks he looks beautiful, and it's *Bella's reaction* that really counts here (thus, altho' Edward is leading most of whole mountain sequence dramatically, as he shows her and tells her what vampires really are, which is really the heart of the *Twilight Saga*, it's always Bella's response to what he's saying and doing that the movie wants us to consider).

The following scene in t continues the mountain reveal sequence with a *lot* of discussion, interspersed with demonstrations of Edward's abilities (high speed, brute strength), and his penchant for clambering in trees like a monkey. The subtext underlined throughout the sequence is *fear* – fear and desire, you might say (fear as the flipside of desire). It's Beauty and the Beast, it's Little Red Riding Hood and the Wolf, it's the Princess and the Monster.

We've been here *many* times, but the *Twilight* movie somehow gets away with it by (1) staging it in a slightly quirky manner, by (2) using

---

47 It's a popular form of staging in Japanese animation.

the hook or gimmick of vampirism, (3) by placing the romance within a very familiar high school setting, and by (4) using the viewpoint of an awkward,[48] plain, teenage girl (with the additional layer that the boy is also feeling clumsy, vulnerable and tongue-tied).

Fear and desire – Edward Cullen emphasizes fear all the way thru the mountain reveal sequence, insisting that Bella Swan should really be afraid of him, that he could kill her at any moment (what the hell kind of romantic courtship is this?! A boy who claims he might kill the girl at any moment!). The anger bubbling away underneath is clear to see in Robert Pattinson's performance, as Edward reveals himself to be a very troubled soul, a lost soul, really, who's furious that the first time he's found someone he really cares for, she happens to be a human.

Bella Swan is already won over – we can see that. Edward Cullen's protestations are mere white noise for her. There's a vital exchange of dialogue here, when Edward confesses that he has killed people, and Bella's response speaks volumes: she says, *it doesn't matter*. Right there, Bella says everything – that, no matter what Edward does now or has done, *she doesn't care*, because she's already totally in love with him (see below). For feminists and detractors of the *Twilight* franchise, Bella's statement condemns her to accept any abuse from her beloved, because she's just said YES to loving a serial killer!

The romance is accomplished in full halfway through *Twilight*: the lovers are seen in a series of clinches and finally lying beside each other in a paradisal realm of flowers. The First Kiss hasn't been seen yet, but that doesn't matter, because both parties have sworn eternal love to each other.

The mountain reveal sequence in t closes with the recreation of the dream that Stephenie Meyer had in June, 2003, which launched the *Twilight Saga* franchise: the meadow dream of a girl and a vampire. The lead-in to the meadow scene is curious and teasing – the camera shoots Bella Swan and Edward Cullen in a two-shot in the boulders and trees; they are very close together, on either side of the widescreen image. This is where the First Kiss would occur (perhaps a kiss was filmed at the time). But then, when it seems as if they are going to kiss, as we'd expect, the camera tilts upwards, into the trees, panning thru them, as if representing their sudden inrush of romantic ecstasy. But also, the movie's saying, 'oh, no, no, ladies and gentlemen, you don't get to see the Big Kiss just yet!'

So the all-important, all-conquering Kiss of Lerrrve is being saved

---

48 Kristen Stewart reacted against being described as 'awkward'. It was the wrong word for her.

for the end of the *Twilight* movie (that is, in the traditional place for the romantic genre), because instead of cutting back to the lovers embracing and smooching, the film shifts to the meadow dream (but there is a 'Let's Trying Kissing' scene in Bella's bedroom, which Edward cuts short abruptly). Without dialogue (but with slushy music, of course), the lovers're depicted lying on the grass, in amongst the mist and the flowers, with Edward's skin glistening, when the sun breaks thru the clouds (it might be a post-coital image – if this were a D.H. Lawrence movie, say). They stare at each other – if this were a Disney cartoon, little, pink hearts would be popping up out of them.

This is essentially Paradise. It's Eden.

The Twilight Saga ends here, really, halfway thru the first novel and the first movie, with the lovers in the meadow, smiling at each other in the sunshine and the mist. Everything that follows is complication and incident, some action and some spectacle, but nothing fundamental changes in the love that Edward Cullen and Bella Swan share in this moment (and of course, the *Twilight Saga* in film form and print form ends back here, too, in the meadow, after three more books and four more films).

Indeed, to underline what we have already seen and know, Bella in voiceover (in her bedroom, contemplating the events) asserts three things::

(1) that Edward Cullen is a vampire;

(2) that Edward thirsts for her blood; and

(3) that she is utterly and unconditionally (unconditionally is a key term in *Twilight)* in love with him.

Watching the first *Twilight* movie being filmed, Stephenie Meyer recalled on her website:

> While watching the playback from a very intense scene with Bella and Edward, the girl next to me literally slid right out of her chair – I think her bones melted. She also may have stopped breathing for a few seconds, too. I know I did.
>
> ❯

Bella Swan is besotted: she is swooningly, gaspingly, quiveringly in lerrrve. So in love, so over the moon, so in unstoppable ecstasy, it doesn't matter to her that her man is a mass murderer! In the mountain scene, Big E. tries to warn Bella off loving him one last time: he's killed people, he tells her. She replies, 'it doesn't matter'.

It doesn't matter?!

What? It *doesn't matter* that Edward has killed people?! Who is this girl? All of a sudden she's Catherine the Great or Lucrezia Borgia!

And in the secret, vampire-only version of the movie, Edward continues: I've conducted disgusting scientific experiments on young children, and the victims all died. And Bella replies, *it doesn't matter.*

And Edward tells her: I visited Germany in 1942 and helped shove people into the gas ovens – the old, the young, male, female, whoever. And Bella replies, *it doesn't matter.*

Twilight (2008), on set.

Twilight (2008), on set.

LOOKING.

Many of the visual compositions in the *Twilight* movie occur in depth – often, as the romance blossoms, characters are watching the lovers from a distance (as in the school canteen, when Bella Swan and Edward Cullen are picking food at the counter, and Bella's chums are watching from their table).[1] It's almost like a scene from a stage version of *Grease*, with the stars down-stage, and the secondary characters (the chorus) stage right, looking on. The filmmakers also make sure that secondary charas like Alice and Jasper are prominent in the background (or Tyler, or Eric, or Angela).

Why Alice and Jasper? Partly because they offer a commentary on the blossoming Bella-Edward romance, as do Mike Newton and Jessica (when we first see Alice and Jasper in the movie, in a medium close-up, walking into the canteen, they are depicted as an item – and Alice is smiling possessively. Thereafter, Jasper and Alice are always seen together).

Alice and Jasper are also a model for Bella Swan of what it would be like to be a vampire couple (as with Emmett and Rosalie, or Esme and Carlisle). And Ashley Greene would've made a fascinating alternative to Bella, had she got the role.

Thus, the romance between Bella Swan and Edward Cullen occurs in a public place – in the midst of the Forks school, with people all around them, watching it develop (and no doubt gossiping about them). So *Twilight* is just like every other high school romance you've ever seen: surely part of its enormous success is precisely because it is so deter-minedly, unashamedly routine + familiar + clichéd. *Twilight* delivers a safe, comfortable form of romance (ignore the vampire/ thriller elements for the moment, and the elements of abuse and coercion – if you can!), and Edward is simply the bad boy that everybody shuns but secretly desires, the kid from the wrong side of the tracks, the biker, the weirdo, the loner, the outsider (traits that Jacob Black also shares – and in the movies, it's Jake who's the biker boy dressed in black).

WOMEN LOOKING AT MEN,

One of the most intriguing aspects of *The Twilight Saga* is that it is about a young woman, yes, and told from a young woman's point-of-view, yes, but it is also about a young woman looking *at young men*. In your typical Hollywood movie scenario, we are looking at women thru men's eyes, or from men's perspective, or within a patriarchal context

---

1 Following the slo-mo entry of the teen vamps in the school canteen, the first vampires that we see in close-up in *Twilight* are two guys: Edward and Carlisle.

which sexualizes and objectifies women. Remarkably, it is the *young men* who are looked at, and who are on display in the *Twilight* series: we are aligned with Bella/ Kristen Stewart, and we are looking at Edward/ Robert Pattinson and Jake/ Taylor Lautner. Not only that, but the young men are eroticized – to the point where the cinematic mechanisms sexualize the young men: using, for instance, slow motion, a typical technique employed when men look at women. Meanwhile, Lautner plays many scenes topless.

I bought a celebrity biography called *Blood Rivals*, about Robert Pattinson and Taylor Lautner. *Blood Rivals* announces on its cover 'choose your side', 'vampire vs. werewolf': are you with 'Team Edward' or 'Team Jacob'? *Blood Rivals* has a great gimmick: it is a biography of two actors that's split into two parts, with the other part printed at the back, upside-down. So you flip the book to join 'Team Jacob' (the device was used for the tenth anniversary edition of *Twilight*).

And of course, the cover shots are both 'smouldering' photos, as Stephenie Meyer would say (Edward 'smoulders' a good deal in the *Twilight Saga*!). Both actors are pin-up gorgeous, of course, and have appeared in numerous magazines and publications aimed at young women and teenage women and depicted as 'hunks' and 'babes'.

THE INTERNET MONTAGE.

There's a cool montage where Bella Swan investigates vampirism online.[2] Taking the cue from the book she bought in Port Washington, she heads off into Google Land. In amongst the images of historical vampires (from India, Egypt, Rome, the Middle Ages), the montage also moves into evocations from the history of cinema (cinema has colonized vampirism in pop culture probably more pervasively than any other medium). For instance, there's a wonderful moment (not in the 2005 book) where Bella imagines herself as a swooning victim on a couch and Edward as Count Dracula (and it's filmed in the heightened, colourful style of a Hammer horror movie of the 1950s-1970s, where Christopher Lee (usually) played the debonair, irresistible bloodsucker).

NOSFERATU.

There're also references to movies such as *Nosferatu*, still for many *the* vampire flick above *all* others (though the 1932 *Vampyre* and the 1931 *Dracula* offer very strong competition!). As Ken Gelder notes (in *New Vampire Cinema*), 'regardless of whether a newer vampire film cites

---

2 There are some in-jokes on the websites – one of the URLs is heathcliff.com. Bella has a nice, shiny, new, Apple laptop (more product placement), not the wheezing, old computer in the books.

it or not... Murnau's film is somehow always *there* in the genre' (80).

Nosferatu, a Symphony of Horror (= Nosferatu, eine Symphonie des Grauens, 1922) is a masterpiece of cinema. It is also unique – there is literally nothing else quite like *Nosferatu.* I urge you to see it (but not on your own in an isolated farmhouse, at night). *Nosferatu* is one of F.W. Murnau's many great movies: the others inlcude *The Last Laugh* (1924) and *Sunrise* (1927). Murnau's other films include the extraordinary, one-of-a-kind *Tabu* (1931), *City Girl* (1930), *The Haunted Castle* (1921) and *Tartuffe* (1925). If you enjoyed the romance in *Twilight,* I highly recommend *Sunrise* and *City Girl*; if you like the Gothic fantasy of *Twilight, Faust* is exceptional.

F.W. Murnau directed 21 feature-length movies. Nine are lost, with only fragments surviving (of three movies). But Murnau has a very high success rate – of his surviving 12 films, 7 are masterpieces.

Nosferatu: Eine Symphonie des Grauens was produced by Albin Grau (who also edited) and Enrico Dieckmann for Prana Film (co-founded by Grau), directed by F.W. Murnau, photographed by Fritz Arno Wagner and scripted by Henrik Galeen. *Nosferatu* is dominated by Max Shreck's incredible performance as the head vampire (called Count Orlok here), in this retelling of Bram Stoker's classic 1897 text.

VAMPIRE SKILLS AND ALICE.

In the *Twihard* books the special skills of each vampire are outlined by Edward to Bella during their numerous conversations about all things vampiric (Edward is the chief exposition character in the t series, along with Carlisle. Someone has to explain all of this stuff!).

Alice's skill is to perceive the future, or *a* future ('Alice *sees* things', says Edward, but the future isn't set in stone and events change). Alice's prophetic ability is in part a dramatic cheat, as prophecy and visions and the like tend to be in ficton, and comes across as that on several occasions. The books and the films use it as they like, creating several gaps in the plotting.

Emmett's skill is brute strength. Esme is passionate love (she is the loving matriarch of the Cullen clan). Rosalie's skill is tenacity/ pigheadedness. Edward's is to hear what people are thinking (but of course he can't hear Bella's thoughts). Jasper's ability is to manipulate the emotions of people around him (usually to create a pleasant mood). And Carlisle's attribute is compassion (*Twilight,* 253/ 269). Carlisle's theory is that vampirism accentuates a skill people had in their former life.

When it came to the *Twilight Saga* adaptations, by far the most dramatic vampire attribute was Alice's: her visions alter the course of the stories many times.[3] Edward's skill was employed in the familiar manner of telepathy (which the Quileute werewolves also share). As for Emmett's brute strength – well, all of the vampires're superhumanly strong. And Jasper's psychological manipulation – potentially powerful – wasn't touched on much, and neither was Rosalie's stubbornness and perseverance (except when it was expressed in her general grouchiness). The compassion and love of the parental figures, Carlisle and Esme, are far less spectacular, tho' perhaps even more important. Meanwhile, Bella's skill, as a shield, was only explored in detail in the final *Twilight* movie of 2012 (tho' it's introduced in the climax of *Eclipse* – when Bella isn't a vampire yet).

THE BASEBALL GAME.

Ashley Greene (Alice) recalled that the baseball game was one of the first scenes that many in the cast filmed, and they weren't sure about it – or the movie. It was 'a little bit chaotic and less structured on set', Greene remarked, and some of the actors couldn't see how it would work (the terrible weather didn't help). Afterwards, Greene said, 'holy shit, it turned out fantastic and I never would've envisioned it on the days that we were shooting it'.

The baseball game was conceived as an intense, high-power sequence, filled with stunts, loud sound effects, and visual effects everywhere. Everything about the scene is over-the-top, and what's so wonderful about it is that it's not really even necessary to the plot. The scene is a bunch of people playing baseball. That's all. Happens everyday in North America and round the world. People playing sport.

Well, sure, agreed, the baseball game *does* include dramatic material: it demonstrates some of the vampires' physical skills (which we've only seen hints of before), it features Rosalie being irritated by Bella (again), and one or two other minor details. But not enough to justify the expense and spectacle lavished on the scene. (The American Nomad vampires encountering the Cullens could've taken place in many another setting.[4] And the fact that they meet in the wilderness is squandered in the end, when the expected smackdown doesn't happen. Which of course looks forward to Big Cheat Battle in *Breaking Dawn*).

But the baseball scene *is* a signature scene in the *Twilight* franchise –

---

3 Alice admits in *New Moon* that the Cullens 'rely on my sight far too much for something that works so imperfectly' (417). Well, we knew that! Alice's visions are used by Stephenie Meyer far too often (and by the movies, which could've cut back on the endless premonitions).

4 Lines came out of rehearsal – such as 'I'm the one with the wicked curve ball', given to Victoria.

after all, it is one area in which the *Twilight Saga* could differentiate itself from all other vampire flicks: it portrays vampires playing baseball! And it's the movies doing what movies very often – they put on a show, a circus act, a skit. The baseball game, in short, is *fun*.

The baseball game should've been set at night, of course. One factor for deciding not to was cost – lighting such a big area is expensive (this's a key reason why many scenes in all sorts of films that ought to be filmed at night aren't). Add to that the unpredictable weather and the higher costs of night shoots, plus the gear needed for the stunts. (Yet another reason is working with minors, who have restrictions on filming at night).

Twilight's baseball game included several stunts – the mid-air collision of Edward and Emmett, for instance; Emmett leaping up into a tree (always with the trees in *Twilight*!); and Edward's high-speed run for the ball.[5] Rosalie gets to bat, but she's struck out as she slides along the wet ground (much to her annoyance – Bella is umpire).[6] Jasper bats, and Carlisle bats (with a Babe Ruth move). Alice is the pitcher (with a typically elegant, Alicean style).

Speed ramping was employed (altering the frame rate within a shot – achieved with a Crazy Horse Rig, using two cameras mounted together and connected by a mirror which films a scene at two different frame rates – 24 f.p.s. and 144 f.p.s., for instance, for the baseball game – so that the ball would reach the batter at a regular speed, then shift to slo-mo for the hit). Some of the baseballs were digital, added to the shots (the image of the ball hurtling into the trees, a nod to *Robin Hood* (1991) was apparently suggested by Rob Friedman of Summit).[7]

As so many visual effects were added to the baseball game, a digital, 'giga-pixel' environment was created of the location (created by Eric Hanson & co.). The key to the baseball sequence was editing, cinema's most explosive and important technical effect (by a long way). DP Elliot Davis said they aimed to make the baseball game like a highlight reel on a TV sports show, with shutter speeds altered to enhance the dynamism.

THE FINALE OF *TWILIGHT*.

In the third act, *Twilight* shifted into action mode, with the romance plot now tied up. That is, Bella 'n' Edward are now a couple, they've been introduced to each other's folks (with all the expected awkwardness

---

5 Edward's high speed run was produced with a 1,000 foot-long cable, with the actor suspended beneath it in a harness. The camera tracked alongside him.
6 Plexiglas (120 feet long) was covered with shuffleboard wax to recreate the base for sliding moves (and covered with leaves to hide it).
7 Cited in C. Hardwicke, 111.

and embarrassments), and they've shared an embrace (instead of a sex scene, the 2008 movie depicted Edward dancing with Bella (a typical stand-in for lovemaking inmovies), followed by a crazy tree-to-tree climbing spree, *à la Planet of the Apes*, climaxing with the lovers standing in a tree overlooking a lake and mountains.[8]

The scene where Bella and Edward try kissing in her bedroom ends when Edward slams himself away from her on the bed, claiming it's too dangerous. (Thus, the tree-climbing and free-running scene at vampire speed stands in for the sex scene that the movie won't deliver at a 'PG-13' rating. One of Stephenie Meyer's provisos for the *Twilight* movie was that it should be rated 'PG-13').[9]

There is a *lot* of fooling around in or under trees in the *Twilight Saga*, as if these are a couple of 8 year-old kids rather than late teens – Edward in the first *Twilight* movie is forever climbing trees [10] – especially during their lengthy discussion up in the mountains. I can't think of a similar sort of movie which conducts a romantic courtship so often in (or around or on) trees! I mean, yes, the Pacific North-West is full of trees and forests, but don't tell me that teenagers spend most of their dates hanging off a stunted oak!

▶

The action finale of *Twilight* seems to come right out of nowhere, and is somewhat uncomfortably bolted onto the 2008 movie in terms of narrative and structure. Oh, sure, there was foreshadowing of the rival group of vampires, James, Laurent and Victoria (killing people in the neighbourhood for food, scenes added to the Stephenie Meyer novel),[11] but the way they stalk into the baseball game[12] and suddenly Bella's the target of a psycho super-tracker/ hunter vampire (with an acute sense of smell),[13] and she's on the run, is just nuts (as soon as the three vampires appear, the level of interest in the movie instantly sags. I know that the baseball game doesn't advance the plot at all, but I'd rather see the Cullens playing baseball (especially when Alice and Rosalie look so cute

---

8 That was invented by Catherine Hardwicke partly to illustrate the vertiginous feelings of being in love: 'I wanted a scene that was like, 'Wow, what does it feel like when you're dizzy, madly in love, and anything's possible?'

9 Rosenberg noted that her sense of humour tended to 'R rated', or older than the 'PG-13' rating the *Twilight* movies had to be.

10 The stunt doubles for Bella and Edward were Helena Barrett and Paul Darnell. They are the ones who're up in the trees overlooking the gorge, flying on wires out of the Cullen mansion onto the trees, and doing plenty of clambering around branches.

11 Tho' what vampire would want to suck the blood of the gnarly, old coots that the rival vamps slay? Why don't they go the blood of juicy, young things? (The usual vampire prey).

12 That the vampires play baseball to let off steam seems sort of bizarre, even tho' it's pure Americana.

13 On top of the usual vampire super-sensitivity.

in their baseball outfits),[14] than the rent-a-villain bad guys).

Indeed, the baseball game in *Twilight* is a big, expensive sequence, filled with showy visual effects, speed ramping, slo-mo, flashes of lightning, wild stunts, elaborate, whooshy sound effects,[15] and music by Muse ('Supermassive Black Hole')[16] – it's *Twilight*'s version of a musical or dance number in a musical movie, that's self-consciously cut like a pop promo for Music Television or a video game. And it has no significant input on the plot of *Twilight* – it's partly about the characters, and about, as Catherine Hardwicke said, the surreal sight of vampires playing baseball – when have you seen that?!

Yes, trying to find something 'new' in the vampire genre is a tall order, so vamps playing 'America's pastime' (as Edward calls it), is delightful.

Back to the face-off: it's seven vampires versus two vampires, as Edward points out (and with Emmett and Jasper, both fearsome warriors, among them!), but they all still flee! Well, I guess the action/ chase finale of *Twilight* puts our lovers in peril, and it offers some *movement* to the 2008 movie, so that the romantic relationship can play out in a bigger dramatic arena, but it was also contrived and fake. We've already seen that Edward is a formidable opponent, who can stop skidding vans slamming into his beloved, and can leap 100 yards thru trees, but you're telling me he's not going to turn around and *face* the psycho bloodsucker James? Oh, please!

(Meanwhile, there are so many other flaws in the construction of the *Twilight* movie's finale. For ex, Bella's Pa Charlie is the Chief of Police, but Bella doesn't ask for his help. We see him cleaning a shotgun on the table (right in the foreground of the shot!), so presumably he's nifty with a gun (and keeps one round the house – and no doubt he's got live rounds, too). And of course, as Police Chief, he'd have lots of contacts (in law enforcement agencies) who could help out in protecting his daughter. But no, Bella doesn't think that far ahead. Instead, she comes up with a series of nasty put-downs to her Daddy to form excuses for her rapid departure from Forks to Phoenix, including using the one her Mom threw at him when she moved out. This is among Bella's cruelest acts in the *Twilight Saga)*.

Altho' Andy Cheng was an action director from Hong Kong, the finale of *Twilight* didn't take a Hong Kong action cinema approach in the

---

14 Wendy Chuck found vintage baseball outfits for the actors, which adds to the charm of the scene.
15 Every movement by anybody is accompanied by whooshy sound effects. Alice raises her leg in slo-mo, and there's a whoosh!
16 The song also featured in British TV shows *Black Mirror* and *Doctor Who.*

baseball scene: in an action movie from any place (and certainly from Hong Kong!), if you brought together your bad guys and your good guys, in a field in the middle of a thunderstorm far away from anywhere, you would *not* have the heroes turn and run! There would be a *ton* of action! (Hong Kong action choreographers would certainly use that enormous waterfall, with characters flying across it. Indeed, Hong Kong filmmakers enjoy nothing more than taking the movie circus to a nearby quarry or patch of land in Canton and inventing 100s of action beats).

Thus, for me, as soon as Carlisle Cullen makes the decision to get Bella Swan out of there, the *Twilight* movie deflates like a lead balloon (altho' he wisely tries diplomacy first with the Nomad vamps). Yes, altho' the camera is shaking, and Edward is yelling at Bella about how nasty James is as they careen thru the forest in a car like frightened deer, and altho' Bella acts very scared, the tension in *Twilight* simply evaporates, and it becomes nothing more'n a routine cop show or thriller that you can see any night on any of 100s of TV channels in the United States of America, or anywhere in the Westernized world.

Boring! James and Bella talking on the phone, and he's the weirdo being creepy, and she's frightened, like the cheapest, tackiest, made-for-TV movie. Boring! The Sullens arranging the elaborate false trail for James. Boring! James running and the vamps running thru the woodland. Boring! Alice, Jasper and Bella holed up in a plush hotel. Boring!

Part of the problem is that the plotting of the t movie, the flow of one scene into another, becomes *mechanical*, becomes the routine plot structure of Any Thriller. Whereas the tension in the Bella-Edward romance is so much more compelling.

But this is a *Hollywood* movie, which has introduced vampires, so it needs to pay off that concept. Polite, civilized vampires standing about talking (the Sullens) is very nice, but it doesn't provide a suitably action-filled ending to a picture. Hence James, Victoria and Laurent.

So in *Twilight*'s finale, we get to see vampires doing their thing – notice how Alice's role is suddenly front and centre as soon as the Nomad vampires show up at the baseball field, influencing the plot (her abilities to see the future are prominent in altering the course of events). Notice how Carlisle states quietly but clearly: I don't want to kill someone. Carlisle, as the clan leader, lays down the rules here: they won't fight, they will flee, and hope that the hunter vampire will lose Bella's scent.

The script also switches the antagonists here: Edward has been something of a threat to the heroine, warning her off falling for him several times. In this version of *Romeo and Juliet*, the obstacles preventing the lovers from pursuing their courtship include the fact that he's a vampire. However, the 'bad' vampires have been introduced early on, too, so that when the switch comes from the 'good' vampires to the 'bad' vampires, it convinces. And this comes after the consummation of the romance plot, in the mountain sequence and the meadow scene.

Remember that the romance elements in *Twilight* are much more significant for the author and the text than the vampire/ action elements. *Twilight* is *first and foremost* a romantic story. In fact, one of the most important aspects of the vampireology featured in *Twilight* is how it relates to a key theme in the romantic story: immortality, how vampires can be lovers in love forever (note the final word of the whole *Twilight Saga*: *forever*).

In *Romeo and Juliet* and similar love stories (such as the *Vita Nuova* by Dante Alighieri and the *Canzoniere* by Francesco Petrarch, the two great Italian poetic cycles), or any Gothic, 19th century novel, lovers are together in death. Stephenie Meyer has reworked the Freudian death drive into total wish-fulfilment: the lovers can be together *in life*. And vampire immortality is the vehicle.

A lot of us are complete softies; we *love* the idea that love can last forever, that lovers can be together for eternity. *Twilight* is a *fantasy* of love, a *dream* of love. If you don't get that (or accept it), none of the rest of it can work.

Or, put it like this, the *Twilight Saga* isn't a vampire story with romance as a secondary plot. No: it's a romance story with vampire mythology as the sub-plot.

❧

The book and the film pit James Witherdale the human slayer against Edward the human protector: but James announces he wants to do what Edward has been struggling to prevent himself from doing: devouring the heroine. It's the Big, Bad Wolf in *Little Red Riding Hood*, and the Beast in *Beauty and the Beast* once again: Edward fights the two drives – to kill and to protect – while James has already decided what he wants (and likely has always fed off humans).

Twilight's finale also takes away agency from Bella Swan: now she's the Princess Who Must Be Rescued once more. Bella is no match for the Big, Bad Wolf, and requires her Knight In Shining Armour to come save her. (From a feminist angle, the action side of the finale of *Twilight* places women back in the subservient role. Bella can't get out of this predicament on her own (she's already rejected her father's aid, and slinks away from her two vampire protectors. As she does, we hear a reprise of her voiceover from the first shots of the film about her own demise). And even tho' she's super-smart, Bella falls for the Big, Bad Wolf's tricks (such as imagining that James has captured her Mom). Here's where being bookish works against Bella: if she'd seen loads of horror movies (as Jessica has), instead of consuming romantic, Victorian novels (where the worst that can happen is tripping over your pretty frock during a waltz at the Duke's mansion), she'd realize that her story has now shifted from a teen romance and become a horror film (and a TV thriller), where the villains often use cunning schemes to snare their prey).

On the plus side, the fights in the finale of *Twilight* in the ballet studio[17] were impressive (it was a room of mirrors – the mirrors having a single purpose, as in a Chinese action movie – so the filmmakers could smash stuff up). The second unit and the stunt team[18] (Andy Cheng,[19] Samuel Le *et al*) certainly provided plenty of smashing, crashing lunges and falls, including having the vampires carve up a hole in the wooden floor (they also use some wirework, which Hollywood has imported from Hong Kong – when the Cullens arrive on the scene, for instance, they fly down from a balcony for no other reason than it looks good).

And of course, James Witherdale makes the fatal mistake that all movie villains make – of explaining to the heroine how he carried out his fiendish plan, wittering on too long, to give the heroes time to Save The Day. (Why do villains always prattle b4 they slay?!).

Hong Kong action movies are without question the finest in world cinema in live-action. The classics of Hong Kong fantasy, such as *The Bride With White Hair* and *A Chinese Ghost Story,* offer the most sophisticated mix of action, spectacle, comedy, melodrama and spookiness in this genre. *Twilight* is enjoyable, but it's not a patch on the *Chinese Ghost Story* or *Bride With White Hair* movies.

If you fancied an ecstatic mix of comedy, action, horror and fantasy, try the *Chinese Ghost Story* movies (1987, 1990 and 1991), starring two of the most beautiful people ever to appear in movies, Leslie Cheung and Joey Wong (sorry, Kristen and Rob!). And the ending of *A Chinese Ghost Story* is a rapturous evocation of genuine tragedy and love-beyond-

17 But how bad guy James lures Bella there with the aid of a video tape is unnecessarily complicated. What is he, a TV editor in his spare time?!
18 The schedule for the ballet school scenes was four days for the first unit and four days for the second unit.
19 Andy Cheng had worked in the Chinese film industry, specializing in action movies, and brought some of that sensibility to the *Twilight* finale. For instance, Hong Kong action, known for its wirework and out-size performances, also takes place entirely in front of the camera, where all of the special effects are practical effects, and the *Twilight* movie had attempted using a practical effects approach too.
Andy Cheng has credits on U.S. movies such as *Rush Hour, Welcome To the Jungle, Shanghai Noon, We WEre Soldiers, Daredevil, Collateral, Mission: Impossible 3, The Amazing Spider-man,* and *Oz the Great and Powerful.*

death.

Once James the hunter has been taken care of, his demise occurs in the background (Alice leaps on his back and twists his head,[20] then he's burnt), because the real drama takes place in the foreground: Edward has to draw out the venom that Bella's contaminated with.[21] She's dying and Edward has to suck just enough blood out to draw out the venom – but not too much blood, or she's gonna die! (Yet, even here, in the finale, the *Twilight* movie was careful not to show much claret at all).

In the book, the finale of *Twilight* is just boring. And the writing is boring, as if the author isn't really interested in it. So Bella goes here, Bella does that, Bella thinks this. So what? Who cares?! Listen to a sample of the prose from the final chapters of *Twilight*:

> I couldn't help myself – I tried to run. As useless as I know it would be, as weak as my knees already were, panic took over and I bolted for the emergency door. (T, 392)

You see? It's the unadorned, plain prose style of airport fiction, a sub-Ernest Hemingway style that's merely functional. But there's no *pleasure* in it, no *jouissance*, no *oomph* to the prose or the scenario.

In the 2005 *Twilight* book, the finale's narrated entirely from our Bella's point-of-view. We see only what she glimpses in her severely wounded state. Instead, Edward fills her in on what happened in the *dénouement* scenes in the hospital room. But he doesn't say exactly what occurred. So the 2008 movie adaptation feels it has to invent a bunch of action for the finale (including the whole of the Edward vs. James fight). Notice, for instance, that it's Alice who provides the killing twist to James's head: in the book, we discover that James is linked to Alice, so it's appropriate that she should kill him (she was a victim that got away from him, when she was in a mental asylum).

Of course, the 2008 American movie could've stayed with Bella Swan's limited viewpoint, but that wouldn't have offered the same all-out duels and stunt gags (although some shots are filmed from her point-of-view, or near it). The Edward—James fight thus ratchets up the action way beyond the 2005 *Twilight* novel, taking it up to the level of big, blockbuster movies where a punch or two isn't enough anymore. No, we must have bodies slamming against walls, stunt guys throwing each other

---

20 The old twisty-head thing, which never convinces me as a way of killing someone (in the 'making of' documentary, Alice twists off the dude's head – but that' too strong for a 'PG-13' rating, so it's suggested with sound effects). However, if it's a vampire doing the twisting, it's more convincing (Ashley Greene can twist my head any time). Decapitation becomes a favourite method for dispatching a vampire in later *Twilight* installments.

21 Of course, it should be Carlisle, being a professional doctor, who should perform this. But he gives some explanation why it ought to be Edward.

around, wire work, elaborate physical effects gags (like the shattering mirrors and glass), and special effects make-up. That's what audiences have come to expect from the finale of a big, Hollywood movie. (The same sorts of finales would occur in each of the subsequent *Twilight Saga* movies, with the last *Twilight* movie staging a huge battle in a snowy field – and that one's a wild invention that isn't in the *Breaking Dawn* novel).

THE HALL OF MIRRORS.

Catherine Hardwicke cited *The Lady From Shanghai* and *Enter the Dragon* as inspirations for the mirrors in the ballet school (but in her notebook, she states 'don't do it, everything is in the shot' [127]). Many films have taken up the memorable finale of *The Lady From Shanghai* (1948), portraying the face-off in a hall of mirrors, between Orson Welles' O'Hara, Rita Hayworth's Elsa and Everett Sloane's Arthur Bannister. It's one of Welles' famous and brilliant set-pieces. As well as a dense montage, an editor's show-piece, the scene is also a visual treat, as the filmmakers include numerous superimpositions – typically, a giant close-up of Rita Hayworth on top of Everett Sloane hobbling past a row of mirrors. The barrage of superimpositions is dense and beautiful. It's astonishing cinema.[22]

As Orson Welles has often explained, that famous ending in the funhouse, with the mirrors crashing around the lovers and the betrayers, was supposed to take place with the sounds of the shattering glass alone. No music: that was added by the studio (Columbia). And Orson Welles hated it (when the clip was shown on a TV chat show later in his life, Welles couldn't watch, and looked away).

The hall of mirrors finale has influenced many movies and TV shows. *Manhattan Murder Mystery* (Woody Allen, 1993) replayed the mirror maze scene in its finale. In *Manhattan Murder Mystery*, the climax took place in an old cinema, behind the screen, surrounded by mirrors, while the hall of mirrors scene in *The Lady From Shanghai* was being projected behind the characters. The two confrontations and shoot-outs – in the 1948 movie and the 1993 picture – were cleverly combined, with the dialogue from the two films interweaving, as well as the gunshots, and the mirrors smashing (again, a triumph not of cinematography, but of montage, of editing).

Other movies have drawn on the mirror scene apart from *Twilight*, including the most famous martial arts movie ever, *Enter the Dragon*

---

22 The hall of mirrors scene is also a triumph of visual effects, as numerous mirrors were rigged to shatter. It was organized by vfx expert Lawrence Butler.

(1973), where Bruce Lee fights in the climax. The shoot-out between James Bond and the villain in *The Man With the Golden Gun* (1975) draws on *The Lady From Shanghai* (but by way of *Enter the Dragon*). TV shows such as *Batman*, *MacGyver*, *The Avengers*, and *Randall and Hopkirk (Deceased)* have used the mirror room. A mirrored room is employed in the *Harry Potter* movie *Harry Potter and the Order of the Phoenix* (2007).[23] *The Lady From Shanghai* has been referenced in films such as *Ghostbusters 2* and *Once Upon a Time In America*.

THE DREAM OF DYING MONTAGE.

To carry us over from the fight in the ballet school and Bella apparently dying to Bella waking up in hospital, the *Twilight* movie shifts into montage mode. A ballad plays ('Let Me Sign' by Robert Pattinson) while the editors put together the most complex montage in the movie (the final scene of *Breaking Dawn* employs the same device, when Bella lets Edward read her mind).

The dream of dying montage was cut together by P.I.C. (they made the titles for *Twilight*). It's common in the business to hire a company specially to do certain sequences like main titles or unusual montages.

The montage acts as someone seeing their life flashing before their eyes as well as a curtain call (and summary) for the whole *Twilight* movie (the closing credits also do that, by selecting takes not used in the final cut, and printing them in b/w).

The near-death montage is highly stylized in places. For example, it seems to flash forward to the future (now we see Bella and Edward in the paradisal meadow but it's snowing); it includes graphic shifts (now we see the figures of Edward and Bella outlined against black); and some of the dissolves between the shots suggest a vision or a dream.

The important part of the finale is not the Cullens vanquishing the villain (which follows exactly the method mentioned earlier by Edward – rip them apart then burn the pieces), but Bella being bitten and the venom doing its work. So, yes – *bite me!* – the heroine *is* bitten by a vampire in *Twilight* (tho' it's not how she imagined it!), and Edward is told by Carlisle to suck it out.

Carlisle Cullen makes two significant moves in the finale: first, he tells Edward to come back to himself and not to kill James, when Edward seems about to do the deed (Carlisle knows that Edward has already murdered people, and he doesn't want his son (he calls him son) to follow that Road To Hell anymore). Secondly, Carlisle pulls back

---

23 The production has the money to use visual effects technology to hide the crew's reflections in the mirrors.

Edward again when he's going overboard on tasting Bella's blood.

PROM NIGHT.

After the mayhem of the James vs. Bella/ Cullens fight, and the near-death montage, and the anxious hospital scene (where Bella is especially distraught over the idea of moving to Florida, as she tells her Mom), and then again when Edward suggests that she goes to Jacksonville and forgets all about him, the *Twilight* movie ends with a sequence of pure romantic fantasy. The setting is a cliché of school stories – the high school Prom – and the mood is self-indulgently romantic. It's hearts and flowers time, it's gooey, girlie time, as the bandstand is festooned with thousands of white bulbs by the DP, the gaffer and the sparks, and our lovers dance slowly. (Bella does ballet as a child but insists now she's 17 that she can't (indeed, won't) dance.)

We even get the lips brushing Bella's throat bit from the very end of the *Twilight* novel, the suggestion of the fabled Vampire Kiss (which some readers thought meant that Bella was being bitten by Edward and transformed). Because this is where Bella broaches the subject of being turned into a vampire, so she can be with Edward forever (this exchange plays out right up to the very final words of the *Twilight Saga* series, where Bella finally gets her fairy tale wish of eternal life and eternal love). And in the subsequent *Twilight* movies, the issue of vampirizing Bella becomes a key bone of contention between the lovers, as well as acting as an important prohibition. Bella expresses the willing vampire victim's mantra: 'bite me!' And Edward replies that he's the good vampire, ma'am, and he couldn't possibly do something so nasty.

The ending of the *Twilight* movie affirms the romantic fantasy storyline[24] – reminding us that this is a love story in which vampires and horror plays a secondary role (rather than the other way around), and a coming-of-age and teen angst story in which neurosis and anxiety is vanquished by a kiss. And – *oh boy!* – not just *any* kiss, but *the* kiss, the Great Kiss, the kiss-of-all-kisses that the movies have been offering as the be-all-and-end-all of all silver screen romances for 120 years!

I mean, isn't one of the reasons that the *Twilight Saga* is such a hit with audiences is precisely because it *is* so old-fashioned, so movie-ish, so corny, so cheesy, so sugary? Don't audiences (not all of them teenage girls!) just love this kind of mushy slush? Isn't this delicious Cheesy Cheese, Romantic Cheese, Lovely Cheese?

It's a shame that Bella's school friends fall away in the second half of

---

24 The brief scene of Victoria observing the lovers on the bandstand was added later, in the re-shoots. It's a standard sequel tease, looking forward to the next movie/s.

Twilight, from the trip to Port Angeles onwards (Bella glimpses them as she rides by in Edward's car – they represent the 'ordinary' life that Bella might've enjoyed if she hadn't fallen in love with a vampire). But the school pals are seen at the Prom night – a final, too-brief appearance, seen from across the room.

Similarly, when Bella wakes in hospital, her Mom's there, but her Pa is only referenced in the dialogue. It's not an essential *dénouement* scene for Charlie (he sees Bella off to the Prom). But it's often the way with movies – there are just too many characters, so they can't all be included in the *dénouement* scenes.

The additional scene where Jacob visits Bella Swan to warn her off dating Edward at the high school Prom is not entirely successful. Yes, it does bring in Jake, who's going to be a major player in *New Moon* (and the subsequent *Twilight* movies), yes it does point up the vamp vs. wolf tension, as well as the erotic rivalry, which will play out in depth in the subsequent movies. But the details of the scene are awkward (such as Jacob delivering a stupid message from his Pa for twenty bucks; Jake being dressed in his school uniform – he is the sort of boy who'd change immediately he got home; and the way that Jake lurks behind the bushes).

DELETED SCENES.

The *Twilight* home releases included some deleted scenes, but, as usual with deleted scenes, none of them are especially crucial to the plot. There's a scene where Bella and Edward discuss vampiredom further (filmed in a continuous shot, where, curiously, they both slip over); a brief scene involving Esmé and Carlisle, watching Edward carrying Bella on his back, as fond parents; a little bit of kissing for the nomadic vampires James and Victoria (portraying their relationship); and an erotic fantasy where Bella wakes up to find Edward in her bedroom and grabs him and embraces him (then she wakes up again and there's no Edward – this scenario was already included in act one).

There are also extended scenes which are slightly longer than the ones included in the 2008 t movie. Again, the extended scenes contain material that's fun to see, but don't need to be in the final cut. (Incidentally, while talking about deleted scenes and extended scenes – DVD and home entertainment releases of movies don't show *all* of the deleted scenes. For instance, the rough cut of *New Moon* (all of the material that was shot from the script put together) was three hours long. The final movie was 130 minutes, and the deleted scenes amount to about 10 minutes. So there is still quite a bit of material that isn't included on the home entertainment releases. And this occurs with many movies. You are not going to be able to see all of the dailies, and every take that was printed of every camera set-up. Even diehard Twi-hards might find it challenging to sit through take after take of every scene).

MY FIRST VIEWING OF *TWILIGHT*. NOT IMPRESSED.

I didn't go for *Twilight* the first time I saw it.

These are my first impressions:

Twilight was Jane Austen[25] for teens, a 19th century-style melodrama for the *Buffy the Vampire Slayer* and *Charmed* generation (tho' nowhere near as satisfying as Austen or *Charmed*). And it was a 'vegetarian' vampire tale (these vampires don't eat humans! They live off the blood of animals! And Bella is a vegetarian). *Twilight* was also, unusually for a vampire story, pretty bloodless (this went beyond keeping to the 'PG-13' rating – filmmakers find all sorts of way of displaying or evoking blood in that particular M.P.A.A. ratings category. But in *Twilight*, the filmmakers were self-consciously avoiding showing the red stuff: these were *good* vampires, 'vegetarian' vampires!).[26]

Twilight was a romantic tale for teenage girls who felt shy, unsure, alienated and disempowered, and their feminized boyfriends (who also felt unsure and unmasculine). Sure: the target audience was envisioned as a thirteen year-old, 'emo' girl with low esteem.

She's a girl, he's a vampire.

She's 17, he's 104.[27]

That was the key prohibition keeping the lovers apart in this teen romance which combined the romantic drama with elements of vampire lore. The vampiric background, tho', coupled with some Native American aspects (the movie was set primarily in the Pacific North-West, and includes Native American characters, principally Jacob Black), was not what this 2008 American movie or 2005 book was about. It was primarily a romance story, a growing up story, a being-a-teenager story (with a bit of a moving-to-a-new-home story/ stranger-in-town story).

One aspect of being a vampire isn't really explored in the *Twilight*

25 No surprise that author Stephenie Meyer was involved with a tribute to Jane Austen in the movie *Austenland*. The plotting of the *Twilight* movies follows Austen closely (the first *Twilight* movie has many echoes of *Pride and Prejudice*, for instance – with Edward as Mr Darcy, of course, and Bella as Elizabeth Bennet). That much of Austen's narrative take place inside numerous conversations, is very much the approach of *Twilight*. The whole franchise can be regarded as boiling down to a series of conversations about romance, livened up with occasional vampire action.

26 Blood is blood, right? So animals' blood should suffice, right? No! We're talking about vampires not hippies! As Edward explains to li'l Bella, it's like having a vegetarian diet, like tofu and soya milk; it doesn't always satisfy (T, 164).

27 In *New Moon*, when the lovers' re-united, Edward says he 109 (NM, 540).

movie adaptations: that they live for a very long time is in there, yes, but that some of them have been together for decades or more. For example, Edward has lived with Carlisle for some 87 years according to the *Twilight* novels.

I read the book by Stephenie Meyer, and got about halfway thru before becoming totally fed up with the utterly banal heroine, Bella the Boring. *Twilight* is written in the first person, and reads like the kind of novel written by a failed author, the kind of writer who writes novels, thinks they're wonderful, then promptly puts them in a drawer. Or goes on and on about them to her circle of friends, or to her creative writing workshop buddies. Everybody hates her work, but nobody's got the guts to tell her. (Published in 2005, *Twilight* rapidly became one of those bestseller phenomena which publishers absolutely *lerrrve*. And which, as with *Harry Potter*, nobody can work out why they are such hits. If publilshers could come up with the exact formula, they would be doing it all the time).

Bella Swan rapidly strikes the reader of *Twilight* as a very irritating, snooty, supercilious, narrow-minded and patronizing kid (the movie sweetens Bella's characterization considerably). She judges everybody around her (they're all lammos in her opinion, thickheads, unstylish, and dumb), puts up with the group of lame-ass friends (they're all dweebs for her), her cop father Chief Swan (he tries, but he's still not good enough for her), but she falls in love head over trembling heart with the gorgeous but aloof vampire Edward Cullen.[28] Yes, even when you're the snottiest bitch in school, and everybody secretly loathes your guts (rigging your truck in the car lot with explosives), you still can't control your hormones.

Continuing with my first impressions of the movie adaptation: in the *Twilight* book, you want to slap Bella and Edward, they're so annoying. In the *Twilight* movie, it's even worse! They are endless close-ups of these idiots! (But weirdly-framed close-ups, as if everything is slightly off-kilter – especially in the key scene in the biology class). As played by Kristen Stewart[29] (b. 1990) and Robert Pattinson (b. 1986),[30] Bella and Edward are exactly what you'd expect from movie producers casting an

---

28 With his meticulously teased hair (courtesy of Mary Valdes *et al* in the hair department), Edward looks like he's walked out of a New Romantic band of the early 1980s. In *Breaking Dawn*, Jessica calls Edward 'the Hair'.

29 I found Kristen Stewart's performance incredibly irritating on the first viewing, with its eye twitching, forehead twitching, and mouth twitching, its self-conscious portrayal of a neurotic girl. However, considering her age (17), Stewart, a tiny, skinny girl, did a fine job, on the whole (in this role that no doubt everybody in L.A. was desperate to nab).

30 Robert Patttinson created an unusual take on the vampire, with downcast looks, pauses and a self-absorption that indicated brooding depths. It's close to parody, but offers a stillness to Stewart's nervy performance style. And Pattinson also grins, at some private joke, at the audience, at Stewart, as if he too is acting in his own movie.

update of soapy, TV fantasy shows like *Buffy* and *Charmed* for a late 2000s, jaded-but-still-interested cel phone generation (meanwhile, Taylor Lautner who plays Jake is even younger (b. 1992), only 16 when filming began).

Pale, wan, with dark eyes (contact lenses!) and permanent glowering, frowning scowls, Bella 'n' Edward are such a couple of drips, you want to fall into a bottomless pit. They spend most of their time angsting and worrying and frowning and whingeing.

Will someone bite somebody please?!

In the revelation scene on the mountain, the camera flies away discreetly from the lovers, as if suggesting a clinch, but then later we see the teens lying next to each other on the grass. Did they? Didn't they?[31] Is that curious camera move to suggest Bella's flights of ecstasy? Is the kiss so incredible (or so passionate) that it can't be shown? Does the camera float away to tease the audience, so we don't quite know if they kissed or not?

As far as the *Twilight* movie and the plot is concerned, we are persuaded to assume that they *didn't* – because the kissing scene crops up later, in Bella's bedroom (but even then they still didn't really – Edward leaps away from Bella, like the good, restrained vampire he is). The filmmakers tease the audience with the Long-Expected Kiss, the culmination of stage one of a romantic story – it should occur at the end of the mountain reveal sequence, really (in a conventional romantic comedy/ drama), but the camera tilts and pans way up into the trees; in the bedroom scene, Edward experiments with kissing Bella, but loses control, and leaps away.

While some critics admired the chemistry between Kristen Stewart and Robert Pattinson (they became a couple not long afterwards, which lasted four or so years), it wasn't enough to lift parts of *Twilight* above a run-of-the-mill, weekday TV drama. Nor were the helicopter shots, the pretty second unit images of the Pacific North-West (and Canada) or the numerous visual effects additions. Some of the stunts and action were clumsily directed, with by-the-numbers staging.

Twilight seemed to be another case of the producers wanting one kind of movie, the director and writers wanting another, the performers going for something else, and the studio and financiers something else again.

Whatever... the formula worked. *Twilight* became a big movie franchise, like the books, so that by the time of the *Twihard* sequels

---

31 And do we give a shit?!

(which came thick and fast, as one would expect), they made tons of $$$$ (a worldwide gross of $402 million from a negative cost of $38m is excellent).[32] To the point where Summit Entertainment and partners took the money-spinning route of splitting up a movie into two parts, as the *Harry Potter* and *Matrix* franchises had recently done (and *The Hobbit* was stretched out over three movies in the pursuit of the Great God Dollar).

Twilight takes itself all very seriously (of course – that's partly what makes it work). But the audio commentary of the DVD release by director Catherine Hardwicke and the stars Kristen Stewart and Robert Pattinson is full of laughter. A pity that some of that laughter at the silliness of this romance-and-vampire tale didn't transfer itself to the screen. Bella Swan, the central character of the book and the movie, is a humourless girl. The only humour she accedes to is snidey sarcasm. And Edward solemnly pouts and glowers in his pale make-up and ruby-red lips enough for both of them (Bella is a 'no make-up' girl,[33] tho' of course that 'no make-up' effect requires make-up to achieve it).

But I changed my mind. And the 2008 *Twilight* movie grows on you. And after seeing all five of the *Twilight Saga* pictures, when you go back to the first movie, it improves. Or you get to appreciate it more. Or you get used to it. And the negative views of that first viewing melt in a breathless sigh and a long, lingering look at glittering skin…

---

32 And *Twilight* looks great on $38 million, like the first *Underworld* movie with $23 million.
33 In the Prom scene, Bella remarks, 'I was very uncharacteristically wearing mascara' (T, 422).

原著超越《哈利·波特》系列荣登全美畅销冠军
就算来自另一个世界
依旧爱你到地老天荒
twilight
暮光之城
11月25日 诱动热血沸腾的浪漫
导演 凯瑟琳·哈德威克 编剧 梅丽莎·罗森伯格 原著 斯蒂芬妮·梅耶 摄影 埃利特·戴维斯
音乐 卡特·伯维尔 演员 克里斯汀·斯图尔特 罗伯特·帕丁森 比利·伯克 彼得·费辛利 伊莉莎白·里瑟
美国巅峰娱乐公司 出品 中国电影集团公司 进口 华夏电影发行有限责任公司 全国发行 上海电影（集团）公司 上海电影译制厂 译制
www.hxfilm.com
上海电影译制厂 上海电影技术厂 数码声制作 洗印加工
独家网络支持： sina新浪娱乐 媒体支持： 电影网

4

NEW MOON, THE MOVIE

'I love a happy ending. They are so rare.'

Stephenie Meyer, *New Moon*

INTRODUCTION.

The first *Twilight* sequel, *New Moon* (Chris Weitz, 2009, a.k.a. *Twilight: New Moon* a.k.a. *The Twilight Saga: New Moon*), was, like all sequels, More Of The Same (yet a little different), plus the usual sequel elements of: more characters, more settings, more complications, and more gimmicks/ gags/ stunts/ whatever (and a bigger budget₁ – $50m – and the worldwide box office gro$$ was enormous – $687m - $709m).₂

Bella Swan was still at the heart of the *Twilight Saga,* and *New Moon* was very much her movie, with Kirsten Stewart in almost every scene – she's in the first shot (tho' thankfully with some of her irritating, hyper-neurotic mannerisms toned down).

I like the *New Moon* movie – it takes the strangest dramatic turns, it's a witty commentary on the *Twilight* phenomenon and on the first *Twilight* movie, we meet Michael Sheen and the Volturi, and there's more of Jacob Black than the other films.

The story of *Twilight: New Moon* was dead simple (if you reduce it to the bare bones), as with the first *Twilight* movie, but with the teeniest twist:

---

1 No doubt the teen actors' asking prices had gone up, after the huge success of the first movie, plus the rights to the books.
2 Product placement in *New Moon* includes Volvo cars and Virgin Airlines.

She's girl, he's a werewolf. (She's 17, he's 16.)

And: She's a girl, he's a vampire.[3]

A girl and a boy: happy ever after, right? Well, yes... And no: it isn't Happy Ever After for Edward Cullen and Bella Swan, following the end of the first *Twilight* movie, where they're dancing and kissing in the light of glowing lamps at the high school Prom.

The 2009 movie replays scenes and motifs from the first *Twilight* movie, but changed around (as often with a sequel). So there are two scenes where a boy enters the girl's bedroom thru a window for a nighttime colloquy, for example, and two sequences of fascination and falling in love.

▶

By the time that *Twilight: New Moon* went before the cameras, the *Twilight Saga* was already attracting pop music fan-style attention (2008 and 2009 were big years for the *Twilight* franchise). Director Chris Weitz remarked that he knew there would be screams during the slow motion shot of Edward Cullen walking up to meet Bella Swan in the school car lot (so he asked actor Robert Pattinson to acknowledge that with a grin).[4] So *New Moon* was put together knowing that the *Twilight Saga* was a major hit with fans. And the main title has a full moon eclipsing down to a crescent moon *slowly*, partly because Weitz reckoned there would be screaming in the theatre (so the movie doesn't start until fans[5] have settled in their seats and stopped screeching).

Jeez, when you've got thousands of fans hollering in the theatre at your movie, you can't lose, right? No! It wouldn't have mattered what happened in the actual movie, in terms of stories and characters, if the anticipation was high enough in the first place. Of course, only a few movies of recent times have received that kind of hysterical, hyped-up attention: *Star Wars* and *Harry Potter* are the two obvious ones. (The *Twilight* movies draw on the same demographic as *Titanic* and *William Shakespeare's Romeo + Juliet*, or romantic comedies such as *You Got Snail* and *Sleepless In New Jersey*).

SOME THEMES.

The first *Twilight* movie could be a stand-alone piece, with a Happy

---

3 In the *Vampires Suck* spoof, Daro (Aro) points out that Becca is already like a vampire – the pale skin, the mopey, miserable attitude.

4 However, a later slo-mo shot, of Bella and Edward frolicking in the forest in the future as vampires drew the wrong kind of laughter.

5 For David Brisbin, *New Moon* was the first time he'd worked on a production with such a fervent and closely-involved fan base: 'it was almost like working onstage – we could feel the audience was right there, in a way I'd never felt before' (NMC, 40).

Ending: Bella Swan gets her man, and Edward gets the girl. But *New Moon* offers some fascinating complications after the ecstatic ending of *Twilight*.

In other words, it all goes wrong. But how could it? The lovers are dancing in the starlight at the close of *Twilight*, and all seems blissful. In short, it's l-o-v-e f-o-r-e-v-e-r.

And about the most compelling aspect of *New Moon* is that it's Bella Swan *herself* who orchestrates the chaos. Yes: in the first act of *New Moon*, prior to the Big Split, Bella is repeatedly harping on about her ageing and dying. She just doesn't want it! Which we can all relate to!

So Bella Swan is a Very Stubborn Girl. She won't die, she won't, she won't, she *won't!*, stamping her little foot). Even when Edward Cullen points out to her patiently that this is the natural course of events in life for the other 7 billion souls on the Planet, Bella doesn't accept it.

Thus, there are several reasons for the Big Separation in *New Moon* – Edward offers some of them, such as Victoria coming after him, and the neighbours asking questions about the Cullens not seeming to age, accidents like Jasper and the blood, and that Bella is not part of their world, the vampire world.

But a key reason is the argument that Bella throws in Edward's face (which she had already started in *Twilight*): *he* won't age, but *she* will. Bella's frustration derives partly from the knowledge that if she were vampirized, they could live together f-o-r-e-v-e-r).

So you could regard Bella as a rebel against life itself – she's Prometheus or Oedipus, defying the Gods or the Furies, or she's Satan (yes, *him*), the rebel angel in *Paradise Lost*, or she's simply a Very Stubborn Girl.

And thus Bella Swan is partly responsible for the agony she suffers: there's no doubt that Bella is her own worst enemy – as we all are (no one can ruin our lives as well as we can). There are many ways to deal with the break-up of a romance, but sitting at home doing nothing after school for months on end is not perhaps the most productive option (and they weren't dating for long – from Spring[6] to mid-September, 2005, five or so months perhaps).

❧

New Moon can be regarded as the flipside of *Twilight*, the version of a romance when it all goes wrong, when the split occurs. *New Moon* is a psychological commentary on *Twilight*, it's the pop psychology inter-

---

6 In the movie's timeline.

pretation of *Twilight*, where the narrative of *Twilight* is deconstructed.

THE PRODUCTION.

In the crew of *New Moon* were producers Bill Bannerman, Marty Bowen, Guido Cerasuolo, Wyck Godfrey, Kerry Kohansky-Roberts, Greg Mooradian, Mark Morgan, Guy Oseary, David Roker and Karen Rosenfelt (8 guys and 2 women). Produced by Temple Hill/ Maverick/ Imprint/ Summit.

Catherine Ircha and Susanna Codognato: art directors, David Brisbin: production designer, Lesley Beale: set decorator, Tish Monaghan: costumes, Norma Hill-Patton: make-up, Thom McIntyre: hair,[7] Peter Lambert: editor, Alexandre Desplat: music,[8] Javier Aguirresarobe: DP, Sean Cossey and Rene Haynes: casting, Mike Toopozian: first A.D., Phil Neilson: 2nd unit director, Scott Hecker: supervising sound editor, Rick Hromadka and Ai-Ling Lee: sound effects designers, Matt Jacobs, Susan MacLeod, Eric Pescarelli, Dottie Starling and Phil Tippett: visual effects supervisors, J.J. Makaro, Gianlucca Petrazzi and Mike Desabrais: fight and stunt co-ordinators, and visual effects were by Wildfire, Prime Focus, Tippet, Frantic and Pacific Title. Released: Nov 20, 2009. 130 mins.

In the cast, in addition to the actors from *Twilight*, were Michael Sheen, Jamie Bower, Christopher Heyerdahl, Tyson Houseman, Kiowa Gordon, Graham Greene, Alex Meraz, Bronson Pelletier, Tinsel Korey, Dakota Fanning, Cameron Bright, and Noot Seear.

There were rumours that Summit Entertainment had disliked Catherine Hardwicke's direction of *Twilight* (or had a problem with Hardwickeherself), but scheduling conflicts and other issues (like, uhh, money), are far more likely as reasons for Hardwicke's departure (Hardwicke cited the too-short pre-production schedule – *Twilight* had benefitted from a long lead-in time). Chris Weitz remarked that Hardwicke 'didn't leave us empty-handed. We still reap the benefits of her amazing casting and the beautiful visual world she created' (indeed, *New Moon* pretty much emulates the approach of *Twilight* in every respect, while adding some flourishes of its own. But it was the first *Twilight* picture which completely defined the look of the *Twilight Saga* in cinema).

Altho' Catherine Hardwicke stepped down from directing the subsequent *Twilight* movies, some of the crew continued to work on them, from producers Mooradian and Godfrey to composer Carter Burwell and editor Nancy Richardson. But many in the crew were new.

The Native Americans were cast by Rene Haynes, who specializes in

---

7 As with *Twilight*, there were a lot of wigs in *New Moon* – for Rosalie, Laurent, etc.
8 Lasse Enersen and Steve Schiltz also composed music.

Native American actors (for movies such as *The New World, Bury My Heart At Wounded Knee* and *Dancing With Wolves*), in collaboration with casting director Joseph Middleton. There was an open casting call – and, due to the popularity of the *Twilight* franchise, thousands of actors applied. Chaske Spencer, a Lakota Sioux, played chief wolf, Sam Uley (an important role – Sam's the guy who stands in Jake's way many times in the *Twilight* series): Spencer was an enthusiastic promoter of the *Twilight Saga*: for him, *Twilight* was 'action, love, loss, fights, and battle scenes – it's what we go to the movies for' (M. Vaz, 2009, 75). The other actors were Hualapai, Cree and Purepecha (Tarasco).

The budget for *New Moon* was about $50 million. The rights to the novel were bought by Summit Entertainment in June, 2007. Summit Ent. wanted the film to be released on Nov 20, 2009, which meant hurrying the production along. Chris Weitz was signed up to direct with only 8 weeks for pre-production (90 days is average for a romance film, but 180 days for an action movie). 'It was a rush, but in a good way' (NMC, 29).

Principal photography for *New Moon* began on March 23, 2009 (about a year after *Twilight*), and ended on May 21, 2009, with six days in Italy (May 25-30, 2009). That's a short schedule for a big, Hollywood movie involving 100s of visual effects shots. (There were about 450 vfx shots in *New Moon*).

Cover sets were often used when the weather didn't co-operate (which was often in the Pacific North-West, as with the production of *Twilight*). Druing filming at the meadow, for instance, when it started to rain then snow, the A unit shifted to a shed and filmed scenes with Jake and Bella in the truck (M. Vaz, 2009, 98).

Jake's costumes were tailored (by Tish Monaghan's team) to enhance his physique, and he was often in Tee shirts (in earthy hues – red and earth tones were used for the werewolves). He wears jeans (and boots – with Kristen Stewart in flat shoes, to make him look taller than her. Differences in height of actors are cheated all the time in movies, for the camera angles, and for the look. In *Twilight*, Stewart is standing on an apple box in some of the scenes with Robert Pattinson).

The colour scheme for Jacob (warm, earth hues, and red), was carried over into his wolf design. Jake, after all, was the key chara among the wolves, and he had to stand out from the others. Jacob's home was dressed with items like a boat, trailers, Native American art[9] (including a hoop drum),[10] and the house was painted red (it was originally green).

9 Did sales of dreamcatchers go up following *New Moon*?
10 A gift from a girl of the Quileute Tribe to the filmmakers when they visited the Reservation.

Make-up artist Norma Hill-Patton took Taylor Lautner's look from fresh-faced teen boy to more mature, bulked-up werewolf by shading and adjusting his jawline, nose and cheekbones, his eyes, the colour of his skin, and his eyebrows (adding mascara).

850 red cloaks were manufactured for the Montepulciano scenes (the last to be filmed in the schedule). The production steered clear of the colour red, so that the finale would have more impact, and also from the first movie's cooler colours. Instead, *New Moon* used earth tones, grays, greens and browns (CFA, 46). Plus oranges, golds, yellow-greens, and neutral tones. Chris Weitz said they'd looked at the Pre-Raphaelite painters for inspiration (including Edward Burne-Jones and Dante Gabriel Rossetti (NMC, 36).[11]

Every time that Robert Pattinson appeared on the Montepulciano set, there would be screaming: 'a chorus of angelic cheering every time Rob stepped out', as Wyck Godfrey recalled: 'You couldn't help but smile and say, 'Oh God, we are in a heightened reality now'' (CFA, 77).

With so many Twi-hards among the extras for the Montepulciano scenes, it was inevitable that the fans would post images online. The next day, producer Wyck Godfrey said he received calls from the studio executives in Los Angeles complaining that the whole scene was on the internet already (flying drones fitted with cameras later became another security problem for high profile productions). Security was especially tight for the wedding scenes in *Breaking Dawn.*

While making *New Moon*, Jackson Rathbone said they were making the *Twilight* movies for the fans:

> We all wanted to come together and make another great piece of art for the fans. It's really about what want to see, because they're the ones buying the tickets.[12]

Many of the locations for *New Moon* were altered from the first movie of 2008. The school was different, and the Cullen mansion was not the location of the first film, the 'Nîke House', but a location in Canada.[13] Bella's house was constructed in Vancouver (and 28th Avenue, Surrey, British Columbia), while interiors were filmed in the studio. Whytecliff Park was used for the cliffs, as well as the Cleveland Dam, B.C. Widgeon Slough, Pitt River, was the setting for the motorbike

11 'We really wanted a wide range of colors and deep blacks, very saturated color, to go away from what is a more contemporary trend to desaturate', remarked Chris Weitz (NMC, 37).
12 Quoted in M. Howden, 71.
13 In *New Moon*, the Cullen house was in West Vancouver, at 118, Stevens Drive (it was designed by Arthur Erickson). The Cullen house was dubbed 'Howl's Moving Castle', as new rooms popped up and others disappeared.

riding scenes.

To make sure that the new locations matched the ones from the first *Twilight* movie, the filmmakers studied the film carefully, 'to see what, at the end of the day, the camera sees', commented production designer David Brisbin. They also used the *Complete Illustrated Movie Companion* for *Twilight*, because it had much better photos than stills lifted from the DVD of the movie (NMC, 50).

Chris Weitz said he wanted to use a different camera movement style for each relationship – handheld for the scenes of Bella amongst her friends, the floaty Steadicam (operated by David Crone), for the Bella and Jake scenes, and linear tracks and dollies for the Edward and Bella scenes (NMC, 38).

Part of the rough cut of *New Moon* was edited on a laptop computer – often when editor Peter Lambert was travelling to view the dailies or to the current location. The rough cut came in at 3 hours long (the first assembly is always longer than the final cut – it's all of the scenes in the script put together. And often everybody hates the rough cut).

There are deleted scenes and expanded scenes included on the home entertainment releases of *New Moon*. As usual, they take up quite a bit of screen time but don't really include anything that isn't found elsewhere in the released cut.[14]

THE STRUCTURE AND SCRIPT OF *NEW MOON*.
New Moon comprises four acts:

Act 1:   Edward leaves Bella.
Act 2:   Bella and Jacob bond.
Act 3:   Jake becomes a werewolf.
Act 4:   Edward and Bella are reunited.

Four acts, not three acts: the four-act model of Kristin Thompson (in *Storytelling In the New Hollywood*), where each act of a movie is 25-30 minutes long, is a much more accurate description of Hollywood-style film narratives. The usual three-act model of movies (introduction; development; resolution) comes partly from theatre, and means that movies end up having middle acts that run to 45m or 60m (i.e., too long, and not useful for analysis in dramatic terms).

That too-long second act in the three-act film script model is actually

---

14 In *New Moon*, a sequence was dropped of Bella rushing home to announce that she'd seen the wolves to Charlie. Editor Peter Lambert said it was more effective cutting straight from Bella in the forest to Bella at home (M. Vaz, 2009, 53).

better regarded as two acts. For instance, in *New Moon* the shift from the second act to the third act occurs when Jacob refuses to answer Bella's calls, and she decides to drive over to La Push. And in the first act, you can see that the scene where Edward abandons Bella climaxes act one (making this particular first act shorter than the usual opening act). Also, halfway thru an act of a movie there is often a dramatic reversal or a turning-point: in *New Moon*'s act one, it is clearly the scene where Jasper Whitlock tries to attack Bella at the Cullens' place.

For Melissa Rosenberg, the first movie established the characters and the settings, so the second movie didn't need to do that – 'now you know the actors, the language, tone, and action' (NMC, 27). Rosenberg began writing an outline for *New Moon* – a 25 page outline 'which was really the hard part' (NMC, 27). *New Moon*'s script was written between June and October, 2008 (while *Twilight* was in post-production).

Working with Chris Weitz for Melissa Rosenberg meant delivering the script to him, which he then polished, being a screenwriter himself (with writing credits including *Antz, The Golden Compass*,[15] *Cinderella* and *About a Boy*).

Melissa Rosenberg said that originally she wrote a big battle for the finale of *New Moon*, with Edward and Alice fighting the Volturi guards. Stephenie Meyer preferred a more modest approach, with only Felix and Edward fighting. OK, fine, keep it modest. But by the time of *Breaking Dawn*, battles that didn't exist in the *Breaking Dawn* novel would be added to the finales of *both* parts of *Breaking Dawn*.

New Moon employs a *lot* of footage from the first *Twilight* movie – as plot point reminders, as the memories of Bella S., and as flashbacks. (It also use some audio from *Twilight*, too – such as Jacob's story on the beach at La Push about the 'Cold Ones'). That's handy, because it means less new footage is required for *New Moon*. This became a staple of the *Twilight* movies – each one recycles earlier footage[16] (as the first movie did when Bella seems to dying, and a montage recycles the movie we've just seen). Indeed, the whole *Twilight Saga* closes with another reprise, this time from all of the movies (thus, you can use montage editing to shorten a movie, but you can also use it to reycle scenes and extend it).

With the filmmakers locked into being 'faithful' to the *Twilight* books, and respecting the provisos that Stephenie Meyer set out (in her

---

15 The team that created the wolves in *New Moon* – Tippett Studio – had worked on *The Golden Compass* with director Chris Weitz.
16 *New Moon* reprises moments from the first *Twilight* movie quite a few times: there're short montages of images from the first movie to remind us of situations like the time that James was destroyed and Edward saved Bella from the venom.

guise as the Twilight Nazi for sticking to the rules), it meant that *New Moon* wasn't conceived structurally like a formulaic romantic fantasy drama. For instance, take the Edward-suicide-Volturi plot, which forms the *action* aspect of the climax of the movie of *New Moon*. It involves the major charas arriving in the villains' lair, exchanging a *lot* of talk, with Edward being knocked around a bit by the henchmen, followed by goodbyes and the heroes exit swiftly. No one is sacrificed, no price is paid (Edward isn't even really hurt), and nobody seems much changed by the experience. (In scriptwriting terms, the action-based finale of *New Moon* is clumsy and very unsatisfying: you wouldn't do it that way if you weren't stuck with staying with the plotting of the 2006 novel, and the other *Twilight* books).

Seen in terms of the *romantic* plot, however, the awkward ending of *New Moon* makes more sense, or has more dramatic pay-off: the heroine gets to rescue the hero (go girl!), and is re-united with him. The hurrying to reach Edward provides some action in *New Moon*'s finale, and Italy delivers some colour and spectacle (and a break from the the gloom of Bella's psychological meltdown), but it's the reunion of the lovers that counts *much* more than any other dramatic element here. (Even so, a screenwriter, creating *New Moon* from scratch, would not bother making the plotting of the finale so complicated, how all sorts of narrative tricks have to be employed to get both the hero and the heroine to meet under that clock tower 5,000 miles away!).

THE PROLOGUE DREAM.

New Moon opened[17] with a dream sequence (like the 2006 novel by Stephenie Meyer – actually, it combined the "Preface" and chapter 1: "Party"), based around the notion of Living With a Vampire: you're going to get old, become your grandma, while your beau stays the same 17 year-old dreamboat. Darn! Why does decay and death have to slay young love?

In fact, Bella Swan's fear of getting old is quite pronounced in the *New Moon* movie, and it's acute in someone so young (it comes out in the dream prologue, and in several scenes thereafter with Edward). As if Bella is already, as she jokes with Jake, 35 years-old. Certainly, Bella is quite a middle-aged (and boring) teenager – she prefers to stay in and read rather than hang out with her friends, for instance (she's an American version of the Japanese phenomenon of the 'shut-in'). (The dream

---

17 Bella's voiceover includes the quote from *Romeo and Juliet* which forms the epigraph to the *New Moon* novel: 'these violent delights have violent ends | And in their triumph die, like fire and power | Which, as they kiss, consume' (II.vi).

sequence also cleverly includes part of the finale set in Italy, as a foretaste or a menu of what's coming up – we see shots of Bella hurrying thru crowds of red-robed people. This isn't explained, but the imagery has all of the hallmarks of a dream, so it works.18 It's from the "Preface" of *New Moon*: 'I felt like I was trapped in one of those terrifying nightmares, the one where you have to run, run till your lungs burst, but you can't make your body move fast enough' [NM, 1]). Thus, altho' we don't know it yet, Bella is hurrying to Save Her Man – so it's a giant flashfoward of two hours.

Bella runs… and ends up in a match cut from sunny Italy (pushing thru red-robed extras) to the meadow of Stephenie Meyer's original vamp-and-girl dream of 2003 (the meadow now looks like a proper-sized meadow, full of purple and white flowers, rather than a golf course in Los Angeles). The dream includes images of Bella as an old woman, a fairy tale mirror from *Snow White* (a similar one crops up soon after in Bella's bedroom,19 next to the bed), and Edward emerging from the trees (a foreshadowing of Edward in his spectral guise20 – this's how we see Edward for much of the movie).

The prologue dream in *New Moon* is played largely without dialogue, in dumb show, focussing on Bella's increasing feeling of anxiety, as she realizes it is a vision of herself in the future, with a perpetually seventeen year-old Edward and herself morphing into someone who looks like her grandmother (Christina Jastrzembska). The scene is thus not about being immortal, or living forever, or even about not dying: it is about ageing and the overwhelming desire for *not ageing*.21 (The lyric, 'hope I die before I get old' from the Who's 1960s yoiuth anthem 'My Generation' comes to mind).

The adaptation of *New Moon* added several premonitions for Bella Swan, which has her acting a little like Alice Cullen. She imagines Edward dying at the hands of the Volturi, for instance. She has flashes of what the Nomad villain Victoria is up to. And her dream in the prologue includes the images of Montepulciano, Italy (which she has never visited).

NEW MOON AND *ROMEO AND JULIET*.

In the first act of *Twilight: New Moon* there were many allusions to the play *Romeo and Juliet* by William Shakespeare (taking the cue from

---

18 The event hasn't occurred yet, and when it does it's not a dream, it's 'real'. So it's not part of a dream world, but more like a vision that Alice has of the future.
19 There's a copy of *Romeo and Juliet* beside Bella.
20 And glittering, too.
21 When Bella mentions 'my ageing' to Edward a little later, he laughs – now *she* is sounding like someone from 1918!

the *New Moon* novel), the ultimate love story of lovers who *should* be together for ever and ever, but who end tragically with a dual suicide (indeed, you could regard *Twilight: New Moon* as a version of *Romeo and Juliet* staged as a teenage, Hollywood romance with vampires).

There's a reference in the *New Moon* movie to the 1968 *Romeo and Juliet* film (in the book, Bella Swan watches it and Edward Cullen watches her watching it). Bella has *Romeo and Juliet* memorized, quips Alice (11); however, it's Edward who is asked to quote some of the last lines (which he does perfectly, of course, having studied it at school in 1924, and again in 1936, and again in 1959). Their teacher, Mr Berty (Russell Roberts in the movie), says that the 1960s film is the best version: it has of course been used many times in schools for studying (tho' the 1996 movie, *William Shakespeare's Romeo + Juliet*, is a finer piece of cinema, and more fitting for the *Twilight* audience, many of whom would prefer it to the Italian/ British version. The 1996 *Romeo + Juliet* is also very *Twilight*-ish with its teen hearthrob Leonardo DiCaprio as its star, a clear forerunner of Robert Pattinson, and Edward Cullen in his pop idol moments).

During the English class, Edward Cullen tells us the ending of this movie, and how he would commit suicide (which is tough for vampires to achieve – jumping off a skyscraper just gives them a mild headache). He would go to the Volturi in Italy, he tells Bella, and await their judgement. Edward thus brings the theme of suicide into the foreground of *New Moon*, where it will become a very disturbing element in Bella's life, too.

In fact, this dialogue about suicide and the other things that Edward says amounts to preparation for the all-important Big Separation scene, where he walks out on our heroine. We can see that, following the birthday party scene at the Cullen mansion, Edward has already decided to leave.

Prior to the English class scene, there's a crucial moment in the school car lot, where our lovers are glimpsed together on screen for the first time. There's no waiting for The Kiss now, as in the first *Twilight* movie – they smooch right away. Just as crucial as seeing our lovers happy and embracing is the appearance of Jacob Black – the *new* Jacob Black, and the *new* Taylor Lautner! Whooo! Check out that look![22] So now Edward has some serious competition! (That Jake just pops up is rather artificial,[23] but it's important to introduce the star (and Jake) early

---

22 Michael Copon (*Scorpion King 2*) was rumoured to be up for the role of the new, larger Jacob Black.
23 But he'd already done that at the end of the first movie.

on, as he plays a huge role later – in story terms, but also in movie terms. Also, it's a better introduction than the next time we see him, when Bella's recovered unconscious from the forest. And Jake's appearance can be explained that he already fancies Bella, and uses her birthday as a chance to see her. He hands her a present, too – a Native American dream catcher, ironically something that Bella could do with at the moment).

The visual framing of the school car lot scene in *New Moon* employs a classic composition for a love triangle that's irresistible to filmmakers (and painters) – of Bella and Jacob standing in the foreground opposite each other, with Edward loitering in the background in between them, scowling. Well, shoot, the old clichés always work, don't they?! (This and similar compositions will be employed throughout the *Twilight* series – I mean, how many ways are there to film three people involved in a love triangle, two guys and one girl?!).

The Stephenie Meyer novel makes much more of Edward Cullen declining alongside of Bella Swan than the movie – he becomes the 'burning man', as Jacob Black dubs him, a lost soul unable to help the one he loves, and torturing himself for contributing quite a bit to this sorry scenario (Edward is the King of Self-Torture in the *Twilight Saga* – and finds his perfect counterpart in Bella, the High Queen of Anxiety).

THE BIRTHDAY PARTY.

The birthday party scene with Bella's clumsy paper cut and the blood crystalizes some of the issues that Edward Cullen has been trying to impress upon Bella: that vampires are dangerous, that it really wouldn't be a good idea if she were changed into a vampire, and that the human world and the vampire world don't mix. (In the course of the scene, as soon as Edward realizes that Jasper is going to go insane with bloodlust, Edward hurls his girlfriend away from Jasper – but with such violence that she crashes into the wall and lands badly on a side table. This seems just a tad OTT! And of course makes li'l Bella shed even *more* blood! I mean, shove Bella out of the way Eddie, old chap, but don't smash her against the wall and break open her arm already!). All of this chaos from a paper cut – it's actually ridiculous, if you think about for longer than 0.00048105 seconds. (The 2009 movie tries to hide the fact that this a really stupid scene – where Bella, among friends, is smashed around because she pricked her finger like Sleeping Beauty – by using plenty of cinematic tricks: slo-mo, whooshy sound effects, scared looks, and ridiculous stunts – Jasper smashes a grand piano! The spoof *Vampires*

Suck sends up this moment hilariously).

Every time that Bella Swan visits the Cullen mansion, something goes wrong: in the first movie, she's already had dinner and the efforts of the Cullens in the kitchen are wasted (Rosalie is especially furious). The second time, she causes pandemonium from cutting her finger.

The birthday party scene in *New Moon* is one of the few times we see the Cullen vampire coven all in the same place, and in a happy moment. That's important – it depicts how Bella is now a part of this family, to the point where even surly Rosalie is giving her a present! (It's a phial of poison. Just kidding.)[24] It also depicts the first sight of Alice in full flight as the unstoppable hostess. Cute!

▶

A birthday party. *Hell* – that means you've gotten a *year older*, right? Oh, Bella is *not* happy! (I mean, even more than usual!). Yes, Bella is one of those people who prefers to duck her head down and shuffle along and pretend that it's *not* her birthday. So people giving her presents – Charlie, her Mom, Alice, Jacob – only underlines the fact that *she is ageing*.

Oh boy, is 18 *so old*?! *Yes*, if you love being a teenager! *Yes*, if you don't want to get old! *Yes*, if you're nuts about your boyfriend and irked that he is younger than you, at 17 (even tho' he's actually 109! Younger *and* older! Eh?!).

Notice, then, the motif of the camera. Charlie gives Bella a camera for her birthday. Cameras… photographs… memories… stopping time… freezing people in photographs… All of the obvious connotations that coalesce around cameras and photography are evoked.

Vanity and ageing – how Bella prints out the photo that Alice took[25] and folds it so she won't appear in it. Just Edward. Bella is one of those people who doesn't like having her photo taken (like some of us!), which's linked, of course, to her anxiety over ageing and mortality.

THE BIG SEPARATION SCENE.

So the climax to act one of *New Moon* was a lovers' separation scene (set in, where else? – the forest yet again – where Bella 'n' Edward have spent their happiest moments). He spurns her (all for good reasons, you understand). And she – well, she goes to pieces.

Completely.

This is the 2009 movie's equivalent of a violent car crash, the kidnapping of the Princess, or an attack on the heroes' stronghold. This is

---

24 Altho' she glumly confesses that Alice chose it.
25 That Alice sneaks the camera out of Bella's bag is a minor but creepy moment.

the Major Dramatic Incident which powers the rest of the movie. It is one of the most significant scenes in the *Twilight Saga*, in book or movie form (it's the flipside of the ecstatic ending of the first *Twilight* movie).

It is devastating – because this is, after all, a romantic fantasy, and here is where the hero walks out on the heroine. Which, in a romantic story, is about the worst thing that happen to the her, apart from the lover's death, or the lover opting for another suitor.

This scene is a literal pop song – it is the embodiment of hundreds of pop song lyrics: *don't go! never leave me!* He turns away from her, then he walks away (of course, being a vampire, he's out of there *very* fast!).

It's a powerful scene, staged very simply (two actors standing and facing each other), and filmed (as usual in the *Twilight* series), with slight variations on simple angles (with the odd over-the-shoulder shot). The editor (Peter Lambert) rightly concentrates on a solid shot-reverse-shot pattern, and the shots selected are rightly cleanly-framed singles.[26] Why? Because fussy camerawork and gimmicky editing would be way too distracting in this critical scene. This is the pivotal scene in *New Moon*, and the audience needs to understand it clearly, and just why the lovers have to be torn apart (when a character is saying something important, it's a good idea to keep the camera steady and not to cut away or include distracting ingredients).

Indeed, the scene is so traditional, it might come out of a movie of forty years ago, or eighty years ago. Of course, there *are* contemporary, 2009-era elements in the acting style, the costumes, the phrasing in the dialogue, how the camera pushes in very slowly, etc. But it's a very familiar scene.

Edward Cullen is leading the scene (literally – he leads Bella Swan into the woods, and she knows that something is up from his behaviour: when she returns home in her truck, she sees him standing near the house, watching her, and acting anything but welcoming).

This is Robert Pattinson's Big Scene in *New Moon*, and he plays it beautifully (thankfully losing a lot of the ticcy, nervy bits of actorly business from the first *Twilight* movie. In fact, Pattinson plays Edward as if he's playing Romeo – but Romeo in a Shakespeare Lite version, a teen angst version of *Romeo and Juliet*).

So Edward talks... and Bella listens: she is reacting to what he is saying. Editor Peter Lambert includes plenty of breathing space between the lines of dialogue, so the audience has time to process the heavyweight

---

26 Later in the scene, the camera rotates slightly, as the reality of what Edward is saying sinks in, and Bella's agitation increases.

information along with Bella. So that the separation scene occurs in something like 'real time' – tho' of course it's a movie version of 'real time', which's so much quicker! (The music, coming in about halfway thru, is supporting the high emotion – and once Edward has disapparated, the music – piano plus traditional orchestra – gets big rapidly. The music is helping to sell the scene).

Edward disappears (quickly); the camera frames Bella as a small figure at the bottom of the screen when it finally cuts to a high angle shot, a wide, crane shot, dwarfed by the trees (the classic way of showing someone alone, with nobody anywhere near them: if it started to rain here, we wouldn't be surprised! Maybe some thunder and lightning, too!).

Bella runs after her lover. Into the forest... then into the night (there is a *very* long fade to black over a long shot of Bella walking in the trees, as if representing all hope draining away from her). She crumples on the ground in the foetal position, weeping, while the camera, on a crane, bears down on her, turning her upside-down on the screen (as her life is turned upside-down).

She is crushed.

He was gone... Love, life, meaning... over. (73)

As the 2006 *New Moon* novel puts it, it's all over. After this, the second act of *Twilight: New Moon* portrays a very lengthy post-romance, manic depression sequence. Bella Swan is a goner – she's lost to herself and to everything around her. For months and months. As her Pa Charlie Swan says, it ain't natural to be so withdrawn (Charlie tells her: he's not coming back).

Kristen Stewart found the break-up scene a challenge, because she felt she had to really deliver emotionally:

before the scene, I was sitting in my car, like, fucking crying – crying so hard you can't breathe, because I was really overwhelmed and intimidated by the scene.[27]

Bella is a Drama Queen *par excellence* – she collapses to the forest floor and remains there for so long a manhunt is instigated by her father! So we need the spoof movie *Vampires Suck*, where Becca lies on the ground kicking and screaming like an angry, spoilt child who doesn't get her own way.

One of the curious elisions in the *New Moon* movie (because the movie follows Bella Swan's point-of-view for the most part), is the

27 In M. Howden, 133.

sudden withdrawal from the story of the Cullen coven. In the separation scene, Edward tells Bella that the Cullens are moving away (we only have his word for this – we don't see any of it). However, we do see Bella repeatedly e-mailing Alice and getting no reply (there is a little voiceover, too, with Bella reading from her messages to Alice. But why doesn't Bella also e-mail Edward, even though she knows he won't reply? But it's enough to suggest the total breach the Cullens have made with her. And she doesn't go over to the house).

We can see that Edward Cullen is not telling Bella everything from Robert Pattinson's performance. But Edward does offer several reasons for them to break up, such as the incident with Jasper, that Victoria the Nomad vampire will hunt him, that people are starting to notice that Carlisle isn't getting any older, and that Bella doesn't belong in the world of vampires. But the full explanations have to wait a long time.

MANIC DEPRESSION IN THE SECOND ACT.

The first *Twilight* movie of 2008 depicted two teenage depressives who find solace in each other's loneliness and alienation. The second *Twilight* movie of 2009 continues that dive into self-imposed melancholizing: altho' Bella Swan is in the foreground, the ghost of Edward Cullen[28] is there,[29] in the manner of Hamlet's ghost, to offer grim warnings (some of which come across more like a parent or a guardian than a friend/ boyfriend (well, he is the Ultimate Older Man – he's 109!). But of course Bella, with her deep-seated and unshakeable father complex, wants just that!).[30]

Drugs, sex, drink, cigarettes, prostitution – people have tried all of these and many more (learning crochet, collecting Pokémon toys) to numb the pain following a romantic break-up (and maybe even watching teen-romance-vampire flicks over and over! How many Twihards suffered a break-up just when *New Moon* came out? And how many have also watched the movies endlessly, even when they're blissfully in lerrrve?!).

Bella Swan's solace is adrenalin, speed, danger (*wait a second* – adrenalin? High risk goofing around? Is that *really* what Bella in the *Twilight* novels would do?! She's a weedy mouse who can't even field a volleyball! I don't buy it – either the movie-Bella or the novel-Bella. She

---

28 When Edward appears in ghostly form, he's wearing a grey, tweed suit, something he might've worn before he was vampirized (M. Vaz, 2009, 107).
29 'That was the challenge of the script, how to keep him alive in the same way the book does and stay true to the book,' Melissa Rosenberg noted. 'I think we found a way to do that.'
30 Edward is superimposed over the images in ghostly, candlelit form, to offer dour warnings or dour advice. In the novel, he's a voice in Bella's mind, tho' he seems to be appearing from outside. (Stephenie Meyer was clear that it was Bella who was conjuring up Edward, and that he wasn't there).

is not a girl who would go for motorcycle rides with bikers or jump off cliffs!).

(A significant aspect of Bella Swan's thrill-seeking in the 2006 novel was left out of the *New Moon* movie: that she becomes immune to the danger. For instance, after the crash on the motorcycle, she continues to learn to ride bikes with Jacob, and gets better. So Edward's voice recedes. In the movie, Jacob insists there'll be no more riding lessons after her tumble, and Bella moves on to the next thrill.)

So Bella Swan takes a motorcycle ride with a grizzled biker callled Chet (Michael Adamthwaite) at night for kicks in Port Angeles[31] (until the ever-watchful ghost of Edward Cullen appears and warns her, 'No!'). And then, ever the tomboy (and so much her Daddy's girl! – the *Twilight Saga* is haunted to the max by fathers and father complex girls) – she teams up with former childhood buddy Jake Black to re-build Harley and Honda motorbikes. (Wait a second – Bella finds some bikes to work on with Jacob?! Is this really the Bella Swan of the *Twilight* novels? Apparently, it is. In fact, the narrative turns that the novel of *New Moon* makes are perhaps the most unusual in the whole *Twilight Saga* – that Bella becomes an adrenalin junkie, and gets into biker culture).

The re-building-the-bike[32] scenes are handled as part-montage[33] and part-short scenes: they are really all about portraying the developing friendship between the heroine and the Second Choice Boy. So that, by the time they get to try out the bikes, and go on a date to the cinema, they are quite far along in their relationship. Tho', Bella, of course, is still holding a candle (in a bejewelled, Victorian sconce, of course) for the long-absent Edward (he's *long* gone – it's been, literally, months!).

The motorcycle sequence (filmed in Widgeon Slough, Pitt River) develops the adrenalin-junkie theme with disastrous results (repeating the pattern of the first speed-junkie scene, when Bella yelps for the biker to stop). The re-appearance of Edward – at several spots on Bella's mad dash towards a crash – is what Bella is seeking. The scene doesn't offer serious jeopardy for the heroine, but she does receive a bloody gash on her head. Her apology about there being so much blood, and Jacob's reply ('it's only blood' – *only!*), is a humorous twist on the scene that helped to persuade the Cullen clan to up sticks and move to Las Vegas (or wherever they've gone!). I mean, jeez, if Bella wasn't be so clumsy, and didn't get cut her stupid finger every damn time she opened a birthday present, Edward might still be there in her life!

---

31 Bad things seem to happen to Bella in Port Angeles.
32 In part they are a tribute to Stephenie Meyer's brothers.
33 There are some self-conscious segues to link the scenes, like the hand-over from a pizza that Bella throws to a spanner that Jacob catches.

In the comedic Port Angeles sequence (the second time we've been to the cinema in the first half of *New Moon* – is this movie secretly sponsored by film distributors trying to get punters back into theatres?), the date turns out to be Bella-plus-Mike-plus-Jake. It is awkwardness embodied, with all three being uncomfortable (Mike just can't win!). And both Mike and Jake deeply resent the other being there.

The filmmakers have fun with providing only the soundtrack of the ultra-violent movie *Face Punch*, which isn't shown (thus neatly getting around the limitations of the 'PG-13' rating for *New Moon*), and the hassle of filming it:[34] instead, the reverse angles reveal Bella sitting awkwardly in the theatre seats between the two guys who like her (Bella looks at their hands waiting eagerly to be held on the armrests).

Mike Newton[35] hurrying into the restroom to throw up after the violent scene in the action movie *Face Punch* is a funny commentary on movie-going, how movies affect people, and about scary/ violent movies (exactly the sort of movies that the *Twilight* movies want to be; note that the vampire and the werewolf elements in the *Twilight Saga*, for instance, are played 99% dead straight and serious. These are meant to be perceived as *real* vampires and *real* werewolves).

The comedy softens up the audience for the following scene in *New Moon*, which is yet another in the long series of scenes depicting the Bella-and-Jacob relationship.[36] The hand-holding, the are-they-or-aren't they? motif, poignantly explores the dilemma of the Rebound Guy, the Surrogate Boyfriend, the boy who's there for the girl (but who remains second in line until the very end).

As soon as lines are marked in the soil, or boundaries are set up, or promises are made, we know they're going to be crossed/ broken/ blurred. Indeed, it happens in this very scene: Jacob promises that he won't ever hurt Bella (what a gentleman!), and that he won't let her down (comparing his form of loving to Edward's, who abandoned her).[37] And what does he do very soon after this, as he experiences the hot flushes that lead towards werewolf transformation? He abandons her!

So, yes, in *New Moon*, Bella Swan is discarded by *two* guys! Ouch! And they're the two guys who're dearest to her! Because right after Jake threatens Mike (played with just the tone of drama-plus-humour – Taylor Launer is terrific here), he storms out, and Bella doesn't see him for

34 Altho' the dialogue still uses 'freakin'', the common, softer stand-in for 'fuckin''.
35 Mike suggests going to see *Tomorrow and Forever.*
36 Spending so much time with Bella and Jacob in *New Moon* does have a downside – we see far less of the Cullens, apart from Alice and Edward.
37 Both boys promise the heroine they will always protect her and never hurt her, and both break their vows.

weeks or months (the movie isn't clear about the amount of time passing here, but there is a montage where Bella is calling Jake several times, leaving messages, and getting no reply). In the 2006 novel, Jake is avoiding Bella, and there're hints of an illness; the movie drops most of that. (Ironically, Newton is a more suitable boyfriend for Bella in some ways).

> What a consternation of soul was mine that dreary afternoon! How all my brain was in tumult, and all my heart in insurrection! Yet in what darkness, what dense ignorance, was the mental battle fought? I could not answer the ceaseless question – *why* I thus suffered... (Charlotte Brontë, *Jane Eyre*, 47)

Bella Swan can't move.

The shocking thing about *New Moon* is its depiction of a bright, independent young girl being floored psychologically and emotionally by losing a guy (and then losing two guys!). To the point where she's repeatedly haunted by nightmares (where she screams in pain), and takes to sitting alone at lunch break, while her (former) friends talk and fool around nearby.[38] To the point where's she sitting in her bedroom doing nothing but staring out of the window. For months on end (a rather fussy, self-conscious 360° Steadicam and motion control shot[39] portrays the months passing by out of the window, and her room getting rattier (it's a fancy version of the usual device in movies to portray time passing with lap dissolves). It's the cinematic equivalent of the part of the 2006 novel where there's a word on a page – 'October' – followed by a blank page, then another page – 'November', and so on. While the girlie tones of Lykke Li sing, 'there's a possibility').[40]

> There's a possibility,
> There's a possibility,
> All that I had,
> Was all I'm gonna get.
>
> There's a possibility,
> There's a possibility,
> All I'm gonna get
> Is gone with your stare.
> All I'm gonna get
> Is gone with your stare.

It's not simply sorrow, it's not a sadness that comes and goes. This

---

38 There are, oddly, no scenes of Bella's chums cheering her up or talking to her about her troubles. In the cafeteria, they leave her alone, and when Bella decides to rejoin their table, there's an awkward silence. However, Bella does go out with Jessica on the town (with disastrous results).
39 The vfx were handled by Prime Focus. The window was enlarged from the first movie.
40 I would imagine that several songs were tried out as temp music here,a s it's a scene where the music is foregrounded.

is a consuming melancholy that is literally drowning Bella Swan. Can young love be that powerful? We like to think so, perhaps. No, wait – *yes*! It should be! It should be Life And Death, right?! *Twilight: New Moon* thrives on romantic clichés, on simple symbols like hearts and flowers (or in this case, in the romantic vampire genre, blood and glittering skin).

> Love is when you suddenly wake up as a cannibal, and not just any old cannibal, or else wake up destined for devourment. (Hélène Cixous, *Stigmata: Escaping Texts*)

But in the *Twilight Saga*, love is also portrayed as an illness which debilitates the heroine, in the melodramatic manner of 19th century literature, when lovers stake *all* on love. Love – or, rather, the loss of love – threatens Bella's life. And if sinking into the abyss of sorrow isn't enough, Bella goes out actively seeking dangerous stunts!

Much of the agony of the lovers' separation in the novel of *New Moon* is depicted in Bella Swan's continuous interior monologue. In the 2009 *New Moon* movie, although a voiceover was perhaps written and recorded, most of the psychology is dramatized in the usual cinematic manner (i.e., by finding scenes which could visualize it, or by having Bella discussing it. There are short voiceovers, however, where Bella addresses Alice in her unanswered e-mails).

The depression scenes resonated with many viewers; 15 years later, director Chris Weitz said he was pleased that the scenes were still being talked about (look at social media, which features accounts of many fans for whom Bella's plight hit home).

New Moon is terrific at depicting the self-absorbed clinging onto romance and romantic themes of the teenage years (which art never grows tired of depicting – and some people never grow out of that time in their lives). It's the adolescent period when love tears apart the integrity of the individual, unbalancing them, creating holes (Bella talks about the hole in her chest – in the book, that's part of her interior monologue). *New Moon* is all about loss and separation, the wound that nothing except that one, particular lover can heal.

Only Edward... Only Bella. (Sorry, Jake!).

> I, too, overflow; my desires have invented new desires, my body knows unheard-of songs. Time and again I, too, have felt so full of luminous torrents that I could burst... (Hélène Cixous)

And the 2009 movie leaves out several scenes we would expect to see

– especially if we've seen the first *Twilight* movie (which we have!). For instance, where oh where is Bella's Mom, Renee? They shared several phone calls in *Twilight*, with her Mom asking about boyfriends when Bella says she'll remain in Sporks instead of visiting Florida (and Mom turned up at the hospital at the end of *Twilight*, travelling from the Sunshine State). So, no calls, and no visits from Mom. Also, Bella's friends seem oddly unconcerned: she leaves them to sit on her own at the Cullen kids' table in the café at school (notice that everyone else avoids it – it's a cursed table!). Maybe Jessica's not bothered – after all, the school idol turned her down. But we'd expect Angelica to offer some support to her friend Bella (isn't that what friends are for?).

THE *TWILIGHT SAGA* AND JULIA KRISTEVA.

We don't need to get into psychoanalytic theory here, because *The Twilight Saga* is vividly clear on exactly what's going on emotionally and psychologically with Bella, Edward and Jacob. But the brilliant writings of the French feminist Julia Kristeva (b. 1941) come to mind in this section on *New Moon*, where Bella Swan is lost in an ocean of depressed subjectivity. As Kristeva puts it in her stunning book *Tales of Love,* in love one assumes one's right to be extraordinary – a great description of being in love:

> Love is the time and space in which "I" assumes the right to be extra-ordinary. Sovereign yet not individual. Divisible, lost, annihilated; but also, and through imaginary fusion with the loved one, equal to the infinite space of superhuman psychism. Paranoid? I am, in love, at the zenith of subjectivity. (1987, 5)

In *Tales of Love*, Julia Kristeva evokes the wildness of love, the loss of self and the eruption of desire:

> Vertigo of identity, vertigo of words: love, of the individual, is that sudden revelation, that irremediable cataclysm, of which one speaks only *after the fact.* Under its sway, one does not speak *of.* ("In Praise of Love", 1987, 3)

Julia Kristeva is right to describe love as the inrush of total subjectivity, an infinity of subjectivity: Bella Swan is drowning in subjectivity in *New Moon* – where Edward Cullen is merely an effect (a pretext) of her isolation and introspection. In Kristeva's psycho-poetic reading, love's the flood of the totally extraordinary, but at the expense of commonsense (as lovers learn, painfully). Bella loses her commonsense, her psychological balance, in several exaggerated scenes, to the point where she is sinking into illness.

One of Julia Kristeva's striking concepts is the semiotic realm, the pre-œdipal realm of the mother. But everyday life is lived in the symbolic realm. You could see Edward as representing the symbolic realm, while Bella is lost in the semiotic realm – Kristeva says that one cannot remain in the semiotic realm, one loses one's humanity. For a woman, that's fatal: she *has to* enter the symbolic realm (which is also linked to the social realm, and to the patriarchal realm and the father).

New Moon also explores the links between love and fear, love and masochism, as Bella Swan's behaviour moves dangerously close to self-harm (or it *is* self-harm): this is certainly one of the more disturbing aspects of *New Moon*, and the *Twilight Saga* as a whole. Self-harm (and one of its ultimate expressions, suicide), are fairly intense topics for what seems to be a romantic drama (tho' they are found in the 19th century melodramatic tradition, and of course in tragic plays (*Romeo and Juliet*) and grand opera, which the *Twilight Saga* certainly gestures towards).

As Julia Kristeva put it in her descriptions of the classic symptoms of love in literature in *Tales of Love*:

> A body swept away, present in all its limbs through a delightful absence – shaky voice, dry throat, starry eyes, flushed or clammy skin, throbbing heart... Would the symptoms of love be the symptoms of fear? Both a fear and a need of no longer being limited, held back, but going beyond. Dread of transgressing not only proprieties or taboos, but also, and above all, fear of crossing and desiring to cross the boundaries of the self... The *meeting*, then, mixing pleasure and promise or hopes, remains in a sort of future perfect. It is the nontime of love that, both instant and eternity, past and future, abreacted present, fulfils me, abolishes me, and yet leaves me unsated... Till tomorrow, forever, as ever, faithfully, eternally as before, as when it will have been, yours... (1987, 6)

Then Julia Kristeva comes to the many functions of art, one of which is, for the artist, to prolong and recapture and rework that which no longer exists. If you can't experience love, then write your way out of your predicament. If the imaginary is 'real', then virtual loving is the same as 'real' loving. Love exists in a nostalgic past or in a never-to-be-attained future. 'The *meeting*, then, mixing pleasure and promise or hopes, remains in a sort of future perfect', comments Kristeva ("In Praise of Love" [in *Tales of Love*, 6]). The only way to deal with the impossibility of love in writing, it seems, is to enter the empire of the metaphor. 'The language of love is impossible, inadequate, immediately allusive when one would like it to be most straightforward; it is a flight of metaphors – it is literature', states Kristeva (*Tales of Love*, 1). She continues, on her 'philosophy of love': '[f]or what is psychoanalysis if not an infinite quest for rebirths through the experience of love...?' (ib.) If the poet has to jump into metaphor, so does the critic or psychoanalyst. They all trade in language. But talking about love, Kristeva admits in *Tales of Love*, 'seems to me different from living it, but no less troublesome and delightfully intoxicating. Does this sound ridiculous? It is mad' (2).

NEW MOON AS A POP PROMO.

New Moon is like an extended pop promo of an indie/ alt rock/ emo love song (you can bet that plenty of emos, Goths and indie kids absolutely adore *Twilight*!).[41] It's certainly filmed like a pop promo, with its swooping camera moves, backlighting, over-use of slo-mo, and slender, pale-faced youths mooning over love and loss. Indeed, in the 2006 book of *New Moon*, Stephenie Meyer acknowledges a host of pop music acts: Muse (her favourite band), Linkin Park, Travis, Elbow, Coldplay, Marjorie Fair, My Chemical Romance, Brand New, the Strokes, Armor For Sleep, the Arcade Fire and the Fray. Meyer has also provided a list of pop music bands to form a soundtrack of her own to the *New Moon* book (not the 2009 movie), and other books. Meanwhile, the *New Moon* movie contains plenty of pop songs (as well as its own more traditional score by Alexandrer Desplat).[42] The soundtrack of *New Moon* included Anya Marina, Muse, Death Cab For Cutie (who composed the lead single, 'Meet Me In St Louis' – I mean, 'Meet Me On the Equinox'), Thom Yorke, the Killers, Editors, OK Go, Black Rebel Motorcycle Club, Hurricane Bells, Sea Wolf, Grizzly Bear, Band of Skulls, Lykke Li, and Bon Iver.

For *Eclipse,* Stephenie Meyer provided a playlist at the back of the book, with a list of pop songs and acts which fitted certain sections of the text. (And elsewhere has provided playlists for the other *Twilight* books).

And yet, incredibly, Bella Swan is *not* a music fan.[43] She doesn't like music! She rarely refers to it (and doesn't have a radio in her Chevy truck).[44] (In the fixing-the-bike montage in *New Moon*, Bella gets up to switch off the music, and says she doesn't care for it anymore – presumably meaning in her post-Edward depression). Mike Newton states it plainly:

---

41 And you can't help noticing that the pop/ rock selected for the *Twilight Saga* tends to be white indie pop (Radiohead, Muse, etc).
42 This was the regular, Hollywood orchestral score (played by the London Symphony Orchestra), recorded in London at Air Studios.
43 Bella tells Jacob at the res that she's gone off music. Guess it's too lovey-dovey for her (but there's plenty of loud, abrasive music out there, too!).
44 That was Emmett's birthday present (which he had already installed).

'How can you not like music?' Mike demanded.
I shrugged. 'I don't know. It just irritates me.' (NM, 209)

How can you *not* adore music? It is the greatest artform humans have invented. I could not live without music, so that Bella's statement – 'music just irritates me' – marks her down in my book as sicker and creepier than Satan Himself! (Or put it like this, if being rejected by Edward has 'ruined' music for her, their romance was *completely worthless*).

IT'S DIVA TIME!

The romance and growing-up and being-a-teenager elements are far more striking than the vampire and horror genre aspects of the *Twilight Saga*. It might be an even more compelling franchise if the vampire and horror elements were played down. Romantic stories don't need them. However, portraying lovers as monsters has worked for eons – because the *Twilight Saga* is essentially *Beauty and the Beast*, the Monster and the Maiden, the Ogre and the Princess, a fairy tale and folklore formula that pretty much always works (it's at least 3,000 years-old). I mean, you can use the *Beauty and the Beast* trope in 1,000s of ways (as writers, artists and filmmakers have done), and the fundamental issue – that the lover is *other* – always seems to work.

Who do you love? *Someone else*. Another person. An *other*.

The *Twilight Saga* depicts the otherness of love, of the beloved, in a high fantasy, campy, Hollywood-and-pop-promo style.

That person you love is *other* than you. They are *not* you. And yet they also *are* you. Or you absorb that person; so the 'two become one', as the cliché has it.

One love – two lovers.

No wonder then that when Edward C. tells her he's walking out of her life – perhaps the key scene in the whole *Twilight Saga* – Bella Swan falls to pieces. Because she thought they were *one*!

We are one, right? You can't leave!

Jilted! *Ouch!* No one dumps Bella Swan!

And thus Edward's departure is couched as a failure – and it replays the failure of Bella's parents, for falling apart and divorcing. And the failure of Bella to make something of her life (in her terms). Here's the motto: fall in love and be disappointed. Love somebody and have your heart crushed. Yes, that's the pessimist's view, the manic depressive's view, the emo's view.

▶

New Moon is nothing but a silly romantic fantasy in which the heroine is fated to choose the Wrong Guy time after time. Yet it is enjoyable, and in its trio of young actors it has an appeal that grows on you. Kristen Stewart, Robert Pattinson and Taylor Lautner may be somewhat bland, safe and predictable as actors, but they are also easy on the eye, and charming (the scenes between Lautner and Stewart are appealing, in their portrayal of an awkward, embarrassing possible romance).

Familiarity – after 2008's *Twilight* movie, where you want to slap Bella *and* Edward, for being such drippy wimps, you kind of get used to their manic depressive, self-absorbed ways. No jokes, and only wry quips to alleviate the so-serious tone, but the *Twilight* movies do grow on you (tho' you still want to slap them. But you know it won't do any good: can you stop someone who's on a self-destructive path? No. You can talk. You can try therapy, and you can try all the other 1,001 miracle/ New Age cures. But if someone wants to spiral down to Hell, your influence on them is limited).

It's no wonder that the *Twilight Saga* should strike a chord with female audiences: it's not only the perfect date movie ('see, honey – this is how girls feel!' you can tell your beau), it's also the perfect nobody-understands-me!–why-is-life-so-horrible?–why-do-I-live-in-such-a-squalid-town? teen drama movie. (True – but if it was a date movie, it was a movie the girlfriends picked to see, not the boys! Plenty of guys complained about being dragged along to the *Twilight* flicks by their girlfriends (they'd rather see a big action movie, I guess, or a gross-out comedy about a spotty doofus who works in a strip club in Las Vegas). Yes, but you could also point that, with its romance, love and magical ingredients, *Twilight* was perfect for getting someone into the mood! After all, what is sexier than a vampire? That was Catherine Hardwicke's goal: she wanted people to see the movie, go home and make out, then go see the movie again!).

▶

Ah, in the teenage years life is sooo *dramatic,* isn't it? Everything is *all* or *nothing.* No in-betweens. It's Diva Time! It's acting out life's thousand-and-one shocks with histrionics and hysteria.

Bella ('I'm Pouting, So What?') Swan acts like she's performing in her own movie of *Romeo and Juliet*: she acts as if there's a camera on her all the time (I mean apart from the ten 35mm cameras, high-speed Arriflexes, Vista Visions, spacecams, cable cams and motion control cameras already trained on actress Kirsten Stewart!). If the class at Forks

High School put on an am-dram show of *Romeo and Juliet*, who would play Juliet? Bella![45] And who would play the Capulet Prince? Edward! (Hell, he's already learnt the lines!).

Poor Jake Black: he might be gorgeous, buff, earthy, warm, kind, sensitive, relaxed, whatever – but he's *not Edward*! (That's his crime – he's not Edward!). For Bella, it's *always Edward*! The romantic triangle is at the heart of *Twilight: New Moon*: this is essentially a relationship movie, but with a vampy/ wolfy twist. A dating/ mating movie: do I choose Edward or Jake? Or neither, and just sit in my bedroom watching the leaves fluttering down? ('the love triangle between Bella, Edward and Jacob is remarkably fragile and volatile', as Ken Gelder put it [2012, 89]). Well, Edward has removed himself from the scene (so noble!), and Jake is right there, offering a super-warm body to cuddle up with in the truck (when you've made a failed suicide/ drowning attempt), someone to go to the movies with (and chuckle over your lame classmates who rush to the restroom to vomit), someone to build motorbikes with, and someone to hang out with.

The 2009 *Cheesy Moon* movie milks the romantic triangle to the max, placing Bella and Jake in ever more intimate settings (in a shed, in the cinema, in her bedroom, in her truck, in the forest). The opportunities for kisses come and go (Jacob Black is a bit of klutz when it comes to not taking advantage of the right moment). Kisses are interrupted with lips inches apart. (The *Twilight* movies don't go further than kissing at this stage: kissing stands in for All That Love Can Be. That is, in the cinematic romance genre, once you've kissed someone, you've crossed that All-Important Moral Line! Oh baby!).

So, no no *no*, Bella Swan *hasn't* kissed Jacob Black by the end of *New Moon*: this Little Red Riding Hood has resisted the (Were)Wolf to the end. And she remains, presumably, a virgin (she yells at her Dad in the third *Twihard* flick, 'I'm a virgin!' during one of those clumsy parent-child conversations about safe sex. Then she hurries upstairs cringeing with embarrassment).

The 2009 movie adaptation of *New Moon* makes much more of the snidey, resentful remarks that Jacob Black expresses about Bella Swan's bloodsucker boyfriend. The movie compresses by its nature the slow-burning romance between Bella and Jacob, and also renders it more hysterical and hyped-up. The slow narrative build-build-build of a Jane Austen, novelistic, romantic structure is Stephenie Meyer's preferred pace in the *Twilight* novels (where each new development in the relationship

---

45 Altho' Jessica would be furious!

between Jacob and Bella is examined in detail), but Hollywood movies are a different kettle of fish bones and decapitated vampire heads. In the movie of *New Moon*, the B.S.—J.B. relationship develops at a rapid pace, and, as is typical of cinema, arguments and confrontations are favoured as representative of the teenagers' relationship rather than reasonable conversations (notice, in drama, how the good times – sharing a pizza, fixing up a bike, riding in the truck – are given short amounts of screen time, while the arguments are explored in more depth. Well, that's drama!).

THE NEXT CHAPTER BEGINS
the twilight saga
new moon
SUMMIT ENTERTAINMENT PRESENTS
"THE TWILIGHT SAGA: NEW MOON" A TEMPLE HILL PRODUCTION IN ASSOCIATION WITH IMPRINT ENTERTAINMENT AND SUNSWEPT ENTERTAINMENT KRISTEN STEWART ROBERT PATTINSON TAYLOR LAUTNER ASHLEY GREENE RACHELLE LEFEVRE
BILLY BURKE PETER FACINELLI NIKKI REED KELLAN LUTZ JACKSON RATHBONE ANNA KENDRICK WITH MICHAEL SHEEN AND DAKOTA FANNING JOSEPH MIDDLETON, C.S.A. ALEXANDRE DESPLAT ALEXANDRA PATSAVAS PETER LAMBERT
JAVIER AGUIRRESAROBE BILL BANNERMAN MARTY BOWEN GREG MOORADIAN MARK MORGAN GUY OSEARY WYCK GODFREY KAREN ROSENFELT "NEW MOON" STEPHENIE MEYER MELISSA ROSENBERG CHRIS WEITZ
PG-13 PARENTS STRONGLY CAUTIONED
Some Material May Be Inappropriate for Children Under 13
Some Violence and Action
11.20.09
www.newmoonthemovie.com
Original Motion Picture Soundtrack Available On Atlantic Records

TOPLESS TAYLOR.

And the Oscar goes to... Taylor Lautner and his amazing body! Oh yes – surely Lautner must take some credit for the success of *New Moon*? But, come on, how many times does Lautner as Jacob Black really *need* to be topless?! (But who's complaining?!).

Bella Swan goes to see Jacob on the Quileute Indian Reservation, and argues with him in the rain – he's topless. She storms over to the res again, has a bust-up with the frat boys, and Jake is topless again. Most teasing of all, Jake visits Bella in her bedroom – and, yes, he's topless! Wow!

Think back to many of your favourite romantic dramas, and very few of them feature the male lead showing off his body to this degree (topless in one scene, maybe, but not in scene after scene).

But Taylor Lautner isn't the only one – all of the wolf boys are shirtless in many scenes. On one level, it's kind of the gender reversal of women in bikinis or lingerie, a common sight in many Hollywood movies – so common it doesn't raise any comments. It's just accepted that in a *James Bond* movie, or a flashy thriller set in Miami or Los Angeles, there will be women in swimwear. Lautner has since remarked that it was uncomfortable for him to keep playing scenes topless (and the scenes were reduced in subsequent *Twilight* films). And there is also the ethical angle of the audience contemplating an under-age actor in objectifying manner (or is the discomfort due to the rare switching of genders? Because women have been sexually objectified in cinema far more often).

One thing is striking about Taylor Lautner's performance – he builds in plenty of pauses, and delivers a lot of his lines s-l-o-w-l-y (this really comes out in the deleted and extended scenes on the home releases, where the sound hasn't been cleaned up, and the scenes don't include music, sound effects and other ingredients). Does the slow delivery come from Marlon Brando or John Wayne, who advised pausing in the middle of lines, so filmmakers can't cut away?

BELLA AND JACOB.

Ain't it always the way?! – Jake Black turns out to be a werewolf! (*Woof! Bite me!*) And these (were)wolves, as in the *Underworld* movie series, have a long-running feud with the vampires! What's a girl to do?! Ah, if only Bella Swan could be happy with the hapless, harmless, goofy Mike Newton! Sure, he's not a pretty, white, boy-band vampire with gelled hair like Edward, but he does have a better sense of humour, isn't morose, and he holds a flame for her, and asks her out on a date (to his surprise, she agrees. But it turns out to be a disaster).

Bella Swan has been actively pursuing Jacob Black (calling him). In her own passive-aggressive way, Bella is quite an active romancer when she wants to be. To the point where she jumps in her truck and hurries over to the Quileute Reservation (a scene we've seen more often with guys pursing girls).

This is an important scene in *New Moon*: it's the first big set-back in the Bella-Jacob relationship. To enhance the drama, it's played out in heavy rain (you can see the actors are really cold).[1] Again, the filmmaking approach sticks to simple singles, over-the-shoulders and the odd two-shot, because the focus is on the dialogue and the heat of the exchange: it is, of course, the mirror of the scene where Edward walks out on Bella (the affinities between the two scenes include filming from the same side, with Bella and Jacob in similar staging, the outdoor setting, and having Jacob turn and walk away from Bella).

So Jacob Black breaks his promises, and lets Bella down, and tells her, as firmly as Edward Cullen did, that she is not going to be a part of his life anymore.

Wow, punched in the face *twice* by guys! First the Beloved, then the Best Friend!

JACOB IN BELLA'S BEDROOM.

The biggest tease in *New Moon* has the hero visiting the heroine in her bedroom at night (and he's… shirtless). The eroticism of the scene is explicit: plenty of girls (and not a few boys) would just *love* it if a semi-naked babe of a boy leapt into their bedroom at night! Yet it's played straight by the actors, and the movie both teases and withholds, like endless foreplay, a movie trailer with no ending. (What is this with beautiful boys suddenly materializing in the heroine's bedroom?!).

The staging of the bedroom scene is curious – how Jacob and Bella stand there at first, how she places her fist on his torso, how he walks past her as he struggles to confess what he is, or to help her remember what he said at La Push.

This is where the 'abstinence porn' (that bizarre term) pops up (again) – how the 17 year-old Bella, after months without a boyfriend, will not succumb to the very obvious charms of young Jacob Black! Even when he presents himself to her at night, in her bedroom, and half-naked! Even a diehard Team Edward fan might be tempted, just to see what the Team

---

1 Lautner loses his wig, to become the familiar Jake.

Jacob groupies have been raving about!

BEST FRIEND.

Jacob Black is on a losing streak at every moment in the *Twilight Saga*, with only a short period just before Edward's suicide attempt in *New Moon* as his Single Hope – when he and Bella Swan are at their closest and nearly-but-not-quite-kissing. By the end of *New Moon*, when Bella tells Jake it was 'always Edward', there is no hope for Jake in that relationship!

> He was my best friend. I would always love him, and it would never, ever be enough. (NM, 219)

- The girl he loves wants someone else!
- And that guy is a vampire, sworn enemy of werewolves!
- When he reappears, she rushes to his side!
- They get engaged!
- They get married!
- They have sex!
- She gets pregnant!
- She becomes a vampire!

Come on, Jake, give it up already! It's never going to happen! The romantic triangle is over by the end of *New Moon* – the triangle that began, remember, about a third of the way thru *New Moon*. The romantic triangle lasts – what? – half a book! (But it continues to be milked in the rest of the *Twi*-pictures).

THE WEREWOLVES.

The wolves were first revealed in the foreground of *New Moon* in the scene where Bella Swan hikes up into the forest to find the beloved meadow (which now looks like her state of mind – decayed and shrivelled).[2] The movie depicts Bella finding the meadow fairly quickly (Bella? *Hiking*?!); in the novel, she spends longer trying to find it (with Jacob); she also haunts the Cullen mansion. (Well, we can't spend ten minutes of *New Moon* with Bella hiking in the wilderlands of the Olympic Peninsula without using a cel phone, the Global Positioning System and Google Maps).

Among the werewolves, cast from First Nations and Native American actors, Chaske Spencer was Sam Uley, Bronson Pelletier was Jared, Alex Meraz was Paul, Kiowa Gordon was Embry and Tinsel Korey was Emily

---

2 Real wolves were used in some scenes – such as Bella's dream.

Young.

The first *Twilight* sequel makes a surprising and abrupt cut from the intense conversation between Bella and Jacob to the paradisal moment when Bella lay beside Edward in the flowery meadow. Subsequently, the meadow idyll is intercut with scenes of Bella hiking in the forest, heightening the contrast between then and now, between Bella at her happiest and Bella in the present tense.

The 2009 movie follows the 2006 novel in having Laurent appear at this point, circling Bells like a shark before coming in for the kill. (Notice that Bella is perversely delighted to see Edward appear, when Laurent moves in closer. She might be just about to die, but she's seen Edward one last time! In her voiceover, heard over the scenes of Bella walking in the forest, she notes that she hasn't seen Edward for some time). Her final words before dying? 'Edward, I love you!' (So cute – because uttering those Three Magic Words makes everything OK, right?).[3]

Just as Laurent raises his paw for the Chop, and Little Red Riding Hood cowers feebly before him, the wolves emerge bulky and fierce from the undergrowth (in an elaborate pull-back shot, while Kristen Stewart reacts with the usual looks of fear/ awe/ surprise/ horror/ whatever, that actors have been doing to non-existent monsters on film sets for a very long time. (*New Moon* cheats, too, a little later: Bella doesn't witness the battle between Laurent and the wolves in the novel, but she imagines it – so we duly cut to slo-mo imagerey of the fight. Also, the movie *doesn't* depict the demise of Laurent at this point, but saves that for the later scene, when Jacob tells Bella what wolves are capable of).

New Moon features many ridiculous scenes, too: as soon as you introduce a pack of ten foot-long wolves, and a battle with vampires, but you want to drag it back to the 'real world', you have scenes like Bella Swan rushing into her home to confront her Pa and Harry Clearwater (with another match cut on movement, which elides several events). Chief Swan listens and acts almost immediately to his daughter's testimony (Clearwater is more sceptical – later we see the old coot hiding the wolves' footprints from Charlie. Clearwater has replaced Billy Black from the first *Twilight* movie as a Native American buddy for Charlie).

Indeed, what's fun about the *Twilight Saga* is that it *does* and *it doesn't* deliver standard or expected horror genre scenarios. It includes vampires, but they can exist among humans and not burn up in the sun. It features werewolves but they're shirtless frat boys. It has immortal characters but they live like (wealthy) high school kids. (Some *Twilight*

---

3 There is a little compassion on Larent's part about killing her. But, shoot, he has to.

fans disliked how Stephenie Meyer discarded some of the 'rules' of the horror genre and the vampire genre. But those literary 'rules', folks, were *not* written in the *Holy Bible*, were not ordained by Gods such as Thor or Zeus, and were not delivered to humans thousands of years ago by tall, green aliens!).

To sell the portrayal of the wolves, the sound team mixed sounds of snarls, grunts, breathing, feet padding, etc, very high, the actors reacted strongly (absolutely vital), and the filmmakers puppeteered parts of the settings to enhance the movements of the beasts.[4] After all, the wolves are just cartoon animals – no different, really, from putting Mickey Mouse or Bugs Bunny into live-action footage. True, the animation is digital (a.k.a. computer-aided animation), rather than cel animation (ink and paint), and – more importantly – it is given a photorealistic look, to blend in with the live-action plates. But it's still basically cartoons. (Notice that terms like 'cartoons' are avoided in contemporary Hollywood cinema, and techie terms like C.G.I. or digital animation are used by the marketing depts of movies. These are 'serious' movies that aim to be 'realistic' or 'believable' – audiences don't want to be reminded that they're really watching products that're essentially no different from putting Jerry the Mouse into live-action).

It's a Big Moment, and it has to work, so there was considerable pressure on the animation team (at Tippett Studio) to pull it off. Even more challenging was the setting: it's full daylight (night scenes can hide all sorts of tricks). It helps to sell the wolves that the scene is a big battle, so the viewer is swept along in the action (without time to contemplate the wolves at length).

There were about 60 wolf shots in *New Moon*, which were animated by ten animators at Tippet Studio. The Jacob-wolf was used as the template in the computer for all of the wolves. The filmmakers at Tippett Studio visited the Wolf Mountain Sanctuary in Lucerne Valley in Cali to study the wolves. The movie-wolves depart from real wolves in many ways, from the look and size to behaviour. The *Twilight* flicks aren't documentaries, and the werewolves are supernatural creatures, after all. They have to work in movie terms.

▶

THE SECOND WEREWOLF SCENE.

Bella Swan isn't totally a wet dish rag: she does exhibit some guts. Most of all in the scene in *New Moon* where she faces off against the group of wolf-guys at the Blacks' place on the res (having driven out

---

4 Like the boat that's smashed by Jake and Paul fighting.

there to confront Jacob for ignoring her phone calls). This is the 2nd big scene at the Quileute Indian Reservation. Not only does Bella force herself past Billy to find Jacob (already this is behaviour far removed from the Bella we know), even more incredibly, the Powerpuff Girl storms up and whacks Paul in the face (of course that punch is *not* in the book!).

Wow! You go girl! This is the big werewolf transformation reveal scene, and Jake acts exactly like Edward would: he defends Bella by attacking (Bella yells at Jake to run, and Jake hurtles towards her, and up into the air,[5] where he shape-changes and fights Paul).[6] So the guys are transforming into werewolves and fighting (as boys do over girls – you know what boys are like!).[7] The visual effects in this sort of scene seem so familiar nowadays they don't dazzle anymore: but this is complex creature animation in full daylight (nowhere to hide the mechanics of it, like trees at night), with tons of fur and details to capture (these shots eat up the visual effects budget by thousands of doubloons per shot).

This is the second werewolf scene at the Quileute Indian Reservation. After it, we see an important scene of the Wolves At Home, and the introduction of Sam Uley's lady, the wolf girl, Emily Young (Tinsel Korey).[8] She sports a very ugly facial scar from a moment when Sam lost it. Thus, this is another abusive relationship, which mirrors that of Edward and Bella, and also illustrates Jacob's warnings to Bella, that he could hurt her in his werewolf transformation.

HOW TO COPE WITH DEPRESSION.

The movie adaptation of *New Moon* exaggerated the scenes where Bella Swan pushes herself towards thrills and chills, in order to make her *feel* something other than total abjection. In the 2006 novel, Bella goes to Port Angeles and visits the cinema with Jessica Stanley. Afterwards, on their way to Maccy D's, Bella hovers around a dive bar, seeming about to enter it and hang out with the bad boys. Altho' Jessica is freaking out behind her, Bella's doing nothing more scary than standing in the road having an internal dialogue with the voice of Edward.

Well, that isn't visual or juicy enough for a movie, is it? (Let alone a Hollywood movie aimed at teens in the 2000s!). So in the adaptation of *New Moon*, Bella rides on the motorcycle with one of the scuzzy dudes

---

5 To make the actors fly, such as Jacob when he transforms into a wolf, the filmmakers used wires suspended from cranes.

6 The wolf transformation wasn't a slow process on screen (where it's often also agonizing in wolfy movies). Instead, it was very rapid (occurring in 8-10 frames).

7 It's markedly different in the novel, where Jacob is defending Bella's honour, but only fighting with Paul, and nobody seems that phased about it.

8 Oh, and there's more kissing, while Bella looks on, embarrassed, and is reminded what's missing.

(there's a suggestion of a rape scenario, as they hare off away from everybody). And Edward appears as a phantom, a much more satisfying prospect cinematically than Bella as Joan of Arc hearing voices. Indeed, friendly ghosts who know the hero appearing to advise them are a staple of cinema – famous examples include the *Star Wars* series. (There's another clever use of images from the first *Twilight* movie, as Bella replays the scenario where Edward rescued her from the bad boys harassing her in Port Angeles, when she visited the town with Jessica and Angela. The replay of the images in Bella's mindscreen here suggests that she is imagining that if she puts herself in danger, Edward will appear from nowhere to save her). Afterwards, Jessica rightly castigates Bella at length Bella for being nuts (Jessica does acknowledge Bella's sadness over Edward here. One of the best things about the girls' night out was that we saw much more of the lovely Anna Kendrick as Jessica. The character of Jessica had been enhanced from the book when the producers saw what Anna Kendrick could do with it. So they gave her the valedictory address at the graduation ceremony, made her the captain of the volleyball team, etc [CFA, 84]).

❿

Suicide and depression: love seems to be nothing but pain in the *Twilight* series: even when Bella and Edward are reunited (at the end of *New Moon*), they act as if they are about to split up in the next five seconds. These are Hollywood movies which spend *far* longer depicting love going wrong, the aftermath of break-ups, and lovers sitting depressed in their bedrooms for months on end, than lovers having a great time! (But, hey, that's drama. A story where the lovers fall in love in a minute and Live Happily Ever After from that moment onwards is a short movie). Except in the first section of *Breaking Dawn*, with the wedding and the honeymoon, the longest stretch in the *Twilight Saga* in between Things Going Wrong (but soon enough, even on the idyllic, too-good-to-be-true *James Bond* honeymoon, the bubble pops).

Depression can lead to suicide, right? Yes – especially when the classic literary text of love and suicide, *Romeo and Juliet*, is used as the thematic template, as it is throughout *New Moon*. Thus, the lovers, separated, opt to try suicide as a lifestyle choice (*New Moon* is unusual among romance tales in depicting *both* lovers going to pieces and following a self-destructive path).

Bella Swan takes her cue from the wild boy werewolves, who cliff-dive for kicks (guess there's not a lot do in the Pacific North-West!). It's tied in to the notion that Bella gets to see an phantasm of Edward when she's about to do something nuts. So, in an effort to see him One More Time, she jumps off a cliff! Into the broiling ocean! Yes, it *is* completely dumb, but, folks, this is Hollywood! This is the movies! This is fantasy!

If I can't have him, I'm gonna kill myself!

Or: *I'm gonna punish him for leaving me by killing myself!*

Yes, the logic of lovers lost in love knows no bounds! You can't reason with such hysterical states of mind.

The masochism in the *Twilight Saga,* if taken literally (and the movies are very literalizing), is disturbing (girls dicing with death). The masochism, if taken symbolically or psychologically, is just as disturbing. (One wonders if *New Moon* led to any copycat attempts, as with *The Deer Hunter* and the infamous Russian roulette scene.[9] Actually, yes, copycat incidents have occurred with the *Twilight* movies and books, including people biting victims and trying to drink their blood (such as a 13 year-old boy from Iowa). And *Twilight* isn't the only vampire flick which has inspired copycat crimes: *Interview With the Vampire* and *Queen of the Damned* are others.)

The cliff-diving sequence in *New Moon* became a major action sequence in its own right: there are high falls and underwater scenes (and, as the documentary about making *New Moon* demonstrated, a huge amount of work in pools and with stunts to achieve it all).[10] However, dramatically and psychologically, the cliff-jumping scene plays exactly as expected: Bella Swan (bless her terminal idiocy) leaps off a cliff seventy feet into the cold, dark ocean and experiences her lover Edward appearing before her (and Victoria is swimming towards her, too. The Pacific is freezing in Malibu, so it has to be even colder a thousand miles up the coast!). She's buffeted about and nearly dies – only to be rescued by – guess who! – Jacob! (Bella is framed in the centre of a shot, after knocking herself unconscious on the rocks when she spots Victoria, with the apparition of Edward on the right, and Jake's arm on the left).

The cliff-and-ocean scene, for all its spectacle and thrills and danger (and high cost), shoots us right back to the romantic triangle which keeps not only this movie ticking along like a Porsche purring along the Italian highways, but the next *Twilight* movie too! (The shot puts Bella in the centre between Jacob and Edward again – but Edward has taken himself out of the running, and is only a figment. Jacob, thankfully, is the real

---

9 The Russian roulette scene in *The Deer Hunter* was associated with 31 incidents involving Russian roulette with handguns between 1979 and 1982, according to Steven Prince in *Screening Violence* (2000). Director Michael Cimino said they did their homework, spoke to 100s of Vietnam veterans, and there were reports of Russian roulette. Besides, Russian roulette with firearms wasn't invented by *The Deer Hunter* – it goes back at least to Napoleonic times.
10 The underwater scenes were filmed at a swimming pool in Vancouver, not the usual tank at a film studio (with partial sets, built by Prime Focus).

thing, a flesh-and-blood guy who can rescue the Arizonan Princess when she acts like a jerk).

▶

The cliff-jumping sequence in *The Moon Really Is Made of Cheese* is excitingly intercut with the werewolf hunt sequence: there's a trade-off that comes with parallel action, of course: it means that both scenes are extended longer, and the suspense of one sequence can be lessened by shifting to the other plot strand. The intercutting works here, tho', and adds a real sense of pace and excitement to the middle acts of *New Moon* (this is the sort of sequence that film editors adore cutting. The song – 'Hearing Damage' by Thom Yorke – is also mixed high).

Thus, the reappearance of Victoria emerges side-by-side with the authorities (led by Chief Swan) hunting down the animals that Bella Swan insists she has seen (where? In the good, ol' forest, yet again! Yes, that forest does a *lot* of dramatic work in the *Twilight* series). The filmmakers push the threat hard, by having the Nomad vampire Victoria (complete with long, Pre-Raphaelite hair!) suddenly materializing right behind Chief Swan (a 'Behind You!' pantomime moment that's not in the book). Harry Clearwater seems to save the day (he senses the vampire), but in the process he suffers a heart attack after she picks him up.

The 2009 movie adds more bits of business in the vampire hunt to the 2006 novel, with elaborate shots with the camera on a cable, overhead shots, speed ramping shots, and an exciting face-off between the Jacob-wolf and the vampire.

Again, Bella Swan doesn't witness any of this in the *New Moon* novel, but the additions to the novel in the film script (and the inter-cutting) pay off with a sacrifice and a death – but not Bella's death, from drowning. (The script puts together life and death in the dialogue, too, when Jake tells Bella, just as she recovers on the beach from nearly drowning, that Harry Clearwater has died).

THE NEAR-KISS IN THE TRUCK.
Events are conspiring against Jacob Black at every moment in *New Moon*! It's 'no fair' being Jacob! No sooner is he cuddling up with Bella Swan in her truck on the way home from the ocean (after helping her back to life on the beach!), when it seems like a kiss is imminent, than the ominous black car of the Cullens looms in the road. And then when the nearly-lovers are in the kitchen alone (while Alice waits outside), and again a kiss seems like a dead cert (it's Kiss Opportunity #51), who

should ring up (always getting in the way!), but Edward damn-his-glittery-skin Cullen! Can't Jake get a break?!

(And Jacob was so close! In the truck, Bella says she'll tell him how special he is when he thinks he might be losing himself. If ever there was an opportunity, this is it! He's just saved her life. Not only from drowning, but being chomped by a vampire! As the camera tracks in, played in a lengthy take, the virtuous princess remembers herself, and her undying lerrrve for Edward Sullen. As if to reward her for her nun-like restraint, who should appear, but Alice! Thus, as in the first *Twi*-movie, it's Alice who ushers in the finale).

THE FOURTH ACT.

The fourth act of *New Moon* (using the 25-30 minute per act model) is clearly announced with the arrival of Alice Cullen at Bella Swan's home in Forks, Washington. Up until this moment, we've been tracking closely the Bella and Jacob relationship-slowly-possibly-becoming-a-romance. We've had the gradual getting-to-know-each-other scenes, the trying-out-the-bikes scene, the cinema-date scene and the sudden-withdrawal scenes.

And when Jacob and Bella seem closer than ever, and're about to kiss in the truck, who should appear, but an emissary of the Cullens – the very 'Cold Ones' and 'bloodsuckers' that Jacob's been warning Bella about! And the re-appearance of Victoria and Laurent is one of the reasons for Jake's transformation.

As soon as Bella spots the upmarket Cullen car, she does a complete turn-about, and Jacob from now on stands *no chance*. No, not a single iota! Not a smidgen! Bella's behaviour switches instantly from repentant cliff-diver, near-suicider and Jacob-admirer to born-again Cullen groupie and vampire lover.

EDWARD AS ROMEO.

Yes – because Edward Sullen is pining away in South America like Romeo's exile in Mantua in *Romeo and Juliet*. He plumps for the ritual 'suicide' of exposing himself as a vampire right at the height of an anti-vampire festival in Volterra, Italy! The heartland of the Volturi! The streets're crowded with 850 extras wearing scarlet robes,[11] and Edward decides to show everyone that's he's a vampire, when the Hand of the Clock of Doom strikes noon. But of course, Bella races to the scene just

---

11 A big job for the wardrobe department, clothing all of those extras. It was easy getting the extras – and most of the people who applied were women.

in time! In a yellow Porsche 911 Turbo convertible![12] So the girl saves her man! Oh boy, you had to be there!

The concept is sort of bizarre, if you consider it for more than a second: someone showing off their glittery skin at a festival (where everybody is dressed up and feeling high from the event anyway) might be interpreted as nothing more'n a splashy Hallowe'en costume. Far better, and more in keeping with the vampire genre, would be to have Edward chomping on some victims in the crowd, or going to the media for a giant kiss-and-tell. Just showing some shiny skin doesn't work for me. (Try showing off your shimmery face at any pop festival! Where it would blend in seamlessly with the Marilyn Manson Goths, the blinged-out, hip-hop home boys, the retro, Clash punks, and the hedonist dancers grooving to a 10,000 dollar-a-night DJ, and where the reaction would be, *duh, whatever!*).

The plotting of the finale of *New Moon* is very patchy, to say the least. For ex, at this point in the *New Moon* movie, there are several too-rapid events which the audience has to buy wholesale. For example, Edward calls the Swan household, only to have Jacob answer the phone (just as he was about to kiss Bella – come on, Jake, leave the phone alone for a moment!). So, Edward thinks that Bella is dead, when Jake mutters darkly about a funeral (he means for Harry Clearwater).

Of course, a couple of phone calls to other people would've told Edward-as-Romeo the truth, that li'l Bells was still alive and fretful as ever (he can call her school, her doctor, her Mom Renee, the police station, whoever).[13] But, no, he's as self-absorbed and lost in his own netherworld as Bella is! (And he crumples his cel phone in rage. *Duh!*).[14] So with one phone call, Edward loses it completely, and travels to Italy[15] to commit *hari kiri*, vampire-style. Or, to put it more bluntly, to make a complete imbecile of himself.

The sudden jolt in the storytelling of *New Moon* looks as if two or three scenes were excised – because suddenly Bella Swan's sitting in Alice's motor, and Jacob Black is pleading with her not to go at the car window (the extras on the home entertainment releases show a little more to these scenes). Playing the scenes intensely, on the part of Alice and Bella, helps to sell this sudden lurch in the direction of the narrative (which is similar to the end of the baseball game in the first *Twi-hard* movie, when it switches pace to become a run-of-the-mill TV thriller).

12 Alice drives the Porsche in a headscarf – a little Euro glam *à la* Sophia Loren or Monica Vitti.
13 In the novel, Rosalie also says that Bella's dead.
14 Handily – so he can't call anyone, and Bells can't call him back and tell him he's a *major jerk!*
15 No, don't point out that it might take Edward longer to reach Italy from Rio than Bella in Forks! (Or that he also has time for an appointment with the Volturi first!).

When Alice Cullen has her visions, the *Twi*-movies don't show us what she sees (until later); instead, we hear what she tells other characters. Many filmmakers would be tempted to feature blurry, dreamy images in a rapid montage, as they often do for visions and dreams of the future.

❧

However, ladies and gentlemen, let's remind ourselves that the plotting in the Greatest Love Tragedy in English literature, *Romeo and Juliet*, also has storytelling in the finale that is both hackneyed and ridiculous (so maybe Stephenie Meyer intended the finale of *New Moon* to be as klutzy as William Shakespeare's 1590s tragedy, or a spoof of Shakespeare). For ex, the Priest's schemes in *Romeo and Juliet* I've always thought were just bonkers: there are so many things that can go wrong with the idea of Juliet playing dead using poison! And things do go wrong! Two kids die (and others. However, *Romeo and Juliet* was played with a happy ending in some productions – such as in the 17th and 18th centuries).

Twilight Saga: New Moon is as stupid but also as understandable, at the emotional level, as the plotting of the ending of *Romeo and Juliet.* Indeed, William Shakespeare's plays are full of just as many (no, way more!) clichés and stereotypes as the *Twilight* books and movies. However, you'd have to admit that Shakespeare was probably, maybe, just possibly a finer writer than Stephenie Meyer!

THE VOLTURI.

When the Volturi are introduced, the *Twilight* movies make them much more the scary, creepy villains of the typical action-adventure movie than they are in the books (where, as Stephenie Meyer explained, they are not out-and-out Bad Guys). Edward Cullen provides the voiceover explaining the Volturi (over the scene where he and Bells contemplate the Mannerist painting in the Cullen mansion), and we are soon shown a Mafia-style execution (as Lord Aro and co. decapitate and tear apart an unfortunate vampire victim).

This reveal of the Volturi occurs in a very complex shot as a painting comes to life, taking us back 100s of years (no, don't ask why Carlisle Cullen would have a painting of the dastardly Volturi in his home!). The scene is important too because it introduces one of the stars of the movie, Michael Sheen. And, as he's playing a super-villain, he's depicted doing what super-villains often do in their introductory scene – he's killing someone (and with his own hands).

The jaunt to Italy in *New Moon* makes a welcome change of scene for the *Twilight Saga*, with some bright, Mediterranean sun washing away the misty greens and greys of the Pacific North-West. With its imagery of a Porsche sports car racing along the dusty roads of Tuscany (driven by Alice in a scarf who looks more'n more like Audrey Hepburn),[16] we might be in a globe-trotting *James Bond* movie. Certainly composer Alexandre Desplat provides a very big music cue to cover up the abrupt shift to Mediterranean climes, warm sun, and a wholly different look from the movie's previous 1h 30m.[17] (The location scouts opted for Montepulciano in Tuscany to act as Volterra, the Volturi's vampire lair. Wherever you put your camera in those gorgeous Italian hill-towns you'll get a great image).

The anti-vampire festival of St Marcus provides a suitably colourful and dramatic setting for the re-uniting of the lovers, where the heroine – can you believe it?! – 'saves' the hero from ritual suicide! The narrative contrivances required to make this happen – by author Stephenie Meyer, by screenwriter Melissa Rosenberg, and by the 100s of filmmakers – are sort of accepted by the audience because, well, shoot, this *is* a romantic fantasy, after all! And it's the finale of a Hollywood movie! Who cares if it doesn't convince on any level 'realistically'! It's a *fantasy*. We all accept that the *Twilight* novels and movies are stuffed with plot holes and things that don't make sense.

The Volturi mob are a bunch of aristocratic, sadomasochistic vampires who're headed up by the totally wonderful Michael Sheen and his insane vampire Lord Aro,[18] and cohorts such as Marcus (Christopher Heyerdahl) and Caius (Jamie Bower), and tiny Dakota Fanning (here playing the vicious bully Jane). These are the sort of people who smile evilly as they torture victims, who take delight in creating mayhem, yet who remain decorous and polite when they're not punishing and maiming. (And they dress and behave like the vampires of movie cliché. Bella expected castles and coffins when she visited the Cullen home in *Twilight*, but here comes the expected look of vampires in cinema. Thus, the Cullens didn't need to be conventional movie-vampires, because the Volturi supplied that).

In the flashback scenes, the Volturi wear breeches, muslin shirts, and florid coats (all in gold hues). In the present day, they appear in judicial robes, with Lord Aro in a black suit (their look suggests the authorities who run the Vatican City and the Italian Government).

16 We have to forget that niggle about vampires showing up all glittery-like in the sunlight.
17 Visually, the transition from the U.S.A. to Italy is clichéd: the camera tilts up from Alice and Bella roaring away from the Swan residence to the sky, then segues into images of a jet (Virgin America!) in a sky that changes from night to day.
18 Hollywood movies have been casting Brit actors as the villains since forever. Of the recent crop concurrent with the *Twilight* movies were Bill Nighy, Ben Kingsley, and Christopher Lee..

MICHAEL SHEEN.

Just look at what actor Michael Sheen does with Lord Aro! He is the great delight of the finale of *New Moon*. On the page in the 2006 novel of *New Moon*, Aro is a strange, pale, eccentric old coot, with a tendency to chuckle (as super-villains often do). Aro's face is described as perfect, with translucent white skin, like the skin of an onion, long, jet black hair, red eyes, with a milky film (NM, 467).

But it's still a rather under-written characterization, as all the characters are in *The Twilight Saga*, bar the golden trio. But the performance by Michael Sheen adds so much: and this is why you hire an actor as skilled and quirky as Sheen, to bring your pedestrian script to life. Sheen of course added that manic laugh – for some viewers, that was worth the price of admission on its own! And altho' Aro chuckles in the novel, he sure doesn't laugh *like that*! And his voice – it's a breathy, high voice that's totally different from the Yanks in the cast. (The scene at Volturi HQ is an ensemble scene, a good scene for studying performance styles: nobody stands a chance when Sheen is in the frame; and here by comparison we can see just how over-cooked (and annoying) Kristen Stewart's nervy, ticcy acting style is).

Michael Sheen said he thought of Lord Aro as a someone 'who played at being a kindly, sentimental romantic – an old grandmother, almost, and yet underneath was a heartless killer' (CFA, 71). Sheen cited the Blue Meanies from *Yellow Submarine* (1968) and the Child-catcher from *Chitty, Chitty, Bang, Bang* (1968) as inspirations.

Michael Sheen (b. Feb 5, 1969, Newport, Wales) has appeared in many theatre productions (*Caligula, Amadeus, Romeo and Juliet, The Seagull, Hamlet, Look Back In Anger, Henry V*, etc), before moving into television and movies (*The Queen, The Deal, Frost/ Nixon, Midnight In Paris* and *Underworld*). Sheen has directed plays, received many awards, and critics have enthused about his performances many times. Of his appearance in *Amadeus* on Broadway, the *New York Times* remarked: 'you start to appreciate the derivation of the term star. This actor is so luminous it's scary!'

THE ACTION FINALE.

By the time we reach the finale of *New Moon*, the filmmakers, as expected, expanded the action and conflict from the 2006 novel up to the level demanded by Hollywood blockbuster movie audiences around the world. The confrontation with the Volturi amounts in the book of *New Moon* to nothing but an extended conversation. Yes, it's talk and more talk in the 2006 novel (rather like the finale of *Breaking Dawn* – *in the book*, that is!).

So, in the 2006 Meyer text: Aro talks… Edward talks… Alice talks a bit… Bella eventually pipes up… Edward is tortured for a moment, then there's more talk… And that's it.

No Hollywood blockbuster movie would be content with that! So Edward isn't just grilled on the floor for a moment by Botticelli-beautiful vampire Jane, he's hurled around the room and smashed about by the heavies. (Listen to the numerous sound effects added to the scenes of Edward and Felix fighting and throwing themselves around, while Bella looks on and screams (as heroines must): they add roars and growls a-plenty to sell the stunts. However, Stephenie Meyer preferred a more modest approach, so some of the ideas were toned down, such as Alice and the others getting into fights. But it might do well to go even bigger than what we see.[19] Indeed, with all of the characters gathered together in the finale of a movie like this, we might expect much bigger action, and many other film teams would opt for a large-scale bust-up).

There *is* a *lot* of talk before the action, however: we learn about Lord Aro's skills, Jane's pain, about the Volturi's set-back, about the relationship between the three high-ranking vampires, and how the Volturi regard the Cullens and Bella Swan (Aro in particular appears fascinated by Bella – whether he fakes interest out of 3,000 years of boredom doesn't matter. Elsewhere we learn that Aro collects people).

There is one vampire dominating the scene: Lord Aro, of course, the King in Stephenie Meyer's vampire world. Here's where the scene in the first act which introduced the Volturi pays off: we saw Aro ripping the head off a vampire victim, so we know what he is capable of. Thus, altho' Aro appears in some respects a politely-spoken, pale, middle-aged Englishman in a dark suit, he also has a tendency to be playful and fey – and red eyes! (Sort of a giveaway, really).

In short, Lord Aro is one of the villains in movies who are the scariest of all: *you don't know what he's going to do*. Kill Bella? Chat with her? Kill her boyfriend and enjoy her shocked reaction? It could go in any direction.

The big action finale in *New Moon* takes place, as usual in Hollywood, blockbuster movies, in the Big, Expensive Set (which's also often, as here, the Villain's Lair. And it often blows up or falls to pieces). The big set is an Italianate design evoking the mediæval and Renaissance

---

19 The Edward vs. Felix fight takes its cue from the first movie's finale: it's close-in, with grabbing, hitting and throwing, and using different running speeds (again, speeding up the movement didn't look right, so slo-mo was employed).

spaces of Italy – the power of the Catholic Church, of the Vatican, of the Medici, of the Italian Government. It was easy to find inspirations for the Montepulciano set, David Brisbin recalled; they used the Duomo in Firenze, for instance, for the look of the marbling (at one time there were around 100 people working on the marble).

Bella Swan knows too much, so the nasty Italian mobsters have to kill her, right? Well, *duh*, if the hero/ine of the whole show isn't being threatened, it isn't a Hollywood, blockbuster movie (or a low budget indie film), right? And of course Edward Cullen intervenes and a fight breaks out. It's essentially a replay of the finale of the 2008 *Twilight* movie, with the stunt team (J.J. Makaro, Gianlucca Petrazzi and Mike Desabrais were stunt co-ordinators) conjuring up some impressive[20] combinations of live-action, multiple film speeds and visual effects to portray vampire velocity and superhuman strength.

There's another reveal - of Bella's ability, before becoming a vampire, of resisting nasty Jane's attacks. A considerable talent, then, after we've witnessed how Jane brought down Edward rapidly (Edward is out-matched by both Jane and Felix).

But *Twilight: New Moon* cops out and looks forward to the next movie, by not dealing with the villains, and not resolving the vampiric issue (of Bella Swan knowing too much and wanting to be a vampire so she can live with Edward f-o-r-e-v-e-r). We know there is another movie on the way – the *Eclipse* novel had been published in 2007, and *Breaking Dawn* in 2008 (before the release of the first *Twilight* movie. Indeed, *Eclipse* was in theatres only seven months later).

So our heroes walk free, and the villains cackle, and Victoria the Nomad vampire is still at large, tho' at least the heroine has been reunited with her beloved. (And, can you believe it?, the villains aren't destroyed even in the final *Twilight Saga* movie! They walk (well, whisk) away with a chortle from a battle that never even happened!).

There's a dramatic cheat here, too: a human full of blood with a beating heart entering right into the inner sanctum of a nest of the nastiest of all vampires! Surely they would rip Bella to shreds! We've already seen Edward, Jasper and others barely able to control themselves when they're near Bella. (Lord Aro does indicate that he thirsts for Bella's blood). However, the vamps know that their underling Heidi (Noot Seear) is bringing along a fresh batch of dumb tourists soon (Marcus mentions it), so maybe they can hold back for another five minutes.

That it's *Alice* who saves the day, and prevents Aro and Felix from

---

20 Impressive by American cinema standards, but compared to a Chinese action movie, ropey.

twisting off poor Edward's skull,[21] is the 2nd of several times when this ruse is used in the *Twilight* movies (it's employed for the colossal cheat in *Breaking Dawn*, for instance). Indeed, the 2009 movie is keen to explore the special gifts of the vampires as well as brute force and speed: so we have Aro commanding Jane to demonstrate her powers, and discovering that Bella possesses a formidable shield (Aro also tries out his mind-reading powers on Bella, Edward and Alice).

Clever little Alice! When the girl in the pixie wig pipes up, insisting to Lord Aro that Bella Swan will definitely be turned into a vampire, the movie features a vision that Alice shows Aro (so now we are in Aro's mindscreen – keep up!): in a rather silly slo-mo sequence unfortunately reminiscent of Hollywood schmaltz like *The Sound of Music* or a shampoo commercial, we see Bella as a vampire with Edward as a vampire romping thru sunlight trees in slow motion (with their skin sparkling in the sun). Surely Aro isn't convinced by this cheesy, greetings card vision of Bella and Edward? Or is Alice conjuring up something which she reckons will convince Aro? If so she opts for something like a chocolate box lid.

By your usual movie-movie rules, the super-villain would shrug but still order the immediate deaths of the three heroes (then there would be a daring rescue by the rest of the Cullen coven, aided perhaps by a new super-vamp character). But the *Twilight Saga* books and movies are *very* reluctant for any character to pay the price (in *Breaking Dawn*, they pretended to kill important charas, then revert to happy smiles and 'it was all a dream'). So, the only significant death occurring in *New Moon* is of the very minor character Harry Clearwater, plus the vamp Laurent (and the victim of the Volturi in the 300-year flashback in act one).

So, out shuffle the heroes from the Volturi Underland in Volterra, sort of triumphant, but actually defeated and morose, passing a bunch of tourists in the endless, curving corridor who soon become victims of the venal vampires (a piece of black humour that deflates the high tension of the action finale of *New Moon*. Often it's a sidekick who delivers a quip: here it's a bunch of innocent people being slaughtered! Yes, a massacre of thirty civilians is played for laughs).[22]

THE EMOTIONAL FINALE.

The Italiano trip and the Volturi confrontation, colourful and fun as it was, is but a mere sideshow to the romantic triangle at the heart of *New Moon* of three American teenagers (for a start, nothing significant altered

---

21 We also see this in an imagined moment from Bella.
22 Incredibly, the *Twilight Saga*, in movie-form, sidesteps many opportunities for black humour.

for the major charas in the Italian jaunt – it amounted to getting told off by a rather severe and weird teacher, and the heroine 'saving' the hero from a not very convincing demise).

For the emotional climax of *New Moon*, there is a very subdued and restrained bedroom scene. After the vampire fight, with its loud clashes and crashes, the Forks bedroom[23] at the Swans' place is remarkably quiet (but Bella wakes up screaming – again – when the movie cuts from the sound of the shrieking tourists to a close-up of Bella in bed – *New Moon* is Kristen Stewart's screamy movie. Lead actresses in the horror movie genre have to scream a lot – it's one of their primary functions).

With the lovers affirming their love, and what idiots they've been, Jacob Black doesn't stand a chance! As Bella tells Jake in the final scene of *New Moon*, it was always Edward for her. (Charlie Swan pops up to have his fatherly talk, and exert his parental authority by grounding his daughter).

Before the final scene in *New Moon*, there's a curious beat where Bella is re-united with the Cullen coven. It's a muted, serious reunion, with no explanations offered of where the Sullens buggered off to, or why they've come back. So, suddenly, they're back (in their mansion). No warm welcomes, either. No time for a glass of wine and a chat.

None of that: instead, we are straight into the meat of the scene: what do they think about Bella becoming a vampire? The Sullens take votes:[24] Edward votes: *no*; Rosalie votes: *no* (no surprise there!);[25] Esme, Alice,[26] Emmett[27] and Carlisle: *yes*. (Carlisle addresses his decision to *Edward*, and *not* to Bella, stepping past her: he doesn't want to lose his son, he says).

On the way back from Cullen Ground Control, once again we're back in the forest[28] for the important showdown between Edward and Jacob, with Bella caught in the middle. Two guys, one girl: someone's got to lose, right? The scenario will be repeated throughout the third *Twilight* movie: Bella in the middle of two attractive guys[29] who are nuts about her (and of course they loathe each other – and there's no need for one to be a vampire and the other to be a werewolf for the animosity to smoulder away!).

Edward C. unexpectedly thanks Jacob B. (partly because he's certain

---

23 Note the deep red bed cover, as if Bella has dried blood on her.
24 Yes, the Cullens are a democracy, compared to the dictatorship of the Volturi!
25 The lines of dialogue that Nikki Reed speaks are the longest in the *Twilight Saga* so far – in the next movie, *Eclipse*, we delve deeper into Rosalie's back-story.
26 Alice is first, hugging Bella.
27 Emmett, refreshingly simple emotionally, grabs Bella in a bear-hug.
28 Yet another helicopter shot.
29 Once again, Jacob is topless, for no reason.

now that Bella has chosen him), and the younger boy tries repeatedly to persuade Bella not to go with Edward, and certainly not to become one of the hated 'Cold Ones'. Bella, meanwhile, asserts that it is *her* choice, not his.

With plenty of growling and glowering, the testosterone-laden confrontation ends with a fight and a transformation: Edward hurls Jake away from him; Jake shape-changes, and snarls. Unfortunately, Bella has chosen Edward, and goes home with Edward, and has told Jake that it has always been Edward. Crushed, Jacob slinks away.

The scene shifts into a new topic, which will be a recurring question for the next film and a half: *when?* When will Bella be transformed? When will she get what she wants? Edward hesitates again (as he will do many more times), repeating Jake's thoughts, that maybe it isn't a good idea.

As the camera holds on extended close-ups of the actors, Bella Swan is stubbornly insistent that she wants to become a vampire. They trade dates. Five years, three years, a year (the *Twilight Saga* sticks to the 'year and a day' sort of schedule of fairy tales).

The last two shots of *New Moon* are a close-up of Edward, then a close-up of Bella, then a cut to black, and the credits roll. But it's what Edwards says here that's been saved for the final beat: 'marry me'. Yes, the *Twilight Saga* is a very traditional, romantic drama, in which words like 'marry me' carry enormous weight. (Notice how the music, with the string section of the London Symphony Orchestra sawing away and the piano plinky-plunking happily, fades to nothing just before the magic words are uttered by the boy-band vampire (as the shot holds and holds): 'marry me'. When we cut to Bella's close-up, she takes a sudden breath, not expecting this particular condition.

▶

Making New Moon.

THE twilight SAGA

eclipse

IT ALL BEGINS... WITH A CHOICE.

SUMMIT ENTERTAINMENT PRESENTS "THE TWILIGHT SAGA: ECLIPSE" A TEMPLE HILL PRODUCTION IN ASSOCIATION WITH MAVERICK/IMPRINT AND SUNSWEPT ENTERTAINMENT KRISTEN STEWART ROBERT PATTINSON TAYLOR LAUTNER
BRYCE DALLAS HOWARD BILLY BURKE AND DAKOTA FANNING MUSIC BY HOWARD SHORE MUSIC SUPERVISION ALEXANDRA PATSAVAS COSTUME DESIGNER TISH MONAGHAN EDITOR ART JONES NANCY RICHARDSON, A.C.E. PRODUCTION DESIGNER PAUL DENHAM AUSTERBERRY
DIRECTOR OF PHOTOGRAPHY JAVIER AGUIRRESAROBE CO-PRODUCER BILL BANNERMAN EXECUTIVE PRODUCERS MARTY BOWEN GREG MOORADIAN MARK MORGAN GUY OSEARY PRODUCED BY WYCK GODFREY KAREN ROSENFELT BASED ON THE NOVEL "ECLIPSE" BY STEPHENIE MEYER
THIS FILM HAS NOT YET BEEN RATED SCREENPLAY BY MELISSA ROSENBERG DIRECTED BY DAVID SLADE JUNE 30 Original Motion Picture Soundtrack Available On Atlantic Records
www.eclipsethemovie.com

5

ECLIPSE, THE MOVIE

My imagination is sadly out of control... I needed therapy.

Stephenie Meyer, *Eclipse* (44).

INTRODUCTION.

The second *Twilight* sequel, *Twilight: Eclipse* (2010), was Business As Usual: a romantic triangle, some high school scenes, vampire duels, embarrassing conversations with parents, visual effects a-plenty, and helicopter shots of trucks/ bikes/ cars driving thru lonely (but pretty) forests. It was the 'same old, same old', as Bella Swan puts it in the 2007 book of *Eclipse;* 'the usual', as Jacob affirms.[1]

The feeling of *déja-vu* is summed up succinctly in the novel of *Eclipse*:

> 'What's up, Bella?' he asked with a big grin.
> I rolled my eyes. 'Same old, same old.'
> 'Yeah,' he agreed. 'Bunch of vampires trying to kill you. The usual.'
> 'The usual.' (E, 420)

For me, the pleasure of the *Twilight* franchise is seriously weakened by the time you reach the third movie (and the third novel). The first film (and the first book) is by far the most compelling, and it works as a stand-alone piece. *New Moon* is fascinating as a commentary on the first outing, with some truly eccentric twists on romantic clichés and a fascinating portrayal of depression and anxiety. In some ways, *New Moon* is the most enjoyable of the five *Twi-Saga* flicks, because of those

---

1 Or as Jimi Hendrix noted, 'S.O.S' = Same Old Shit.

unusual narrative turns.

But what do I know? – because *Eclipse* opened to incredible business, and sell-out midnight screenings. (Box office gross: domestic: $300,531,751. International: $405,570,004).

Eclipse was produced by Temple Hill/ Maverick/ Imprint/ Sunswept/ Summit. Producers: Wyck Godfrey,[2] Karen Rosenfelt, Bill Bannerman, Marty Bowen, Greg Mooradian, Mark Morgan, Isaac Klausner and Guy Oseary (7 guys, 1 woman); Melissa Rosenberg wrote the screenplay;[3] Javier Aguirresarobe was DP; Paul Denham Austerberry was production designer; Tish Monaghan oversaw the wardrobe; Charles Porlier was make-up designer; Gina Sherritt was key hair stylist; John Stoneham, Layton Morrison, Larry Lam (uncredited) and Jonathan Eusebio were stunt and fight co-ordinators; E.J. Foerster was second unit director; casting by Stuart Atkins, Sean Cossey and Rene Haynes; Art Jones and Nancy Richardson were the editors; Justin Muller was first A.D.; Stuart Provine and Mandell Winter were sound effects editors; Howard Shore[4] composed the score (Muse provided the main single: 'Neutron Star Collision (Love Is Forever')); Jeremy Ball, Phil Tippett, Eric Leven and Jon Cowley were vfx supervisors; Alex Burdett was mechanical fx supervisor. Visual effects were by Rodeo, Image Engine, Tippett Studio, C.I.S. Hollywood, C.I.S. Vancouver, Animatrik, Wildfire, Prime Focus, Lola Visual Effects, Make, Proof, Hammerhead, Hatch and Plug. According to co-producer Bill Bannerman, the total crew for *Eclipse* was between 600 and 800 people. Released: June 30, 2010. 124 mins.

Eclipse starred Kristen Stewart, Robert Pattinson, Taylor Lautner (the three top-billed stars), Bryce Dallas Howard, Billy Burke, Ashley Greene, Kellan Lutz, Nikki Reed, Peter Facinelli, Xavier Samuel, Anna Kendrick, Michael Welch, Justin Chon, Jackson Rathbone, Elizabeth Reaser, Sarah Clarke, Christian Serratos, Gil Birmingham, and Dakota Fanning (but, alas!, no Michael Sheen!).[5] Notice the *very* short period between the releases of *New Moon* and *Eclipse*: Nov, 2009 and June, 2010 (so *Eclipse* was in pre-production while *New Moon* was in post-production).

Principal photography began on Aug 17, 2009 and ended on Oct 29, 2009. The reported budget was $68 million. The film opened in over 4,468 theatres worldwide. *Eclipse* won awards for Teen Choice, Scream,

---

2 One of the entertaining aspects of the DVD release of *Eclipse* is the audio commentary by Godfrey and Stephenie Meyer.

3 For the director David Slade, Melissa Rosenberg said he wasn't a writer, but a visual director, who preferred to think in terms of the visual aspects of a scene.

4 Some of Shore's cues sound very much like reworkings of cues he wrote for the *Lord of the Rings* movies.

5 Partly because Aro and the chief Volturi can't be bothered to travel out of Italy. But they do for the final *Twilight* film! For a non-existent battle!

People's Choice, and M.T.V. Movie Awards.

Among the companies involved with the marketing of *Eclipse* were Burger King (offering raw cow meat, and real blood instead of ketch-up), and fashion label Nordstrom. Among the publicity jaunts were *The Oprah Winfrey Show* and the M.T.V. Movie Awards.

Eclipse's production filmed in Vancouver, Canada for the usual reasons anybody goes to the 'Hollywood of the North' – saving money and available studio/ office space, along with scheduling. Like many movie productions of recent years, the *Twilight* series took advantage of the financial gains of filming in Canada (such as the exchange rate), basing itself out of Vancouver Film Studios (filming also took place at the Canadian Motion Picture Park Studios in Burnaby). British Columbia in Canada stood in easily for the Pacific North-West – in fact, it's not very far from the Olympic Peninsula and Forks (altho' the shoot was often very cold on location, as it so often is, wherever you film. Even if you pick a spot that seems to be warm or even hot, somehow it soon turns cold). The Seattle scenes in *Eclipse* were filmed in Vancouver (as well as the Forks scenes).

Eclipse's a violent movie, as the Parental Guide written by the Screen It website pointed out: 'Violence consists of people being bitten, attacked, manhandled, tossed considerable distances, decapitated, and eventually torn apart. Some of that has only slightly bloody results in order to avoid an R rating'. Screen It lists in detail the problematic areas portrayed in *Eclipse* for parents, such as: swearing,[6] alcohol use, blood and gore, sex and nudity, scary scenes, and bad attitudes.

ADAPTING THE *ECLIPSE* NOVEL.

The 2010 movie version of *Eclipse* completely alters the dramatic structure of the 2007 text by Stephenie Meyer, which's essentially a series of conversations: Bella-Charlie, Bella-Edward, Bella-Jacob (and, later, Bella-Alice, Bella-Rosalie, etc). That's what the *Twilight Saga* is, really: it's a girl talking to her Dad in her home in a small, All-American town... a girl talking to her boyfriend in a car or in her bedroom... a girl talking to her best friend on a beach...

One chat after another.

Well, *shoot*, that *isn't* enough for a big, blockbuster Hollywood movie! Actually, it *could* be, it *could* be enough: you *could* have a Hollywood, blockbuster flick which's presented as a series of conversations (*à la* Jane Austen, George Eliot and Charlotte Brontë). But, no,

---

6 At least 2 asses, 1 damn, 1 hell and 1 use of "Oh my God.".

no, *no*! Those movies don't usually generate $200 million in theatrical rentals! So, out come the visual effects, the stunts, the special make-up, the shaky camerawork, and the loud alt.rock music.

But if you know the *Twilight* books, and if you know the novel of *Eclipse,* you'll see instantly that the 2010 movie version of *Eclipse* is a *very* different form and story from the 2007 text. We're not just talking about all of the thousands of shifts in narrative form between literature and cinema, we're talking a *big* shift away from what the book of *Eclipse* is, in its tone, its content, its story, and its characters.

Eclipse the novel is about a young woman negotiating between three men in her life: her Father, her Boyfriend and her Best Friend. That's really what it is: a girl and three guys. Secondary characters flit in and out (Alice, Rosalie, Carlisle, Billy, Angela, etc), but essentially the *Eclipse* tome boils down to a young woman and her choices in life (which guy?, which college? and even which life? – immortal or human?).

Well, the 2010 film adaptation of *Eclipse* only captures *some* of that, and reworks it in a very different sort of narrative form, where the teenage romance is sometimes sidelined in favour of action sequences. The *book* of *Eclipse,* for example, opens with a series of lengthy conversations in the Swan residence in Forks about being a dutiful, obedient daughter and girlfriend (a *long* talk with Charlie Swan, and then a *long* talk with Edward Cullen). But the *movie* of *Eclipse* opens with a Gothic action sequence where a shadowy, scarily speedy 'something' tackles an unfortunate young man who accidentally crosses its path, turning him into a vampire (the first shot of *Eclipse* is actually of Riley Biers exiting a bar alone in a downpour at night).

The scene in a rainy,[7] nighttime Seattle is really from a completely different movie – a John Carpenter or Dario Argento flick about scary things in modern, North America, say. And when the movie-*Eclipse* keeps returning to Riley and Victoria and the hapless, unruly newborn army, it wilfully misrepresents the *Eclipse* novel. You can see how the eight film producers and one screenwriter have done what they did in the first *Twilight* movie – bumped up the signficance of the vampire threat. In *Twilight,* that meant bringing the three Nomad vampires forward in the timeline. In *Eclipse*, it means cutting back to Riley and newborn army from time to time. (We get back to more familiar *Twilight Saga* territory when, after the Seattle prologue and the main titles (with, as usual in the *Twilight* movies, and in many another movie, no other credits

---

7 The production employed two cranes carrying forty rain towers to simulate the heavy downpour in the alleys and dockside area of Vancouver.

whatsoever, apart from 'Summit Entertainment' and the film's title),[8] we visit Bella Swan and Edward Cullen in the sunny, dreamy meadow. By rights, the meadow scene, which also ends the 2010 movie, should be the first scene – to introduce the stars and some of the issues they'll be tackling in the picture).

▲

For screenwriter Melissa Rosenberg, *Eclipse* was about choices – having Bella Swan examining her choice of Edward or Jacob closely:

> The whole movie is really about choice and consequences, and I think that requires some very delicate handling. You're talking about some very subtle emotions and you really have to track that, and it comes to looking at both these guys as a viable option.[9]

And for Stephenie Meyer the issue of choice is absolutely central. Meaning, not only which lover do you choose, but the *consequences* of your choice, and *living* with your choice (if you choose one thing, it automatically cuts out all of the other options). If you choose Edward, get used to it, honey! Because it means you're going to have to lose Jacob! (You could point out that the issue of Bella choosing Edward or Jacob was *already fully resolved* in the previous movie! At the end of *New Moon*, the heroine chooses the vampire; or, rather, their romance is re-affirmed after going thru a shaky patch).

There's an important aspect to the question of choices in *Eclipse*, however, which both Jacob and Edward miss, and so do the marketing teams of the *Twilight Saga* movies who emphasize 'Team Jacob' versus 'Team Edward'. And that is: Bella's *own life*, her life not in relation to this or that boy (i.e., 'Team Bella' – which we, as viewers, all belong to whether we like it or not. And you're are in 'Team Bella' *first*, before you rush over to join the rowdy, earthy lads in 'Team Jacob' or the solemn, polite, too-pretty vamps in 'Team Edward').

Bella Swan gives a short but very important speech at the end of the 2010 movie of *Eclipse:* it isn't just about wanting to live with Edward forever and ever, for her, it is also about wanting this particular lifestyle, where she feels she fits in, where she feels she can make something of her life. Issues such as marriage/ weddings/ rings, etc, are only part of the deal for Bella, and Edward himself is not the entire picture (so it's not all about me? he jokes. This is also what Rosalie warns Bella about: the romance with Edward is only part of what Bella will experience when

---

8 The Summit logo has rain streaked over it, emulating the alterations to the Warners Brothers' shield in some recent films.
9 Quoted in M. Howden, 109.

she's vampirized. Because being one of the undead brings with it a whole bunch of issues which you don't face as a human being. For Rosalie, it's not perfect and blissful being a vampire – there are plenty of aspects of being human which she misses).

▲

The movie of *Eclipse* drops numerous characters from the novel, of course. One of the most significant is Angela (Christian Serratos) – precisely because the Angela-and-Bella scenes in the *Eclipse* book are so everyday and unspectacular. Bella goes to Angela's house and they fill in addresses for the school Prom announcements. There's some girlie talk about boyfriends, but it's a scene which's strikingly lacking in much of the meat of the *Twilight Saga* in both print and celluloid form (it was filmed, but dropped from the final cut – you can see it in the deleted scenes).[10] Oh, Bella *does* interact with girls of her own age, but the *Twilight* movies play those scenes down in favour of the romantic and horror scenes. (Jessica Stanley is great value, as played by Anna Kendrick, tho' the scenes are played more for humour, and Bella interacts with Alice, who *isn't* your typical, same-age girlfriend!).

By the usual guidelines of romantic dramas, the wedding would be the *end* of the *Twilight Saga. Eclipse* would close with the wedding, and the lovers would ride off into the sunset in their flashy car. Even if everything goes wrong for them as a married couple, the audience couldn't care less: they've had their romantic dream, and the *Twilight Saga* would work just as dandy as a trilogy: *Twilight, New Moon* and *Eclipse.*

THE PRODUCTION.

Kristen Stewart was given a new set of clothes for *Eclipse* (even tho', Tish Monghan admitted, Bella Swan would probably not have bought anything new!). But the cast and the wardrobe dept 'were tired of those clothes!'.

Edward's silhouette was bulked up by costume designer Tish Monaghan, so actor Robert Pattinson would look suitably strong next to Taylor Lautner, who spends part of *Eclipse* shirtless. (Charles Porlier was the head make-up artist on *Eclipse,* aided by assistants Patricia Murray, Lise Kuhr and Michelle Hrescak; JoAnn Fowler was head make-up, 2nd unit.)

To create vampire speed, sometimes the actors were pulled along by a

---

10 The Bella-Angela scene is touching and modest (covered with simple reverse angles and a two shot). The filmmakers tried to put it into the movie in at least two places, but it slowed the movie down (according to director David Slade).

truck on a conveyor belt set-up (which the filmmakers dubbed the 'magic carpet'); there was also a treadmill rig pulled by a large quad bike (the actors ran on the treadmill).

The Cullen mansion (two stories of it) was built on a stage in Vancouver (and packed up for the later *Twilight Saga* movies). The set included an outdoor area, with greens and a driveway. It was built in the studio partly because so many scenes were set in and around the house. (And the filmmakers duly showed off the set by having the camera tracking around the exterior – for the shot that introduces the Graduation Party, for instance). The village set for the Quileute Tribe flashback was constructed near Squamish, North of Vancouver, at an inlet.

The mountain set altered the topography of the real location on Mount Seymour[11] – no one notices, because no one cares about that stuff anyway![12] But also, when the characters emerge from the tent, there's been a snowfall, and the setting looks very different.

The mountain set included real trees, fake snow, and foam rocks cast from real rocks. The set was backed by green screens to which skies, matte paintings of mountains, and set extensions were added by the vfx companies.

The wolves in *New Moon* had drawn on the look of the actors playing them; for *Eclipse,* the filmmakers shifted back towards more 'realistic' animals (altho' they are of course very movie-movie creatures, with enormous bodies and numerous tweaks and adjustments from real wolves). The wolf models featured 4 million hairs, which grew to millions more.

The battle at the end of *Eclipse* was filmed in a gun range: the production added trees and greens, plus cranes and rigs for wirework. The battle took four weeks to shoot. The newborn vampires were played by 21 stunt people, and were costumed in regular, off-the-rack clothes.

The *Twilight* movies are costly productions, in which the film crews go overboard in trying to deliver high quality visuals. For instance, for the quarry scene in *Eclipse,* Technocranes (giant camera cranes) were trucked down to the location outside Vancouver, and promptly sank in the soft earth. But you don't need a Technocrane to film someone riding on a horse! Hollywood has done just fine since 1910 with a small, wooden Pathé Studio camera and a wooden tripod! (And you can film mega-epics with a tiny, wooden camera – like *Intolerance,* 1917). Similarly with the wolves: no one in the global audience will notice if a

11 Mount Seymour was the setting for the mountain scene (the crew shot for only one day).
12 Except those oddballs who spend hours listing all of the 'mistakes' and 'bloopers' in movies; they have obviously never made a film.

digitally animated wolf has one million or four million separate hairs on its body! But the filmmakers were adamant they wanted digital animals with 4-8 million hairs!

STYLE.

In terms of direction, storytelling and performance, *Twilight: Eclipse* seems a little more subdued than *New Moon* or *Twilight*, a little more by-the-numbers, with the comedy less assured,[13] and the high drama lacking intensity (or maybe that's because *Eclipse* comes after the hysterics and manic depressions of *New Moon*). *Eclipse* is a little too much like coasting along, as we visit the familiar locations (the forest meadow, the Cullens' mansion, the Quileute Indian Reservation, the rainy city streets), with the same actors delivering the same dialogue in the same way (it's 'Same Old, Same Old').

Thankfully, the second unit (led by second unit director E.J. Foerster) stages some fine action sequences in *Eclipse,* and the central romantic ▲ [triangle] still holds attention (even if the obstacles for the lovers are diminishing by the minute: we know, for ex, that Jake B. doesn't stand a chance! – Bella S. tells him so; and we know that Bella's resistance to (Edward's proposal of) marriage is crumpling. Indeed, by the end of *Eclipse,* Bella's agreed to let Alice Cullen off the leash and go to town organizing the Wedding of the Century – the *21st century,* that is!).[14]

However, for some fans, *Eclipse* is lighter and frothier than the previous two *Twihard* movies. Maybe the comedy *is* finer honed in *Eclipse,* or maybe it's that we've seen and heard all of the comical turns that the *Twilight Saga* has explored already. You have to admit that by the *third* installment in an on-going movie franchise, you have seen all of the best bits, the best jokes, the best action sequence, and the best characters that the filmmakers can think up. This applies to many movie franchises. (Luckily, in 2010, when *Eclipse* was released, the wonderful send-up movie *Vampires Suck* was on its way! *Vampires Suck* (released six weeks after *Eclipse,* on August 18, 2010) was a so-necessary antidote to the mock seriousness of the *Twilight* franchise).

In the movie of *New Moon,* much was made of the literary references to *Romeo and Juliet.* In *Eclipse, Wuthering Heights* is used as a key intertext by the 2007 novel, but the movie dropped it (too complicated? Too self-conscious? Unnecessary? Or too much of a repeat of *New Moon*?

---

13 There is far less comedy in the Edward-Bella scenes, for instance. Edward really is not much fun in *Eclipse.*
14 Alice, of course, has been champing at the bit and waiting for the green light from Bella!

Or because *Wuthering Heights* isn't as well-known as *Romeo and Juliet*?).

THE OPENING SCENES.

The 2010 movie *Eclipse* opens with two conflicting desires: in the meadow, Bella asks, 'Change me' (but she should say, as she does in the novels, 'Bite me!'), and Edward, ever the somewhat prissy, old-fashioned suitor, replies, 'Marry me'. This summarizes the drama:

- *Bite me*
- *Marry me*
(I'll bite you if you marry me — I'll marry you if you bite me)

Edward Cullen's acting in a D.W. Griffith melodrama of the 1910s – well, that was his era! He imagines Bella as Lillian Gish as the swooning, virginal heroine, and he's the dashing hero. Edward thinks he's in *Hearts of the World* (1918), *The Great Love* (1918) or *Broken Blossoms* (1919).[15]

Meanwhile, Bella Swan's acting in a rom-vamp version of *Pride and Prejudice* or *Jane Eyre* filmed for M.T.V. in 2010 (Bella's rewritten Bram Stoker's novel *Dracula* as a girlie romance in which she *wants* the vampire, and she wants to *be* a vampire). And yet, because bugger all has changed in Hollywood cinema in 100 years, the melodramas of the 1910s still play just fine in the 2010s (or to put it the other way around: the melodramas of the 2010s aren't much different from the melodramas of the 1910s. Also, the models for Hollywood films of the 1910s and 1920s (and particularly those of D.W. Griffith) were 19th century fiction, just as Victorian literature is a model for the *Twilight Saga*).

The cinematic link into the meadow scene is Bella's voiceover: yes, it's another quote (this time from American poet Robert Frost, another high school class favourite), and when we cut from the obligatory helicopter shots of trees and mountains, we see that Bella is *really* reading aloud – as she revises for her English Language course. (What a good, geeky student Bella is! She takes her homework out on a date in a sunny forest!).

> Some say the world will end in fire,
> Some say in ice,
> From what I've tasted of desire
> I hold with those who favor fire.

Caught in low angle, back-lit close-ups and medium close-ups, we see the Money on the screen – the two stars, Robert Pattinson and Kristen Stewart. The issues they raise will resonate throughout this movie (and

15 In those great days, Griffith was directing three or four feature movies a year.

the next one... and the one after that). The choices are intriguing – vampirism or marriage, undying or mortality (a vampire kiss versus a human kiss). But nothing is resolved here... instead, there is plenty of kissing! *Don't bite me! Kiss me!* (Thus, the romantic part of the story is already over in the *Twilight Saga* – it was over by the first act of the first *Twilight* movie, when Bella Swan fell head over jeans in love with Edward Cullen, and he with her. The vampirism motif, and the vampirism vs. werewolf issue, are, in the end, colourful but merely sideshows.)

Much juicer by far (or bloodier?) is the romantic triangle structure of *Eclipse,* which was such an important part of the previous *Twilight* movie, *New Moon.* In *Eclipse,* the erotic triangle is pointed up in neon in the school car lot scene, and is subsequently explored in multiple variations throughout the movie, including either side of the battle with the newborn vampire army (just before the battle, there's the Big Kiss With Jacob scene, for instance, and right after it, yet another Bella⬦Jacob scene, swiftly followed by a Bella⬦Edward scene).

The two scenes that open the *Eclipse* picture are striking in contrasts: one is nighttime, rain-soaked, dangerous – basically, it's a horror movie. The second is bright, summery, peaceful, and romantic, evoking familiar pairings: the city vs. the countryside, night vs. day, horror vs. romance. pain vs. ecstasy, and the two oposing views of vampirism. In one scene, a guy is attacked by a vamp and bitten, undergoing a very traumatic experience. In the second scene, a girl asks to be bitten (in between lots of kissing. And there's a gender reversal: a woman bites a boy, and a girl begs a man to bite her.)

In amongst the many discussions about vampiric transformation in *Eclipse (*and into *Breaking Dawn*), it's worth reminding ourselves that Bella Swan has *already* been bitten by a (male) vampire (James the Hunter). And she was quite far-gone in the transformation. (Yet that very horrific moment has sunken into oblivion, and is seldom mentioned in the movies).

VICTORIA.

Disappointingly, exasperatingly, the second movie sequel in *The Twilight Saga* brought back flame-haired,[16] bitch-vamp Victoria yet again as the arch villain. She still wants payback on the Cullen coven (and Bella Swan) for wasting her beloved mate, James Witherdale (does anybody even remember him? That's two films ago!). Even tho' Victoria

---

16 Howard has long, curly ginger hair, a blue vest, a dark coat with extra-long sleeves, and dark pants.

is targetting Bella, she ought to be aiming for the Cullens, who're the ones who actually did the deed. Bella is clearly not capable of physically defeating a vampire. (Better to have finished off Victoria in *New Moon* (as with Laurent), and invented a new super-villain for *Eclipse*, even though that would've – Heaven forfend! – deviated from the *Holy Bible* of Stephenie Meyer's books).

Victoria (now played by Bryce Dallas Howard (daughter of director Ron Howard),[17] much to actress Rachelle Lefevre's consternation – and some of the *Twilight* fans), is a woman widowed and ticked off who breeds an army of 'newborn' vampires in Seattle, Washington to take on the Cullen Clan. Meanwhile, back in Sporks, the Cullen vampires make an uneasy alliance with the Quileute werewolves so they'll have sufficient numbers to withstand the assault (quite a bit of fiddly, tiresome narrative work was required by Stephenie Meyer to make this happen convincingly in the novel of *Eclipse,* and by screenwriter Melissa Rosenberg and the producers in the movie – but it's worth it mainly because of the pay-off of seeing Jacob and Edward grudgingly shift towards accepting each other, with Bella literally in between them, in the tent scene on the mountain – the key scene in *Eclipse.* And there is an action pay-off, of course, in seeing vamps and wolves fighting alongside each other, which provides the big action part of the finale).

I think *Eclipse* is disappointing, because after the introduction of the Volturi mob in film two of 2009, *New Moon*, like a high camp, blood-sucking version of the Italian Mafia combined with the decadent, corrupt wings of the Vatican Council, Victoria and her makeshift New Model Army of newborn vampires is a bit of a let-down – especially when the Volturi were such fun, and led by the incredible Michael Sheen! (Coming up with bigger and bigger villains in each movie is a huge challenge in Hollywood action franchises (the familiar problem of dramatic escalation). We've all seen *James Bond* movies and thought, eh?, is *that* weedy guy the Final Boss?). And that Victoria wants vengeance for an act that took place two flicks back also lacks a certain heat in dramatic terms (I mean, we've already forgotten about that, haven't we? Because the romantic story in the *Twilight Saga* is far more engrossing).

Disenchanting on another level: because Victoria's goal is so *secondary* to everything: we know, for ex, that no major character is going to be seriously threatened, let alone sacrificed (not on Stephenie Meyer's watch!), and that Edward and Bella and Jacob ain't *never* going to be dispatched (and certainly not by Victoria or Riley!). That, at most,

17 Howard had been considered for the first *Twilight* movie as Victoria (she was Stephenie Meyer's choice), but had had a baby at the time.

one or two werewolves will bite the dust, and maybe one of the lesser Cullens (but, of course, in the end not even a minor Cullen hits the dirt, in the books or in the celluloid adaptations. And not a hair on their pretty heads is out of place).

Well, OK, the Volturi coven do turn up: like the Mafia and the Vatican (and like governments and cops and teachers), they take it upon themselves to stick their noses in (to police vampire behaviour, they claim); if vampires are acting up and drawing attention to themselves, they will take action, just like the crime syndicates. So the Volturi materialize in Seattle like *very* unwanted guests at a girlie party, have a look at the naughty, youthful, newborn vampires, and decide to do... *absolutely nothing!* Tiny Dakota Fanning (as Jane) glowers with her creepy, red contact lenses, huffs and haughs about a bit, peers into the gloom from a parking garage, then decides to walk away. *Duh!* In narrative terms, it's feeble. It's another non-event in the *Twilight Saga*. (And, what a pity, Lord Aro declined to make the Atlantic crossing, so we don't get to see Michael Sheen). The same strategy of non-events occurs in *Breaking Dawn 2*, when they Volturi turn up, have a chat, then leave! (Though the movie added a huge, non-existent battle, as if rewarding the Twihards who made it that far, and suffered through several damp squibs).

That the Volturi travel 5,000 miles to the American North-West *twice* stretches belief. That they arrive an hour after the battle shows that their information gathering is useless (even tho' they can sense that a newborn vampire army is being bred in Seattle – all the way from Italy).

On the plus side, Victoria does provide the basis for the exciting chase sequence halfway thru *Eclipse*'s first act. Conceived rather like a car chase (and performing the same function of livening up the movie with a change of pace), it offered another view of the high-speed of the vampires (this time most of the Cullen clan), and allowed Emmett and Jasper to strut their stuff. And it allows Howard Shore to wind up the orchestra to maximum, with a strong piece of music (called 'Victoria').

True, this sort of second unit sequence, with its elaborate stunts, its slo-mo, and its many visual effects, does seem to come from a different movie. (There is a teensy bit of narrative juice squeezed out of the chase, tho' – the vamps violate the Treaty, as Jacob angrily explains to Bella in the school car lot. Jake's fury aligns itself with his overall animosity towards Edward, of course (he exploits it several times!). But he's also irked because, altho' it isn't mentioned much in *Eclipse,* more kids are becoming werewolves in response to the vampire threat to the Olympic

Peninsula).

Victoria is sooo amazing, she can out-run six vampires, plus some wolves, who chase her in the early action scene in *Eclipse*. But at the end, she is bested by Edward single-handed – with a li'l help from a werewolf (Seth), who takes on Riley.

THE ROMANTIC TRIANGLE.

Anyhoo, Victoria is, as with the other villains in the previous *Twilight* movies, a mere sideshow to the central plot of *Eclipse* – which is to milk that romantic triangle to the max! (Even tho', to repeat, it is completely over and done with at the end of the previous installment!). And to add some guff about souls and Edward's reluctance to 'change' Bella into a vampire (so she can live with him forever).

So it's Bella… and Edward… and Jake…

A girl… a vampire… and a werewolf…

No, Jacob Black is not giving up! He remains as devoted to Little Miss Miserable as ever. Unfortunately, being a younger, less sophist- icated and somewhat dim guy (compared to Edward Cullen's high culture and refinement – you can bet that Jake doesn't listen to wussy Claude Debussy and play the piano!), he makes more girlfriend-boyfriend mistakes with Bella. Like losing it when she tells him she's going to be bitten after graduation. Like grabbing a kiss from Bella (after so many missed opportunities in *New Moon*!). She slugs him, and sprains her wrist, in an over-done but comical moment[18] (more is made of her injured hand in the *Eclipse* novel, as well as the bracelet with a wolf on it that Jake gives her for a Graduation gift).

And, jeez, this is a giant, blockbuster movie grossing hundreds of millions of dollars worldwide?! Do people really want to see this immature, dumb, soap opera stuff? Girls hitting guys when they sneak a kiss?! I guess they do! (Nothing's moved on since the 1930s in Hollywood cinema, where this scene might play in an early Marx Brothers movie, as Harpo chases ladies across the set). As Jacob quips in *Breaking Dawn*, it's 'like I was in some Goth version of a bad sitcom' (BD, 170).

Indeed, I would say that the appeal of *The Twilight Saga* and a chief reason for its enormous success is precisely in these stupid-but-lovable scenes, these clichéd and *very* old-fashioned moments – the romance of loving the Wrong Guy… the cringeworthy talk with Dad about safe sex

---

18 It's amusing in *Eclipse* when Jacob Black confesses that he tried to kiss Bella and she hit him and broke her hand and Charlie seems mildly amused (Charlie is more Team Jacob than Team Edward).

in the kitchen... Edward insisting on *not* Doing It when they're alone in the house together (*not tonight, baby!*)... Jake hoping that Bella will stay human for longer (so he might be in with a chance)... Jacob chucking a spanner when he hears something from Bella he doesn't like... and the two boyfriends growling and glowering at each other while a skinny, little girl stands between them... (this last scenario, carried over from *New Moon*, occurs with the regularity of a breaking dawn in *Eclipse*. Every few scenes we have another shot of li'l Bella standing in between Edward and Jacob, and trying to prise them apart).

Altho' the vampirey bits of the *Twilight* flicks, like the slo-mo/ hi-speed duels, or the will-he-won't-he-change-Bella-into-a-vamp-chick? issue, are appealing, I reckon it's the sheer familiarity and comfort and safeness and repetitiveness of the romantic emotions and the soap opera scenes that really gel with an audience (the novel of *Eclipse,* for example, barely features any high speed vamp action, and nothing in the books works in slow motion!).[19]

Oh, for sure, these are *not* 'great characters' of world literature, like Romeo or King Lear or Don Quixote or Cleopatra (!).[20] And the *Eclipse*'s story is *not* at the level of *The Changeling, War and Peace* or *The Odyssey* (!). But neither is it meant to be. This isn't 'great art'. And it's not 'great cinema' (it's *not* on the same level as *Sunrise, Faust, The Last Laugh* or *Nosferatu* – to pick four masterpieces directed by F.W. Murnau in the 1920s).

But *The Twi-Saga* is not pure junk, either. It's populist, certainly, and clichéd, and dumb, and very predictable (as Mike Newton puts it in the early scene where the kids discuss Jessica's Graduation speech, you have to embrace clichés. And Hollywood cinema is masterful at that). The *Twilighting* plots groan under the weight of stereotypes and familiarity (and creaky plotting). It's flashy, and self-conscious, and mock-serious (and mock-comical).

But *Eclipse is* entertaining. You can't entice millions of punters into movie houses at eight bucks[21] a ticket (!) unless *they want to see the movie!* So it's not 'hype', either, or mass marketing, or PR: because if a movie stinks, word travels rapidly, and down it goes faster than the *Hindenburg* in 1937. If the *Twilight* movies were 'opening weekend movies' – which opened wide in theatres but sank fast – they wouldn't have become a cultural phenomenon (or grossed billion$ solely in theatres).

---

19 Except the pace.
20 They are explicitly compared with charas from *Wuthering Heights, Romeo and Juliet* and *Pride and Prejudice* in the 2007 novel.
21 The average price for a cinema ticket in 2010 was $7.89.

MORE ON THE ROMANTIC TRIANGLE.

Talk about milking a romantic triangle! ▲▲▲ The filmmakers of *Eclipse* work hard to include as many confrontations between Edward-and-Jacob, or Edward-and-Bella, or Jacob-and-Bella, or Bella-and-Edward vs. Jacob, as they can. Nobody can miss the fact that, as in *Romeo and Juliet* (and pretty much every romantic tale ever), the lovers spend more time *talking* about love (or whingeing about it) than actually loving. There *are* kisses, and intimate moments in *Eclipse,* but these're far out-numbered by the griping and the gassing (it's easy to see from reading the *Twilight* books that author Stephenie Meyer likes nothing better than to set up a scenario where two people can talk at length, and then to let them talk. And talk. And *talk*... Or, Meyer describes something happening – and after it, there's more talk, and analysis, and picking over the bones. The talky scenes in the *Twilight* series go on and on and on, and some book editors (including me) would surely prefer to prune some of them. But those conversations are actually where the beating, bloody heart of the *Twilight Saga* dwells).

The romantic triangle is much clearer and more obvious in the movie of *Eclipse* than in *Eclipse* the book, at least in the first third of the story. There's no doubt that Jacob Black is just as crazy about Bella Swan as Edward Cullen, but the novel doesn't play the romantic triangle as a mass of seething sexual jealousies. The movie of *Eclipse* is much clearer about the erotic triangle, however, and makes much more of Jacob and Edward glaring at each other, and several times just about to start fighting. (And there's Edward's envy over any time that Bella chooses to spend with Jake, or that Jake gets to give Bella a Graduation present, which she wears – and Edward eventually responds with a bracelet gift of his own).

The 2010 movie of *Eclipse* ramps up the drama much quicker and with more exaggeration than the 2007 novel. The *Eclipse* flick can't wait to get to the confrontation scenes in the love triangle, but the *Eclipse* novel is *much* slower, and it takes *many* pages of dialogue before the relationships are brought to boiling point (much of the time, for instance, Edward and Jacob are kept apart, physically, tho' of course neither wastes an opportunity to put their rival down in dialogue). In the book of *Eclipse,* Edward insists that jealously doesn't play a part – he simply thinks that werewolves are very dangerous, and that Bella shouldn't go anywhere near La Push. Prompted by Jacob, Bella begins to see that Edward is perhaps envious.

Is it me or does Robert Pattinson play many scenes in *Eclipse* in a grumpy, frowny fashion, as if Edward is seriously threatened by the mere presence of Jacob Black? (Or is he constantly contemplating the prospect of turning Bella into a vampire?). Gone is the Smiley Edward of the first movie, where he looked about to break out in a grin every moment. Indeed, would Bella fall in love with Edward if he'd been like this? And, compared to Taylor Lautner's Jacob, Edward seems a much whinier, unglowing prospect. (We know that Pattinson thought very little of the *Twilight Saga* – perhaps his ambiguous attitude towards it was coming thru in his performance).

You have to admire Jacob's persistence in pursuing romance with Bella, even though she told him plainly at the end of *New Moon* that it was always Edward. Or you feel sorry for him, and how he can't move forward, and step way, way past Bella Swan.

MOM AND DAD.

So in *Eclipse* Bella's Mom Renée finally turns up, after being absent for a whole movie (*New Moon*), when Bella was falling completely to pieces and really needed her (Renée's absence in *New Moon* is very obvious). Bella visits Florida and shares some mother-daughter time which's mercifully free of vampirey gloom. However, Edward tags along, and Mom comments on how he's keeping a beady eye on her all the time. (We don't see how Edward negotiated getting from the airport to a taxi or a bus or a rental car without glittering up a storm in the Sunshine State. 260 sunny days per year in Florida! Not a great place for bloodsuckers).

The quilt that Bella's Mom gives her came about when the film-makers wanted to enhance the relationship between Bella and her Mom/family, and what she would be giving up when she became a vampire (CFA, 84). Or was that to make up for Renée's strange absence from *New Moon*?

Meanwhile, Chief Swan has grounded Bella (she has to be back from the meadow, for example, for 4 p.m.), and would prefer it if Bella saw far less of Edward Cullen – or even better, jilted him (he's just too good-looking, too cool, and too well-off for Charlie's liking. Certainly, he's not your typical regular guy from Sporks. Or as Charlie might put it to his drinking buddies: he's not one of us).

The two parental scenes in the first act of *Eclipse* are important in reminding us that Bella Swan is still a young girl, only recently 18, that she lives with Dad, and keeps in touch with her Mom. (Many storytellers would dispense with the parents, for all the obvious reasons.)

VAMPIRISM HURTS.

Inevitably, how people become vampires in the *Twilight* series is not pretty. Jasper Whitlock's involved in a vaguely sadomasochistic relationship with a vamp-queen, Maria (played by Catalina Sandino Moreno, uncredited); Rosalie was the victim of a gang rape scenario in the Big, Bad City (Rochester, New York) involving her fiancé Royce King (Jack Huston); Emmett's attacked by a grizzly bear; Esme suicided off a cliff; and Edward was dying of Spanish influenza.

No, folks – turning into a vampire can't possibly be a gentle, peaceful affair, conducted consensually between two calm adults in a sunny garden. It has to be blood, guts and violence. Well, that's drama, eh? Always with the yelling, the kicking and the screaming! In which case, Bella Swan's request to become a vampire is understandably alarming to vampires: who'd want to choose this life? (Or, rather, this un-life?).

And when Bella herself is transformed into a Vamp Princess, it's not, as the lovers might've decided, in the meadow on a sunny day, but as she's dying in childbirth! (With only two useless boys to help her!).

ALICE AND JASPER.

Jasper Whitlock has more to do in the second sequel (*Eclipse*), as does Alice Brandon. Both are good value. Alice is Bella's closest friend in the Cullen coven (aside from Edward): she offers a friendly, feminine friendship in contrast with Edward's rather snooty, arrogant attitude (the book of *Eclipse* includes Angela – and Jessica – among Bella's friends, but unfortunately they're seldom seen in the 2010 movie. Yet in the *Eclipse* novel, Alice irritates Bella as much as she delights her).

It's Alice who's up for a party, or baseball, or a wedding, or a flight to Italy to stop her brother from making a tit of himself. Even Chief Swan takes a shine to Alice (well, as played by Ashley Greene, like a spoilt, rich girl with a touch of Audrey Hepburn about her, she is very attractive. And in the suburban, truck-stop, lumber-yard somnolence of the teeny town of Sporks, super-glam Alice stands out a mile!).

Jasper Whitlock/ Hale, meanwhile, turns out to be the cool, older brother type who's acquired (thru hardship) the knowledge to train the Cullens and the wolves against the newborn vampire army. In *Eclipse*, Jasper is described as 'the tall, blond vampire who looked like a brooding movie star' (E, 251). (Movie star references abound in the *Twilight* series in the novels – the perfect way, of course, to describe the charisma of the Cullens).

More Jasper means more Jackson Rathbone – and he's terrific.

Rathbone has several big scenes in *Eclipse,* including the training scene, the final battle, and of course the American Civil War flashbacks.

THE FLASHBACKS.

As *Twilight: Eclipse* was the central installment in a four-book, five-movie set, there was time for some back-story and flashbacks, in act two (in the three-act model of movies) of your typical Hollywood flick (altho' four acts is more accurate, as it is here, in *Eclipse*). So we got to see the back-stories of characters such as Jasper Whitlock (the American Civil War), and Rosalie Hale (in 1930s Rochester, New York). Rose's back-story was due to appear in *New Moon.* Emmett (not shown) was the victim of a bear attack, and near-dead he was taken by Rosalie to Carlisle.[22]

Unfortunately, easily the most intriguing 'origins' story in the *Twilight Saga* books is that of Carlisle Cullen, the oldest amongst the Cullen clan, but this isn't shown in any of the *Twilight* movies, apart from a brief appearance in the Volturi flashback in *New Moon*, and the even shorter scenes of Carlisle transforming Esme and Edward in *Twilight* (there's an exciting witchfinding scene (related in the novel of *Twilight* [290]), where Carlisle is bitten by a vampire, which cries out to be filmed).

And Alice Brandon's origins story is also interesting – it involves mental illness, an institution, an older vampire, and the vamp villain from the first *Twilight* film, James Witherdale. (Three of the winners of the short film competition run by Lionsgate/ Volvo/ Tongal/ Facebook depicted Alice's back-story: *The Mary Alice Brandon File, The Groundskeeper* and *We've Met Before*).

THE JASPER FLASHBACK.

Jackson Rathbone as Jasper Whitlock was dressed in a Confederate, Texas cavalry costume bought from a company that made costumes for Civil War re-enactments. And very fine he looked indeed! In scenes staged day-for-night in a quarry[23] near Vancouver (this was actually the first day of principal photography of *Eclipse*), we see the debonair, politely-spoken Jasper on horseback and soon encountering three vampires posing as helpless women (for Jasper, this is such rotten luck).

Jasper narrates the flashback in voiceover, and the 2010 movie cuts back a few times to Bella Swan asking the appropriate questions for the

---

22 Well, as in the book, a grizzly bear attack isn't as interesting, and doesn't contain the necessary psychological aspects, as the back-stories of Jasper or Rosalie.
23 So many film productions use quarries, for all the obvious reasons.

audience (this occurs at the end of the training session, when Bella asks Jasper how come he knows so much about newborn vampires).

We see Jasper training newborn vampires for Maria, the Countess Dracula of the back-story, in a dusty, old barn (they appear to be hillbilly types), as if this is a slice of Old Americana with a twist of vampiric, black humour. Things get even uglier when Jasper is ordered by Maria to destroy some of the newborn vampires, which he isn't keen on doing (the novel of *Eclipse* adds much more of Jasper's life after Maria – it includes lengthy periods of depression and drifting, which lasts until he meets Alice Brandon in the 1940s. In the movie, suddenly Alice was there, Jasper explains. And, when we cut to the present tense, yes, there she is again – cosying up to Jasper and smooching him, embarrassing Bella once more. It's understandable that we don't get into Jasper's sad life following Maria, as the flashbacks stick only to the key points of the back-stories in the novel, but it's a pity, I think, that we don't see Jasper meeting Alice in the diner in Philadelphia. And Alice's back-story, of course, was also left out of *Eclipse*. That's for the TV series of the *Twilight Saga*, perhaps).

The rustic setting, the barn, the menacing but glamorous vampire leader using coercion and erotic desire, and the very sinister goings-on in Maria's newborn army might be a spoof of American religious cults (of which there are many).

Anyhoo, as well as fleshing out Jasper Whitlock's characterization (Jasper has been, up to now in the *Twi*-series, left on the sidelines somewhat), the flashback to Civil War Texas is also included in *Eclipse* because it bears directly on the newborn vampire plot,[24] developing in Seattle, WA (and it also gives us an idea of what our heroine will undergo when she is turned from Emo Heroine into Vamp Princess). To the point that, in a dream (I mean, a nightmare), Bella Swan realizes that what happened with Jasper is now occurring in Seattle, and *femme fatale* vamps are behind both scenarios! So the dream intercuts Maria whispering in Jasper's ear like a demon on his shoulder with Victoria.[25] (So now Bella has prophetic visions *à la* Alice. Thus, Bella has some impact on the newborn vampire part of the plot in *Eclipse,* by suggesting (to Edward) that Victoria is hiding behind someone (so that Alice can't see her). Because, after all, Bella has little to do in combating the newborn vamps, other than to smear her blood on trees to create a scent trail (she's not going to fight a vampire one-on-one).[26] And she *is* the

---

24 It also evokes the romance of Jasper and Alice, which is another mirror of Bella and Edward.
25 This occurs differently in the book of *Eclipse*; Bella works out that Victoria has created the newborn vamp army and is coming for her.
26 A reprise of what the Cullens did in film one to put James off the trail.

heroine of this movie, so bumping up her input helps, and also turns her from useless, screaming victim (the horror movie staple) into pro-active heroine).

The manipulative, masochistic relationship of Victoria and Riley not only echoes that of Maria and Jasper in the Texan, 19th century flashback, it also provides a commentary on the Bella-Edward romance (a moral lesson on how vampire relationships can be as twisted and damaging as human ones).

THE ROSALIE FLASHBACK.

Nikki Reed's big scenes in the movie of *Eclipse* involve Rosalie Hale's back-story, related by her to Bella Swan. The 2010 movie starts the sequence with Bella approaching Rose to ask her about her dislike of her (it's taken three films for us to find out why Rosalie has been so anti-Bella! Or maybe it's taken that long for Bella to work up the courage to ask the prickly Rose!).

Anyway, Rosalie is a seriously disenchanted soul, someone who resents intensely having her life taken away from her. It's great to finally see Nikki Reed's Rosalie leading a whole scene, without the distractions of other characters (for instance, there are several pages of dialogue to set up the flashback, by Rosalie: gazing out over the dusky landscape of Washington State, Rosalie talks and Bella listens).

The Rosalie Hale flashback in *Eclipse* offers another version of *Little Red Riding Hood* combined with *Beauty and the Beast*: don't trust men – or as fairy tale literature puts it, watch out for wolves! Yes, men are brutish, insensitive, boorish, loud, smelly – you name it! Rosalie's romantic dreamy bubble is burst in a horrendous fashion, with a gang rape just before her wedding.[27] The first scene in the flashback features Rosalie and Royce King walking in a busy park in daylight (filmed in Vancouver); while Rosalie chatters, King is already eyeing up a woman passing by. As the scene where the drunken Royce latches onto Rosalie shows, this man is a total heel.

It's an over-simplified revenge story, like a Victorian melodrama of the penny dreadful kind (such as *Sweeney Todd*), combined with some archaic proto-feminism: wearing her wedding dress, like an insane Mrs Havisham from *Great Expectations*, Rosalie wastes her oppressors one by one, saving Royce King for last.

However, this being a 'PG-13' flick, we don't *see* Rosalie kill anybody: the rapists are dispatched in Rosalie's voiceover. We don't see

---

27 In the novel, however, Rosalie also disparages her rather shallow ambitions, to have a husband, a house and children; in the movie, Rosalie plays it straighter.

the violation of Rose, either, only part of the lead-up to it. When the movie cuts to Royce King, we see a bunch of cops guarding him outside a room, in a corridor. Again, nothing is shown: we hear gunshots and screams (over a close-up of the doors), and then Rosalie storms in, the picture of female fury. King cowers on the carpet (bottle in hand), and the movie cuts away, back to Nikki Reed's lovely face in medium close-up, serene and platinum blonde on the Cullen balcony in the present tense. (We don't see Carlisle finding Rosalie, either, or her transformation into a vampire, or that Rosalie didn't like either Carlisle or Edward at first, all related in the *Eclipse* book).

Primitive sexual politics and vaguely sadomasochistic themes are part of both flashbacks in the *Eclipse* movie: in the Jasper Whitlock flashback, a man is ensnared by an evil, scheming, very dangerous woman (right out of a fairy tale); in the Rosalie Hale flashback, a similarly fairy tale-ish story unfolds with sexual abuse at its heart.

Both flashbacks, as well as the Quileute Tribe and wolf origins flashback, bear directly on Bella Swan: the themes of sexual coercion and exploitation in both the Jasper Whitlock and the Rosalie Hale flashbacks throw a disturbing light on the Bella-Edward relationship, where the undercurrent of violence is always present (he tells her, repeatedly, that he is dangerous). And at the end of Rosalie's flashback scene, she tells our 18 year-old, American heroine that there is something more than even Edward that she will crave as a vampire, something that she will kill for – yes, it's the thing that the *Twilight Saga* in book or movie form is reluctant to show: *blood*. (By revealing less of it, it becomes more powerful – the taboo or magical element in the *Twilight Saga*).

THE QUILEUTE TRIBE FLASHBACK.

The all-important back-story of the werewolf group in *Eclipse* is related in the 2010 *Twilight* movie, here couched in the context of a Native American council around an open fire at night, with the tribal elders gathered to ponder on events. So we see the werewolves and Native Americans' interpretation of the 'Cold Ones', the vampires. In the flashbacks, the vampires are white, aristocratic (European) types, viewed as outsiders who have come to the New World as invaders – and murderers, with the werewolves aligned with Native Americans protecting their homeland and people (the elder sums up the philosophy they should adopt in one word: *courage*). It's thus an alternative History of America, a fantasy Founding of America, with a fictionalized account of the formation of the U.S.A. seen from the viewpoint of First Natoins (As if everything went wrong for the Americas – South America as well as North – when the white man set foot on the land).

The Quileute Tribe flashback sequence in *Eclipse* involves a series of scenes which are intercut with the storytelling of Billy Black in the present tense around the camp fire:[28] we see the Spanish 'Cold One' (played by Pete Murphy of British New Romantic band Bauhaus – surely it should've been a member of Muse?)[29] standing over the corpses of some Native Americans. He soon bites the dust as two Quileute tribesmen phase into wolves and chomp him up (the 'Cold One' dispatches the first wolf).

In the much bigger scene set in a village in a creek,[30] we see the vamp's mate going on the rampage, decimating the villagers (who're fleeing in all directions). The village Chief transforms into a werewolf and battles the vampire: the tussle is won when the Chief's third wife[31] bravely stabs herself, distracting the vamp with fresh blood.[32] The wife's crucial quality, Billy Black tells us, is courage (yes, that is certainly one of the most important qualities anybody can ever have).

The Quileute Tribe village sequence is filmed with loose, often handheld camera; plenty of movement as the villagers try to escape the hysterical 'Cold One'; and there's no dialogue – instead, plenty of screaming! (Billy Black provides the narration).

There is much more of the werewolves' back-story in the 2007 book of *Eclipse,* including elements that move into wholly mythical territory, which the 2010 movie cut. Instead, the movie concentrated on the rivalry between wolves and Cold Bloodsuckers.

The depiction of vampires as exotic outsiders – literally 'aliens' – decadent, debauched, aloof, Old World and white – is part of the vampire genre. In some (postmodern) readings of vampire lore, vampirism is a disease, aligned to plagues (the links between vampires and plague-carrying rats), and to Eastern European immigrants, to the influx of Eastern Europeans into Western Europe and the U.S.A. Vampirism has also been analyzed in the light of AIDS and blood-related diseases, to syphilis, STDs, drug addiction, etc (vampirism is a multi-purpose metaphor/ analogy/ trope/ image/ whatever for anything you like).

Thus, the *Twilight Saga* offers a simplistic ideology for your

---

28 This was a night of constant rain, apparently, difficult conditions. Again, just when it's supposed to be a warm night around the camp fire!
29 Maybe the connection here is that Bauhaus appeared briefly in the mundane vamp flick *The Hunger* (1982).
30 It is, admittedly, a rather clichéd portrayal of a Native American, creekside settlement.
31 Kristen Stewart was tried out in the wife's costume here, so it would link up with the finale.
32 We've already seen in previous *Twilight* movies how insane vamps get when they see/ smell blood!

delectation: it depicts the Native American werewolves defending North America (their homeland) against the influx of white, European, Old World, degenerate aristocrats – people who've become so in-bred and psychologically unstable (like ageing, corrupt families), they prey upon other humans for their blood. The werewolves and their First Nations culture are portrayed as in touch with the Earth, spirits of the forest, sensual, warm, in opposition to the other-wordly, frigid, over-educated and overly intellectual, aloof, inhuman (or anti-human) vampires.

In this view, vampires are so disconnected from the natural world they see it simply as food, something to be used (they are rapists, exploiters, killers), whereas the werewolves (and the Native Americans) live in harmony with the planet. (The Quileute Tribe flashback in *Eclipse* also includes a piece of foreshadowing, when the third wife distracts the female vamp for a moment by stabbing herself; Bella uses the ruse in the finale of *Eclipse* against Victoria.[33] Because nobody thinks to give her a gun, a sword, a spear or even a darn knife! Yes, even the Cullens, for all their hi-tech, switched-on cleverness and resourcefulness, don't think they need to give a single weapon to Bella! I mean, surely a machine gun with armour-piercing shells is going to have some effect on a vampire at close range?!).[34]

Another example of dramatic foreshadowing occurs in the conflab in the garage on the Quileute res, where Jacob Black explains to Bella how imprinting works – a scene where the erotic subtext is glowing in neon. It is related in reference to Sam and Emily, but will play out big time in the subsequent *Twilight* movies.

BREE TANNER.

There's a young vampire in *Eclipse,* too, called Bree Tanner (played by Jodelle Ferland) – Twilighters know her well because Stephenie Meyer published a side story about Bree, entitled *The Second Short Life of Bree Tanner* in 2010 (Meyer recalled that it was partly her talks with screenwriter Melissa Rosenberg that encouraged her to flesh out the side plot).

Bree Tanner of course offers a mirror to Bella Swan: a white, teen girl who becomes a vampire (tho' against her will, like the rest of the newborn vampire army). 'I stared at her, mesmerized, wondering if I were looking into a mirror of my future', Bella muses in the finale of *Eclipse,* in prose which uses a hammer (I mean, a wooden stake) to hit home the

---

33 Tho' in the book she doesn't cut herself.
34 Her Dad gives her pepper spray in *Twilight*! In a funny aside, Charlie offers Bella pepper spray again in *Eclipse*, when Bella's going out with Edward.

message (E, 506). The *Eclipse* movie doesn't feature Bree much, but she is given a little dialogue, and has several close-ups (interacting with Riley), to identify her in amongst the army of newborn vampires. And she is the sacrifice in the action finale. (Notice that it's Esme and Carlisle who first realize that Bree is not an ordinary newborn, and might prove worth saving, because Esme and Carlisle are the kindly mother and father figures among the Cullens; it's a pity that super-bitch Jane wouldn't allow them to keep Bree alive – then we would see Carlisle's rehabilitation of humans-as-vampires in the present tense, rather than in the back-stories of Edward, Esme, Rosalie, Alice *et al*).

TRAINING.

The second act of an action/ fantasy/ adventure movie often contains the same scenes we have in *Eclipse:* training scenes, flashback scenes, moral discussions and the like, all of which set up the finale.

The uneasy alliance between the vamps and the wolves is broached at the Graduation Party at the Cullens' place (the party is a very welcome change of pace in *Eclipse*, where the cast can let their hair down).[35] But, as usual with celebrations in the middle of a movie with plenty of serious drama and cheesy romance to deliver, the merry-making is swiftly replaced with more plot. Bringing together several scenes from the 2007 book – Alice's vision of the newborns in Seattle, Jake & co. visiting the party (and apologizing to Bella), a discussion between the Native Americans and the Cullens – the storytelling and decision-making is rapid (despite Bella's repeated protests).

Memorably, we see Jake asserting himself in a nest of vampires – Jacob B. in the ascendant is enjoyable (in any part of the *Twilight Saga*). Over Bella Swan's objections, which she raises many times after this, too (and Edward's grudging acceptance), Jacob reminds her, 'this is what we do'. Indeed, why else are young kids in La Push being turned into werewolves if not to combat vampires?! In the typical ensemble scene which includes Carlisle in the *Twilight Saga*, it's usually the elder vampire to whom everybody else defers, and it is so here, with Carlisle welcoming Jake's offer of help. Carlisle is the voice of reason, of experience (he's been a vamp longer than all of the others present), and of concern - he knows what a threat the newborn vampires can be (as does Jasper). There are several meaningful looks and nods exchanged in this scene (as also in the training scene).

The training sequence in *Eclipse* reprises the mood and tone of the

---

35 Tho' not the fashion-plate perfect Cullens, who never have a hair out of place, even after wild training sessions.

baseball game in film one of two years earlier (in the *Eclipse* book, they take place at the baseball field). Here, the Cullens demonstrate how vampires fight to the visiting wolves. The pairings of each duel follow the established characterizations and the back-stories: so Edward and Carlisle fight, Jasper and Emmett fight, Jasper and Alice fight, etc (Esme, as the den mother, is rightly left out – and actress Liz Reaser didn't enjoy filming the violent scenes). Each character is given their moment to shine, as well as demonstrating their fighting style (graceful for Alice, rough-and-tumble for Emmett, quick and efficient for Jasper, and so on).

It's entertaining to see Jasper Whitlock finally getting to drive a scene in a *Twilight* flick, as he oversees the training sessions, explaining about the newborn vampires and helping to set up the finale of the movie. Jackson Rathbone is impressive as the suave and confident Jasper (well, he is from Texas, ma'am!). And, as we soon see in the flashback, Jasper has already trained a newborn army (and for another uncaring, cruel female vampire).

In the *Eclipse* book, the training sessions occur at night, so that they can work away from onlookers; the movie really should follow the novel here – vampires and night (and werewolves and night) go together like burgers and fries. Maybe cost was an issue again, and under-age actors – Lautner was 17 (if so, why not film the training scene on a forest set, because sets filmed for night can hide the fact they're sets easily?). Same with the finale.

BEDS AND TENTS.

The *Eclipse* filmmakers have Jake Black (topless, as ever!) carrying Bella Swan for no particular reason thru the forest (oh yes, something to do with the scent, to ensnare the newborn vampires – a boring element in the book of *Eclipse,* and it's boring in the movie, too. But it does mean an opportunity for yet another Bella-and-Jacob discussion).

The idea is to camp in a tent on a mountain. But what's wrong with staying in a nearby Best Western or Days Inn? Much warmer and cosier! (Camping in a plastic tent with no heating with just a sleeping bag up in the mountains would be *incredibly cold*.[36] Kristen Stewart really sells the cold – but, ironically, as we're in the studio in Vancouver, it was probably really hot).

It was a scene which, as the documentary on *Eclipse* showed, was tough on Taylor Lautner, having to carry Kristen Stewart in take after take. A rig and harness had been developed but it didn't look right. (Bella

---

36 I've done it.

gets carried a lot in the *Twilight Saga*!). And Jacob carries Bella again later in *Eclipse*.

That shows, tho', how American actors in movies like this are spoiled rotten – because if this movie had been produced in most other places on Earth, an actor would be told to pick up the girl and carry her. Simple as that! No complaining, just do it! (And for take after take!).

The filmmakers have Jacob B. taking Bella home in the truck, and Edward C. too (in his car – a flashy, black Volvo given to the production as product placement). They have Bella visiting Jake on the Quileute Indian Reservation, and Bella visiting the Cullen mansion.

The filmmakers also wind up the romantic-erotic tension with some titillating scenes. Like when Bella Swan spends the night at the Cullens' place, when everybody is away[37] (Alice, smiling, reckons she's doing Bella a favour. This opportunity is partly orchestrated by Alice in her Fairy God-mother role as an all-purpose matchmaker). Plenty of teenage couples in many a story would take advantage of a parentless, unchaperoned night to do what they like (which's what Bella wants to do in the book; she tries to be as seductive as possible, in her clumsy, naïve, haven't-got-a-clue manner). Not Edward! He is so 'old school' (a hundred years 'old school'!), he withdraws from the romantic clinch with our Bella on the bed (she is clear that she wants more – the scene follows the embarrassing, comical encounter where Bella tells her Dad she's a virgin). Edward goes all formal and prissy, a man from a bygone era, preferring to wait until they're married! He has the ring and all! He says he'd court her, they'd be chaperoned, like in the old days, when he grew up a hundred years ago. (Here's where Edward goes down on bended knee to propose formally to his beloved).

It's a postmodern-yet-archaic take on ancient mating rituals. Edward opts to do things by the book (yes, *that* book! That four thousand year-old, Middle Eastern book!): the *Twilight Saga* has plenty of fun with feminizing the man in the romantic relationship, so that it's Bella who's often the aggressive or 'masculinist' one. (Stephenie Meyer said she liked the idea that a man could adhere to courtly principles, that he wouldn't let lust overwhelm him. Which sort of makes Edward a 'one in a million' guy).

The seduction scene is played over lingering close-ups (as always in the *Twilight Saga* – and in pretty much all romantic dramas. Has a romance of any kind been filmed *entirely* in long shots?). DP Javier Aguirresarobe provides suitably romantic lighting (soft, reflected light),

---

37 The Big Kiss Scene between Bella amd Edward occurs in a common place, just before the finale starts (before the vampire army leaves Seattle).

and the setting is a huge bed with a canopy (looking forward to the love scene in *Breaking Dawn, Part 1*, and a call-back to Bella's remark in film one: 'no bed', when she enters Edward's domain in the Cullen residence). The scene was one of the last to be filmed in *Eclipse,* and both actors were nervous about it (getting the tone and mood just right is challenging).

✍

And then there's the tent scene, the central scene in *Eclipse* for the soap opera part of *The Twihard Saga* (and Stephenie Meyer's favourite scene of any she wrote [CFA, 85]). How can you get your teenage characters into bed without them really having sex, in a 'PG-13'-rated movie and a Young Adult novel? Oh yes, by using 'Survival 101', as Jacob Black calls it: he's a hot-blooded werewolf, so he climbs into Bella's sleeping bag, as she shivers near death, to warm her up (Edward is of course *very* reluctant to allow such a thing). It's a very amusing scene, with Edward, the 'Cold One', unable to contribute anything useful.[38]

So the dialogue in the tent scene in *Eclipse* does have Jake and Edward grudgingly growing to accept each other a little more (while Bella may or may not be asleep – tho' in the *Eclipse* book she is definitely awake, but sleepy. She has to be awake, because the Twilight Goddess has doggedly insisted on a first person point-of-view throughout. But it's better not to explain every darn thing, and leave it open whether Bella is awake or asleep). But the blocking of the scene – Jake lying next to Bella in the sleeping bag while Edward looks on, hating every moment – says it all (the *Breaking Wind* movie sent-up the scene, inevitably, with the expected humping – which simply makes explicit the subtext of the scene in the *Eclipse* novel: Jacob gets to have Bella while Edward looks on, helpless).

Edward admits that he's glad that Jacob's there to help out, and if they weren't sworn enemies, he might like Jake. The werewolf acknowledges that – 'maybe if you weren't a disgusting vampire who was planning to suck out the life of the girl I love... well, not even then.' (E, 446) In the movie, it comes over strongly that it's *Jacob* who is leading this scene, *not* Edward.

THE ENDING.

If there's an army of newborn vampires being bred in Seattle, we know there's going to be a big battle, right? Of course! ('Same old, same

---

38 Well, Edward: use your imagination, there *are* ways you can warm up an 18 year-old girl. And also take her mind off impending danger! But, Edward is Mr Old Skool, a prissy, restrained personality, and he certainly won't take advantage of being in a tent alone with Bella on a mountain at night.

old'! – this is a contemporary, Hollywood movie, after all. Hollywood is a business which really excels at selling audiences the same stuff, but in new packaging. This is what the entire media – no, the entire Western, capitalist system – does).

The plotting of the action finale of *Eclipse* is both simple *and* unduly complicated (that is, altho' the key element is a villains-versus-the-heroes smackdown, there is still plenty of to-ing and fro-ing, and Bella and Edward being separated from the others, so that they can have a skirmish of their own with Victoria and Riley, which departs from the 2007 novel, of course, where Edward never lets our Bella out of his sight (or his smell)). Part of a novella that Stephenie Meyer wrote about one of the newborn vampires, the young girl Bree Tanner, was included in the movie (*The Short Second Life of Bree Tanner* was given to the actors, so they had more back-story for the characters they were playing).

Anyway, the main thing in *Eclipse* was we got to see the Cullen clan in full-on, battle mode, and plenty of rival vampires were wasted in as many ways as second unit director E.J. Foerster and the stunt team[39] could think up (this was their big scene). An ample, triple burger serving of decapitations, arms being ripped off, people being strangled, and mauled by werewolves (all of this was added to the 2007 *Eclipse* novel, which stays with Bella upon the mountain for the duration of the battle, with Edward adding a teensy bit of commentary via mind-reading).

And no blood! Yes, once again in the *Twilight* movies it's a vampire battle with no tomato ketchup on the screen. Yes, because, like, these vampires are sort of brittle, frozen ash or crystalline underneath, their bodies and skulls shattering like glass (handily scooting around the 'PG-13' limitations: and, being crystalline stuff, the *sound* the decapitations and severings make isn't the gloopy sound fx of the 'R' rated horror genre, but a sort of pingy, metallic sound.[40] And, anyway, we've all seen gory, bloody battles 1,000s of times).

The gags come thick and fast in the action finale of *Eclipse,* and it's exciting stuff. The only disappointing aspect is that it's full daylight: a battle such as this calls for nighttime in the midst of a lightning storm (the training sessions with Jasper, for instance, occur at three a.m. in the *Eclipse* book, for obvious reasons). A vampire vs. werewolf battle with no blood and in bright daylight – it's as if the filmmakers are doing their best to try for something new in the genre.

The stunt team have thought up gags for each of the Cullens to

---

39 John Stoneham, Layton Morrison, Larry Lam (uncredited) and Jonathan Eusebio were stunt co-ordinators.

40 One wonders how much the sound effects team ummed and ahhed about just what sound a vampire makes when its head has been smashed off. Ping? Zing? Kerrching? Wham?

perform (as with the training sequence): Jasper is the most fearsome by far among the Cullens, running at full speed and punching and wasting newborn vampires as he goes. Emmett hurls himself into the fray with his usual recklessness (there's a beat where he works in tandem with a wolf, and another features a head-butt). Alice, ever the graceful pixie-elf-fairy, gets to spin and float like a deadly dancing doll. Esme and Carlisle work together as husband and wife – Esme holds a victim so that Carlisle can behead it with a punch.

(The newborn vampires somehow travel the 140 or so miles from Seattle to Forks unnoticed (if they go by sea (!) it's a lot further). Having them enter the ocean is a cool image, but the practicalities of their journey are completely elided by the most powerful tool by far in movies – the editor's cut.)

Meanwhile, up on Mount Seymour (but actually on the large, snowbound, indoor set in Vancouver), Edward once again protects his fiancée from annihilation (for the third time in the *Twilight Saga*! What a man!). The ending of *Eclipse* is a foregone conclusion, of course: how can Riley Biers, Victoria's lieutenant, who's been manipulated by the red-haired, Nomad vamp, possibly emerge victorious? And how could Victoria, cast in the rather thankless role of the villain in the 'B' plot in this romantic fantasy (in a wholly predictable role which's also woefully under-written, so actress Bryce Dallas Howard seems unable to do much with it except smoulder and pout),[41] make any mark upon our unsullied heroes? (Beyond the odd scratch applied by a diligent make-up asstistant – in the book of *Eclipse*, Edward emerges with nary a bronze lock of hair out of place! He's as cool as James Bond after trouncing 55 henchmen).

In a movie stuffed with silly moments, perhaps the dumbest in *Eclipse* had Victoria scampering up a tree! To escape Edward. (What is it with the *Twilight* movies and characters climbing in trees?!).[42] Well, I guess Victoria's not much of a fighter – she prefers to retreat at the first sign of trouble (altho', as the earlier forest chase showed, she's a helluva runner, jumper and dodger, a berserker sort of free-runner). So Edward simply pushes over the tree, and the fight continues!

But a much more satisfying moment had Edward Cullen (a little earlier) taunting Victoria as she retreats, when Riley's been attacked by the wolf Seth[43] (when Bella Swan would probably prefer to let that psycho-vamp go!), with the details of her mate James's demise (altered

---

41 Other actors, with under-written villain roles, have been able to flesh out the role far more than this.
42 That's what they do in the god-awful *Hunger Games!*
43 In the novel, Edward works with Seth, but that's dropped for the movie.

from the 2007 *Eclipse* book, which focusses more on Victoria being used by James as tool in his hunting, just as Victoria uses Riley). So Victoria, driven to fury, launches herself at Edward.

This is where the Quileute Tribe flashback pays off, with Bella (playing the wife/ princess/ victim who stands on the fringes of a fierce fight feeling useless – always the thankless part to play in an action movie – though the easiest to achieve, and you don't get covered in bruises) thinking of something contribute: she cuts herself as the Chief's third wife did (curiously, about the only blood we see in *Eclipse* – and in the *Twilight Saga* as a whole – is that of our Bella).44 It's enough to distract the two vamps, who have Edward in a headlock. There are several more beats to the duel (including some curious over-the-head moves), before Edward dispatches Victoria by biting off her head, going for her neck (thus hommaging the customary motif of the vampire genre).

✏

In the Big Kiss scene in *Eclipse,* where Bella Swan and Jacob Black finally get to smooch big time, the 2007 *Eclipse* book adds a *Lord of the Rings*-style vision of Bella seeing her future with Jake, including a couple of moppets that she would have shared with him. The 2010 movie elided that, instead going for the *Gone With the Wind* romantic novel approach, and filming 27 set-ups of kissing (and more kissing… and *more* kissing!) against a lovely backdrop of mountains and skies (presumably filmed at Mount Seymour). Howard Shore duly delivers a suitably r-r-romantic cue.

When two people kiss, a novel can do things that cinema can't – the *Eclipse* novel narrates the Big Kiss from inside Bella Swan's point-of-view (as with everything else in the *Twilight* series). So that we experience the violence and domination of Jacob Black's kiss, and Bella's gradual submission to the feeling. The 2010 movie doesn't really do that: it isn't the same sort of kiss. (But the camera does linger on Bella afterwards, as if she's thinking, Hell, did I choose the wrong guy? It's the effect on *Bella*, ultimately, *not* Jacob, that the movie foregrounds).

And right after the kiss, there is a short but crucial duologue between Edward and Bella, where *he* says, 'you love him' (so Edward has finally faced up to it!). But her reply is what he wants to hear: 'I love you more' (I see, right, so it's OK, then?).

✏

And then, with poor Jacob Black injured by a vampire, the path is clear now in *Eclipse* for the romantic plot to advance. Indeed, Stephenie

---

44 Even here, there isn't a close-up of Bella's cutting her arm with a stone, it's elided (there's a sound effect instead). And, no, Bella doesn't smash a sharp pebble into her belly like the third wife of the Chief did!

Meyer takes Jacob out of the picture a couple of times – here where he's wounded by a newborn vampire (as he rushes in to help Leah), and later when he flees in a major sulk after receiving the wedding invitation (shown at the beginning of the next movie, *Breaking Dawn*).

Eclipse closes with a visit to the injured Jake, played in a whispered, muted manner (Jacob once again states his case in the Romance Game, and Bells once again resists), and the mirror of the meadow scene that opens the 2010 movie. Altho' Jake is effectively out of the running, with his severe injuries, he is still, in his doped-up and painful state, bringing the conversation with Bella back to the romantic issue. It would be easy as breathing with me, he tells Bella.

Stephenie Meyer related that the idea for *Twilight* came from a dream she had on June 2, 2003, about 'a vampire and a woman talking in a meadow'.

> It sounds cheesy but it was a great dream. The meadow scene in the movie is basically the dream that I had. When I woke up, I wanted to know what happened to those characters.45

In the meadow, a lot has happened since the beginning of the film, tho' the characters don't seem much altered.46 However, Isabella Marie Swan has consented to marry Mr Old-Fashioined, and now they're discussing a date for the wedding,47 August 13th, a month before Bella's birthday (she is keen to be transformed before she gets another year older).

It's here that Bella makes an important speech about what *she* wants, about plumping for the vampire lifestyle because it feels right for her, because she feels like she'll fit in (so it's not all about Edward, or about choosing between Team Edward and Team Jacob). Notice that Charlie (and Renée) are absent from the *dénouement* scenes in *Eclipse* – the last time we see Chief Swan, for example, is before the finale starts).

Curiously, it's a sunny day in the meadow but Edward's skin isn't glistening: in the documentary about *Eclipse,* there's a cloth hung above the actors, for shade. Why? Perhaps because the glittering skin effect might be too distracting with the intimate scenes played so much in close-ups (and cost might be a factor: that glittery visual effect isn't cheap!). That's in the second scene; but in the first meadow scene, Edward is glittering.

In the *Twilight Saga*, the 'B' plot in each movie – assorted vampires

---

45 Quoted in M. Howden, 27.
46 The two meadow scenes would probably have been filmed at the same time, hence the similarities.
47 With Edward unsure about letting Alice loose on organizing the dress, the ceremony, the guest list... Bella's response is practical: does it matter?

threatening Bella Swan, with Edward fending them off in the finale – is used to provide the action climax. All of that vampire vs. vampire stuff, entertaining as it is, is the secondary plot: the 'A' plot is the romantic plot, the romantic triangle plot, the soap opera/ melodrama plot.

Thus, the action finale of *Twilight 1* comprised Edward protecting Bella from another guy (the psycho vampire James). The action finale of *Twilight 2: New Moon* was the same: Edward protecting his beloved from the nasty Volturi, as well as Victoria. In the third *Eclipse* movie, More of the Same. And in the fourth movie. And in the fifth, their daughter Renesmee.

It's Stone Age, grunt-grunt stuff, isn't it?: it's along the lines of a Sid Caesar or Mel Brooks sketch featuring prehistoric men arguing about a woman,[48] that they're dragging along by her hair:

'Mine! My woman!'
'No, Ugg. *Mine*. Give me woman, Ugg.'

At the end of *Eclipse*, Bella Swan tells Edward Cullen (in the meadow scene, mirroring the opening scene) that it's not simply a choice between him and Jacob Black: it's also about her *wanting* to be a vampire. It may be a helluva life, and fraught with danger, but it's one she gravitates towards. And Edward is her magic key to vampire existence.

Thus, the *Twilight* series is not simply about falling in love with a vampire (i.e., falling for the so-wrong guy!), it's also about Bella finding her way in the world, and deciding, no, she doesn't want marriage (she resists it), and she doesn't want to go to college or university, and she doesn't want to spend four decades in some crummy job... No, she wants to be a vampire. And do whatever vampires do. Which is...? What, exactly? Errr – apart from sucking blood, hanging upside-down, sleeping in coffins – it's 'be vampires', I guess! (And immortality and *not* dying and *not* ageing are also vital for Bella).

Thus, the *Twilight* series is also a coming-of-age story, a search for identity story, a growing-up story (with *choice* as the main topic of discussion). Like millions of others. The question is simple: what are you going to do with your life? Where are you going to live? What is your life going to be like? What job are you going to have? (In a late capitalist society like North America, working is mandatory – and you only get 14 days a year paid vacation (and that's after 5 years in a job)! So *BITE ME!*).

48 Like the terrific Stone Age skit in *The History of the World, Part One.*

The question, voiced ever more clearly in *Eclipse* is: what about the choice between being human and being vampiric? What about losing connections to family and friends? The scenes with Bella and her divorced Mom Renée and Dad Charlie rub that in.

ADDITONAL SCENES.

Among the scenes filmed but dropped from *Eclipse* were the Angela-Bella conversation while they fill in school Prom announcements; a short moment between Bella and her Pa after the Graduation ceremony, when he beams as the proud father; Victoria being a nasty S.O.B. hijacking a car and its drivers; and visions of Alice and Edward working for the Volturi (where they are shown mopping the blood off the floor in the Great Hall wearing Hello Kitty headscarfs. Just kidding).

A scene that was partially filmed for *Eclipse* but not included had Alice and Edward working for the Volturi – Edward read Lord Aro's mind and knew he had designs on them. This would've been inserted in the discussion at the Cullen mansion about the newborn vampire army in Seattle, and Edward wonders if the Volturi are behind it.

The extended scenes included on the *Eclipse* home entertainment releases included Rosalie narrating her back-story in a slightly different way (and being introduced holding someone else's baby); more of the scene where Edward plays the possessive boyfriend (and Bella shuts then opens her window in anger); more of the scene where Jake and Edward argue over Bella, and she stands in between them and says, 'I'm Switzerland' (eh?); and more of Edward's reproachful attitude towards Bella following the Bella-and-Jacob kiss.

Making Eclipse.

6

BREAKING DAWN: PART 1,
THE MOVIE

THE PRODUCTION.

So *Breaking Dawn* was split into two movies (2011-2012), a practice of recent times that only the biggest, most lucrative film franchises can afford to do. The *Matrix* movies, the *Harry Potter* flicks, the *Hunger Games* series, and *Kill Bill* were split into two productions (and most notoriously, *The Hobbit*, a short fantasy book for kids, was chopped by a dwarf's axe into *three* movies!). The aim is simple: to make money. Oh, sure, the filmmakers and the money men and the studios might talk about the source material being 'long' books (such as the last *Twilight* novel or the last *Harry Potter* novel), and requiring a longer running time. Rubbish! They just want even more $$$$! By that logic, an adaptation of *Great Expectations* or *The Count of Monte Cristo* should be five movies in length!

With the luxury of two movies each around 1h 55m long, the *Twilight Saga* could slow down (or slow down even more!). The pace of *Breaking Dawn, Part 1* was, to say the least, leisurely. For a Hollywood blockbuster movie, that is. So leisurely, it didn't have a single action sequence until Edward argues with Bella over who's driving to the mall (Edward breaks the car window in frustration). Because *Breaking Dawn: Bite 1* is the Wedding and Honeymoon *Twilight* movie (before it all goes wrong).

✚

The producers of *Breaking Dawn* were Wyck Godfrey, Karen Rosen-felt and Stephenie Meyer; Marty Bowen, Guy Oseary, Mark Morgan and

Greg Mooradian were exec producers; Bill Bannerman, Roberto Bakker, Isabelle Tanugi and Carlos Paiva were associate/ co-producers (8 guys, 3 women); Summit Entertainment/ Temple Hill produced the movies; Melissa Rosenberg[1] wrote the script;[2] Bill Condon was director; the DP was Guillermo Navarro (best-known for his work with Guillermo del Toro – the *Hell-Boy* movies and *Pan's Labyrinth*); Debra Kane was casting director; Virgina Katz[3] (who has worked Condon several times) was editor (co-editing with Ian Slater for *Part 2*); Richard Sherman was production design; Carter Burwell was composer (back from the first *Twilight* movie);[4] Alexandra Patsavas was music supervisor; Robert Burger was music producer; Lorin Flemming was art director; David Schlesinger and Jan Blackie-Goodine were set decorators; Justin Muller was first A.D.; Jean Black was make-up head; Rita Parillo and Beatrice De Alba supervised the all-important hair; Michael Wilkinson (*300, Watchmen*) designed the costumes; Dane Davis was sound designer; John Bruno[5] (*Terminator 2, Titanic, Avatar*), Phil Tippett, Eric Leven, Terry Wendell and Ken Kokka were visual effects supervisors; John Rosengrant was special make-up effects supervisor; Peng Zhang, Jeff Imada and Scott Ateah were the stunt and fight co-ordinators; vfx were by Tippet Studio, Comen, Legacy Effects, Modus, Lola Visual Effects, Digiscope, Spin, Halon, Prologue, Method Studios, Hydraulx, Mr X, Pixel Magic, Image Engine, Soho, and Wildfire.

In the cast of *Breaking Dawn, Parts 1* and *2* were the principals from the previous *Twilight* movies, plus: Mackenzie Foy (as Renesmee), Lee Pace (Garrett), Casey LaBow (Kate/ Katrina), Noel Fisher (Vladimir), Joe Anderson (Alistair), Cameron Bright (Alec), Angela Sarafyan (Tia Rami), Rami Malek (Benjamin), Christian Camargo (Eleazar), Mía Maestro (Carmen), Judith Shekoni (Zafrina), Charlie Bewley (Demetri), J.D. Pardo (Nahuel), Wendell Pierce (J. Jenks), Marlane Barnes (Maggie), Guri Weinberg (Stefan), Erik Odom (Peter) and Lisa Howard (Siobhan).

Breaking Dawn, Part 1 was released: Nov 18, 2011. 117 mins.

1 Melissa Rosenberg wasn't sure if she would return to the *Twilight* franchise for the final movie. Rosenberg described working with Bill Condon as 'the most enriching to me as a writer' in the series (M. Vaz, 2011, 19). Condon recalled that his most intense collaboration was with Rosenberg, over several months, during pre-production.
2 Rosenberg asked Condon if he wanted to rewrite the script, but he declined: he would be the director (M. Vaz, 2011, 19).
3 Katz noted that the Bella scenes were cut slower, while the rhythm of the Jake and wolf scenes were 'snappier and faster' (M. Vaz, 2011, 130).
4 Kevin Teasley also composed music.
5 Visual effects supervisor for *Breaking Dawn 1* was John Bruno, a veteran going all the way back to *Poltergeist*. Bruno worked on *Ghostbusters, The Abyss, Batman Returns, Cliffhanger, True Lies, X-Men, Rush Hour 3* and *Kingsman*.
　John Bruno's directorial debut was *Virus* (1998), an enjoyable sci-fi/ horror hybrid with a dead simple premise: an alien entity enters the mainframe of a Russian research ship via the Mir space station which the ship was tracking. *Virus* becomes a haunted house scenario, with the hapless cast being picked off by assorted *mecha* and a giant super-robot, Goliath.

Breaking Dawn, Part 2 was released: Nov 16, 2012 (in the U.S.A.). 116 mins.

B.D. *Part 1*'s budget was $110 million.

B.D. *Part 2*'s budget was $120 million.[6]

(Some estimates are higher. Budgets are difficult to estimate and check, because film studios are not always transparent with accounts. A movie such as *Star Wars: The Force Awakens* (2015) was reported in the press as costing $245-300 million. But it actually cost a colossal $533.2 million. Filming the *Star Wars* sequel in Britain, using the new Film Tax Relief scheme of 2007 from the British Government, enabled the studio, Disney, to claim back part of its corporation tax as long as it spent some of its production money in the country. One reason we know more accurately how much the *Star Wars* movie sequels cost is because in Britain accounts have to be filed publicly (and accounts for *The Force Awakens* were still being filed in 2023, 8 years after the film was released)).

Breaking Dawn had amazing opening weekends at the box office, and went on to generate global grosses of $712m and $832m (probably more than if it had been a single movie). It was also released in an I.M.A.X. version. (The films are in widescreen – 2.35: 1). Filming in 3-D was considered (being popular among high budget movies at the time), perhaps using 3-D to portray Bella's new experience as a vampire ('okay she wakes up as a vampire, now let's see the world differently', as Bill Condon put it).

The *Breaking Dawn* production[7] began the 101 days (50 for each film) of principal photography on Nov 1, 2010 with 4-5 days[8] in Rio de Janiero and the environs for the honeymoon sequence, followed by the interiors in Louisiana (until mid-Feb, 2011), and the exteriors (including the wedding), filmed over 38 days in British Columbia (including Squamish and Vancouver Island).[9] The last day in Vancouver was April 15 (when it snowed). A final day in St Thomas, U.S. Virgin Island, was filmed in April at the Easter weekend (for the honeymoon scene, with Bella and Edward in the ocean). Principal photography wrapped on April, 22, 2011. The production team reconvened a year later, in April, 2012, for re-shoots.

The *Breaking Dawn* production was based for much of the shooting schedule in Baton Rouge in Louisiana. Why? Usually, it's money, but it's also sometimes scheduling, and the availability of studio space.

6 Quite a step up from the $38m of *Twilight* and the $50m of *New Moon*.
7 Pre-production lasted 15 weeks, instead of a more usual 20 weeks.
8 Bill Condon said it was two weeks in South America.
9 Condon said about a third of the schedule was based in Vancouver.

(Some States in North America offer tax breaks and financial incentives to film productions). The production also filmed in Vancouver, the Hollywood of the North, as before (again for financial reasons), and in other sites in Canada. In Louisiana the crew filmed in New Orleans – which of course has its own powerful magical and spiritual traditions (including vampire fictions – those of Poppy Z. Brite and Anne Rice, for instance). And New Orleans stood in for other places (such as Seattle and London).

101 days is a short schedule for two big Hollywood movies. But when you think about it, a good deal of both *Breaking Dawn* movies is actually people talking in a room – at the Cullen mansion, or on the Reservation, or in the forest, or at Isle Esme. (But a good proportion of the two movies was created in computers at the 16 vfx companies).

The wedding was filmed last because it was meant to be August, and the movie needed dry weather. Much of the wedding and the reception was filmed near Squamish, British Columbia, at an outdoor location which included the Cullen mansion next to a river. (Bella's house was about 100 miles away). Security, for the wedding scenes in particular, was tight.

And many parts of *Breaking Dawn 1* and *2* were produced in L.A. – this is where the production companies (Summit, Temple Hill, etc) were based, where elements like casting, costume fittings, etc, took place, where visual effects were created, and so on. There were 700-950 vfx shots in *Breaking Dawn, Part 1*.

Why shoot two films at the same time? There are several reasons, not all of them to do with money. One is scheduling: it can be easier to get the actors and crew together in one place; another is keeping the crew and cast together, so they don't drift off to other jobs; another is the second movie can be released soon after the first one (the *Twilight Saga* was committed to a yearly release schedule); another is the efficiency of using resources, of hiring equipment and studios, and of using locations.

It is a rare but not unknown form of production. Famous examples include the two *Superman* sequels, the two *Back To the Future* sequels, the two *Pirates of the Caribbean* sequels, the last *Harry Potter* film, and the three *Lord of the Rings* films. (So you can see how the studios and the producers have considered the success of the first movie and ordered up two more, saving costs by filming them back-to-back).

Filming two movies at the same time meant the schedule was back and forth, out of continuity. In two days Kristen Stewart 'went from the married Bella to pregnant Bella to vampire Bella, with major make-up changes going on all the time', producer Bill Bannerman noted (M. Vaz, 2011, 35). Stewart's vampire make-up took two hours, and pregnant Bella, with the prosthetics, took three hours.

Much of the two *Breaking Dawn* movies take place at or near the Cullen mansion. The Cullen residence in *Breaking Dawn* was much expanded from the location in film one – now we see the back of the building, and the area used for the wedding, as well as Carlisle's office and Alice's bedroom. However, the choice by Catherine Hardwicke and James Lin of the 'Nike house' defined the Cullen mansion for all of the subsequent *Twi*-movies. (The third storey was added digitally). Green screens were employed around the set in Baton Rouge, with background plates of the forest filmed by John Bruno and Mark Weingartner in Canada added later (Terry Windell and co. filmed the plates for the Brazilian island scenes). The Cullen mansion and other sets were built inside a warehouse (not a soundstage) in Port Allen, over the Mississippi River from Baton Rouge. (There are some fun props in the Cullen mansion – like the full-size, wooden Cross in the hall, just in case the Sullens fancy a spot of crucifixion).10

ONE BOOK, TWO MOVIES.

In splitting the *Breaking Dawn* novel into two parts, the film producers felt obliged to rework the text in order to convert it into a suitable narrative for a Hollywood franchise. So the antagonism between the vampires and the werewolves was bumped up, to add action and jeopardy for *Part One*,11 as well as the climax; and the immortal children/ Volturi plot was enlarged in film two, plus of course the battle-that-never-happened, a truly audacious piece of show business. Stephenie Meyer was amenable to either possibility:

> I was always open to either one or two movies – which told the story the best way. There were pros and cons to both versions. (M. Vaz, 2011, 68)

One can imagine how *Breaking Dawn* would've played as a single movie – we have the three previous *Twilight* movies as guides. For a start, *Breaking Dawn* as one film would be much pacier, with far fewer slow scenes and meanderings (the first act of *Breaking Dawn, Part 1* features scenes with plenty of pauses and air, for example, added by editor Virgina Katz, as Bella steels her nerves before the ceremony, or says goodbye to her folks. Film editors can add plenty of 'air' (or breathing

10 Maybe if they managed to snag a Volturi or two.
11 The threat of the wolves was enhanced considerably to provide the necessary obstacles for the movie script of *Breaking Dawn, Part 1*.

space and pauses) in scenes, or they can really tighten them up, so they play super-fast). The vamps vs. wolves conflict wouldn't be necessary in *Part 1*, because the Volturi-plus-immortal children plot would be enough to act as the main threat/ action sequence (and the climax); the gathering of the witnesses and the training sessions would be covered with a single montage for each (or two much shorter montages for the training, like the montages in film one for the internet search and the back-stories); the wedding might stay as long (though with some of the hugs, speeches and pauses trimmed), but the honeymoon would need clipping;[12] and the extended end credits (saying *sayonara* to the cast from all five movies) would probably be dropped (or reserved for the three principals).

Because, as a single movie, *Breaking Dawn* still has plenty of material to explore: the wedding; the honeymoon; pregnancy; birth; and vampirehood. For writer Melissa Rosenberg, a single movie would've meant rushing the wedding, and the 2nd half of the book would have to be condensed too much.[13]

The cover of the book of *Breaking Dawn* is a chess piece. Why? Because it's a novel about clever manœuvring (*à la The Merchant of Venice*): 'the end of the story was not going to be a great big huge battle scene', as Stephenie Meyer put it. But the movie went ahead and added one anyway! (and in the second part!).

STORY AND STRUCTURE.

Structurally, *Breaking Dawn 1* is divided into four acts, with a 117 minute running time. Act one is the wedding (and the run-up to it). Act one ends with the newly-weds leaving for Rio de Janiero. Act two is the honeymoon. Act two ends with the set-back of the pregnancy, and Bella's dialogue hook: 'Thing?' (responding to Edward announcing that Carlisle will be able to get that 'thing' out of her). Act three of *Breaking Dawn, Part 1* comprises the return to Forks, Washington; the next threat comes from the wolves, and from Bella's illness. Act three climaxes with a re-affirmation of the love story: Edward can hear the baby (cue tearful hugs). Act four, the finale, begins when Jacob (who's been prominent in act three), meets with Carlisle and Esme and decides to do something.

The dramatic structure of *Breaking Dawn, Part 1* is a little like Jean-Luc Godard's maxim – that a movie should have a beginning, a middle and an ending, but not necessarily in that order.[14] So the wedding, which might usually round off a (romance) story, comes at the start. Structur-

12 The honeymoon, even some diehard Twi-hards would have to admit, does run on and on.
13 *Breaking Dawn, Part 1: The Official Illustrated Movie Companion,*, 17.
14 Condon remarked of the 2008 *Twilight*: 'everything that got set up there gets resolved here. I think you'll find that there are stylistic and other nods to that film'.

ally, *Breaking Dawn, Part 1* is dissatisfying – snapping the narrative bones of the novel into two parts isn't wholly successful, requiring action scenes to be invented to fulfil the demands of a contemporary, Hollywood franchise movie. Two action sequences were invented to climax *Part 1* and *Part 2* of *Breaking Dawn* – the werewolf vs. vampire smackdown in *Part 1* and the imagined battle in *Part 2*.

Ignore the vampire and werewolf elements in *Breaking Dawn, Part 1*, and you have a soapy melodrama in which a young woman faces some of the benchmarks and challenges of moving from childhood to adulthood: marriage, sex, pregnancy, motherhood, etc.

As director Bill Condon put it, Bella Swan gets married, has sex for the first time, gets pregnant, dies and is reborn – and that's just the first *Breaking Dawn* movie! (Yes – and that's also why the first *Breaking Dawn* movie is far more satisfying than the second movie!). *Breaking Dawn, Part 1*, as Condon pointed out, is all about Bella, while the second movie was a big battle involving vampires from around the world (M. Vaz, 2011, 21).

Producer Wyck Godfrey commented that *Breaking Dawn* contained events that many readers hadn't experienced yet:

> for a lot of readers, they hadn't gone through those things: married at eighteen, immediately pregnant, having a baby, and then marital strife. For our actors, too, they were having to play characters going through life events they hadn't gone through, either. (CFA, 109)

With Jacob Black recovered but bitter and bitching on First Beach about Bella Swan, and parents and family left far behind, much of *Breaking Dawn, Part 1* focussed entirely on Edward and Bella during their honeymoon on an island retreat in South America. (There's a minor scuffle when Jake turns up at the wedding, and he reacts badly (again!) to Bella's decisions – but that hardly counts as action in Hollywood blockbuster movie terms).

✛

Breaking Dawn, Part 1 doesn't convince at the usual levels (we don't really believe that these characters are there, in those places, doing those things), but it doesn't want to: this is an interiorized movie, a movie about a young woman wondering whether she's doing the right thing.

Does she want to get married? Yes.

Does she love Edward? Yes.

Does she want to leave her family and friends behind? Much more difficult to say.

The issue of becoming a vampire is merely a fantasy literature motif tacked on a psychological story that's already full of dilemmas. (And the dilemmas are the stuff of Agony Aunt columns in women's magazines, the stuff of TV chat shows, or newspaper gossip columns, of people everywhere:

Should I marry him? What about the other guy? What will my parents think? And so on.

Indeed, parts of the *Breaking Dawn, Part 1* come across like a movie version of an article in *Cosmopolitan* or a letter to an Agony Aunt: 'so, like, my honeymoon was going so well, until, like –' blah, blah, blah).

✢

Elements which didn't make it into the 2011-12 celluloid adaptation of *Breaking Dawn* included Edward bizarrely suggesting to Jacob Black that he fathers a child with Bella Swan, so she can have a real human baby instead of the freak he put inside her (BD, 168). Edward does appeal to Jacob in the movie, but only to try talking some sense into Bella. The subplot of Rosalie Hale craving Bella's baby wasn't really a part of the 2011-12 movies (there's a beat where Bella calls up Rosalie on her cel at the Rio airport – it stretches credibility a lot that Bella would have Rosalie's number on her phone!).[15] Rose does stand in the way of Jake a couple of times (but it isn't really made clear that Rosalie covets the baby because she never had the chance to have children of her own, and also that she doesn't even care particularly if Bella expires during childbirth – it's the baby she wants).

The birth scene was different from Stephenie Meyer's book, lacking the fight between Rosalie and Jacob (the sparring between Jake and Rose is very amusing in the 2008 novel, and might've added some humour to act three of *Breaking Dawn, Part 1*). The scene of Jake fleeing the Cullens' place in an Aston Martin for some fresh air and a new perspective proved to be a dead-end in the novel, and (rightly) didn't appear in the movies – we've already seen that, anyway, when Jacob hurtles out of his home after seeing the wedding invite in the opening shots of the movie.[16]

As a 'date movie', *Breaking Dawn, Part 1* sucks big time for guys going along with their girlfriends – there's a wedding (boring!), a honeymoon (boring!), sex (mildly amusing!), a pregnancy (boring!), an illness and horrible pregnancy (boring and icky!), and arguments about

---

15 Or that she's even got a phone!

16 However, Jake is certainly an attractive guy in the books and in the movies, so it does stretch disbelief a tad that there aren't a few girls/ boys who fancy him.

babies and monsters (boring!). From a regular boys' point-of-view, the first half of *Breaking Dawn, Part 1* might be hard to sit thru (wedding and honeymoon), and the second half is not much better (pregnancy and illness). You have to wait a *long* time for some action, for instance – and even then it's the artificial antagonism between the vamps and the wolves. (But the film producers had a very clear idea of who their audience was for the *Twilight* movies by the time of *Breaking Dawn* – the *Twilight* fans! They even turned up at the locations during filming! Or to put it in a nutshell, the audience for the *Twilight* movies is 80% female).

STYLE.

Style-wise, *Breaking Dawn, Part 1* happily dives into the warm end of the colour spectrum, with earth and cream tones (as if to emphasize Bella's last moments of being human, of having blood run thru her veins instead of some crystalline vampire venom). The warm greens and whites of the wedding scenes continue into the South American honeymoon, with a house filled with big-leaved plants (as if they've brought the forests from the Olympic Peninsula with them, or as if everywhere they go, it's forested). The beach, the sand, the waterfall, the sea, the island – numerous motifs here connote Paradise, a South Seas idyll (it's Stephenie Meyer's version of the Garden of Eden, with the apple, the woman, the snake and all the rest. The first quote in the *Twi-Saga* is from *The Book of Genesis*, 2:17).

Many of the clothes for *Breaking Dawn* were bought by Michael Wilkinson and his team from stores in Tinseltown. The racks of clothes in the wardrobe dept were used to start dialogues about the characters between the filmmakers and the actors about what the costumes might be (M. Vaz, 2011, 24). *Breaking Dawn, Part 1* is a film with several important costumes. Well, one above all – the Wedding Dress (others include Alice's divine flapper-style dress, the Cullen boys in Italian suits, and Bella's blue dress as a vampire).[17]

Kristen Stewart changed costume some 60 times in the two *Dawns* (which the Bella in the novels certainly doesn't do!). Ironically, Bella's loose, modest clothing when she's pregnant (old, grey sweat pants) is how she appears in Stephenie Meyer's novels (but she's only allowed to dress like that in a Hollywood movie when she's severely ill!). For the honeymoon, Alice has packed cute shorts and tops for Bella, along with very skimpy lingerie (the kind of outfits that Bella would never, ever

---

17 In some scenes, Jake becomes the All-American Biker Boy – wearing a leather jacket, with his hair in something close to a quiff. Edward is once again clad often in blue colours.

buy, or would never contemplate wearing!). Somewhere along the way, in the days before the wedding service, Alice has persuaded Bella to leave all of the clothes shopping to her and Bella, against her better judgement, went along with it!

There is plenty of music (by Carter Burwell and Kevin Teasley) slipping in and out of the scenes in *Breaking Dawn, Part 1*, but much of its passes by the ear without making much of an impression (you quickly get tired of *yet another* tinkly piano piece plinking in the background. It's as if Edward from film one is scoring this movie). Far better, I reckon, would've been to include at least one or two classic pop music numbers, rather than the bland pop songs featured here – which included Sleeping At Last, the Features, the Joy Formidable, the Belle Brigade, Christina Perri, Iron & Wine, Imperial Mammoth, Mia Maestro and the Noisettes. Bruno Mars was the lead single ('It Will Rain' – a dependable weather forecast for Sporks). (The first movie was more successful in allowing lengthy sequences to run on *without* music. *Breaking Dawn*, both parts, is far too frightened to allow more'n 42 seconds of silence. This dogged insistence of plastering movies with burbling underscore – now it's everywhere in Hollywood – often spoils them).

The structure of the editing has some awkward moments in *Breaking Dawn, Part 1*: for instance, part-way through the lengthy honeymoon sequence (which takes up all of act two), the movie abruptly cuts to La Push beach back in the Olympic Peninsula[18] and a scene of Jacob Black whingeing. It reminds us that Jake is still in the mix (and of course he's not happy!), and of other minor points (like the antagonism btn Jacob and Sam Uley, and that Jake has his own circle of cohorts – which sets us up for the wolfy split in act 3. And in a close-up of Leah, with Jake in the background out of focus, Leah makes the important point that it's miserable loving someone who's chosen someone else).

However, the editing of *Breaking Dawn, Part 1* is livened up by several impressive montages: some for Jacob (imprinting on Renesmee, and calling the wolves together); some for Bella (as she prepares for her honeymoon night, and as she dies); some for Edward (as a killer in the 1930s, and as he researches immortal children); a montage for the dinner speeches;[19] a montage for the wedding invitations; and many montages for the lovers (during the honeymoon there are chess montages, waterfall/ swimming montages, and even Bella in lingerie montages).

Editors love putting montages together – it is pure filmmaking, pure cinema (no talking heads, it's not theatre, it's not still photography or

---

18 Filmed at Way Beach, Vancouver Island.
19 There are jump cuts, too.

radio, painting, etc). And composers love montages, because their music is allowed to run on longer, and unbroken, and (usually) without fighting against sound fx and dialogue.

Act 3 of *Breaking Dawn, Part 1* corresponds to the *Jacob* chapter in the 2008 novel. However, the filmmaking remains objective, and doesn't get into Jake's subjective experience much (except in two striking instances: in the rapid montage where Jake, in werewolf form, is haunted by Bella's decayed state, and calls the wolves together, and when he experiences imprinting).

We *need* Jacob Black in the middle of *Breaking Dawn, Part 1* – he's about the only character who's outspoken emotionally. His anger and frustration are vented several times: he yells at Edward, gets angry with the Sullens, imagines biting off Edward's head, and, in an extravagant and satisfying gag, kicks his motorbike into the trees (haven't we all wanted to do that!). Edward isn't allowed to lose it ever in the movies – except once, and it's shocking to see Edward yell at Bella and storm out (especially upsetting because Carlisle's just told her that she can be saved).

REPLAYING THE FIRST *TWILIGHT* MOVIE.

Director Bill Condon noted that *Breaking Dawn, Part 1* was a replay of the first *Twilight* movie in some ways. So self-conscious *hommages* and motifs from the first movie were integrated into the 2011 movie (including the music by Carter Burwell – Burwell scored *Breaking Dawn*, and had composed the music for the first *Twilight* movie. Condon had worked with Burwell on five other movies).

Breaking Dawn, Part 1 reprises the first *Twilight* movie yet again by having a montage of online,[20] research images – this time it's Edward Cullen searching for information on half-vampire/ half-human children (famous paintings, such as Henry Fuseli's *The Nightmare* (1782), a favourite with filmmakers, is prominent, plus the usual suspects like Hieronymous Bosch. We also see the phrase 'immortal children', foreshadowing the second *Breaking Dawn* movie).

Does Edward expect to find an official, Government-endorsed website dedicated to half-human-half-vampire children?! Sure – everyone's heard of it, along with E-Bay and Facebook!

Breaking Dawn, Part 1 emulated the first *Twilight* movie by having another montage of images from the movie – and from all of the *Twilight Saga* movies. The scenario is actually the same: in the ballet school,

---

20 With Yahoo receiving product placement.

Bella's dancing and her life flashing before her eyes; the same thing occurs in *Breaking Dawn, Part 1*, as Bella is dying and being reborn as a vampire (however, the montage is considerably longer – and much fussier and tricksier, as more vfx were added to morph and blend scenes together, some of which shift into b/w).

MALE NUDITY.

In *Breaking Dawn*, the shirts were back on! (Boo-hoo! cry some of the Twi-hards): according to director Bill Condon, Taylor Lautner's agent had insisted that his boy (his walking cash machine) only take his shirt off once. Surely some of the audience (80% female) were miffed about not seeing Lautner half-naked! Plus the gang of werewolf boys ('four really big half-naked boys', as *New Moon* puts it). As Edward bitchily quips in *Eclipse*, 'doesn't he have a shirt?' (*Meow*!).

> He grinned. 'Does my being half-naked bother you?'
> 'No.'
> Jacob laughed again, and I turned my back on him to focus on the dishes. (E, 192)

Thus, the *Twilight* movies were unusual in portraying more male nudity (or partial nudity) than female nudity (altho' Kristen Stewart is depicted partially undressed many times in *Part 1*, particularly during the honeymoon, as if making up for all of the scenes where Taylor Lautner is topless).

INTRODUCTIONS.

The first of two movies adapting the 2008 *Breaking Dawn* novel (released Nov 18, 2011 in the New World) opens with a montage of wedding invitations (which cleverly re-introduces some of the key charas such as Renée, Charlie, Billy, etc). Jacob Black, understandably, goes ballistic – surging out into the forest on the Quileute Indian Reservation in the opening scene, to go A.W.O.L. in the rain for weeks (this was the epilogue of *Eclipse*, and it might've been a scene inherited from *Eclipse*; but it makes more sense to put it here – to introduce one of the three chief stars in *Breaking Dawn, Part 1*. It's twenty minutes before Jake returns, at the wedding. And this is the only time in *Breaking Dawn* that Taylor Lautner takes off his shirt! *So bite me!*).

But the introduction of the other main characters in *Breaking Dawn* is amazingly under-stated for a giant movie franchise: instead of the glowing meadow scene of *Eclipse*, or the slo-mo shot in the car lot of

Edward in *New Moon*, we have Bella and Alice[21] discussing high-heeled shoes on the porch of the Cullen mansion (the cut to a C.U. of Bella's shoes and then to A. and B. in a two-shot is incredibly casual and low key), and a Bella point-of-view shot of Edward upstairs, as he stares pensively out of the window (pre-wedding nerves for the bridegroom? Only a little later, when Edward visits Bella in her room at home, are the lovers seen together. So, like, no glowing, slo-mo shots of Edward? And no really decent intro shot for Bella?).

THE WEDDING.

Oh, but let's not forget the wedding!

The w-e-d-d-i-n-g, folks!

As organized by Alice Cullen (who else could it be?! – she's the go-to-girl for Parties For Any Occasion), the wedding was a *Hello!*-style[22] bash in the grounds of the Cullen clan's luxurious forest home in the Pacific North-West (no need to hire a fancy palace when you live in one). Given the opportunity for taking a much longer sojourn with the wedding sequence due to the luxury of two movies to tell one story, the filmmakers indulged themselves with including every detail of pre-wedding nerves, pre-amble, anxiety, and planning, plus squeezing every ounce of romantic/ dramatic/ emotional/ spectacle out of the day itself.

The Dress. The Shoes. The Hair. The Make-up.

The Jewellery. The Invitations. The Table Settings.

We had the lot! Hell, even bitter Rosalie Hale stuffs her antsy harrumphs into her jeans and gets down with the girls, offering to do Bella S.'s hair (as per the book).[23] For this scene, we're in Alice's bedroom, of course! (Just look at the size of those closets, and how many outfits and shoes dear Alice has!).[24] Weddings are gifts to dramatists, of course (if you can't create a good wedding scene, you are a truly dreadful writer!), and the filmmakers of *Breaking Dawn, Part 1* spared no expense in milk-milk-milking this much-anticipated installment in the *Twilight Saga* (after all, this is the Big Pay-Off Scene in the romantic narrative form. And many romantic tales would opt to stop right here, with the caption, '*And they lived happily ever after*'. As indeed they do – except in *Twilight*, it's the word *forever* that's the mantra. Edward uses it in his speech, while looking longingly at his bride. And what most of the assembly don't realize is that Big E. really means it literally: f-o-r-e-v-e-r

---

21 Alice is in her element organizing the wedding.
22 And, like a *Hello!* celebrity rag wedding, there were photographers (and helicopters) keen to get a glimpse of The Dress (the producers were adamant that security on this show would be high).
23 Which of course sets up the subplot of Rosalie coveting the baby, which was lost in the movie.
24 Ashley Greene is radiant in a purple flapper-style dress with 1930s-era beading.

– by which time, everybody at the ceremony will be long dead).[25]

Production designer Richard Sherman cited *A Midsummer Night's Dream* as an inspiration for the glade in the trees for the wedding (*A Midsummer Night's Dream* is one of the intertexts of of the *Breaking Dawn* novel. Presumably, that means the play by Shagspur, not one of the many film or theatrical adaptations). In the *Breaking Dawn* book, the dancing takes place outdoors, but the nuptials are celebrated in the main room of the mansion. The movie's solution was to Alice-fy the Cullen mansion even more than Alice herself did in the novel: benches and tables constructed from wood and branches, as if the furniture has grown out of the forest; huge clusters of small, white lamps that hang in ribbons; and 500 cascades of wisteria vines.

For the wedding, there was an immense amount of interest in The Dress (notice how Alice Cullen teases us with The Dress – it's in a bag). Stephenie Meyer wanted the designer Carolina Herrera; the costume designer Michael Wilkinson worked with Herrera to create the Most Important Costume of *Breaking Dawn* (and of the whole *Twilight Saga*) – an old-fashioned dress in white satin, with long sleeves, and an open back edged with French Chantilly lace (copies of the Wedding Dress was later sold by Herrera for $35,000 each). The Dress[26] was revealed gradually, as Bella Swan walked along the aisle (it took a long time for Bells and her Pa to stroll down the aisle – tho', thankfully, it wasn't in slo-mo).

For Michael Wilkinson, designing the costumes for the wedding, the highpoint of the *Twilight Saga*, was a big deal. Wilkinson and Carolina Herrera created an outfit incorporating vintage elements (Edwardian/ Victorian) with contemporary ones: long sleeves, an open back with French lace, a flared train, a skirt down to the floor, a scooped neckline, and mainly in white silk. The shoes came from Manolo Blahnik. The hair comb from the Gilded Lily. The men's suits were from Brioni. (Note the prevalence of Italian designers, reflecting the Italian influences on the *Twilight Saga*).

A wedding is a handy dramatic format for introducing all of the major players, and *Breaking Dawn* is no exception: the filmmakers make sure that most of the secondary charas are present and correct, and now seen in a new guise, smartly dressed in tuxes and evening dresses (and there's time for the minor charas to have short bits of business – because after this, many of them vanish).

Members of the film crew had cameos at the wedding, including

---

25 Hmm, that is an odd thought: the guests who're vamps will out-live everyone else present.
26 It was locked up, wrapped in cloaks, and assigned its own vampire bodyguards.

Stephenie Meyer, Wyck Godfrey, Bill Bannerman and Melissa Rosenberg. There's a look shared between Meyer and her heroine. So cute!

The wedding introduces teensy bits of plot which'll pay off later in *Breaking Dawn* – like the introduction of the Denali coven[27] and Irina (Maggie Grace) and a reprise of the vampire versus werewolf rivalry (and Laurent's demise).[28] Note Billy Black's gloating smile in these scenes – his lads demolished Laurent (and Jessica's quip about Mike drooling over the Denali girls).

The dinner speeches were amusing, captured in a montage structure (and staged in *tableau*-style), with Bella's Mom's embarrassing song, Emmett's joke that gets no response (about Bella not sleeping for a while!), Jessica's catty quips (about being a much more eligible girlfriend for the Hair than Bella), Charlie's muttering about being a cop, etc.

There was time for a sweet scene between Jake and Bella at the wedding (this is a crucial scene, because it introduces Jake in the foreground interacting with his beloved, and one of the three stars of the movie). Altho' Jacob wishes her well, he's probably a blockhead to turn up at all! Like, rub it in, Jake! Like, feel *even worse*, Jake, than seeing the woman you love in her wedding dress at her nuptials!

But that's part of the romance genre, isn't it? In this respect, and pretty much every other respect, the *Twilight* movies are first and foremost part of the romance genre. After the big battle at the end of *Eclipse,* the *Twi-hard* series shifts wholly into the romance genre (and even Edward's admission that he preyed upon humans in his youth, in the 1930s, doesn't convince either the audience or Bella. She brushes it aside, as many in her shoes might do (but not me) – 'like, so what? So, like, you're a mass murderer? *Phooey*! Marry me already!').

Jake B. appearing at the wedding also re-introduces a motif that has kept the *Twilight* movies ticking over happily towards a worldwide gross of several billion dollars: the romantic triangle. So, yes, it's yet another replay of the Edward versus Jake versus Bella baloney.

The stag night is sweet: Edward is yanked away from Bella's bedroom by his brothers, Emmett and Jasper. (As Bella and Edward talk in the room, you can hear the vampires yelling, 'BORING!' Here the guys act like jocks, like the dates that've been dragged along to see *Breaking Dawn* by their Twi-hard girlfriends, voicing their thoughts: '*Borrring!* ').

There is a montage[29] of Edward Cullen Doing the Vampire Thing

---

27 This departs from the book; in early drafts of the script, the Denalis would've appeared in *Part 2*, with their back-story explained in a flashback.
28 Played in flashcuts.
29 The movie shifts from colour to black-and-white here, echoing the *Frankenstein* film.

with a bunch of victims, who are all, apparently, criminals – nay, killers. So it's OK, then! Yes – bite those hoodlums, Ed! They're all men, so they don't count! (In the film-within-a-film scene, in a packed theatre, *The Bride of Frankenstein* (1935) plays to a thrilled crowd, and Edward follows a man out of the auditorium as he pursues a woman).

According to Bill Condon, these scenes came about from discussions with Rob Pattinson about the back-story of Edward (and lines from the first *Twilight* novel), and were not originally part of Melissa Rosenberg's script. So they were added to the schedule. (The choice of *Frankenstein* evokes several layers of meaning – one is the most well-known horror novel of the 19th century, along with *Dracula*; another is the many film adaptations of *Frankenstein*, which links to the *Twilight* series; yet another layer is that Condon had directed *Gods and Monsters*, about the director of the *Frankenstein* films at Universal, James Whale; yet another is that while the audience in the theatre innocently watches a horror movie, there is a real monster in their midst, Edward).

Edward C. becomes a murderer preying upon other murderers; he's a sort of undead superhero prowling the city, Spider-man with fangs. There are further images of Edward biting victims in dark alleys (but, Hell, would you want to suck the blood of a serial killer, a rapist or a child molester? And this is the guy that Bella's marrying! She might well complain: don't kiss me with *that* mouth!).

And then, after Edward's related his nasty past, Bella simply says, like a dumb kid, looking up at him with her so-innocent face, but those guys were murderers, right? You probably saved more people from dying. It's this kind of cock-eyed, naïve sentimentality that has critics banging their heads against walls.

Bella Swan really is an idiot in *The Twilight Saga*.

✠

In the run-up to the wedding in *Breaking Dawn, Part 1*, there are many scenes of characters (principally Bella Swan) looking into mirrors, examining themselves thoughtfully (in the 2008 novel, Bella studiously *avoids* mirrors – ah, but cinema is absolutely besotted with mirrors). There are teary scenes (Bells weeps plenty in the novel). There are ominous dream sequences (in one, Bella's married to Edward in a white-on-white setting,[30] but has slaughtered all of the guests! So they are piled up in a mound below her, while Edward and Bella stand above them. The Volturi appear as their sinister selves, too (in an ironic touch, standing where the Priests would be at a wedding ceremony. The nightmare

---

30 But wearing a different wedding dress.

handily reminds us of the Volturi, because they aren't seen for some time after this. At one time, Melissa Rosenberg considered bringing the Volturi in earlier, using the necklace gift as a dramatic device [M. Vaz, 2011, 19]). In another dream, Jacob imagines himself ripping off Edward's head (very satisfying!), which he's probably fantasized doing several times. In another vision, Bella's lying in a coffin in her wedding dress, while her Dad Charlie looks on. In the 2008 book, the only dream/ nightmare that Bella has is of the immortal children).

The question, 'Do I want to marry a vampire?', is way secondary to the questions everybody can relate to: 'Do I want to get married?' Or: 'Do I wanna get hitched to *this* guy?'

In this particular Hollywood movie, marriage means saying goodbye to your parents, to your former life, and embracing a new life. Leaving your friends behind, and becoming devoted to one person. (The vampiric element, as always in the *Twilight* series, enhances feelings and views that already exist). The first time that Bella really weeps is when she's hugging Jake, and he reminds her of all she will miss when she's vampirized.

On the plus side, it's not all introspection and self-questioning: there is *plenty* of kissing and cuddling in the first two acts of *Breaking Dawn, Suck 1*. And when our loving couple embrace at the altar, they imagine themselves alone (as per the novel), with everybody in the congregation disappeared (as opposed to slaughtered!). Yes, two lovers do create a whole world around themselves, and everything else fades away. They don't *need* parents, siblings, friends, family, anybody. They are a world unto themselves. (And the camera makes the obligatory circular move around the lovers. It's written in the D.G.A. rulebook that the circular, Steadicam shot must be included in 80% of all Hollywood movies).[31]

The Priest launches right into the vows, missing out the usual preamble to any wedding service. (No vicar, reverend or church official misses an opportunity to wax lyrical to a captive audience).

I missed the input of Bella Swan's school friends, though, before and during the wedding – Bella preparing for the day took place at the Cullen stronghold, in amongst the dysfunctional and very weird vampire family. Much more fun, I reckon, would've been to place Bella with her school chums. The 2011 movie also missed a proper farewell with Jessica, Mike, Angela, Eric and company.[32] (However, the *Breaking Dawn* book does

---

31 Actually, that shot also became a visual effects shot, because Stewart had a wrist brace from an accident which had to be covered up.
32 There is a brief exchange between Jessica and Angela at the wedding, when the possibility of Bella being pregnant is mooted (after all, she's marrying at 18, too young in the opinion of a character like Jessica).

keep Bella with her Pa then with Alice, and later her Mom, so that Jessica, Mike, Angela *et al* don't get a look-in).

THE HONEYMOON.

The mystery honeymoon in *Breaking Dawn, Part 1* was a slice of romantic fiction done in Jackie Collins-style (Collins being the High Queen of Glitz and Romance). So we had flights to... Rio de Janiero... to the funky streets of Rio (where everybody grooves, and it's always carnival time![33] – these scenes were added to the novel)... to a moonlit boat[34] ride to the idyllic island getaway...

James Bond, Mills & Boon, rom-coms, 'chick flicks' and other forms of fantasy fiction and romance fiction love to indulge the audience with such lavish, jet-set vacation spots. Start saving those dollars and cents, girls, and you could have a vacation here too![35]

Well, our Bella Swan *is* marrying into money (we have to assume that the Cullens, not the Swans, are financing this jamboree! And they *own* this island getaway (Isle Esme)! So altho' it's a 'traditional' wedding, it's not *that* traditional! The family of the bride don't seem to contribute much to the wedding except to turn up!). Bella's the girl who 'done good', the girl who snagged the wealthy husband – *and* he's good-looking! – *and* he's an animal in the bedroom! Whooo!

The only downside of Cinderella clinching her Prince Charming is that, well, he's a *vampire*! A cold, stony, dangerous guy (and mass murderer!). And, in a regurgitation of numerous romance genre clichés, the honeymoon takes a sudden slide into drama when Bella Swan finds herself pregnant.

✤

Breaking Dawn's honeymoon depicted the End of the Dream: Edward gets what he wants: Bella. And Bella gets what she wants: her man, Edward (the Vampire Change being put on hold for the moment). But, as Thomas Hardy noted often in his classic, 19th century novels, a wedding is the *start* of the problems, not the end or the solution to them! (At his most nihilistic extreme, in *Jude the Obscure*, Hardy asserted, via the character of Widow Edlin, that 'weddings be funerals'!).

Well, altho' the *Twilight Saga* is based on a 19th century, melodramatic model (with Jane Austen[36] as the Goddess of this form of relationship and romance story), and even though it is filled with

---

33 These were the first shots of principal photography (in the Lapa district).
34 The scenes were watched by 100s of people on the harbour.
35 Did *Breaking Dawn* influence real weddings and honeymoons? Very likely!
36 Bella is of course a big Jane Austen fan – her book of the works of Austen has been read many times (T, 128).

vampires pouting gloomily, it is never as bleak and pessimistic as Thomas Hardy's novels! (For miserabilism – usually in rainy, church cemeteries – Hardy is King!).

So, no, the honeymoon of Bella Swan and Edward Cullen isn't a disaster. But also, it can't run smoothly. It can't be hearts and flowers and multiple orgasms all round. The first obstacle in the honeymoon is unusual: it's sex. They both want it (they're on their honeymoon, after all), but they know that it might have dire consequences. It's a twist on Biblical injunctions about intercourse (that book, the *Holy Bible*, looms over all of the *Twilight Saga*). But, come on! This isn't sex before marriage! They're married now. And Bella is a virgin! (As she loudly informs her Daddy). Which ought to satisfy stern, long-bearded religionists and arch conservatives of any church, sect or faith. (No, the *Twilight* movies do not suggest for a moment that Edward is (or must be) virtuous too! The double standards of patriarchy are upheld. The novel seems to suggest, however, that Edward really *is* a 104 year-old virgin. And in the 2011 movie, Edward simply laughs when the question is posed – the best response to such enquiries).

When the much-anticipated lovemaking in *Breaking Dawn, Part 1* occurs, it's played pretty much as expected (tho' with some welcome humour beforehand, as Bella Swan prepares for the All-Important Night in a frantic, nervous montage of bathing/ washing/ shaving, taken directly from the 2008 *Breaking Dawn* book). And some humour afterwards – with the room and the bed wrecked, and feathers floating down.[37]

Stephenie Meyer might not be a fan of erotic fiction, and claimed to be uninterested in reading *Fifty Shades of Cullen*, but there are at least two scenes of intercourse in the honeymoon section of *Breaking Dawn, Part 1* (along with several other intimate scenes which were pushing at the 'PG-13 rating).

Yes, the *Twilight* series only nods towards feminism (and only to second wave feminism), because most of the time it's thoroughly traditional and totally patriarchal. She's a virgin (he might be a virgin), there's a wedding, a honeymoon, she becomes a wife, she has sex, she gets pregnant, she has a child, she becomes a mother, etc. It's no different from 100,000 romances and melodramas. (and some feminists complained that Bella is portrayed as a masochist, happy to have her body bruised in the controversial 'morning after' scene).

Yet *Twilight* does have a sexually-assertive young woman at its heart, which's intriguing and unusual. Before the wedding, and during the

---

[37] The funniest room-wrecking-sex-scene-aftermath occurs in *Love and Death* (1975).

honeymoon, it's Bella who's often the most aggressive sexually. And Bella does question the institution of marriage (questions it, but still goes ahead with it). But she is also a dutiful wife and Mom. In short, she becomes Mrs Cullen (and the Mrs Cullen that Edward wants.[38] So *Breaking Dawn* can be regarded as anti-feminist, pro-patriarchal and very conservative).

Shots of a box of Tampax and a character talking about menstruation (right after the heroine's thrown up in the bowl!) are certainly rare in romantic dramas with action and thrills (many film studios would probably prefer it if references to women bleeding did *not* get a mention anywhere in their money-spinning movie franchises. Yes, they'll happily stage nasty decapitations and grotesque, gory violence, and war-mongering on a psychotic scale, but not the natural menstruation that happens to millions of women every day, oh no!). Notice how Edward in these scenes stands back, feeling useless, a cliché of the awkward, embarrassed, helpless man (in fact, that is Edward's default position in much of *Breaking Dawn, Part 1*).

'THEY KISS'.

The honeymoon does benefit from the romantic chemistry that Kristen Stewart and Robert Pattinson display. So that when the script says, 'they kiss' (for the 55th time), we believe it.

For Kristen Stewart, some of the romantic/ erotic elements written into the *Twilight* scripts were too much:

> From the third one on, we're constantly kissing! Sometimes it felt a little redundant and weird, especially when every scene is written around the climax of a kiss. It's like 'A-a-a and... here it comes!' (CFA, 121)

Kristen Stewart's right: there's far more kissing in the *Twilight Saga* than in many romantic dramas or rom-coms. (But, apart from the actors at the time, who's complaining?).

In *Breaking Dawn* Kristen Stewart displays her body in numerous scenes: Bella in lingerie, Bella in a bikini, Bella in a towel. This returns the *Twilight Saga* to the familiar conventions of Hollywood cinema, where women are objectified by the camera. (And for Robert Pattinson fans, there's quite a bit of Rob partially-clothed).

In terms of editing, the honeymoon used a lot of music to create short montages: a chess-playing montage... a Bella-in-lingerie montage... a waterfall/ swimming montage... When lovemaking is off the menu, the

---

38 He calls her 'Mrs Cullen'.

newly-weds take to exploring the island vampire-style, with leaps off waterfalls and hiking thru the jungle.

AND THEY NEARLY 'LIVED HAPPILY EVER AFTER'.

Part 1 can be summed up as: *they nearly lived happily ever after*. And *Part 2* is: *they lived happily ever after*.

After the more tightly-plotted narratives of the previous three *Twilight* movies, you have to admit that the storytelling in *Breaking Dawn, Part 1* is not only rather sedate and lacking dramatic momentum, it also doesn't seem nearly enough of anything for a Big Hollywood Movie. Oh, the wedding (preamble, experience and aftermath) is interesting, and the (very) lengthy honeymoon episode has its moments, but nearly an hour of *Breaking Dawn, Part 1* sails by without (1) a major action or dramatic scene, (2) any departures from the expected ingredients of a fairy tale-style, romantic drama: we have a wedding, a honeymoon, and a conception. Much of *Breaking Dawn, Part 1* is so much like 'ordinary life' as to not warrant being turned into a movie, let alone a lavish, Hollywood production (or a movie that millions would flock to see). I mean, if there were Busby Berkeley dance numbers to enjoy along the way, or some comical set-pieces, or some wild vamp vs. wolf action, or *something*, it might be worth our attention.

The truth, as far as a romantic drama is concerned, and as a fairy tale is concerned, and as the genre and form of the *Twilight Saga* is concerned, the story was *over* at the wedding. The nuptials signal the *end* of a romantic tale: '…and they got married and lived happily ever after'.

That's *it*. It's *over*. We're *done*.

To continue *past* the marriage of the hero and the heroine in a romantic drama means… well, it means that the storytellers are forced to invent new obstacles and new challenges for the characters to face. So, they have sex (despite the possibility of pain)… so, the woman conceives (but it's not a normal pregnancy)… so, the werewolves oppose the procreation of a vampire child/ monster… and so on.

The werewolf plot challenging the heroine's pregnancy is one of a number of parts of *Breaking Dawn* that seem too obviously contrived. Cleverly, it puts Jacob Black in the middle, in between the rival camps, and once again links up Edward, Bella and Jacob (as they – what a surprise! – fight for her survival yet again!), but it seems rather awkwardly handled, requiring (once again), a *lot* of manœuvring by Melissa Rosenberg and the filmmakers to make it convince (M. Vaz, 2011, 19).

Really, *Breaking Dawn, Part 1* is a woman's movie even more'n the previous three *Twilight* movies. The guys are reduced to supporting players in the saga of *The Life and Times of Bella Swan* – as she struggles with intercourse, pregnancy, marriage, living with in-laws and disease.

Meanwhile, there isn't an action sequence until the last third of *Breaking Dawn, Part 1*! Oh, halfway thru, there's the 'talking wolves' scene (scene 92, dubbed 'the lumberyard scene'),[39] where the filmmakers desperately attempt to inject some momentum into the 2011 movie by having Jacob, Leah, Seth, Sam and the other werewolves hurtling thru the forest and the mountains (cue the busy music, the rapid cutting, the speedy camera moves). But, folks, all these werewolves're doing is *rushing* to... a committee meeting!

Well, yes, there *are* dramatic elements in the 'talking wolves' scene: a split in the werewolf community, with Jake, Leah and Seth breaking off from Sam's pack (the highpoint is where the Jacob-wolf faces up against the Sam-wolf). But that is very much a *minor* plot in the grand scheme of the *Twilight Saga* (because Bella has *already* married her man! She chose *Edward*! Not *Jake*!). (And the 'talking wolves' scene, no matter how much money was spent on it, how skilful the animation was, how great the sound fx and music were, is the hokiest scene in the *Twilight* series).

Breaking Dawn sticks to the Bella point-of-view in the main. For the phone calls, for example – when Bella and Edward talk to the Cullens in North America, we stay with Bella and Edward (and ditto when Bella speaks to Rosalie). However, the movie also steps away from Bella many times: we see Jacob in wolf-form talking to Sam's pack; we see Jake, Leah and Seth as the breakaway pack; we see short scenes btn Jake and Seth, and Jake and Leah; we see the Cullens talking to Jake; and Jake making the crucial decision to act, with Esme and Carlisle (however, importantly, we *don't* follow Alice and Jasper at all – they're only referenced in dour dialogue).

Significantly, *Breaking Dawn, Part 1* cuts away from the idyllic, erotic honeymoon in South America halfway through to the rainy, windy Pacific North-West and the beach at La Push (two beach settings, but look at the contrast in the light). Here, Jacob is whingeing to all who'll listen about his beloved Bella being transformed into – *uggh!* – a bloodsucker. The dramatic content is represented by the blocking of the scene: Jacob, Seth, Leah and co. are sitting in one group, while Sam Uley, Paul and their girls are in another group (some of them are kicking

---

39 The plates were filmed at a logging camp near Squamish.

a ball around). No matter what the dialogue might be (Jacob's complaints), the staging and the cutting pattern does all of the expressing necessary (how Jacob and his chums glare at the others, for example).

THE ABORTION ISSUE.

Critics noted the abortion debate elements of *Breaking Dawn, Part 1*: the central dilemma was Bella Swan's conception and the discussions of abortion. Well, shoot, you can bet that most of these Old World, conservative, Republican-voting vampires are going to be anti-abortion! They're like reactionary Roman Catholics in all but name (and the Volturi act like the Vatican Council, and have an HQ right out of the Catholic regime). Bella S. asserts, in the key group discussion scene (at the Cullens' mansion, when Jake arrives), that it's *her* decision alone. Well sure, but Jacob Black has a point, if the baby inside her is going jump out and start feeding! (Jacob voices the wolves' opinion throughout, that the baby bloodsucker is a nasty critter. And it's literally killing his beloved Bella!). Alice calls it a 'foetus'; Rose corrects her (twice): 'it's a *baby*'.

(The staging of the discussion scene in *Breaking Dawn, Part 1* illuminates how Bella's pregnancy has become everybody's issue – they are gathered together and all looking at her – and also how it has split the Cullens: Bella sits on the couch (the centre of attention); Rose stands possessively in between her and Jacob; Alice and Jasper sit to one side, anxious; Emmett is relegated to a back seat (as his girlfriend Rosalie tries to take over); Carlisle and Esme stand nearby, concerned; and Edward hovers. The static presentation of the group scenes in the Cullen family home are echoed in the next movie, when the vampire witnesses arrive. As screenwriter Melissa Rosenberg put it: 'How do you make a visually compelling movie about someone who is lying there, dying of a pregnancy? It's gruesome, depressing, and *static*, something that would work for a theatrical play' (M. Vaz, 2011, 108).)

This part of the *Twilight Saga* can be seen as one of thousands of movies about terminally ill patients, which are a whole genre in cinema (*Love Story, Philadelphia, Cat On a Hot Tin Roof, Terms of Endearment*, etc. The director of *Twilight 1* – Catherine Hardwicke – made one in 2015: *Miss You Already*). Remember that one of the chief reasons for Bella Swan choosing vampirism is to *avoid* death. That is, not solely to be immortal, and to spend the rest of her existence kissing Edward Cullen, but *avoiding dying*. So perhaps we have to see what Bella is trying to evade (however, this section of the *Twilight Saga* is also pretty miserable).

Act 3 is full of modest scenes between two actors: Jacob and Seth, Jacob and Leah, Jacob and Bella, Jacob and Edward, Edward and Bella, Carlisle, Edward and Bella, all filmed in the simplest manner: close-ups, with the occasional two-shot or over-the-shoulder shot (occasionally trickier shots are used – crash zooms, for example, to portray Jacob and Edward communicating via telepathy). DP Guillermo Navarro provides lighting that resembles a permanently overcast and very boring Wednesday in Nowheresville.

Inevitably, sometimes the music for these scenes is the all-purpose sound of all Western cinema and television for sorrowful scenes: plinky piano (every composer for film and TV knows that at some point the film producers will ask for raindrop piano. I'm not sure when teardrop piano became the go-to music for emotional scenes of any kind, but I wish it would sink into the Abyss, never to be heard again. Sure, *proper* Chopin, Liszt or Debussy is truly divine music composed for the piano, but these piano cues for TV and film are synthetic, miserable muzak, and how they are used is horrible).

STEP FORWARD, JACOB BLACK.

Apart from the wedding sequence, most of the secondary characters fall away from the narrative of *Breaking Dawn, Bite 1*, which focusses very much on the newly-weds. Only Jacob Black, back in the Pacific North-West (after a long sojourn in North Canada in wolf-form – though off-screen), is kept prominent in the story (and other minor characters, who relate directly to Jake, such as his Pa Billy, and Leah and Seth, his new disciples). The decision is partly an editorial one: to keep the 2011 movie fixed on the married couple, instead of dissipating interest by cutting away to other scenes.[40]

But when it all goes horribly wrong during the South American honeymoon, and the 2011 movie shifts back to North America, the secondary charas have more to do. First up is to introduce some action – principally by resurrecting the age-old vampire vs. werewolf rivalry. Thus, the obstacle and challenge of Bella's unnatural pregnancy is connected with the werewolves: their goal is to destroy the child. And if that means killing Bella too, so be it.

This is where Jake B. takes centre stage, which's delightful (taking its cue from the *Jacob* section of *Breaking Dawn*). The novel had shifted the point-of-view to Jacob, and the Jacob-oriented scenes are the movie's

40 Thus, the telephone conversation where Bella speaks to Alice, also included footage of Alice and Carlisle. But it was decided the sequence was more effective by staying with Bella and Edward.

version of that. For most of the *Twilight* movies, the focus is always on 'Team Bella'. But now it steps over to 'Team Jacob': Taylor Lautner has *a lot* to do in acts 3 and 4 of *Breaking Dawn, Part 1* (particularly in act 3), and he rises to the challenge. (However, the movie doesn't really capture the first person narrative aspects of the Jacob chapters in the 2008 book).

So Jake Black starts to grow up big time, rebelling against Sam Uley and his leadership of the Quileute Tribe wolf pack. Jake asserts himself (but he also has a couple of devotees – Seth and Leah, as in the book – tho' the book adds *plenty* more of interaction and dialogue with this second, smaller wolf pack. For example, there's a scene where Jacob and Leah talk, with Leah begging to be included, now that she too has abandoned Uley's pack. Scenes such as this would not be scripted or filmed at all if the novel had been adapted as a single movie).

There is a very expensive, intricate sequence, relying heavily on digital animation of the wolves (courtesy of Tippet Studio),[41] in which Jacob faces off against Sam Uley and the other wolves. There were 16 wolves in *Breaking Dawn*.[42] The filmmakers opted to use voiceovers, so the wolves could be communicating with human voices, as well as plenty of growls and snarls.[43] It wasn't wholly successful – now you're into talking, animated animals (tho' moving mouths were left out). It is a key scene in the *Breaking Dawn* novel, however, and necessary partly so that Jacob can legitimately hole up at the Cullen mansion; it also, of course, brings back Jacob into the picture. Because, by rights, his story was over at the end of *Eclipse,* when Bella chose Edward not him (or, if you prefer, by the end of *New Moon*, when B. and E. were re-united).

NOT A BUNDLE OF LAUGHS.

In the second half of *Breaking Dawn, Part 1*, we seem to spend ages in and around the Cullen house, having despondent, hushed conversations concerning: What To Do About Bella? Indeed, *Breaking Dawn, Part 1*, after the honeymoon comes to an abrupt end, is really the story of a terminally ill character (and the heroine really does die!). The heroine's declining in health, and nobody can save her. Everyone gathers around with long faces. And, being vampires, they're very buttoned up and

---

41 Tippet Studio began storyboarding and previzing the *Breaking Dawn* movies in mid-2010. They provided 150 shots for *Part 1* and 380 shots for *Part 2*.
42 16 wolves were required for *Breaking Dawn, Part 2*, a step-up from the six needed for *New Moon*. Some of the wolf shots were fully animated by hand. On set, to line up camera angles and give the actors something to work with, plastic standees of the wolves were used.
43 The sound crew are working for every cent of their fee in this sequence – electronically treating the actors' voices, and adding a huge number of sound effects (not only the sounds of the wolves, but also their interaction with the riverside).

restrained and motionless (and emotionless), with only Jacob as our lifeline to something human-like and warm. Brief respites, like the blood drinking (a genuinely creepy, gross-out moment), or Bella and Edward hearing voices from the womb, can't stem the sad, downward drift of the narrative. Every time we cut to Kristen Stewart, she looks worse – thinner, drawn, exhausted.[44]

Breaking Dawn, Part 1 is not, then, a bundle of laughs (there is *very* little humour to be found anywhere in the 2011 movie).[45] The marriage and the sex and the honeymoon now seem like a death sentence: it's pretty glum, actually, as desolate as terrible movies of the same period like *Wolverine: Origins* and *Snow White and the Huntsman*.

Of course, we know that the hero and the heroine *won't* be sacrificed, and we know too that the second half of *Breaking Dawn, Part 1* is following the usual formula of placing more'n more obstacles in front of the protagonists, and also pushing them down psychologically as far as they can go, so that when they bounce back, they bounce up all the higher. Thing is, this part of a movie (typically at the end of the second act, or the beginning of the third act, using a 3-act model), isn't usually this long! It's 10-15 minutes tops. Here, we have lengthy *longeurs* of Bella suffering more'n more pain, and the vamps and the *ronin* wolf being unable to offer much help.

> Jeez, how did anyone stand living with him? It was really too bad he couldn't hear Bella's thoughts. Then he'd annoy the crap out of her, too, and she'd get tired of him. (BD, 231)

A key scene in the Jacob<–>Edward rivalry occurs in act 3 of *Breaking Dawn* when Edward confesses to his adversary that if Bella dies he will give him the satisfaction of ending his life. That Edward has reached a suicidal place reprises the agony Edward endured in *New Moon*, when he believed that his beloved had died. Jake in the novel of *Breaking Dawn* characterizes Edward as a 'burning man', a spectral husk of the person he used to be.

It was compelling to see Edward lose it a little – his character is sooo buttoned up (to the point where often he says nothing at all, but offers merely a blank, pale face), it was a pleasure to witness him unleashing a little rage at the prospect of losing Bella Swan (in the Carlisle's clinic scene). That the anger was unexpected and also directed at her was part of the surprise, because Edward has always been nothing but tender towards

---

44 But loving the attention, no doubt! Yes – Bella (and Stewart) can be diva-ish at times!
45 The two *Breaking Dawn* movies certainly delivered in terms of drama, melodrama, soap opera drama, and other forms of drama. They were a little weaker in humour. Some of the attempts at comedy fell flat, and they weren't enough of them.

her (and especially when she's near death), and playing the part of the devoted, caring husband (needless to say, that anger isn't in the 2008 novel, where Edward becomes a shell, a 'burning man', broken and beaten. The movie, as movies tend to do, compresses the emotion, then heats it up to hysteria).

Poor Jake Black! To love Bella Swan, and to lose her. She was always Edward's Girl. It's sad, it's hopeless, it's depressing to see such a lively, sensitive guy devote himself to a lost cause. How, for instance, Jake hangs around after Bella and Edward return from the disastrous honeymoon. Jake's on hand to warm Bella up (in a touching scene on the couch), because Bella's a girl who's often cold.[46] But Jake's devotion goes way beyond that of a concerned friend. Again and again, the movies remind us of the choices that Bella has made, and the presence of the other two in the love triangle. And in the pairings of monogamous marriage of the Western world, there's always going to be a loser in the romantic triangle.

THE BIRTH SCENE.

So to the icky birth scene in *Breaking Dawn, Part 1.*[47]

Fans and audiences wondered whether the movie version would emulate the graphic depictions of the *Breaking Dawn* book – i.e., the blood, the blood! The answer was: no (because these are deliberately largely bloodless vampire flicks). Again, no: because the target audience meant delivering a 'PG' or 'PG-13' rating. So, no blood. Well, not too much (but who decides what's 'too much blood'?! Hell, all humans are filled with 8 or so pints of blood![48] What's so darn scary?!).

The idea that the portrayal of one of the most important and fundamental experiences in human life (birth) should need to be 'R' rated or censored or shielded from some viewers is truly weird. Birth is not only completely natural, without it there wouldn't be any humans at all!

But there *is* some ketchup – around Bella Swan as she lies on the gurney, on Ed's front and face, on Jake, and over the baby.

Well, if the birth wasn't too bloody in *Breaking Dawn, Part 1*, it was certainly scary, and it was high drama – a girl's dying! 'Get it out of me!' yells Bella Swan (or something like that). Yes, we all know that feeling! Yet even here there was humour (not strictly intentional). For instance, how the vampires hovering around in the birthing room freak out when they see blood. Poor Rosalie can't take it, and has to be hurried

---

46 And when she's a vampire, she's permanently cold! She goes from Arizonian gal to cold-as-death vamp.

47 It was filmed in Louisiana in January, 2011.

48 Not vampires, though!

out (by Alice)! (In the book of *Breaking Dawn*, there's a long-festering antagonism between Rosalie and the two boys, which erupts big time in the birthing scene, with Jake attacking Rosalie and shoving her out of the room – go Jake!).

Thus, as the birth is all going completely wrong, it's down to two teenage guys, no less, to save the day! And it just *has to be* Edward and Jacob, right?! Two boys! – The girls have fled at the sight of blood! So, instead of the usual midwives and nurses and old witchy figures clucking around the mother like old hens, and shoo-ing the men outside, in your typical birthing scene, it was two boys. And it's two boys[49] who don't have a clue about what to do about giving birth! And *of course* the man they really need – Doctor Carlisle Cullen – is A.W.O.L.! Darn, bad timing or what? Someone's got a life-threatening illness and the good Doctor is absent. Oh dear. (This is a Big Plot Hole: there are *six vampires* in the house, no less, who can pop out and hunt: Alice, Jasper, Emmett, Rose, Esme and Edward. They could catch and kill a deer or a bear and bring it back (or at least a couple of squirrels!), so Carlisle can stay with the patient. In addition, I'm sure that Jacob in his wolf-form could rustle up a big mammal or two, and Seth and Leah could help out).

Of course, the birth scene was played for Hysterical, High Drama, with both Jake and Edward in agony over seeing their beloved Bella Swan fade away before their eyes, and die. Even though we know that there is not a chance in Hell that the heroine of the entire *Twi-lite* series is going to be sacrificed; maybe, at the worst, someone else might be injured or expire. But not our Bella! Oh no! (And of course, once a baby's been delivered, no way is that kid going to croak!).

Jacob Black exits the house and weeps (these are sensitive, feminized boys!). That he doesn't smash Edward Cullen to pieces reveals just how much he has matured – in this movie especially, but also in the previous movies (in the *Breaking Dawn* book, Edward says that when Bella's heart stops beating, he will die, and Jake assures him he will do the job quickly).[50] So he is altogether a more thoughtful and tactful Jacob. Instead, the wolf boy departs with a bitter remark that Edward doesn't deserve to die – he deserves to live with killing his bride. (In the novel, Jacob shuffles away from the birth-now-death room like a 'crippled old man', finding Rosalie and the baby on the couch, and determining to slaughter the abomination. In the movie, Jacob crumples to the ground as the camera cranes above him, one of the standard cinematic forms for portraying despair, a mirror of the forest scene with Bella in *New Moon*).

49 Edward may be 109, but he hasn't learnt anything about assisting with a birth.
50 There's a brief fantasy of Jake's of him in wolf-form killing Edward.

The imprinting scene in *Breaking Dawn*, which occurs soon after this, is covered from Jacob's point-of-view. Eyes, as usual in *The Twilight Saga*, are the focus (the camera trucks into and out of eyes), with a rapid montage sequence introducing the baby as she grows rapidly. The montage depicts Renesmee at several ages,[51] with an emphasis on the girl looking at the viewer – that is, at Jacob. *Breaking Dawn, Part 1* thus throws us years into the future, and it evokes Jake's future life. The montage also features the rather finicky visual effects which have been applied to actress Mackenzie Foy, so she can appear at several ages).

The most striking aspect of the birth scene is perhaps the cinematic approach: this is really a film editor's scene: the sequence is cut to ribbons by editor Virgina Katz in numerous very brief shots, a few feet or less in length (a little like a movie trailer), plus the editor's bag of filmic tricks: fades to black, and black leader, and step-motion (removing frames or optically printing selected frames), and coloured frames, and short bursts of dialogue. Meanwhile, the camera takes up a position close to Bella's vision, so that we see what she sees (when in doubt in the *Twilight* movies, shifting to Bella's subjective point-of-view usually works). And as this is a highly stylized, impressionistic and even abstract approach to drama, there are also several top shots. (It's so heightened, that when the movie cuts to a more objective, long shot, from the other side of the windows of Carlisle's office, when the baby's born, it seems strange). As Bill Condon explained:

> let's have her give birth and only see what she can see. So it's all from her point of view, right? And for me, that allows us to do things like, oh my God, he's coming back into frame and he's got blood on his teeth! He just bit through something. And if you know what he bit through then you know, but if you don't, you don't, you know?

Some viewers found the birth scene upsetting physically – it was one of those scenes with flashing effects which seemed to trigger adverse reactions from some punters (including epileptic seizures), placing *Breaking Dawn* in the company of flicks such as *The Exorcist* and *Alien*, which caused some audiences to react badly (and of course *The Sound of Music,* which has 'em retching in the aisles).

To depict Bella's illness, traditional practical effects and special make-up were employed, alongside digital effects, overseen by vfx supervisor John Bruno, John Rosengrant of Legacy Effects, and Ola Visual Effects (who had aged down Ian McKellen and Patrick Stewart in *X-Men 3*, 2006). The decay of Bella was created in three stages, from

---

51 Photos of actress Mackenzie Foy were used as reference material for the visual effects teams.

gaunt and under-weight to her birthing size, when special make-up was added (such as a pronounced collarbone, sunken chest, hands and cheeks.).

A lifesize doll was made of Kristen Stewart, for the final stages of her illness (the puppet was used for the scene where Bella collapses, as well as Bella on the operating table). A partial puppet was used for the birth scene, for the lower half, with Stewart lying underneath the table.

✦

So the change from human to vampire, which Bella Swan has hungered for ever since she got to know the Cullen coven, occurs in the traumatic scene of a woman dying in childbirth. So it's yet another twist on 19th century melodrama (where a woman expiring in childbirth is a common motif in literature of the period). Thus Bella dies in childbirth like a 19th century heroine, and, thru power of fantasy, is revived, like Snow White or Sleeping Beauty in a fairy tale (with her Prince literally kissing her back to life – bitting the venom into different parts of her body).

What can bring someone back to life in a vampire movie? Well, vampirism, of course! So the scene has Edward chomping Bella, hoping to hurry up the girl-becomes-vamp transformation with his venom. But vampirism in the *Twilight Saga* is one of several metaphors for love, of course: ultimately, it's love that revives Princess Bella.

And naturally it works. And that is the final image of the first part of *Breaking Dawn* – Bella's eyes opening as a vampire. All covered in slow, mobile close-ups, as the filmmakers milk the scene for every ounce of suspense possible. (This is where the *Jacob* book and the *Bella* book end and begin in the novel of *Breaking Dawn*). Just b4 Bella wakes, there are quick cuts to each of the Cullen couples, and Jacob (all looking pensive).

Bella Swan is dead for quite some time, however. *Definitely* dead. *Very* dead. Both Jake Black and Edward Cullen try to revive her, and Edward persists after Jacob storms out. Edward leaves subsequently to fight the werewolves. Digital animation depicted the interior of Bella's body (*Fantastic Voyage*-style), the blood, the arteries and the cells (with the customary goopy, weirdo sound effects – I mean, everyone's body sounds like that inside, right?!). We see, too, the effects that Edward's vampire blood/ venom has on Bella, resurrecting her, re-fusing bones. (With the visual effects make-up, the special prosthetic make-up and the practical effects combining to produce a slick resurrection scene – re-animation scenes are of the key scenes in fantasy and science fiction cinema, with *Frankenstein* as the foundation for all of them. And the vampire Bella is babed-up, too, with a self-consciously elaborate make-up emphasizing her rebirth as a glamour girl. This is Vampire-Bella, even more glamorous than Bride-Bella at the beginning of the movie).

✠

Talking about the 'PG-13' rating for *Breaking Dawn* and the birth and sex scenes: we have *already* seen plenty of violence and horror in the first *Twihard* movie, so *Breaking Dawn* doesn't need 'R' rated material in the birth scene or the sex scenes: the 'PG-13' category is malleable, and can slide around. Remember the 2008 *Twilight* movie? In that flick, we saw Bella being slammed against a wall, being injured in the head and the leg and the arm, being threatened with death, being bitten by a vampire (the pain was screamingly agonizing), plus we saw two men beating the Hell out of each other, and a man having his head ripped off and being burnt.

It's all hypocrisy, tho': for example, consensual sex is heavily censored in contemporary cinema, so that in a 'PG-13' rated flick only suggestions of lovemaking can be depicted. Yet violence, gore and horror are portrayed in detail. In *Breaking Dawn*, for instance, we see a vampire having his skull split open slowly and painfully. *Ouch!* But we can't see something such as, for instance, Edward performing oral sex on Bella! Why is, say, a guy licking a woman's clitoris so offensive, or even the birth of a baby, when we can see numerous decapitations, limbs being snapped and severed, victims being electrocuted, stabbed, burnt, and mauled by wild animals?

VAMPIRES VERSUS WOLVES (AGAIN).

So, what does the November, 2011 movie *Breaking Dawn, Part 1* climax with? Only yet another sequence where Edward Cullen (and Jacob Black this time) is protecting Bella Swan! Just like each of the previous *Twilight* movies!

Protect Bella! Don't let them get Bella!

The siege/ attack is not in the 2008 *Creaking Dawn* novel, but the movie required some Big, Dramatic Scenes which would articulate some of the issues at stake, but also provide the necessary quickening of the blood, that most Hollywood blockbuster movies employ in the final act (the filmmakers acknowledged that this part of *Breaking Dawn* had been invented for the movie). However, to be even braver, *Breaking Dawn, Part 1* could've gone the other way, and left out the rivalry with the wolves and the siege, and focussed entirely on Bella, Edward, Jacob and the birth. Jacob didn't need to be a Rebel Wolf to be part of the action at the Cullens' house: Bella could've demanded that he be there for her last days, and Edward would've been happy to oblige, as he is in the novel.

But the confrontation between the werewolves and the vampires in *Breaking Dawn, Bite 1* does provide a suitably visceral slice of super-charged action,[52] with the remaining vampires (Alice, Jasper and Edward) grappling with the wolves (there was an earlier action sequence, essentially a chase and skirmish in the forest, as Carlisle, Esme and Emmett go hunting, which, again, was added to the novel. In that brawl, once again it is the woman (Esme this time) who is cornered and threatened by a werewolf. It's Emmett who dives to Esme's rescue).[53]

For the vampires versus werewolves battle, once again, the stunt team conjure up a variety of ways in which the two sides can hurl themselves at each other in the close quarters of the back of the Cullen mansion: Alice fights off wolves on her back on the ground... Seth and Leàh dive in to help... there's a last minute rescue when Carlisle, Esme and Emmett re-appear from their feeding trip... Emmett climbs a tree[54] and punches a wolf... Edward and Jacob have their moments to shine (Jacob transforms[55] for the last time in *Breaking Dawn, Part 1*).

Peter Zhang co-ordinated the stunts for the fight. 80 shots were filmed over five nights. The battle rightly occurred at night, in contrast to the vampires vs. werewolves finale of *Eclipse*.

The siege of the Cullen mansion doesn't make much sense if you stop and think about it. For ex, why did the werewolves stage a frontal assault? If their aim was to nobble the newborn baby, why didn't some of them attack from the other side? Also, why didn't they head off the returning vampires – they knew they were hunting (as Paul yells at Jacob, 'you played us!'). Also, why didn't they use firearms to snipe some of the Cullen crew while in their human form? I bet some of the wolfy boys would have access to a pistol or two (but guns have been carefully kept away from the mix in the confrontations in *The Twilight Saga*, of course). Also, in their human form the wolves could've achieved much more than simply spying on the Cullens: there are booby traps, for instance, which both sides could've implemented. (Similarly, the Cullens, despite their technology, medical equipment, flashy cars, and methodical approach to life, didn't have back-up plans for feeding (but they have blood for Bella to drink), and oddly they don't seem to possess any firearms either).

---

52 It was filmed in Squamish, Canada, in late April, 2011.
53 There are call-backs to earlier movies, when the vampires escape by leaping over a river.
54 Trees become part of the stunts.
55 Why does Jake leap into the air to phase? So he won't get in anyone's way? No – because it looks cool! (And it's a call-back to *New Moon*, when we first saw Jacib transforming).

Attacking as a group all at once from the same direction, tho', is dramatically more efficient: it brings all of the charas together, stages the action in the same spot, so that the action and the outcome can be wound up quicker.

However, notice that, altho' the fighting at the conclusion of *Breaking Dawn, Part 1* is intense, nobody appears to be killed, or even severely injured. Indeed, once Jacob Black has transformed into wolf-form, the fighting stops, and the Jake-wolf and the Sam-wolf confront each other. This time, the 'talking wolves' approach was dropped (just too silly), and Edward handily translates the snarls and grunts for us: Jake has 'imprinted' on Renesmee, and thus the li'l tyke is sacred in Wolf Law. (The imprinting motif is the *deus ex machina* script device that Saves the Day in *Breaking Dawn, Part 1*. The explanation of imprinting, tho', goes back to *New Moon*, when Jake explained it to Bella at the Reservation. Yes, it's rather contrived, and is as artificial as the vampires vs. werewolves conflict – but it does mean that, in a way, it's Jake and Renesmee who come to the rescue).

In sum, the werewolves vs. vampires action-filled additions to the *Breaking Dawn* novel were necessary, perhaps, to spice up the narrative of the 2011 adaptation, but the end result is yet another of Stephenie Meyer's predilections for confrontational scenes in which some action occurs, but the talk is far more significant. And *no one* is sacrificed. Like the Big Battle at the end of the final *Twilight* movie, there's plenty of action but no one is dispatched – or even injured! No price is paid at all! Instead, there is a *lot* of talk! (Call it 'intense' talk, or 'dramatic' talk, but it's still darned talk! Indeed, over the course of the whole *Twilight Saga*, very few characters die, or are injured permanently, or are punished. And even someone who definitely *does* die – Bella Swan – gets to be reborn!).

▲

THE CRITICS.

And the critics? By now, we don't need to consult them anymore, because the critical responses for *B.D. 1* were the same as they were for the previous *Twilight* movies. Bloated, too long, too depressing, not enough story for a proper movie, 'joyless', 'tedious', 'bland slow and boring', 'a boring mess', 'so-so', 'worst yet', 'insipid', and it's for *Twilight* fans only, blah blah blah…

As with many fantasy, sci-fi, action-adventure, horror and other genre pictures, it's a mystery why newspapers and magazines bother to send along critics to review movies they know will be panned.

What's the point? To be impartial? To prove that they are responsible members of the world press and thus cover everything? To review segments of popular culture in a fair and even-handed manner? If something's popular, do they have to consider it?

But newspapers and magazines send out journalists knowing that they will almost certainly trash these sorts of movies! Reviews of this kind of Hollywood movie in the press are a complete waste of everybody's time. Instead of a 500-word review, newspapers, magazines and online platforms should just print one sentence: *we hated it*.

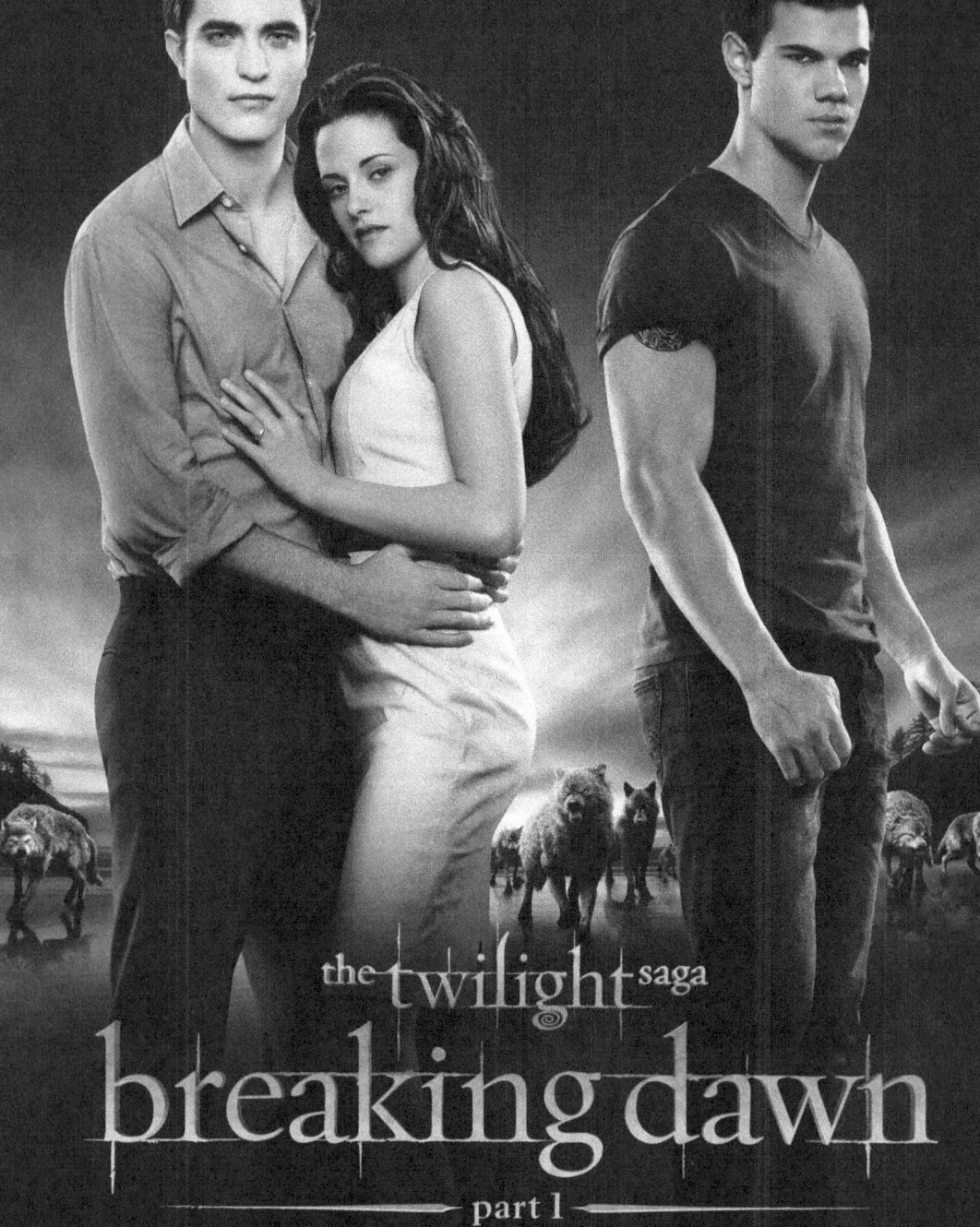

FOREVER IS ONLY THE BEGINNING

the twilight saga
breaking dawn
— part 1 —

11.18.11
BreakingDawn-TheMovie.com

JOIN THE WORLDWIDE COMMUNITY ON f FACEBOOK.COM/TWILIGHT   #BREAKINGDAWN

Making Breaking Dawn, Part 1

7

BREAKING DAWN: PART 2

'In truth, young Bella, immortality does become you most extra-ordinarily,' he said. 'It is as if you were designed for this life.'

Stephenie Meyer, *Breaking Down*

INTRO.

So, the story of Bella Swan and Edward Cullen is all over by the very beginning of *Breaking Dawn, Part 2*: this is the Happy Ending of fairy tales, right here (altho' the story was already over at the end of *New Moon* – or by the end of act one of *Twilight*). The imagery is sunny, glowing, smiley; it is a literal rebirth, as Princess Bella comes back to life. The images of renewed vision, of seeing the world for the first time (tho' using the motif of vampiric sensitivity), accentuate this rebirth. And it takes place at dawn, the symbolic renewal of the day, of life itself (waking from the simulated 'death' of sleep, as William Shake-speare often noted). And then, she sees her lover,[1] and the lovers are reunited.

He says, 'you are so beautiful,' and she replies, 'I love you' (everything is beautiful when you've woken from the dead, right?). Cue the kissing! And that's our Happy Ending: Bella has got her man, got what she wants (vampirehood and foreverdom), and has become a wife and mother into the bargain. In the world of fantasy you *can* Have It All (indeed, you *should* Have It All! I mean, why not? This is a fantasy! And the *Twilight Saga* has never pretended to be anything other'n an out-and-out romantic fantasy).

---

1 The out of focus shot was apparently one that DP Guillermo Navarro had always wanted to do – of taking off the camera lens (there's even a suitable sound for the moment).

So it's smiles and kisses all round in *Breaking Dawn, Bite 2*. The *smugness* is close to insufferable, too – for every character. These are super-smug people! With their white, comfy, middle-class lifestyle, their glossy, fashion-plate appearance, and their deep-seated, un-changing, unchallengeable beliefs that they are good and totally in the right.

Thus, the emphasis from critics on sexual abstinence in the *Twilight* franchise is contradicted directly in the *Twilight* movies numerous times: the soft, golden *light* is very sensual (look at the way that Kristen Stewart is lovingly photographed throughout the series); the stars are attractive; the lifestyle (flashy cars, gorgeous clothes, trips to Italy and Rio) is sexy; Stewart has beautiful boys visiting her bedroom at night; and actors are kissing and cuddling all over the place (including Stewart and Pattinson – and, yes, Stewart and Launter!). And there are two sex scenes.

In addition, when Bella Swan is reborn in *Breaking Dawn*, it's a very sensuous experience: she sees the world anew, so that everything she has taken for granted is rejuvenated. She sees the world as if for the first time. She sees sunlight as if for the first time. And if that isn't a sensual, orgasmic experience, I don't what know is.

Before the Volturi plot kicks in as *Breaking Dawn, Part 2* unfolds, there are scenes of Bella Swan being a New Vampire: going hunting with her mate (holding back from chomping a (male) mountaineer in order to wrestle a mountain lion instead)... meeting Jacob in her new vampy guise... meeting and bonding with her daughter Renesmee... discovering that Jacob has imprinted on her baby... arm-wrestling with Emmett... enjoying vampire lerrrve with Edward... and meeting her Pa Charlie as she pretends to be human... (Notice how Bella mentions that she isn't ageing anymore – a *very* big deal for Bella – and Stephenie Meyer. Ironically, the hankering after immortality nearly always types charas in movies as villains. But not here).

When Bella resurrects as a vampire, she's clad in a blue stretch dress (the 'hunting dress'), a new colour for Bella, symbolizing her renewed leash of life, as Michael Wilkinson (costume designer) explained (actually, it's a call-back to Bella's 'rebirth' at the end of *Twilight,* when, fresh out of hospital, she wore a blue dress to the school Prom). It's odd, tho', that the Sullens opt to put a dress on Bella for her funeral, a girl who's lived her life in jeans and sweat pants.

Bella Swan as a newly-born vampire is an important experience for the audience to see in *Breaking Dawn, Part 2*: it's what she has been harping on about for four movies, after all! So we have to see it: to see Bells waking into the new world of acute perception (with a montage of extreme close-ups, crash zooms and spot sound effects); we see Bella and Edward running at high speed (and in slo-mo) in the forest (always with the forests in *Twilight*!); we see Bella's super-human powers (leaping over rivers, ascending sheer mountains like a monkey);[2] and we see Bella's first kill.

There is also some gender reversal in the birth-of-a-vampire sequence: now Bella S. is the strongest gorilla on the block, grabbing her man roughly and kissing him, and trouncing the he-man vampire Emmett at arm-wrestling. Bella becoming Action Girl is one of the audience-pleasing aspects of *Breaking Dawn 2* – especially after playing the Princess Who Must Be Rescued and the eternal victim throughout the series (and undergoing that traumatic pregnancy and birth).

However, as with Sarah Gellar in *Buffy, the Vampire Manicurist* and Kate Beckinsale in *Underworld*, it takes some suspension of disbelief that tiny, skinny Kristen Stewart is capable of kicking ass action-wise in *Breaking Dawn*. Stewart is famous for swearing and griping on set, but she seems completely harmless.

Another montage occurs in *Breaking Dawn, Part 2* as Jacob Black 'imprints' on the moppet Renesmee: the images comprise a series of flashforwards to Renesmee as she ages, becoming a pretty, young woman. So here's Jake's Consolation Prize: not Bella, but her daughter! (Why does Renesmee age so fast – yes, you guessed right![3] – so that Jacob can have that special girlfriend he's always wanted without waiting 18 years! When he would be – what? – 36?).

A couple of love/ sex scenes follow, with the lovers now both vampires, in their new/ old cottage on the Cullen Estate. Vampire sex is like regular sex in movies – close-ups (faces, hands, legs only, and no parts of the body in-between), back-lit, staged and edited to fit into the agreed 'PG-13' classification (accompanied by the mandatory slow pop ballad – 'Fire In the Water' by Feist). The filmmakers assigned a group of artists (at Prologue Films) to create the vampire sex montage, which featured plenty of visual effects (including a C.U of Bella with sparkles around her – an image used in Japanese *animé* to evoke orgasm). Indeed, the *Twilight Saga* is very fond of short, montage-style movie-making – for Jacob imprinting on Renesmee, for Bella thinking back over her life as she dies in *Twilight* (repeated again in *Breaking Dawn*), for Jake being tormented by Bella's illness, for Edward researching immortal children, for Bella in her post-Edward depression in *New Moon*, and for the closing credits and shield sequence in *Breaking Dawn, Part 2*, etc (film editors

---

2 The rock clilmbing sequence was filmed near Squamish, at Stowamus Chief cliff.
3 Things have to happen *quickly* in movies.

Virginia Katz and Ian Slater have taken up the example of editor Nancy Richardson in her use of montages in the first *Twilight* installment, and placed montages throughout the two *Breaking Dawn* pictures).

The lovers even get their own dream home, complete with open fire, in the woodland (with the interior design overseen by – who else?! – elf-like Alice Cullen). And that, folks, wraps up the whole Bella-and-Edward story, which has been central to this fantasy romance movie franchise from 2008 to 2012 (they can say *f-o-r-e-v-e-r* now, or at the end of the movie – it makes not the slightest bit of difference).

Because after this, the plot that consumes most of *Breaking Dawn, Part 2* – of the Volturi and associates waging war on the Cullens and witnesses – with li'l Renesmee as one of the objects of dissension – is a foregone conclusion. We have seen that the finales of each *Twilight* movie have featured some attempt to threaten and/ or kill Bella, and each one has been thwarted by Edward, Jake and the Cullens. Why would this sequel be any different?

There is no way, in the Manichean (or Mormon) moral universe of *The Twilight Saga*, and in this type of Hollywood, blockbuster flick, that the Volturi brood could possibly be victorious. They are typed as the villains thru and thru (altho' there *are* genuine motivations/ reasons for some of the stuff they do).

Thus, *Breaking Dawn, Part 2* had a far less dramatic appeal for me: we know what's going to happen, and now that attention has shifted from the love triangle, and from the Bella-Edward (and Bella-Edward-Jacob) relationship, the show becomes much more a by-the-numbers, action-oriented movie. Nothing wrong with that, tho', if the action is impressive (and it is).

The issue under dispute for the Volturi nobles is the immortal child, Renesmee' but, actually, it's more a clash of cultures and lifestyles: the Volturi are a traditional, right-wing and very ancient clan, wallowing in their power, and they despise the bourgeois, modern, liberal, 'vegetarian' ways of the Cullen clan (and they consort with werewolves, too, vampires' mortal enemies).

▲

STYLE AND APPROACH.

TALKY SCENES.

In order to liven up the many talky scenes in the Cullen mansion (*Breaking Dawn, Part 2* contains a *lot* of these! And so does *Part 1*! – if you took out the talky scenes in the mansion from both *B.D.* films, they'd be reduced to half-an-hour), the filmmakers increase the speed of the vampires. So now, when Jasper hurries over to li'l pixie Alice when she's troubled, he doesn't walk, but is a blur of speed.

However, the issue of depicting the Cullens isn't wholly satisfying in *Breaking Dawn, Part 2*. In many, many scenes, the Cullen coven are portrayed watching TV, or maybe reading, or just standing there. The Cullens are great when they're being movie-ish vampires, or in a melodramatic scene, but for most of the time they are, well, *boring*. They're just like regular folk. They watch TV, they read books (or maybe business reports), and mess about on their laptops.

One can imagine the discussions between the director and the actors when they reach the set: so it's another day on the Cullen mansion set in Louisiana (on the call sheet it says: shooting Scene 209, for ex), and the filmmakers have another 5/8ths of a page of the script to work through today.

Actor:	'What shall I do in this scene?'
Director:	'Err, how about reading a book?'
Actor:	'I did that last time! And the scene before that!'
Director:	'OK, well, watch TV, then.'
Actor:	'Boring… Can't I strike some cool poses by the window? How about I dance around the table or practice my Tai-Chi?'
Director:	'No. Just stand there. Motionless. Check the Twilight Queen's book! Meyer says that's what vampires do!'
Actor:	(*mumbles*) 'Crap.'
Director:	'What did you say?'
Actor:	(*kneeling*) 'Nothing, my Master.'

There are many ways of filming the most basic dramatic scene in cinema – people talking in a room – but you have to admit that the many of the solutions offered by *Breaking Dawn 1* and *2* were indifferently directed and staged. The acting style in both *Breaking Dawns* is muted,[4] restrained, held back – which works fine for some scenes, but not everything. The *Twilight Saga* is not by-the-book television, and you hope for something special.

CLOSE-UPS.

Nobody would pretend that the direction of *Breaking Dawn* is of the class of, say, Orson Welles or Tsui Hark. But there *are* moments where it

---

4 Robert Pattinson reverts to the very quiet, reserved Edward again, after the melodramatics of *Part 1*. Meanwhile, Kristen Stewart gets to let fly a little as the new vamp on the scene.

is genuinely or unusually cinematic. The depictions of vampire speed throughout the *Twilight* series, for example, are pure cinematic trickery, of the kind that early film pioneers such as Géorges Méliès and D.W. Griffith might admire.

The visual effects in the *Twilight* movies do have their show-offy, look-at-us-aren't-we-clever? side to them, as well as being subtle and invisible when necessary. But audiences love that. They love that T-Rexes don't exist in our day and age[5] but you can see them terrorizing bratty, white kids in the *Jurassic Park* movies. They love that UFOs blow up the White House in *Independence Day* or wreck Las Vegas in *Mars Attacks!* (*ack ack!*). They love it when little Yoda hobbles around the corner to take on Christopher Lee as Count Dooku in *Star Wars: Attack of the Clones*.

But some of the greatest cinematic effects in *Breaking Dawn* rely on much simpler (tho' not necessarily cheaper!) means: there's a modest scene in the living room of the cottage between the lovers that's filmed in giant close-ups – the kind of close-ups that cut off the forehead, you're in so close, and they look simply massive on a cinema screen (the *Twilight* movies are filmed in 2.35:1 ratio). The filmic approach is employed later, in the final scene of *Breaking Dawn, Part 2*, in the meadow.

Here the special effect is the human face, and great actors. After all, what can beat the human face for mystery and marvels? Like, nothing! (OK, maybe a Summer night filled with stars… or the ocean…).

And this is why you spend the money to hire good actors, precisely for these simple, intimate and important moments. (And great make-up artists (Jean Black – make-up; Rita Parillo – hair),[6] because you have so much time to examine every inch of those faces.[7] And DP Guillermo Navarro certainly knows how to make these actors look beautiful).

And the numerous montages in the two *Breaking Dawns* are authentically cinematic. They also change the sometimes too-stately pace of the storytelling in the movies.

THE BOOK AND THE MOVIE.

Breaking Dawn added thousands of elements to the 2008 novel, as movies usually do. We followed the action to Egypt, for instance, and saw Benjamin being a magician. The movie added a Happy Ever After epilogue, depicting the grown-up Renesmee as Jacob's girlfriend. There was more interaction between Garrett and Kate (and their flowering

---

5 Apart from in New Jersey.
6 Once again, wigs and hair-pieces were a big part of the hair and make-up job on *Breaking Dawn* (around 40 were needed for the principals).
7 Condon wanted to pull back on the pale make-up for the vampires.

romance).

Sections of *Breaking Dawn* were redundant, as director Bill Condon admitted: the introduction of numerous vampires, for example, as the Cullens gather witnesses to the rainy Pacific North-West (but really it's a battalion, as Lord Aro quips – because he's acutely sensitive to any threat to his power). Altho' entertaining (tho' not as much as other movies have made of introducing a bunch of new characters – again, plenty more humour would've been welcome), the extra witness characters didn't require such detailed scenes (if *Breaking Dawn* had been one movie, such scenes would likely be a short montage). However, you could argue that assembling an army, and moving into training sequences, are part of the action genre. We've seen them in numerous movies (in the fantasy genre in recent times, *X-Men, The Avengers, Lord of the Rings,* etc).

Except this isn't what made the *Twilight Saga* entertaining or special in the first place (these are romantic/ dramatic/ fantasy films with action added, but they're not fundamentally action movies). Indeed, the final two acts of *Breaking Dawn, Part 2* (or three acts, if you use the more accurate four-act-per-movie model), were a mere sideshow to the *Twilight* enterprise. Because Bella had already got the man, become a vampire, and even had time to have kids!

The story was over.

NOTES ON SOME SCENES.

The first act of *Breaking Dawn, Part 2* culminates with an important but modest scene: Bella Swan, on her own in the forest, stands in some God-rays in the forest, and notes (in voiceover) that this is All She Ever Wanted. Yes, she's got (1) vampirehood, and (2) her man, and (3) a child (and (4) a new family. It's a scene very much in the spirit of Stephenie Meyer's *Twilight* concept: it has Bella alone, the voiceover, the first-person narration, the forest, and being a vampire. If the *Twilight Saga* were made as single movie, this would be one of the final scenes. (Bella also narrates the gathering of the witnesses sequence).

This scene occurs in the usual point for the end of the first act in a conventional movie: 29 minutes (most acts in feature-length movies are 25-30 minutes long). After this, the immortal child/ Volturi plot kicks in, pretty rapidly. So quickly, in fact, *Breaking Dawn, Part 2* appears as two movies: (A) Bella enjoying vampiredom, her home, her man, her family and her child, and (B) Bella, the Cullens and the witnesses versus the Volturi posse.

The sudden switch in the plots was so abrupt, the filmmakers didn't even bother to hide it, or to prepare for it by building in dramatic foreshadowing in the first act of *Breaking Dawn, Part 2*. The 2012 movie simply switches over to thriller mode. So that, when *Breaking Dawn* was cut into two pictures, you can see how much of the additional material (detractors would call it 'padding' or 'filler') was added to the last two-thirds of *Breaking Dawn, Part 2* (i.e., the middle two acts). So we have the gathering of the vampire witnesses sequence, the training sessions, and the scenes of the Volturi making visits of their own (to Londinium). Had *Breaking Dawn* been a single movie, a good deal of this material would've been squashed into a single montage (with voiceover from either Bella or maybe Carlisle to explain what's going on).[8]

There's no doubt, tho', that the middle acts of *Breaking Dawn, Part 2* are somewhat flabby, narratively and dramatically. In the first *Twilight* movie, the thriller plot involving the American Nomad vampires didn't really kick in until their arrival at the baseball game (and even there, it seemed to come from a different movie – altho' it was foreshadowed by two murder set-pieces). *Breaking Dawn, Part 2* wants to stage a giant war between the two sides in the vampire world, so it brings in the threat much earlier, at the start of act two. Unfortunately, maintaining the suspense from there to the battle is a tough challenge, which the movie doesn't always solve.

On the plus side, the arrival of each new vampire witness in *Breaking Dawn, Part 2* does offer the opportunity for some new faces, new fashions, new settings (London, Seattle, Cairo, Alaska), a few new issues (tho' they're very minor ones) – and some new visual effects (like the Amazon warriors' virtual reality jungle, Katrina's electrical jolts, and Benjamin's elemental, Ancient Egyptian magic).

❏

Bella Swan's vampire power is a shield (i.e, defensive, protective, motherly). A tricky thing to visualize on celluloid (or pixels), but sound effects and music and a bit of acting help. It's thematic, of course: Bella protecting her children and her loved ones, and being able to direct her shield during the battle, to aid others (the Battle That Never Happened, I mean). It's also, initially, about Bella not letting people in, being withdrawn and closed-up, and about Edward Cullen not being able to read her thoughts (which's his power). In the final scene of *Breaking Dawn, Part 2*, Bella allows Edward into her mind, offering a montage summary of the whole movie franchise, just as Bella nearly dying at the end of the first *Twilight* movie featured a similar montage. That memorialization of

8 There is quite a a bit of narration, however, from Bella.

the *Twilight Saga* as a franchise continues in the credits, as all of the key charas are credited, from each of the five pictures. The producers certainly know their audience well, because the end credits are perfect in paying tribute to the cast. Of course, to *really* be an *hommage*, the credits should also include the producers, screenwriter and directors, plus of course the Queen of the *Twilight Saga* herself, Stephenie Meyer).

❏

Alice Brandon's visions are used a few too many times in *Breaking Dawn 1* and *2*: quicker than narrative devices such as a phone call, or someone popping in with news, the Alice-visions allowed the filmmakers to leapfrog over a ton of exposition or tricky narrative gaps. You can simply have Alice seeing something, and everybody reacts to it as if it's the Gospel Truth. Alice is thus a major plot changer in the *Twilight Saga*, an in-built plot twist or reversal, altering the course of the movies several times.

The most outrageous use of previsualization is of course the battle sequence in film five, a conceit whereby the filmmakers have their cake and eat it.

But Alice Brandon's visions are also used far too much throughout the *Twilight Saga*, with many key sequences pivoting around them (like Alice being able to visualize what hunter vampire James Witherdale is up to with his elaborate snare at the ballet school in Phoenix in film one). It lessens suspense and surprise when you have a character simply tell you what's going to happen. Alice's one of my favourites characters, but as soon as she starts up with the visions, it becomes just silly.

❏

The father subplot in both parts of *Breaking Dawn* was a little awkwardly and disappointingly handled. Charlie Swan had been such an enjoyable character in the *Twilight* series, but in *Breaking Dawn*, after the farewell at the wedding, he fades into the background (as Bella's Mom does, too. In fact, Renée is notably absent from the sequence where Bella is re-united with her Dad – not even a phone call to Florida. Instead, there are references to Renée in the dialogue).[9] The frantic, teary phone calls from South America (and later from the Cullens' home), were as one would expect. But the reunion of father and daughter at the Cullens' residence (at the end of act one of *Part 2*), didn't have the emotional punch it deserved (it's under-played by both Kristen Stewart and Billy Burke, like so many scenes in both *Breaking Dawns*).[10]

---

9 A mother might've twigged that all was not right with her daughter! (Like, what's with the glam make-up, and the contact lenses?!).
10 As if Burke and Stewart decided to 'play it real' – i.e., as subdued as possible.

Because we have to buy it that Charlie Swan is so relieved to see his li'l Bells back again, he overlooks her vampiric appearance, her cold body, and her refusal to tell him everything that's happened. It's *a lot* for an audience to accept on faith: this is Charlie's scene, not Bella's, and Billy Burke does a fine job. But this is a cop! One of the primary figures of authority in the Western world! Well, Hell, we just have to accept that Charlie is really a softie at heart, that he has been missing Bella so badly,[11] he'll welcome her as she is, without questions, without wanting to know more.

However, the Charlie Swan subplot did turn up one of the most bizarre scenes in the whole *Twilight* series: Jacob Black undressing in the forest in front of Charlie! A weird scene on so many levels, it also could've used a little more humour (but Billy Burke plays it straight, with all of his focus on going to see Bella). Meanwhile, Jake's idea that changing into a werewolf is going to help is typical of his rather blunt methods![12] (The scene takes Stephenie Meyer's pedantry to a striking degree. Nobody *cares* what happens to outfits when a character transforms into an animal or monster in movies. But Meyer had the wolf-boys carrying clothes).

❏

The excursion to Seattle, to meet J. Jenks (Wendell Pierce), isn't especially interesting: it amounts to a long chat in a restaurant topped and tailed by second unit shots of a car on a highway. It's a sequence which likely wouldn't have even been scripted, let alone filmed, had *Breaking Dawn* been a single movie. (It does serve to emphasize how much Bella values Alice's visions: that the passports provided by the sly fixer Jenks are for Jake and Renesmee only).

There's a Christmas-At-The-Swans' Residence scene, where we get to see Charlie and Sue, Jacob and his pack, and the new family of Edward, Bella and Renesmee at home. Rightly, this is about the last scene before the Big Battle (because this depicts what our heroes're fighting for. Yes – they're fighting for the Great American Dream, the idea of the family, of tradition, of community).

❏

That Lord Aro opts to deal with the Cullens and their 'immortal child' is silly, if you think about it (so... *don't!* It's a mooovie!). And that he accepts Irinia's evidence immediately. However, there are clearly other issues involved (some're suggested in the way that Michael Sheen plays Aro): boredom, perhaps above all: Aro is *very* old, and the tedium

---

11 He looks shabby.
12 Edward digs at Jake that his real motive is to keep Bella in Forks.

of endless repetition must play a part. That Aro is using the 'immortal child' issue as a pretext or an excuse to move against the Cullens is obvious. There is an element in Aro of existence as a game, of doing things because they are naughty (witness his child-like grin as he burns the 'immortal child', gloating at its creators in the Middle Ages flashback).

The *Twilight* books flesh out these issues: that Lord Aro was never happy that Carlisle Cullen chose to leave the Volturi, for instance, or that Aro has always regarded the idea of vampires feeding off livestock as ridiculous. Aro likes to 'collect' people and their skills, too (some characters reckon that he's after Alice for her foresight. We've already seen, in *New Moon*, how Edward refused to join the Volturi's oper-ation. But to stage a full-scale assault just to nab Alice doesn't convince either).

❏

We see the Volturi leaders running down yet another victim – in London (yes, there's a long shot of Big Ben and the Houses of Parliament. And, yes – it's in another dark alley! Well, a back alley is of the prime sites in all action-adventure or thriller stories set in cities (is there an urban thriller that doesn't use a dark alley?). Garrett is also introduced in a dark alley). We see Alec's special skill of nasty black fog/smoke in action, and the poor sod is engulfed (that he is Japanese may be significant – how many North American businesses would love to tear apart East Asian companies, which're out-matching them on every level).

That Lord Aro himself would be personally overseeing such minor information gathering and executions is absurd (the equivalent of the U.S. President or a Chinese Emperor dealing with an underling's betrayal personally), especially when we know his dislike of travelling – but it does show the villains being villains, and shows the Volturi guard dogs doing what they do. Also, the scenes act as foreshadowing for the Big Cheat Battle. (Do Aro and the boys really mince around London dressed like that?! They might've wandered out of the tourist hotspots such as London Dungeon or a Jack the Ripper Tour. In the *Twilight Saga*, it's always Hallowe'en).

❏

Modest but significant scenes (in act 3 of *Part 2* of *Breaking Dawn*) depict Bella bonding with her daughter: reading her a bedtime story, for ex (one day she will tell Renesmee *The Fairy Story of Twilight*), and huddling in the tent.

The pre-battle camp-fire is a potentially entertaining scene which is squandered. Many scenes in the two *Breaking Dawn* films are like this:

there is potential for insight, for back-story, for humour, but Melissa Rosenberg plays down the comedy. So it's another talky scene where cold vampires sit around a roaring fire, and swop boasts about wars and rebellions.

The 2012 *Twlight* movie is so stuck on the plot there seems to be little time to kick back: the camp-fire scene could be a *lot* more compelling: for ex, Amun is actually about the oldest of all the vampire on show in the *Twilight* movies, as is Kebi, yet nobody asks them anything about what life was like in Ancient Egypt. Come on, we'd *love* to hear about life in ancient Thebes or Alexandria from someone who was actually there! (The Denalis mention Constantinople, Garrett the American Civil War, and the Oirish their Rebellion – all fascinating, but we want to hear about colossal battles involving Pharaohs and Ancient Egyptian Gods!).

Much more successful is the simple two-hander between Edward and his father, standing near the fire: once again, it's played very under-stated by Rob Pattinson and Peter Facinelli, but there's a sweetness about Edward thanking Carlisle for everything. (These scenes are important, however, in reminding us what is at stake: that each vampire group has 'something to fight for'.)

RENESMEE.

While most film productions opt to have the casting director search for babies and kids who look like the older actors, the *Twilight* movies, so visual effects-heavy already, chose to use digital animation. So baby Renesmee had a digital face,[13] as did the other kids playing her at different ages (as well as digitally animated additions to the body). A real baby, three-weeks old, was also used (the blood was Philadelphia cream cheese mixed with strawberry jelly), and yet another puppet. Director Bill Condon remarked that it took *a lot* of work to get the face of Renesmee right (that is, a lot of sending tests and footage back and forth between the production office and the vendors, and many costly hours at computer workstations – visual effects are *very* expensive because the people who create them are well paid).

Which begs the question: why didn't they do what everybody else does, and cast a bunch of tots who looked similar? Oh, I guess because the production team wanted the li'l tyke to *act* (Renesmee is a magical child, remember). Well, you could coax out similar performances from

13 Author Stephenie Meyer had wondered if visual effects could portray a convincing human. The answer here was: no. It's much easier for audiences to buy monsters or creatures or dinosaurs or aliens in computer animation. Humans are the toughest challenge.

real children (and, with selective editing, and sound effects, you could achieve the task much quicker and cheaper). Also, the production had cast Mackenzie Foy as their lead Renesmee (for scenes where she interacts most with the actors), so the children were all made to look like Foy, either younger or older. But somehow the digital animation approach fitted with the nature of Renesmee as a half-vampire, half-human baby.

Poor Mackenzie Foy isn't allowed to do a single kiddish thing in *Breaking Dawn* – she is always Bella Swan's daughter, never a child, always Renesmee, a function of the movie's plot, never a real girl who watches TV, plays with her cel phone, eats candy, etc. She is of course friendless, and has no interactions whatsoever with other children. She's the prize child, a thematic motif.

THE IMMORTAL CHILDREN.

So it's Bella Swan, once again, who's at the centre of the conflict between the vampire clans, with her daughter as the target of their animosity (Renesmee, by extension, is a young Bella dramatically as well as in other ways). The notion of 'immortal children' (i.e., similar to gods) was intriguing. As the exposition in *Breaking Dawn, Part 2* showed (delivered by Doctor Carlisle, yet again – he often performs the vampire lore explanations), immortal children act like demons or changelings, driven by unbridled and untameable hunger and libido. (The issue of just *why* vampires would seek to create a super-weapon like an 'immortal child', when they have plenty of special powers themselves, and the 'immortal children' are so difficult to control, isn't really addressed).[14]

The *Twilight* movies want to have things both ways, of course: they depict, in a montage-style flashback, the Volturi mobsters solving the issue of a particular immortal child[15] by killing him (and his creators. It's a boy because of course girls simply wouldn't be so destructive, would they?). If the immortal children are mass murderers, laying waste to entire villages (the flashback takes place in a standard, fantasy movie burning village in some rural, mediæval setting),[16] then presumably putting a stop to that is useful. Yet the Volturi are also painted as the villains, smiling (in repeated shots) as they torture and kill victims (the alternatives to dealing with an immortal child aren't explored. And anyway, s-l-o-w solutions are not given much consider-ation in flash-bang, Hollywood flicks that thrive on rapid action. There might be other solutions to

14 Again, there is more in the books, and in the *Twilight* guides.
15 He has the blond look of a neo-fascist kid out of sci-fi movies of the 1960s (like *Village of the Damned*).
16 With tulip-domed buildings in the background, it's presumably either Russia or Eastern Europe.

dealing with out-of-control monsters, but simply killing them is the quickest method in contemporary Hollywood movies of this kind – and it provides spectacle, of course).

The trouble is, the immortal children plot feels heavy-handed in how it's added onto *Breaking Dawn, Part 2*: it introduces a new obstacle/ threat (a dramatic necessity in each new sequel of this kind) which seems too obviously contrived. Well, yes, if Bella Swan has a baby, it's expected that the child will be threatened as well as Bella (if Bella is now a Mom, then her motherhood will be put under threat). The concept of immortal children is needed if the Volturi are going to get involved (and it'll take something seismic to prise them out of their Italian, hilltop lair – they wouldn't travel all the way to boring, rainy Washington State for nothing!).

Does Lord Aro *seriously* believe that the Cullens have 'manu-factured' an 'immortal child'? Of course not! But he *will* use the concept as a pretext for things he fancies doing. One is collecting vampires with special skills: in the movie, it's assumed that he's after Alice.

Going to war with the Cullen family also fulfils several other functions for the Volturi: it breaks the boredom of thousands of years; it acts as a demonstration of political power to the rest of the vampire world; and it satisfies the need to quash alternative vampire lifestyles.

The immortal children flashback does of course introduce the Volturi into *Breaking Dawn 2*, and they are always good value. It's a different movie when they show up, but we go along with that. Also, *Breaking Dawn, Part 2* gives Edward Cullen several Important Things To Do: one is, Edward realizes that the Volturi think that Renesmee is an immortal child. Another is: Edward delivers a key speech in the Cullen mansion, where he says he will fight (which rallies some of the vampires present, including those who were on the verge of abandoning the cause).

Considering how passive Edward Cullen is in many sections of both *Breaking Dawns*, it's good to see Edward taking charge. Yet all of this – the Volturi, the immortal children, Edward giving war-like speeches, the gathering of witnesses – emphasizes just how much Bella is a bystander in her own story. For instance, it's Edward who suggests the use of witnesses, and says he will take on the Volturi if necessary. Because Bella's journey is already over: she's got everything she wanted (Edward, marriage and that crucial vampiredom) – and a super-adorable child into the bargain. (So there's nothing *new* for Bella *to do* – except of course to protect what she has from outside threats. Hence the introduction of the Volturi plot).

THE VAMPIRE WITNESSES.

The themes that *Breaking Dawn* drew upon from *The Merchant of Venice* included bearing witness, and Portia's quick wits, in avoiding catastrophe by 'her cleverness and by using the right words' (TS, 42). The reference to *The Merchant of Venice* is also a hint that things will turn out well. *A Midsummer Night's Dream* was an influence on the concept of imprinting ('the magic of setting things right – which doesn't happen in the real world, which is absolutely fantasy', Stephenie Meyer said).

Most of the large array of vampire witnesses in *Breaking Dawn* were given a little bit of business to do, or a bit of dialogue, to illustrate their personalities and backgrounds. But not much: even split into two movies, *Breaking Dawn* didn't get far beyond paper-thin, cartoony characterizations. So we saw:

• the Amazon warrior women (real Amazons!), played by Judith Shekoni (Zafrina) and Tracey Higgins (Senna), transforming Washing-ton State into a jungle;

• the Irish coven (Liam, Maggie and Siobhan – Patrick Brennan, Marlane Barnes and Lisa Howard) sitting on one side quietly, and talking about their rebellion;

• the creepy, kooky Romanians Vladimir (Noel Fisher) and Stefan (Guri Weinberg), and their millennia-long grievance with the Volturi (they're itching for payback. Vlad and Stef, who steal every scene they're in, get to have an action sequence where they turn into Japanese ninjas, flying thru the trees, trumping Jacob and the werewolf guards);

• Garrett (Lee Pace)[17] the rugged North American Nomad/ adventurer who gets to have a romance with Kate (Casey LaBow) of the Denali coven ('I would follow you anywhere, woman', he tells her just before the battle). Introduced snacking in a dark alley, Garrett complains that he hated the first British invasion and he hated the second! (His unlucky victim is a musician);

• Alistair (Joe Anderson), the solitary, cynical Brit (whose function seems to be to watch from the sidelines (or a handy tree) and pour scorn on everything. However, as *The Official Illustrated Guide* shows, Alistair has a colourful past going back to the reign of Edward II in Ye Olde Englande – sort of *Braveheart* meets Aleister Crowley [TS, 272f)). Alistair's life is one of the back-stories that would be a delight to see;

• the Egyptians,[18] who included wunderkind Benjamin (Rami Malek), the so-serious Amun (Omar Metwally), his mate, Kebi (Angela

---

17 Pace was the King of the Elves in the *Hobbit* series.
18 Yes, there is a shot of a camel in the Egyptian scenes.

Gabriel), and Ben's mate, Tia (Angela Sarafyan);[19] we get to see some of Benjamin's magic (and Benjamin is one of the most upbeat of the vamps in the *Twilight Saga* – he actually smiles a lot!). Benjamin also performs a turning-point in the Big Battle, by shattering the Earth;

• and the Denali coven from Alaska[20] with their blonde, high fashion look: Katrina/ Kate (Casey LaBow), Tanya Carmen (Mía Maestro) and Eleazar (Christian Camargo); Katrina has the special skill of zapping victims with electricity (which she demonstrates on Edward, while Bella tries to learn to control her shielding ability).

Garrett, Alistair, Eleazar, Kate and the two Romanians make the biggest impression among the vamp visitors to the Olympic Peninsula. (Eleazar, for instance, is given several pieces of exposition). The scenes of the special skills of the vamps of course foreshadows how the vamps fight in the Big Cheat Smackdown.

The visit to Alaska to the Denali clan (in deep snow) offers a little bit of action, too (in a section of the film which became a little bogged down in plot), when the Denalis tussle with Edward over the nature of their daughter. The Denali family is another foreshadowing of how the vampire world will react to the issue of the immortal child, and how the Volturi will deal with it.

THE BIG CHEAT BATTLE IN *BREAKING DAWN, PART 2.*

According to Stephenie Meyer, it was during a dinner at a steakhouse[21] while producing *Eclipse* that she and Melissa Rosenberg worked out how to make the ending of *Breaking Dawn, Part 2* more cinematic. Either Meyer or Rosenberg came up with the idea, and they both said, 'That's it! That's gonna work!' (Meyer said she would've killed a few more Cullens).

According to Mark Cotta Vaz (in the *Breaking Dawn* movie guide), the outrageous concept of a mass battle between the rival vampire clans was cooked up by Stephenie Meyer and Melissa Rosenberg (when they met in Vancouver). For Rosenberg, the lack of a juicy confrontation between all sides in the *Breaking Dawn* novel was a major problem.

The fake battle was the toughest assignment for the *Breaking Dawn* scripts for Melissa Rosenberg (most of which were complete by August, 2009):

> The final battle sequence is a big challenge because it lasts 25 pages. It's almost an entire three-act story in and of itself. You have to track

---

19 The Egyptian women make very little impact in the movie.
20 They actually have origins in Slovakia and Spain, tho' the movie doesn't delve into that.
21 But isn't Meyer vegetarian?!

hundreds of characters. It's an enormous challenge to choreograph on the page and for Bill Condon to choreograph on the stage.

The finale of *Breaking Dawn, Part 2* delivered a cheat the likes of which hasn't been perpetrated on a global audience since the dreadful movies of M. Night Shyalaman! *What balls*, as Captain Willard avers in *Apocalypse Now* – what balls to stage an entire battle in the snow (with 900 shots! 100s of stunts! Gazillions of visual effects! Millions of dollars!), and then to have whole thing be naught but a vision that Alice has!

The final installment of the *Twilight* series solved the problem of the ending of the book 'with an audacious *Dallas*-style device that had audiences laughing, gasping and groaning, generally WTF!?-ing, all at the same time', as critic Mark Kermode put it (21).

This is one of the most outrageous examples in recent cinema of 'having it both ways', or 'having your cake and eating it', or staging an colossal action sequence then pretending it was all a dream!

I couldn't believe it when I saw it.22 There are so many flaws in the concept – you know what they are – it's not even worth bothering to mention them. (OK, how about a couple of flaws: that Alice's vision is of *one* possible future is probably the most obvious weakness. Because that isn't the future, is it? The future that actually happened is the future where everyone agrees it's better not to fight and walks away! (This is outlined in the first *Twilight* book, when Edward tells our Bella that 'Alice *sees* things', but also that 'the future isn't set in stone' [T, 253]). Another fault with the Big Cheat Battle is that the notion of 'bearing witness' (*pace The Merchant of Venice*) is lost, because a Hollywood-style battle takes over (Carlisle mentions the witnesses, but Lord Aro dismisses the issue). Another flub is that Aro accepts what Alice shows him, and walks away. That is, he believes what the enemy has shown him! In a vision! That Aro and his crew would come all that way and *not* fight is hooey.23 Another defect: having seen how the battle will play out, Aro can simply re-arrange his strategy! Another flaw: why does Alice have to show the battle in such detail, beat for beat, lasting 10 minutes?! A shorter version might've convinced just as well. Why not just show the part where Aro loses his head? That's the only bit he *really* cares about! He doesn't mind if his lieutenants or cohorts like Caius, Alec, Jane *et al* are toppled. Meanwhile, what is everyone else doing for the ten minutes

---

22 It seems even more ridiculous than the haunted house dreck *The Others* (2001), where everyone turns out to be a ghost. Or, most agonizing of all, *The Sixth Sense* (1999).
23 In the novel, the Volturi bring along their wives – Suplicia and Athenodora; dropped for the movie.

it takes to show this l-o-n-g vision? Just waiting? Oh yes, they *are* vampires, so 10 minutes in the cold and snow is nothing to them. Presumably Alice's vision was condensed into a single visionary moment for Aro's benefit).24

Cheats of this magnitude are a big finger to the audience. They tell the audience: guess what?, everything you have been watching was fake, a lie, a dream, a vision! Including, by extension, the movie itself (but we knew that). It devalues the whole fantastical enterprise, the suspension of disbelief, of art, of show business, of entertainment. It rams home that everything we consume in media and entertainment is faked. (But there *are* some successful examples of 'it was all a dream' in movies – perhaps the most famous one is in a much-loved picture, *The Wizard of Oz*. But the context there is very different from *Breaking Dawn*: *Oz* is a family-oriented, fairy tale fantasy movie, a cartoony musical where the heroes link arms and sing).

However, the battle itself in *Breaking Dawn, Part 2* didn't disappoint as spectacle. It was certainly big and splashy and visceral. It was introduced with ærial images of mountains and snow and a thunderous music cue from Carter Burwell (percussion, of course, and strident brass – and an extravagant choral cue, with pounding timpani, when the two sides gather. As the sequence develops, the sound team add many layers of sounds – those sounds which are in between sound effects and music: scraping, uneasy drones, for example).

The Big Cheat Fight isn't unique: many movies have attempted similar narrative twists. Time travel plots, for example, deliver similar sorts of possibilities for the future and 'what ifs?' The dramatic device allows filmmakers to do two things: to destroy the world but not to destroy it. For example, in the movie *Next* (2007), based on a Philip K. Dick short story, Los Angeles is blown up by an atomic bomb set off by terrorists. Yet it isn't – that was one possible outcome (in *Next*, Nic Cage plays a character who can see into the future, like Alice, but only a very short time).

The filmmakers employed *plenty* of time to build up the suspense (shots of our heroes (in their small groups), more ærial shots, more images of feet, the arrival of Volturi, and the first of many talky beats). Time is stretched out – so that when Edward walks from one side to the other to meet Aro, it takes 60 shots and 90 seconds (or that's what it felt

24 To be really faithful to the concept of *staying with Bella*, which the *Twilight* books do throughout (aside from the Jacob Black chapters), the 2012 movie should actually remain with *Bella and her family*, standing in the snow, while they watch Alice and Aro locked hand-to-hand from afar! Then we might've had Bella and Edward chatting about domestic stuff: 'Did you put out the trash, hon?' 'Uhh, yeah.' 'You didn't, did you?' 'Uhh, no.' 'OK, we're doing a chores list when we get home.'

like). Yes, and we know that all of the vamps here can *ziiip* 100s of yards in a milli-second! (Which they do when they disappear at the end of the battle). Whatever – the build-up is actually the most significant section of a Big Battle. So, as long as we get to enjoy something juicy and exciting, we don't mind sitting thru the mandatory reaction shots of everyone present.

(Indeed, this is one of the most striking aspects of the Big Cheat Battle scene in *Breaking Dawn 2* – it is full of 100s of close-ups as every character, including most of the secondary characters, receive close-ups. Or several. In addition, the sequence features numerous point-of-view shots – the viewpoint of Alice and Jasper looking at the Cullens as they walk past them, for example. The scene required a lot of planning to ensure that every character was covered).

That Irinia is executed by the Volturi brigade is expected (war-monger Caius is especially itching for some action, and the snitch will do in the meantime) – tho' the way our heroes prevent the Denalis from seeking vengeance was clever: at Edward's urging, the two Amazons (Senna and Zafrina) take away the sight of the Denali coven.

None of this happens in the *Breaking Dawn* novel, of course – which gives the producers more licence in portraying the Big Battle (because it's a conflict that never happens). But the inventions stick to the tried and tested formula of giving each of the main and secondary charas something to do, which relates to their special skills, and to their relationships. So we see Alice's acrobatics, Emmett's punches, Bella's shield, Kate's electrical jolts, Benjamin's nature magic, Alec's black fog, Jane's pain, and Edward's genius for making cappuccinos[25]

There's a terrific face-off between Carlisle Cullen and Lord Aro, where, John Woo-style,[26] they race towards each other, colliding up in the air (but then, no! Not Carlisle! Not Carlisle dead!). When Aro lands, holding Carlisle's head, there's a gasp from the audience (as director Bill Condon recalled at a preview screening). It's gutsy when a Hollywood movie sacrifices some of its major, well-loved characters. But very rare. However, the last installment in a five-flick set is the time to do it (especially if you've evoked models like William Shakespeare, *The Merchant of Venice* and *Romeo and Juliet*, where multiple deaths in the last act are a given).

When we cut to Esme's reaction shot, the filmmakers use one of the most effective of all cinematic devices (and it costs nothing!): *silence*

---

25 Even in the snow in the wilderness.
26 John Woo's incredible action movies have influenced so many moments in recent Hollywood cinema.

(instead of the expected scream). But Liz Reaser's acting – and Robert Pattinson's shocked expression, too, standing next to her – does all of the expressive work here (we cut to Esme and Edward because Carlisle means most to them).

That moment – the death of the caring, loyal, father figure Carlisle Cullen (it's probably the most significant on-screen death in the whole *Twilight Saga*, apart from Bella's demise) – is the act that instigates the *real* start of the vampire versus vampire battle. Carlisle was selected as 'the most shocking' character to kill (as Melissa Rosenberg put it), someone who is much loved, and the one who brought all of the vampire witnesses together.

Now, incensed, our heroes hurtle towards the Volturi mob, with Edward[27] in the lead (with the customary clash of two running armies filmed from side-on – mandatory in any big combat scene).[28] Because, you have to admit, there was *a lot* of preamble before warfare was commenced. A *lot* of talk.[29] You sat in your seat, thinking, OK, sure, so, like, *when* are they going to start ripping each other to pieces? Can we see some blood already? OK, not blood, then at least some bloodless but crystally-crunchy decapitations?

The snowbound brawl included some terrific gags – most marvellous being Benjamin splitting apart the Earth's crust, with the villains (mostly) toppling down into a fiery abyss. Edward, apparently falling to his doom like a rebel angel into Hell (much to Bella's dismay), zooms back and sticks it to an enemy.[30] Alice gets to kick Lord Aro *very* high. (This is the initiation of hostilities[31] – after it, Carlisle dashes into the fray – to his doom). And of course Bella gets to use her shield – to help her husband Edward, and some others, such as Jasper (thankfully, the filmmakers, tho' probably tempted, didn't make what Bella did too super-human, and they also generously gave plenty of screen time to other characters. However, Bella does get hurled far into the air – by Aro, and enjoys several moments of action). Esme has her own struggle over the chasm, too (saved by a werewolf who tumbles to its doom). Alice gets to nobble the very nasty Jane (aided by Sam Uley the werewolf, who

27 Edward is given several beats to lead and to shine in the battle.
28 Who did that first? – the running, the yelling, and the crunching meeting of the two sides? It was probably John Woo or another Chinese action movie! (Note that our heroes are moving from left to right – there's a psychology of screen direction which favours certain sides).
29 It's a chess game (one of the minor motifs in the series), and not the first time a battle has been depicted as chess (the high angles of the black figures against the white snow emphasizes that). One of the more amusing moments, and a favourite with some critics as well as director Bill Condon, was Michael Sheen's mad giggle when he meets li'l Nessie.
30 Lovers watching their beloveds die (or nearly die) is a recurring motif: Alice and Jasper, Carlisle and Esme, and Bella and Edward.
31 It's a curious act, tho' – does Alice kick Aro knowing that she couldn't beat him in the middle of the Volturi, so it will buy her companions (and herself) some time? Far better, tho' to sacrifice herself and go all-out and try to kill Aro. After all, no one dies anyway, 'cos this is a vision!

performs the final, ripping kill), in an extended sequence of girlie action, hammering away assailants as she hurls herself at Jane (Jane was one of the vamps who took out her beloved Jasper by injuring him with her beam of pain). World-weary Marcus groans, 'finally!', when two vamps (Vlad and Stef) close in on him to tear off his limbs (vengeance for the East Europeans, beaten by the Volturi clan centuries ago). Tanya and Kate corner Caius and rip his skull open (payback for Irina). And each of the other characters has their moment to shine: Emmett, Rosalie, Alec, Caius, etc.

Meanwhile, Jacob's given Something Significant To Do (because you can't forget each of the three principal characters): whisk Renesmee away to safety (that, too, can't be a simple act of Running Away – the pair're pursued by vamps thru the snow-filled forest, and Jake gets to kill the hunters). Alas, there's no Taylor Lautner in the chase – it's just animation, of Jacob in his wolf-form (so Lautner isn't really part of the finale of *Breaking Dawn*). Instead, it's down to Mackenzie Foy to do play the customary role of Frightened Princess (a role in cinema going back to the early 1900s).

And, finally, the Demise of the Chief Villain, accompanied by a giant, choral music cue: it should be Bella Swan who takes out the freak Lord Aro.[32] The 2012 Hollywood movie included Edward in that grapple too: after all, it was their daughter they were protecting (thus B. and E. become a bizarre husband-and-wife killing team – a very odd tag team move has Edward spinning Bella and hurling her at Aro). An important villain does require two people to kill him: so Bella pins Aro while Edward smashes at his body and performs Aro's decapitation, which signals the end of the Alice-vision (the camera takes Aro's point-of-view as his shocked eyes see the flaming torch thrust towards him, and the screen fills with flames).

When we match cut from Lord Aro's immolation to Aro's shocked response at Alice's vision of his death, the frenetic battle is over. There is some more talk (always with the talk!), but as soon as Aro's left, everybody sort of shuffles away. Vladimir and Stefan berate the vampire witnesses (as expected) – they should attack now! while the Volturi're on the run! But no one's interested. Apart from some smug smiles, hugs and the kisses, the Cullens and company. seem a bit embarrassed – as if they're thinking, did we *really* do that to the movie audience?!

So what a let-down, a come-down, an all-out shocker when it's revealed, after seeing all of that carnage and wild stunt work and gross-

32 Rosenberg: 'Of course, Bella and Edward had to be the ones to kill Aro. That was the ultimate, and that they do it together felt really right. I really wanted to see Bella just rip his frickin' head off'.

but-fun gags and countless visual effects shots (costing millions of dollars, folks!), that it was all a dream, just an Alice-vision… a trick played *on us*. (Notice that the filmmakers include quite a bit of 'air' here, as editors call it – that is, a series of reaction shots, before the storytelling continues. They probably anticipated that audiences would be stunned or wowed to find It Was All A Dream. If an audience is going to chatter about what they just saw, it's here).

To be truthful and honest to the audience, the filmmakers should've included a big red caption: THE NEXT TEN MINUTES IS ALL A VISION THAT ALICE IS SHOWING ARO!

OK, so the vision of our Alice Brandon *was* signalled, tho' in a pretty subtle fashion! How many in the audience twigged, on first viewing, that this was all a vision? And how many groaned with disbelief when it was revealed as a glimpse into the future, with the villains simply slinking away? More than one or two, I bet.[33] (The signal that it's a vision is Alice's reaction to Aro, when she says he'll fight whatever happens).

Well, the Big Cheat Fight in *Breaking Dawn, Part 2* did allow for the filmmakers to have it both ways (as entertainers and artists *love* to do!): to show the heroic (or, for the enemy, welcome) deaths of numerous characters (including Carlisle, Jasper, Jane, Alec, Marcus, Caius and of course Lord Aro), and to *not* show them. To demonstrate that our heroes would fight to the death, and yet they didn't! To have the war and the violence but no consequences. Thus, it was a literally bloodless conflict. Like going from 'R' rated gore to 'G' rated peace and love, from the nastiest scenes in *The Texas Chainsaw Massacre* to the pastel-hued niceness of *101 Dalmatians*.

No blood was shed in the making of this movie.

Yes, the Big Cheat War in *Breaking Dawn, Part 2* allowed the filmmakers to act as the ultimate parent, the oh-so-sensitive mother figure, the kind-hearted auntie, who tells its wide-eyed, fearful offspring, looking up with those big, Bambi eyes, 'oh no, dear, that *never happened*, it was all a dream!'

Another flaw with the fake snow battle in *Breaking Dawn, Part 2* is that it takes agency away from Bella Swan, the heroine of the *Twilight Saga* – so that she is simply a pawn, really, in a big chess game (remember the chess pieces on the cover of the novel). Bella doesn't get to *do* much in the battle, apart form protect her loved ones with her

---

33 However, director Bill Condon said that scene had tested well with (preview) audiences – from the thrill of the action to the shock of seeing major characters have their heads ripped off: Carlisle and Jasper.

magical shield (OK, yes, she does smash some vampires around, she is kicked for miles by Lord Aro, and she does destroy Aro at the end, with the aid of Edward).

But this *isn't* what the *Twilight Saga* is about, is it? The *Twilight* series, as many fans would agree, is a romantic fantasy story in which vampires and action are *secondary* to the main themes of love and romance (and issues like being a teenager, growing up, discovering your identity, and avoiding dying if you can manage it).

In relation to Stephenie Meyer's four *Twilight* books, the Pretend Battle is way off the point.

Another issue with the cheated combat in *Breaking Dawn, Part 2* was this: no price was paid. Well, yes, that *is* typical in a Hollywood-style narrative. The villains die, the heroes're triumphant, the conflict's resolved, and everybody's smiling afterwards. Scuppering the impact of the conflict and its multiple deaths and turning it into a dream/ vision meant that nobody paid any price. Instead, arch villain Lord Aro simply whisks away with a final, gloating quip and his tail between his legs. (The battle's *dénouement* is unsatisfying dramatically: there's a (simu-lated) whip pan between Alice and Bella, and Aro sighs about missing such a wonderful prize).

One of the only losers was Jacob Black. But in Alice Brandon's vision (not *another* Alice-vision?!), in the final moments, he's depicted standing on a beach[34] next to the grown Renesmee, with her head on his shoulder. So he Gets The Girl after all, tho' it's The Girl's Daughter (!). That's still second best. (Yes. It's a clever solution to the problem of the eternal love triangle, as Bill Condon noted, but it's still the Consolation Prize).

And Bella Swan was even reconciled with her parents (well, Charlie at least), after we'd been told, repeatedly (and with much sorrowful music and lingering close-ups), that once our Bells was a vampire she would no longer be in her parents' orbit.

So our heroes got to have their (vegetarian) cakes and eat them (again: *no blood was shed in the making of this movie!*).

MORE ON THE BATTLE.

The battle was filmed over six weeks in Baton Rouge, with green screens on three sides of the studio. The snow was paper. The smackdown was an enormous undertaking for the many visual effects companies. It required extensive storyboarding and pre-visualization (for the stunts, for

---

34 Presumably we're still in Washington State, and Jacob hasn't whisked Renesmee away to Hawaii.

the wolves, for the digital animation, etc). The warfare also meant plenty of work for film editors Virginia Katz and Ian Slater (it is a showpiece for the editors, the kind of sequence that editors love to get their fangs into).

The production scouted many fields in Louisiana to find the perfect spot to stage the invented smackdown in *Breaking Dawn*. In the end, it was decided that there were too many variables to control by filming on location (weather, lighting,[35] stunt rigs, access, and all of the back-up facilities like make-up, hair, costumes, props, catering, etc), so the field was recreated on a soundstage in Baton Rouge. Thus, the *Twilight Saga* moved from being a mainly location-based movie in the first *Twilight* production, to an entirely green screen undertaking.[36]

One might expect the battle to take place at night – and the familiar wild, rainy, stormy night of horror and action cinema. Also, night can hide all sorts of tricks that filmmakers use. Setting the battle during the day would be a practial decision in part – wrangling so many actors and complicated visual effects is easier to do if it were outside. Also, if the combat had been filmed outdoors, that would mean six weeks of night shoots. (But once it had been decided to film in a studio, it could be switched to night).

Technically, the battle in *Breaking Dawn, Part 2* is very impressive. Filming in snow with plenty of visual effects, stunts and gags, and with such a large cast of principals, is a big challenge for everybody involved (even if the snow and the environment is fake). *Breaking Dawn* fared better than other productions which filmed open-air battles on green screen stages (such as *The Golden Compass,* the *Star Wars* prequels, *Alice In Wonderland,* and *The Hobbit*). *Breaking Dawn* recreated the great outdoors of a giant, snow-covered field convincingly (the lighting – by Guillermo Navarro, his gaffer and the lighting team – really helped to sell the feeling of being outdoors in the mountains). But the snow, as always in movies, looked fake: whether it's salt, paper, foam, plastic, whatever, artificial snow always looks fake in cinema. It's one special effect that movies, even using the latest technology, can't get right.

Breaking Dawn managed to give everyone their moment to shine, while the second unit team (headed up by E.J. Foerster) explored even more ways of trouncing a vampire (with decapitation still the number one choice). As usual, there were more stunts and gags filmed that didn't make it into the final cut (such as Alice and some of the women going into Action Girl mode). But this was the sequence where the stunt team

35 Continuity with lighting is a key consideration.
36 The actors staged their own dance-off (the Breaking Dawn Dance Battle, they dubbed it) – to break the monotony of filming the finale week after week on the green screen stage. (Everyone knew about it except director Bill Condon: 'God, I've never been surprised on a set like that ever').

and the second unit really shined (partly because the entire episode was invented, so the limits of what could be shown were loosened a little).

MICHAEL SHEEN AND LORD ARO.

The famous laugh that Lord Aro emits in *Breaking Dawn* came about spontaneously, on the set, Michael Sheen explained. A lot of people enjoyed it, and it does help to express the madness that lies not far from the surface among the Volturi clan (and, besides, because Caius and Marcus (and, well, everybody else), are so uptight and grim, it's great having Aro be so delighted with life in his own, mad way).

Michael Sheen is incredible in the battlefield scene. This might be the best thing about it – more Michael Sheen. There is some excellent acting talent in the *Twilight Saga* movies, but when Sheen is on screen, nobody else stands a chance. Sheen's acting also shows just how paper-thin the performance styles of even Kristen Stewart and Robert Pattinson are.

The Volturi mob are pure camp, from one angle, a bunch of degenerate aristos who dress up in Hallowe'en versions of regal, Catholic finery ('matching Goth clothes', as Stephenie Meyer puts it in *The Short Second Life of Bree Tanner* [76]). But then, if you've got a bunch of Italian vampires, they have to be costumed in high-fashion-meets-Hammer-horror (plus a dash of Italian horror movie-making *à la* Dario Argento and Mario Bava). And the actors play the Volturi barely this side of camp, with Michael Sheen's Lord Aro a mix of amused insanity and polite weirdness.[37] Aro is one of those creepy bad guys who never loses his cool, never raises his voice, and only enters the fight when absolutely necessary (even tho' Aro heads up the Volturi battalion at the Big Face-Off in the snow, he's the most reluctant to enter the fray, sending everybody else in first, like a General in the First World War. Indeed, it's the sight of his own demise that persuades Aro to buy into Alice's vision and order his troop home to Italia, rather than, say, seeing lieutenants such as Jane or Alec being destroyed).

No need for the wonderful *Scary Movie* team, or *Saturday Night Live*, or *The Simpsons* to parody the *Twilight* movies, because they are already pretty self-conscious about the amount of camp and silliness they are perpetrating on the global cinema audience. However, the *Twi-hard* films don't wink at the audience, and they manage, like the *Pirates of the Caribbean* movies or the *Harry Potter* flicks, to stay just this side of send-up and parody. But you can be sure that many times in the

---

37 He's been around a *long* time, so, one reasons, he's developed this wackiness.

production of the movies, from 2007 to 2012, the filmmakers and the actors were acutely conscious of just how completely bonkers much of the stuff they were producing was.

THE *DÉNOUEMENTS.*

Breaking Dawn, Part 2 closes with a series of *dénouement* scenes, which resolve not only this one movie, and the two-part movie, but also the *Twilight* series. Sunny, warm farewell scenes, next to the river. Smiley looks from Alice to Jasper. The reuniting of the family of four – Bella, Edward, Renesmee and Jake (in casual clothing, Bella in a simple, grey top – back to her 'emo', Goth girl outfits after the fashion-plate look of her new vampirehood). The guys stand there, hands in pockets, while Bella embraces Renesmee and affirms that they will always be together. A moving vision of an older Renesmee (courtesy of Alice's prophecies as she contemplates this cute family scene), together with Jake (so he gets the Consolation Prize of the daughter of his beloved), on a beach, with Bella and Edward. It's a sweet glimpse into more of a Happy Ever After future for our heroes (because lerrrve is *forever*, right? Oh baby, yes, yes, yes!).

And so to the final scene of *Breaking Dawn, Part 2*: back to the meadow, the Garden of Eden (sprinkled, as ever, with purple flowers), featuring just the two lovers (it's handy that Renesmee always has someone to look after her when needed). The *Twilight* series was always about Bella and Edward, finally, and it's right that they should round off this fantasy romance movie franchise (the close-ups are enormous, with some trickery of a lens or formatting, evoking the C.U.s in a Cinemascope epic movie from the 1950s). The dialogue isn't that crucial, this is more about the sunshine,[38] the purple bouquets, the glowing close-ups, their heads an inch or two apart. Yes, there's plenty of kissing! Always with the kissing in the *Twilight* series!

Filmmakers sometimes like to include short montages of the highpoints of their movies near the end. Here in *Breaking Dawn, Part 2*, it's couched within the terms of Bella lowering her shield to include Edward in her thoughts. Whatever – the main reason is for the film producers to show a montage of images from all five movies, with each sequence focussing on the star of the show, Bella Swan.[39] (Accompanied by a song[40] from Christina Perri ('A Thousand Years'), which emphasizes love lasting a thousand years).

38 Without the sparkly effect.
39 As Bill Condon explained, these shots were often outtakes from scenes, not the footage used in the final cuts (i.e., another way of including new material).
40 One can imagine that several songs were tried for this crucial montage.

Forever...

Breaking Dawn, Part 2 closes with a very unusual device, something so corny and obvious you can't believe they did it, but it's possible that Stephenie Meyer had something to do with the idea: the final words of the whole *Twilight* movie franchise emphasize *forever*.[41] And what does the movie do? – it cuts from Bella and Edward in their all-time favourite place (the flowery meadow) to the last page of the novel of *Breaking Dawn*. With black-and-white visual effects (the field turns to b/w, and the words're reversed, white out of black), the camera picks out the last lines (and that last word, *forever*).

Well, you can also bet that many writers would *love* to have their books celebrated in that fashion! But the only books that get to be seen on screen in their own movie adaptions are fairy tales (in the Walt Disney manner of opening a movie on a close-up of an olde worlde fairy tale volume, as the pages turn and the jolly, old narrator introduces the story).

Breaking Dawn's end credits feature a curtain call of the characters – across all five movies (again using the design element of black, white and red), accompanied by the music of Christina Perri (followed by Green Day, Ellie Goulding, Reeve Carney and Paul McDonald/ Nikki Reed). Even charas that had few lines and barely make an impression get their smiley or moody close-ups (and both actresses who played Victoria are rightly featured). The word-to-screen idea was reprised in the credits, for the three principal actors (taken from their introductions in the *Twilight* novel), who take pride of place as the last three actors in the curtain call. (The two closing montages are indulgent, but they work – they are all about the magic of Hollywood, the magic of movies).

THE CRITICS.

Among the critical reaction to *Breaking Dawn, Part 2* was, 'Thank God! It's over!' Meaning the *Twilight* movie franchise. Five movies which were Hell to sit thru for many critics (poor, poor things! Oh, the poor dears! Medic! *Medic!* Get this film critic a brandy!). Yet there *were* some critics who enjoyed the *Twilighting* flicks (even if they used phrases like 'guilty' enjoyment – as if everybody should really be watching *Shoah* (1985) or Ingmar Bergman's solemn movies or learning Latin and Greek). No, not all movies have to be 'serious' or 'meaningful', or to 'make ideological statements' (which they do anyway, even if they don't intend to. Politics is built-in to everything). Not all movies have to be *The Passion of Joan of Arc* or *Bicycle Thieves*. In fact, as any good

41 Edward also closes his wedding speech with the word *forever*. In fact, *forever* pops up all over the place in Melissa Rosenberg's *Breaking Dawn* script.

film critic knows very well, the Hollywood film industry in general pumps out popcorn and schlock, remakes of sequels of 'reimaginings' of 'reboots' of remakes of something that might once upon a time have been 'original'.

In short, film critics are *not* the audience of *Twilight*, nor of most mainstream Hollywood movies. (Critics go to see movies for free at special preview screenings in cities like L.A., New York, London, Paris and Tokyo), where the audience consists of other film critics, who seldom laugh, gasp, yell, throw popcorn or even titter. They don't see movies with a rowdy full house on a Friday night).

THE EPIC FINALE THAT WILL LIVE FOREVER
the twilight saga
breaking dawn
part 2
SUMMIT ENTERTAINMENT "THE TWILIGHT SAGA: BREAKING DAWN - PART 2" A TEMPLE HILL SUNSWEPT ENTERTAINMENT KRISTEN STEWART ROBERT PATTINSON TAYLOR LAUTNER BILLY BURKE PETER FACINELLI
ELIZABETH REASER KELLAN LUTZ NIKKI REED JACKSON RATHBONE ASHLEY GREENE MICHAEL SHEEN DAKOTA FANNING DEBRA ZANE, C.S.A. MICHAEL WILKINSON CARTER BURWELL ALEXANDRA PATSAVAS
VIRGINIA KATZ, A.C.E. RICHARD SHERMAN GUILLERMO NAVARRO, A.S.C. BILL BANNERMAN MARTY BOWEN GREG MOORADIAN MARK MORGAN GUY OSEARY WYCK GODFREY KAREN ROSENFELT STEPHENIE MEYER
PG-13
"BREAKING DAWN" STEPHENIE MEYER
11.16.12
MELISSA ROSENBERG BILL CONDON
BreakingDawn-TheMovie.com

Making Breaking Dawn, Part 2

8

VAMPIRES SUCK

I felt like – like I don't know what. Like this wasn't real. Like I was in
some Goth version of a bad sitcom.

Stephenie Meyer, *Breaking Dawn* (170)

The *Twilight Saga* spawned many spoofs in many media.[1] Two are worth
noting: *Vampires Suck* (2010), from the Friedberg-Seltzer team, and
Breaking Wind (2012), written and directed by Craig Moss. Both were
superlative comedies which were enjoyed by many viewers, but which
were (predictably) decimated by film critics (the poor crrritics hated
Vampires Suck, and loathed *Breaking Wind* even more!).

Ironically *Vampires Suck* and *Breaking Wind* delivered more
satisfying versions of many scenes from the four Stephenie Meyer books
than the 'official' *Twilight* movies produced by Summit Entertainment
(yes, altho' the scenes were couched in a comedy format, they were
actually more fulfilling versions of the scenes in the books.[2] You could
argue that *Vampires Suck* is a more successful adaptation of the *Twilight*
books than the 'official' versions, even if it's a comedy).

Vampires Suck (Regency/ Fox) was a brilliant and very funny send-
up of the *Twilight Saga* – not only the movies, but the whole cultural
phenomenon of the *Twilight* series[3] (the other *Twilight* spoof, *Breaking
Wind,* was released in 2012).

1 *Twilight* has been parodied in fan fiction, in novels, and many other forms. Musical parodies of
Twilight include: *Twigh School Musical, The Hillywood Show,* and The *Twilight: The Musical.*
2 *Vampires Suck* was striking in just how closely it could replicate so many of the familiar images
and scenes from the *Twilight* movies – it had the school, the truck, the Cullen house, and
thousands of other elements down to a T.
3 *Vampires Suck* was a movie that guys might enjoy, after being dragged along to see the *Twilight*
movies by their dates.

Vampires Suck is without question one of the great parody movies of recent times, and it is certainly one of the great parodies of a massively popular franchise (every giant movie franchise should have one – we're still waiting for the ultimate, full-length parody of *Star Wars* (of the newer *Star Wars* movies, that is – we haven't forgotten about *Space Balls,* the Mel Brooks spoof movie), *Barry Trotter, Lord of the Rings, Batman, Avatar* and *The Avengers*).

Vampires Suck was produced by Peter Safran, Jerry P. Jacobs, Hal Olofsson, Jason Friedberg and Aaron Seltzer, exec. prod. by Arnon Milchan, and written and directed by Friedberg and Seltzer. It was made by Regency Enterprises and released by 20th Century Vole. The budget was $20 million, and the global box office gross was $80.5 million.[4] Released: August 18, 2010. 82 mins.

In the crew of *Vampires Suck* were: Christopher Lennertz (m.), Shawn Maurer (DP), Nancy Foy (casting), Peck Prior (ed.), William A. Elliott (prod. des.), Kevin Hardison (art dir.), Alix Hester (costumes), Jamie Hess and Matthew W. Mungle (special make-up), Silvina Knight and Douglas Noe (make-up), Michael Moore (hair), Keith Adams (2nd unit dir.), Jon Title (sound design ed.), Anna MacKenzie (sup. sound ed.), and vfx by Pixel Magic, Rez-Illusion, W.M. Creations and Laser Pacific. (Many in the team were regulars in the Friedberg and Seltzer Circus). Like the later *Twilight* movies themselves, *Vampires Suck* was based in Louisiana (it filmed in Bossier City, Shreveport and Minden).

Vampires Suck starred Jenn Proske, Matt Lanter, Christopher Riggi, Anneliese van der Pol, David DeLuise, Kelsey Ledgin, Dave Foley, Jeff Witzke, Crista Flanagan, Nick Eversman, Zane Holtz, Stephanie Fischer and Ken Jeong.

Whatever you think of the previous spoofs directed by Jason Friedberg and Aaron Seltzer (some of us are *big* fans!), such as *Date Movie, Epic Movie* and *Disaster Movie*, they sure hit the spot with *Vampires Suck*. It's probably their most satisfying comedy.

Vampires Suck features all of the elements of a Jason Friedberg and Aaron Seltzer movie that we know and love:
 • crazy puppets (the vampirized squirrel);
 • dumping junk on the star (Becca's pounded by falling rubble in her bedroom);
 • pin-up/ semi-nude girls (Becca in rubber);
 • gratuitous violence for laughs (shooting Alice, kicking Becca's Pa, Frank, and Bobby and Frank play-fighting);

---

4 The top 5 movies globally in 2010 were *Toy Story 3, Alice In Wonderland, Barry Trotter and the Deathly Hallows, Part 1, Inception* and *Shrek Forever After.*

- numerous stunts;
- a guy's kicked in the crotch;
- silly signs (Becca's parking spot);
- spoof books;
- cheapo ways of getting around expensive visual effects (Edward's bling; vampire speed; Jacob running on wires);
- fart jokes;
- joke products (like Becca's I-Pod playlist);
- dummies (Becca when she's been drained of blood; Frank's sex doll);
- joke props (the giant cactus);
- fat people (John in the deleted scene);
- pops at gay culture (the camp werewolves);
- dancing (the werewolves dancing to 'It's Raining Men').

The parody flicks of Jason Friedberg and Aaron Seltzer are regularly criticized for scorning and not loving the movies they're spoofing. This is not the case. And it is not the case with *Vampires Suck*: the 2010 parody picture reminds us why we enjoy the *Twilight Saga*, even tho' it is cheesy, badly written, awkwardly cast, and downright offensive politically (certainly it's toxic in terms of feminism of any kind).

If you know the *Twilight Saga*, you will love *Vampires Suck*! If you *loathe* the *Twilight Saga*, you will love *Vampires Suck*! If you secretly enjoy the trashy, dumb and completely irritating and yet compelling *Twilight* movies and books (but won't admit it to anybody), you will love *Vampires Suck*!

The writers and filmmakers have captured so many aspects of the *Twilight* craze, it's hilarious and remarkable:
- the silliness of the whole vampire premise;
- teenage girls and vampires;
- depressed, angst-ridden teen girls;
- the new girl at school;
- the boy band hair styles (including a *bad* wig[5] for Becca);
- the ridiculous over-use of s-l-o-w m-o-t-i-o-n;[6]
- the preposterous costumes;
- the mock-serious voiceover;
- vampire speed;
- blood (Becca's paper cut[7] spouting blood like a Sam Peckinpah

---

5 Is your hair from Fantastic Lesbians? one of the girls carps in the egging scene.
6 With a sly dig at Catherine Hardwicke, director of the first *Twilight* movie in the dialogue. The send-up of slow motion is dubbed here 'Hardwicke 101' – cheesy and predictable! (So Becca does a *really slow* turn of the head to look at Edward in the school canteen). It's also a rare reference to a fellow filmmaker.
7 Reminding us that the paper cut beat in *New Moon* is a loony scene!

movie);

- the rivalry of fans in Team Jacob and Team Edward;[8]
- the Native Americans;[9]
- Jacob undressing for contractual reasons;[10]
- the homoerotic undertones of the butch, topless werewolves;
- vampires having sex (and Becca sexing up in lingerie);
- the annoying sidekicks (Becca's mates at school);
- Becca losing her boyfriend;
- the visions of Alice/ Iris (and the plot confusions they create);
- the over-inflated, pretentious, mock-Shakespearean dialogue;
- the switch in casting of Victoria (which irked some Twi-hards);[11]
- the irritating but adorable but actually irritating personality of mouthy Jennifer;
- and the music: indie, portentous, cloying.

Even the cast and crew of *Twilight* knew they were really making a plate of steaming cheese during shooting in March, 2008, not a hip, cool vampire flick for teenagers, and *Vampires Suck* humorously reveals that.

I wish the studio (Regency Enterprises/ Fox) had allowed the filmmakers of *Vampires Suck* to have an 'R' rating instead of a 'PG-13' rating.[12] It's ironic that the original *Twilight* movies (also rated 'PG-13') are more graphic in some areas (like gore and violence) than the spoof movie (albeit not with sexual issues). It wouldn't be until *Best Night Ever* that Friedberg and Seltzer entered 'R' rated territory.

Among the reasons that *Vampires Suck* is a more satisfying parody venture than some of the previous flicks directed and written by Jason Friedberg and Aaron Seltzer is that the story is strong, and cleverly combines the first two *Twilight* movies.[13] Instead of providing a loose framework for a series of self-contained movie or pop culture spoofs (like *Disaster Movie*), *Vampires Suck* follows a single storyline and one bunch of characters, making it so much more focussed (but the filmmakers found plenty of things to spoof along the way). Similarly, *Meet the Spartans* is a strong film structurally because it follows the plot of *300*.

But *Vampires Suck* cut down considerably on the pop culture

---

8 Introduced in the prologue.
9 There's a great send-up of the scene where Charlie and Billy josh around in the background, beating each other up.
10 The toplessness was criticized after *New Moon*, and was consciously reduced in subsequent *Twilight* movies.
11 When Bryce Dallas Howard replaced Rachelle Lefevre.
12 The filmmakers saved the single use of the word *fuck* allowed in 'PG-13' movies by the M.P.A.A. for the *Twilight* credits, for the moment when Becca becomes a vampire (the transformation pre-empted the movies by two years. A single expletive is allowed in a 'PG-13' film: the single use of the word *fuck* in 'PG-13' films *Titanic, Minority Report* and *Armageddon*. Any more, and it becomes an 'R' film.)
13 Actually, it's a romantic story, like *Date Movie*.

references that're a staple of Friedberg and Seltzer's films: so there's no Jacko, no celebrity lookalikes, no TV game show spoofs, no joke commercials (and no half-naked supermodels), which further reduces the scattershot approach of previous parody movies like *Epic Movie* and *Disaster Movie.*

> 'This looks like a horror movie waiting to happen,' I snickered.
> (Stephenie Meyer, *Twilight*, 424)

Vampires Suck combined the storylines of the first two *Twilight* movies, *Twilight* (2008) and *New Moon* (2009) (with swipes at the third one, *Eclipse*, 2010). But it also references the *Twilight Saga* books, and author Stephenie Meyer,[14] and the famously intense fans.[15] The script of *Vampires Suck* wittily and skilfully fuses the two *Twilight* books and movies, retaining the key narrative beats while also spoofing them. In short, *Vampires Suck* is a great comedy and a great parody largely due to the script (which's true of most parody movies, and most comedy movies: it's one reason that writers love comedies, because they foreground screenwriting).

Altho' much of *Vampires Suck* is a parody of the first two *Twilight* movies and novels, it does also use elements from the later books: it climaxes with Edward biting Becca, for ex, from *Breaking Dawn.* The *Eclipse* movie was released on June 30, 2010, so there wasn't much time for last minute additions about *Eclipse* to be included in *Vampires Suck* (released on Aug 18, 2010). All of the books were fair game, tho' (the last one, *Breaking Dawn,* was published on Aug 2, 2008).

Some enterprising folk have edited together the *Twilight* movies and the *Vampires Suck* spoof movie and put them online. When the original film and the parody're intercut, the jokes seem even funnier, and the spoofers have got so much of the original movies wickedly dead-on. The cut-together movies remind us that *Twilight* on its own is ridiculous, and the best spoof you could make of *Twilight* would be... to simply show *Twilight.*

The first two *Twilight* movies (well, all of them, really) use a tried and tested narrative structure: one girl, two guys. The romantic triangle has worked for 1,391,845 other movies, so it'll work just fine in a spoof flick. And the other narrative ingredients, like the new girl in a new school and a new town, or *Beauty and the Beast* (a girl and a vampire), are also traditional plots which have been proven to work in countless stories (many horror movies are fundamentally versions of *Beauty and the*

---

14 *Vampires Suck* quotes from Meyer on her Twitter account.
15 'Fan' comes from 'fanatic', as pop star Prince used to point out.

Beast). So *Vampires Suck* can be seen as successful dramatically, without adding the humour and the spoofs. Which helps the comedy no end. (And, yes, *Vampires Suck does* work as a comedy without the viewer knowing a jot about the *Twilight Saga* franchise).

There is so much juice in the vampire genre, too, which movie-makers can grab hold of (*Vampires Suck* isn't the first vampire spoof; there have been many. A wonderful one is *Dead and Loving It* (1995), the Mel Brooks send-up of 1992's *Bram Stoker's Dracula* (and other *Dracula* flicks) starring Leslie Nielsen. Other famous vampire movie spoofs include *The Fearless Vampire Killers* (1967), *Love At First Bite* (1979), *The Little Vampire* (2000), *Dark Shadows* (2012), and of course the *Scary Movies*).

Also, the pop culture phenomenon of *Twilight* had so many aspects to it that were gifts to spoofers (not least the scarily devoted teenage fans). And, as movies, the *Twilight* pictures are already completely ludicrous and ultra-camp, they almost defy sending up. Yet there's enough 'reality', of li'l Bella Swan living in Forks in contemporary North America, that the filmmakers can use to work *against*. (Yes, she's a plain, dowdy, anxious and boring girl who somehow has guys swooning over her).16

Meanwhile, the three leads of *Vampires Suck* (Jenn Proske, Matt Lanter and Christopher Riggi) delivered wonderful impersonations and riffs on the golden trio of the *Twilight* movies, Kristen Stewart, Robert Pattinson and Taylor Lautner. Proske as Becca Crane was especially good at capturing Stewart's maddening ticks and Method acting quirks,17 her wild over-acting of a nervous, angsty 16 year-old (right down to the badly-fitted wig – cruel but fun!). Proske simply has to repeat one or two of those quirks and it becomes funny, reminding us just how affected and mannered Stewart's acting style was in the *Twilight Saga*. (Proske is so good she would make a great Bella if Stewart needed replacing). And Proske does some brave turns – in the sleepwalking scene, for instance (there is more in the deleted scenes).18

Vampires Suck could've gone even further with some of the *Twilight* material: it could've added more to the irksome aspects of Bella Swan's personality, for instance. Such as her snooty, superior attitude, her pretentious cultural aspirations, and her condescending attitude towards

---

16 Daro points out that Becca is already like a vampire – the pale skin, the mopey, miserable attitude.

17 The filmmakers kept Proske performing like that throughout *Vampires Suck*, reminding us of just how irritating Kristen Stewart's approach to acting was, which took itself *so* seriously.

18 The deleted scenes of *Vampires Suck* include more of Jennifer's romantic subplot (another letter from John, and meeting John at the Prom); more of Jennifer angling for votes for Prom Queen; more of the Zolturi menacing students (such as Eric/ Derric); and much more of Daro's monologue.

her friends. (But the 'official' *Twilight* movies steered clear of Bella's patronizing treatment of some of the kids at school, which might've made her somewhat unlikeable. And there's no doubt that in the *Twilight* books Bella reckons she's *very* smart – she's a girl who reads Jane Austen for pleasure).

Matt Lanter was great as Robert Pattinson's pin-up, pale vamp (the pale, trashy, heroin chic look), with the morose, moody scowls, and the fashion plate aspects of Edward's appearance and attire, the hair spray and hair gel, and his all-consuming narcissism (his hair in curlers, the powdering of the cheeks; make-up designers Silvina Knight and Douglas Noe also gave Lanter bright red lipstick).

Matt Lanter has captured, too, some of Robert Pattinson's distinctive, very self-conscious actorly bits of business (like the attempts at exquisite, oh-so poignant expressions of romantic suffering). And of course the hair acting that Pattinson does all the time in the *Twilight Saga*.[19]

Christopher Riggi as Lanter's hunky, Native American werewolf rival Jacob White was spot-on, too (Lanter, Proske and Riggi are nice to look at – Riggi without his joke chest hair and nipples make-up is buff!). Also, Anneliese van der Pol was right on the nail as the bratty, irritating, arrogant, desperate-to-be Prom Queen, Jennifer. (A character like Jessica is a gift to comedy writers).

One of the most successful aspects of *Vampires Suck* is invisible: the score by Christopher Lennertz.[20] The Budapest Symphony Orchestra played the score, conducted by Géza Török. It's a brilliant job of satirizing the over-blown orchestral scores of the *Twilight Saga* (and many similar Hollywood movies). But Lennertz also under-scores many of the scenes with appropriate music – slightly off-kilter, suspenseful strings, for instance, for scenes where Becca's becoming fascinated by Edward.[21] And there are some specially written quasi-indie/ alt. rock songs. And some hiphop, the go-to sounds for all Friedberg and Seltzer movies. (The soundtrack of *Vampires Suck* included Alana D., Magicwandos, Miss Righty 6, Barnetta, Revival Chiefs, Marilyn Manson, Dandielle Barbe, and the Weather Girls).

Some of the songs in *Vampires Suck* parody the emo/ Goth/ indie music that *Twilight* is full of (Stephenie Meyer's beloved Muse, Placebo and Foo Fighters. Meyer included playlists for the *Twi-hard* books). It's

19 Pattinson preens and plays with his hair *a lot* in the *Twilight* films.
20 Michael T. Ryan was supervising music ed.; Rebekah Touma was music coordinator; Dave Jordan and Jojo Villanueva were music supervisors.
21 'I was consumed by the mystery Edward presented. And more than a little obsessed by Edward himself.' (*Twilight*, 57)

the white, angst-ridden rock of the alienated, disaffected youth of Middle America. The song 'My Panties'[22] by Magicwandos include the lines:

> I feel so lonely,
> Nobody gets me,
> I am so unhappy.

I loved the entry into the town of Sporks, where every store is vamp-related and even the bums will work for blood; I loved the playlists on Becca's I-Pod which include playlists entitled 'I Hate Life', 'Loathe Ya' and 'Teen Angst' (genius!);[23] I loved Bobby White and Frank beating each other up in the background of the early scene where Becca meets Jacob;[24] I loved Edward in a biohazard suit[25] in the biology class; I loved Edward juggling an apple, bowling ball and baby; I loved the 'Angst-o-Meter', which Becca's Pa Frank (Diedrich Bader) uses to measure his daughter's anxiety level in the nightmare scene; I loved Jacob's teabag – the 'rebound guy';[26] I loved Jacob and the wolves demolishing the last Nomad vampire; I loved Edward stripping down to bling jewellery and a mirrorball for the 'suicide' reveal[27] (and for the diamond skin reveal); I loved the kids in the car lot throwing stuff at sad, loser new girl Becca, dissing her tomboy clothes and her hair and the cheerleaders kicking her;[28] I loved the giant cactus that Becca takes to Sporks; I loved the bedroom scene where Edward drools over Becca asleep, murmuring about how just the fact that she's breathing gives him joy, and she farts (he topples out of the window); I loved Becca sleepwalking; I loved Edward showing his killer instincts with a squirrel!;[29] I loved Becca in her sexy outfit (pre-empting scenes in 2011's *Breaking Dawn*); I loved Becca's interior monologue about wanting 'to hump the shit' out of Edward; I loved the other voice appearing in the pretentious voiceover (spouting dialogue as inane as in *Twilight*); I loved Becca's Dad Frank training Becca in self-defence (and getting maced and beaten up); I loved Becca kicking and screaming like a baby[30] when Edward leaves her;[31] I loved the stupid self-help books for lonely, jilted teenagers that Becca consults; I loved the

---

22 Heard when the Becca and her Pa enter the town in the cruiser.
23 There is more of the emo song in the deleted scenes.
24 Including their sarcastic versions of fake male camaraderie prior to the bust-up.
25 Such a suit is mentioned in the *Twilight Saga* as something that Bella might wear against the weather.
26 'He was my best friend. I would always love him, and it would never, ever be enough.' (*New Moon*, 219).
27 Reminding us how silly the 'suicide' scene in *New Moon* is!
28 When someone stuck a 'Kick Me' sign on her back.
29 Edward shoots Alice to demonstrate his killer instinct (this was probably a late addition to the script because the Walt Disney *Alice In Wonderland* movie was released in Mch, 2010).
30 'He was gone... Love, life, meaning... over' (*New Moon*, 73).
31 This could've gone further, with a series of failed suicide attempts.

couples walking outside Becca's place, dressed like Edward, and with Edward's stupid pop idol hair (even children, and dogs!); I loved Frank keeping Becca's room as it was when she was a kid; I loved Becca's Pa with his sex doll as her new Mom; I loved the running battles between Team Jacob and Team Edward fans; and I loved Iris/ Alice (Crista Flanagan) guiltily trying to explain why Edward would try to do something crazy (exposing the holes in the plots of the *Twi-hard Saga* revolving around Alice and her visions).

There are cel phone jokes, too – about online and social media guff like Facebook and Twitter. And the mandatory jokes about Canadians: they slip over the borders, come here and do the awful jobs that Americans are too lazy to do, and now they're eating our people – yup, Canadians.[32] Or is it Mexicans? (For some comedians, they are interchangeable; it's Mexicans in the deleted scenes).

The bedroom scene in *Vampires Suck* is marvellous – it takes a familiar scenario of farce comedy – the eager teenage girl and the reluctant guy in a room – and runs with it. The scene in *Twilight* (the book and the film) is already very close to parody; in *Vampires Suck,* the script exaggerates Becca's desire in very amusing ways. And it adds unexpected twists, like Edward's boyish delight after the kiss (he's never even got to first base). And, this being Seltzer and Friedberg, the seduction scene can only end in multiple slapstick beats – Edward hurling Becca thru the ceiling by accident, and Becca being pounded by debris.

The filmmakers of *Vampires Suck* have got so many aspects of the *Twilight* movies spot-on, with uncannily accurate recreations of so many iconic moments from the films, plus of course their own alterations and additions. They got Bella Swan's house, the bedroom, the school,[33] the car lot, the forest, the town, the beat-up truck, and the cast of secondary characters dead-on (the location managers[34] and the casting director did a fine job sourcing all of this, and the DP, production designer, set decorator, props guy, the costume designer,[35] the hair and make-up people, too). There are helicopter shots of piney terrain, and of course the mandatory images of cars on country roads, which comprise 80% of the running time of each *Twilight* movie.

Indeed, some of the scenes in *Vampires Suck* are *superior* to those in the *Twilight* series: the school Prom Night, for example, is a far more satisfying scene (not least because it features more dancing and more

32 Director Aaron Seltzer is Canadian.
33 Sporks High School, Home of the Bloodsuckers.
34 Gregory McNamara was location scout.
35 Every frame of *Twilight* was examined very closely, and skilfully replicated in the parody version. Look at the dark green top that Bella wears in the lab scene – the spoof reproduces it perfectly.

music, which's one of the specialities of the Friedberg-Seltzer approach to movie spoofs, and also because that's where (improbably but logically)[36] they stage the finale). Yes, parody movies *can* improve on the original movie. Why? Because they can see what the original film did, and develop it (thus, *Vampires Suck* can also be regarded as a sequel movie to the 2008 *Twilight*).

The attention to detail in *Vampires Suck* is remarkable, too: the spoof emulates not only the scenes but also some of the same shots. The filmmakers have clearly seen the *Twilight* movies many times, printed out stills (screen shots, not on-set publicity photos), and studied every aspect of the *Twilight* productions to get their spoof movie dead-on.

It's the fans, the Twi-hards, the Twilighters, the fanpires, who carry the first joke in *Vampires Suck,* when it opens with an amusing spoof of the finale of *New Moon*, with Becca hurrying thru crowds of red-robed extras[37] in a sunny, Italianate square. The rabid Team Jacob and Team Edward fans converge and beat each other up. Edward strips down to nudity (complete with mirrorball over the genitals). Best of all, the ridiculous Zolturi hover about.

In *Vampires Suck,* the post-cinema scene from *Twilight* (where Jessica rants about the zombiefest *Dawn of the Dead*, 1978) used *Breaking Dawn* (of course), due to be released the year after *Vampires Suck* (in 2011). Loudmouth Jennifer shoots off about how predictable *Breaking Dawn* is, and uses a spoiler gag: 'I never thought they'd get married and have a kid!' And one of the many Twi-hards in the theatre queue yells, 'thanks for the spoiler, dipshit!'[38]

▲

One of the dumbest sections of a recent film franchise is the part of *New Moon* (the book and the movie) where the heroine sinks into suicidal depression. As the 2006 *New Moon* novel puts it, when Edward leaves, it's all over. The second act of *Twilight: New Moon* portrays Bella Swan as completely lost to herself and to everything around her. For months. As her Pa Charlie Swan says, it's not natural to be so withdrawn (Charlie tells her: he's not coming back. As Frank tells his daughter in *Vampires Suck,* that was the best piece of ass she'll ever get, and she won't get it again).

Being manically depressed is one thing, but La Meyer's *New Moon* novel has the jilted heroine becoming an adrenalin junkie – riding

---

36 The film combines the Prom night with the Italian escapade.
37 And in *New Moon*, many of those 850 extras were played by Twi-fans who'd travelled to Montepulciano in Tuscany (most of them were women).
38 *The Simpsons* employed this gag – about Darth Vader being Luke Skywalker's father in *The Empire Strikes Back,* during a Homer flashback sequence.

motorcycles recklessly, hanging out with scary biker dudes, and even jumping off cliffs.

Come on! This is a mousey, timid, weedy girl who can't even return a volleyball! And she's going to ride motorbikes now and leap off cliffs into the freezing sea? This completely preposterous scenario in *New Moon* was a gift to comedy writers – *Vampires Suck* has Becca happily snipping the brake lines on a motorbike, and riding blindfolded, and on one leg, and singing with a guitar. (*Vampires Suck* didn't bother with the cliff-jumping sequence – too costly and too much hassle. And the point had already been made with the motorcycle gags).

▲

The finale of *Vampires Suck* combined the ends of *Twilight* and *New Moon*, so that the school Prom was fused with Edward at Volterra. In *Vampires Suck,* though, it's a scene where many characters can be brought together for a curtain call (they don't appear like this in the *Twilight* movies, such as Becca's Pa Frank). The finale also includes the highpoint of *Breaking Dawn*, of Bella becoming a vampire.

The finale of *Vampires Suck* adds plenty of action to the novels, as the Zolturi converge on Edward, and also a Friedberg and Seltzer speciality: dancing and music. You can't have too much music in a Friedberg and Seltzer movie, so as Edward and Daro tussle, they bump into the DJ booth (repeatedly), causing the needle to jump, leading to several musical numbers, including 'The Hustle' by the 26th Street Boyz, 'On Fire' by Classic and 'All Thru the Night' by Tony Lyndsay (all on one vinyl album!).

Ken Jeong delivers a silly, campy version of Michael Sheen's even sillier turn as the venal vampire overlord Aro Volturi in the *Twilight Saga* (there is more of Jeong's Daro in the deleted scenes).

▲

Vampires Suck was wonderful in the way it exposed the subtexts in the *Twilight Saga*, the subtexts that the whole of contemporary, Hollywood cinema trades on, but likes to pretend aren't there. For instance, the powerful sexual attraction that Becca has for Edward (down to her wearing black lingerie with flashing stop-and-go lights in the bra cups!, and seducing her man), and for Jacob (when he rips off his shirt and sits on her bed), and she, of course, bites her lip and can't stop staring at him; and the homoerotic subtext of the topless werewolves.

There is some clever stepping around budgetary issues, too in *Vampires Suck*: for instance, the digital werewolves in the *Twilight* flicks are *incredibly* expensive to produce (and involve teams of well-paid visual effects folk). The solution is *Vampires Suck* is simple: Jacob soars through the air to save Becca from the Nomad vamp and transforms into... a tiny chihuahua dog! Followed by his buddies, four shirtless guys who launch into a camp boy band routine for 'It's Raining Men' by the Weather Girls (which Friedberg and Seltzer had already used in *Meet the Spartans*). Meanwhile, for vampire speed, which involves cables, special rigs, and plenty more costly visual effects in bigger budget flicks, *Vampires Suck* simply has Edward riding a Segway (and it uses exactly the same techniques that *Twilight* employed – hiding rigs and the like behind logs).[39] And Jacob runs like the apes in *Planet of the Apes* (2001) – on wires).

The budgetary issue is interesting, because the *Vampires Suck* crew delivered a movie pretty much the same as the first two *Twilight* movies, but for half the price ($20 million for *Vampires Suck* as against the $38m that the first *Twilight* movie cost, and $50 million for *New Moon*). It's true that there aren't as many locations in *Vampires Suck* (no ocean scene,[40] for instance, or – *duh!* – Italy), not as many pricey visual effects (but there are many visual effects), not as many extras in the crowd or at school (tho' quite a few), and no stars (but the *Twilight* movies didn't really have many stars, apart from, say, Michael Sheen).

So what made the first *Twilight* flick twice as expensive as *Vampires Suck*? One factor is the cost of the rights to the Stephenie Meyer books. Plus costs like locations, visual effects,[41] music rights, and extras. And of course the talent. By the time of the second *Twilight* movie, everybody's fees would've gone up (the budget of the second *Twilight* outing, *New Moon*, for instance, was $50 million).

Clever guys, Jason Friedberg and Aaron Seltzer – *Vampires Suck* also included witty and intelligent deconstructions of the recent vampire phenomenon (and there are swipes at *The Vampire Diaries*,[42] *Buffy*, *Dracula*, *True Blood*,[43] etc). And analyses of just why the *Twilight Saga* should appeal to teenage girls (the attraction to Edward plus the prohibition of getting it on with him). *Vampires Suck* is thus not only a parody of the *Twilight Saga*, it also takes on vampire cinema, and contemplates how vampire mythology has become popular once again.

Vampires Suck was another movie written and directed by Jason

---

39 The build-up to the reveal of the Segway includes shots exactly like those in *Twilight*, where the mechanics of cinema are hidden behind trees.
40 In the first *Twilight* film, that scene was shot in one day – a day of such terrible weather that the backers imagined the production would cancel it. They didn't, they ploughed on.
41 Yet *Vampires Suck* achieved a glittering diamond effect for Edward, as well as wirework.
42 A book in the science class.
43 *True Blood* is on a bottle label.

Friedberg and Aaron Seltzer which was panned by critics, loathed by critics, denounced as the Spawn of Satan by critics. It's juicily ironic, because those same critics had also scorned the *Twilight* movies. (Yet, even tho' the *Twilight Saga* was regarded by film critics as witless junk for lonely, teenage girls, that wasn't enough for the critics to enjoy *Vampires Suck*).

'This movie sucks more,' summed up *Rolling Stone*'s Pete Travers, in a famous review.

I've tried to find a major movie critic who *likes* the movies helmed by Jason Friedberg and Aaron Seltzer, but I haven't found one yet! Owen Gleiberman (*Entertainment Weekly*) is one of the very few critics who admits to enjoying them (tho' others have confessed to guilty chuckles). Instead, there is an astonishing amount of poison directed at these directors. C*rr*itics accuse Friedberg and Seltzer of all sorts of odious crimes:

- like (1) feeding off other people's efforts (what, like, critics don't do that?!),
- like (2) pouring scorn on the movies they spoof (what, like, critics don't pour scorn on every frigging thing they see?!),
- like (3) making cheap jokes at other people's expense (what, like, critics don't do that?!),
- like (4) dumbing down popular culture (what, like, 99% of Hollywood's output each year doesn't do that?!),
- like (5) pandering to the lowest common denominator (what, like, 99% of Hollywood's output each year doesn't do that?!),
- like (6) somehow damaging the film industry itself with their nasty, crude attempts at 'entertainment' (what, like, critics don't do that?! like, *duh*, 99% of Hollywood movies aren't doing that?! The notion that a handful of parody movies could 'damage' the vast, global entertainment business is ridiculous!).

And many audiences loved it: these quotes are from Metacritic:

This was the Best Movie Ever! it was hilarious! ... I heard almost all of the people laughing like hell in the movie theatre.

-

Yes, it's a stupid movie. Yes, it's a bad movie. But it's still so funny!!

-

I could not stop laughing after seeing this movie. It was absolutely PERFECT for people like me who couldn't stand the *Twilight* franchise and it was a movie that needed to be made.

9

BREAKING WIND

Breaking Wind (Craig Moss, 2012) was a send-up of *Breaking Dawn, Part 1* (Bill Condon, 2011), as well as many other moments from the *Twilight Saga*. It was produced by Bernie Gewissler and Craig Moss, and written and directed by Moss for Lionsgate. It starred Heather Ann Davis, Eric Callero, Danny Trejo and Frank Pacheco. Released: Jan 13, 2012. 82 mins.

This was the second *Twilight Saga* movie spoof released in theatres (the first being *Vampires Suck* in 2010). With a higher M.P.A.A. rating than *Vampires Suck* (an 'R', which the *Twilight* movies themselves should've been), *Breaking Wind* was keen to explore cruder jokes. Fart jokes (a *lot* of fart jokes!), blowjob jokes, gay sex, sex toys – *Breaking Wind* was very much in the vein of the Jason Friedberg and Aaron Seltzer and Zucker-Abrahams-Zucker spoof movie mold.

Heather Ann Davis gave a spirited version of Kristen Stewart's emo victim girl in the *Twihard Saga*, and Eric Callero (as Edward) and Frank Pacheco (as Jacob) offered plenty of fun moments. The spirit of *Breaking Wind* was delightfully silly: it's always great to see a movie which doesn't take itself seriously *at all*. Because even those American movies that are classed as comedies still want to tell a story and create drama (romantic comedies are a good example: they typically want to be funny and lighthearted, but they also want the audience to invest in the characters and the romantic themes).

In most recent North American movies, there's a point where they *stop* and won't go any further. They explore close to the edge, but then they recoil, and return to base, to home, to safety, to the Great American Dream. No matter how *crazeee* a typical Hollywood movie is, it will come back to base and it will re-affirm the family, the law, marriage, education, the military, capitalism and money, and the American Way of Life.

And after a while you get *sick* of that. Like, is that *all* there is? Only the American Way of Life, for anybody living anywhere in the world? So at the end of a Big, Loud Action Movie, or a fantasy blockbuster flick featuring weirdos with pointy ears, or a romantic comedy about a smug, self-satisfied New York couple, there will always be the scene, the shot, the facial expression, the music, the sound, the visual effect or the image which expresses that Return Home, that re-affirmation of Good Ol' American Capitalism, to send its audience out of the theatre happy and self-assured, back to their cars, to the shopping mall, to the bar, to the subway…

❄

Once again in a spoof movie, *Breaking Wind* didn't need to do much except replay some of the key scenes in *Breaking Dawn, Part 1* to expose just how preposterous the whole vampire genre is, and how lame the *Twilight Saga* is when you examine it closely (yes, you have to admit, *Twilight* is a very lame, very dumb, very useless franchise! But that's partly what we love about it! And it is also, in its own way, compelling and even great).

I loved Rosalie so resenting Becca in *Breaking Wind* that she attempts to kill her a number of times, whinges about her being so fucking irritating, and kicks her over a balcony where she crashlands on a table: 'Jesus Christ, why don't you die, bitch?!' I loved the 'Team Jacob' and 'Team Edward' stickers that Jacob and Edward plaster on people at school.[44] I loved the werewolves as overweight guys, with Jacob perpetually snacking, and always referring to his priceless abs (a wonderful send-up of the gym-honed bodies that male stars desperately try to develop for the cameras). I loved Becca's Pa blethering on about gay sex. I loved Carlisle trying to show the group gathered for training about the newbie vampires on his laptop computer, but not being able to get past the idiot captcha password.[45] I loved the mini versions of the Sullens. I loved the send-up of the ridiculous tent scene in *Twilight*, with Jacob humping Becca in the sleeping bag (and Becca's wide awake and loving it).

And more: I loved the filmmakers in *Breaking Wind* turning Becca's sexual desire (which's what powers so much of the *Twilight Saga* along), into something explicit: so she's got dildos in her cupboards, porn mags

---
44 *Breaking Wind* saluted the fans, too, with snippets at the end of the film of fans.
45 We all hate those!

on her bed (big black men, of course!), and falls asleep reading *The Art of Fellatio* (meanwhile, she has nightmares of her granny going down on Edward, in a send-up of the opening scenes of *Breaking Dawn, Part 1*, and *New Moon*).[46] Later in the 2012 parody movie, Becca's dressed as a stripper, gyrating around a pole, to get Edward in the mood (echoing *Breaking Dawn, Part 1*, where our Bella tries to turn on Edward wearing lingerie. But *Breaking Wind*, like *Vampires Suck*, is *far* superior in this regard, and many others).

And even more: I loved the use of the same helicopter shot, over forests and a lake, towards a snowy mountain. I loved the *Twilight*-style voiceover over those images, including Becca wittering on about absolutely bugger all for 60 seconds, and also Becca using her vibe to masturbate, before she realizes the mic's on.

And more and more: I loved the werewolves' flashback, where we see four of the famous characters that Johnny Depp's played in recent movies, including Edward Scissorhands, Willy Wonka (from *Charlie and the Chocolate Factory*), the Mad Hatter (from *Alice In Wonderland*) and of course Jack Sparrow (from *Pirates of the Caribbean*), standing in for the dreaded vampires who attack some Native Americans in a very silly, OTT fight scene.

Sure, *Breaking Wind* was a lower budget production than the movie it was lampooning (by some way! *Breaking Dawn Part 1*'s budget was at least $110 million). But it didn't matter: *Breaking Wind*, like *Vampires Suck,* reminded us once again that if you take away the vampires and the werewolves in the *Twilight Saga*, you've got nothing more'n another story about kids and high schools and dating and the 10,000 Agonies of Being a Teenager. That's all.

And *Breaking Wind*, in the flashback, with the Johnny Depp characters, reminded us that a movie is simply just that: people dressing up and acting out stories. That's all. Cinema is just storytelling. And it doesn't make the slightest bit of difference to the audience if the storytelling costs $20,000 or $2 million or $200 million. Who gives a hoot? It's just a story! And who cares if it was written, directed, acted and produced by well-known, multi-talented and highly-paid show business veterans, or by a bunch of actors and crew paid at the S.A.G./ Equity day rates? It's just a goddam story! It's just storytelling!

There are limits to low budget versions of high budget Hollywood fare, and that's of course in elements such as stars, exotic locations, 100s of extras, and visual effects. But a lot of the vampire visual effects in the

---

46 The nightmare repeats, with Edward humping granny.

Twilight Saga were achieved with editing and sound effects, two cheap ways of making something look and sound good (a rapid cut, or speeding up film, plus a whooshy sound effect). But putting werewolves on screen, that means millions of $$$$$. While *Vampires Suck* got around that by using a chihuahua dog, *Breaking Wind* didn't bother – no need, you just ignore the issue, and stick to your fat slob pack of guys, and add more fart sounds.

THE HILLYWOOD SHOW

The Hillywood Show produced several brilliant musical spoofs of the *Twilight* franchise. *The Hillywood Show* was founded in 2006 by two sisters, Hannah (b. 1986) and Hilary 'Hilly' Hindi (b. 1990) on the YouTube channel and similar media outlets. The Hindi sisters lead a bunch of friends and enthusiasts in their entertaining spoofs of pop culture franchises. Working out of Las Vegas, the Hindis created elaborate, amazingly detailed parodies with very low budgets (complete with impressive costumes, make-up, hair, sets, etc), taking on franchises such as *Harry Potter, Supernatural, Batman, The Vampire Diaries* and *The Lord of the Rings*, and pop stars such as Lady Gaga. For *Twilight*, the Hindis choreographed their send-up and *hommage* with mass dances (to the sound of Katy Perry's 'Hot N Cold'),[47] focussing mainly on the cafeteria scenes, but including many other iconic scenes from the first *Twilight* film. *The Hillywood Show* went on to parody the rest of the *Twilight* movies, with each spoof becoming more elaborate (and longer). The girls were delighted when *Twilight* director Catherine Hardwicke praised their parody.

---

47 The lyrics – 'you're hot, then you're cold, you're yes, then you're no', suit Edward's personality.

ALCUNE SAGHE NON MUOIONO MAI.

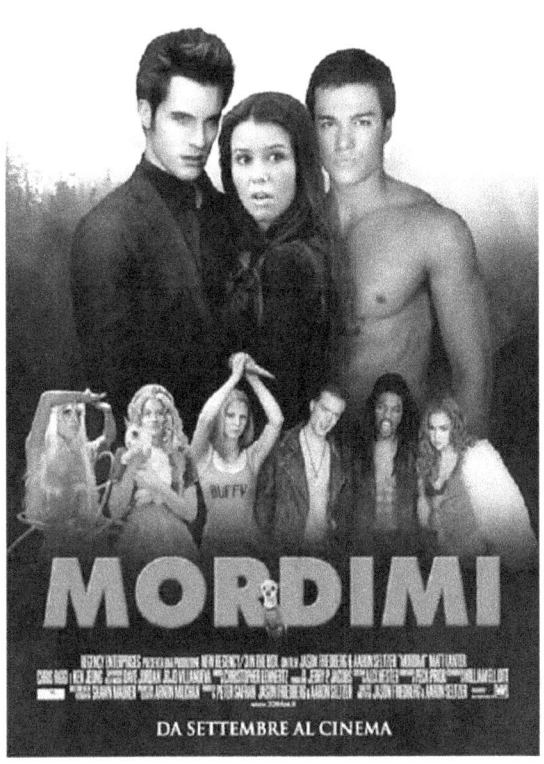

Vampires Suck (2010)

ERIC CALLERO FRANK PACHECO HEATHER DAVIS EMMA BELL DANNY TREJO

breaking wind
Part 1

JACOB

DVD VIDEO

THE LINGER IS ONLY THE BEGINNING

15

Breaking Wind (2012).

APPENDIX

MOVIES LINKED TO
THE *TWILIGHT SAGA*

THE HUNGER GAMES

The Hunger Games (Gary Ross, 2012) was a piece of adolescent claptrap cobbled together from *Lord of the Flies, The Truman Show, Westworld, The Running Man, Battle Royale,*[1] reality TV and Ancient Rome. Based on the 2008 book by Suzanne Collins, *The Hunger Games* comes over as a third-rate TV movie but far less fun (too fucking long and no ad breaks! It is an excruciating 142 minutes). A limp, bloodless satire on North America's slack-jawed consumption of reality television (and the media in general), and groups of people lost on islands, and a bunch of silly games in which death is the only way out.

How this abysmal movie ever grossed over $400 million[2] is a complete mystery. Further installments inevitably appeared in 2013 (*Catching Fire*) and 2014 and 2015 (*Mockinjay, Part 1* and *2* – the studio (Lionsgate/ Color Force) took the $uper-cynical *Harry Potter* and *Twilight* route of splitting the last movie into two).[3] And a 5th outing arrived in 2023: *We Fooled You Four Times Before, Now Here's More!*

Many, many aspects of *The Hunger Games* rankled *avec moi:*

Let's start with the deeply irritating New Agey music, with the female singer (Mariana Tootsie)[4] cooing plaintively (James Newton Howard was composer). This was simply *horrible.*

---

1 Have a look at the *manga* of *Battle Royale* if you fancy seeing a *really* grossly violent version of this sort of story. *Battle Royale* is also a 1999 novel (and later movie) by Koushun Takami.
2 And the movie franchise as a whole grossed $2,968 million.
3 Like *The Maze Runner* and *Twilight, The Hunger Games* led to a book series, and a movie series.
4 What a stupid name!

The idea that Westerners will suddenly descend into near-savagery over the course of a few decades in the near future needs a more convincing set-up and explanation. Atomic bombs usually do the trick.

Katniss Everdene as played by Jennifer Lawrence is an 'emo' teenager, a sister to Bella Swan in the *Twilight Saga* and Anastasia in *50 Shades of Grey*. Desperately unappealing, always sombre, seldom smiling, and taking herself *so* seriously, Katpiss was the sort of character, like Bella, that you want to *slap*. So drippy, so useless. (The rest of the cast included Woody Harelson, Liam Hemsworth, Josh Hutcherson, Stanley Tucci and Donald Sutherland).

It's the same audience as the *Twilight Saga* (and the *Harry Potter* movies): girls in their teens and the dates (or brothers) they persuaded to come along to the theatre to watch a tomboy girl show a weedy boy how to kick ass and survive in the wilds.

A girl with a bow and arrow!

Well, *hell*, it makes a change, I guess, from Jean-Luc Godard's 'a girl and a gun'.

She's a girl with a bow and an arrow! She hunts deer for her family! (Oh, for *fuck's sake*!). And Peter's[5] always *lerrrved* her from afar! Well, smash me over the head with a brick! Gouge out my eyes with rusty knitting needles! Don't make me sit thru this junk!

There are so many irritating moments in *The Hunger Games*, so many scenes which don't convince on any level whatsoever. But this humourless piece of dreck is played so stinkingly earnest and desperate to be 'worthy' or 'meaningful', you can't even laugh *at* it.

Actors walk and walk thru endless landscapes – one of the surest signs of clueless filmmakers. Listen, guys, if you're going to use RAPID EDITING in some scenes, apply that quick cutting to these BORING, second unit shots of performers trudging thru woodland. Cut, cut, cut these scenes!

I could point out hundreds of dopey incidents in *The Hunger Games*. One will suffice: a group of nasty teens chase our heroine up a tree (!). Yes, a bloody tree! The bad guy climbs the tree but falls. They shoot two arrows, then give up and go to sleep! Now I'm sure that any kid from the past 100,000 years, from the ages of four to eighteen, could figure out plenty of ways of killing someone who's immobile in a freaking tree!

I can't resist mentioning a couple more clunkers in *The Hunger Games*:

• In this feeble satire on the U.S.A.'s obsession with television (an

---

5 Even the spelling of his name is irritating: 'Peeta'. Just call him 'Peter' already!

addiction of four hours a day is average for Americans), the heroine's good, old boyfriend back home asserts: if people didn't watch it, it would wither. Yes – and you can start by not producing lame movies like this!

• We are told that exposure can kill quicker and surer than a knife in the training sequence. True: exposure to the elements debilitates or kills quicker than going without food or water. So what does our heroine do? She sleeps in a sodding tree! Any kid knows that a tree is a really dumb place to rest up: no shelter, no security, it's freezing, and you can be seen for miles!

• Suicide in *The Hunger Games* is by eating berries! This is like an idiotic eleven year-old's version of a Japanese romantic epic. *Hari kiri* with fruit!

The casting in *The Hunger Games* is bizarre – far odder than the colourful hair and make-up jobs (by Linda Flowers – head of the hair department and Ve Neill,[6] head of the make-up department).[7] Woody Harrelson's alcoholic slacker is acting in a completely different movie (a Seattle grunge-a-thon, perhaps), and Donald Sutherland looks mildly bemused (which, after all, is one of the things that Sutherland can do so well).

The action is simply woeful in *The Hunger Games*. It is filmed in the impressionistic manner of so many recent North American movies, with the camera and lens in far too close, the cutting too rapid, so that you get a series of shots which have no impact, and no dramatic value. Is this to get around the 'PG-13' rating? No! Because plenty of 'PG-13s' have crunching action scenes.

The shaky camerawork – *so fake!* Who invented this kind of camerawork!?: it is in focus, it is well-lit, it is well-composed by the camera operator, but it is shaky. Coupled with rapid editing (with five shots of a single action where one would do just as well), this kind of camerawork is sickening to watch for long periods of time.

If you were *really* going to simulate a 'documentary' feel in cinema, the camerawork would go in and out of focus all the time, the light would blow out the lens or be so dark you couldn't see aught, the framing would be all over the place, important bits would be missed as film/ tapes/ discs/ data/ batteries ran out or failed, and the camera would be *far* shakier than this as the operator tries to keep someone running in the crosshairs.

Also, the sound would be all over the shop: to be authentically 'documentary-like', the sound would dip out or be distorted; it would be

6 Neill is the make-up artist who creates all those wacky looks for Johnny Depp.
7 Or the stupid names – Haymitch Abernathy, Trexler Hoverhound and Peeeeta Mellark.

muffled; there would be wind noise, planes, cars, etc.

In fact, the sound would be like Jean-Luc Godard's 1960s movies, where Godard asked the sound recordist to include everything in a scene with a uni-directional mic. So, in a café scene in *Vivre Sa Vie* or *A Band Apart*, you have *very loud* pinball machines, clattering of plates and cups, the sound of traffic outside, and the sound of people talking. Have you ever sat in a café and *listened* to the sound? It can be deafening! (Try recording a conversation in a busy café).

To be a true 'documentary', recreating filming something that's 'really happening', you'd have to include numerous other technical and stylistic elements. Such as: actors talking *over* each other. This occurs in real life *all the time*, but it's one of the fakest things about cinema (and all drama, theatre, radio, etc), that actors wait for their moment to speak their lines.

Right. Enough. Life is too short for *The Hunger Games*.

SNOW WHITE AND THE HUNTSMAN

Kristen Stewart followed up the *Twilight Saga* with *Snow White and the Huntsman*. A complete flop, *Snow White and the Huntsman* (Universal, 2012) was one of a number of recent movies inspired by fairy tales and reworking them as live-action fantasy movies (others include *Beauty and the Beast*, *Gretel and Hansel*, *Red Riding Hood* and *Alice In Wonderland*).

Among the cast of *Snow White and the Huntsman* were Kristen Stewart, Chris Hemsworth and Charlize Theron, with production by the incredible Joe Roth, L. Boccaccio, G. Borders, H. Hayden, S. Mercer, P. Patel and S. Bradshaw and direction by first-timer Rupert Sanders. Filmed mainly in Britain (based out of Pinewood Studios), *Snow White and the Huntsman* cost an astonishing $170 million.

What a waste of money!

Snow White and the Huntsman is… a series of empty shots, a fairy tale eviscerated of all magic. There's literally *nothing here*, nothing going on. I wait and wait for *something* to happen. But it doesn't.

What a *waste* of time!

Snow White and the Huntsman isn't 'bloated' or over-done or OTT (some of the usual accusations against current blockbuster flicks), it's not 'done' at all (it's uncooked). It's just empty. There really is nothing there at all.

Fairy tale expert Jack Zipes agreed with me: 'a disgrace to filmmaking', he wrote to me in an email.

Oh, sure, *Snow White and the Huntsman* was technically adept – it was in focus, the sound was recorded (or looped) clearly, the visual effects (consuming $$$$$ of the budget) were fun in parts, the second unit shots were pretty,[8] and the creative departments delivered a handsome-looking production. But the direction was indifferent, the acting was so-so or just plain dull, the music (by James Newton Howard) was undistinguished (except for that bizarre choral cue for the wedding ceremony), and…

Oh, who cares?!

We know why *Snow White and the Huntsman* was a total dud: it was *the script*, folks. Yet *again*! The writing credits went to Hossein Aminni, Evan Daugherty and John Hancock. Well, the script, yes – plus the concept, the direction, the staging, the acting, and some of the casting.

After 30 minutes in *Snow White and the Huntsman,* still *nothing* had happened. And they had already spent *$40 million!*

Thirty minutes equals $40 million of the $170 million budget! Imagine giving $40 million to a host of companies around the world, and asking them to come up with a compelling 30 minutes of entertainment! I'm sure Cirque du Soleil, any firework manufacturer, any Las Vegas show, could put on a glorious slice of entertainment lasting 30 minutes for $40 million! (And in Hong Kong cinema, you could have *thirty* new movies for $170 million!).[9]

But this Hollywood movie *can't.* Even when it is spending $1,400,000 *a minute*, it *still can't* make a movie entertaining! ($40 million for 30 minutes is higher than the budget of the TV shows of the Oscars or the Grammys, surely!). Incredibly, a sequel appeared in 2016.

Who was *Snow White and the Huntsman for*? *Twilight* fans desperate for more Kristen Stewart? Not family audiences – it was too violent and too downbeat for them. For middle-aged audiences? No! They've seen this movie 100,000 times! For twenty-somethings, then? No, it was too slow and too boring for them. It must be for girls aged 12-16, and the dates or brothers or friends that they could fool into coming along to the theatre. Plus maybe some lonely, older 'emo' girls.

What a waste of time!

---

8 Wales and the Lake District were among the locations.
9 Give that 170 million bucks to 170 new filmmakers, one million each, to make a *new, original* movie.

Charlize Theron played the Wicked Queen (Ravenna) as a shouty, frowny, wannabe diva. But Theron is about as threatening as a villain as a cup of tea. Yet this should've been *her* movie. (Meanwhile, despite all of her efforts, like all villains in Hollywood flicks, she is still a miserable S.O.B.)

Movie villains often have a fatal flaw. They don't *do* anything. I mean beyond acting as movie villains, and antagonists, providing the obstacles and oppositions which help to drive the plot.

Apart from that, they are fatally left without anything to do. Evil Queen Ravenna in *Snow White and the Huntsman* is a good example: every time we see her, she is in her big circular tower. Doing nothing. Occasionally she slinks out to the balcony, to gloat over her queendom.

Jeez, she *really* needs to find something to do! Get a job, girl! If she was as busy as everybody else in the realm, she wouldn't have the time (or energy!) to angst about her fading beauty. Or is this a portrait of a middle-aged woman who's been surgically detached from her cel phone and has no idea what to do?

Snow White and the Huntsman is couched very much in the model of the Hallmark adaptations of literary classics (they did *Snow White* with Kristen Kreuk in 2001). Launched by the Halmis, Hallmark Entertainment delivered a series of family-oriented TV specials and movies based on classic texts, with fairy tales and fantasy prominent, such as *Gulliver's Travels, Snow Queen, 20,000 Leagues Under the Sea* and *Alice In Wonderland.*

You cast a pretty, young, North American actress as Snow White, an older-but-still-attractive middle-aged woman as the Queen (Miranda Richardson in the Hallmark *Snow White*), and a bunch of character actors for the dwarfs. You add tons of action and visual effects, edit it at TV pace, and update the story and dialogue.

Snow White and the Huntsman is a Hallmark or TV movie-style production, with more expensive visual effects, a few more extras, and costlier costumes and sets, but why it cost $170 million is a mystery.

And *Snow White and the Huntsman* was fatally humourless.[10] Hell, why is every fantasy action movie of recent times about as humorous as waking up in a morgue over Christmas? Why does everyone have to look so bloody morose? Not just the villains and their creepy, vaguely incestuous relationship (Brother Dork and Sister Vamp), but everyone else? Oh yes, I forgot: when Ravenna attained the throne, the land was laid to waste.

---

10 The only attempts at humour occurred with the dwarfs. But not much, and not very well done anyway.

What a waste of energy!

22 year-old Kristen Stewart is an appealing, intense Snow White. Not a Princess at all, more a glowering, skinny, 'emo' late teenager with buck teeth. Stewart throws herself into the role, but she seems to be playing Bella Swan in the *Twilight* series. (And *Twilight* fans were outraged with their Bella was seen kissing the middle-aged director of the movie, Rupert Sanders, in public, apparently betraying the dearly beloved Robert Pattinson).

This is a movie where the heroine escapes from a heavily-guarded castle in daylight by diving down a culvert, wading thru water, and jumping into the sea. And not one of the guards pursuing her follows her into the drain! [11] (This is a movie, also, where the heroes stage a ridiculous cavalry charge on a castle along a beach! Haven't they seen *El Cid*?!).

TRUE BLOOD

True Blood was a Home Box Office TV series that launched in 2008 about vampires and humans in present day Louisiana (where parts of the later *Twilight* films were made). Executive produced by H. Deutsch, R. DesHotel, M. Hudis, A. Robinson, A. Woo, N. Oliver, R. Tucker, G. Finberg, A. Ball, B. Buckner and an coven of 17 other assoc./ co. and assist. producers. It was based on Charlaine Harris's *Southern Vampire Mysteries* series (2001-2013), and created by Alan Ball.

Famous for its sex scenes and bad language (i.e., it's a typical Home Box Office production, where cable/ satellite TV outlets can get away with more than network TV), *True Blood* was actually conventional and traditional. Yes, and it even had a romance between a special girl and a handsome vampire at the heart of it.

True Blood portrayed a scuzzy, lived-in, trailer park *milieu* of the American South, where the nights are loud with bugs, and everybody gathers at a diner. No one shaves, everyone slouches, and the sarcastic, antsy dialogue (masking deep-seated hostilities) is the best part of the show.

True Blood shared many affinities with the *Twilight Saga*: vampires in modern-day North America; a romance between a young woman and an

---

11 Not only that, this bleeding obvious flaw in the castle's designs is employed during the climactic battle to let the dwarfs in.

older vampire; mind-reading; sexed-up vampires (the *Twilight Saga* contains just as much S/M as *True Blood*!); and there was even the real-life relationship between Anna Paquin and Stephen Moyer (as the leads), reflecting that of Robert Pattinson and Kristen Stewart in the *Twilight Saga*. (However, nothing in the pilot episode of *True Blood* persuaded me to watch any more).

THE VAMPIRE DIARIES

No need for a TV version of *Twilight* – *The Vampire Diaries* has already done it.

The TV series *The Vampire Diaries* (2009-2017) looked as if a business mogul in Gotham or L.A. had seen in the media trades how much $$$$ the *Twilight* movie had made, and summoned his lackeys to a meeting, telling them from behind his giant oak desk:

'Get me one of these.'

If you didn't know that *The Vampire Diaries* had started out as a book series first published in 1991 (authored by L.J. Smith), you might be forgiven for thinking it had been cooked up by some television executives at one of the U.S.A.'s numerous TV stations in direct response to the massive succe$$ of the *Twilight* novels and the first *Twilight* movie.

The Vampire Diaries was adapted from some books for teens, sure, but it was produced in the wake of the *Twilight* phenomenon (and it certainly benefitted from surge of interest in supernatural romance yarns that the *Twilight* phenomenon spearheaded). Created by Kevin Williamson (best-known for *Scream* and *Dawson's Creek*) and Julie Plec, plus an undead brigade of 47 other producers (co-., assoc., sup. and exec-producers)[12] for C.B.S./ Warner (a.k.a. the C.W. channel),[13] scripted by a ghoul army of 43 screenwriters (including Brian Young, Matthew D'Ambrisio, Neil Reynolds and Caroline Dries), and directed by a zombie battalion of 46 directors (inlcuding Marcos Siega, Michael Allowitz, Joshua Butler and Chris Grismer), *The Vampire Diaries* ran for eight series (171 shows) and also led to some spin-off series (*The Originals* and *Legacies*).

---

12 47!
13 Along with Alloy/ Outerbanks/ Bonanza.

The Vampire Diaries is a classy production with a really striking number of similarities with the *Twilight Saga*. By halfway through the pilot episode (tx Sept 10, 2009), we've already seen these scenes filched from the *Twi*-series: cars driving in forests at night; a vampire attack; a high school; plenty of cute girls and cute boys; a mysterious, smoulderingly handsome vampire (who's also a transfer student – and a stalker); an introspective heroine (and would-be writer – she's the diarist of the show), played by Nina Dobrev; witty, pop culture-drenched dialogue among groups of girls; romantic triangles; a girl with prophetic abilites; classroom scenes; corridor and locker scenes; the small-town environment; and plenty more.

The Vampire Diaries also shares many other affinities with the *Twilight Saga*, outside of the story and the characters, such as the production values, the visual approach, the indie/ alt. rock soundtrack, the casting choices, and even some of the same locations (the series was based in Vancouver and Georgia).

The casting of *The Vampire Diaries* was troublesome, as with *Twilight* – Paul Wesley said he auditioned 15 times (15!) before landing the role of the vampire Stefan Salvatore (finding young actors who can play vampires seems to be very challenging. Indeed, producer Kevin Williamson was adamant that Ian Somerhalder played the rival vampire, Damon Salvatore, to the point where he said he would walk if Somerhalder wasn't cast).

I haven't read the many *Vampire Diaries* books or watched the whole 8 series, but you can tell from the pilot episode that *The Vampire Diaries* was going to be a hit – particularly with a young audience hungry (bloodhungry) for more romantic vampireology in between the releases of the *Twilight* movies. *The Vampire Diaries* has the young, attractive cast, the adorable, vulnerable, sensitive Princess (she writes! she knows her literature!), her sad situation (she's recently an orphan), the fashionable clothing, the high school setting, the cuts from pop/ indie music, the slick filmmaking, and the horror movie tropes, including the mandatory vampire speed and stunts.

(Even so, there are some clunky ingredients in the pilot episode of *The Vampire Diaries* – some of the secondary charas, for example, don't compel much (true, they are developed as the series progresses, as the audio commentary from the creators and director informs us). The subplot of the mopey, out-of-control younger brother Jeremy (Steven McQueen) is tiresome. And some of the ex-boyfriends and ex-girlfriends seem interchangeable.)

FANS ON *TWILIGHT* (2008)

INTERNET MOVIE DATABASE

I was blown away and it exceeded my expectations in every respect.

•

This is the best movie I've seen that has stayed the closest to the book as much as it could.

•

I LOVE *Twilight* very much and I will admit I had high expectations going into the movie and I don't think it disappointed.

•

As a film aimed towards teenagers it was very appealing and beautifully filmed. The cinematography was breathtaking. I could not get over the emphasis on eyes and facial expressions. It was sensual in a non provocative way.

•

I was so highly impressed by the film that I bought the book today.

•

I have seen the movie 4 times and am reserving to get the DVD.

•

I am a huge fan of the *Twilight* series, and was very pleased with the movie.

•

I always love going to the first showings of a movie. The true fans come out to those ones. The atmosphere is awesome. When Jacob, Edward, Carlyle, and the other vampires made an entrance, the crowd was screaming and cheering.

•

...a very shallow, tiring, detestable film.

•

I absolutely hated this movie.

•

What a huge disappointment. After the movie ended I wanted my money back.

-

...the most boring film I have seen in a long time.

-

The character of Bella bored me to death in this film. Robert Pattinson was probably the worst actor in this film.

-

I want to say something nice about this movie, but I can't. To say one positive word about this movie would be equivalent to treason. I can't describe how terrible this movie is without inventing new words for it.

FROM METACRITIC

Truly a masterpiece of its genre.

-

I don't care if other poeple hate this because I totally love *Twilight.*

-

One of two: you either love to hate it or you hate to love it.

-

Is it different? Yes. Stupid? Yes. Dull? Yes... but it's my guilty pleasure. I enjoy bad movies.

FROM AMAZON U.S.A.

This is still my favorite movie ever... I loved the books and the movies!

-

Love this movie.

-

Loved everything.

-

I love *Twilight.* Love love love. It's my comfort movie.

-

I love this movie and the characters.

-

This was a beautiful (cinematography), cringey movie romanticizing a psychopathic killer who is abusive to a girl with social problems... The writing and plot were also pretty weak and lame. Lots of bad acting...

-

The beginning is almost unbearably boring, with Edward and Bella exchanging stares and stuttering.

-

Stephenie Meyer just needs to get laid.

CRITICS ON *TWILIGHT* (2008)

A genuine love story might be difficult for a young audience to handle, but this fantasy is blissful madness - an abstinence fable sexier than sex. (*The New Yorker*)

•

As a life lesson for teenage girls, *Twilight* (excuse the pun) sucks. As a parable for the dark side of female desire, it's weirdly powerful. (Dana Stevens, *Slate*)

•

On screen, *Twilight* is repetitive and a tad sodden, too prosaic to really soar. (*Entertainment Weekly*)

•

Despite questionable casting, wooden acting, laughable dialogue and truly awful makeup, nothing is likely to stop young girls from swarming to this kitschy adaptation of Stephenie Meyer's popular novel. (Claudia Puig, *U.S.A. Today*)

•

At times, the dialogue is laugh aloud bad - almost to the point of being hilarious. (*Reel Views*)

•

Watching *Twilight*, I was floored by how earnest all of this was, how seriously everyone involved took what is clearly a horrible, unhealthy, doomed relationship. (*Consequence*)

•

I struggle to remember another 12-certificate [PG-13] film being quite this twisted. (Mark Kermode, *Hatchet Job*, 21).

•

An underwhelming vampire romance long on camp but short on emotional insight. (*Hollywood Reporter*)

FILMOGRAPHY

TWILIGHT

Released: November 21, 2008. 122 mins.
Prod. by Temple Hill/ Maverick/ Imprint for Summit Entertainment.
Prod. by Greg Mooradian, Mark Morgan, Wyck Godfrey, Karen Rosenfelt, Marty Bowen, Guy Oseary and Michelle Stabile.
Scr. Melissa Rosenberg.
Dir. Catherine Hardwicke.

NEW MOON

Released: Nov 20, 2009. 130 mins.
Prod. by Temple Hill/ Maverick/ Imprint/ Summit.
Prod. by Bill Bannerman, Marty Bowen, Guido Cerasuolo, Wyck Godfrey, Kerry Kohansky-Roberts, Greg Mooradian, Mark Morgan, Guy Oseary, David Roker and Karen Rosenfelt.
Scr. Melissa Rosenberg.
Dir. Chris Weitz.

ECLIPSE

Released: June 30, 2010. 124 mins.
Prod. by Temple Hill/ Maverick/ Imprint/ Sunswept/ Summit.
Prod. by Wyck Godfrey, Karen Rosenfelt, Bill Bannerman, Marty Bowen, Greg Mooradian, Mark Morgan, Isaac Klausner and Guy Oseary.
Scr. Melissa Rosenberg.
Dir. David Slade.

BREAKING DAWN, PART 1

Released: Nov 18, 2011. 117 mins.
Prod. by Summit Ent./ Temple Hill.
Prod. by Wyck Godfrey, Karen Rosenfelt, Stephenie Meyer, Marty Bowen,

Guy Oseary, Mark Morgan, Greg Mooradian, Bill Bannerman, Roberto Bakker, Isabelle Tanugi and Carlos Paiva.

Scr. Melissa Rosenberg.

Dir. Bill Condon.

BREAKING DAWN, PART 2

Released: Nov 16, 2012. 116 mins.

Prod. by Summit Ent./ Temple Hill.

Prod. by Wyck Godfrey, Karen Rosenfelt, Stephenie Meyer, Marty Bowen, Barbara Kelly, Mark Morgan, Greg Mooradian, Bill Bannerman and Guy Oseary.

Scr. Melissa Rosenberg.

Dir. Bill Condon.

BIBLIOGRAPHY

STEPHENIE MEYER

Twilight, Atom/ Little, Brown, London, 2007
New Moon, Atom/ Little, Brown, London, 2007
Eclipse, Atom/ Little, Brown, London, 2007
The Host, Sphere, London, 2009
The Short Second Life of Bree Tanner, Atom/ Little, Brown, London, 2010
Breaking Dawn, Atom/ Little, Brown, London, 2010
The Twilight Saga: The Official Illustrated Guide, Atom Books, London, 2011
Life and Death, Atom/ Little, Brown, London, 2015
The Chemist, Little, Brown, 2016

OTHERS

R. Abele. *The Twilight Saga: The Complete Film Archive*, Little, Brown, 2012
L. Albert. *Stephenie Meyer*, Enslow Publishers, 2009
R.C. Allen, ed. *Channels of Discourse: Television and Contemporary Criticism*, Methuen, London, 1987
R. Altman, ed. *Sound Theory, Sound Practice*, Routledge, London, 1992
—. *Film/ Genre*, British Film Institute, London, 1999
G. Anatol, ed. *Bringing Light To Twilight*, Palgrave Macmillan, 2011
D. Andrew. *The Major Film Theories*, Oxford University Press, Oxford, 1976
—. *Concepts In Film Theory*, Oxford University Press, Oxford, 1984
K. Anger. *Hollywood Babylon*, Dell Publishing, New York, NY, 1975
L. Aronson. *Screenwriting Updated*, Silman-James, Los Angeles, CA, 2000
J. Arroyo. *Action/ Spectacle Cinema*, British Film Institute, London, 2000
A. Assister & A. Carol, eds. *Bad Girls and Dirty Pictures: The Challenge To Reclaim Feminism*, Pluto Press, London, 1993
J. Aubrey, J. Stevens, E. Behm-Morawitz, and M.A. Click. "The romanticization of abstinence: Fan response to sexual restraint in the Twilight series", *Transformative Works and Cultures*, no. 5, 2010
W. Aycock & M. Schoenecke, eds. *Film and Literature*, Texas University Press, Austin, TX, 1988
L. Badley. *Film, Horror and the Body Fantastic*, Greenwood Press, Westport, CT, 1995
—. *Writing Horror and the Body: The Fiction of Stephen King, Clive Barker and Anne Rice*, Greenwood Press, Westport, CT, 1996
M. Barker, ed. *The Video Nasties: Freedom and Censorship In the Media*, Pluto Press, London, 1984
—. & J. Petley, eds. *Ill Effects: The Media/ Violence Debate*, Routledge, London, 1997
—. *From Antz To Titanic*, Pluto Press, London, 2000
P. Bart. *The Gross: The Hits, the Flops: The Summer That Ate Hollywood*, St Martin's Press, New York, NY, 1999
—. *Who Killed Hollywood?*, Renaissance Books, Los Angeles, CA, 1999
L. Bawden, ed. *The Oxford Companion To Film*, Oxford University Press, Oxford, 1976
M. Beja. *Film and Literature: An Introduction*, Longman, London, 1979

E. Bell *et al*, eds. *From Mouse To Mermaid: The Politics of Film, Gender and Culture*, Indiana University Press, Bloomington, IN, 1995

H. Benshoff. *Monsters In the Closet: Homosexuality and the Horror Film*, Manchester University Press, Manchester, 1997

J. Bernardoni. *The New Hollywood*, McFarland Press, 1991

M. Bernstein, ed. *Controlling Hollywood: Censorship & Regulation In the Hollywood Studio Era*, Athlone Press, London, 2000

P. Biskind. *Easy Riders, Raging Bulls: How the Sex 'n' Drugs 'n' Rock 'n' Roll Generation Saved Hollywood*, Bloomsbury, London, 1998

—. *Down and Dirty Pictures: Miramax, Sundance and the Rise of Independent Film*, Bloomsbury, London, 2004

C. Bloom, ed. *Gothic Horror*, Macmillan, London, 1998

D. Bordwell & K. Thompson. *Film Art: An Introduction*, McGraw-Hill Publishing Company, New York, NY, 1979

—. *Narration In the Fiction Film*, Routledge, London, 1988

—. *Making Meaning*, Harvard University Press, Cambridge, MA, 1989

—. & N. Caroll, eds. *Post-Theory: Reconstructing Film Studies*, University of Wisconsin Press, Madison, WI, 1996

—. *The Way Hollywood Tells It*, University of California Press, Berkeley, CA, 2006

D. Breskin. *Inner Voices: Filmmakers In Conversation*, Da Capo, New York, 1997

A. Britton *et al*. *American Nightmare: Essays On the Horror Film*, Toronto, 1979

C. Brontë. *Jane Eyre*, Penguin, 1966/ 85

P. Brophy. "Horrality – The Textuality of Contemporary Horror Films", *Screen*, 27, 1, 1986

S. Bruzzi. *Undressing Cinema*, Routledge, London, 1997

N. Burch. *Theory of Film Practice*, Secker & Warburg, London, 1973

G. Burt. *The Art of Film Music*, Northeastern University Press, 1994

M. Bygrave. "Hollywood", *Daily Telegraph*, Mch, 1998

N. Carroll. *Mystifying Movies: Fads and Fallacies of Contemporary Film Theory*, Columbia University Press, New York, NY, 1988

M. Carter, ed. *Dracula: The Vampire and the Critics*, UMI Research Press, Ann Arbor, MI, 1988

D. Cartmell *et al*, eds. *Trash Aesthetics: Popular Culture and Its Audience*, Pluto Press, London, 1997

—. & I. Whelehan, eds. *Adaptions: From Text To Screen, Screen To Text*, Routledge, London, 1999

J. Caughie, ed. *Theories of Authorship: A Reader*, Routledge, London, 1988

—. & A. Kuhn, eds. *The Sexual Subject: A* Screen *Reader In Sexuality*, Routledge, London, 1992

R. Chapman & J. Rutherford, eds. *Male Order: Unwrapping Maculinity*, London, 1988

G. Chester & J. Dickey, eds. *Feminism and Censorship: The Current Debate*, Prism Press, Bridport, Dorset, 1988

Hélène Cixous: *A Hélène Cixous Reader*, ed. Susan Sellers, Routledge, London, 1994

—. & Catherine Clément: *The Newly Born Woman*, tr. Betsy Wing, Manchester University Press, Manchester, 1986

B. Clarke, ed. *The Cinematic City*, Routledge, London, 1997

W. Clayton & S. Harman, eds. *Screening Twilight*, Tauris, 2014

V. Clemens. *The Return of the Repressed*, State University of New York Press, Albany, NY, 1999

Melissa A. Click *et al*, eds. *Bitten by Twilight: Youth culture, media, and the vampire franchise*, Peter Lang, New York, 2010

C. Clover. *Men, Women and Chain Saws: Gender In the Modern Horror Film*, Princeton University Press, Princeton, NJ, 1992

S. Cohan & I.R. Hark, eds. *Screening the Male: Exploring Masculinities In Hollywood Cinema*, Routledge, London, 1993

J. Collins *et al*, eds. *Film Theory Goes To the Movies*, Routledge, New York, NY, 1993

D.A. Cook. *A History of Narrative Film*, W.W. Norton, New York, NY, 1981, 1990, 1996

L. Cooke & P. Wollen, eds. *Visual Display*, Bay Press, Seattle, 1995

P. Cook, ed. *The Cinema Book*, British Film Institute, London, 1985

R. Corman. *How I Made a Hundred Movies In Hollywood and Never Lost a Dime*, New York, NY, 1990

F. Couvares, ed. *Movie Censorship & American Culture*, Smithsonian Institution Press, Washington DC, 1996

C. Craft: ""Kiss Me With Those Red Lips": Gender and Inversion in Bram Stoker's *Dracula", Representations*, 8, Autumn, 1984

B. Creed. *The Monstrous-Feminine*, Routledge, London, 1993

T. Cripps. *Making Movies Black*, Oxford University Press, Oxford, 1993

C. Degli-Esposti, ed. *Postmodernism In the Cinema*, Berghahn Books, New York, NY, 1998

B. Denberg. *"The Twilight Saga*: Is it promoting abstinence?", Moviefone, November 18, 2009

N. Denzin. *The Cinematic Society*, Sage, London, 1995

C. Derry. *Dark Dreams: A Psychological History of the Modern Horror Film*, Thomas Yoseloff, 1977

D. Desser & G. Jowett, eds. *Hollywood Goes Shopping*, University of Minnesota Press, Minneapolis, MN, 2000

A. De Vaney. *Hollywood Economics*, Routledge, 2004

V. Dika. *Games of Terror: Hallowe'en, Friday the 13th and the Films of the Stalker Cycle*, Farleigh Dickinson University Press, Rutherford, 1990

L. Doan, ed. *The Lesbian Postmodern*, Columbia University Press, New York, NY, 1994

J. Donald, ed. *Fantasy and the Cinema*, British Film Institute, London, 1989

S.C. Dubin. *Arresting Images: Impolitic Art and Uncivil Actions*, Routledge, London, 1992

A. Dworkin. *Pornography: Men Possessing Women*, Women's Press, London, 1984

R. Dyer, ed. *Heavenly Bodies: Film Stars and Society*, Macmillan, London, 1987

—. *Only Entertainment*, Routledge, London, 1992

—. *Stars*, British Film Institute, London, 1998

J. Dyson. *Bright Darkness: The Lost Art of the Supernatural Horror Film*, Cassell, London, 1997

M. Eagleton, ed. *Feminist Literary Theory: A Reader*, Blackwell, Oxford, 1986

A. Easthope, ed. *Contemporary Film Theory*, Longman, London, 1993

M. Eisner with T. Schwartz. *Work In Progress*, Penguin, London, 1999

R. & P. Engelmeier. *Fashion In Film*, Prestel, Munich, 1997

P. Ettedgui. *Production Design & Art Direction*, RotoVision, 1999

P. Evans. *Terms of Endearment: Hollywood Romantic Comedy of the 1980s and 1990s*, Edinburgh University Press, Edinburgh, 1998

J. Eszterhas. *The Devil's Guide To Hollywood*, Duckworth, London, 2006

C. Finch. *Special Effects*, Abbeville, 1984

J. Finler. *The Movie Director's Story*, Octopus Books, London, 1985

—. *The Hollywood Story*, Wallflower Press, London, 2003

C. Fleming. *High Concept: Don Simpson and the Hollywood Culture of Excess*, Bloomsbury, London, 1998

J. Fletcher & A. Benjamin, eds. *Abjection, Melancholia and Love: The Work of Julia Kristeva*, Routledge, London, 1990

G.E. Forshey. *American Religious and Biblical Spectaculars*, Praeger, Westport, CT, 1992

K. Fowkes. *Giving Up the Ghost: Spirits, Ghosts and Angels In Mainstream Comedy Films*, Wayne State University Press, Detroit, MI, 1998

K. French, ed. *Screen Violence*, Bloomsbury, London, 1996

H. Geduld, ed. *Filmmakers On Filmmaking*, Indiana University Press, Bloomington, IN, 1967

K. Gelder. *Reading the Vampire*, Routledge, London, 1994

—. & S. Thornton, eds. *The Subcultures Reader*, Routledge, London, 1997

—. ed. *The Horror Reader*, Routledge, London, 2000

—. *New Vampire Cinema*, British Film Institute, London, 2012

J. Gelmis. *The Film Director as Superstar*, Penguin, London, 1974

C. Gledhill, ed. *Stardom: Industry of Desire*, Routledge, London, 1991

T. Gold. *The Guardian*, Nov 16, 2012

J. Gordon & V. Hollinger, eds. *Blood Read: The Vampire As Metaphor In Contemporary Culture*, University of Pennsylvania Press, Philadelphia, PA, 1997

B.K. Grant, ed. *Film Genre*, Scarecrow Press, Metuchen, NJ, 1977

—. ed. *Planks of Reason: Essays on the Horror Film*, Scarecrow Press, 1984

—. *Film Genre Reader II*, University of Texas Press, Austin, TX, 1995

S. Gravett. *From Twilight To Breaking Dawn*, Chalice Press, St Louis, MO, 2010

E. Grosz. "The Body of Signification", in J. Fletcher, 1990

—. *Volatile Bodies*, Indiana University Press, Bloomington, IN, 1994

E. Grove. *Raindance Producers' Lab: Lo-To-No Budget Filmmaking*, Elsevier, Oxford, 2004

J. Halberstam. *Skin Shows: Gothic Horror and the Technology of Monsters*, Duke University Press, Durham, NC, 1995

C. Hardwicke. *Twilight: Director's Notebook*, Atom, London, 2009

D. Harries. *Film Parody*, British Film Institute, 2000

S. Highfill. "Ashley Greene", *Entertainment Weekly*, Feb 24, 2022

C. Hill. *Video Violence and Children*, Oasis, London, 1983

D. Hogan. *Dark Romance: Sex and Death In the Horror Film*, McFarland, NC, 1986

J. Holte. *Dracula In the Dark*, Greenwood Press, Westport, CT, 1997

M. Howden. *Blood Rivals*, John Blake, London, 2009

L. Hutcheon. *A Theory of Parody*, Methuen, New York, 1985

—. *A Poetics of Postmodernism*, Routledge, New York, 1988

D. Hughes. *Comic Book Movies*, Virgin, London, 2003

R. Huss & T. Ross, eds. *Focus on the Horror Film*, Prentice-Hall, Englewood CLiffs, NJ, 1972

E.L. James. *Fifty Shades of Grey*, Arrow Books, London, 2012

D. Jones. *Horror: A Thematic History In Fiction and Film*, Arnold, London, 2002

S. Jones & K. Newman. *Horror 100 Best Books*, Xanadu, 1988

G. Jordan & C. Weedon. *Cultural Politics*, Blackwell, Oxford, 1995

B.F. Kawin. *How Movies Work*, Macmillan, New York, NY, 1987

P. Keough, ed. *Flesh and Blood: The National Society of Film Critics on Sex, Violence, and Censorship*, Mercury House, San Francisco, CA, 1995

M. Kermode. *Hatchet Job*, Picador, London, 2013

A. Kibbey *et al. Sexual Artifice: Persons, Images, Politics*, New York University Press, New York, NY, 1994

P. Kirkham & J. Thumim, eds. *Me Jane: Masculinity, Movies and Women*, Lawrence & Wishart, London, 1995

S. Klein. *"Twilight"*, *Forbes & Fifth*, University of Pittsburgh, Fall, 2015

H. Knowles. *Ain't It Cool? Kicking Hollywood's Butt*, Boxtree, London, 2002

R. Kolker. *A Cinema of Loneliness: Penn, Stone, Kubrick, Scorsese, Spielberg, Altman*, Oxford University Press, New York, NY, 2000

P. Kramer. *The Big Picture: Hollywood Cinema From Star Wars To Titanic*, British Film Institute, London, 2001

—. *The New Hollywood*, Wallflower Press, London, 2005

J. Kristeva. *Powers of Horror: An Essay on Abjection*, tr. Leon S. Roudiez, Columbia University Press, New York, 1982

—. *Desire in Language: A Semiotic Approach to Literature and Art*, ed. Leon Roudiez, tr. Thomas Gora, Alice Jardine & Leon Roudiez, Blackwell, Oxford, 1982

—. *The Kristeva Reader*, ed. Toril Moi, Blackwell, Oxford, 1986

—. *Tales of Love*, tr. Leon S. Roudiez, Columbia University Press, New York, N.Y., 1987

—. *Black Sun: Depression and Melancholy*, tr. L.S. Roudiez, Columbia University Press, New York, NY, 1989

C. Lake. *Terror and Everyday Life: Singular Moments In the History of the Horror Film*, Sage, London, 1994

R. Lapsley & M. Westlake, eds. *Film Theory: An Introduction*, Manchester University Press, Manchester, 1988

John Lechte: *Julia Kristeva*, Routledge, London, 1990

E. Levy. *Cinema of Outsiders: The Rise of American Independent Film*, New York University Press, New York, NY, 1999

J. Lewis, ed. *New American Cinema*, Duke University Press, Durham, NC, 1998

—. *Hollywood v. Hard Core: How the Struggle Over Censorship Created the Modern Film Industry*, New York University Press, New York, NY, 2000

—. ed. *The End of Cinema As We Know It: American Film In the Nineties*, New York University Press, New York, NY, 2002

L. Lewis, eds. *The Adoring Audience: Fan Culture and Popular Media*, Routledge, New York, NY, 1992

J. Leyda. ed. *Film Makers Speak: Voices of Film Experience*, Da Capo, New York, NY, 1977

S. Macdonald. *A Critical Cinema: Interviews With Independent Filmmakers*, University of California Press, Berkeley, CA, 1988

R. Maltby. *Harmless Entertainment: Hollywood and the Ideology of Consensus*, Scarecrow Press, Metuchen, NJ, 1983

—. *Hollywood Cinema*, 2nd ed., Blackwell, Oxford, 2003

Elaine Marks & Isabelle de Courtivron, eds. *New French Feminisms: an Anthology*,

Harvester Wheatsheaf, Hemel Hempstead, 1981

G. Mast *et al*, eds. *Film Theory and Criticism: Introductory Readings*, Oxford University Press, New York, NY, 1992a

—. & B Kawin, *A Short History of the Movies*, Macmillan, New York, NY, 1992b

T.D. Matthews. *Censored*, Chatto & Windus, London, 1994

J. McCarthy. *Psychos: 80 Years of Mad Movies, Maniacs and Murderous Deeds*, St Martin's, New York, NY, 1986

—. *The Modern Horror Film*, Citadel, New York, NY, 1990

D. McClintock. *Indecent Exposure: A True Story of Hollywood and Wall Street*, W. Morrow, New York, NY, 1982

R. McKee. *Story: Substance, Structure, Style and the Principles of Screenwriting*, Methuen, London, 1999

M. Medved. *Hollywood vs. America*, HarperCollins, London, 1992

S. Mendelson. "Why the *TwilightSaga* Film Franchise Mattered", *Huffington Post*, Nov 14, 2012

F. Miller. *Censored Hollywood: Sex, Sin and Violence On Screen*, Turner Publishing, Atlanta, 1994

T. Miller *et al*, eds. *Global Hollywood*, British Film Institute, London, 2001

E. Muller & D. Faris. *That's Sexploitation! The Forbidden World of "Adults Only" Cinema*, Titan Books, London, 1996

J. Natoli. *Hauntings: Popular Film and American Culture 1990-92*, State University of New York Press, Albany, NY, 1994

—. *Speeding To the Millennium: Film and Culture 1993-1995*, State University of New York Press, Albany, NY, 1998

—. *Postmodern Journeys: Film and Culture, 1996-1998*, State University of New York Press, Albany, NY, 2001

S. Neale & F. Krutnik. *Popular Film and Television Comedy*, Routledge, London, 1990

—. & B. Neve. *Film and Politics In America*, Routledge, London, 1992

—. & M. Smith, eds. *Contemporary Hollywood Cinema*, Routledge, London, 1998

—. *Genre and Hollywood*, Routledge, London, 2000

—. *Genre and Contemporary Hollywood*, Routledge, London, 2002

K. Newman. *Nightmare Movies*, Harmony, New York, NY, 1988

—. ed. *The BFI Companion To Horror*, Cassell, London, 1996

—. & J. Marriott. *Horror! The Definitive Companion To the Most Terrifying Movies Ever Made*, Carlton Books, London, 2013

J. Orr. *Contemporary Cinema*, Edinburgh University Press, Edinburgh, 1998

C. Paglia. *Sexual Personae: Art and Decadence From Nefertiti To Emily Dickinson*, Penguin, London, 1992

—. *Sex, Art and American Culture*, Viking, London, 1992

—. *Vamps and Tramps: New Essays*, Penguin, London, 1995

M. Parke & N. Wilson, eds. *Theorizing Twilight*, McFarland & Co., Ltd, 2011

D. Parkinson. *The Rough Guide To Film Musicals*, Penguin, London, 2007

W. Paul. *Laughing Screaming: Modern Hollywood Horror and Comedy*, Columbia University Press, New York, NY, 1994

C. Penley, ed. *Feminism and Film Theory*, Routledge, London, 1988

R. Prendergast. *Film Music*, W.W. Norton, New York, NY, 1992

S. Prince. ed. *Screening Violence*, Athlone Press, London, 2000

D. Quinlan. *The Illustrated Guide To Film Directors*, B.T. Batsford, London, 1983

—. *Quinlan's Illustrated Directory of Film Comedy Stars*, B.T. Batsford, London, 1992

T. Reeves. *The Worldwide Guide To Movie Locations*, Titan Books, London, 2003

R. Rickitt. *Special Effects*, Aurum, London, 2006

B. Robb. *Screams and Nightmares*, Titan Books, London, 1998

J. Robertson. *The British Board of Film Censors*, Croom Helm, 1985

J. Romney & A. Wootton, eds. *Celluloid Jukebox: Popular Music and the Movies Since the 50s*, British Film Institute, London, 1995

Melissa Rosenberg. "Exclusive Interview", with Ryan Turek, Coming Soon, Aug 19, 2008

—. "Q & A: Melissa Rosenberg", *The Seattle Times*, Mch 18, 2010

— Interview, *Collider*, by C. Radish, Nov 15, 2012

—. "Women and Hollywood", Nov 20, 2012

M. Rubin. *Thrillers*, Cambridge University Press, Cambridge, 1999

R. Ruiz. *The Poetics of Cinema*, Dis Voir, Paris, 1995

M. Russell & J. Young. *Film Music*, RotoVision, 2000

V. Russo. *The Celluloid Closet: Homosexuality In the Movies*, Harper & Row, New York,

NY, 1981

B. Rux. *Hollywood vs. the Aliens*, Frog, Berkeley, CA, 1997

A. Sarris. *The American Cinema*, Dutton, New York, NY, 1968

—. ed. *Interviews With Film Directors*, Avon, New York, NY, 1969

T. Schatz. *Hollywood Genres,* Random House, New York, NY, 1981

—. *Old Hollywood/ New Hollywood,* UMI Research Press, Ann Arbor, MI, 1983

—. *The Genius of the System: Hollywood Filmmaking In the Studio Era*, Pantheon, New York, NY 1988

Screen Reader I: Cinema/ Ideology/ Politics, Society for Education in Film & TV, 1977

Screen Reader II: Cinema and Semiotics, British Film Institute, London, 1982

C. Seifert. 2008. ""Bite me! (or don't)": Stephenie Meyer's vampire-infested Twilight series has created a new YA genre: Abstinence porn", *Bitch Magazine,* December 17, 2008

S. Seltzer. *"Twilight", Huffington Post*, Aug 9, 2008

C. Sharrett, ed. *Crisis Cinema*, Maisonneuve Press, Washington, DC, 1993

B. Sheen. *Stephenie Meyer*, KidHaven Press, 2010

T. Shone. *Blockbuster: How the Jaws and Jedi Generation Turned Hollywood Into a Boom-Town,* Scribner, London, 2005

E. Showalter, ed. *The New Feminist Criticism,* Virago, London, 1986

R. Shuker. *Understanding Popular Music*, Routledge, London, 1994

—. *Key Concepts In Popular Music,* Routledge, London, 1998

S. & B. Siegel. *American Film Comedy*, Prentice Hall, 1994

D. Siering. "Taking a bite out of *Twilight*", *Ms. Magazine*, 19, 2009

N. Sinyard. *Filming Literature: The Art of Screen Adaption*, Croom Helm, Beckenham, Kent, 1986

D. Smith. *American Filmmakers Today*, Blandford Press, Poole, 1984

G. Smith. *Epic Films*, McFarland, Jefferson, NC, 1991

L. Spencer. *Love Bites: The Unofficial Saga of Twilight*, E.C.W. Press, 2010

J. Stacey. *Hollywood Cinema and Female Spectatorship*, Routledge, London, 1994

P. Steven, ed. *Jump Cut: Hollywood, Politics and Counter Cinema*, Between the Lines, Toronto, 1985

G. Stewart. *Between Film and Screen: Modernism's Photo Synthesis*, University of Chicago Press, Chicago, IL, 1999

J. Still & M. Worton, eds. *Textuality and Sexuality: Reading Theories and Practices*, Manchester University Press, Manchester, 1993

M. Stokes & R. Maltby, eds. *Identifying Hollywood Audiences*, British Film Institute, London, 1999

J. Storey, ed. *Cultural Theory and Popular Culture*, Harvester Wheatsheaf, Hemel Hempstead, 1994

J.M. Straczynski. *The Complete Book of Scriptwriting,* Titan Books, London, 1997

J. Stringer, ed. *Movie Blockbusters*, Routledge, London, 2003

C. Tashiro. *Pretty Pictures: Production Design and the History Film*, University of Texas Press, 1998

Y. Tasker. *Spectacular Bodies: Gender, Genre and the Action Cinema*, Routledge, London, 1993

—. *Working Girls: Gender and Sexuality In Popular Cinema*, Routledge, London, 1998

S. Teo. *Hong Kong Cinema*, British Film Institute, London, 1997

K. Thompson & D. Bordwell. *Film History: An Introduction*, McGraw-Hill, New York, NY, 1994

—. *Storytelling In the New Hollywood*, Harvard University Press, Cambridge, MA, 1999

D. Thomson. *A Biographical Dictionary of Film,* Deutsch, London, 1995

—. *The Big Screen*, Allen Lane, 2012

S. Thrower, ed. *Eyeball: Compendium: Sex and Horror, Art and Exploitation*, FAB Press, Godalming, Surrey, 2003

C. Tohill & P. Tombs. *Immoral Tales: Sex and Horror Cinema In Europe 1956-1984*, Titan Books, London, 1995

E. Traube. *Dreaming Identities: Class, Gender and Generations In 1980s Hollywood Movies*, Westview Press, Boulder, CO, 1992

J. Trevelyan. *What the Censor Saw*, Michael Joseph, London, 1973

J. Twitchell. *Dreadful Pleasures: An Anatomy of Modern Horror*, Oxford University Press, Oxford, 1985

J. Ursini & A. Silver. *The Vampire Film*, Limelight, New York, NY, 1993

M.C. Vaz. *Twilight: The Complete Illustrated Movie Companion*, Atom/ Litle, Brown,

London, 2008

—. *New Moon: The Official Illustrated Movie Companion,* Atom/ Little, Brown, 2009

—. *Eclipse: The Complete Illustrated Movie Companion*, Atom/ Litle, Brown, London, 2010

—. *Breaking Dawn, Part 1: The Official Illustrated Movie Companion,* Atom/ Little, Brown, 2011

H. Vogel. *Entertainment Industry Economics*, Cambridge University Press, Cambridge, 1995

C. Vogler. *The Writer's Journey: Mythic Structure For Storytellers and Screenwriters*, Pan, London, 1998

J. Wasko. *Movies and Money*, Ablex, NJ, 1982

—. *Hollywood In the Information Age*, Polity Press, Cambridge, 1994

A. Weiss. *Vampires and Violets: Lesbians In Film*, Penguin, London, 1993

E. Weiss. & J. Belton, eds. *Film Sound: Theory and Practice*, Columbia University Press, New York, NY, 1989

P. Wells. *The Horror Genre*, Wallflower, London, 2000

S. Willis. *High Contrast: Race and Gender In Contemporary Hollywood Film*, Duke University Press, Durham, NC, 1997

E. Wistrich. *'I Don't Mind the Sex It's the Violence': Film Censorship Explored*, Marion Boyars, London, 1978

M. Wolf. *The Entertainment Economy,* Penguin, London, 1999

R. Wood. *Hollywood From Vietnam To Reagan... and Beyond*, Columbia University Press, New York, NY, 2003

—. & R. Lippe, eds. *American Nightmare: Essays On the Horror Film*, Festival of Festivals, Toronto, 1979

—. "Burying the Undead: The Use and Obsolescence of Count Dracula", *Mosaic*, 16, 1, Spring, 1983

T. Woods. *Beginning Postmodernism,* Manchester University Press, Manchester, 1999

J. Wyatt. *High Concept: Movies and Marketing In Hollywood*, University of Texas Press, Austin, TX, 1994

E.C.M. Yau, ed. *At Full Speed: Hong Kong Cinema In a Borderless World,* University of Minnesota Press, Minneapolis, MN, 1998

J. Zipes. *Breaking the Spell: Radical Theories of Folk and Fairy Tales*, Heinemann, London, 1978

—. *Fairy Tales and the Art of Subversion: The Classical Genre for Children and the Process of Civilization,* Heinemann, London, 1983

—. *Don't Bet on the Prince: Contemporary Feminist Fairy Tales In North America and England*, Methuen, New York, NY, 1986

—. *The Brothers Grimm: From Enchanted Forests To the Modern World*, Routledge, New York, NY, 1989

—. ed. *The Oxford Companion To Fairy Tales*, Oxford University Press, 2000

—. *Breaking the Spell: Radical Theories of Folk and Fairy Tales*, University of Kentucky Press, Lexington, 2002a

—. *Sticks and Stones: The Troublesome Success of Children's Literature from Slovenly Peter To Harry Potter*, Routledge,, London, 2002b

—. *The Enchanted Screen: The Unknown History of Fairy-tale Films*, Routledge, New York, NY, 2011

—. *The Irresistible Fairy Tale*, Princeton University Press, Princeton, NJ, 2012

WEBSITES

StephenieMeyer.com
kristenstewart.com
twilightlexicon.com
thetwilightsaga.com
Fickle Fish Films   ficklefishfilms.com
carterburwell.com

JEREMY ROBINSON has published poetry, fiction, and studies of J.R.R. Tolkien, Samuel Beckett, Thomas Hardy, André Gide and D.H. Lawrence. Robinson has edited poetry books by Novalis, Ursula Le Guin, Friedrich Hölderlin, Francesco Petrarch, Dante Alighieri, Arseny Tarkovsky, and Rainer Maria Rilke.

Books on film and animation include: *The Akira Book* • *The Art of Katsuhiro Otomo* • *The Art of Masamune Shirow* • *The Ghost In the Shell Book* • *Fullmetal Alchemist* • *Cowboy Bebop: The Anime and Movie* • *The Cinema of Hayao Miyazaki* • *Hayao Miyazaki: Pocket Guide* • *Princess Mononoke: Pocket Movie Guide* • *Spirited Away: Pocket Movie Guide* • *Blade Runner and the Cinema of Philip K. Dick* • *Blade Runner: Pocket Movie Guide* • *The Cinema of Donald Cammell* • *Performance: Donald Cammell: Nic Roeg: Pocket Movie Guide* • *Pasolini: Il Cinema di Poesia/ The Cinema of Poetry* • *Salo: Pocket Movie Guide* • *The Trilogy of Life Movies: Pocket Movie Guide* • *The Gospel According To Matthew: Pocket Movie Guide* • *The Ecstatic Cinema of Tony Ching Siu-tung* • *Tsui Hark: The Dragon Master of Chinese Cinema* • *The Swordsman: Pocket Movie Guide* • *A Chinese Ghost Story: Pocket Movie Guide* • *Ken Russell: England's Great Visionary Film Director and Music Lover* • *Tommy: Ken Russell: The Who: Pocket Movie Guide* • *Women In Love: Ken Russell: D.H. Lawrence: Pocket Movie Guide* • *The Devils: Ken Russell: Pocket Movie Guide* • *Walerian Borowczyk: Cinema of Erotic Dreams* • *The Beast: Pocket Movie Guide* • *The Lord of the Rings Movies* • *The Fellowship of the Ring: Pocket Movie Guide* • *The Two Towers: Pocket Movie Guide* • *The Return of the King: Pocket Movie Guide* • *Jean-Luc Godard: The Passion of Cinema* • *The Sacred Cinema of Andrei Tarkovsky* • *Andrei Tarkovsky: Pocket Guide.*

'It's amazing for me to see my work treated with such passion and respect. There is nothing resembling it in the U.S. in relation to my work.'
(Andrea Dworkin)

'This model monograph – it is an exemplary job, and I'm very proud that he has accorded me a couple of mentions… The subject matter of his book is beautifully organised and dead on beam.'
(Lawrence Durrell, on *The Light Eternal: A Study of J.M.W. Turner*)

'Jeremy Robinson's poetry is certainly jammed with ideas, and I find it very interesting for that reason. It's certainly a strong imprint of his personality.'
(Colin Wilson)

'*Sex-Magic-Poetry-Cornwall* is a very rich essay... It is a very good piece… vastly stimulating and insightful.'
(Peter Redgrove)

CRESCENT MOON PUBLISHING

web: www.crmoon.com e-mail: cresmopub@yahoo.co.uk

ARTS, PAINTING, SCULPTURE

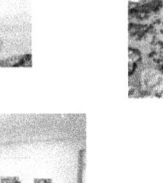
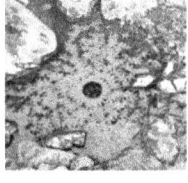

The Art of Andy Goldsworthy
Andy Goldsworthy: Touching Nature
Andy Goldsworthy in Close-Up
Andy Goldsworthy: Pocket Guide
Andy Goldsworthy In America
Land Art: A Complete Guide
The Art of Richard Long
Richard Long: Pocket Guide
Land Art In the UK
Land Art in Close-Up
Land Art In the U.S.A.
Land Art: Pocket Guide

Installation Art in Close-Up
Minimal Art and Artists In the 1960s and After
Colourfield Painting
Land Art DVD, TV documentary
Andy Goldsworthy DVD, TV documentary
The Erotic Object: Sexuality in Sculpture From Prehistory to the Present Day
Sex in Art: Pornography and Pleasure in Painting and Sculpture
Postwar Art
Sacred Gardens: The Garden in Myth, Religion and Art
Glorification: Religious Abstraction in Renaissance and 20th Century Art
Early Netherlandish Painting
Leonardo da Vinci
Piero della Francesca
Giovanni Bellini
Fra Angelico: Art and Religion in the Renaissance

Mark Rothko: The Art of Transcendence
Frank Stella: American Abstract Artist
Jasper Johns
Brice Marden

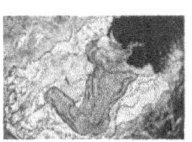

Alison Wilding: The Embrace of Sculpture
Vincent van Gogh: Visionary Landscapes
Eric Gill: Nuptials of God
Constantin Brancusi: Sculpting the Essence of Things
Max Beckmann
Caravaggio
Gustave Moreau
Egon Schiele: Sex and Death In Purple Stockings
Delizioso Fotografico Fervore: Works In Process 1
Sacro Cuore: Works In Process 2
The Light Eternal: J.M.W. Turner
The Madonna Glorified: Karen Arthurs

LITERATURE

J.R.R. Tolkien: The Books, The Films, The Whole Cultural Phenomenon
J.R.R. Tolkien: Pocket Guide
Tolkien's Heroic Quest
The *Earthsea* Books of Ursula Le Guin
Beauties, Beasts and Enchantment: Classic French Fairy Tales
German Popular Stories by the Brothers Grimm
Philip Pullman and *His Dark Materials*
Sexing Hardy: Thomas Hardy and Feminism
Thomas Hardy's *Tess of the d'Urbervilles*
Thomas Hardy's *Jude the Obscure*
Thomas Hardy: The Tragic Novels
Love and Tragedy: Thomas Hardy
The Poetry of Landscape in Hardy
Wessex Revisited: Thomas Hardy and John Cowper Powys
Wolfgang Iser: Essays and Interviews
Petrarch, Dante and the Troubadours
Maurice Sendak and the Art of Children's Book Illustration
Andrea Dworkin
Cixous, Irigaray, Kristeva: The *Jouissance* of French Feminism
Julia Kristeva: Art, Love, Melancholy, Philosophy, Semiotics and Psychoanalysis
Hélene Cixous I Love You: The *Jouissance* of Writing
Luce Irigaray: Lips, Kissing, and the Politics of Sexual Difference
Peter Redgrove: Here Comes the Flood
Peter Redgrove: Sex-Magic-Poetry-Cornwall
Lawrence Durrell: Between Love and Death, East and West
Love, Culture & Poetry: Lawrence Durrell
Cavafy: Anatomy of a Soul
German Romantic Poetry: Goethe, Novalis, Heine, Hölderlin
Feminism and Shakespeare
Shakespeare: Love, Poetry & Magic
The Passion of D.H. Lawrence
D.H. Lawrence: Symbolic Landscapes
D.H. Lawrence: Infinite Sensual Violence
Rimbaud: Arthur Rimbaud and the Magic of Poetry
The Ecstasies of John Cowper Powys
Sensualism and Mythology: The Wessex Novels of John Cowper Powys
Amorous Life: John Cowper Powys and the Manifestation of Affectivity (H.W. Fawkner)
Postmodern Powys: New Essays on John Cowper Powys (Joe Boulter)
Rethinking Powys: Critical Essays on John Cowper Powys
Paul Bowles & Bernardo Bertolucci
Rainer Maria Rilke
Joseph Conrad: *Heart of Darkness*
In the Dim Void: Samuel Beckett
Samuel Beckett Goes into the Silence
André Gide: Fiction and Fervour
Jackie Collins and the Blockbuster Novel
Blinded By Her Light: The Love-Poetry of Robert Graves
The Passion of Colours: Travels In Mediterranean Lands
Poetic Forms

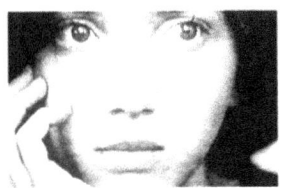

The Light Eternal is a model monograph, an exemplary job. The subject matter of the book is beautifully organised and dead on beam. (Lawrence Durrell)
It is amazing for me to see my work treated with such passion and respect. (Andrea Dworkin)

CRESCENT MOON PUBLISHING
P.O. Box 1312, Maidstone, Kent, ME14 5XU, Great Britain. www.crmoon.com

cresmopub@yahoo.co.uk   www.crescentmoon.org.uk

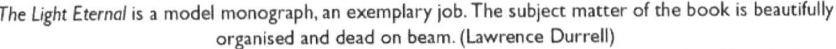

www.ingramcontent.com/pod-product-compliance
Lightning Source LLC
Chambersburg PA
CBHW071246220526
45468CB00001B/12